INVITATION TO
PSYCHOLOGICAL RESEARCH

INVITATION TO PSYCHOLOGICAL RESEARCH

James D. Evans

Lindenwood College

HOLT, RINEHART AND WINSTON
New York Chicago San Francisco Philadelphia
Montreal Toronto London Sydney
Tokyo Mexico City Rio de Janeiro Madrid

Juna Blūma
1985.

Library of Congress Cataloging in Publication Data

Evans, James D.
    Invitation to psychological research.

    Bibliography: p.
    Includes indexes.
    1. Psychology—Research.   I. Title.
BF76.5.E9   1985   150′.72   84-12855

ISBN 0-03-063602-7

CBS COLLEGE PUBLISHING
Holt, Rinehart and Winston
The Dryden Press
Saunders College Publishing

To Lois and Laura,
Charlotte and LeRoy,
and Patricia

PREFACE

During the past ten years, teachers and students of psychology witnessed the emergence of many fine textbooks on research methods. Most of these volumes are more comprehensive than their predecessors, in the sense that they cover correlational and applied research designs, as well as the experimental method. And much to the relief and enjoyment of both students and instructors, many of these texts are easily read and understood.

In spite of the wide range of favorable options, I often found it difficult to select one textbook for the research methods course that I offer annually at Lindenwood College. In fact, I usually resorted to requiring two textbooks, for several reasons. For one, it seemed that the texts that were readable, and even enjoyable, tended to lack sophistication and systematic organization. These delightfully written works would often whisk the student into the "how to" aspects of research without first providing a pragmatic philosophy of science. Further, the logical underpinnings of research design and statistical analysis were either ignored or covered in a cursory fashion. On the other hand, I found that most of the systematic texts were too narrow in content, too difficult, or lacking in interest value for the average student in my classes. It was this dilemma that led me to write the present text.

I created *Invitation to Psychological Research* with the aim of addressing the diversity of issues and approaches in today's psychological research. It was also my desire to combine the best pedagogical characteristics in a single research methods book. These characteristics include:

1. *Readability*. I wrote *Invitation* as a transcription of my research methods lectures. The language and conceptual level are geared to the academic capabilities of the typical college junior. The text contains numerous, easy-to-relate-to examples, and the tone is conversational. I frequently address questions to the student, just as I do when presenting a lecture. Throughout the book, I have tried to speak directly to the reader.

2. *Comprehensive Coverage*. It is becoming very clear that the wave of the future in research methods will include a variety of techniques and strategies that are not laboratory-based or strictly experimental in nature. The comprehensive topical coverage of *Invitation* reflects this anticipation of the near future (now the present). Although the book covers the experimental method as thoroughly as most other research methods texts, many of the nonexperimental approaches, including field techniques, case-study research, developmental methodology, and program evaluation, are also presented.

3. *Logical Order of Presentation*. Basic research concepts and procedures are presented in a systematic fashion. Part 2, "Five Phases of Scientific Inquiry," epitomizes the systematic character of the text by presenting the logical steps and operations of scientific research in the order in which they actually occur during the investigative

process. Not only are these five pivotal chapters carefully linked together, but they also explicitly form the conceptual bridge between Part 1 (philosophy of science) and Part 3 (methods).

4. *Emphasis on Understanding*. I have never found it very satisfying or educationally sound to simply present information to students for their unquestioning consumption. Thus, in composing *Invitation*, I have taken care to explain why certain procedures are preferred (or necessary) in scientific research; I have also made an effort to de-mystify difficult concepts. I think it is important for students to understand the relationship between imperfect correlation and "regression toward the mean," the rationale behind psychology's code of research ethics, why science favors "parsimonious theories," what makes correlated-groups designs more "powerful," and so on.

5. *Integration of Research Design and Statistics*. The current trend in research methods books is to compromise severely on the matter of statistical analysis and logic. In many texts, statistical matters are either largely omitted or relegated to an obscure appendix or two. Yet any social scientist with much research experience knows that it is unrealistic and impractical to consider research design independently of statistical theory and procedure.

This text does not attempt to teach basic statistics. However, I have tried to blend statistical concerns with design considerations where appropriate. At the outset, I make it clear to the reader that measurement and statistics are inseparable parts of the research process. This theme is carried through the text, in almost every chapter. Chapter 6 serves as an overview of the rationale involved in extracting statistical relationships from a set of raw data, with emphasis on the use of statistical tools to identify relationships rather than on mathematical concerns. That chapter also presents statistical logic as a basic step in the sequence of scientific investigation, which is a realistic portrayal of the subject matter. Chapter 8 casts the idea of statistical significance in a similar role.

Several chapters in Part 3 end with a brief consideration of certain statistical tests that are most appropriate for the particular research designs covered in the respective chapters (for example, ANOVA is considered in conjunction with experimental designs). My treatment of statistics doesn't assume that the reader has had a statistics course. Because of the approach used, however, even the student who has had such a course should profit from the statistical material.

A QUICK LOOK INSIDE

Invitation should require no supplements under most circumstances. An eclectic philosophy of science is presented in the first two chapters. Chapter 3 rounds out Part 1 by discussing both the rationale and the procedures of ethical conduct in research with human subjects. Part 2 gives a detailed account of most of the prerequisites to sound research: how to formulate researchable questions; where to get research ideas; a comparison of the five basic research designs used by psychologists; the logic and construction of measurement devices; the internal-versus-external-validity issue; the interfacing of research design and statistics; the purpose of probability sampling; the meaning of statistical significance.

Part 3 provides step-by-step instruction on the use of systematic-observation, case-study, psychometric, survey, and experimental approaches in conducting psychological investigations. Attention is also given to special problems in applied research and archival investigations.

Part 4 consists of a chapter on constructing a research report. I have attempted to put together a chapter that will be genuinely helpful to the students in their efforts to master this sometimes frustrating art. The chapter includes not only carefully laid out instructions on the mechanics of writing the report but also a complete sample research paper that illustrates the various points. You will also find an emphasis on good organization and scholarship.

INTENDED AUDIENCE

Invitation was written for juniors and seniors who are taking their first course in research methods. Although the book was written with the psychology major in mind, its comprehensiveness makes it suitable as the principal text for research methods courses in other areas of the social sciences as well.

LEARNING AIDS

I have incorporated several features to enhance the effectiveness of this book as a teaching tool. An outline at the beginning of each chapter provides an "advance organizer" to make the material more meaningful as the student reads along. All terms set in boldface type are listed alphabetically and defined in the Glossary at the end of the book. The chapter summaries and review questions should also prove helpful when the student is preparing for class and reviewing for exams.

Most chapters contain "boxed" material. Those titled "Issues in Science" boxes are designed to bring the student's attention to current controversies in science and present a realistic picture of the scientific enterprise. Additional "Highlight" boxes present extended discussions of studies, examples, or clusters of concepts mentioned in the text.

INSTRUCTOR'S MANUAL

If this text does its intended job of clearly and thoroughly presenting research methods, then users should have ample class time for the development of discussion and class exercises. Accordingly, the *Instructor's Manual* that accompanies *Invitation* contains several suggestions for discussion topics and student-involvement projects. In addition, the manual lists the concepts introduced in each chapter and provides multiple-choice items for assessing student mastery.

ACKNOWLEDGMENTS

As is true of every textbook writer, I am indebted to many people for the support and advice they so generously provided during the development of this book.

From start to finish, the editors and staff of Holt, Rinehart and Winston were enthusiastic and helpful in all respects. In particular, I would like to thank Rosalind Sackoff, my developmental editor, conscience, and guide, for her steadfast commitment to the goal of making this text the best possible teaching device.

Several of my colleagues reviewed all or several parts of the manuscript and made many useful suggestions for improving it. Endless thanks to: Jeffrey Berman, University of Texas; William Brown, University of Central Florida; Roy Connally, University of Central Florida; Jeanne Maracek, Swarthmore College; Stuart Miller, Towson State University; William Pope, Mary Washington College.

I am grateful to the Literary Executor of the late Sir Ronald A. Fisher, F. R. S., to Dr. Frank Yates, F. R. S., and to Longman Group Ltd. London, for permission to reprint Tables IV and VII from their book, *Statistical Tables for Biological, Agricultural and Medical Research* (6th edition, 1974).

I also wish to express heartfelt appreciation to my unusually understanding family and coterie of friends, who cheered me on at each stage of the project, waited patiently when I began to repeatedly initiate the "author's litany" ("just one more month, just one more month . . ."), and generously sacrificed in countless ways so that I could complete my work. To all of those dear people, let me now say that the reports of my permanent disappearance were greatly exaggerated.

Last but not least, whatever is best in this book is to be credited to my students, who have taught me much about learning, teaching, and research methods.

J. D. E.

CONTENTS

PART 4

COMMUNICATING SCIENCE   375

PART 1

ASKING WHY AND WHITHER

1

GETTING THE SCIENTIFIC ATTITUDE

A ten-month-old boy investigates his world:

> Laurent is lying on his back but nevertheless resumes his experiments of the day before. He grasps in succession a celluloid swan, a box, etc., stretches out his arms and lets them fall. He distinctly varies the positions of the fall. Sometimes he stretches out his arm vertically, sometimes he holds it obliquely, in front of or behind his eyes, etc. When the object falls in a new position (for example on his pillow), he lets it fall two or three times more on the same place, as though to study the spatial relation; then he modifies the situation. (Piaget, 1963, p. 269)

A sixth-grader works on a personal problem:

> Joyce has several small warts on both hands, a condition that she finds embarrassing at times. Her health teacher, Ms. Mullins, told the class that warts are caused by viruses. She wonders if "sterilizing" her hands with rubbing alcohol will get rid of the ugly bumps. She is puzzled by Ms. Mullins' statement, though, since her brother says that he always removes warts by rubbing onions on them and then eating the onions. To make matters even more confusing, Grandma Dykes swears that the secret to wart removal is to rub one half of a new potato on each wart and then bury the potato halves in the back yard after sundown. To find out who is right, Joyce begins applying alcohol to her left hand every evening at bedtime. Once a week, she uses Grandma's potato regimen on the right hand. Disappointingly, after five weeks all of the warts are still present and appear to be thriving. Tears streaming down her cheeks, Joyce sits alone on the back porch, munching the last of several onions, confident that the remaining cure is the right one.

A mechanic performs his work:

> The motorcycle refuses to start, but Mike has a theory about troubleshooting internal combustion engines: Fuel must get to the carburetor chamber, the spark plugs must discharge, and compression must build in a timely fashion to make the fuel ignite. Mike's quick check of the gas tank, fuel lines, and carburetor float bowls verifies the presence of fuel. Since the bike is new, he seriously doubts that it has compression problems, but removes the spark plugs and runs a compression check anyway. All is okay there. Now that the fuel system and engine compression have been "absolved of guilt," he knows that the problem is electrical. After installation of new spark plugs fails to bring the beast to life, he examines the breaker points. Clean as a pin, and they give off ample spark when opened. The next step is to trace through the ignition system with a continuity light.. . .

A scientist investigates a new treatment for cancer:

> Dr. Ederer leans intently toward her data sheet. She is both fascinated and puzzled by the results of her two-year study on a psychological treatment for cancer victims. Earlier investigations by other researchers suggested that a cancer patient's use of positive visual imagery might prolong life or, better yet, lead to a remission of the disease. But Dr. Ederer's results are not that straightforward. It is clear that her imagery-using patients gave more favorable self-reports on their health than the "control" group of patients. But the death rate and the indexes of disease progression are the same in each group. Just when she decides to set aside her data and review the previous studies for possible procedural differences, something on the last sheet catches her eye. There it is! During the course of their "special treatment," 40% of her imagery patients apparently elected to terminate their chemotherapy. The corresponding figure for the control patients is only 10%. Could it be that the use of positive imagery benefits patients to the point where some of them begin to ignore medical treatment? Do the negative effects of avoiding chemotherapy then cancel out the positive effects of imagery? The scientist picks up her phone and dials her assistant. "Bill, I think you would be interested in looking at the data on our cancer patients. I think we'll need to do some extra analyses of these results—and probably some more data collection!"

These excerpts portray the activities of four people of diverse ages and backgrounds as they pursue their usual interests and concerns. Yet they all seem to be doing the same sort of thing, something I suppose could be called "problem-solving." It would be easy for you to think of many examples of such behavior in your own life, since much of your time is spent attempting to reduce the discrepancy between what you presently know and what you must know to handle new circumstances—that is, problem-solving. Not only is the need to acquire knowledge adaptive, it is also exciting, motivating, and capable of producing much personal fulfillment (Berlyne, 1966, 1967; Maslow, 1970; Rogers, 1963). Although this need is not unique to human beings, our preoccupation with knowledge acquisition has made us a distinct species (White, 1960).

There are many paths to knowledge, and an even greater number of problem-solving strategies. In this book you will explore the path called *science*. I selected the above excerpts of problem-solving behavior because they nicely illustrate certain aspects of the scientific method that we all use quite often. They also suggest that, to a degree, science is an extension of an important human need.

SCIENCE: A WORKING DEFINITION

Science is often thought of as a particular body of knowledge that is somehow more factual or believable than knowledge that is not "scientific" (Standen, 1950). However, scientists themselves prefer to view science as a logical set of rules and procedures that they use to answer questions and solve problems (Oppenheimer, 1956). Specifically, science is a *method of inquiry that generates knowledge about the natural world through the development of falsifiable theories that are both based on and evaluated by objective observation.* In a general sense, anyone who uses the scientific method to obtain knowledge is a scientist.

Several ideas in the above definition require further comment. First, you should note that it is the particular *method* used to obtain knowledge, rather than the subject matter studied, that sets scientific knowledge apart from other types of information. Furthermore, scientific knowledge is believable and factual only to the extent that the logical set of rules and procedures defining science has been successfully applied to a question or problem.

A second point to note is that the primary and essential aspect of the scientific approach is *objective observation*. The scientist's theories, which represent his or her present understanding of particular natural phenomena, typically begin with observations. And ultimately they must be validated or disconfirmed by additional observations. Accordingly, theories must be *falsifiable*, that is, capable of being disproved through observation. Theories that fail to meet this criterion, though they may be interesting, have little scientific utility.

The qualifier "objective" represents an important ingredient of scientific observation. At one level, objectivity means that the scientist makes observations without imposing personal biases on the data-collection process. At a more practical level, this means that scientists who study a particular phenomenon must be able to agree among themselves on what is being observed, how "it" is to be observed, and what "it" should be called (Oppenheimer, 1956). This process of *consensual validation*, or community agreement, on matters of scientific interest serves to average the biases of individual researchers so that, overall, a neutral (i.e., objective) perspective can be achieved. As will be explained in Chapter 2, scientists use special rules, concepts, and techniques of inquiry to help them realize the goal of objectivity.

PEOPLE AS SCIENTISTS

Some Comparisons

Let's reconsider the anecdotes that opened this chapter. What did the problem-solving activities of the infant, the sixth-grader, and the mechanic have in common with the formal research endeavors of Dr. Ederer? Recall that all of the problem-solvers appeared to be developing *hypotheses* (that is, educated guesses) about how certain environmental events are related to other events. And they generated *evidence* to test their hypotheses. All were attempting to exercise some control over the conditions under which the evidence was collected: the infant by systematically varying the position of his arms, the sixth-grader by treating her hands in different ways, the mechanic by setting up a carefully planned sequence of test operations, and the scientist by using a control group. And all of the problem-solvers ultimately were trying to isolate the *causes* of the outcomes they were observing. The infant, the sixth-grader, and Dr. Ederer were trying to establish *inferences*, or general conclusions, about regularities in nature. The mechanic was faced with a somewhat different challenge, however, in that the laws of nature that concerned him already had been established. His task was to *logically deduce tests* from a widely accepted *theory*—a procedure that is also a common part of the scientific method. Perhaps the most general theme in the problem-solvers' behavior was that of *reduction of uncertainty*, defined as developing a general idea that can summarize or explain a complicated situation. Uncertainty reduction is also the overall theme of science.

The idea that scientific methods are a direct extension of the problem-solving side of human nature has received considerable, though far from unanimous, support from both philosophers of science and scientists themselves (see Singer, 1971, for a review of the arguments). For example, many years ago Sir Ronald Fisher, who is well known for his work in applied statistics, stated that the scientific experiment is but a systematic refinement of people's general tendency to learn through experience. He thought that the scientist's work is more carefully planned, systematically related to existing knowledge, and accurately recorded (Fisher, 1966). More recently, Argyris (1980) wrote that "the theory individuals use to make sense out of, and to manage, their everyday lives is consonant with the theory of actions (but not necessarily the espoused theory) that the scientists employ when conducting rigorous research" (p. 2).

Some Research

The similarities between everyday problem-solving strategies and the methods of science have led to some intriguing research on the extent to which nonscientists use principles of scientific inquiry.

Scientists, Yes. Robinson (1980) found that, like scientists, college students are more likely to believe a hypothesis when it is supported by several independent sources of evidence than when it is supported repeatedly by the same source. The unwillingness of modern scientists to accept the validity of extrasensory perception stems, in part, from the lack of independent evidence for the phenomenon (Hansel, 1966, 1980). That is, the few instances of consistent evidence for ESP were produced by just two or three laboratories, with many other laboratories failing to reproduce the effects.

Well, Almost. At this point you may feel like asking: "Okay, if people in general naturally behave like scientists, then why is formal study of the scientific method necessary?" An interesting series of studies by Kahneman and Tversky (1972, 1973; Tversky & Kahneman, 1971) provides a response to that question by indicating some critical flaws in our natural "scientism." Their research showed that, like scientists, nonscientists are quite capable and willing to make predictions under conditions of uncertainty. ("Uncertainty" in the scientific sense simply means that an element of chance is involved because the person doing the predicting has only partial information to go on.) But nonscientists apparently ignore important information that scientists are trained to use routinely. Specifically, nonscientists tend to disregard (a) the overall probability, or likelihood, that a particular type of event will occur and (b) the reliability, or dependability, of the evidence from which the prediction is made. For example, Kahneman and Tversky gave students a brief description of a bright, studious young man. They then asked the students to rate the likelihood of the young man's entering graduate school in each of nine areas of study. The results? The raters gave the "subject" a better than 50-50 chance of entering medical school. Since only a tiny percentage of bright, studious people make it to medical school, the raters' predictions clearly were in violation of all reasonable odds. The element of probability had largely been ignored. What's more, the students made the same type of prediction error even when told in advance that the information before them had been produced by unreliable sources.

So what do lay people usually base their predictions on? Kahneman and Tversky's results suggested that in everyday life we make predictions and draw conclusions on the basis of how things *should* work out in a world where our private theories and personal stereotypes are mostly valid. But, of course, many of our private theories are not valid. Indeed, the need to protect ourselves from our own erroneous beliefs and fallible logic was a major reason for the development of the objective techniques of science.

Getting Better. The upshot of available arguments and research, then, is that you and I can be considered scientists in a general, functional sense, even before we formally study the scientific method. By nature we are curious, find problem-solving rewarding, make predictions, formulate theories, and accumulate observations that pertain to those theories. But if we relied solely on what comes naturally, most of us would not be very efficient researchers. Fortunately, formal training in the scientific method helps us to refine our native scientism. From this training, we learn to make our theories more precise and testable, perform systematic empirical tests of those theories, set up controlled conditions for those tests, systematically search for relations among the variables tested, and formulate explanations of those relations that reflect the observed facts rather than otherworldly·or fanciful notions (cf. Kerlinger, 1964).

In turn, such refinements in our problem-solving techniques help us to attain a higher sense of mastery as problem-solvers, and to approach a keener, more realistic understanding of the regularities in nature. And that includes human nature. What's more, when we study the philosophy and methods of science, we take a vital step toward becoming productive contributors to the knowledge-acquisition process.

Since you are reading this book, I assume that you have more than a passing interest in understanding psychological phenomena. Perhaps you plan to make a career of psychology or a related field of the social sciences. Or perhaps you are simply an avid "people watcher" who is interested in the field of psychology from a consumer's point of view. In either case, you will benefit from improving your grasp of topics covered in this book. Most of my colleagues in the field would agree with my claim that a science of psychology offers the most exciting, efficient, and promising approach to understanding behavior. To find out why we feel this way, read on.

WHY A SCIENTIFIC APPROACH?

As mentioned earlier, there are many paths to knowledge. With regard to human behavior and experience in particular, the clergy obtains knowledge through faith, doctrine, and revelation; philosophers through rational methods; artists and writers through creative inspiration and insight. As you will see, scientists use most of these paths to knowledge to some extent. But they place great emphasis on controlled observation and quantification (versus purely rational or logical analysis), skepticism (versus faith), simplicity and parsimony[1] (versus fanciful or otherworldly explanations), and public repetition and scrutiny of research efforts (versus private knowledge and special revelation). These characteristics constitute a demanding system of checks and balances that allows science to correct itself in the process of knowledge acquisition. In fact, the self-correcting nature of science is what sets it apart from most other approaches to knowledge (Kerlinger, 1964).

What are the special advantages of these checks and balances in the study of behavior and experience? I believe there are three main advantages. First, scientific inquiry helps to liberate us from dogma, deeply ingrained preconceptions, and personal biases as we attempt to learn more about the most complicated subject available—ourselves. Second, the methods of science often suggest unforeseen possibilities that otherwise might escape notice, comprehension, or use. Third, the scientific method simply has proved to be the most efficient means we have for verifying relationships among variables and establishing a knowledge of cause and effect.

Science as Liberator

Taking Wisdom to the Cleaners.   The social sciences have a peculiar status among academic disciplines: They overlap and compete with a number of other fields in their attempts to understand people—fields such as philosophy, theology, and the humanities. Since theories of human behavior developed by these other disciplines have existed for hundreds of years,[2] many of them are widely accepted in our culture, oftentimes by scientists themselves. The scientific method provides an independent check on these older conceptions of humanity.

The checking function of science was aptly illustrated by some of the earliest studies in educational psychology. These investigations were objective tests of the age-old notion that the human mind consists of a few general "faculties," such as linguistic ability and logical aptitude, that underlie all specific intellectual skills. This classical philosophy, known as the "doctrine of formal discipline," served to justify requiring grammar school students to take Latin and geometry. It was widely thought that students could strengthen their general mental faculties by steeping themselves in these basic disciplines. Educators further presumed that students who had taken Latin and geometry, for example, would improve in most other school subjects. After all, what school subject doesn't involve the application of either linguistic ability or some type of logic?

Of course, most students today are not required to take Latin and geometry (although many high schools still recommend these subjects to their college-bound students). They owe one to the late E. L. Thorndike and his colleagues: Rather than accept what seemed like a reasonable, if timeworn, approach to education, Thorndike and associates conducted a series of empirical studies on the transfer of training from one mental skill to another.

In the true scientific spirit, these investigations consisted of making objective observations under controlled conditions. Thorndike's aim was to find out if human behavior was consistent with the prevailing beliefs about formal education.

In the first of the investigations, Thorndike and Woodworth (1901) set out to see if training in the skill of estimating the areas of rectangles would transfer to the task of estimating the areas of other geometric figures, such as triangles and circles. The basic strategy was as follows:

> *Step 1*, pretest a group of college students on their accuracy in estimating the areas of several different kinds of geometric figures; *step 2*, thoroughly train the students to accurately estimate the areas of rectangles; *step 3*, posttest the students on the area estimation of the figures used in the pretest.

The researchers controlled the length-to-width proportions of the rectangles used in training, the order in which stimuli were presented, and the amount of training that each participant received. They also carefully observed and recorded the amount of error in each estimate given by each participant.

Contrary to conventional wisdom, the data obtained by Thorndike and Woodworth showed that "training the mind" through the estimation of areas of rectangles did not appreciably improve the students' skill in estimating the areas of other geometric figures. However, the training session did improve the students' ability to estimate the areas of a new set of rectangles.

After examining the mismatch between a respected theory of education and the observations of student performance that they had collected, the researchers concluded that there is no such thing as a general mental faculty that can be trained for use in a variety of situations. Rather, training in Task A will aid the performance of Task B only to the extent that the two activities contain "identical elements"—that is, require some of the same specific skills and components of knowledge.

Thorndike was acutely aware of the possibility that his negative findings on the doctrine of formal discipline may have been unique to the particular estimation tasks he and Woodworth used. Perhaps the intellectual functions taught in a Latin course would, in fact, transfer to other school subjects.

To test the relevance of his initial findings to the actual school situation, Thorndike (1924) moved his research team to the classroom. His subjects in this investigation were 8,564 high school students. Using the I.E.R. tests of Selective and Relational Thinking, he pretested the students on general academic intelligence at the beginning of the school year. At the end of the year, he employed the same measure to posttest the students. He then compared the intellectual gains of students who had taken a Latin curriculum that year with gains shown by students who had concentrated their studies in other curricula, such as chemistry or bookkeeping.

Despite expectations based on the prevailing educational theory, the Latin students showed only an average amount of intellectual growth when compared to students who had pursued other disciplines during the same period of time. And what of geometry? Although the intellectual gains of geometry students were somewhat better than average, even those gains were numerically lower than the improvements shown by chemistry and bookkeeping students! What's more, *no particular curriculum seemed to produce much of a difference in general academic ability.* Again Thorndike's conclusion was that training in a specific area will have positive transfer effects on performance of a new skill only to the extent that the training and transfer tasks share identical elements.

Subsequent to these pioneering works in the transfer of training, dozens of other researchers independently examined similar questions in the field of education. Most of those studies yielded results that supported Thorndike's findings and conclusions (cf. Grose & Birney, 1963). As a result of this line of investigation, the classical approach to formal education gradually came to be supplemented by new educational philosophies emphasizing the transfer of specific skills. Such significant changes in public and professional viewpoints and related technologies seem to occur with fair frequency when scientists dare to test long-held beliefs. Thus, similar effects of scientific checks on conventional wisdom are well documented in many other areas, such as mental health (Garfield, 1981; Reisman, 1966), sex differences (Hyde, 1981), industry (Schultz, 1970), and medicine (Glasser, 1976), to name just a few.

Transcending "Everyman's Psychology."   Related to the peculiar status social sciences occupy among academic disciplines is the fact that everybody, regardless of background, has considerable experience with the behavior of people and their institutions. Consequently, almost every individual feels like something of an expert on psychological and social problems, even though similar expertise would not be assumed regarding problems in the physical sciences (Bartz, 1968). The danger in this attitude is that all people, including scientists, construct commonsense theories of psychology. Worse yet, they are apt to feel confident that their private views are mostly valid. Yet many of the lay person's theories are nothing more than individualized versions of cultural stereotypes or personal hunches based on coincidental events in one's life. A major value of the methods of science is that they allow us to temporarily free ourselves from the tyranny of what Sanford (1965) called "everyman's psychology."

One interesting, if unsettling, result of scientific objectivity is that many of our popular beliefs are discredited. You may be surprised to know, for example, that fat people tend to be *less* "jolly" (that is, more irritable) than slim people (Schachter, 1971), that higher pay may not produce higher productivity in employees (Herzberg, 1966), that people often will do more for less pay (Brehm & Cohen, 1962; Yukl, Wexley, & Seymour, 1972), and that having sex frequently during young adulthood is associated with good sexual ability in old age, rather than sexual "burnout" (Pfeiffer, 1975). These examples should make it clear why most graduate schools require their clinical-psychology students to become scientists before they become practitioners.

Science as an Eye-Opener

In addition to providing an objective means of correcting our preconceptions, the scientific method often reveals possibilities that otherwise might go unnoticed. In short, scientific research has a way of continually expanding our mental horizons. This characteristic seems to result from the combination of two pivotal aspects of scientific inquiry: the intense examination of natural events coupled with the constantly evolving, progressively more sophisticated research technologies used by scientists.

A relatively recent "eye-opener" in the field of psychology began in the animal laboratory at Rockefeller University. It was there that Neal Miller launched a systematic empirical attack on a generally accepted distinction between the type of learning studied by B. F. Skinner (operant conditioning) and the type studied by Ivan Pavlov (classical, or respondent, conditioning). Miller (1969) contended that the distinction was unnecessary, and that the underlying processes were the same in both types of learning.

Part of Skinner's rationale for differentiating between respondent and operant conditioning was as follows: While the salivation of Pavlov's dogs was controlled by the reinforcing stimulus (meat powder) that *preceded* it, the pecking response of Skinner's pigeons was controlled by the reinforcing stimulus (grain) that *followed* it. Thus, respondent behaviors were said to be controlled by their antecedents, whereas operant behaviors were said to be controlled by their consequences (Skinner, 1953). Also, respondent behaviors often are glandular or visceral responses—salivation or blood pressure, for example—governed by the autonomic nervous system. In contrast, operants generally fall into the class of motor responses mediated by the "skeletal" nervous system, which is involved in deliberate and precise movements of body parts (cf. Hulse, Egeth, & Deese, 1980).

At the level of everyday conversation, respondents represent involuntary responses of the body to various stimulus conditions, and operants are "voluntary" responses, in the sense that people and animals make selected movements in order to achieve particular consequences. And, since time immemorial, almost everyone has known that organisms can "will" their legs to slow down, but not their hearts. Right?

Miller found little comfort in this common knowledge. Consequently, he planned and conducted several rigorous empirical tests of the hypothesis that visceral respondents cannot be controlled by their consequences. He undertook these tests in spite of his research assistants' conviction "that I was assigning them an impossible problem" (1969, p. 1025). The results of these studies were truly startling and ultimately opened up an unforeseen field of behavioral medicine.

In one of the earliest successful investigations in this area, Miller and DiCara (1967) set out to see if laboratory rats were capable of regulating heart rate when rewarded for doing so. To render their hypothesis falsifiable, they first had to devise a way to subject visceral respondents to an operant-conditioning procedure.

One initial problem was to control the rats' "voluntary" muscles, since bodily movements do affect heart rate. This control was accomplished by injecting the rats with doses of curare that were large enough to temporarily paralyze all of the rats' voluntary muscles. So complete was the paralysis that the subjects had to have their breathing assisted by respirators (that's right, rat-sized respirators!).

Another problem was how to reward paralyzed rats. This was achieved by delivering mild electrical current to a small brain structure called the medial forebrain bundle. Rats seem to find stimulation of this structure rewarding, as they have been known to make thousands of lever-pressing responses per hour in order to get this kind of stimulation (Olds & Milner, 1954).

Miller and DiCara's general procedure went as follows: The curarized rats' heart rates were monitored as the rats lay on a table. To control for specificity of effects, half of the rats were rewarded for increasing their heart rates, and half for decreasing their heart rates. Precise stimulus control was demonstrated by delivering rewards for correct performance only when a "time-in" stimulus was on.

The rats cooperated beautifully by exhibiting heart rate changes averaging 20 percent, in the appropriate directions, across a 90-minute interval. Thus, visceral respondents had been controlled by their consequences. So, in effect, these visceral responses were behaving as operants. What's more, additional experiments of this type showed that rats could rather precisely influence intestinal contractions, kidney functioning, blood pressure, and even blood volume in their ears, when rewarded for it.

While these findings were interesting in their own right, and supportive of Miller's general learning theory, they also suggested new possibilities for behavioral control of certain medical problems. Perhaps for the first time, physicians, medical researchers, and psychologists interested in behavioral medicine began to seriously entertain the idea that well-motivated humans could be trained to exercise control over critical internal functions. Research with human subjects showed that indeed people are capable of learning how to control functions ranging from brain waves and blood pressure to anal sphincter muscles (e.g., DiCara et al., 1974; Schwartz, 1975). The result was that the now rapidly growing field of biofeedback came into being. And while biofeedback technology is still in the experimental stages, its potential for relief of suffering and prolongation of life is nothing short of phenomenal.

Science as an Efficient System

It is fair to say that "science is conspicuous among other human endeavors by its rate of forward progress" (Singer, 1971, p. 1010). In other words, scientific disciplines generate new knowledge faster than unscientific fields. The methods of science were constructed and refined with the express aim of *efficiently identifying relationships among natural events and the conditions that control these relationships.* The tremendous success of these methods is reflected in the huge technological advances Western culture has enjoyed since the scientific revolution of the seventeenth and eighteenth centuries. Prior to that time, human technology had progressed little since the Stone Age. It was this very fact that led Snow (1963) to note that the agricultural and scientific revolutions "are the only qualitative changes in social living that men have ever known" (p. 28).

The scientific revolution has indeed revolutionized our lives. And it seems that people judge both science and scientists in terms of the impact scientific research has on society and the quality of life. But should the worth of a research project be evaluated mainly in terms of its promise of producing technological advances? Let's consider the issues behind this question.

BASIC VERSUS APPLIED RESEARCH

Much of the research you hear about and read about is high in "relevance" and immediate social value. Research having these qualities is referred to as **applied research**. It is often contrasted with **basic research**, which is undertaken for the sake of generating new knowledge—period. But actually, applied research is an intermediate step between basic research and technology. The sequence goes something like this. Basic research, the backbone of science, typically involves years of hit-and-miss groping, order alternating with disorder, and unexpected setbacks mercifully intermingled with occasional insights. The usual question asked by basic researchers is "What if?" Once a problem has been researched heavily by basic scientists, applied scientists set up "how to" studies to determine the best way to use the new evidence for a socially valuable purpose. Thus applied research is much more focused than basic research, and also tends to follow a rigid time schedule not possible in basic research (Thomas, 1981). Once applied researchers have established the social relevance of the new findings, as well as the necessary conditions for their use, technologists enter the picture. Their function is to devise the means for mass production and dissemination of the "product."

Many people, including some government officials (Schaar, 1979), are impatient with basic research. They take a dim view of such activities as tinkering with cell cultures, monitoring the intestinal contractions of rats, and laboratory studies of distraction. Often the feeling is that such research projects are both dull and a type of frivolous self-indulgence that scientists use to justify their existence. This opinion implies that scientists should embark only on research projects that have clear and immediate pertinence to pressing social needs (see Box 1–1). However, these same critics may applaud the appearance of new vaccines, the development of clinically effective biofeedback techniques, and the implementation of new safety measures for automobile drivers—as though these "technological breakthroughs" emerged from a vacuum.

Value of Basic Research

If you find it hard to understand the concept of "research just for the sake of knowing," consider the following points. First, if researchers were restricted to investigating only relevant and socially important matters, most of what we presently label "basic research" simply would not get done. And, as odd as it may seem, the progress of applied research would thereby be severely curtailed. This is because most applied research projects are the offspring of long years of basic research (TRACES, 1969). For example, Salk's testing and final perfecting of poliomyelitis vaccine could not have occurred without Enders's previous research on cell cultures (Thomas, 1981). Likewise, a sophisticated technology

Box 1–1
ISSUES IN SCIENCE
Who Has the Right?

There is a vocal and powerful element in our society that would attempt to decide for scientists what topics are important to research. This element is most clearly represented and championed by U.S. Senator William Proxmire, who chairs the Senate committee that oversees government funding of large research projects. In an attempt to discourage the funding of particular investigations that he deems "wasteful," Proxmire began issuing his infamous "Golden Fleece" awards. In targeting a research project, or the supporting agency, for the "award," he proclaims the project wasteful and/or silly and thus not worthy of the federal government's research monies. When presenting a Golden Fleece award, he typically defends his choice with inflammatory remarks.

One psychologist tagged with Proxmire's award in 1974 was Ronald Hutchinson. Hutchinson's project, which was being funded by three federal agencies, was designed to find out what factors lead to outbursts of aggression. Proxmire sarcastically described the research as an attempt to determine "under what conditions rats, monkeys and humans bite and clench their jaws" (Schaar, 1979, p. 13). Hutchinson later won a libel suit against Proxmire when the U.S. Supreme

Court made a landmark decision in Hutchinson's favor.

In 1975 Proxmire attacked the National Science Foundation's funding of several psychological investigations of "falling in love." He referred to the studies as the federal version of "The Love Machine" (NSF, 1975). Of one of the studies on love, he said, "I'm against it because I don't want the answer" (NSF, 1975, p. 73). Speaking of NSF support of studies in social psychology in general, Proxmire set forth the following warning: "If they continue to have absurd areas of study, there will be more and more questions raised about whether their whole budget couldn't be cut substantially" (*APA Monitor*, May 1975, p. 6).

While Proxmire may come across as a "heavy" in his attack on the freedom of scientific inquiry, it should be understood that his job requires him to be a watchdog for the taxpayer. His attitude also should serve to remind us that the value system of scientists must coexist with conflicting value systems (see Shaffer, 1977). With reference to this point, psychologist Richard Atkinson, former deputy NSF director, once remarked, "I don't think society would provide much support for science if it were just an intellectual activity" (*APA Monitor*, June 1980, p. 5).

built up over decades of basic research on perception made possible the applied work in person-machine relations being conducted by today's human-engineering psychologists (Landy & Trumbo, 1980).

A second point is that it is impossible to predict which of today's research efforts will have social relevance in the distant future. Some young psychologists of the 1930s must have found B. F. Skinner's preoccupation with the behavior of pigeons most curious. Today, however, many of those psychologists' protégés use Skinner's principles of operant conditioning in their daily work with clients. Similarly, when Miller (1969) pioneered the fascinating biofeedback movement, he didn't mean to! He was simply trying to experiment with rats in order to test a theoretical question in the psychology of learning.

In Perspective

Both basic and applied research are necessary components of science: basic research to open up possibilities, and applied research to extend those possibilities and test their limits. Moreover, both kinds of research generally rely on the same set of scientific principles. In fact, the basic/applied distinction is more a function of the researcher's purpose than anything else. And it is not hard to find scientists who like to do both kinds of research.

THE PLAN OF THIS BOOK

I developed the present chapter for the purpose of conveying to you the spirit of the scientific movement as it applies to psychological investigation. My intention was to help you appreciate the relevance of scientific problem-solving to your powerful need to know and understand; also, to help you see the advantages offered by a scientific approach to human behavior and experience. In addition, I hope that some of your initial questions about applying science to psychological topics have been dealt with. Above all, I hope that your curiosity about what lies ahead has been stimulated. I firmly believe that students of any field learn and retain more when they start out with a sense of perspective and purpose.

Just as this chapter represents the spirit of science, Chapter 2 describes the body of science: its special characteristics and terms, its objectives, and its conceptual and methodological tools. Chapter 3, which completes Part 1 of this text, expresses the conscience of science through a consideration of research ethics. Although not a formal part of the logic of scientific inquiry, knowledge of ethical principles and practices is indispensable to responsible research.

To continue the analogy, Part 2 of this book (Chapters 4 through 8) can be likened to the mind of science. These chapters detail the successive phases of the process of any scientific inquiry. They are designed to help you develop a solid understanding of the conceptual foundations of scientific methods. Without such an understanding, the procedures of psychological research, no matter how highfalutin they might be, are almost entirely worthless. Meaningful and useful research begins and ends in your gray matter, not in laboratory technology.

Part 3 (Chapters 9 through 15) represents the behavior of science. These chapters will assist you in transforming the conceptual basis of psychological research into research activities. That is, they will tell you how to use a variety of research and statistical procedures to investigate psychological and social problems.

Finally, Part 4 (Chapter 16) will help you to activate the voice of science. You will learn how to communicate your research to others via the most important and permanent medium available to researchers: the research manuscript.

REVIEW QUESTIONS

1. Briefly describe two problem-solving situations in which you behaved like a scientist. What specific aspects of your problem-solving techniques also characterize scientific inquiry?

2. According to Sir Ronald Fisher, how are the layperson's "experiments" like the scientist's experiments? How are they different?

3. Kahneman and Tversky's research showed that nonscientists tend to ignore critical information that scientists use routinely. What kind of information were they referring to? Give an example.

4. What are three major advantages of the scientific path to knowledge?

5. What is the *major* difference between basic and applied research?

6. Develop arguments both for and against allowing scientists to pursue "impractical" lines of research.

Notes

[1]Scientific parsimony means: Given several explanations of an event that are equally consistent with the evidence, the explanation involving the fewest concepts is preferred.

[2]In contrast, scientific psychology is just over a century old.

AN ANATOMY OF SCIENCE

Now that you have had a chance to think about the "why" of science, let's take a look at the "what" side: the special vocabulary, traits, and concepts of science and how they relate to one another. Perhaps you already have run into some of the ideas covered in this chapter, either in previous courses or through some personal reading. All the better! Now you will have a chance to review these essential ideas and see how they mesh with some new concepts to form a working philosophy of science.

Technical concepts and definitions, as well as a special language, are a necessary part of any discipline. The sciences are no exception. But keep in mind that the language of science is not just so much jargon developed to establish a unique identity. Each technical term and concept serves a significant function. Referring to these technical meanings, Snow (1963) wrote that when "the scientists do cheerfully use words in senses which literary persons don't recognize, the senses are exact ones, and when they talk about 'subjective,' 'objective,' 'philosophy' or 'progressive,' they know what they mean, even though it isn't what one is accustomed to expect" (p. 19).

TRAITS OF SCIENCE: THE PROTECTIVE SHIELD

In Chapter 1, I stated that the objective methods of science were developed to protect us, meaning scientists too, from our biases and erroneous personal beliefs. The characteristics of science that serve to check the distorting influences of personal interpretations include: *empiricism, skepticism, parsimony, publicness, tentativeness,* and the combination of *induction* and *deduction.*

Science Is Empirical (and Quantitative)

Empirical versus Rational. **Empiricism** refers to a reliance on observation rather than theory or purely logical analysis to answer questions. To say that science is empirical is only partly true, in two respects. First, there are **rational sciences**, like mathematics and some branches of philosophy, that answer questions largely through logical analyses and rational arguments. Second, even the empirical sciences make use of theory and logical derivations in interpreting some observations and predicting others. But empirical sciences give priority to observation and data collection[1] over purely theoretical explanations. So when you argue with your friends about which political candidate is the voters' logical choice, you are behaving like a rational scientist. When you survey the candidate preferences of a representative group of voters, you are using the empirical method.

Why does psychology prefer to be an empirical science? Mainly because psychologists must deal with the world of phenomena—real events, real things, behavior, people. Thus, any conception of behavior ultimately needs to be checked against actual behavior. When many independent observations of behavior are consistently out of line with a theory, is it more reasonable to change the theory or to attempt to change the "real world"? So far, the first alternative has proved more effective. For this reason, empiricism is the cornerstone of the scientific method. To state the matter bluntly but realistically, if something cannot be observed, it has no scientific existence. And if a theory is not supported by observations, scientists place little confidence in its truthfulness.

Quantification. Scientists typically convert their observations to numbers, or **quantify** them. (You will learn how to do this when you get to Chapter 5.) So you may read in a research report that the experimental group averaged 80 percent on a memory test, whereas the control group averaged only 65 percent. Or that the average IQ of people in a sample was 112. Or that the obese subjects ate 1.5 times the amount of food consumed by slim subjects.

There are good reasons for quantifying your observations. One is that by converting the observations to numbers, you can summarize your results, using the rules of simple arithmetic. The arithmetic summaries then help you to get a clearer picture of the average (or overall) trend in the data. This simplifies interpretation of the results in almost any study. A second reason for quantification is that it allows you to perform statistical tests on the data to see if your results are likely to represent more than just chance happenings. (See Chapter 8 for further discussion on this point.)

Science Is Skeptical

Scientists are trained to be doubters. This reflects their underlying doctrine of **skepticism**: Because perfect knowledge is impossible and even partial knowledge is elusive, we should doubt the truthfulness of any assertions of knowledge. You may find this doctrine puzzling, if not utterly discouraging. It seems to run counter to the optimistic technology that has been derived from scientific research. But skepticism serves the objectives of science very handily, for it forces the continual gathering and checking of evidence.

What's more, a skeptical attitude helps to protect science, and ultimately all of us, from pat explanations based on popular beliefs and spectacular coincidences. It also discourages deception. A good example of these points is the case of Uri Geller, a "psychic" entertainer who has gained much popular appeal. Geller made believers out of much of the international public by using his "psychic powers" to make crude reproductions of line drawings that had been sealed in envelopes, to make broken watches run, to bend keys and spoons, and to receive ESP messages. Two skeptical New Zealand psychologists, however, found that college-student volunteers could perform the line-drawing and watch-repair feats with the same degree of success as Geller (Asher, 1976). The students said they could literally see many lines in the drawings because they were faintly visible through the envelopes. What about resurrection of dead watches? Jewelers informed the investigating psychologists that almost any warm hand could start some malfunctioning watches by thinning the oil in the watch mechanisms. Further, the psychologists themselves gave convincing demonstrations of "psychic" key bending. Their secret? Sleight-of-hand and brute strength. Geller's ESP ability is still a question—one best approached with a skeptical frame of mind.

Science Is Parsimonious

A fourteenth-century English philosopher named William of Ockham set forth the idea of **parsimony** in scientific theories: Other things being equal, the simplest explanation of a phenomenon is preferred over more complicated accounts. The simplest explanations are those involving the smallest number of concepts.

This rule of thumb for scientists came to be known as "Occam's[2] Razor." A reflection of the skepticism doctrine, the rule is applied almost routinely in most sciences. Its rationale is that the laws of nature are simple; therefore, the simplest explanations are most likely to approximate the way things "really are." In fact, *the chief criterion of scientific understanding is being able to explain a complicated body of data by means of a simple principle.*

Science Is Public

Detecting Research Errors.   Scientists are expected to make their research public and are rewarded for doing so. Typically, researchers communicate their methods, findings, and conclusions to the scientific community by publishing their research in professional journals or presenting papers at professional meetings.

Making your research efforts public is necessary because scientific knowledge is established and continually revised through a process of "consensual validation." This means that your methods, findings, and conclusions are examined carefully by other researchers for flaws and inconsistencies. When inconsistencies between methods, findings, and conclusions are discovered (as frequently happens), a **research error** has been committed (Underwood, 1957). The presence of a research error opens up the possibility that hypotheses other than the one you proposed may account for your results. As Webb et al. (1966) put it, "Backstopping the individual scientist is the critical reaction of his fellow scientists. When he misses a plausible rival hypothesis, he can expect his colleagues to propose alternative interpretations" (p. 9).

Replication.   Often scientists will try to repeat, or **replicate**, a previously conducted study to see if they get the same results as the initial investigator. Successful replication increases confidence in the original research. Failure to replicate suggests that either the initial results were a fluke of chance or some contaminating variable was operating in the original study. When, for complex reasons, the scientific community does not attempt to replicate certain "landmark" studies, the progress of scientific understanding can be affected severely. See Box 2–1 for two classic examples of this point.

Science Is Tentative

Reflecting the skeptical attitude, scientific understanding is tentative and ever-changing. Thus, theories and conclusions constantly are undergoing revision as additional data are accumulated. The replacement of Newtonian physics with relativity theory and quantum mechanics is the classic example of this. In Newton's day, his view of the universe was *the* truth. But *the* truth changed rather quickly with the appearance of new accounts that could explain more.

Similarly, psychologists long considered a small brain structure, the lateral hypothalamus, to be a center for the initiation of hunger and thirst motivation. However, new research began to identify this structure simply as one neurological communication route in a more general motivation system (Stricker, 1976).

Science Combines Induction and Deduction

Logical Methods.   Logical reasoning proceeds in two directions: (*a*) from particular observations to general conclusions and (*b*) from general theories to statements about particular events. If you were to observe the published results of course evaluations at your school, note that most of the psychology teachers get low ratings, and conclude that psychologists make poor teachers, you would be using **inductive logic**—drawing a general conclusion from particular observations. Suppose, on the other hand, you have developed a theory about the relation between characteristics of academic disciplines and the effectiveness of teachers in those disciplines. Further suppose that your theory leads you

Box 2–1
ISSUES IN SCIENCE
Oops! Did We Forget to Replicate?

Failure to attempt replication of scientific studies is most likely to occur when prestigious researchers report findings that are supportive of the prevailing theories and beliefs of the scientific community. Such seems to have been the case in two historically influential research episodes.

In the first episode, J. B. Watson, often referred to as the Father of Behaviorism, reported the successful conditioning of fear in a male infant called Little Albert. Using an experimental technique similar to that employed in Pavlov's work with dogs, Watson apparently was able to condition Albert to show signs of fear in response to a tame rat. (Albert had initially exhibited a liking for the animal.) Watson also claimed that Albert's conditioned fear generalized readily to other furry objects, such as a Santa Claus beard (Watson & Rayner, 1920). The significance of this investigation is that it was eagerly embraced by the field of psychology as the prototypical model of emotional conditioning in human beings. It also became one of the most widely cited investigations in psychological literature, thus playing a major role in the education of generations of psychology students.

The problem is that Watson's demonstration of emotional learning in an infant has never been replicated. Few have tried to duplicate the feat, and those who have tried have been unsuccessful (Samuelson, 1980). The seriousness of the absence of replication in this case is enlarged by the fact that Watson and Rayner's published report contained inconsistencies and contradictions, and, of course, was based on a sample of only one person.

The second research "episode" of interest here spanned more than two decades and involved studies of the heritability of general intelligence. Cyril Burt, a venerated British psychologist, claimed to have administered intelligence tests to several dozen pairs of identical twins. In each case, the members of each twin pair supposedly had been separated from each other early in life and raised by different families in different social-class environments. Burt's unusually "neat" data showed that, in spite of the apparent lack of common environmental experiences, members of the respective twin pairs were remarkably similar to their co-twins in general intelligence. Burt's (1966) conclusion was that about 85 percent of the trait we call intelligence is accounted for by heredity.

A colossal and heated controversy was touched off in 1972 when Arthur Jensen, an American psychologist, published a book that argued in favor of a genetic basis for racial differences in general intelligence. (On standard IQ tests, Asian Americans score higher than Caucasian Americans on the average. The group average for black Americans is lower than that of Caucasians.) Although Burt's twin studies had served as a principal empirical basis for Jensen's contentions, Jensen had not attempted to replicate those studies (Samuelson, 1980).

Here's the rub: In the midst of a stormy debate ignited by Jensen's writings, Burt's data were found to be grossly tainted. Not only were there numerous statistical oddities and "errors" in the twin data, but it also appeared that Burt had fabricated some of his results (Evans, 1976). In fact, Jensen and many other psychologists had proceeded to theorize prolifically about the origins of general intelligence on the strength of findings that had not been checked by the critical replication process. Further, as in the case of Watson's landmark study, thousands of psychology students had been exposed to Burt's findings—under the assumption that the data were valid representations of the facts about intelligence. Again, we are reminded of the serious consequences that can beset a scientific field when replication is overlooked.

to conclude that psychologists are poor teachers, and therefore that Dr. Wilhelm Pavlov's psychology class would not be worth taking. In this case, you would be using **deductive logic**, that is, predicting a specific event from some general ideas that you started out with.

Combining Methods. The ongoing enterprise of science relies on a meshing of the inductive and deductive methods. Figure 2-1 illustrates how the two methods work together. Note that the sequence of events in researching a problem is represented along a time dimension that proceeds from left to right in the figure.

> At Point 1: The researcher starts out by making some initial observations of a behavior that interests him. Suppose he notices that bystanders often fail to help a victim of violence (see Latané & Darley, 1970).
> At Point 2: It seems to him that the larger the number of bystanders, the less likely it is that help will be rendered. At this point he has *inductively* derived an initial hypothesis (a proposed relationship between events) from some particular observations. On the basis of this general hypothesis, he *deductively* predicts that the proposed relationship between number of bystanders and likelihood of a victim's being assisted will hold true in a specific laboratory experiment.
> At Point 3: He tests the prediction by making several observations of helping behavior in a laboratory setting.
> At Point 4: Based on his particular experimental observations, he uses the *inductive* method to draw some general conclusions about bystander intervention. His tentative conclusions lead him to formulate an additional hypothesis—say, that the bystanders want the victim to be helped but do not feel personally responsible for helping when many others are present. This general hypothesis leads *deductively* to further specific tests.
> At Point 5: Tests of the hypothesis are conducted, etc.
> At Point 6: The researcher draws the results of his inductive and deductive methods together into an initial theory about bystander intervention. Most likely, the theory will suggest additional hypotheses and tests, and will be revised and expanded indefinitely as new observations are added to the process.

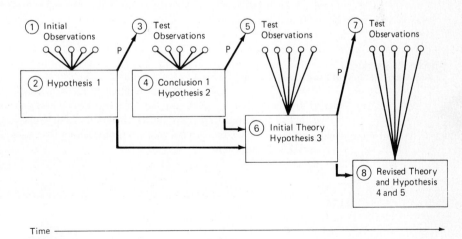

Time ——→

FIGURE 2–1

Science is both inductive and deductive. Note that the circled numbers indicate the temporal sequence in scientific investigation and that the letter P stands for predictions made by the scientist.

ASSUMPTIONS OF SCIENCE

The goals, tools, and procedures of scientists rest on three assumptions about nature, including human nature. These assumptions are **order**, **determinism**, and **finite causation**.

Order

It is assumed that the universe functions according to an inherent order. Thus, natural events are not capricious but, rather, follow a discoverable set of laws. Moreover, these laws tend to be simple and straightforward, in contrast to the complex appearance of natural phenomena. Since human behavior is a part of nature, researchers in the social sciences assume that it too is "governed" by discoverable principles.

Determinism

The basic rule of order in nature is assumed to be determinism: All events have causes; further, if all the causes of an event could be discovered and "set in motion," then the event would occur inevitably. If most natural events occurred spontaneously or as a result of "free will," science's objective of discovering invariant laws would be impossible. For this reason, determinism is the most fundamental assumption of the scientific enterprise. It is the basis of the concept of reliability in measurement (see Chapter 5) and the underlying rationale for requiring public replication of studies. The assumption of determinism also gives rise to the expectation of predictability in human behavior. To reject this assumption is to repudiate the scientific approach.

Science has moved away from the notion of **absolute determinism**, the idea that perfect prediction and control are possible. Because it is not feasible to observe or control all things that determine an event at any one moment, modern scientists advocate a **probabilistic (or relative) determinism**: Given that conditions A, B, and C are set up, behavior X has a known probability of occurring. But X will not occur every time conditions A, B, and C are present.

Finite Causation

Underwood (1957) pointed out that, in addition to assuming that events have causes, scientists must also assume that the number of causes of any event is limited. If every event in nature had an infinite number of causes, than everything would be a function of everything else. And hence, the psychologist's aim of isolating the major determiners of a behavior would be hopeless.

GOALS OF SCIENCE

Scientists attempt to **describe**, **understand**, **predict**, and **control** events in nature. I will discuss these goals within the framework of a classic question in social psychology: How does the presence of other people affect the individual's performance on a task?

Triplett (1897) performed the first experiment in social psychology. He had 40 children of various ages wind in fishing line under two conditions: working alone; winding in the line while standing beside another child who was performing the same task. The results of his experiment showed that the children reeled faster when working together than when they performed the task alone. Accordingly, he concluded that the physical presence of others can free energy that normally is not used. This study stimulated a series of investigations that will serve as a convenient illustration of how scientists pursue the goals listed above.

Description

Scientific description involves the labeling, definition, and classification of natural objects, events, and situations; it also includes a statement of observable relationships among these things. Description is always the first goal of science, but, like most aspects of scientific inquiry, it is constantly subject to revisions and additions.

Triplett labeled performance in the presence of others "competition." Later investigations of similar situations resulted in a definitional distinction between two conditions involving the presence of others (Zajonc, 1965):

1. *Audience Conditions*: Research subjects perform in the presence of passive spectators.
2. *Coaction Conditions*: Research subjects perform in the presence of others who are involved in the same activity.

While Triplett used the label "latent energy" to refer to the internal state presumably caused by the presence of others, the same presumed state later was labeled "arousal." And though Triplett dubbed the relationship between the presence of others and performance "positive stimulation," subsequent researchers referred to the relationship as "social facilitation."

Understanding

From your own experience you know that when you truly understand something, it is fairly easy to summarize it in your own words. This is also true of scientific understanding. Consistent with the doctrine of parsimony, the goal of understanding is achieved to the extent that a large body of apparently complicated observations can be explained by a simple principle or theory. These explanatory principles usually take the form of *tentative* statements of cause-and-effect, subject, as always, to revision in light of new evidence. Understanding is the most important goal of science. Description opens the door to eventual understanding, and prediction and control index the accuracy of our understanding.

Zajonc's (1965) extensive review of research on social facilitation illustrates what is meant by scientific understanding. His review revealed that the two dozen or so studies done on social facilitation were split about evenly on the conclusions they led to; half showed a positive effect of others and half indicated that the presence of others hinders performance. The general results of his review are summarized in Table 2–1. Before reading on, examine the table and see if you can formulate some general idea that would account for the conflicting results.

Zajonc's examination of the large mass of findings on social facilitation led him to make the observation that when people are required to make well-learned responses, the presence of others helps them; but when they are learning a *new* response, they are hindered by the presence of others. He went on to explain that when we are trying to learn

TABLE 2–1

Summary of the Effects of the "Presence of Others"*

Audience Conditions	*Coaction Conditions*
Helped Performance in These Tasks:	*Helped Performance in These Tasks:*
College students following a revolving target.	Rats, dogs, and chickens eating.
National Guard trainees monitoring a signal.	Children winding fishing line.
College students doing simple arithmetic.	Ants excavating earth.
	College students canceling vowels.
	College students making word associations.
Harmed Performance in These Tasks:	*Harmed Performance in These Tasks:*
College students memorizing nonsense syllables.	Cockroaches learning a maze.
College students learning a finger maze.	Finches and parakeets learning visual discriminations.
	College students solving verbal problems.
	Rats learning to avoid shocks.
	College students learning to avoid shocks.

*Based on Zajonc's (1965) review of the research literature on social facilitation.

a new behavior, the "correct" response is relatively weak and is easily dominated by stronger habits. Once a behavior pertinent to a situation is well learned, however, it is a dominant response in that situation and is not readily overpowered by competing behaviors.

At this point, Zajonc introduced the additional concept of "arousal" to label the inferred internal state brought about by the presence of other people. He then proceeded to offer a simplifying principle to explain the body of conflicting data. There were two parts to his principle:

1. The presence of others is motivating, that is, produces heightened arousal.
2. Highly aroused organisms emit dominant responses, which may or may not be pertinent to the task at hand.

If this analysis is correct, you would expect well-learned or simple behaviors, like eating or monitoring a light, to be boosted by the presence of others. However, mastery of tasks involving new learning, such as memorization of nonsense syllables or negotiating a maze, would be impaired by the emergence of competing, dominant responses that are irrelevant to the task. As you can see by reviewing Table 2–1, the research literature is entirely consistent with Zajonc's explanation. His model, then, exemplifies what is meant by the goal of understanding: A large and diverse body of observations is accounted for by a simple cause-and-effect principle.

Prediction

Scientists want to be able to predict events for two reasons. First, accurate prediction can have practical value, as when weather or success in a course of training is forecast. Second, and perhaps more important to basic scientists, prediction affords a test of understanding. That is, when accurate predictions of outcomes can be logically deduced from explanatory principles, the validity of those principles is supported.

Take an example from social facilitation research. Zajonc's explanation of social facilitation effects led him to make the following prediction: If the presence of others is arousing, then certain biochemical changes associated with arousal should also be associated with the presence of others. Zajonc then marshaled some convenient evidence that supported his prediction. He cited several studies in which the blood serum level of hydrocortisone was shown to increase in animals as a function of living with other animals versus living alone. Hydrocortisone, a product of the adrenal glands, is known to be oversecreted under conditions of heightened arousal.

Note that it was perfectly legitimate for Zajonc to derive a "prediction" of existing findings from his theory and then use the "prediction" as support for the theory.[3,4] You should also note, however, that more confidence in a theory is gained when it correctly predicts new outcomes than when it "predicts" known outcomes.

Control

Control of outcomes is a goal of science, but it has different meanings depending on whether the researcher takes a basic-research perspective or an applied/technological outlook.

Control in Basic Research. The main advantage of the laboratory experiment is that it permits the experimenter to exercise strict control over most factors that would influence the results. Specifically, the experimenter wishes to control:

1. the events that take place in the experiment
2. extraneous variables that could contaminate the results
3. the assignment of subjects and groups to experimental treatments
4. the order and timing of the experimental treatments
5. when and how the behaviors of interest will be measured (Weick, 1965)

Control in Applied Research. Applied scientists desire to use well-tested principles for improving the productiveness or quality of life. When technological controls are successfully applied to the environment, the underlying theory also receives support.

Zajonc's analysis of social facilitation suggests application of the following control: Factory workers who perform overlearned, repetitive actions should be allowed to work in the presence of other people rather than in individual rooms or cubicles. However, the design engineers of the same firm should be encouraged to work in privacy.

Does it bother you that the findings of social scientists might be used to control certain areas of your life? Well, you're not alone! The issue of scientific control of human behavior has been debated by psychologists themselves ever since psychology became a science. Take a look at Box 2–2 for a review of the arguments.

TOOLS OF SCIENCE

In their quest for better understanding, scientists use a number of specialized conceptual tools. These tools are what will tie your research activities to the traits and assumptions of the scientific approach. Importantly, they will help you to move freely between the inductive and deductive stages of research.

Box 2-2
ISSUES IN SCIENCE
To Control or Not to Control: That Is the
Question

The controversy surrounding the use of psychological understanding to control human behavior is as old as scientific psychology itself. In fact, Wilhelm Wundt, the German founder of experimental psychology, chastised a few of his own students for their efforts in applied psychology. Wundt felt that psychology's goal should be to understand the "generalized adult mind," and definitely not to dabble in technology and application (Boring, 1950).

In 1956, humanist Carl Rogers and behaviorist B. F. Skinner debated the issues of scientific control of human behavior (Rogers & Skinner, 1956). Their classic exchange clarified the principal considerations in the controversy, which continues today.

Skinner's position was that since people are controlled by environmental factors anyway, why not harness these existing contingencies through scientific understanding. That way, the deliberate application of behavioral principles could be used to steer people in appropriate directions for a better life, including more personal happiness.

Rogers' rebuttal was that any type of behavioral control requires "managers" who would select particular values and behaviors and apply controls in the service of those values and behaviors. And what people or agencies can be trusted to make decisions for the rest of us? Rogers concluded that science ought to be attempting to "free" people by helping them to realize their inherent potentials, not trying to shape and control those potentials.

Where do you stand?

Variables

In doing empirical studies, you always will be dealing with variables and noting their interrelationships. A **variable** is anything that can take on (i.e., change to) different values or qualities. Variables stand in contrast to **constants**, which take on only fixed values. So while the time required for water to boil on your stove is a variable, the temperature at which the water boils is a constant. And while generic sex is a variable (male versus female), the number of ribs in a normal human being is a constant. Other examples of variables are height, weight, length, width, environmental stress, ego strength, social class, fear of success, frustration, aggression, deprivation, etc. In short, almost anything can be a variable, because most things and processes in nature express themselves at various levels or in different qualitative states.

Quantitative variables, like length or Intelligence Quotient, theoretically vary by degree along a number scale and often can take on an indefinite number of values. But we think of **qualitative variables**, like sex or presence versus absence of a disability, as varying in an either-or fashion—that is, in *kind* rather than in degree. For example, suppose you investigate the effects of three different kinds of psychotherapy on the scores that patients make on a standard test of "psychological adjustment." In this case, the three *kinds* of psychotherapy would be a qualitative variable, and the scores on the test of psychological adjustment, which vary by degree on a single dimension, would represent a quantitative variable.

For purposes of experimental control, researchers often force a variable into a constant value so that the "pure" effects of other variables can be studied. It is not unusual, for instance, to hold intelligence constant in order to investigate the relative effectiveness of different methods of teaching concepts to children.

Most research projects focus on the relationship between two types of variables: independent and dependent.

Independent Variables.   Variables that are thought to influence, determine, or cause changes in other variables are called **independent variables**. When you conduct an experiment, the conditions that you systematically manipulate are the independent variable. You expect this manipulation of conditions to bring about some change in the subjects' behavior. To refer to a previous example, the deliberate use of three different kinds of psychotherapy in an experiment represents manipulation of an independent variable. It is important to note that *each type of therapy is only one value of the independent variable*. The three therapies together make up the single independent variable. In general, *you must use at least two values or kinds of something to call it a variable*.

There are two classes of independent variables in the field of psychology:

1. **Environmental independent variables** are conditions that are external to the persons serving as subjects in a study. These conditions include variations in the physical or social setting of the study, the stimuli or instructions that are presented to the subjects, and the task dimensions employed (i.e., type or difficulty of task). Since these conditions are external to the subjects, often they can be *directly* manipulated or controlled by the researcher. This makes the effects of environmental variables relatively easy to interpret. That is, if you hold all other variables constant while systematically changing only variable X, and if your subjects subsequently sprout thick hair on their tongues, you can be fairly certain about what effect variable X has!

2. **Organismic independent variables** are traits or characteristics of subjects (i.e., organisms) that you cannot alter during the course of your study: characteristics such as intelligence, sex, age, social class, having been a Boy Scout, religion, etc. It is not feasible to manipulate organismic variables; you can only "exploit" their present existence. For example, you wouldn't be able to randomly assign college students to male-versus-female conditions for the purpose of studying the effect of sex on concept-learning ability. But you could randomly sample 100 males and 100 females from a college-student population and compare the groups on concept learning. Likewise, you cannot manipulate a person's age or intelligence for experimental purposes the way you could manipulate the kind of stimuli or tasks you expose that person to. But you could select people from existing age or intelligence groups and compare their behavior.

Although between-group comparisons allow you to investigate the "effects" of sex or age or having been a Boy Scout, interpreting the effects of organismic variables is generally very hard to do. The interpretation problems arise from the fact that each variable of this type is "contaminated" by a cluster of uncontrolled variables. And any one or any combination of these contaminating factors may be responsible for your results.

Consider this example. In general, teenage males score higher on standardized math tests than teenage females (Westoff, 1979). Thus the "effect" of the sex variable is very clear in this case. But what does such an effect mean? Is it the result of genetic combinations, hormonal differences, social expectations, upbringing . . . ? Do the results clearly suggest any specific explanatory principle? Similar interpretive problems attend the investigation of any organismic variable. (For thorough discussions of these problems, see Baron & Treiman, 1980; Underwood, 1957.)

Dependent Variables.   The specific behavior of subjects that you observe or measure is called the **dependent variable**, because you think it depends on the independent variable in your study. Thus if you carry out a well-controlled experiment and you record significant changes in your subjects' behavior following manipulation of the independent variable, you logically conclude that the independent variable produced the behavior change. In other words, you conclude that changes in the independent variable caused the changes in the dependent variable.[5]

Let's return to the example of an experimental investigation of the effects of three kinds of psychotherapy on psychological adjustment. The variable that you manipulate, type of therapy, is the independent variable. The variable that you record, scores on a test of psychological adjustment, is the dependent variable. You expect the adjustment scores to depend on type of therapy.

Operational Definitions

Psychology is an empirical science. Consequently, the variables studied by psychologists must be defined, at some point, in terms of observables. An **operational definition** specifies the operations used in observing and measuring a variable. By formulating an operational definition, you translate a verbal or conceptual definition into observables. This makes it possible for you to use the empirical methods of science to investigate the variable.

"A feeling of dejection and hopelessness" is a conceptual definition of depression. "Scores on the Depression Scale of the Minnesota Multiphasic Personality Inventory" is an operational definition of depression. It specifies how the factor of depression will be measured. Of course, a complete operational definition of depression would also specify how the Depression Scale of the MMPI was constructed and validated, and how it is administered and scored. Fortunately, however, many measurement operations in psychology have become so standard that a simple reference to their label often suffices as an operational definition. The amount of detail required for your definitions will depend on how familiar other researchers are with the kind of measurement operations you use. The best way for you to test the adequacy of your operational definitions is to have another researcher read them and then tell you exactly what you did to measure your research concept.

You should avoid falling into the trap of **narrow operationism**: the idea that a particular set of observation procedures is *the* definition of a variable. To the contrary, many variables studied by psychologists may be defined by several different sets of measurement techniques, all (ideally) converging on the same conceptual definition. For instance, "memory" may be defined by a free-recall test, a cued-recall test, a reproduction test, a recognition test, or a reaction-time test. Having several independent measures of the same variable is desirable, because multiple measures enhance the concept's generalizability. The principal requirement is that any measurement operations you select be logically related to the concept you are investigating.

Purposes of Operational Definitions.   Underwood (1957) listed three functions served by operational definitions:

1. They force scientists to clarify concepts and tighten up research designs.
2. They promote parsimony in science, because operational definitions of a new concept must differ from operational definitions of existing concepts.
3. They facilitate communication among scientists.

To these I would add a fourth function:

    4. They make possible the essential process of replication.

Above all, remember that if your variables cannot be specified in terms of observable events, they have no link to the real world and, hence, are outside the realm of science.

Further Examples.   Intelligence may be operationally defined as your score on the Wechsler Adult Intelligence Scale. Hunger may be operationally defined as the number of hours that you have been deprived of food. Now, can you think of at least three operational definitions of romantic love? (Think "observables.")

Constructs

Paradoxically, although scientists must work with observables, their chief interest lies in unobservable (hypothetical) characteristics of people and things. The clinical researcher who analyzes relations between loss of appetite, sleeplessness, and scores on a personality scale isn't interested primarily in these tangibles, but rather in a hypothetical state of mind called depression. Similarly, the researcher who spends hours scoring free-recall tests isn't obsessed with discrete words or with counting but is more likely to be charting a very interesting (but unobservable) process called "short-term store."

These inferred characteristics that form the conceptual content of theories are called **hypothetical constructs**, or simply **constructs**. In psychology they represent educated guesses about what must be going on inside people or animals. Other examples of constructs include anxiety, ego, cognitive dissonance, learning, arousal, and attention. In fact, almost all variables studied by psychologists are classified as constructs. This is true of other scientific disciplines as well. Prior to the advent of the electron microscope, for example, both the gene and the atom were hypothetical constructs.

Why do scientists bother with these abstract inferences? Because they make scientific research interesting, help scientists to logically tie together diverse observations, and lead to the formulation of new hypotheses and empirical tests. But I emphasize that *the only useful constructs are those that can be linked to observables* either directly or indirectly. Some constructs, like Hull's (1943) concept of Drive, are tightly anchored by the measurement of both independent and dependent variables. Constructs that are operationally defined on both the "cause" and "effect" sides of relationships are known as **intervening variables**. For Hull, Drive was the inferred psychological state that intervened between hours of deprivation and a rat's running speed in a straight alley.

Relationships and Hypotheses

One of your primary tasks as a researcher is to discover reliable relationships among variables (Argyris, 1980; Walizer & Weiner, 1978). A **relationship** is simply an association between two variables, such that a change in the value of one variable is at least partially predictable from a change in the other variable. The inverse association between supply and demand is a **negative relationship**: As supply goes up, demand tends to go down, and vice versa. The association between social class and annual income is a **positive relationship**: High levels of income go with the higher social strata, and low incomes are associated with the lower classes. If you knew that a person had moved from a lower to a middle social stratum, you could predict with confidence (but not certainty) that his income also had moved up.

Almost all of the relationships investigated by social scientists are imperfect. That is, the variables involved *tend* to vary together in a predictable way; but the value of one variable can be predicted from the value of the other only part of the time—and then only approximately. In Chapter 6 you will learn how to extract relationships from observations and how to represent them empirically; in Chapter 7 you will encounter the task of interpreting relationships.

Hypotheses are proposed relationships. For instance, on the basis of his interpretation of social facilitation research, Zajonc proposed that students would do better on classroom exams if they studied alone and were tested publicly. Normally such propositions are subjected to an empirical test, and the relationship is either supported or disconfirmed. Although many hypotheses imply cause-and-effect relationships, others merely postulate an association, leaving open the question of causality.

Principles and Laws

Principles are simple statements that summarize a body of evidence. Typically a principle will incorporate or "explain" several relationships in terms of a higher-level relationship. Thus Zajonc summarized a mountain of social facilitation data by combining the concepts of arousal and response competition into a succinct explanation.

Scientific laws are principles that are widely accepted in the scientific community. The main thing that advances a principle to the status of a law is an informal consensus of opinion among scientists as to the generalizability of the principle. Ebbinghaus' "forgetting curve" is an example of a law in the field of psychology. It shows that the rate of forgetting newly learned material decreases as a function of time.

Theories and Models

Scientists use theories and models to represent the natural world and thereby guide the planning of studies to investigate natural phenomena. A **theory** is an internally consistent network of assumptions, constructs (i.e., variables), operational definitions, relationships, and principles. A theory helps you to organize and interrelate principles and findings; summarize and explain natural events; develop new hypotheses and predictions—that is, generate new research. Common examples of psychological theories are Festinger's theory of cognitive dissonance, Maslow's hierarchical theory of motivation, Rogers' theory of client-centered counseling, and Tolman's theory of learning.

Models are abstract conceptual frameworks (worldviews) that help to stimulate and guide theory development. Models are broader than theories, and one model usually spawns a number of theories (see Box 2–3). For example, the "organismic model" of development (Reese & Overton, 1970) is the basis of theories put together by Piaget, Erikson, Maslow, and many others. Models differ from theories not only in level of abstractness but also in the sense that models have no relation to the world of real events. Scientific theories, however, must make contact with the real world. And they do so through their operational definitions.

Theories are evaluated in terms of their accuracy in explaining and predicting natural phenomena. But the most important criterion for evaluating a theory is its "fruitfulness," or how much research it generates. Even an inaccurate theory can be a useful one if it stimulates considerable research (Hall & Lindzey, 1970).

Box 2–3
HIGHLIGHT
The Nature of Scientific Models

Two general models that give rise to several psychological theories are characterized below. Note that models are "worldviews," or general ways of thinking about nature—in this case, human nature. Although abstract, they are useful analogies that aid the process of theory development. Each model described here possesses a characteristic philosophy and associated assumptions about how the universe of phenomena works. Each also leads logically to particular implications about human nature that often are concretized in the form of psychological theories.

Mechanistic Model[6]	*Organismic Model*
Analogy: Machine. Movement by any part completely determined by antecedent movements of other parts.	*Analogy*: Organism. Change and movement produced autonomously, as a result of organism's active commerce with the environment. Organism constantly develops toward higher levels of functioning.

Mechanistic Model	*Organismic Model*
Philosophy: Newtonian. Deterministic. Reductionist. Universe consists of "pieces" and events that combine additively to produce current states of existence.	*Philosophy*: Leibnizian. Teleological. Holistic. Universe consists of spontaneously active and developing wholes.
Implications: In principle, person's behavior is completely determined and predictable. Present behaviors are explainable on the basis of past events. People are basically reactive; behavior is determined by forces outside the individual's control.	*Implications*: Strict prediction of person's behavior is precluded by spontaneity of behavior and nonadditive development; new stages of development are qualitatively different from preceding stages. People are basically active entities that are autonomously propelled.
Theories: Skinner's operant conditioning, social learning theories, conditioned-reflex theories.	*Theories*: Stage and humanistic theories, such as Piaget's, Maslow's, Rogers's and Erikson's.

Populations and Samples

When a scientist conducts an investigation, she usually is not interested primarily in the characteristics of the particular people, settings, time frames, and stimuli she actually observes. Rather, she will want to *generalize* her results to a much broader spectrum of people and situations. This total set of people and situations that the scientist is interested in understanding is called a **population**. Some examples are all college students, all Americans, all people over the age of seventy, all members of the American Psychological Association, and so on. But since it is normally infeasible to observe an entire population, scientists most often must settle for observing a subset of a population, called a **sample**, and hope that the sample fairly represents the population of interest. As you'll see later, the samples that best represent, and hence generalize to, the chosen populations are those that are randomly selected from those populations.

SUMMARY

Science has its own system of assumptions, philosophical traits, and technical terms and concepts; these elements of scientific inquiry are designed to increase objectivity and facilitate efficient discovery of invariant relationships in nature.

The *traits* of science include: empiricism, skepticism, parsimony, publicness, tentativeness, and a combination of inductive and deductive reasoning.

Scientific inquiry rests on the *assumptions* of order, determinism, and finite causation.

The *goals* of scientific inquiry include: description, understanding, prediction, and control of natural phenomena.

Scientists use several specialized conceptual *tools* to transform their assumptions, goals, and philosophical traits into research activities. The most important tools are independent and dependent variables, operational definitions, constructs, relationships, hypotheses, principles, laws, theories and models, and populations and samples.

REVIEW QUESTIONS

1. What is the advantage of psychology's being an empirical science?

2. In what sense is the doctrine of skepticism a philosophical basis for the scientific traits of empiricism, parsimony, publicness, and tentativeness?

3. Make up an example of inductive reasoning. Of deductive reasoning.

4. Define the three major assumptions of science.

5. How do the goals of description, prediction, and control serve the ultimate goal of understanding?

6. Give three examples of quantitative and qualitative variables.

7. Briefly describe a scientific study you would like to do. Identify the independent and dependent variables, and give the reasoning for your classification of variables.

8. What are hypothetical constructs? Why are they of interest to scientists?

9. Devise an operational definition of "a good attitude in the classroom."

10. Distinguish between relationships and hypotheses; principles and laws; theories and models.

11. What are the principal functions of a scientific theory?

12. In what way can an inaccurate theory be a "good" theory?

Notes

[1] The term "data" (singular, da*tum*) often is used interchangeably with "observations," but sometimes it refers to the scientist's final compilation of all observations in a study or to the numbers that represent that compilation.

[2] "Occam" is a common version of Ockham. Metaphorically, the rule serves as a razor in cutting out theoretical excesses.

[3] Einstein's General Theory of Relativity gained additional respect when it logically "predicted" that the planet Mercury's rotation should have 43 seconds more arc than could be accounted for by the gravitational effect of other planets. The existence of the excessive amount of arc had been known for hundreds of years prior to its being "predicted" by Einstein's theory (Coleman, 1958).

[4] Unless the existing evidence predicted by the theory was also the data base from which the theory was developed originally—which would be "circular" reasoning.

[5] Even in poorly controlled studies that do not permit cause-and-effect conclusions, the terms independent and dependent variables often are used. In many of these investigations two variables have been measured and found to be related to one another—for example, high school grades and college grades. The behavior known to have occurred first (i.e., high school grades) is called the independent variable, because causality is assumed to work forward in time. In investigations where time precedence cannot be established, theoretical considerations may be used to designate one factor as the independent variable.

[6] These comparisons are based in part on Reese and Overton (1970).

3

ETHICS IN PSYCHOLOGICAL RESEARCH

Can you vividly remember an instance in which you paid a hefty price for a defective piece of merchandise and then found that you could get neither an adequate exchange nor a refund on the item? What feelings did you experience? Did you feel "taken," deceived, frustrated, angry, hurt? Did your self-esteem suffer, perhaps just a little, because you were naive enough to be sold a "lemon," and because you felt unable to recoup your loss?

Now use your imagination to place yourself in each of the following scenarios, both of which are based on true incidents:

SCENARIO 1: You sign up for participation as a subject in a perception experiment. Arriving at the appointed time and place, you are met not by the experimenter but by two other subjects whose appointments were scheduled to occur before yours. About ten minutes later the experimenter arrives and, without greeting or explanation, marches past all three of you and enters the laboratory. A few minutes later, the experimenter pokes her head out and snaps, "Higgins." The first-scheduled subject dutifully scampers through the lab entrance to begin his participation. Since you have a second engagement in 45 minutes, you grow restless and wonder whether this commitment was a wise decision. Forty minutes pass, two more subjects have arrived, and at last you are summoned into the lab. While examining a data sheet, the steely-voiced experimenter rattles off the instructions to you in a disinterested monotone: You are simply to report all letters and words that appear on the screen in front of you. The task begins and, to your embarrassment, your performance is *lousy*. The stimuli simply come and go too quickly. After 20 minutes, the experimenter abruptly tells you that you may go. You ask if she would explain the purpose of the study and how you did at the task, but she replies that there simply isn't time for that. In fact, she practically runs over you as she rushes to the door to call the next name on her list. Later, while walking across campus, more than half an hour late for your engagement, you take a solemn vow never again to volunteer for research.

SCENARIO 2: You read an ad in a local newspaper in which a prominent psychologist, Dr. Laser, offers to pay $10 to anyone who will participate in a study on learning. This seems like easy money to you as well as an opportunity to learn something new about the psychology of learning, so you decide to sign up. A few days later, you arrive at Dr. Laser's laboratory on the campus of the prestigious Metropolitan University. After signing a research contract, you are told that the experiment concerns the effect of electrical shock on the memorization of simple verbal associations. Your job is to play the role of "teacher" and administer shocks to another subject—a friendly, middle-aged man—whenever he makes mistakes during the learning task. To your dismay, in order to honor your agreement with Dr. Laser, you end up shocking the poor man several times during the study. When it's all over, and you're wiping the perspiration from your brow, Dr. Laser informs you that the study wasn't really about learning at all, but concerned obedience to authority—his authority, in this case. You also learn that the other subject wasn't actually shocked; his screams were a ruse. Still, you are shaken by the fact that you willingly inflicted what you thought to be pain on another human being. For several weeks thereafter, you find it hard to sleep.

What do these two unhappy research episodes have in common with the example of a "bad deal" purchase that opened this chapter? They share a character of wrongful manipulation and exploitation, unfairness, and violation of personal rights. And their damaging impact goes beyond material loss and penetrates the victim's self-concept and self-esteem, producing long-lasting emotional aftereffects.

Why do we immediately view such experience as fundamentally "wrong," "bad," and "harmful"? The answer lies in the assumptions that human beings carry with them when they enter into relationships with other people. In many ways, our dealings with others, whether they be primarily commercial or primarily social, involve an implicit social contract (Schuler, 1982; Thibaut & Kelly, 1959). The "contract" is based on the assumption that there will be a fair exchange of costs and benefits between the parties in the relationship. In exchange for giving time, services, or material items, each person expects to receive something of approximately equal value. Also, she expects that she won't be required to give up more than is expressly agreed upon or implicitly understood, either now or later. The ethical norm governing this universal "contract" has been referred to by various names, such as the "norm of social obligation" and the "golden rule" ("Do unto others . . .").

When this basic norm is violated, five consequences can be expected: (a) The "loser" in the transaction will incur undesirable and inequitable costs relative to her "benefits"; these costs include both tangible and intangible, psychological ones. (b) The "loser," as well as some other people who are aware of the injustice, will be angry, perhaps outraged. (c) The "loser" will experience increased mistrust in human relationships in general. (d) The "loser" will come to greatly distrust the particular kind of contract or relationship that led to feelings of having been exploited. (e) The "loser" will be very reluctant to enter into other relationships of that particular type. Obviously, widespread violation of the "norm of social obligation" would lead to chaotic social conditions.

Since psychological research with human subjects always involves either an implicit or an explicit social contract between the researcher and the subject, the ethical norm of social obligation applies fully to that research. As members of the human community, psychologists have an obligation to honor and safeguard the rights of other human beings, including those who happen to serve as subjects in their investigations. As members of a profession that has pledged itself to ". . . respect the dignity and worth of the individual and strive for the preservation and protection of fundamental human rights" (*American Psychologist*, 1981), psychologists have an extraordinary obligation to ensure that their research participants are treated ethically. The primary motivation for psychology's intense concern with research ethics is the sense of moral responsibility that is part of the field's human-service orientation. But there are practical reasons as well. In the words of Baumrind (1971), "By misusing the trust that society has traditionally accorded the researcher, he invites society to withdraw its support" (p. 896). By this Baumrind means that if we treat our research participants unethically, we will lose society's goodwill and monetary support. Further, we will soon be unable to find people willing to participate in our investigations.

Since you are both a researcher and a potential "subject," it is extremely important for you to be sensitive to the significance and complexity of ethical issues and procedures in psychological research. In this chapter, you'll learn about these matters and how psychologists have dealt with them. I hope that you will apply what you learn.

THE ORIGIN OF ETHICAL CONCERNS IN RESEARCH WITH HUMAN PARTICIPANTS

The Cost/Benefit Orthodoxy: Please Don't Tip the Scale!

Ethical problems arise in research with human subjects because such research represents fertile soil for the emergence of value conflicts. A few of the basic value conflicts include:

1. protection of individual rights versus freedom of scientific inquiry
2. protection of individual rights versus the scientist's professional obligation to seek new information

3. protection of individual rights versus society's need for scientific and technological advances
4. the scientist's right to advance in her career versus society's norms of humane treatment, personal freedom, and protection of privacy

Why do there have to be value conflicts in psychological research? Some have argued that there need not be. Baumrind (1971), for example, has emphatically stated that if a research design potentially threatens the subject's rights or well-being, it should be abandoned in favor of a new design that is ethically acceptable. Others have suggested that ethical problems can be avoided by asking people to play the roles of research subjects instead of actually undergoing research procedures that may infringe on their rights (e.g., Forward, Canter, & Kirsch, 1976). Neither of these proposed solutions to ethical dilemmas has yet been embraced by a majority of research psychologists. The reason is that, for some research questions, valid data can be obtained only through the manipulation of powerful independent variables (e.g., fear stimuli), the observation of "sensitive" phenomena (e.g., cheating, embarrassment), and the use of deception. Furthermore, some types of program-evaluation research require that potentially beneficial treatments be withheld from "control" groups (cf. APA, 1982). So long as the interests of society and the scientific community require the occasional use of research procedures that may infringe on subjects' rights, value clashes and ethical dilemmas will exist in psychological research.

The question is, how are those ethical dilemmas to be handled? Clearly, neither society nor the scientific community would be well served by granting psychologists a "blank check" on the treatment of subjects. Since 1973, the American Psychological Association has followed an ethical philosophy that might be called the **Cost/Benefit Orthodoxy**. The basic idea behind this philosophy is that the researcher has serious, ongoing obligations to his profession, to the pursuit of truth, and to society on the one hand, and equally important obligations to his subjects on the other hand. Thus the guiding principle in the researcher's ethical evaluation of his work is to carefully balance the obligations on one side against those on the other side.

In theory, this is how the Cost/Benefit Orthodoxy is supposed to work: When planning an investigation, you should consider all of the potential costs and benefits that are likely to accrue to both the subject and society as a result of the investigation. (From this point on, the term "society" will be used to refer to all of the "supraindividual" interests for which the researcher is responsible—e.g., truth, her profession, and society in general.) Potential *benefits* to the subject include material rewards (if he is paid), course credit or fulfillment of a course requirement, increased knowledge or understanding of psychology, himself, or the scientific method, and satisfaction derived from contributing to science. Some potential *costs* to the subject include his time and effort, relinquishing some personal freedom and self-determination, psychological or physical distress, and being subjected to deception or invasion of privacy. On the other side, society may benefit from the furthering of its interests in scientific knowledge, increased understanding of human nature, practical or technological spinoffs from the research, and the continued employment of its scientists (!). Society may incur costs from a scientific procedure when that procedure severely violates its ethical norms, wastes the taxpayer's money, or leads to the development of a harmful or destructive technology. Presumably, each potential cost and benefit to the subject and society has a "weight" that varies from one investigation to another. Thus, each investigation you conduct should be individually evaluated in terms of its ethical acceptability.

Although the Cost/Benefit Orthodoxy is the dominant ethical philosophy within the field today, many social scientists don't think that the philosophy is adequate. See Box 3–1 for alternative viewpoints.

A Study That Unleashed the Furies

Ethical concerns have repeatedly arisen and been debated by psychologists for decades. Indeed, as early as 1952, the American Psychological Association (APA) saw a need to assemble a committee to formally review ethical problems in the field and make official recommendations regarding ethical standards. Since then, the amount of attention afforded ethical questions and violations within the profession has steadily grown.

In 1966, the APA deployed a special committee which was to focus specifically on ethical issues and practices in research—the Ad Hoc Committee on Ethical Standards in Psychological Research. A review of the APA's major professional journal, the *American Psychologist*, through the early and middle 1960s suggests that one series of studies, in particular, was very influential in stimulating the formation of the research-ethics committee. In any case, the initial investigation in the series certainly caused considerable, and

---

Box 3–1
ISSUES IN SCIENCE
Is Striking a Balance Enough?

The prevailing ethical doctrine in the behavioral sciences is based on the idea that some potentially unfair or harmful treatments may be administered to subjects as long as the scientific or social benefits of the research balance the subjects' personal "losses." But several social scientists have carefully analyzed this doctrine and found it to be unjust to subjects.

Schuler (1982) has suggested that the Cost/Benefit Orthodoxy in the social sciences may be inherently biased against subjects. He notes that usually there is a great power and status differential between the subject and the researcher: The subject has been excluded from the planning of the study and, not knowing the full meaning of the research situation, must effectively surrender control and regulation to the researcher. This arrangement is patently unbalanced against the subject's interests because "the experimenter calculates the possible profit or loss before beginning a series of experiments and will carry them out only if the balance is positive for the experimenter. The subject, on the other hand, has to be satisfied with very uncertain expectations" (p. 50). It is for this very reason that

Kelman (1968) has advocated the practice of having the subjects of an investigation participate in the planning of the investigation. He also has urged that, instead of using deceptive manipulations, researchers fully inform their subjects of the nature and meaning of the research procedures and then have them role-play how they think uninformed subjects would respond to the experimental conditions.

Baumrind (1971) has also taken a stern position of opposition to the Cost/Benefit Orthodoxy:

The risk/benefit approach that the [APA Committee on Ethical Standards in Psychological Research] has adopted may have the effect of justifying [violations of the rights of the subject] by offering to the investigator appealing rationalizations for risking the subject's welfare based upon the anticipated "benefits" to society of the proposed research. (p. 887)

Like Kelman, Baumrind advocates employing subjects in an informed, collaborative role.

sometimes heated, debate among psychologists. I'm referring to the now classic study of "obedience to authority" conducted by Stanley Milgram (1963; also, see Milgram, 1974, for a review of the complete series of investigations). Since Milgram's original study highlights some critical ethical concerns, I'll review it in some detail. In later sections of the chapter, I'll refer to this investigation in connection with particular ethical principles or issues.

Milgram's motive for conducting his controversial studies of obedience was a socially valuable one. He wanted to find out if mindless and destructive obedience to authority figures—such as that shown by Nazi guards in World War II concentration camps—is something that the *average person* is capable of. He was interested not only in the percentage of his sample that might blindly obey an authority figure's command to harm another person, but also in finding out what conditions produce such extreme obedience and what variables might reduce the tendency to obey. Clearly, this type of information could be both scientifically and socially useful.

Milgram (1963) recruited a wide range of adult male subjects for his obedience experiment by running an ad in a New Haven, Connecticut, newspaper offering $4.50 per hour to anyone who would participate in a "study of memory." Upon their arrival at a laboratory at Yale University, subjects were greeted by *Dr.* Milgram, who was wearing a white lab coat and looking quite authoritative.

Milgram told each subject that the experiment concerned the effects of punishment on learning. Subjects served in pairs, one member assuming the role of "teacher" and the other the role of "learner." The learner's task was to memorize a lengthy list of word pairs, that is, to be able to give the correct verbal response to each stimulus word that was presented. The teacher's job was to present the stimulus words, record the learner's response, and *"punish"* the learner for each incorrect response by administering an electric shock. The learner, Mr. Wallace, who was actually Milgram's *confederate*, was led into a cubicle and ceremoniously strapped into a chair. As the teacher (the *real subject*) watched, shock electrodes were attached to Mr. Wallace's wrist. Then the cubicle door was closed, and the learner was out of the teacher's view for the remainder of the experiment.

The apparatus that supposedly would transmit the shocks to the learner had an ominous appearance. It had 30 toggle switches, all labeled with different shock intensities ranging from 15 to 450 volts, in 15-volt steps. There were descriptive labels below each switch ranging from "Slight Shock" to "Danger: Severe Shock" and, finally, "XXX." Milgram instructed the teacher to administer the lowest-intensity shock following the learner's first error and to increase the intensity by 15 volts for each succeeding error. Although *no shock was actually delivered to the learner in this experiment*, the real subjects (the teachers) believed that they were, in fact, shocking another human being.

Once the "learning trials" were under way, the learner began making a number of errors. Most of the teachers dutifully administered the shocks in graded steps, as instructed. At 120 volts the learner began to complain that the shocks were too painful. As more errors were made and the shock intensities climbed further, the learner first demanded to be set free, then yelled out that he would give no more answers (omissions were treated as errors!), and after 300 volts, began to scream in anguish. After 330 volts was reached, the teacher heard nothing but an ominous silence from the cubicle, perhaps thinking that the learner had fainted or died.

During the course of the learning trials, the typical subject would pause and, showing signs of distress, ask Milgram whether he should go on. In response, Milgram would stand next to the subject and insist that the experiment be continued, with such statements as "Please continue," "The experiment requires that you continue," "It's absolutely essential that you continue," and "You have no other choice, you *must* go on"

(p. 374). In most cases, the real subject was visibly disturbed and anxious, but Milgram was unflinching in his demands.

The surprising result of this investigation was that 65 percent of Milgram's subjects obeyed the experimenter all the way to 450 volts. This result was surprising in several respects. First, Milgram's subjects were not pathological sadists. They were normal, everyday people—people such as those you and I regularly work and associate with. Second, at the insistence of an authority figure, the subjects persisted in their macabre task, despite the anguished pleading and screaming of their victim. Third, when the study was described to a panel of 40 psychiatrists, they predicted that only about 2 percent of the subjects would obey through the highest shock intensities.

Milgram's findings are more than surprising. They're a valuable addition to our understanding of factors that contribute to destructive and deadly acts of obedience. But his method of obtaining the information raises a number of ethical issues which we shall consider throughout the remainder of this chapter.

PSYCHOLOGY'S RESPONSE TO ETHICAL DILEMMAS

The Development of an Ethical Code

In response to various ethical concerns that had accumulated through the years, the APA's Ad Hoc Committee on Ethical Standards in Psychological Research prepared an ethical code for psychological researchers. These carefully developed standards were based on a distillation of input from several thousand APA members regarding ethical issues and dilemmas in behavioral research. The resulting 104-page document, first published in 1973, was titled *Ethical Principles in the Conduct of Research with Human Participants*. The manual set forth and discussed 10 cardinal principles to assist psychologists in their evaluations of proposed research procedures as well as in their professional conduct toward human subjects.

Since 1973, *Ethical Principles* has been the official ethics guide for psychological researchers who employ human subjects. More than that, the document serves as a reference for special APA committees charged with investigating possible ethical violations in research with human participants.

In 1978, the APA's Board of Scientific Affairs set up a Committee for the Protection of Human Subjects in Psychological Research. This body was assigned the task of recommending revisions in *Ethical Principles* following the first five years of the document's existence. As a result of that committee's work, the second edition of *Ethical Principles* was published in 1982. It differs little in substance from its predecessor, which apparently was a very complete and adequate document.

Now let's take a look at the 10 guidelines that make up the core of *Ethical Principles* and consider how you might implement them in your research.

The Researcher's Ten Commandments

The principles reprinted below summarize the fundamentals of ethical research practices. Study them well, and keep them in mind as you plan your investigations. I will discuss the practical implications of these principles in the remaining sections of this chapter. If you're serious about a career in psychology, however, I heartily recommend that you purchase a copy of *Ethical Principles* and study it in its entirety. For information on the current price of the manual and shipping charges, write to the American Psychological Association, Inc., 1200 Seventeenth Street, N.W., Washington, D.C. 20036.

Research with Human Participants[1]

The decision to undertake research rests upon a considered judgment by the individual psychologist about how best to contribute to psychological science and human welfare. Having made the decision to conduct research, the psychologist considers alternative directions in which research energies and resources might be invested. On the basis of this consideration, the psychologist carries out the investigation with respect and concern for the dignity and welfare of the people who participate and with cognizance of federal and state regulations and professional standards governing the conduct of research with human participants.

A. In planning a study, the investigator has the responsibility to make a careful evaluation of its ethical acceptability. To the extent that the weighing of scientific and human values suggests a compromise of any principle, the investigator incurs a correspondingly serious obligation to seek ethical advice and to observe stringent safeguards to protect the rights of human participants.

B. Considering whether a participant in a planned study will be a "subject at risk" or a "subject at minimal risk," according to recognized standards, is of primary ethical concern to the investigator.

C. The investigator always retains the responsibility for ensuring ethical practice in research. The investigator is also responsible for the ethical treatment of research participants by collaborators, assistants, students, and employees, all of whom, however, incur similar obligations.

D. Except in minimal-risk research, the investigator establishes a clear and fair agreement with research participants, prior to their participation, that clarifies the obligations and responsibilities of each. The investigator has the obligation to honor all promises and commitments included in that agreement. The investigator informs the participants of all aspects of the research that might reasonably be expected to influence willingness to participate and explains all other aspects of the research about which the participants inquire. Failure to make full disclosure prior to obtaining informed consent requires additional safeguards to protect the welfare and dignity of the research participants. Research with children or with participants who have impairments that would limit understanding and/or communication requires special safeguarding procedures.

E. Methodological requirements of a study may make the use of concealment or deception necessary. Before conducting such a study, the investigator has a special responsibility to (1) determine whether the use of such techniques is justified by the study's prospective scientific, educational, or applied value; (2) determine whether alternative procedures are available that do not use concealment or deception; and (3) ensure that the participants are provided with sufficient explanation as soon as possible.

F. The investigator respects the individual's freedom to decline to participate in or to withdraw from the research at any time. The obligation to protect this freedom requires careful thought and consideration when the investigator is in a position of authority or influence over the participant. Such positions of authority include, but are not limited to, situations in which research participation is required as part of employment or in which the participant is a student, client, or employee of the investigator.

G. The investigator protects the participant from physical and mental discomfort, harm, and danger that may arise from research procedures. If risks of such consequences exist, the investigator informs the participant of that fact. Research procedures likely to cause serious or lasting harm to a participant are not used unless the failure to use these procedures might expose the participant to risk of greater harm or unless the research has great potential benefit and fully informed and voluntary consent is obtained from each participant. The participant should be informed of procedures for contacting the investigator within a reasonable time period following participation should stress, potential harm, or related questions or concerns arise.

    H. After the data are collected, the investigator provides the participant with information about the nature of the study and attempts to remove any misconceptions that may have arisen. Where scientific or humane values justify delaying or withholding this information, the investigator incurs a special responsibility to monitor the research and to ensure that there are no damaging consequences for the participant.

    I. Where research procedures result in undesirable consequences for the individual participant, the investigator has the responsibility to detect and remove or correct these consequences, including long-term effects.

    J. Information obtained about a research participant during the course of an investigation is confidential unless otherwise agreed upon in advance. When the possibility exists that others may obtain access to such information, this possibility, together with the plans for protecting confidentiality, is explained to the participant as part of the procedure for obtaining informed consent.

BASIC ETHICAL ISSUES

The 10 principles presented above pertain to 7 fundamental ethical issues:

1. moral and ethical responsibility (Principles A and C)
2. harm avoidance (Principles B and G)
3. undoing or alleviating harm (Principles H and I)
4. informed consent and fairness (Principle D)
5. the use of deception and concealment (Principle E)
6. curtailment of personal freedom (Principle F)
7. confidentiality (Principle J)

Accordingly, I'll discuss the practical implications of the 10 guidelines within the context of these underlying issues.

Moral and Ethical Responsibility (Principles A and C)

Principle A: General Responsibility of the Principal Investigator.   The principal investigator is the person who is responsible for designing, initiating, and supervising a research project. The principal investigator may or may not actually interact with subjects or collect data; assistants or collaborators may perform these functions. Nonetheless, the principal investigator is responsible for weighing the advantages and disadvantages of a proposed study, and for the fair and humane treatment of subjects.

    As the principal investigator in your own research projects, you must carefully assess the probable benefits and costs that your study will bring to both the subjects and "society." The official position of the APA (1982) is that when an investigator is evaluating the pros and cons of a research procedure, priority must be given to the subject's welfare rather than to what the investigator or society might gain from the study.

    It is always desirable to seek the advice of others in the planning stages of your research. A primary reason for this practice is that most investigators cannot be completely objective in weighing the scientific or social merit of their proposed studies relative to the subjects' costs. The opinions of people who are not professional scientists or researchers may be especially helpful for correcting your biases.

Principle C: Responsibility for Collaborators and Assistants.   If collaborators or assistants help you collect data, then you are responsible for ensuring that they are informed concerning the ethical issues posed by the research. It is also your responsibility to ensure that your co-researchers are properly trained in the ethical treatment of subjects, and to verify that subjects are, in fact, receiving courteous and fair treatment.

It is important to remember that collaborators and assistants shoulder the same degree of responsibility as the principal investigator. Thus, even if you are "merely assisting" a psychologist in the data collection process, you are every bit as obligated to the subjects and society as is the psychologist. This consideration leads to another important point: If, while serving as a research assistant, you decide that you are morally opposed to a research procedure or uncertain about its ethical status, it is unethical for the principal investigator to pressure you into conducting the procedure.

The Role of Institutional Review Boards.   To ensure that investigators are meeting their responsibilities in research with human participants, many organizations sponsoring such research maintain Institutional Review Boards (IRB). The typical IRB is a formally constituted body consisting of both scientists and nonscientists. Its function is to examine the ethical implications of a proposed study and rule on its acceptability, especially as regards provisions for protecting subjects from harm. If your institution or organization has an IRB, you may be required to submit a description of your proposed research projects to that group (check with your research supervisor). If the IRB rules that your research would involve unjustified costs to your subjects, then you will have to revise your proposal and resubmit it.

It is worth noting that the federal government's Department of Health and Human Services requires that all federally funded research organizations employ IRBs. Failure to do so will result in the withdrawal of all federal monies from the negligent organization.

Professional Responsibility in Face-to-Face Interactions with Subjects.   If you have ever served as a subject in a study run by an inconsiderate or discourteous researcher, then you are already aware of the importance of professionalism in dealings with subjects. Most subjects, especially those who are first-timers, tend to be apprehensive about being in a psychology experiment. Your role, as researcher, should be to calm them down and reassure them. Treating them like objects or lower forms of humanity has exactly the opposite effect—it increases their apprehension and often riles them. And what degree of external validity would you expect your data to have if they were obtained from emotionally unsettled subjects? More important than external validity, however, is the fact that treating subjects unkindly is totally unprofessional and ethically unacceptable.

The most common mistake that beginning researchers make is to not allow sufficient time for the unhurried conduct of individual experimental sessions. You should budget at least 15 minutes more per session than your pilot study indicated you would need. This allows you to accommodate subjects who are a few minutes late for their appointments with you and provides sufficient time, in most cases, for adjusting equipment and answering unanticipated questions that some subjects will have. Also, budget plenty of time for "debriefing" the subject at the end of the session (see "Undoing or Alleviating Harm," below). A few of your participants will require longer-than-average explanations.

Don't be late for appointments with subjects. And don't be afraid to be friendly and natural with them. The more "real" you are, the more relaxed and genuine they are likely to be. Try to make requests instead of directives. Finally, always communicate your appreciation of the subject's help. Not only are the subject's well-being and dignity at stake, so are yours and the profession's.

Harm Avoidance (Principles B and G)

Principle B: Consideration of the Degree of Risk to Subjects.   The ethical code of the APA recognizes two categories of "risk" in research with human participants: "subject at minimal risk" and "subject at risk." Many, perhaps the majority, of psychology experiments fall into the "subjects at minimal risk" classification. This means that it is very unlikely that the participants will experience any appreciable distress, and that the likelihood of physical or psychological harm to them is virtually zero. Most experiments that simply require subjects to memorize words or pictures or, perhaps, make simple perceptual judgments represent what is meant by "minimal risk."

Procedures that clearly have a greater than zero probability of causing psychological or physical stress fall into the "subject at risk" category. Milgram's obedience study is an extreme example of "subject at risk" research. Latané and Rodin's (1969) investigation of bystander intervention, which is described in Chapter 8, is a somewhat less extreme example of "risky" procedures. Obviously, then, there are various degrees of the "subject at risk" factor within psychological methodology. Often Institutional Review Boards can serve a valuable consultative function in rendering an opinion on the degree of risk to subjects posed by a procedure. Assuming that the IRB approves your study, it is then up to you to judge whether the risk of harm to your subjects is really justified by the likely scientific or social merit of the investigation.

Principle G: Protecting the Subject from Discomfort, Harm, and Danger.   The vast majority of psychological investigations do not induce appreciable physical or psychological stress in subjects. But some areas of research, such as studies of cheating, failure experiences, or obedience, may require short-term induction of unpleasant psychological states. Other topics, such as pain perception or the effects of drugs, can hardly be researched in a controlled fashion without the creation of physical discomfort or the risk of some danger. But in undertaking research that will almost certainly involve at least temporary harm or distress, you incur special obligations to your subjects. The greatest obligation is to take all reasonable steps to minimize the level and duration of distress. Your other responsibilities include:

1. obtaining complete information and advice from clinical and medical experts regarding the tolerable levels of stress, proper safeguards to implement, and the likely degree and duration of negative effects of the procedure
2. screening especially vulnerable subjects from the pool of participants, when possible
3. apprising the subjects of the likely levels of discomfort and possible long-term effects connected with the procedure (Milgram's study loses points here: His subjects did not anticipate appreciable stress at the outset of the study.)
4. ensuring that the subjects are aware of their right to terminate their participation at any time
5. proceeding only after you have the subject's *informed consent*, acknowledged in writing
6. monitoring for unforeseen or unintended stressful conditions during the course of data collection
7. "debriefing" the subject after the experimental session to alleviate as much of the stress as possible, as soon as possible
8. conducting follow-up assessments of subjects at periodic intervals to ensure that the effects of the stress do not persist.

Above all, before you decide to undertake any type of stress-inducing study, be sure to review possible alternatives to the procedure that may allow adequate examination of the research question without the deliberate creation of unpleasant experiences.

Undoing or Alleviating Harm (Principles H and I)

When a research procedure that you're using causes a subject to suffer psychological or physical discomfort, it is imperative that you make every effort to "undo" or at least reduce the intensity of the subject's distress as soon as possible. A major tool for implementing harm alleviation is the **debriefing session**, which should take place immediately after the subject has completed her participation. Basically, "debriefing" means that you "level" with the subject, fill her in on important aspects of the research that you could not reveal in your initial description of the project, and answer any questions she might have. Even if the procedure falls into the "subject at minimal risk" category, it is part of your ethical responsibility to educate the subject with regard to the true and complete purpose and significance of the research, and to expose any deception or concealment that was employed.

Besides providing the subject with interesting and useful information, there are two additional aspects to the debriefing process: (a) *dehoaxing* the subject, by correcting any misinformation or incorrect knowledge that she may have derived from participation in the study; (b) *desensitizing* the subject, by lessening or removing negative feelings (i.e., embarrassment, guilt) that she may have about her behavior in the study (Holmes, 1976).

Principle H: Dehoaxing the Subject.   Debriefing the subject will involve "dehoaxing" whenever you have employed deception or concealment in a study. Deception can be by *omission* or *commission*. Deception by omission occurs when, in your preexperimental explanation to the subject, you withhold some information about the study's purpose or about a procedural step that the subject will undergo. In some investigations of memory, for example, subjects may be informed initially that the purpose of the investigation is to examine short-term memory—which may be true. But the study may also assess long-term memory via an *unexpected* "final free recall test," which is "sprung" on the subject after all of the short-term memory trials have been completed (e.g., Jacoby & Bartz, 1972). The nature of the investigation may require that the subjects not be informed at the outset about the eventual test of long-term memory; this aspect of the procedure is simply *omitted* from the initial explanation. It then becomes the investigator's responsibility to include in the debriefing session a clarification of the purpose of the final memory test, and to explain why the deception had to be used.

Deception by *commission* is used when you simply lie to the subject about the purpose of the study or about what he will be required to do. For example, you might tell the subject that the study concerns the effect of punishment on learning, when, in fact, the study actually is designed to assess factors in obedience to authority. Thus, deception by commission is exactly what Milgram employed.

Though there are exceptions to this statement, deception by commission is generally considered to be more harmful than deception by omission. The reason is that deception by commission is likely to make the subject feel stupid or gullible for having been so completely taken in by the ruse. Also, this type of deception may have an impact on the subject's general trust in human relationships; after all, you have intentionally told him an outright lie that perhaps has made him look weak, silly, or naive. Therefore, if you plan to use this brand of deception in your studies, you should also carefully plan and implement a thorough and convincing debriefing that satisfactorily explains why you did what you did to the subject. Moreover, if your deception is likely to make the subject feel bad about his behavior in the experiment, be prepared to "desensitize" him as well as dehoax him.

Principle I: Desensitizing the Subject.   Desensitization during the debriefing session helps subjects who were led to engage in socially unacceptable or embarrassing behavior to cope with their shame, embarrassment, anger, or guilt. In effect, an adequate desensitization procedure calms the subject down and reassures him of his "normality" and integrity.

Holmes (1976b) has reviewed two general strategies for desensitizing subjects:

1. Suggest to the subjects that their "questionable" behavior was a result of situational determinants (e.g., "demand characteristics") within the study rather than of the subjects' personality or "real" motives; further, that the subjects' behavior isn't relevant to what they would be likely to do outside the laboratory. As Holmes points out, these reassurances put the researcher in the ironic position of disavowing the external validity of her research. They may also amount to false statements if the results are externally valid. The rationale, however, is that the subjects' well-being takes precedence over other considerations.

2. Point out that the ". . .subject's behavior was not abnormal, unusual, or extreme" (Holmes, 1976b, p. 868); further, that most other subjects in the experiment behaved the same way.

In view of these desensitizing strategies, it is interesting to consider how Milgram handled his subjects' feelings in the debriefing sessions. After Milgram dehoaxed a subject, and the unharmed "learner" came forward to shake the subject's hand and reassure him, Milgram proceeded with a thorough desensitization:

> The experiment was explained to the defiant subjects in a way that supported their decision to disobey the experimenter. Obedient subjects were assured of the fact that their behavior was entirely normal and that their feelings of conflict or tension were shared by other participants. . . . In some instances, additional detailed and lengthy discussions of the experiment were also carried out with individual subjects.
>
> When the experimental series was complete, subjects received a written report which presented details of the experimental procedure and results. (Milgram, 1964, p. 849)

Informed Consent and Fairness (Principle D)

Informed consent and "fairness" are at the heart of research ethics. Both concepts are based on the idea that ethical research should always rest upon a nonexploitative, mutually agreed upon *social contract* between the subject and the researcher. As much as is possible, the costs, risks, and benefits to the subject should be explicitly stated prior to the subject's participation. Furthermore, the researcher should honor any commitments he makes to the subject, such as the promise of money, extra course credit, or a full report of the findings. Deplorably, it is not hard to find instances reported in the research literature in which psychologists have failed to honor explicit commitments to subjects. Most commonly, such cases involve researchers' using promises of monetary rewards as part of their experimental manipulation. In the debriefing session, however, the subjects are informed that the monetary incentive was simply a deception designed to influence their motivation, and that the researchers actually have no funds to award. This type of deception violates the fairness norm and is rarely, if ever, justified.

Consent Forms.   The most common and, perhaps, most satisfactory way to implement the informed consent idea in your research projects is to prepare a "Verification of Informed Consent" form, such as the one that appears in Box 3–2. The form requires that you explain to the subject, as fully as possible, (a) the nature and purpose of your study, (b) exactly what the subject will be asked to do, (c) the subject's benefit or compensation

---

Box 3–2
HIGHLIGHT
Sample Consent Form

VERIFICATION OF INFORMED CONSENT

I, _____ (Please Print Full Name), voluntarily give my consent to serve as a participant in the study titled:

_____

I have received a satisfactory explanation of the general purpose of the project, as well as a description of what I will be asked to do and the conditions that I will be exposed to. I realize that it may not be possible for the researcher to explain all aspects of the study to me until after I have completed my participation. In return for my service in this study, I will receive:

_____ .

It is my understanding that the researcher is responsible for any risks that I may sustain in this study. I have been informed of the following risks or potentially unpleasant experiences:

_____

_____

It is my further understanding that I may terminate my participation in this study at any time, and that any data obtained will be confidential.

_____   _____
Signature of Participant   *Researcher Prints Name Here*

_____   _____
Date   *Signature of Researcher*

for participating, (d) the possible risks to the subject, if any, and, *importantly*, (e) that the subject is free to terminate his or her participation at any time. This type of form fulfills an important portion of your obligation to the subject, reassures the subject, and expressly protects the subject's autonomy and freedom in the situation (see Ozar, 1983). Remember, the consent form should be read and signed by your subjects before they render their service, not during the debriefing session.

The Question of Consent Competence.   In some cases, your subjects may not be legally or functionally competent to give informed consent. This may be true, for instance, if you are working with children, prisoners, or mentally disabled people. In these cases, you will need to obtain the written consent of the persons who are legally responsible for the subjects. Even if your subjects are not "competent" to sign a consent form, however, you are obligated to explain the study to them as best you can within the limits of their ability to understand (APA, 1982; also see Miller & Gordon, 1978).

When Informed Consent Is Impossible, Impractical, or Unnecessary.   In some varieties of research, such as naturalistic observation, informed consent before the fact would defeat the purpose of the study. In survey-type research, informed consent may be *implied* by the subject's agreeing to answer the interviewer's questions, or by the subject's completion and return of the questionnaire. And in some kinds of archival research that involve obtaining information from records available to the general public, informed consent may be unnecessary. Thus, while the principle of informed consent is a central compo-

---

Box 3–3
HIGHLIGHT
Exemptions from the Policy of Informed
Consent?

The federal government's Department of Health and Human Services has composed a set of strict regulations that are to be adhered to in research with human participants. Compliance is mandatory for organizations and institutions that receive any kind of federal funding. Informed consent and restricted use of deception are among the most important guidelines handed down by the department. But, according to the department's revised regulations, which appeared in the January 26, 1981, *Federal Register*, the following kinds of research projects are exempt from the guidelines:

1. Research conducted in educational settings, such as instructional strategy research or studies on the effectiveness of educational techniques, curricula, or classroom management methods.
2. Research using educational tests (cognitive, diagnostic, aptitude and achievement), provided that subjects remain anonymous.

3. Survey or interview procedures, except where *all* of the following conditions prevail:
   a. Participants could be identified;
   b. Participants' responses, if they became public, could place the subject at risk on criminal or civil charges, or could affect the subjects' financial or occupational standing;
   c. Research involving "sensitive aspects" of the participant's behavior, such as illegal conduct, drug use, sexual behavior, or alcohol use;
4. Observation of public behavior (including observation by participants), except where all three of the conditions listed in #3 above are applicable.
5. The collection or study of documents, records, existing data, pathological specimens or diagnostic specimens if these sources are available to the public or if the information obtained from the sources remains anonymous.

nent of research ethics, there are justifiable exceptions to this general requirement. Box 3–3 lists several categories of research that, according to the Department of Health and Human Services, may often be exempt from the requirements of informed consent and debriefing (*Federal Register*, January 26, 1981).

The Use of Deception (Principle E)

Rationale of Using Deception in Psychological Research.   To the extent that deception is used in a study, the principle of informed consent is violated. Most psychologists realize this. Why, then, is deception tolerated by the profession? The simple, if somewhat unsatisfactory, answer is that in the case of some research questions "valid data could not be obtained if the participant were fully informed about the purpose and procedures of the research and the experiences to be anticipated" (APA, 1982, p. 35). Essentially, the use of deception at the expense of informed consent is rationalized on the basis of the Cost/ Benefit Orthodoxy, which was discussed early in this chapter. Sometimes the probable social or scientific worth of a study that employs deception is seen as balancing the extra psychological and social costs of using deception. Under such circumstances, the considered opinion of the principal investigator and her colleagues is that the validity and, hence, value of data would be considerably reduced if the deception were not employed.

As an illustration of why deception is sometimes necessary, consider an investigation by Resnick & Schwartz (1973) which examined the effect of "verbal conditioning" under two levels of informed consent. In this study, each subject was presented with a series of verbs and, on each trial, was to use the presented verb and one of six pronouns (I, We, You, They, She, or He) to construct a sentence. The subject was free to select any pronoun he or she wished in making up each sentence. But the experimenter rewarded the subject with verbal approval (e.g., "okay" or "good") only when the subject used "I" or "We" in the sentence. The objective was to try to "verbally condition" the subjects to increase the frequency with which they selected the target pronouns in preference to the alternative pronouns. A host of earlier studies had demonstrated that such conditioning effects are easy to accomplish.

The other variable in the study was the amount of information subjects had about the experimenter's purpose and hypothesis. Half of the subjects were fully informed on these matters, whereas the other half were given information only on the procedure, not the purpose. What results would you expect? Resnick and Schwartz found that the "uninformed" (i.e., deceived) group performed as people typically do in verbal conditioning experiments. They gradually increased their use of the target pronouns. But the "fully informed" group actually decreased their frequency of using "I" and "We." That is, their behavior flatly contradicted the principles of learning and conditioning that had been established across prior decades of research. Thus, within the framework of current knowledge, the data of the fully informed subjects were invalid.

It is clear, then, that the methods presently available to psychological researchers will sometimes require the practice of deception for the sake of obtaining useful data. But any practice of deception in your studies increases your obligation to the subjects. Specifically, your responsibilities are to (a) carefully consider, in consultation with others, whether the deceptive aspects of the study are justified by the probable value of your data; (b) consider possible alternative procedures that may yield equally useful information with less reliance on deception; (c) make sure that your subjects are thoroughly debriefed as soon as possible (APA, 1982).

Invasion of Privacy. The strongest objections to deceptive research practices emerge when the procedure threatens to invade the subject's privacy. By invasion of privacy, I mean obtaining information on the subject's intimate behavior or lifestyle that he would not knowingly make public. Believe it or not, examples of such covert incursions into private lives occasionally appear in the research literature. For example, in an attempt to get valid data on "egocentricity in conversations," the observers in one study resorted to hiding under dormitory beds so that they could eavesdrop on the conversations of college students (Henle & Hubbell, 1938). One wonders whether there might not have been several simpler and more ethically acceptable methods of obtaining data on egocentric speech, even in the 1930s.

In another case of invasion of privacy, psychological researchers set up a hidden periscope in a public restroom and observed and recorded various aspects of urination exhibited by American males (Middlemist, Knowles, & Matter, 1977). The researchers were interested in the effect that invasion of "personal space" has on emotional arousal, as measured by latency and duration of urine flow. As might be expected, they found that the presence of another man standing in front of the adjacent urinal resulted in a delayed onset of urination and a quick ending to the act. Both of these outcomes were interpreted to mean that invasion of personal space increases emotional arousal. Again, one might well question the necessity of using this extremely invasive technique to study the particular theoretical question of interest.

Fortunately, invasion of individuals' privacy to the extent illustrated by these studies is relatively rare in psychological research. To be sure, any investigator who chooses to violate people's constitutional rights to that degree for the sake of scientific progress must assume an unusually onerous ethical burden. Furthermore, he should proceed with his study only after thorough consultation with colleagues regarding possible alternative methods that would be less objectionable.

Is It Ethical to Be Unobtrusive? The examples of invasion of privacy considered so far have involved covert observation of people's behavior in *private* situations or during *private* acts. But most studies that employ unobtrusive, or "nonreactive," observational methods focus on less sensitive and less intimate behaviors in situations that are typically accessible to the public eye. Nonetheless, these observations are made covertly without informed consent and, thus, constitute acts of deception on the researcher's part. Additional ethical complications arise when field-observational studies include staged researcher interventions that may take up the subjects' time or cause them some unpleasantness. Consider the following examples that were among several summarized by Silverman (1975):

> 1. Persons selected at random are phoned. The caller pretends that he has reached a wrong number, using his last piece of change, and that his car is disabled on a highway. The party is requested to phone the caller's garage and ask them to come for him. The garage number is actually the caller's phone and another experimenter, standing by, pretends to take the message (Gaertner & Bickman, 1972).
>
> 2. Automobiles, parked on streets, look as if they were abandoned. (License plates are removed and hoods are raised.) Experimenters hide in nearby buildings and film people who have any contact with the cars (Zimbardo, 1969).
>
> 3. People sitting alone on park benches are asked to be interviewed by an experimenter who gives the name of a fictitious survey research organization that he claims to represent. At the beginning of the interview, the experimenter asks a person sitting nearby, who is actually a confederate, if he wouldn't mind answering the questions at the same time. The confederate responds with opinions that are clearly opposite to those of the subject and

makes demeaning remarks about the subject's answers; for example, "That's ridiculous"; "That's just the sort of thing you'd expect to hear in this park" (Abelson & Miller, 1967).

Should these research situations be considered invasions of privacy? A substantial minority of the general public thinks so. When Wilson and Donnerstein (1976) asked a representative sample of 174 citizens for their opinions on studies such as those described above, 32 percent said that psychologists' unobtrusive techniques constitute an invasion of privacy, and 41 percent thought that such studies should not be conducted. On the basis of their findings, Wilson and Donnerstein concluded that it would be the better part of ethical wisdom to consult with some of the potential subjects of unobtrusive observation prior to deciding to conduct studies like those summarized above. "By finding out from the subject pool the aspects of the method that are objectionable, the researcher can explore other viable alternatives, possibly even with the aid of members of the subject pool" (Wilson & Donnerstein, 1976, p. 772).

The APA's Committee for the Protection of Human Subjects in Psychological Research (1982) recognizes that unobtrusive observation without informed consent is sometimes necessary if data obtained in natural settings are to be externally valid. In the opinion of that committee, your primary responsibility in using nonreactive observation is to ensure that subjects remain anonymous.

Alternatives to Deception.   Many psychologists feel that deception procedures, in their conventional forms, can often be avoided and alternative methods used in their place. Forward et al. (1976), as well as Kelman (1967, 1972), advocate a **role-playing approach** to research projects that normally would require the use of deception. In the role-playing approach, the subjects are fully informed concerning the nature of the research question, the variables involved, and the types of manipulations or situations that would be employed if a deception approach were to be used. Then the subjects and experimenter collaborate on the development of their respective "scripts," which include the systematic variation of independent variables and a specification of the proposed dependent measure. Finally, either the scripts are "acted out," with data being collected in the usual fashion, or else the subjects simply say what they probably would do if the agreed upon experimental conditions were actually carried out. Interestingly, at least one researcher (Mixon, 1972) has replicated and extended Milgram's obedience studies using the role-playing technique.

Forward et al. argue not only that the role-playing approach is more ethically acceptable than deception studies, but also that the role-playing model produces more realistic results. The basis for the latter claim, according to Forward et al., is that role-playing situations allow human choice and "self-presentation" to determine behavior, just as is true of everyday life. In contrast, deception studies attempt to remove these important elements from the subjects' behavior.

Critics of the role-playing approach point out that it is the "self-presentational" aspect of role-playing that is likely to produce invalid data (e.g., Cooper, 1976). The critics' argument is that some role-playing subjects who wish to please the researcher will yield to the clear "demand characteristics" of the role-play, whereas other subjects who wish to present themselves in a good light (science be damned) will act out only socially desirable behaviors. In neither case would the real effects of the independent variable be apparent.

Another alternative to deception is the use of **assumed consent** (Berscheid, Baron, Dermer, & Libman, 1973). In this procedure, the researcher conducts a type of pilot study to assess how "acceptable" a deception procedure would be to subjects. A complete and detailed description, which includes a specification of the deception that is to be used, is given to a group of potential subjects. If a majority of the potential subjects indicate that they wouldn't mind participating in the study despite the deception, then it is assumed that the actual subjects (who will be deceived) would also find the procedure acceptable. This approach doesn't eliminate deception, but it does lighten the researcher's ethical burden.

Curtailment of Personal Freedom (Principle F)

Schuler (1982) has noted the typically huge discrepancy between the status and power of the experimenter on the one hand and those of the subject on the other. Such a discrepancy opens up a real possibility of coercion and exploitation. Although the consent form signed by the subject prior to her participation in the study is designed to ensure that she retain her right of self-determination, many feel that this measure is not, in itself, a sufficient safeguard. Let's consider why this might be true.

Milgram Revisited. To what extent were Milgram's subjects free to control their fate? True, his subjects had freely offered their service in return for a small monetary reward. They were also free to terminate their participation at any time, and, in fact, 35 percent of them did just that. But consider the following facts: Milgram had staged the research session such that the power and status differential between him and his subjects would appear maximal. He employed a device that is frequently used in psychological research: deception. And how much personal freedom and choice remain for a person who doesn't understand the true nature and meaning of a situation in which he finds himself? Milgram also used "maximal goading of subjects" (cf. Schuler, 1982) with such demanding statements as "You have no choice but to go on." Beyond that, Milgram's subjects probably felt an obligation to fulfill the social contract that they had struck with the experimenter—especially because they were to be paid for it.

Although Milgram's investigation certainly is an extreme example, many of the coercive elements of his procedure are found to varying degrees in a variety of psychological studies reported in the literature. Perhaps we typically overestimate the amount of freedom our subjects have.

What You Can Do. What steps can you take to ensure that your subjects retain as much of their right of self-determination as possible? The APA (1982) offers many suggestions on this matter. Three of the most important are: (a) Consult with other people who are experienced in ethical matters to obtain advice on any likely curtailment of freedom that may be associated with your method of recruiting subjects, the type of subject population you will employ, or your experimental procedures. (b) Communicate your subjects' rights to them prior to their participation, and have them acknowledge those rights in writing. (c) Be alert to any distress shown by your subjects during their service, and be ready to help them ease out of their commitment, if that seems to be in their best interests.

Confidentiality (Principle J)

All data obtained in your research projects are confidential, unless you and the subject have agreed in writing to waive confidentiality. In most cases, subjects' names should be separated from their data as soon as possible after data collection. When feasible, names should not appear on the data sheets to begin with. If you need to be able to identify your subjects for purposes of collating data across several tasks or multiple research sessions, it may be possible to use a coding system or a set of logos (fictitious, usually humorous or outlandish titles or names, such as "Charlie Brown" or "Captain Hook," which are easy for subjects to remember). You will need to enlist your subject's help in implementing the coding system. An effective coding system protects the subject's data from being identified by anyone without the subject's assistance.

SUMMARY

Because psychological research projects involve a social contract between the researcher and her subjects, ethical norms and ethical considerations are important aspects of such investigations. The primary motivation for psychology's intense concern with the ethical treatment of research participants is the sense of moral obligation that is central to the field's human-service orientation. But there is also a practical reason for treating subjects ethically: If we don't consider the subjects' interests, we soon will have no subjects to observe, for society will withdraw its support of psychological research.

The primary guiding philosophy behind psychology's research-ethics code is what might be called the Cost/Benefit Orthodoxy. The basic idea behind this philosophy is that the benefits and costs that society might derive from a study must be balanced against the subjects' potential costs and benefits, with priority ultimately being given to the subjects' interests.

In response to the various ethical issues and dilemmas that arise in the context of research with human beings, the American Psychological Association developed and published a manual entitled *Ethical Principles in the Conduct of Research with Human Participants*. This document sets forth 10 cardinal principles that pertain to the following 7 issues:

1. moral and ethical responsibility of the investigator(s)
2. harm avoidance
3. undoing or alleviating harm
4. informed consent and fairness
5. the use of deception
6. curtailment of personal freedom
7. confidentiality

REVIEW QUESTIONS

1. In what sense does the psychological investigation involve a social contract? What is the nature of that contract, and who are the parties to the contract?
2. Describe some of the value conflicts that give rise to ethical dilemmas in psychological research. How is the Cost/Benefit Orthodoxy used to deal with these dilemmas?
3. Describe the general ethical responsibilities of the principal investigator. What are her responsibilities concerning her co-researchers and research assistants?
4. What are your obligations as principal investigator when your procedure may cause the subjects some physical or psychological stress?
5. What is the "debriefing session"? Why is it useful and often necessary? What is the difference between "dehoaxing" the subject and "desensitizing" the subject?
6. Define or describe: informed consent, consent forms, consent competence. Under what circumstances might informed consent not be feasible or necessary?

7. Summarize the usual "justification" given for using deception in psychological research. Describe two alternatives to deception.

8. For what reasons is the subject's personal freedom so vulnerable in psychology experiments?

9. Why is it important that subjects' data be kept confidential? What might be some consequences of breaches in the confidentiality policy?

10. Analyze Milgram's study of obedience to authority in terms of the seven basic ethical issues reviewed in this chapter.

Notes

[1]From APA, *Ethical Principles In the Conduct of Research with Human Participants*. Washington, D.C.: American Psychological Association, 1982. Reprinted by permission.

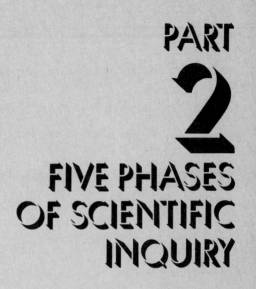

PART

2

FIVE PHASES
OF SCIENTIFIC
INQUIRY

In the next five chapters I will discuss the sequence of activities that you will go through in conducting a scientific investigation. I will emphasize the logic and function of each phase of inquiry, but will also include various "how to" suggestions where appropriate.

The first thing you need to do as a researcher is clearly formulate the question or questions you want to ask. This includes "operationalizing" your questions by translating them into an appropriate research design. The design you develop will be a function of the nature of your question, practical considerations, and your purpose in doing the study.

Once your question has been formulated and operationalized into a research design, the next step is to measure the behavior of interest—that is, observe your subjects under specified conditions and convert their responses to numerical data. In phase three, you will extract relationships from your data through the use of logic and statistics. Interpreting relationships in phase four will involve consideration of the theoretical implications, as well as the *theoretical limits*, of your findings in light of the research design you used. In the final phase of a research project your task will be to decide how generalizable your findings are and to make general assertions, to the extent that they are justified.

4

FORMULATING QUESTIONS

Believe it or not, the most challenging part of becoming a psychological researcher is learning how to ask the right kinds of questions: questions that are both nontrivial and manageable. Nontrivial questions are those that have important substance because they pertain to unexplored areas of behavior and experience, constitute a new test of a theory, or are relevant to a practical problem. Manageable questions are those that are clear and precise enough to be operationalized into a "doable" research project.

√

ASKING THE RIGHT KIND OF QUESTION

Asking Useful Questions

Determining what is a "useful" question in scientific research is a difficult task. For one thing, the criteria of usefulness are largely dependent on current social norms in science— the *Zeitgeist*, or spirit of the times—and so are always a somewhat arbitrary matter. And norms can be blinding. For example, eminent scientists of Mendel's day discouraged him from researching the "useless" question of the independence of inherited traits because the idea conflicted with prevailing scientific notions (Barber, 1962).

Bearing in mind that it is easy to become closed-minded about what constitutes a useful question, I humbly make the following recommendations.

Do:

1. Ask questions about relatively unexplored areas of behavior and experience. Often we are intimidated by the prospect of entering virgin territory in science, because there are so many practical problems and unknowns. But the gold is there for the dauntless. A good example of researching unexplored areas is Singer's (1974, 1975) work on daydreaming. Until the 1970s, psychologists had avoided investigating this phenomenon because it is so subjective and "common." Nonetheless, Singer proceeded to develop several questions and measures pertinent to daydreaming and ended up building an impressive program of research around the topic.

2. Ask questions that lead to tests of a theory. To many scientists, research questions designed to test an existing theory are the most useful type of query. Why? Because theoretically guided research efforts generally have the greatest potential to increase understanding. Take an example: Is the ability to be hypnotized related to one's susceptibility to classical conditioning? Salter's (1949) theory of hypnosis clearly predicts such a relationship. Can you think of a way to empirically test this question? If so, your data could significantly enhance our understanding of hypnosis.

3. Ask questions that address a practical problem. Practical questions typically lead to applied research but may also be theory related. Consider some examples of practical questions: Does marijuana interfere with memorizing textbook material? What are the determiners of helping behavior in a crisis? On which work shifts are police officers most likely to be killed? What are the characteristics of nursing-home residents who suffer falls? Do programs like Project Head Start help disadvantaged kids to catch up academically?

Avoid:

1. "Reinventing the wheel." That is, unless your only intent is to get experience in data collection, it is usually an empty exercise to pose a research question that already has been tested numerous times with consistent results.[1]

2. Asking questions with obvious answers. Do you really want to spend your valuable time finding out if people get angry when insulted, or if there is more cheating during

unsupervised final exams than during exams that are monitored? It is another matter, however, if you propose to investigate the relationship between amount of anger expressed and the social status of the "insulter"; or the kind of student-teacher relationships that minimize cheating during exams.

Asking Manageable Questions

Many intriguing questions are difficult or impossible to research in their present form because they are too broad in scope. It is common to start out with general questions, as curiosity tends to express itself in general thoughts. Also, interesting research problems often have wide ramifications. But before you can begin a scientific study, your original question may need to be analyzed into several smaller questions. As you then ponder which of the smaller questions to research, you will need to ask yourself: (a) Which question best fits my original aim? (b) Can I translate the variables of my smaller question into observables? (c) Can the selected question be researched within the limits of my population of subjects, the time available for doing the study, and the money I have to spend?

Consider the question "Why do people become jealous?" Is this a manageable question? That is, could we conduct an empirical study based on the question as stated? The question seems to be asking: "What factors contribute to jealousy?" Even worded this way, however, the query is not yet in a researchable form. Let's take a look at what would have to be considered and done before we could carry out an empirical test.

Deciding on an Independent Variable. By "factors," do we mean developmental events, personality traits, or social circumstances? If we are referring to personality traits, then we will want to narrow our question down to one or two specific traits, say "self-confidence" and "paranoia." After we have chosen the target traits for our independent variables, it is then necessary to select an operational definition of them. And there may be literally dozens, ranging from scores on personality tests through peer ratings to situational behaviors.

Choosing a Population. Does the word "people" refer to children, college students, people in love, relatives, or adults in general? The target population should be specified clearly in our final research question. Let's suppose the population of interest is college students.

Specifying a Dependent Variable. Jealous of what? Possessions, lovers, social position? If we mean romantic jealousy, the next step is to select or develop an operational definition of romantic jealousy so that it may be measured and its empirical relation to self-confidence assessed.

Thus, the original question, "Why do people become jealous?" now becomes, "Is there a relationship between self-confidence and romantic jealousy in college students?" or, more precisely, "Is there a correlation between scores on measure X of self-confidence and measure Y of jealousy, for a college-student population?" (And, if so, what are the theoretical implications?)

SOURCES OF RESEARCH IDEAS

Where Psychologists Get Their Ideas

After reading about a clever and interesting psychology experiment, do you find yourself thinking, "How neat! How did she ever come up with that idea?" The genesis of research ideas almost always seems mysterious, elusive, and even awe-inspiring to people who are relatively new in a field. But there actually is very little magic involved, save those (very) rare moments of creative insight that catch us by surprise. Most of the time psychologists rely on several standard idea "sources" for creation of their research questions (McGuire, 1973). Earlier I mentioned two of those sources: existing theories and practical problems. Let's now consider some additional ones.

The Case Study.   An intensive study of an individual or an organization is called a case study. While isolated cases rarely constitute conclusive support for a hypothesis, the single case may be used as a source of ideas for larger-scale, better-controlled investigations. For example, most of the experimental investigations of motivated forgetting, or "repression," were designed to test Freud's psychoanalytic model (e.g., Holmes, 1972; Zeller, 1951). Freud's conception of repression was both based on and demonstrated by his classic case studies of Victorian-era neurotic patients.

Another example of research stimulated by case studies comes from Wolpe's research on systematic desensitization psychotherapy (Wolpe, 1969). Wolpe experimented with "graduated counterconditioning" to overcome phobias. The procedure involves a gradual reduction in the subject's psychological distance from the feared object as his fear is progressively reduced. Wolpe developed the idea for this research partly on the basis of Jones's (1924) case studies of childhood phobias.

The Paradox.   The existence of paradoxes, or apparent contradictions, in human behavior quite naturally sparks our curiosity and leads to speculative explanations, some of which may be converted to testable hypotheses and investigated. One example of this was Latané and Darley's (1970) observation of bystander behavior. The paradox they noticed was that crisis victims were less likely to receive help from bystanders when there were many onlookers than when there was only one bystander. Latané and Darley attempted to account for this oddity by developing a diffusion-of-responsibility hypothesis: the idea that each bystander's feeling of personal responsibility for helping diminishes in proportion to the number of other people present. Their extensive experiments on this hypothesis gave it considerable support.

Conflicting Results.   Science abhors inconsistencies. Therefore, when different investigators conduct similar experiments on the same problem and report results that do not agree, seeds for a variety of additional studies have been sown. The additional studies typically are designed to do one of two things: either expose a research error that can account for the discrepant findings or suggest a superordinate principle that will reconcile the conflicting results. Zajonc's (1965) analysis of the initially puzzling data on social facilitation (reviewed in Chapter 2) represents the second type of resolution. You will recall his hypothesis that the increased arousal caused by the presence of others facilitates the performance of easy tasks but hinders the performance of hard tasks. Thus, task difficulty was the apparent key to reconciling the discrepant results. How would you set up an investigation to test Zajonc's proposal?

Hypothetico-Deductive Method.   Sometimes fruitful research ideas emerge from the logical combination of two lines of inquiry. McClelland and Atkinson's (1953) original studies of achievement motivation exemplify this hypothetico-deductive approach to deriving hypotheses. Their research on achievement motivation grew out of Freud's view that motivation is expressed in fantasy, combined with Edward C. Tolman's theory that performance is a joint function of *motivation, expectancy* (one's subjective probability of succeeding), and *incentive* (perceived value of the goal). The convergence of these two lines of theorizing resulted in a brand-new deduction that was ripe for empirical testing. The chain of reasoning went something like this:

1. Hypothesis 1 (from Freud): If you ask a person to tell a story about an ambiguous picture containing human figures engaged in some activity, the fantasies expressed in the story will reflect the degree to which the storyteller is preoccupied with (i.e., motivated by) achievement thoughts. The achievement-fantasy score on this projective test is called the Motive to Succeed (*Ms*).

2. Hypothesis 2 (from Tolman): Motivation is expressed in performance only to the extent that the person has an *expectancy* of succeeding in the achievement of a goal, and only to the degree that the goal has *incentive value*. Expectancy of success could be defined as one's subjective probability of success (*Ps*). In turn, the incentive value of success is the complement of the likelihood of success, or $Is = (1 - Ps)$. In other words, easy goals are less valuable than improbable goals.

3. McClelland and Atkinson's *deduction* based on the combination of hypothesis 1 (Freud) and hypothesis 2 (Tolman): The motive to succeed (*Ms*) will be expressed in a performance measure—called the Tendency to Approach Success (*Ts*)—to the extent that the probability of success and the incentive value of success approach their optimal values. Specifically, the Tendency to Approach Success will be a *multiplicative* function of the fantasy-based measure of *Ms* times the situationally determined values of *Ps* and *Is*. Thus, McClelland and Atkinson's predictive formula: $Ts = Ms \times Ps \times Is$.

From this hypothetico-deductive model, McClelland and Atkinson were able to predict subjects' performance in achievement-oriented tasks.

Commonsense Analysis.   Research proposals often originate from a commonsense assessment of how people function on a daily basis to produce a particular behavior. I always have been fascinated by the ability of some individuals to remember trivia—obscure names, dates, and events—and have noticed that most people who are good at the trivia game tend to be outgoing and talkative, that is, extroverted. I also know that oral rehearsal of newly learned material strengthens its accessibility in memory (Gates, 1917). Is it possible that extroverted people are generally better "trivia players" than introverted people because, as extroverts, they frequently verbalize their recently acquired tidbits? How could I test this commonsense idea?

Extending Existing Data.   Practically speaking, a sizable proportion of the research done in any field of science is designed primarily to extend previous findings and conclusions to new settings, procedures, or populations. It is in this way that limits on the generalizability of findings are established. As an example, consider a fascinating line of research on "hunger motivation" in humans. Most of us feel that we eat primarily because we need the nourishment to keep our bodies healthy and fully functioning. But there is considerable evidence that many obese humans eat mainly in response to the sight of food or food-related stimuli rather than because of physiological need. Nisbett (1968), for instance, found that the number of sandwiches consumed by overweight subjects was a function of how many sandwiches were in clear view. (Extra sandwiches were available for the taking in a nearby refrigerator.) Obese subjects who could see three sandwiches ate substantially more than obese subjects who initially had only one sandwich in their visual field. In contrast, the amount consumed by subjects of normal weight was not affected by the visibility of the food.

Ross (1974) extended these findings using a different procedure. He found that obese humans eat twice as many cashew nuts when bright lights are focused on the nuts than when the lighting is dim. His slim subjects were not affected by the lighting. Rodin (1975) further reinforced the thesis of cue-dependent eating in the obese with still another approach. When obese subjects were exposed to a mouth-watering description of food, they ate much more than their slim counterparts who had heard the same description.

Where to Look for Ideas

Even though you are now familiar with the diversity of ways in which psychologists come up with research hypotheses, you may still be wondering just where you should look for some general ideas, just to get started. Fortunately, many "thought starters" are close at hand.

Listening to People.   Don't overlook the questions that students ask in class—including those you ask. Questions like "Are females more responsive than males to nonverbal communications?" and "Why didn't Dr. Sloggenbottom include this condition in his study?" often contain implicit research ideas. Also, your professor's lectures may contain many promising directions for research projects. One thing to remember, though, is that *the person who suggests a research idea has first "dibs" on it*. So be sure to get the originator's permission to borrow her idea for your study. This is an important ethical practice.

Textbooks.   Try leafing through texts that you have used in your social science courses. Many times you will run across a line of research that intrigued you while you were taking the course. Perhaps you will be able to devise a new test of an old hypothesis or develop a study that extends previous findings. Or, better yet, you might be able to deduce a completely original hypothesis by combining two existing theories or principles.

Introductory textbooks are a good place to start because they contain simplified descriptions of a variety of theories and findings. Once you have settled on a general idea or area of research, advanced texts in that area will provide further details on your subject. However, because of the considerable time lag involved in writing and publishing a text, it will be necessary for you to do some additional searching through current periodicals. A thorough familiarity with recent research that bears on your hypothesis is a prerequisite to meaningful inquiry.

Popular Periodicals.   Of course, newspapers and magazines written for the general public sometimes prove to be valuable sources of hypotheses, so don't overlook them. More specialized publications geared to scientific interests are an even better bet. My students have found the following periodicals to be quite helpful: *Psychology Today, Human Behavior, American Scientist, Scientific American, Science, Discover.*

Journal Articles.   Scientific journals are the principal means that researchers use to communicate their efforts to the scientific community. Therefore, each issue of every journal is teeming with potential ideas for new research. Even if you obtain your hypothesis elsewhere, you will want to consult recent issues of particular journals to see what, if anything, has been done in your area of interest. Ask your librarian for a list of journals in psychology and related fields. You will be astounded by the great number available.

Now, two caveats about digging into the journal literature. First, scientific journal articles are written for experienced researchers, and the prevailing norm is succinctness of expression. So be prepared for encountering a tight writing style, some unfamiliar technical terms, and sophisticated statistical analyses. (You may need to consult your instructor or a good statistics book in some cases.) Also, sometimes a good piece of research is communicated in a dry fashion. Stick with it! A difficult article may turn out to be the one containing the information you need. What's more, learning how to read professional journals can be a rewarding intellectual experience.

A second caveat is that you may be overwhelmed by the sheer number of journals that pertain to your research topic. In some cases there are dozens. Given your time constraints, it may be impossible to search through just the last two years of the relevant periodicals. Mercifully, there are more efficient ways to find the literature you need.

Literature Retrieval Systems. You can dramatically reduce your literature search time, while increasing its thoroughness, by taking advantage of commonly available literature retrieval systems, such as *Psychological Abstracts, Science Citation Indexes*, and computerized reference services.

Summaries of research articles, books, and technical reports in psychology and related disciplines are available in *Psychological Abstracts*, which is published monthly by the American Psychological Association. Although there is an index at the end of each issue, you will save time by working with the semiannual *cumulative indexes*. Each cumulative index covers the literature summarized in six issues (approximately 13,000 abstracts!). Index topics are arranged alphabetically, and each one refers you by *article number* to the summaries related to that particular topic. The next step is to examine the summaries to determine which of the described publications pertain to your research idea. Since the summaries include complete references, it should then be a simple matter for you to track down the articles you are interested in.

Many researchers find the *Science Citation Index* (SCI) to be a convenient supplement to *Psychological Abstracts*. The SCI lists articles published in a broad range of physical, life, and social sciences. Each time period covered by the SCI is represented by three cross-indexed volumes: a *subject* index (the one you start with), a *source* index, and a *citation* index. Even though the SCI provides less complete coverage of the field of psychology than *Psychological Abstracts*, it has a special advantage: Once you track down a particular article through the subject and source volumes, you may consult the citation volume to locate most other articles and books that have cited your article during the specified time period. Thus, you normally gain easy and rapid access to a gold mine of additional sources related to your topic. The *Social Science Citation Index* may be used in the same way as the SCI.

In addition to the standard indexes described above, many libararies also provide a *computerized information service*. One such program is the Bibliographic Retrieval Service, which offers over fifty literature data bases. When you use this system or a similar one, the first step is to provide the reference librarian with a key word (e.g., "addictions"), key phrase (e.g., "opponent-process theory"), or an author's name. Using a data terminal to communicate with the computer, the librarian will feed the key terms into the search system. The computer will do your search for you, and, often in a matter of minutes, the line printer will produce a sizable list of references related to your key terms. You can then use the references as leads to the documents you need.

OPERATIONALIZING YOUR QUESTIONS

After you have *conceptualized* a research question, you will need to select a method for testing it empirically. That is, you will need to *operationalize* your research problem.

The various research designs used by scientists are described below. Which one you choose will depend on three criteria: (a) the nature of your question, (b) practical considerations, and (c) the purpose of the study. Cause-and-effect questions, for example, usually require some version of the experimental method. One the other hand, hypotheses that merely address the existence of a relationship are amenable to virtually any design. On the practical side, the experimental method cannot be used to investigate some questions, such as the relationship between child-rearing practices and honesty. Likewise, it usually is impractical to administer psychological tests when the research setting is a tavern!

The purpose of the study is still another matter to be considered. Some applied-research topics require use of the case study or the single-case experimental design. If your aim is to generalize findings, systematic observation, the survey method, or a field experiment may be most appropriate.

Internal and External Validity

Ideally, the task of science is threefold: to find invariant relationships among variables, to interpret those relationships in a cause-and-effect (theoretical) framework, and to generalize them beyond particular studies. Finding relationships is least difficult, and any method of research will allow you to do this. But choice of method will bear critically on the remaining tasks.

Interpreting relationships and generalizing relationships represent the issues of internal validity and external validity, respectively. An investigation has **internal validity** *to the extent that changes in your independent variable can be deemed responsible for changes in your dependent variable*. Although today's scientists often skitter around the word (Wolman, 1971), this is the "causality" question. The **external validity** issue addresses a different question: "To what populations, settings, treatment variables, and measurement variables can this effect be generalized?" (Campbell & Stanley, 1966, p. 5). As you will see, in the field of psychology there tends to be a trade-off between internal and external validity. Research methods designed to maximize one type of validity frequently fall short on the other type of validity. Historically, research psychologists have focused their efforts on increasing internal validity, usually to the detriment of generalizability. Recently, however, psychologists seem to have turned more attention toward the generalizability question (Argyris, 1980; Hersen & Barlow, 1976; Sommer, 1977). See Box 4–1 for one point of view of this matter.

Criteria of Causality.   You may evaluate the internal validity of an investigation by applying the standard criteria of cause-and-effect used by scientists. Generally speaking, three commonly accepted conditions must exist to support the claim that a change in variable X brought about a change in variable Y (Kenny, 1979):

1. *Covariation*. This means that a relationship, or *correlation*, must exist between the variables, such that a change in variable Y can be "predicted" from a change in variable X. A correlation between two variables does not suffice, by itself, to support a statement of cause-and-effect. But if the variables do not covary to some extent, then one cannot be influencing the other.

2. *Time Precedence*. Scientists assume that causal processes work forward in time. Therefore, if X is a cause of Y, then it must be shown that, when both variables are being observed, a change in X always precedes a change in Y. If Y sometimes changes first, then doubt is cast on the hypothesis that X is causing Y.

3. *Nonspuriousness*. In an analysis of cause-and-effect, nonspuriousness means that "plausible rival hypotheses" have been ruled out. A rival hypothesis would be that some

Box 4–1

ISSUES IN SCIENCE

Lab to Life: The Great Chasm?

Since psychology's birth as a science a little more than a century ago, psychological researchers have almost single-mindedly pursued better methods of controlling variables. The intent of improving controls is to increase the internal validity of findings. The principal way of achieving this has been the use of laboratory studies. But hasn't our obsession with the laboratory setting exacted a tremendous price in terms of the generalizability of our knowledge about people? Robert Sommer (1977) thinks so. He views the prevalence of laboratory studies in psychology as a case of the proverbial tail wagging the dog. That is, the controlled laboratory study began as a means of reaching a better understanding of human behavior. Now, however, control of variables seems to have become an end in itself, even though it may limit severely our understanding of "natural" behavior. In attacking what he sees as an overreliance on the experimental method, Sommer states that "we have developed a science of psychology based largely on behavior in the laboratory and have hedged on the issue of generalization" (p. 7).

In the interest of generalization, Sommer recommends the use of naturalistic observation, participant observation, and field experiments as first steps in investigating psychological questions. He also feels that even research topics suited to the laboratory should be studied under field conditions as well. Why? If "no analogues to the behavior exist in nature, then one must raise questions about the importance of the topic" (p. 7).

Sommer described how he and his students studied "social facilitation" effects in a natural setting:

My students and I visited each of the pubs in a middle-sized city, ordered a beer, and then sat down and recorded on napkins or pieces of newspaper the consumption of lone and group drinkers. We found that group drinkers consumed more, not because they drank faster, but because they remained longer in the pub. The longer people remained, the more they drank. (p. 7)

Sommer's interesting results were submitted for publication. However, the consulting editor gave the study a negative review because it lacked appropriate controls!

uncontrolled *third variable* (Z) is responsible for the relationship between X and Y; that changes in Z somehow are causing X and Y to change together, with X having no influence on Y. For example, the consumption of ice cream and the incidence of drownings covary positively—that is, increase and decrease together. But if you claimed that eating ice cream causes drowning, you would be faced with the task of ruling out at least one rival hypothesis: that variable Z, summer heat, is responsible for the relationship between ice cream consumption and drownings.

Interestingly, "faith" also figures into causal analysis. See Box 4–2 for an explanation.

Confounded Variables and Criterion 3.   The "nonspuriousness" criterion of cause-and-effect is the most difficult condition to satisfy. Indeed, it represents the Achilles heel of most research designs. This is because most methods of gathering data fail to control for possible contaminating variables (associated with variable X) that could produce changes in variable Y, even if X has no effect on Y whatsoever. These contaminating factors are called **confounded variables**. A classic example is the case of two introductory psychology teachers who use different teaching techniques but test with the same exams. If one class does better on the exams than the other class, you might attribute the outcome to

Box 4–2
ISSUES IN SCIENCE
Cause, Effect, and "Faith"

Covariation, time precedence, and nonspuriousness are the formal criteria of cause-and-effect in science. But there is an implicit fourth criterion that somehow supersedes the first three. Kenny (1979) referred to this as "an active, almost vitalistic process" (p. 4); I prefer to think of it as the element of "confidence," "belief," or "faith" that scientists have in a cause-and-effect link. This notion reflects Hume's (1748) widely accepted assertion that cause-and-effect processes cannot be directly observed. Thus, even when the scientist satisfies the covariation, time-precedence, and non-

spuriousness conditions, what she ultimately winds up with is a *theory* about how X might influence Y. The degree of confidence the scientific community has in that theory certainly depends on the extent to which the three formal conditions of causality have been met. But general confidence in the scientist's causal statements is also influenced by prevailing views in the scientific community, the professional standing of the investigator, and even the religious beliefs of her colleagues (Barber, 1962).

teaching technique. But since teaching technique is *confounded* (i.e., contaminated) by personality of the teacher, time that the class meets, and possibly the intelligence level of the students, your original causal inference could well be wrong. Any one of the uncontrolled variables could be producing the differences in test scores.

The concept of confounded variables is right at the heart of the internal validity problem, and it plays an important role in both the selection of research designs and the interpretation of relationships. In Chapter 7, I'll describe the most common sources of confounding as well as some effective ways to minimize it.

Criteria of Generalizability.   Methods of research are also selected and evaluated on the basis of the amount of generalizing they allow. Three criteria of external validity are commonly applied in determining the extent to which findings can be generalized beyond a particular research episode:

1. *Representativeness of the Sample.* You probably would have more confidence in the generalizability of responses obtained from a randomly selected group of research subjects than in the generalizability of responses given by a group of volunteer subjects. Obviously, subjects who select themselves for research participation may not fairly represent the natural diversity in a population of people.

2. *Representativeness of Investigative Conditions.* College students tend to behave more naturally outside the psychology laboratory than inside it. Thus, results obtained through unobtrusive observation of behaviors between class sessions should be generalizable to many other settings. In contrast, the results of a laboratory study may apply mainly to situations in which the students are aware of being studied.

3. *Representativeness of Tasks and Responses.* Variables that affect the memorization of a list of nouns may have only limited relevance to the retention of textbook concepts. In general, a number of activities and materials used in laboratory settings for reasons of convenience and control may not fairly represent many conditions of everyday life.

The problem of external validity is covered at length in Chapter 8.

Overview of Research Designs

In this book, you will learn about five basic research designs that psychological research-ers use to operationalize their questions and hypotheses. The methods differ from one another in the degree to which the researcher intervenes in, and changes, the environ-ment of his subjects. The major objective of researcher intervention is to control variables that bear on the internal validity of the findings. Efforts to control variables also influence external validity, however, and not always in a desirable way.

Here I will briefly preview the basic methods and compare them on the two validity dimensions. To aid the process of comparison, I will present examples of how each method might be used to investigate an interesting question, the "frustration-aggression hypothesis" (Dollard, Doob, Miller, Mowrer, & Sears, 1939), which states that a frus-trated organism is always more likely to respond aggressively than an organism that is not frustrated. Thus the independent, or "cause," variable is frustration, and the dependent, or "effect," variable is aggressive behavior.

Systematic Observation. Of all the research designs, systematic observation generally in-volves the smallest amount of researcher intervention. Its simplest form is **naturalistic observation**, in which the researcher unobtrusively records the behavior of unaware sub-jects in their natural environment. The overriding goal of naturalistic observation is to develop an accurate description of the behaviors and relationships that operate when peo-ple or animals are not reacting to circumstances of "being observed."

Normally, systematic observation studies produce results with good external validity. But internal validity is hard to establish. To illustrate the internal validity problem, let's consider a hypothetical study of the frustration-aggression hypothesis. Suppose you as-sume an inconspicuous post at a busy intersection and observe horn honking (aggression) among drivers before and during rush hour (frustration) in a metropolitan setting. You are likely to find that during the presumably frustrating conditions of rush-hour traffic, there are more horn honks than during an equivalent period before rush hour. But can you be confident that frustration is producing the increased honking? Rush hour is not only confounded by time of day but also by the number of cars on the road; more cars mean more honking regardless of frustration. Also, consider the possibility that honking the horn might be a necessary part of the strategy involved in negotiating a traffic jam. In short, it is just plain hard to rule out plausible rival hypotheses with the minimal control available in simple observational studies.

The Case Study. A case study is an intensive investigation of an individual or an organi-zation. The idea of a case study is to focus on important present behaviors, query the in-dividual extensively on events in his past, and try to find out how past events are related to the present behaviors. Freud's psychoanalytic case histories represent this method.

Case studies involve a little more intervention and control than most systematic obser-vation studies. Because the subject of the case study is acutely aware of being examined, and because the investigative conditions may be somewhat atypical (e.g., the analyst's of-fice), the external validity of this approach generally is only moderate. (External validity may, in fact, be low if observations are based on only one subject.) For a variety of rea-sons (discussed in Chapter 10), the internal validity of the case-study method is highly questionable.

To return to the frustration-aggression hypothesis, let's suppose that a counselor of male adolescents observes that his cases of adolescent aggression often involve clients who had deprived (i.e., frustrating) childhoods. How solidly do these observations support the hypothesis that frustration caused the aggression? Is it not possible that the clients who suffered deprivation in childhood came from lower-class neighborhoods? Consider this possibility in light of the well-documented evidence concerning social class and aggression: Direct physical expression of aggression is a coping mechanism that is nurtured in lower-class male children (Gouldner & Gouldner, 1963; Miller & Swanson, 1960). Thus the clear possibility remains that child-rearing practices, rather than deprivation per se, were responsible for the high levels of aggression. In general, case studies fail to control for a host of potentially confounding factors.

The Psychometric Method.   Both the psychometric approach and its first cousin, the survey method, involve more intervention and control than the case study. For one thing, subjects in psychometric studies are asked to respond to a *standard set of stimuli* (questions and statements). Also, the standard stimuli usually are administered by a person who clearly assumes the role of an investigator, as opposed to a counselor, therapist, or consultant.

In the psychometric method a sample of people is given one or more psychological tests and is measured on two or more psychological traits. Then the investigator performs a statistical analysis on the test scores to see if there is a relationship (i.e., correlation) between the scores on one trait and the scores on another trait.

Since there are tests of aggression and tests of frustration, you could use the psychometric approach to see if aggression is related to frustration. But since correlations are not solely sufficient to infer causation, the internal validity of your findings would be suspect. That is, a third variable could responsible for the observed relationship.

The external validity of the psychometric approach depends on how representative your sample of subjects is and the extent to which your test scores predict behavior outside the testing situation. Normally, psychometric studies have only low to moderate generalizability.

The Survey Method.   Social scientists conduct surveys with samples of people for the purpose of generalizing to a whole population. Properly conducted sample surveys—those based on techniques of random sampling—possess high external validity (see Chapter 12). That is, the sample's results also apply to the population. The generalizability of findings from such surveys is conveniently demonstrated by the success that professional pollsters have in predicting the outcomes of national elections.

The principal steps in conducting a survey-type study are:

1. Define the population of interest and the characteristics (i.e., variables) you wish to study in that population.
2. Draw a representative subset, or *sample*, of people from that population.
3. Measure the target variables in the sample of people.
4. On the basis of the sample's characteristics, attempt to make general statements about those same characteristics in the original population.

Like the psychometric approach, the survey method offers little in the way of internal validity. For example, Campbell (1947) surveyed a representative national sample of white, non-Jewish Americans to investigate factors associated with negative attitudes toward Jews. He found that the more economically frustrated people were, the more they expressed aggressive attitudes toward Jews. This outcome appears to support the notion that frustration produces aggression. But take a more critical look. It has been determined that having negative attitudes toward minority groups is associated with having little formal education (Bettleheim & Janowitz, 1964). Therefore, it is entirely possible that certain variables related to amount of education affect *both* a person's economic situation and his attitudes toward Jews. Economic frustration itself may have no influence on aggressive feelings. We simply cannot be very confident about the causal role of frustration, because the survey method doesn't permit the logical elimination of plausible rival hypotheses.

The Experimental Method. The experiment is the most efficient method available for assessing cause-and-effect hypotheses. The logic of the experimental method is simple: Only one independent variable[2] is manipulated while all other potential influences are held constant. The behavior of interest, that is, the dependent variable, is carefully observed and recorded. If the subjects' behavior changes significantly, the change logically can be attributed to the one thing that was deliberately varied—the independent variable.

Because potentially confounding variables are held constant, the internal validity of properly carried out experiments is high. The usual way that control is exercised in an experiment is through random, or chance, assignment of subjects to experimental treatments. As Campbell and Stanley (1966) put it, "The true experiment differs from [other methods of research] just because the process of randomization disrupts any lawful relationships between the character of antecedents of the subjects and their exposure to X [a level of the independent variable]" (p. 65).

You could do an experiment to test the frustration-aggression hypothesis by adapting a procedure used by Barker, Dembo, and Lewin (1941). Using 50 children as subjects, you would first randomly assign 25 children to each of two conditions: Frustration or No Frustration. Most of the time, random assignment will make the two groups "statistically equivalent" on all potentially confounding variables. Next you would manipulate the independent variable by treating the two groups differently in just one way: You frustrate one group but not the other.

Frustration would be varied in the following manner. Every child in the experiment would be led into a room where old broken toys are piled up in the middle of the floor. Behind a screened partition in the room there would be a display of brand-new toys. In the Frustration condition the child would not be able to get to the desirable toys because the door on the partition would be locked. However, each child in the No Frustration condition would have full access to the desirable toys, as the door would be unlocked. Children in the first group would be considered "frustrated" because their goal-directed behavior toward the visible toys would be blocked by the locked barrier.

Your dependent variable, aggression, would be measured by counting the number of times each child cried, uttered an angry statement, or abused the broken toys.

If the Frustration children showed significantly more aggressive responses than the No Frustration children, you would be fairly confident that the frustration variable had produced the difference. Why? Because random assignment of subjects to levels of the independent variable very likely equated the groups on everything else that could have affected their aggression.

Before you rejoice in having been led to the "perfect" design, consider the following limitations of the experimental method. I mentioned earlier that many problems of interest to psychologists cannot be studied via the experiment. Beyond this, many experimental studies have poor external validity. There are several reasons for the generalizability problem: In most experiments, subjects are keenly aware of being "experimented on" and, therefore, may behave atypically; the laboratory setting often has an artificial atmosphere about it; laboratory tasks tend to be highly contrived and may not have real-life counterparts; for reasons of control, experimental stimuli frequently are unrealistically simple.

In Search of a Method

Table 4–1 gives a summary comparison of the five basic research methods along the dimensions of internal and external validity. The designations "high," "moderate," and "low" represent typical situations but would not be accurate for all applications of the designs.

At this point, you may be frustrated (but, one hopes, not aggressive) regarding the problem of which research design to use. It seems that they all have problems—and they do. Even if your research question is amenable to the experimental approach, the problem of generalizing your findings looms ahead.

The hard fact is that there is no single method solely sufficient for researching all, or even the majority, of psychological topics. And because many areas have been only sparsely investigated and many aspects of our research technology are still crude, there is no particular method that is universally preferred in psychology.

At present, then, how can you deal with the dilemma of internal versus external validity? Both "triangulation of methods" and "hybrid methods" offer possible solutions to this problem.

Multiple Converging Methods.   Most hypotheses and problems that psychologists study can be approached through a variety of research designs. You already have seen how the frustration-aggression hypothesis could be tested with all of the basic methods. Even such traditionally experimental areas as memory and perception can be investigated through a number of different operations (Brunswik, 1956; Hermann & Neisser, 1978). Using multiple methods to converge on a single problem is referred to as "triangulation" (Denzin, 1970), a term borrowed from the surveying profession. The advantage of triangulation is that a deficiency in either the internal or external validity of one research method may be compensated for by using other methods to follow-up on the initial study. For example, Thompson (1980) employed a combination of systematic observation and the psychometric method to assess the external validity of memory phenomena that had been observed almost exclusively in experimental settings. His interesting findings are described in Box 4–3.

Hybrid Methods.   Some hypotheses can be approached via methods that combine the advantages of two or more basic designs. **Field experiments**, for instance, are well-controlled studies conducted in natural settings. Sherif and Sherif's (1956) experiment on the

TABLE 4–1

A Comparison of Research Methods Along Two Dimensions of Validity

	Validity	
Method	*Internal*	*External*
Systematic Observation	Low	High
Case Study	Low	Low to Moderate
Psychometric	Low	Low to Moderate
Survey	Low	High
Experimental	High	Low

Box 4–3
HIGHLIGHT

Naturally Occurring Memories: A Lesson in Triangulation

Laboratory experiments on memory, often employing very simple materials under rigidly controlled conditions, have consistently produced the following results: (a) people remember material they generate themselves better than material that is given to them for memorization; (b) very meaningful items are forgotten at the same rate as less meaningful items; (c) rehearsal of material increases performance on an immediate memory test, but does not slow down the rate of forgetting over time.

To find out if these timeworn memory phenomena hold true outside the laboratory, Charles P. Thompson (1981) had 16 college students systematically observe and record unique events in their lives and in the lives of their roommates. The unique events were recorded all semester, and the roommates were not aware of the study until the end of the term. Using a type of psychometric procedure, the event recorders also rated the meaningfulness of each happening. At the end of each week, the recorders turned in that week's event descriptions to Thompson.

At the end of the semester the existence and nature of the investigation were revealed to the roommates. Both the recorders and their roommates were then given various psychometric-type tests of memory for the events.

Consistent with the findings of laboratory experiments, the results of Thompson's study showed that the more meaningful events were forgotten at the same rate as less meaningful items. That is, there was no correlation between the meaningfulness of material and how quickly it was lost from memory.

Some other findings flatly contradicted the outcomes of laboratory experiments. First, the recorders' rated memory for the events was no better than that of their roommates, in spite of the fact that the recorders had generated the event descriptions themselves. Second, contrary to prior lab data, events that Thompson's participants thought about (i.e., rehearsed) a lot were forgotten at a slower rate than events they had rehearsed less.

Thus, by creatively adapting classical questions about memory to systematic observation and psychometric methods, Thompson was able to examine the real-world validity of some long-standing experimental findings. The results were instructive indeed. Appropriately, he concluded, "It is not a foregone conclusion that results collected in a neatly designed and carefully executed laboratory study will transfer to the messy domain of memory for naturally-occurring events" (p. 20).

creation of intergroup hostility exemplifies this hybrid approach. To maximize the naturalness of investigative conditions, the Sherifs carried out the study in a summer-camp setting. Twenty-two preadolescent boys, who thought they were there to study camping methods, were divided into two matched groups—the Rattlers and the Eagles. The investigators induced intergroup competition through a series of contests between the Rattlers and the Eagles. One result of this competition was the development of extremely bad feelings between the groups. In a second phase of the experiment, the researchers reduced the hostility by setting up a number of problem situations that required cooperation between the rival groups. This classic study produced much useful information on the conditions that affect prejudice (Ashmore, 1970). Because of the way it was conducted (i.e., matched groups in a natural setting), it is considered to be both internally and externally valid.

SUMMARY

The greatest challenge for the beginning researcher is learning how to ask researchable questions. This involves a two-phase sequence: conceptualizing a specific problem or hypothesis and then "operationalizing" it into a research design.

Questions that are most useful to scientists are those that test a theory, explore a new domain, or address a practical problem. Broad questions must be narrowed down to be researchable. Several sources of possible research questions were reviewed in this chapter.

Once conceptualized, a research question must then be operationalized by converting it to a *research design*. The five basic designs are systematic observation, the case study, the psychometric method, the survey, and the experiment. Which design is used for investigating a particular question depends on certain practical considerations and the relative importance of *internal validity* versus *external validity*. Since all of the fundamental research designs tend to be deficient in either internal or external validity, social scientists frequently use several different methods to investigate a particular phenomenon.

REVIEW QUESTIONS

1. What criteria should be considered in determining whether a research question is "useful"? Why is the usefulness of a question sometimes difficult to evaluate?

2. Consider the question "How does old age affect sexual behavior?" Is this question a researchable one? If not, what would you have to do to it before you could conduct an empirical test?

3. List at least five sources of research ideas commonly used by psychologists, and give an example of each.

4. What is *Psychological Abstracts*? What information does it contain, and how would you use it?

5. What are the three chief criteria that determine choice of a particular research design?

6. Distinguish between internal validity and external validity.

7. Summarize the main characteristics of each major type of research design used by psychologists.

8. Compare and contrast the five basic research designs on the dimensions of internal validity and external validity.

9. State the rationale (logic) of the experimental method. (Hint: How does the experiment allow us to draw cause-and-effect conclusions?)

10. Define: confounded variables; triangulation of methods; hybrid methods.

Notes

[1]This statement should not be interpreted as a recommendation against attempts to duplicate recent or otherwise unreplicated studies.

[2]In some experiments, more than one independent variable is manipulated, but the manipulation is conducted in such a way that none of the independent variables is confounded with any other independent variable.

5

OBSERVING
AND MEASURING

Observation and measurement are fundamental to the empirical sciences. **Observation** occurs when you systematically note or record instances of behavior that fall into a preselected behavioral category. **Measurement** involves using an unambiguous set of rules to convert observations to a numerical scale.

In measurement theory, the numbers assigned to observations are meant to represent either (a) the *presence or absence* of an attribute, state, or process in the person observed (for example, schizophrenic = 1, "normal" = 0) or (b) the *amount* of an attribute, state, or process in the person observed (for example, IQ = 127).

Observation is the first step in the measurement process and, therefore, must be carefully planned and conducted. In any study you do, both your technique of observing and your measurement rules will be a function of the specific operational definitions and research design that you use. The operational definitions and research design, in turn, should accurately reflect your original research question and the theoretical concepts of interest. Thus, a logical consistency should bind the stroke of your data-recording pen to the conceptual underpinnings of your project.

That, in a nutshell, is what this chapter is all about: the logic and procedures used in translating psychological concepts into observables, and then into numbers that can be subjected to statistical analysis. First, we'll look at the difference between clear and unclear rules of measurement and why it is important to use clear measurement rules. Second, we'll consider two dimensions that are central to the *quality* of measurement: reliability and validity; we'll also review some ways to increase the reliability and validity of measurement. Third, we'll survey the most frequently used measurement techniques in psychology. Finally, we'll consider the problem of how to get "honest" measurements from people.

DEVELOPING CLEAR MEASUREMENT RULES

In devising a measure of something, the main initial consideration is that the rules for assigning numbers to observations be clear as to their application (Kerlinger, 1979; Nunnally, 1967). To illustrate this point, I'll use the example of book-carrying behavior in college students.

Numerous investigators have reported sex-related book-carrying styles (e.g., Hanaway & Burghardt, 1976; Jenni and Jenni, 1976; Scheman, Lockard, & Mehler, 1978). The basic finding in these studies was that males tend to carry books down at the side (about hip level) in one hand, whereas females tend to carry books against the abdomen or chest, frequently securing them with both hands.

Now suppose I have a hunch that, in addition to gender, the "masculine book-carrying style" is related to college students' major areas of study; further, that I wish to test this hypothesis through a systematic observation approach. Assuming that I have devised a means of ascertaining each subject's college major, how might I measure "masculine book-carrying style"? I have specified the unit of observation (college students) and the characteristic that I wish to measure, so I now need to state a rule for converting observations of book-carrying behavior to a numerical scale.

An example of an *unclear* rule is as follows:

> The book carrier will be rated on a 5-point scale representing the extent to which books are carried "down at the side."

You probably see a lot of problems with this rule. Just a few questions begged by this ambiguous formulation are: What specific scale values are to be used? Do they range from 0 to 4 or from 1 to 5? What are the descriptive anchor points on the measurement scale? Is "at the chest level" the opposite extreme from "down at the side"? Or is it "on the head"? Is the highest number on the scale to be assigned to the "down at the side" anchor point or to its opposite? What specific *behavioral criteria* will the rater(s) use to assign scale values to book-carrying styles?

Obviously my measurement rule, as it stands, is not sufficiently clear to permit a consistent assignment of numbers to observations. A less ambiguous statement of my measurement rule might take the following form:

> The book carrier will be rated on a 5-point scale representing the extent to which his/her behavior approximates the "masculine book-carrying style." The scale values range from 1 to 5, where 1 means "least masculine" and 5 means "most masculine." The following behavioral criteria will be used to assign ratings:
>
> 5—Books are held down at one side, resting in the carrier's hand; the cover of one book is almost flush against the carrier's hip, and the books are approximately parallel to the body's vertical axis.
>
> 4—Books are down at one side, resting on the carrier's forearm and hand; the ends of the books are resting obliquely on the carrier's hip and are approximately at a 45° angle to the body's vertical axis.
>
> 3—Books are pressed against the carrier's abdomen and chest, secured by one hand and forearm; the books are approximately parallel to the body's vertical axis.
>
> 2—Books are held against the carrier's abdomen with both hands; books' ends are supported by the abdomen, and the books are approximately at a 45° angle to the body's vertical axis.
>
> 1—Books are pressed against the carrier's abdomen and chest, secured by both hands and both forearms; the books are approximately parallel to the body's vertical axis.

In contrast to the unclear measurement rule considered initially, the clear rule spells out the precise criteria for assigning numbers to observations. This must always be the case if measurement rules—and operational definitions in general—are to be useful.

Even the clearest measurement rules need to be refined and adapted to specific circumstances. In the case of the second rule given above, for example, some decision would have to be made regarding occasional book-carrying styles that do not fit the rating scheme. Also the possibility of assigning midpoint ratings (e.g., 3½) to "in-between" styles might be considered. And the physical layout and format of the scale would need to be selected.

It is best to iron out these small problems during a **pilot study**, which is a type of practice run that precedes the actual study. It is a good idea to do a pilot study prior to undertaking any type of investigation, but this is particularly true of research projects that require the training of raters.

RELIABILITY AND VALIDITY

Once you develop an unambiguous measurement rule, you have a measuring device. But there is an important distinction between measurement per se and the quality of measurement (Kerlinger, 1979). The quality of your measurement procedure is established by evidence that it is (a) measuring something consistently and (b) measuring what it is supposed to measure. These two concerns represent the issues of **reliability** and **validity**, respectively.

When used as criteria for assessing the quality of a measurement procedure, the concepts of reliability and validity can be looked at from three angles. First, you can consider their definitions and logical significance. Second, you can view them within the context of two kinds of measurement error. Third, you can look at reliability and validity operationally—that is, in terms of the procedures used to evaluate each of them.

Definitions and Rationale

The Question of Trustworthy Data.   Reliability refers to the consistency of results produced by a measure. When a reliable measurement operation is administered to the same group of people more than once, the individuals being measured tend to retain the same ranks in the group from one measurement episode to the next. The expectation of such consistent outcomes stems from the assumption that psychological characteristics are relatively stable across time. Thus, if the instrument being applied is measuring any trait at all, the ranks it assigns to persons should not fluctuate wildly from time to time. In short, the results should be replicable.

Conversely, when the expected stability of outcomes is almost entirely absent, the measurement instrument is really measuring nothing more than random, or chance, processes—as in the roll of a die. In such a case, you would have little faith in the data. When assessed for reliability, most psychological measures show evidence of some stability, though often the stability is far from perfect. In any case, the greater the consistency of data produced by a measurement procedure, the more confident you are that something more than chance is being measured, and the better the quality of your measurements.

The Question of Relevant Data.   To be useful, measures must be not only reliable but also valid. A measurement procedure is valid to the extent that what it measures is *relevant* to what it is supposed to measure.

To get a better feel for the concept, consider a hypothetical situation in which valid measurement is questionable. Imagine you are taking a course titled "Applied Statistics," and that both the textbook content and the classroom lectures emphasize the use of statistical procedures in applied situations. But suppose that every exam in the course consists mostly of problems requiring you to develop mathematical proofs of statistical formulas. Further, none of the test items asks for a demonstration of what is stressed in the course—namely, ability to apply statistical procedures to data sets. Are the tests relevant to mastery of the course material? Certainly not. Therefore, if we assume that the purpose of classroom exams is to assess content mastery, then the exams used by the hypothetical statistics instructor would be considered invalid.

The same type of measurement problem exists when personnel officers use selection tests that are irrelevant to success in the jobs applied for. To be a valid criterion for hiring a job applicant, a selection test must be shown to be a good predictor of job performance: People who get high scores on the test should receive better on-the-job performance evaluations than those who get lower test scores. In fact, it is a violation of federal law to use selection tests lacking empirically demonstrated relevance to job performance (Howell, 1976).

There are two major reasons that psychological researchers worry so much about the validity of measurement. First, they cannot justify theoretical statements about data unless they know what psychological processes the data reflect. Second, it is possible to speak of individual differences on a psychological trait only to the extent that measurements of individuals can be shown to represent that trait.

In most scientific investigations, the researcher attempts to ensure the validity of her measures in advance of data collection. This is done by carefully considering the logical, theoretical, and empirical relationships between the measurement operations employed and the constructs that the investigator wishes to study.

Unreliability Limits Validity.   In a sense, the problem of developing a valid measure "piggybacks" on the reliability of measurement. Put simply, a measure that is unreliable cannot be a valid measure of anything. A more practical statement is that the validity of a measurement operation is limited by the operation's reliability. By using stable measures of your variables, you increase the potential for obtaining valid results. As is explained below, however, high reliability does not guarantee valid measurement—but it does make valid measurement possible by minimizing the amount of random error in your data.

Two Types of Measurement Error

Unsystematic Error.   The ideal in a two-variable investigation is to obtain two error-free numerical indexes, or "scores," for each participant in the study. The scores would represent the subjects' *true* relative standing on each of the variables under investigation. Then the researcher could examine the scores of all subjects on both variables to see if the variables are systematically related—for example, people with high values on variable A might tend to obtain low values on variable B—and then attempt to interpret the relationship within the context of a theory.

In this ideal situation, a person's score on measure A could be represented as follows:

Subject's Score = | True Score on Measure A |

The "true score" shown in the figure is the score a person would receive if the measuring device were completely free of random error.

Unfortunately, many measures are not error-free. Random, or **unsystematic**, error may contaminate the measurement process in the case of one or more variables in a study. Random errors result from such factors as confusing instructions to the subject, momentary distractions, a fluctuating mental or physical state of the subject, equipment errors, unsystematic recording errors on the researcher's part, etc. And it is these random errors that lower the reliability of measurement. Consequently, a person's score on measure A might be visualized more realistically as:

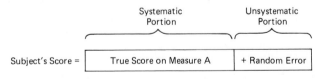

Note that *the true-score portion of the measurement contains the valid part of the measurement.*

With a very unreliable measure, the picture looks like this:

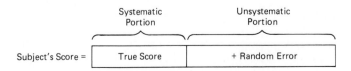

It probably is obvious to you by now that the greater the random error in a measurement, the less room there is in a subject's score for the valid component of the measurement. It is in this sense that the reliability of a measure places a limit on the measure's validity.

Systematic Error.   The problem of measurement error extends beyond the random influences that create unreliability in measures. All too often, measurements are also beset by a second type of error that is of a *systematic* nature—that is, does not vary randomly from time to time—and actually exists as part of a subject's true score. Even if your method of measurement is perfectly reliable, so that subjects' obtained scores equal their true scores in every instance, part of each score may represent something that is irrelevant to the construct you are attempting to measure. This is because not all of the stable part of a measurement is necessarily a valid representation of the variable of interest (Brown, 1976).

If you find this idea a bit strange or puzzling, consider the following example. Suppose you are interested in identifying social blunders that induce severe guilt. To conduct this program of research, you develop an almost perfectly reliable test of guilty feelings. After you have published a couple of interesting research reports on guilt induction, other researchers obtain your permission to use the guilt test in their own research. Much to your surprise, you later discover that your test has been successfully employed as a measure of "interpersonal anxiety"! In addition, one investigator reported that when interpersonal anxiety was controlled, your guilt test was only weakly responsive to guilt-induction techniques. In light of the evidence, you realize that scores on your extremely reliable instrument are far from perfectly valid indicators of guilt as a "pure" construct. In fact, you conclude, true scores on your test probably represent this situation:

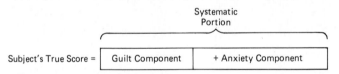

In constructing items for your guilt index, it is likely that you systematically, but erroneously, incorporated much material that is relevant to anxiety. Thus, as a measure of guilt per se, your instrument is partially invalid.

The above example illustrates the point that *reliability is necessary but not sufficient for validity.* While high reliability reduces the influence of *random* measurement errors, thereby permitting valid measurement, enough systematic error may still exist to invalidate the measurement procedure.

Procedures for Assessing Reliability and Validity

Another way of approaching the concepts of reliability and validity is to consider some operations typically used to assess the quality of measurement. (Since I discuss these techniques in detail in Chapter 11, at this point I'll describe only two techniques for each concept.)

Reliability Assessment.   The most easily understood operation used to evaluate reliability is the **test-retest method.** To use this approach, you administer a measurement procedure to one group of subjects on two occasions, let's say today and a week from today.[1] Then you compare the measured values obtained on the first occasion to those obtained the second time around to see if your subjects tended to retain their individual ranks in the group from one time to the other. To the extent that people keep the same standings from the first measurement episode to the second, the measurement procedure is said to be reliable. It produces stable results.

You can get a clear picture of the test-retest method by studying Table 5–1. Note that seven people have been measured twice with a fairly reliable measure, Measure A, and twice with an unreliable device, Measure B. Each person's rank in the group is given for each measurement occasion.

You can see that when Measure A was used, the subjects' respective ranks changed very little from the test to the retest. But when Measure B was used, it would have been impossible to predict the retest results from the initial test outcomes. There was simply too much instability in ranks across time.

Researchers often employ the **linear correlation coefficient**, symbolized by r, as a numerical index of reliability and validity. When the r coefficient is used to index the degree of positive correspondence between two sets of ranks, its value can range from 0.00 (no correspondence between ranks) to 1.00 (perfect correspondence between ranks).[2] Rarely does r equal 1.00. But the closer it gets to 1.00, the stronger the pattern of correspondence it represents. (See Chapter 6 for information on the computation of r.)

When the linear correlation coefficient is utilized to measure the stability or consistency of a measurement procedure, it is called the **reliability coefficient**, and is symbolized by r_{kk}. A general rule of thumb is that reliability coefficients should be at least .80 for measures of personality traits and at least .90 for measures of aptitudes and intelligence. But there are many exceptions to the guidelines (Brown, 1976).

When applied to the data shown in Table 5–1, $r_{kk} = .93$ for Measure A, but only .29 for Measure B. Thus, Measure B is like a fair-weather friend: It can't be counted on from one day to the next. In contrast, the first reliability coefficient tells us that Measure A is trustworthy.

A second procedure commonly used to evaluate reliability is referred to as the **interrater**, or **interscorer**, method. Just as a measurement procedure should produce consistent results across time, so should it yield consistent outcomes across different researchers who are measuring a particular group of people at the same time.

TABLE 5–1

Hypothetical Sets of Ranks Produced by a Reliable Measure (A) and an Unreliable Measure (B)

Person	Measure A[a]		Measure B[b]	
	Rank on 1st Measurement	Rank on 2nd Measurement	Rank on 1st Measurement	Rank on 2nd Measurement
Jane	1	1	1	3
Sue	2	3	2	4
Kate	3	2	3	6
Lonny	4	4	4	1
Bill	5	5	5	2
Mack	6	7	6	7
Doug	7	6	7	5

[a]$r_{kk} = .93$
[b]$r_{kk} = .29$

To assess interrater reliability, you and another researcher would simultaneously observe a group of subjects and *independently* convert their responses or observable characteristics to numerical data. For example, both of you could rate the physical attractiveness of 10 college students, using a 7-point rating scale. Then you and the other rater would compare your attractiveness scores to find out if the 10 subjects tended to be rated similarly by each of you. As in the case of test-retest reliability, you could compute a reliability coefficient to index the degree of correspondence between the two sets of ratings.

It is especially important to establish interrater reliability when the research project entails the use of (a) rating scales, (b) open-ended questions (e.g., What is your opinion of the Equal Rights Amendment?), or (c) thematic or essay-type responses on the subjects' part. In general, interrater reliability becomes a significant consideration to the degree that the measurement or scoring process invites scorer subjectivity or scorer error.

Validity Assessment.   The most intuitively obvious approach to evaluating the validity of a measurement operation is **content validation**. This involves inspecting the psychological content apparently tapped by the measure and judging whether that content is relevant to the trait or process you are attempting to investigate (APA, 1974). In putting together a true-false test of self-esteem, for instance, an investigator probably would include statements such as "I like the sex I am" and "I'm as competent as most people." But in terms of establishing the test's content validity, the test constructor would be hard pressed to justify inclusion of the statement, "I would rather own a Jaguar than a Cadillac." In situations where content validity is a concern, as it is with independent and dependent variables in most experiments, the theoretical appropriateness of the measurement operation usually is *ensured in advance*, via "expert judgment," rather than empirically assessed after data collection (Nunnally, 1967). Within the framework of your own research projects, you, your co-researchers, and other investigators with kindred research interests are the "experts."

It would be comforting if the discussion of validity could end here, embedded in the blissful simplicity of content validation, but validity is a complex notion taking many forms and approached from diverse angles. Often the apparent content of a measurement procedure is of secondary importance; in these cases, what the measure correlates with is of primary importance. A good example of this point comes from some research on the measurement of intelligence. Most people would be justifiably skeptical if they were told that their IQs could be measured via a simple line-judgment task. The content of such a task seems irrelevant to the concept of general intelligence, yet there is preliminary evidence suggesting that IQ is strongly correlated with the speed of judging which of two straight lines is longer (reported by Cohen, 1982). If these findings hold up under independent replication, then the line-judgment task would be considered a valid measure of IQ and , perhaps, the underlying construct of general intelligence.

Thus, a second operation used to validate measurement procedures is to demonstrate empirically that they are correlated with appropriate criteria. If a measure is designed to tap general intelligence, then scores on the measure should correspond regularly to scores on an accepted criterion of general intelligence. This is one type of **criterion-related validity** (APA, 1974). In most cases, the linear correlation coefficient is used to index the strength of relationship between the measure and its criterion or criteria. When applied in this way, the r statistic is termed the **validity coefficient**, and is symbolized r_{XY}, where X represents the measure and Y the criterion. It is noteworthy that a measure can have good criterion-related validity even though it may seem to lack content validity.

Consideration of criterion-related validity brings us back to the relationship between reliability and validity: Poor reliability greatly restricts the degree to which a variable can correlate with any other variable. So if either the measurement procedure or its criterion is unreliable, criterion-related validity will be difficult to establish.

Ways to Maximize the Reliability of Measurement

Experienced researchers use a variety of strategies and procedures to ensure and improve the reliability of their measurement operations. Here are a few steps that you can take to maximize the reliability of your data:

Choosing and Constructing Measurement Procedures.

1. Devise an unambiguous measurement rule. This matter was discussed at length earlier in this chapter.

2. If you are constructing your measurement procedure from scratch—that is, not using a tried and true procedure—it would be wise to conduct a pilot study for the express purpose of testing the measure's reliability.

3. In studies that employ systematic observation, select and define standard behavioral categories prior to beginning the observation process. An example of this strategy was given in the early part of this chapter, in connection with the observation of book-carrying styles. The use of predetermined checklists, in which response categories are anchored by clear behavioral criteria, yields much more reliable data than a ''decide as you go'' method of observing.

In general, it is a good idea to use behavior-based measures rather than subjects' self-reports or researcher ratings. Available evidence strongly suggests that data derived from observable behavior are considerably more reliable than subjectively generated data, such as data based on ratings of traits or characteristics (Fiske, 1979).

Presenting the Stimulus Situation.

1. Make sure that instructions and stimuli are presented to subjects in a clear and straightforward fashion. Questions or statements on a self-report device should be brief and stated in plain language. Each item should ask for only one piece of information or one judgment on the subject's part.

2. Standardize the treatment of subjects. With the exception of manipulation of the independent variable, all aspects of an experiment should be constant across subjects. In psychometric or survey studies, all subjects should receive the same instructions and explanations, as well as a standard set of statements or questions presented in a uniform fashion.

Collecting the Data.

1. Get a large sample of the subject's behavior. As a rule, a measurement operation becomes more reliable as you increase the size of the sample of behavior obtained from subjects. The reason? Large behavior samples tend to yield more precise estimates of subjects' true scores than do smaller samples (Nunnally, 1967). Larger behavior samples also will result in a greater range of subject scores on the dependent measure. This, too, increases reliability of measurement (Brown, 1976). So use many trials in an experiment, and many items to measure each dimension tapped by a test or questionnaire.

2. When subjective ratings or subjective scoring must be used, employ more than one rater or scorer. Averaging data across several observers provides a much more stable result than does the best effort of a lone observer (Strahan, 1980).

3. Monitor the functioning reliability of equipment.

Ways to Maximize the Validity of Measurement

While a measure's validity is usually more difficult to establish than its reliability (see Chapter 11), there are several techniques that you can use to increase the likelihood of obtaining valid results. A few of the more common procedures are described here.

Manipulated Variables.

1. Critically evaluate the logical relationship between your experimental manipulations and the psychological process you wish to manipulate. Obtain the critical opinion of co-researchers.

2. Use postexperimental interviews to determine how the experimental manipulations affected the subjects' psychological state. Asch (1956), for example, subjected college students to social pressure to get them to misjudge the length of straight lines. About 37 percent of them yielded to the pressure and gave verbal judgments that conflicted with information from their visual systems. Had social pressure actually changed their perception of length, or had they merely gone along with the group to avoid being embarrassed or ostracized? Asch's postexperimental conversations with his subjects revealed that a desire to conform to the group, rather than a perceptual alteration, accounted for most of the misjudgments.

3. Incorporate adjunct dependent measures into the experimental design to check the effect of manipulations. For example, if you are studying the effect of anxiety on affiliation (the main dependent variable), you might have your subjects in the different anxiety conditions rate their anxiety in the situation (e.g., Schachter, 1959). These ratings would serve to validate the effect of your anxiety manipulations.

Nonmanipulated Variables.

1. If you construct an original test or attitude scale, conduct pilot studies to establish the reliability and validity of the measure.

2. When constructing questionnaire or interview items, check the content of the items for their logical or theoretical relationship to the psychological variables you desire to measure. Solicit the opinion of others regarding what kind of information the items seem to be asking for. Do the same in developing items for an attitude scale or any other type of paper-and-pencil measure.

SCALES OF MEASUREMENT

Measurement is carried out at several levels of logical and mathematical sophistication. It is conventional in scientific disciplines to distinguish among four levels of measurement and to refer to them as **scales of measurement** (Wartofsky, 1968). Going from lowest to highest mathematical sophistication, there are **nominal, ordinal, interval,** and **ratio** scales. The higher scales meet all of the logical requirements and assumptions of those that are mathematically lower, and also satisfy some additional assumptions (Brown, 1976).

It is important to know what scale of measurement you are using because it will determine what mathematical and statistical operations you can perform on your data. For example, there is virtually no limit on the mathematics that can be applied to ratio-scale data. In contrast, there are severe restrictions on data representing nominal or ordinal measurement.

Nominal Scales

When you sort observations into categories that represent *differences in kind*, and nothing more, you are using a nominal scale. Examples include classifying people as depressed versus "normal," female versus male, recipients of psychotherapy A versus psychotherapy B; or classifying responses as assertive versus aggressive versus submissive, mature versus regressive, and so on. Note that a nominal scale of measurement makes only qualitative distinctions among events. All observations that share a common characteristic are placed in the same category, and there is no indication of differences in magnitude or quantity in the measurement operation.

Since the use of quantitative distinctions is usually not appropriate for a nominal scale—for example, being male is in no way "more" or "less" than being female—some authorities do not consider classification procedures to be measurement in the usual sense of the word (see Nunnally, 1967). But categorical differences frequently are assigned "dummy quantities" for purposes of statistical analysis. Thus, if a researcher wishes to study the correlation between eating habits and personality traits, each subject who is a vegetarian could receive a dummy quantity of 1, with nonvegetarians being scored as 0's.

The most common arithmetic operation applied to nominal data is to simply count the number of observations that fall into various categories. Once the tallying is complete, it is possible to use statistical procedures that apply to frequency counts.

Nominal scales, then, represent the lowest level of measurement. A researcher who chooses to use qualitative measures is greatly limited in terms of the possible mathematical and statistical treatments that can be applied to the data. For this reason, it is prudent to devise a higher scale of measurement when it is possible and realistic to do so.

Ordinal Scales

As the label implies, ordinal scales permit an ordering of observations according to magnitude. Ordinal scales include information provided by nominal scales—distinctions in kind—as well as information on the *ranks* that individual observations assume in the total set of observations. In short, they provide information on "more" or "less" as well as on "same" or "different."

Ordinal scales are quantitative since they allow the meaningful assignment of numbers to observations to represent different amounts of a trait or attribute.

Conventional classroom grading systems that involve the assignment of letter grades ranging from A to F exemplify ordinal measurement. The various grades represent not only differences in kind but also differences in the relative amount of course mastery shown by students: A final grade of B reflects a higher level of mastery than a C but less than an A.

Note, however, that this type of scale does not indicate the amount of distance between B students and C students on the dimension of course mastery. Without further information on how the grades are assigned, we can't assume that the knowledge differential between B and C students is equal to the knowledge differential between A and B students. Depending on the teacher, the amount of course mastery needed to move from a C rating to a B rating might be much more or much less than the amount required to advance from B to A. In the final analysis, all we have here is a ranking of students from highest to lowest, with many tied ranks. Thus, although ordinal scales provide information on the relative positions of observations on a measured dimension, they don't include information on the distance between observations.

It is important not to confuse values, or scale points, on an ordinal scale with the **numerical ranks** that correspond to these values. An example will clarify this distinction: A researcher could rate three subjects on an 11-point scale of extroversion, such that Mario, Sam, and Saleh receive ratings of 11, 10, and 7, respectively. Since the researcher feels that numerical differences between scale points are not accurate representations of actual amounts of difference in the trait of extroversion, he assumes only an ordinal scale. Accordingly, he converts the scale scores to ranks. Since Mario received the highest rating, his numerical rank is 1; likewise, Sam's rank is 2 and Saleh's is 3.

Since an ordinal scale lacks information on the distance between observations, it makes little mathematical sense to add or subtract scale points. For instance, it wouldn't be accurate to assert that $(10 - 8) = (8 - 6)$ in a situation where you can't be confident that two units represent the same amount of something all along the scale. For the same reason, it is not legitimate to multiply or divide ordinal-scale points by one another. Nonetheless, the numerical ranks representing the relative standings of observations often can be subjected to some of the usual arithmetical operations for purposes of statistical analysis. Table 5–2 lists most of the statistical treatments that can be applied to a set of ranks.

Interval Scales

In addition to possessing all of the properties of nominal and ordinal measurement, interval scales provide information on the distance between scale points in terms of equal scale

TABLE 5–2

Permissible Mathematical Operations and Applicable Statistical Procedures for Four Scales of Measurement

Scale	Permissible Mathematical Operations	Applicable Statistical Procedures
Nominal (Categories)	None	Counts, proportions, percentages, chi square, phi correlation coefficient, contingency coefficient, sign test, Z and t tests for proportions
Ordinal (Ranks)	Determination of inequalities	All of the above; simple ranks, percentile ranks, median, interquartile range, rank-order correlation, median test, Mann-Whitney U test, Kruskal-Wallis K test
Interval (Equal scale intervals)	Determination of inequalities; addition and subtraction of scale points and scale intervals; multiplication and division of scale intervals	All of the above; arithmetic mean, variance and standard deviation, standard scores, Z and t tests for means and mean differences, analysis of variance and covariance, Pearson r, Eta
Ratio (Equal intervals plus absolute zero)	All of the above; multiplication and division of scale points by one another	All of the above

units. That is, *each scale unit is equal to every other scale unit all along the measurement dimension*. Consequently, no matter what part of the dimension you are working with, score differences of a given magnitude always represent the same amount of difference in the attribute being measured. When temperature is measured with a Fahrenheit thermometer, for example, the difference between 110° and 100° equals the difference between 10° and 0°. Both scale differences represent exactly the same amount of difference in temperature.

Behavioral-science researchers prefer to employ interval scales rather than nominal or ordinal scales because interval scales permit a wider variety of mathematical operations. With interval scales, permissible operations include addition and subtraction of scale points and multiplication and division of scale intervals. For example, if you have equal intervals, it is accurate to say that $(9 - 7) = (5 - 3)$ and that $(9 - 7)/2 = (5 - 3)/2$. Recall that such operations are not meaningful when you have only an ordinal scale.

This mathematical flexibility leads to further advantages. You may apply a large number of useful statistical indexes and powerful statistical tests to interval-scale data (see Table 5–2).

What you can't do with interval-scale data is divide or multiply scale *points* by one another (Nunnally, 1967). This limitation stems from the fact that interval scales do not have absolute-zero points. For instance, $100/50 = 2$ only if the lowest value on the scale is truly zero. Otherwise the equality does not hold true. Certainly the above equation would not be accurate for the Fahrenheit thermometer, since, across much of the northern hemisphere, temperatures often plummet below the arbitrary zero point. In the same vein, it is absurd to assert that a person whose IQ is 160 is twice as intelligent as a person with an IQ of 80. Since no one has been able to identify or define an absolute zero for general intelligence, attempting to form ratios between scale points is an exercise in self-deception.

How can you know when you have an interval scale of measurement? In the case of most psychological variables, you can't—at least not for sure. In the behavioral sciences it often is impossible to prove directly that scale intervals are equal (Nunnally, 1967). The most widely adopted rule of thumb, therefore, is to *assume* an interval scale when you are reasonably confident that your scale at least approximates interval properties (Brown, 1976; Ghiselli, 1964). If the assumption of equal intervals leads to research results that are theoretically or practically useful, then your assumption is justified.

Ratio Scales

Ratio scales represent the highest level of measurement. They possess absolute-zero points in addition to having equal intervals. Therefore, all of the usual mathematical operations, including multiplying and dividing scale points by one another, can be carried out with ratio-scale data.

Although many physical measures, such as time and length, are on ratio scales, scaling at the ratio level is relatively rare in the field of psychology. Most psychological ratio scales are found in the area of perception. However, some investigators have succeeded in applying ratio scaling to personality and social-psychology variables (e.g., Gescheider, Cattin, & Fontana, 1982; Wright, 1968). Fortunately the difficulty of constructing ratio scales for many variables does not severely hamper psychological research, as interval-scale data serve just as well as ratio-scale data for most statistical treatments and most theoretical and practical uses.

SPECIFIC TECHNIQUES OF OBSERVATION AND MEASUREMENT

Data may be generated by the activities of the observing researcher or through subjects' self-observations and self-reports. Examples from each of these perspectives will be considered.

Researcher-Produced Data

Qualitative Recording.   Many valuable data in psychology are not in a directly quantifiable form. Rather, they exist as systematic verbal descriptions, or **anecdotes**, of behavior patterns. This approach to data collection is quite common in naturalistic observation and case studies. Piaget's (1963) data on the problem-solving behaviors of children, for example, were almost always presented in a qualitative form, as the following passage illustrates:

> At 1; 6 (23) for the first time Lucienne plays with a doll carriage whose handle comes to the height of her face. She rolls it over the carpet by pushing it. When she comes against a wall, she pulls, walking backward. But as this position is not convenient for her, she pauses and without hesitation, goes to the other side to push the carriage again. She therefore found the procedure in one attempt, apparently through analogy to other situations but without training, apprenticeship, or chance. (p. 338)

Notice that even though this verbal account does not lend itself to numerical representation, it is carefully anchored by references to observed behavior. Once critical behaviors are recorded in such a systematic fashion, they serve as the basis of inductive theorizing and hypothesis construction. And it is often possible to develop quantitative measures of constructs developed from qualitative research and then subject the theory to rigorous empirical tests, as some researchers have done with Piaget's ideas (e.g., Gruen, 1965).

If you are quick with a pen or pencil, you can carry out qualitative recording the old-fashioned way by writing down the most significant behaviors during an observational episode. Or you may choose to observe now and record later from memory. But, when possible and ethical, it is usually more convenient and accurate to augment your observational powers through the use of automated devices, such as video recorders.

Counting Responses.   One of the oldest and most reliable measurement methods consists of simply counting the number of times that a particular type of response is made. There are tens of thousands of examples of this measurement mode in the psychological literature.

Historically, response frequency has been the dominant dependent measure in the fields of learning, operant conditioning, and memory. In Tolman's classic experiments on "place learning," for instance, the dependent measure was a count of the number of times that rats turned right or left in a "cross maze" (Tolman, Ritchie, & Kalish, 1946); in other studies, Tolman counted the number of errors made by rewarded and unrewarded animals as they negotiated more complicated mazes (Tolman & Honzik, 1930). Likewise, for decades, Skinner and his intellectual descendants have relied on cumulative responses over time to index the degree of operant learning in a variety of organisms.

In some of the earliest experiments on memory, Ebbinghaus (1885) meticulously kept track of the number of study trials required to learn or relearn serial lists of "nonsense syllables" (e.g., XOQ). Present-day memory researchers continue the tradition of response counting. For instance, they often record the number of stimulus words correctly recalled or recognized and then convert the numbers to "percent correct recall" or "percent correct recognition."

The usefulness of response-count measures certainly isn't limited to the fields of learning and memory, however. This type of index frequently takes the form of counting the number of people in a natural setting who exhibit a certain response or characteristic, or perhaps the number of times that a response is exhibited by subjects under varying social circumstances. Research on social facilitation of drinking behavior provides an illustration of the latter use of response counting. By actual count, people polish off more glasses of beer when drinking in groups than when imbibing alone (Sommer, 1977).

Time Measures.   There are two varieties of time measure: latency and duration. **Latency** is the amount of time it takes a subject to respond to a stimulus situation. **Duration** is the amount of time that subjects engage in a particular response.

Latency of responses has been used to measure the motivation of laboratory animals (Bolles, 1967). The general finding is that latency of operant responses decreases as motivational states increase. In reaction-time studies, latency of response has been employed to index the efficiency of the central nervous system as a function of age (Birren, 1964).

Duration measures are commonly used to examine preferences in human beings and animals. The duration of mutual eye contact, for instance, is considered to be one measure of mutual liking and attraction (Cook, 1977).

Intensity Measures.   With some imagination on the researcher's part, the force with which subjects respond can be utilized as a measure of certain constructs. In his empirical investigations of personality structure, Allport (1933) regularly included intensity indexes, such as voice intensity, writing pressure, and pressure of the resting hand. Interestingly, these variables clustered together statistically and appeared to represent a stable "expressive" trait of personality. It seems that some individuals are characteristically more intense than most other people.

Another example of intensity measurement comes from the research of Gescheider et al. (1982). Employing a special device called a hand dynamometer, these investigators asked college students to use force of hand grip to express their perception of the seriousness of 22 crimes and the severity of 14 jail terms. Subjects were also asked to give subjective numerical estimates of crime and punishment magnitudes. The subjective estimates corresponded very closely to the intensity of hand grip. Moreover, the judged seriousness of crimes corresponded closely to the perceived severity of the jail terms normally resulting from those crimes. So, in the minds of some college students at least, the punishment does seem to fit the crime.

Rating Attributes.   The observation and measurement techniques considered thus far are classified as *behavioral measures.* They all depend on the observation of specific responses or on physical scales that directly reflect specific responses. But psychological researchers regularly step outside the realm of specific behaviors to rate or judge general characteristics of people.

Sometimes the "rating scale" consists of a simple checklist of characteristics. For example, Bales (1970), a social psychologist, used the following kind of checklist items to assess the dominant personality types of individuals as they interacted in task-oriented groups:

1. Does he (or she) seem to *receive a lot of interaction from others?*
2. Does he seem *personally involved in the group?*
3. Does he seem *valuable for a logical task?* (p.6)

There were 26 characterizations on Bales's checklist. As each individual was considered, the observer checked "yes" or "no" for each item on the list.

Other rating scales have multiple points. In an investigation of the effect of physical attractiveness on dating behavior, Walster, Aronson, Abrahams, and Rottman (1966) rated each of their subjects on the following type of scale:

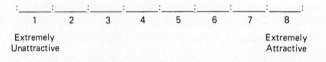

A major advantage of **multi-point rating scales** is that they tend to produce more reliable results than two-point scales.

When several rating scales are used to measure one trait, the ratings may be either summed or summed and averaged to yield a single value on the dimension of interest.

Self-Observation

Investigators often rely on their subjects to generate data directly—in a sense, to be both the observer and the observed. When self-observation measures are applied, the subject attempts to systematically record his or her behavior. The investigator then codes, analyzes, and interprets the behavioral data submitted by the subject. The two most common self-observation techniques are diary-keeping and response monitoring.

Diaries.   Research participants have been asked to keep diaries, logs, and journals to document a diversity of behaviors, including night-dream frequency and content, food-consumption patterns, study habits, and sexual behavior.

Although the content of research diaries may be primarily qualitative, sometimes the researcher is able to extract quantitative information from the entries. By examining the content of subjects' dream journals, for example, you could determine the relative frequency of anxiety dreams, dreams with sexual themes, and so on.

Response Monitoring.   Much applied research in the field of behavior modification depends on subjects' self-observation. One of the most useful techniques of self-control is to count the number of times per day that one engages in a desirable or undesirable habit. Thus, participants in programs designed to help them quit smoking keep careful records of the number of cigarettes smoked per day (Kazdin, 1975). This procedure gives the participants feedback on their progress and provides the researcher with data for evaluating the effectiveness of the behavior-modification technique.

In other research situations, subjects may be asked to record the amount of time they spend engaging in a particular kind of behavior, such as studying course assignments or watching television.

Self-Reports

One of the most widely used data-generation procedures consists of asking subjects to describe how they feel about or perceive something. The "something" might be a sensory stimulus, a word, a picture, a social issue, another person, or even the subjects themselves. The description might take the form of agreeing versus disagreeing, estimating magnitudes, selecting a multiple-choice alternative, filling out a rating form or question-naire, or writing a story. Collectively, these subject-produced descriptions are referred to as **self-reports**. Several examples are discussed below.

Estimation.   One of the basic aims of psychologists who study perceptual processes is to find out how the magnitutude of subjects' impressions of sensory stimuli varies as physical magnitude is increased or decreased. Though there are numerous ways to get this type of information, the most commonly used procedure is **magnitude estimation** in which the subject is given a stimulus and is asked to represent its magnitude on a physical or numerical scale (Stevens, 1956).

Bruner and Goodman (1947) used this technique to investigate how personal values affect size perception. They instructed boys from well-to-do families and poor families, respectively, to estimate the size of coins of various denominations. The subjects' task was to adjust a circular patch of light, by turning a knob, so that the diameter of the light patch matched that of each coin presented. Bruner and Goodman's data showed that both groups of boys gave overestimates. However, the "poor" subjects overestimated the size of coins to a greater extent than the "rich" subjects. Bruner and Goodman's much-disputed conclusion was that the poor boys' size estimates were greater because poor boys value money more than rich boys do.

There is a lot more to perceptual scaling and estimation techniques than can be presented here. If you wish to pursue these topics further, see Nunnally (1967), Corso (1967), or Dember and Warm (1979).

Attitude Scales.   Self-report instruments used to measure attitudes typically consist of a set of written statements or questions to which the subject responds. The form of the subject's response—for example, checking an alternative or assigning a number—is predetermined by the researcher. But the specific nature of the response to a statement (e.g., assigning high, moderate, or low ratings) is up to the subject, and presumably reflects his or her attitude toward something. Usually, the subject's responses to a number of items are summed and averaged to get a single numerical index of his or her overall attitude toward a group, issue, or situation.

Occasionally items on an attitude scale appear in a two-alternative format, such as:

I think that every female should have the right to have her pregnancy aborted.

(Check one)

———————   ———————
Agree   Disagree

This format is usually found on questionnaires and opinion surveys.

But many researchers feel that they can obtain more precise estimates of attitude by using a multi-point rating scale such as:

Politicians should not be allowed to use the television networks to promote their campaigns.

(Check one)

| ———————— | ———————— | ———————— | ———————— | ———————— |
| Strongly Agree | Agree | Not Sure | Disagree | Strongly Disagree |

For scoring purposes, "Strongly Agree" would be assigned a value of 5, "Agree" a value of 4, and so on. This type of device is referred to as a "Likert scale."

If you use attitude scales in your research, you should be particularly careful about wording, as the way you phrase the statements can influence the subject's response. Ambiguous wording can produce haphazard or arbitrary responses. You should also be aware of the fact that phrasing an item negatively (i.e., using "not," "no," "never") can change its meaning somewhat (Nunnally, 1967). Finally, avoid "double-barreled" statements that essentially ask the subject to express an attitude on two different matters: for example, "We should do away with welfare programs and all other socialistic commitments."

There are many other methods of constructing attitude scales. For information on these, consult Nunnally (1967) or Sahakian (1972). Also, see Chapter 12 of this book.

Psychological Tests.   There are hundreds of standardized, commercially published self-report measures commonly referred to as psychological tests. Since the use and interpretation of these instruments often require a professional level of expertise, you would be able to use them for research purposes only under the direct supervision of a qualified person.

Many psychological tests are designed to measure *typical performance*. That is, the items ask the respondent to indicate what she typically would do in a certain situation, how she normally feels about herself or other people, or what her usual traits and preferences are. Measures of typical performance include attitude, vocational-interest, and personality tests. You might use a test of typical performance to study the relationship between two or more traits, or the relationship between a trait and a set of behaviors. For example, researchers have exerted considerable effort in an attempt to isolate personality traits that predict "hypnotizability" (cf. Barber, 1976).

There are dozens of personality tests that have been used for research purposes. They vary considerably in the populations they are designed for, the type of response required of the test-taker, and the traits that they measure. Some have "objective" response formats, such as agree/disagree or multiple-choice, whereas others require an open-ended oral or written response that must be scored subjectively. The well-known inkblot tests exemplify the latter. While most personality inventories assess a number of traits in a single sitting, others, such as the Manifest Anxiety Scale (Taylor, 1953), are designed to tap a single characteristic.

The best-known personality test is the Minnesota Multiphasic Personality Inventory (MMPI), which was devised to provide information for making clinical diagnoses of psychiatric problems (Hathaway & McKinley, 1967). The test is made up of 550 self-descriptive statements, such as "I am a nervous person," "I sometimes hear voices that others can't hear," etc., to which the test-taker is to respond "Yes," "No," or "Cannot Say." Various subsets of the 550 items pertain to particular diagnostic categories—for example, depression, schizophrenia, hypochondriasis—10 in all. A person's score on each diagnostic scale is a function of how many scale items he responds to in the "keyed" direction. If he answers most of the "schizophrenia" items as a schizophrenic would, for instance, he receives a high score on that scale.

Other personality inventories are intended for use with "normal" populations. One such test is the California Psychological Inventory, which measures traits like "responsibility," "sociability," and "dominance," rather than pathological trends. The Jackson Personality Inventory also falls into this class of personality test. It assesses such traits as "tolerance" and "conformity."

The advantage of using published personality tests, rather than constructing your own, is that most published tests come with considerable information about their reliability and validity. But there are disadvantages as well. First, the reliability coefficients of many personality tests are not very impressive (Brown, 1976), which, of course, raises legitimate questions about how valid the scales can be. Second, traits measured by a test that someone else has constructed may differ in crucial ways from the characteristics that you wish to measure. Because trait labels can be misleading, it pays to study the validity data well to determine what the test actually seems to be measuring—labels notwithstanding.

A second general category of psychological tests is made up of measures of *maximal performance*. They assess how well you can do when you are making your best effort to retrieve information from memory and to solve problems. These measures include aptitude and intelligence tests. The Scholastic Aptitude Test is one example that most college students are painfully familiar with. Measures of maximal performance are most useful when your research project requires the measurement of cognitive abilities.

The list of aptitude and intelligence tests is quite long. Currently available measures of both maximal and typical performance are described in the *Mental Measurements Yearbook* (Buros, 1978).

KEEPING THEM HONEST

The Problem of Reactivity

If you have ever been a research subject, then you know that the awareness of being observed and measured can cause subjects to behave atypically. This phenomenon is referred to as **observational reactivity** (Rosenthal & Rosnow, 1975). Though naive researchers sometimes assume otherwise, human subjects are not passive responders to the research situation. Rather, they are active problem-solvers who seek to serve one or more purposes in their research participation (Orne, 1962). While the list of possible motivations for behaving atypically in a research setting is potentially very long and somewhat speculative, some of the more common ones include:

1. furthering the progress of science (by behaving as an ideal subject should!)
2. performing well enough as a subject to deserve extra points in a psychology course
3. deciphering the researcher's hypothesis, or "the real purpose of the study." (Many subjects expect to be deceived.)
4. protecting self-esteem by putting one's best foot forward
5. pleasing the researcher
6. sabotaging the study

The importance of observational reactivity is that it threatens the external validity of behavioral research. If subjects are dishonest in their responses to the research situation, then the findings may well be relevant only to circumstances in which people are "putting on a show" for an observer.

Dealing with Reactivity

What can you do to minimize observational reactivity? The answer depends on the particular type of measurement procedure you are using. Jourard (1969) has suggested that a good general strategy is to be as honest as possible with subjects. His assumption is that people will dissimulate less if they trust the researcher. Certainly this policy is to be recommended, but it isn't a complete remedy (see Orne, 1962). Fortunately, there additional ways to reduce reactivity.

Archival Data.   Archives are records that are routinely kept and preserved by individuals and organizations. These records may occasionally be consulted to verify self-report or behavioral data. For example, if you conducted a survey for the dean's office to find out what kinds of books college students read for enjoyment, you might get some rather surprising responses, especially at a school where students are constantly reminded of the institution's reputation for academic excellence. Let's suppose that 40 percent of your sample claims to be reading classical works in the arts and sciences. However, a check of the paperback sales records at the college bookstore might well reveal a different trend in leisure-time reading.

The reason that archival records represent "nonreactive" data is that such records are compiled for reasons unrelated to behavioral research. We'll explore the use of archives further in Chapter 15.

Unobtrusive Measures.   Unobtrusive measures are data-gathering techniques that conceal the process of observation (Webb, Campbell, Schwartz, & Sechrest, 1966). A clever study by Rosenhan (1973) serves as an example. Rosenhan and seven co-researchers gained admission to various psychiatric hospitals by appearing at the admissions office and reporting that they had been hearing voices. Subsequent to being admitted, they ceased any suggestion of abnormal behavior and conducted themselves as "sanely" as the hospital environments permitted. In spite of their immediate resumption of normal behavior, the pseudopatients were detained at the hospitals for an average of 19 days (one as long as 52 days), and all were discharged with a diagnosis of "schizophrenia in remission."

Rosenhan's team kept notes on their hospital experiences. A major finding was that the hospital environment conferred a sense of depersonalization and powerlessness. When the pseudopatients initiated contacts with ward personnel, for instance, only 4 percent of the psychiatrists and 0.5 percent of the nurses bothered to stop and talk. Another interesting statistic was the number of pills administered to the eight pseudopatients—about 2,100 in all.

Rosenhan's observational technique was nonreactive. The subjects being observed—that is, the hospital staff—were unaware of their status as research participants so they behaved in their usual fashion. The results were startlingly informative. Starkly different, and less valid, findings undoubtedly would have emerged had the pseudopatients presented themselves as systematic observers.

In general, field-observation methods, such as that used by Rosenhan, lend themselves very well to nonreactive measurement, so long as the observer can conceal her true role in the situation.

Validity Scales.   Personality inventories, such as the MMPI, invite observational reactivity because the test-taker has the option of selecting any response he desires, regardless of how accurately it describes him.

Many subjects are motivated, for a variety of reasons, to paint false pictures of themselves. Depending on their individual interpretations of the testing situation, some subjects may want to appear disturbed, "sick," or abnormal and will attempt to "fake bad" in their selection of responses. But a more common tactic among dissemblers is to "fake good"—to choose what they consider to be socially desirable alternatives (Edwards, 1957).

The tendency to select test-item responses for the purpose of presenting an invalid image of oneself is referred to as a **response set**. Test constructors try to deal with response sets by including **validity scales** in the test itself. The MMPI, for example, contains three validity scales.

The Lie Scale of the MMPI consists of several socially ideal self-descriptions, such as "I have never told a lie." Honest responders would agree with very few statements of this type. Essentially, the Lie Scale is designed to detect attempts to fake good.

The MMPI's F Scale is based on the same rationale as the Lie Scale but is designed to identify those who are faking bad. The K Scale is the third validity scale, and it represents a measure of test-taking defensiveness.

If a subject scores too high on a validity scale, either her results must be discarded or she must be asked to retake the test—with no guarantee that honesty will prevail the second time around.

Instrumentation.   Under some circumstances, self-reports may be supplemented by physiological responses measured via special instruments. A convenient example is provided by research on the effectiveness of "aversion therapy" in the treatment of sexual perversions (Feldman, 1966). Since the goal of aversion therapy is to make the patient dislike the object of his perversion, treatment usually entails administering a very unpleasant stimulus in the presence of the object—for example, shocking the patient as he reaches for his favorite fetish. Unpleasant treatments of this kind not infrequently lead to a patient's falsely reporting an early "cure" in order to avoid further treatment. One technique of validating the "cure" is to use a special camera to measure pupil size as the patient focuses his eyes on a picture of the inappropriate sex object. If his pupils dilate in response to the picture, chances are the patient is still "in love," despite his self-report to the contrary.

The use of physiological measures to supplement self-reports is but one example of a more general strategy for dealing with reactivity, which is to employ more than one measure of the dependent variable. The rationale for using multiple dependent measures is that it is difficult for a subject to fudge his responses in a consistent direction across two or more measures. Thus, agreement between the different measures increases confidence in the validity of the data and, conversely, disagreement between measures signals the need for cautious interpretation of the results.

Bogus Pipeline.   Short of actually measuring the subject's physiological reactions, you can lead her to believe that you are doing so (Jones & Sigall, 1971). For instance, you could attach some lifeless wires to the subject and tell her that the wires are connected to a polygraph (lie detector); further, that the mechanism will pick up any dishonest responses as she is filling out an attitude questionnaire.

Since the wires wouldn't really be connected to a functioning device, the information pipeline they represent is "bogus," or fake. But if the subject believes that any attempt to dissimulate will be detected, she may well be intimidated into giving frank answers to the questionnaire. Of course, there are always ethical drawbacks associated with any technique that relies on intimidation, even in the name of Science.

SUMMARY

Observation and measurement are fundamental to the empirical sciences. *Observation* occurs when you systematically record instances of preselected behaviors. *Measurement* is the process of converting observations to numerical indices according to a set of rules.

The main initial requirement is that the measurement rule be unambiguous as to its application. After that, the *quality* of a measurement procedure is determined by its *reliability* and *validity. Unsystematic*, or random, errors in the measurement process contribute to unreliability, whereas *systematic*, or constant, errors pose problems for the measure's validity.

Two common ways to assess reliability are the *test-retest* method and the *interrater* method. The validity of a measure often is evaluated through an inspection of its *content*; another method of validation involves determining what *criteria* the measure correlates with. Several methods of increasing reliability and validity were reviewed in this chapter.

Measurement takes place at various levels of sophistication, called *scales of measurement*: nominal, ordinal, interval, and ratio.

Data can be generated by the activities of the researcher or those of the subject. But in many situations, subjects have been known to manifest *observational reactivity*: They behave atypically when aware of being studied. Techniques for minimizing reactivity include the use of *archival data, unobtrusive measures, validity scales, instrumentation*, and the *bogus pipeline*.

REVIEW QUESTIONS

1. Define *observation* and *measurement*.

2. Make up an example of an ambiguous measurement rule, and tell how it could be made unambiguous.

3. Distinguish between the concepts of reliability and validity; then describe how they are related.

4. Relate the concepts of reliability and validity to measurement error.

5. Summarize two methods of assessing reliability and two methods of validating a measure.

6. List at least three steps that you can take to maximize the reliability of measurement.

7. Compare and contrast nominal, ordinal, interval, and ratio scales.

8. Make up or refer to examples of the following techniques of observation and measurement: qualitative recording, response counting, time measures, intensity measures, ratings, self-observation, and self-reports.

9. Define observational reactivity. Why is it considered a problem in psychological research?

10. Summarize at least four methods of minimizing observational reactivity.

Notes

[1] The test-retest interval can vary from a few seconds to several years. Most commonly, the time lapse between testings is between one week and one month. The choice of interval will depend on practical considerations, the purpose of the research, and how stringent a test of stability the investigator wishes to conduct. In almost all cases, the stability of test scores declines as the test-retest interval is increased.

[2] The linear correlation coefficient can also carry a negative sign; $-r$ means that the two sets of ranks bear an inverse correspondence to one another, such that people with high ranks on one measure have low ranks on another, and vice versa (see Chapter 6 for a complete discussion of this). But when used as an index of reliability, r is always positive.

6

FINDING RELATIONSHIPS

Once the research question has been formulated, the research design implemented, and the data collected, you are ready to search for relationships.

You will experience an indescribable excitement as you look over a fresh data-summary sheet; it is just possible that your careful planning and your long hours of data collection have yielded some important information about the lawfulness of behavior. In scientific disciplines, lawfulness is revealed by empirical relationships. And the numbers on the data sheet, which represent measurements on the variables of interest, very likely will show a relationship between those variables, if any exists. But before relationships can be detected in a set of data, you have to know how to organize and treat your measurements so that the information you seek can be extracted from them.

SEEING RELATIONSHIPS IN DATA

An empirical relationship can be defined in several ways. It is:

1. "a 'going together' of two variables: it is what the two variables have in common" (Kerlinger, 1979, p. 22)
2. "a patterned mutual change between variables. That is, as X changes, Y changes in a patterned way" (Walizer & Wiener, 1978, p. 60)
3. a connection or association between two variables, such that a value of variable Y is at least partially *predictable* from the corresponding value of variable X

For present purposes, a **relationship** between two variables exists to the extent that research subjects' classifications or positions on variable Y correspond in some regular fashion to their classifications or positions on variable X.

It is important to bear in mind that most of the relationships studied in the behavioral sciences are far from perfect. Thus, if variables X and Y are related, the values of Y will *tend* to correspond in a regular fashion to values of variable X, but usually there will be many exceptions to the pattern of correspondence. Of course, the stronger the relationship, the fewer the exceptions to the general pattern.

The data collected by psychological researchers come in many forms—for example, percentages, groups of test scores, and so on. It is desirable, therefore, that you learn how to spot relationships in a variety of data contexts. In this section, you will encounter examples of relationships within the frameworks of frequency counts, categorical percentages, mean differences between groups, and matched pairs of scores.

Frequency Counts

Several years ago, my colleagues and I developed an interest in Fear of Success (FOS) motivation. This construct, originally researched by Horner (1968), supposedly represents a stable disposition to avoid being successful at important scholastic and vocational endeavors. According to Horner, persons who possess a high level of this trait anticipate incurring negative social consequences if they are successful. Horner theorized that the trait would be most common in populations that, through experience, have learned to associate disapproval and social rejection with outstanding achievement. Although much of Horner's research suggested that FOS motivation is more prominent in white, middle-class females than in their male counterparts (Horner, 1970), gender differences in this regard have been difficult to replicate (Zuckerman & Wheeler, 1975).

A major criticism of Horner's FOS construct was that she had failed to demonstrate that the "motive" could be influenced by the conditions that supposedly create it: negative consequences resulting from achievement. So my co-researchers and I decided to find out if FOS could, in fact, be affected through systematic variation of the social consequences of competent performance (Evans, Nelson, & King, 1979).

Our subjects were 32 female college students who volunteered to participate in a study of "the relationship between verbal intelligence and creative-writing ability." Sixteen subjects were randomly assigned to each of two conditions: Social Rejection of Achievement Behavior versus Social Acceptance of Achievement Behavior.

All subjects first competed with a male "subject" (actually an accomplice of the experimenters) on an anagram task, which involved unscrambling letter sequences to form words. The outcome was staged so that all subjects in both experimental conditions did much better on the task than their male partner. The experimenter always commented on the subject's superior performance but, depending on which condition a subject was in, her competence elicited either negative (i.e., rejecting) or neutral (i.e., accepting) reactions from her partner.

In the final phase of the experiment, the experimenter asked the subject and the accomplice to write creative themes in response to the cue "After many long years of work, Mary has become nationally recognized in her profession." The theme-writing task was actually a projective test of FOS fantasy and was similar to the fantasy-based measures of FOS motivation used by Horner. We wanted to find out if social rejection for being successful at the anagram task would increase the incidence of FOS imagery in the themes.[1] Thus, Social Reaction was our independent variable, and Presence versus Absence of FOS Imagery was our dependent variable.

When we scored the themes for FOS fantasy, we found that 10 of the 16 subjects in the Social Rejection condition had produced themes containing FOS imagery. In contrast, only 3 subjects in the Social Acceptance condition showed evidence of such imagery.

Is there a relationship to be found in these data? To answer this question, it is useful to arrange the data in a **contingency table**, as shown in Table 6–1, to help reveal any statistical dependence, or contingency, existing between two nominal-scale variables.

Note that the contingency table clarifies the variables involved: Variable X = Social Reaction, with two levels, Rejection versus Acceptance; Variable Y = FOS Fantasy, with two levels, Present versus Absent.[2] Through combining the two levels of Variable X with the two levels of Variable Y, we produced a 2 (levels) × 2 (levels) table, with four cells. Each cell represents one of the four possible outcomes in the experiment: (a) Rejection

TABLE 6–1

Fear of Success as a Function of Social Reaction to Competence: An Example of Frequency Counts Arranged in a Contingency Table

| | | Social Reaction (X) | | |
		Rejection	Acceptance	Totals
FOS Fantasy (Y)	Present	10	3	13
	Absent	6	13	19
	Totals	16	16	32

subjects show FOS fantasy, (b) Rejection subjects show no FOS fantasy, (c) Acceptance subjects show FOS fantasy, (d) Acceptance subjects show no FOS fantasy. The number in each cell is the observed frequency of the outcome that the cell represents.

When arranged this way, do the data indicate that variables X and Y "go together"? Is a particular level of Y associated more often with one level of X than with the other level of X? Can the incidence of FOS fantasy be predicted, to some degree, from a knowledge of how the male accomplice reacted to the subject's achievement? The answer to all three questions is yes. The presence of FOS fantasy was observed relatively more often in the Rejection condition than in the Acceptance condition, and the absence of FOS fantasy occurred more frequently in the Acceptance condition. So there is a *numerical* relationship between variables X and Y in this case. However, the statistical reliability of the relationship would have to be judged on the basis of a test of statistical significance. **Statistical reliability** means that the outcome of a statistical test leads us to expect that the same pattern of results would occur if the study were repeated (see later sections of this chapter; also, Chapter 8).

If no relationship existed between Social Reaction and FOS fantasy, the frequency of occurrence of FOS themes would have been more equally distributed across the two levels of Social Reaction, as illustrated in Table 6–2 (fictitious data).

You will find that with contingency tables that are larger than the 2×2 tables shown in Table 6–2, more skill is required to detect relationships on the basis of a visual examination of the cell frequencies. In a 4×5 table, for example, 20 cells would need to be considered. In that type of situation, the investigator typically conducts a statistical significance test for the whole table first. If the test indicates the existence of a reliable relationship, the next step is to compare particular cells within the table, both visually and statistically, to determine the specific nature of the relationship (Snedecor & Cochran, 1980).

Percentages as a Function of Category

Table 6–3 shows the results of a class project carried out by a team of my students. These researchers used systematic observation to study the relationship between gender and book-carrying styles in a college-student population. Book-carrying styles were defined as follows:

A: Books are carried down at the hip in one hand.
B: Books are carried out from the side of the body, in one arm.
C: Books are carried against the chest or abdomen, secured with one arm.
D: Books are carried against the chest or abdomen, secured with both arms.

TABLE 6–2

Example of a Contingency Table Showing No Relationship Between Variables X and Y (fictitious data)

		Social Reaction (X)		
		Rejection	*Acceptance*	*Totals*
FOS Fantasy (Y)	Present	7	6	13
	Absent	9	10	19
	Totals	16	16	32

TABLE 6–3

Gender and Book-Carrying Styles: Frequency Counts Arranged in a Contingency Table

		Gender (X)		
		Male	Female	Totals
Book-Carrying Style (Y)	A	148	21	169
	B	5	9	14
	C	1	33	34
	D	20	124	144
	Totals	174	187	361

The sample of students observed consisted of 174 males and 187 females. The results, as presented in Table 6–3, show the frequency of book-carrying style (the dependent variable) as a function of gender (the independent variable). Since the males favored style A by a large margin, and the females clearly preferred style D, there is a numerical relationship between variable X and variable Y. To an appreciable extent, you could predict values of the dependent variable on the basis of gender classification. But how important are book-carrying styles other than A and D? It's difficult to say, because the relative importance of particular cell frequencies is clouded by the large samples and the fact that the female sample was not the same size as the male sample. In such cases, researchers often will convert the cell frequencies to **proportions** or **percentages** to facilitate interpretation of the data. In this example, percentages may be obtained by dividing each cell frequency by its *column total* and multiplying the result by 100. For instance, when the number of males who exhibited book-carrying style A is divided by the total number of males, the result is $148/174 = .85$. This proportion is then multiplied by 100 to transform it to a percentage: 85 percent of the males used style A.[3]

The data are presented as percentages in Table 6–4. A clearer picture of the relationship emerges when percentages are used in lieu of raw frequencies, because conversion to percentages places both the male and the female data on a standard numerical scale ranging from 0 to 100.

Mean Differences

Much of the data in psychological research does not take the form of simple frequency counts. Consider the case in which the dependent measure is a numerical score or value

TABLE 6–4

Percentage of Males and Females Showing Each of Four Book-Carrying Styles

		Gender (X)	
		Male	Female
Book-Carrying Style (Y)	A	85	11
	B	3	5
	C	1	18
	D	11	66
	Totals	100	100

rather than an either/or classification. In this situation, each subject would have a **raw score**, that is, a particular numerical value on some measured dimension. If there are two or more groups of subjects, where each group represents a different level of the independent variable, the data sheet would consist of two or more columns of raw scores, with each column representing the outcomes of a particular treatment group. An example of a two-group data sheet is shown in Table 6–5. These fictitious data simulate the results of a study of the effects of teacher expectations on the intellectual development of elementary-school children.[4]

When such investigations are actually carried out, the procedure involves randomly assigning the children in a classroom to two treatment groups that, on the average, have approximately equal potential for intellectual growth during the school year. Then the unwitting teacher is told that, based on information provided by psychological testing, he can expect one group of children (the "experimental" group) to show rapid intellectual gains. The resulting teacher expectations have been shown to have a significant impact on IQ changes over the school year, especially in the first and second grades: Despite the initial equivalence of the two groups, the children expected to get smart faster show larger IQ increments than the "control" children (Rosenthal & Jacobson, 1968).

Let's suppose that the raw scores in Table 6–5 are the IQ gain scores for a class of 10 first-grade students. Note that a gain score is shown for each student in the study. The scores in the Experimental Group column are those of students who were expected to show substantial intellectual growth.

Do these data reveal a relationship? To get a preliminary answer to this question, it is helpful to bear in mind how the two variables under examination are arranged in the table. The independent variable, teacher expectations, is represented by the column labels. The dependent variable, IQ gain, is represented by the raw scores under the column labels. When you inspect the size of raw scores as a function of column, it does appear that the dependent variable varies in value from one level of the independent variable to the next. That is, the gain scores of the Experimental Group appear to be substantially larger.

But raw scores set into columns, especially when they are numerous, usually don't present as clear a between-group difference as you see in this simplified example. Consequently, the recommended procedure is to compute an **arithmetic mean** for each group, with the formula:

$$\overline{X}_j = \Sigma X_j / n, \text{ where}$$

$\overline{X}_j$ is the arithmetic mean of group 1 or 2 (j = 1 or 2),
Σ is the symbol meaning "sum" or "add up,"
X_j is the symbol for raw scores in the jth group, and
n is the number of observations included in the sum.

The equation instructs you to add up the raw scores in each column and divide by the number of observations in the column.

When this formula is applied to each column in Table 6–1, the resulting means are 27 for the Experimental Group and 12 for the Control Group. And the **mean difference** = $(\overline{X}_1 - \overline{X}_2) = (27 - 12) = 15$.

The advantage of converting the data to a difference between group means is twofold. First, this statistic gives an unambiguous picture of the overall effect of the independent variable, which often is obscured by individual differences on the dependent measure. Second, mean differences can be subjected to tests of statistical significance to find out if the numerical differences are statistically reliable.

Computing mean differences to find relationships in data sets is not limited to the two-group situation. The logic and procedure are regularly extended to research designs

TABLE 6–5.

Raw-Score Gains in IQ as a Function of Teacher Expectations (Fictitious Data)

	Experimental Condition (X)	
	Experimental Group	*Control Group*
	30	7
	24	10
	27	14
	32	17
	22	12
	$\Sigma X_1 = 135$	$\Sigma X_2 = 60$
	$\overline{X}_1 = 27$	$\overline{X}_2 = 12$

involving several groups. In such designs, it is often the case that patterns of mean differences must be considered in order to identify the nature of any relationship present.

An example of the multigroup data sheet appears in Table 6–6. Note that the independent variable is the amount of caffeine ingested by the research subjects. The dependent variable is performance on an anagram-solution task. Are there mean differences among the four conditions? Is there a relationship between caffeine dosage and performance? If so, how would you describe the relationship?

Pairs of Scores

It is not uncommon to encounter studies in which each subject has a pair of raw scores: one on variable X and another on variable Y. This situation would exist, for example, if a researcher administered two personality tests in an effort to determine the extent of relationship between two traits. Just such a data set is shown in Table 6–7 (fictitious data).

By examining the table, you can see that each of 10 subjects (a through j) received a score on a self-esteem test (variable X) and a score on a test of neuroticism (variable Y). Note that the arrangement of data is critical for assessing any relationship that may exist between the two traits. That is, each subject's letter designation, score on X, and score on

TABLE 6–6

Performance on an Anagram Task as a Function of Caffeine Dosage, in Milligrams
(Fictitious Data)

	Caffeine Dosage (X)			
	0 mg.	*100 mg.*	*500 mg.*	*1000 mg.*
	3	15	11	7
	5	12	10	5
	3	5	15	3
	7	10	5	5
	7	8	9	5

TABLE 6–7

Self-Esteem and Neuroticism: Ordered Pairs* of Raw Scores for Ten Subjects (Fictitious Data)

Subject	Self-Esteem (X)	Neuroticism (Y)
a	27	25
b	32	18
c	40	16
d	33	20
e	24	24
f	35	21
g	20	28
h	21	29
i	36	17
j	26	26

*Note that each subject has a value on X and a value on Y, and that each subject's X score is paired up with his or her Y score.

Y are set into the same row of the data sheet. The two scores of each subject are literally "paired up." For instance, subject c's value on X was 40, and his value on Y was 16.

Do the subjects' self-esteem scores correspond in some regular fashion to their neuroticism scores? Notice that subject c had the highest value on self-esteem and the lowest value on neuroticism; also that subject g, who was lowest in self-esteem, ranked second from the top on neuroticism. Could it be that the traits are inversely related, such that low scores on one trait predict high scores on the other? Perhaps so. But mere visual inspection of paired data leaves much to be desired, especially when an investigation involves, say, several dozen subjects. It is for this reason that you will want to use graphs to help you detect and define regular patterns in your data.

GRAPHING RELATIONSHIPS

Graphs are pictures that summarize data. They facilitate the discovery of relationships by accentuating general trends and reducing the "visual noise" inherent in large sets of raw scores.

A graph, or figure, as illustrated in Figure 6–1, occupies a space defined by the intersection of two perpendicular lines called "coordinates." By convention, the horizontal axis, referred to as the **abscissa**, represents values of variable X, and the vertical axis, or **ordinate**, represents values of Y. The short lines attached to each axis mark off the various scale units on X and Y, respectively. Within the graph, values of Y are plotted as a function of corresponding values of X. Depending on the nature of the data set, the Y values may be in the form of raw scores, means, frequencies, or proportions.

The Scatter Diagram

When data are arranged as ordered pairs, the plot of raw scores on Y against the X values that they match up with produces a **scatter diagram**. This type of graph has been set up

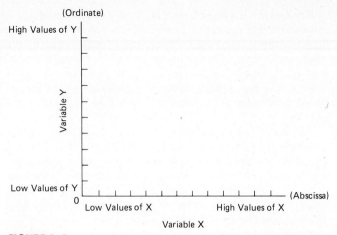

FIGURE 6–1

General Two-Axis Structure Used in Graphing Empirical Relationships

for the paired self-esteem and neuroticism scores listed in Table 6–7, and the resulting graph is presented in Figure 6–2. The dispersed pattern of dots illustrates why this kind of graph is called a scatter diagram.

Each point in the figure represents the numerical intersection of the two scores belonging to a single subject. Hence, with 10 subjects, there are 10 points altogether. To construct this graph, a dot was placed at the exact point where each subject's self-esteem score came together with his neuroticism score. Consider subject c, for instance. His X value was 40, and his Y value was 16. As shown in the figure, the dot representing subject c lies right at the spatial intersection of 40 on X and 16 on Y. (To verify this, draw perpendicular lines from 40 on the X axis and 16 on the Y axis. They will meet at subject c's dot.)

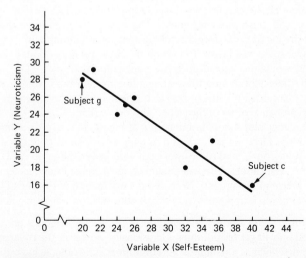

FIGURE 6–2

Scatter Diagram Showing Neuroticism Scores as a Function of Self-Esteem Scores

Based on this scatter plot, what can be said of the relationship between self-esteem and neuroticism? The covariation between X and Y is much easier to see in the graph than in the paired raw scores. Values of neuroticism decrease regularly as values of self-esteem increase, and vice versa. In fact, the pattern of covariation is so distinct in this scatter diagram that a straight line drawn through the dots serves as a good summary of the relationship. The line, referred to as the **regression line**,⁵ or **line of best fit**, has been included in the figure to emphasize that the variables are related in a **linear**, or straight-line pattern.

The line of best fit in Figure 6–2 was statistically derived, which is always the most accurate way to determine it (see Hays, 1981). But there is nothing wrong with estimating the line visually if you simply want to get a rough indication of the form of relationship between your variables. When you draw the line on the basis of visual examination alone, try to estimate the "best-fitting" line by tracing a central path through the configuration of dots so that the pattern of points is fairly well balanced on each side of the line. The line should be smooth and unbroken.

Types of Relationship

Scatter diagrams are excellent tools for illustrating the many different kinds of relationship that may exist between two variables. While these succinct pictures of data may not be worth a thousand words, they do provide a wealth of information, including indications of: (a) the direction of the relationship, (b) the form of the relationship, and (c) the strength of the relationship.

Direct and Inverse Relationships.   Two variables have a **direct**, or **positive**, relationship when high scores on variable Y tend to be associated with high scores on variable X. In other words, as X scores change in a particular direction (higher or lower), corresponding scores on Y tend to vary in the same direction. This type of relationship exists between scores on the verbal aptitude section of the Scholastic Aptitude Test (SAT) and college grade-point average. Students with relatively high SAT-verbal scores tend to make higher-than-average grades, whereas students with below-average aptitude scores tend to get grades that are also below average; and it is generally true that students of moderate aptitude tend to get moderate grades. This positive relationship is the statistical rationale behind the use of SAT scores by college admissions committees. At many schools, applicants who score well below average on the SAT are not admitted, because it is unlikely that they would maintain an adequate grade-point ratio.

The scatter plot of a positive, straight-line relationship is shown in Diagram *a* of Figure 6–3. Note that the line of best fit is oriented from the lower left-hand corner to the upper right-hand corner of the graph. This shows that as X increases, so does Y.

The scatter plot shown in Diagram *b* of Figure 6–3 suggests a different kind of linear relationship. Here, variables X and Y tend to change in opposite directions, such that higher values on Y tend to be associated with lower values on X. This is an **inverse**, or **negative**, relationship. You will recall that, in an earlier example, neuroticism was related to self-esteem in this fashion. Note that the orientation of the line of best fit for the negative relationship is opposite that of the positive relationship shown in Diagram *a*.

Curvilinear versus Linear Relationships.   The scatter diagrams presented so far have illustrated only linear relationships. Occasionally, however, the covariation of X and Y can best be described as a nonlinear, or **curvilinear**, function. A hypothetical scatter plot of this type of relationship appears in Figure 6–4.

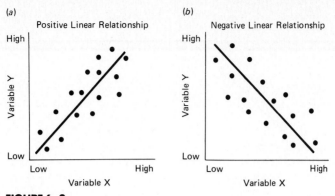

FIGURE 6–3

Scatter Diagrams of Positive and Negative Linear Relationships

By examining the figure, you can see that the dots clearly define a relationship between X and Y. But the way that Y changes as a function of X varies as X values go from low to high: As X increases, Y first increases, then levels off, then decreases. The general pattern is one of an inverted U. Such is the association between performance on certain tasks (variable Y) and the level of subjects' motivation (variable X). It is sometimes found that performance increases with motivation up to a point, but further increases in motivation do not improve performance. And even greater increments in level of motivation lead to a decline in performance (Beck, 1978).

Other types of curvilinear relationships appear in behavioral data. With a little imagination, you'll be able to think of some.

Strong, Moderate, and Weak Relationships.   The strength, or magnitude, of a relationship is reflected by the degree to which dots in the scatter diagram deviate from the line of best fit. Figure 6–5 shows how the scatter plots differ for strong (Diagram *a*), moderate (Diagram *b*), and weak (Diagram *c*) relationships. In general, as the relationship between X and Y gets weaker, the pattern of dots gets "fatter." This means that it is difficult to

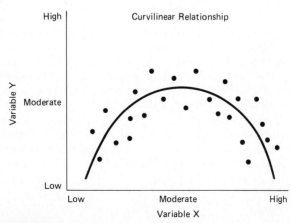

FIGURE 6–4

Scatter Diagram of a Curvilinear Relationship

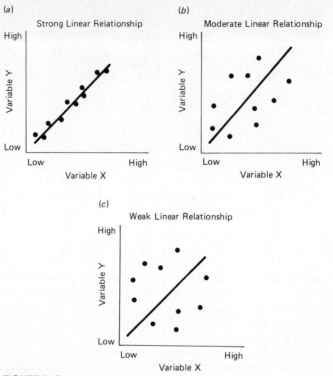

FIGURE 6–5

Scatter Diagram of Strong, Moderate, and Weak Linear Relationships

predict Y values from X values when the variables are weakly associated, because Y can assume a diversity of values at any one level of X. In contrast, when there is a nearly perfect relationship between X and Y, the dots in the scatter plot "hug" the line of best fit. In the latter case, Y can be accurately predicted, since, for a given level of X, Y will almost always be close to a particular value.

Null Relationships.   Sometimes two variables that you think might be associated with one another turn out to be essentially unrelated. The nonexistence of a relationship is referred to as a **null relationship**. It may be interpreted to mean that, for all practical purposes, we can predict nothing about variable Y from a knowledge of variable-X values.

A null relationship may mean that Y varies unsystematically relative to X, as is illustrated in Diagram *a* of Figure 6–6. Notice that the scatter diagram is roughly circular in form; the dots deviate maximally from the line of best fit. This is the type of result you would get if you repeatedly rolled two dice simultaneously and plotted the outcomes of one die against those of the other. In other words, this kind of scatter plot is indicative of the complete independence of two variables.

A null relationship doesn't always show up as a circular scatter diagram. In fact, it may assume the guise of a strong-looking linear relationship. Consider the example shown in Diagram *b* of Figure 6–6. The dots representing the intersection of variable-Y and variable-X values do form a straight-line pattern and don't deviate very much from the line of best fit. Why, then, is this a null relationship?

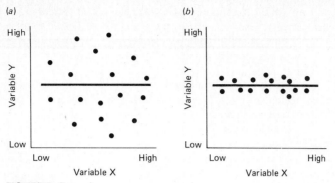

FIGURE 6–6
Scatter Diagrams of Null Relationships

Isn't there something odd about the straight line that summarizes the pattern of scatter? Indeed, it is parallel to the horizontal axis of the graph. It lacks **slope**. Conceptually, *slope refers to the average amount of change in Y for every unit change in X*. If two variables are linearly related to one another, then Y must increase or decrease regularly as X increases (refer back to Figure 6–3). And this is the key to the puzzle presented by Diagram *b* of Figure 6–6: Variable Y tends not to change in any way as variable X increases. Consequently, the two variables cannot covary. This example demonstrates that the narrowness of the dot pattern in a scatter plot is not a sufficient criterion for judging the strength of a relationship. The slope of the pattern must also be considered.

The situation represented in Diagram *b* of the above figure is but one example of a more general problem in the statistics of relationships. That problem, called **restriction of range**, means that, for a particular sample of observations, the range of values on variable Y, variable X, or both is so small that one variable cannot possibly show much systematic change as the other variable increases or decreases. The problem in Diagram *b* is that the range of values on variable Y is too narrow.

Restriction of range creates difficulties of interpretation because it artificially forces two variables into a weak or null relationship, even though they may be substantially related under other circumstances. Either of two situations can cause narrow score ranges. One is the use of a sample of subjects who, for one reason or another, are too homogeneous on one or both variables. It would be unwise, for example, to use a sample of graduate psychology students to examine the relationship between IQ and creativity, as these subjects would be too much alike on the IQ dimension. Thus, IQ could not vary enough to show a systematic association with creativity.

A second cause of restricted score ranges is unreliable measurement. In Chapter 5, it was pointed out that reliable measures produce considerable variation within a sample of observations (assuming that the subjects are *heterogeneous* with respect to the trait measured). Conversely, an unreliable measure tends not to differentiate very well among subjects possessing different levels of the trait under examination.

Other Graphing Techniques

Up to this point, the only graphing technique considered has been that which applies to matched pairs of raw scores. Many data sets do not come in a matched-pair format, but nonetheless, the data can be graphed, and it is often informative to do so.

Consider the situation in which variable X is an independent variable in an experimental design, and its "values" are nominal-scale classifications represented by two or more treatment groups. The dependent variable, Y, is some measure of performance that was assessed at an interval-scale level of measurement. Such a situation existed in the hypothetical study of teacher expectations and IQ that was reviewed earlier in this chapter. You'll recall that those data were not in the form of ordered pairs; rather, they appeared as two columns of IQ-gain scores (variable Y), where each column represented an independent treatment group (i.e., a level of variable X).

How should this type of data be graphed? The usual technique is to plot the *mean* of variable Y as a function of classifications of X. This has been done for the IQ-gain data in Table 6–5, and the resulting **line graph** of the means appears in Figure 6–7.

Recall that the Experimental Group mean was 27 and the Control Group mean was 12. To construct the line graph, you:

1. Set up a vertical axis to represent the units of the dependent variable.
2. Set up a horizontal axis to represent classifications of the independent variable.
3. Place dots where the mean scores on Y intersect with their corresponding classifications on X (for example, where 27 intersects with Experimental Group and 12 intersects with Control Group).
4. Connect the dots with a straight line.

This procedure yields a picture that clearly summarizes the mean differences between treatment groups. Note that although the graph shows how Y varies as a function of X, it is not a scatter diagram. In a line graph, the various Y values are reduced to a single point (the mean) for each level of X.

Graphing means in this way is easily extended to data sets representing more than two treatment groups. For practice, you may wish to construct a line graph of means for the data listed in Table 6–6.

Frequency-count data may also be graphed. Most of the time, however, it is preferable to present frequencies in tables rather than in graphs (APA, 1974).

THE STATISTICS OF RELATIONSHIPS

Sifting through raw data, sums, percentages, and means gives you a feel for your results and comprises the first step in arranging your data for graphical presentation. Graphing the data, in turn, simplifies the results and often makes numerical relationships in the data stand out in bold relief. But even the best laid out data sheet and the clearest graphs often fall short of providing certain pieces of information that are critical to the interpretation of your findings.

What sorts of information am I referring to? Evidence for the statistical reliability of the data is one; another is the computation of a numerical coefficient that precisely indexes the strength of relationship between variables X and Y.

Testing for Statistical Significance

No matter how impressive your data and graphs look, any relationship between variables they suggest may be more apparent than real. Especially when your sample of observa-

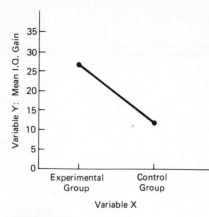

FIGURE 6–7
Line Graph of Means

tions is quite small, let's say between 10 and 30, even large percentage or mean differences between experimental conditions may represent a fluke of chance. In such situations, your results would be unreliable; you wouldn't be likely to get the same pattern of findings if the study were repeated with a completely new group of subjects.

Since it is not usually feasible or practical to quickly carry out several independent replications of a research project, investigators try to reach a decision about the reliability, or "realness," of their findings through tests of **statistical significance**. If a relationship proves to be statistically significant, then it is likely to be reliable: We would expect the relationship to hold up under replication.

The logic of tests of statistical significance is simple. If the data suggest that there is a relationship between two variables, you compute an appropriate **test statistic** on the basis of your sample data. (If you've had a statistics course, then you are familiar with test statistics such as Z, t, and χ^2.) You then compare the numerical value of your test statistic to a mathematically derived set of values that would be expected on the basis of chance alone, where chance is defined as random processes. Since each of the chance values has a known probability of occurring, you can determine how likely the value of your test statistic would be if only chance were operating to produce your data. If your test statistic turns out to be a rare event in the set of chance values, then you declare it to be non-chance, or statistically significant; the relationship in question is judged to be statistically reliable.

A statistically significant outcome, then, is merely *a rare event in a set of chance events*. But how is rareness defined? By convention, a test statistic is significant if its numerical value would occur by chance alone only 5 percent of the time or less. A more stringent standard is sometimes used by which an outcome is declared significant only if it would occur 1 percent of the time or less due to chance processes alone.

Note that even a statistically significant relationship may be a result of chance. When the 5 percent criterion of significance is applied, the theoretical likelihood of this is 5 in 100. It is so unlikely to be solely a chance outcome, however, that you are willing to take the small risk involved in declaring that your data represent more than chance processes. In short, the statistical test has given you confidence in the faithfulness of your findings. (See Chapter 8 for a more complete discussion of hypothesis testing and statistical significance.)

Indexing the Strength of Relationship

When a test statistic is declared significant, it is probable that a reliable relationship exists between variables X and Y. However, most test statistics do not directly provide information on the strength of the relationship. This is an important consideration because when exceptionally large samples of observations are analyzed, even a weak relationship will be statistically significant (Bakan, 1966). Beyond this, information on the magnitude of a relationship is interesting and important in its own right.

Fortunately, many of the relationships investigated by psychologists approximate a straight-line function. Therefore, a convenient index of linear association can often be employed to measure the degree to which two variables covary.

Pearson's r. The most widely used index of relationship strength is the **Pearson Product-Moment Correlation Coefficient**, commonly referred to as the Pearson r (named for its British developer, Karl Pearson). It can be applied to any data set in which the relationship between variables X and Y can be assumed to be essentially linear. When used to describe the magnitude of a relationship in a sample of data,[6] r is "scale free." This means that it can be applied to data based on any scale of measurement, including nominal and ordinal data (Hays, 1981).

The Pearson r has other advantages. It ranges between two fixed values, 0.00 (a null relationship) and 1.00 (a perfect relationship). It is generally true that the more r departs from 0.00 and approaches 1.00, the stronger the relationship it represents. Thus, relative to the crude indication that may be gleaned from visual inspection of a scatter diagram, r provides a precise and readily interpretable measure of relationship magnitude.

In addition to indexing the strength of a relationship, r also contains information on the direction of the relationship. The positive or negative sign of the index is the tipoff. For example, when $r_{xy} = +.60$, you know that Y varies *directly*, or positively, as a function of X. In contrast, an r_{xy} of $-.60$ indicates an *inverse* association—Y decreases as X increases. It is important to remember that the information on direction is independent of the information on strength. Hence, $r_{xy} = -.60$ reflects the same magnitude of association as $r_{xy} = +.60$. The two correlations differ only in the direction of covariation between X and Y.

The Pearson r is the statistical essence of straight-line relationships. It is a *standardized index of the extent to which subjects' relative positions on one dimension (Y) bear a patterned correspondence to their relative positions on a second dimension (X)*. To get a feel for what this means, examine the three patterns of rankings shown in Figure 6–8.

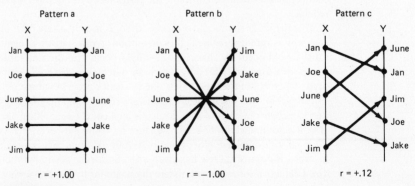

FIGURE 6–8
Examples of Patterns of Correspondence Between Ranks on Two Dimensions

Pattern *a* shows the relative positions of five people on dimensions X and Y, respectively. Note that there is a direct pattern of correspondence between the ranks held on X and those held on Y. In this case, $r_{xy} = +1.00$. Ranks on Y are perfectly predictable from ranks on X.

In Pattern *b* there is also a perfect correspondence between ranks on the respective dimensions, but the pattern of correspondence is inverse. Nonetheless, errorless predictions of positions on Y can be made from a knowledge of positions on X. In this case, $r_{xy} = -1.00$.

In contrast to the first two situations in Figure 6–8, Pattern *c* represents something close to a null relationship. It would be very difficult to predict a person's rank on Y, even if we knew his or her rank on X. The two sets of ranks seen here have no patterned correspondence linking them together. In this case the correlation between the two sets of ranks is only $+.12$.

When r is applied to behavioral data, the result almost always falls between the extreme outcomes illustrated in the figure. But the important point here is that the size of r directly reflects the degree to which subjects' ranks on one variable vary in a systematic, linear fashion with their ranks on a second variable.

Computing r from Raw Scores.   In most courses on research methods, it is convenient to have available an easy-to-use formula for computing r. Although there are several ways to do this, I'll present only the *raw-score formula*, as it is the simplest one to apply. Other approaches to the computation of correlation coefficients can be found in most standard texts on statistics.

The formula for r that may be applied directly to raw scores is:

$$r_{xy} = \frac{n(\Sigma XY) - (\Sigma X)(\Sigma Y)}{\sqrt{n(\Sigma X^2) - (\Sigma X)^2} \ \sqrt{n(\Sigma Y^2) - (\Sigma Y)^2}} \text{, where}$$

r_{xy} is the linear correlation between variables X and Y,
n is the number of *pairs* of scores in the data set,
ΣXY is the sum of the products of X values times the Y values that are paired up with them
    $(XY = (X) \cdot (Y))$,
ΣX is the sum of the X values,
ΣY is the sum of the Y values,
ΣX^2 is the sum of the squared X values $(X^2 = (X \cdot X))$,
ΣY^2 is the sum of the squared Y values $(Y^2 = (Y \cdot Y))$,
$(\Sigma X)^2$ is the squared sum of X $((\Sigma X)^2 = (\Sigma X) \cdot (\Sigma X))$,
$(\Sigma Y)^2$ is the squared sum of Y $((\Sigma Y)^2 = (\Sigma Y) \cdot (\Sigma Y))$,
$\sqrt{\ }$ is the "radical sign," indicating that you must find the square root of the value under the sign.

The easiest way to use this formula is to set up a six-column worksheet, such as that shown in Table 6–8. You will recognize these data as belonging to the study on the relationship between neuroticism and self-esteem. Since the scatter diagram of these data (Figure 6–2) clearly indicated that X and Y are linearly associated, the Pearson r will serve as an accurate index of relationship strength.

To better understand the meaning of the numbers in each column, consider subject a. Column (1) gives his letter designation. Column (2) shows his score on X (27), and column (3) shows his score on Y (25). Column (4) contains the square of subject a's X value ($27^2 = 729$), and column (5) shows the square of his Y value ($25^2 = 625$). Finally,

TABLE 6–8

Worksheet for Computing the Pearson r

(1) Subject	(2) X	(3) Y	(4) X^2	(5) Y^2	(6) XY
a	27	25	729	625	675
b	32	18	1024	324	576
c	40	16	1600	256	640
d	33	20	1089	400	660
e	24	24	576	576	576
f	35	21	1225	441	735
g	20	28	400	784	560
h	21	29	441	841	609
i	36	17	1296	289	612
j	26	26	676	676	676
	$\Sigma X = 294$	$\Sigma Y = 224$	$\Sigma X^2 = 9056$	$\Sigma Y^2 = 5212$	$\Sigma XY = 6319$

column (6) gives the result of multiplying subject a's X score by his Y score $(27 \cdot 25 = 675)$.

When these entries are arranged in the appropriate columns for each subject, you are ready to sum each column and apply the equation for r. Thus, for this sample of $n = 10$ pairs of scores,

$$
\begin{aligned}
r_{xy} &= \frac{10(6319) - (294)(224)}{\sqrt{10(9056) - (294)^2} \ \sqrt{10(5212) - (224)^2}} \\[2mm]
&= \frac{63190 - 65856}{\sqrt{90560 - 86432} \ \sqrt{52120 - 50176}} \\[2mm]
&= \frac{-2666}{\sqrt{4124} \ \sqrt{1944}} \\[2mm]
&= \frac{-2666}{(64.22)(44.09)} \\[2mm]
&= \frac{-2666}{2831.46} \\[2mm]
&= -.94
\end{aligned}
$$

As the scatter diagram of these data suggested, there is a very strong inverse relationship between neuroticism and self-esteem in this sample.

The equation for r can be used whenever data are in the form of paired scores, and it is reasonable to assume that the relationship between variables is linear. The use of a hand-held or desk calculator greatly increases the accuracy and speed of computing r. In fact, some calculators contain a program for r, so that all you have to do is enter the raw scores on X and Y and press the r key. For large samples of observations, however, the utilization of a high-speed computer is recommended, especially if you have several correlations to compute. Ask your instructor about the availability of computer services at your school.

Pearson's r: What Does It Mean?

The linear correlation coefficient may be interpreted according to a number of different standards. Generally speaking, each approach to interpreting r considers a unique type of information. Therefore, it is usually wise to evaluate a correlation from several vantage points, including its magnitude, its statistical reliability, and its practical significance.

Magnitude Interpretation. The first characteristic of r that a researcher scrutinizes is its size. It is meaningful to assess the strength of association between X and Y on the basis of the numerical value of the correlation coefficient, because r can vary only between two fixed bounds.

Magnitude interpretations of r typically follow a scheme such as:

If r is between:	The relationship between X and Y is:
.80–1.00	Very Strong
.60–.79	Strong
.40–.59	Moderate
.20–.39	Weak
.00–.19	Negligible

Such an interpretive scheme is a good starting point, but it has its limitations. For one, the boundaries of the strength intervals must be arbitrarily set. It would have been just as legitimate, for instance, to specify .75–1.00 as the range of "Very Strong" relationships. Also, the meaning of the size of r varies with the area of research and the type of data under consideration. For example, an r_{xy} of .40 might be considered a strong validity coefficient for a personality test but a weak validity coefficient for certain standardized intelligence tests.

Another problem with interpretations based on the size of r alone is that the factor of sample size is not taken into account. The "strength intervals" shown above make sense when there are 100 or more pairs of observations in the sample, but they would be misleading when sample size equals, say, 15. In the latter situation, a correlation of .40 could not be taken too seriously, despite its respectable size. The reason is that, with only 15 pairs of observations, an r of .40 has a fair likelihood of occurring solely as a result of chance. Hence, it would not be considered statistically reliable, and any attempt to attribute importance to the correlation because of its size would be unwarranted.

Statistical Significance Interpretation. As noted above, not all correlations that look big represent real relationships. Especially with very small samples—for example, where n is between 3 and 20—even sizable coefficients may be chance outcomes. As a general rule, for an r of a given magnitude, the likelihood that the relationship is reliable decreases with sample size. This rule is graphically represented in Figure 6–9, which assumes that an outcome is statistically significant, hence reliable, if it would occur as a result of chance alone 5 percent of the time or less. Examination of the significance curve in the figure reveals that while a correlation coefficient of .40 would be judged statistically reliable for a sample size of 30 or greater, the same coefficient would be declared a chance event when sample size equals 10 or 20.

Because correlation size can be misleading, tests of statistical significance are almost routinely applied to r, usually before more specific interpretations of the relationship are attempted. The particular way that the significance test is carried out depends on what assumptions are met by the data set (Hays, 1981). Under certain circumstances,[7] the test consists of merely comparing the computed r to a set of r values expected on the basis of chance to determine the theoretical likelihood that the computed r is just a random

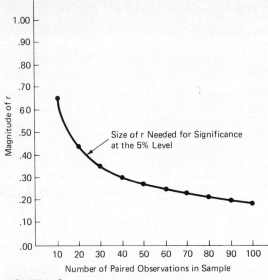

FIGURE 6-9

Statistical Significance of r as a Function of Sample Size (5 percent Level of Significance)

event. But regardless of how the statistical reliability of r is assessed, the significance test always takes the sample size into account.

Practical Significance Interpretation.   Now that I've emphasized the interpretation hazards posed by small samples and downplayed the importance of correlation size per se, I'm going to do an about-face on both matters, but for good reasons.

When samples consist of several hundred pairs of observations, r's of almost any size will be statistically significant. When n = 500, for instance, a correlation of .09 could be declared reliable, even though a relationship this weak is trivial. Consequently, it is prudent to consider the **practical significance** of a relationship. As the term is used here, practical significance refers to *the amount of information conveyed by the correlation.*

One way to assess the practical significance of r is to ask how much of the variance in variable Y is accounted for by variance in X. **Variance** is an abstract statistical concept that often stands for the individual differences among values in a data set. Thus, if there is wide variation among the raw scores, the data show a lot of variance. Conversely, if raw scores differ very little from one another, there is little variance in the sample.

It can be shown mathematically that the squared correlation coefficient equals the proportion of variation in Y values "accounted for" by variation in X values (Hays, 1981; Snedecor & Cochran, 1980). If $r_{xy} = -.60$, for example, then the proportion of variance accounted for equals $r_{xy}^2 = (-.60)^2 = .36$. This means that, in the sample, 36 percent of the variation in Y values was *covariation* with X values. Hence the remaining 64 percent of the variance represents change in Y that was independent of change in X.

The advantage of using "variance accounted for" to evaluate empirical relationships is that it often serves to put small, but statistically significant, correlations into proper perspective. An example of this point comes from research on sex differences. Over the years, much has been written concerning rather consistent gender differences in mathematical and verbal ability (cf. Maccoby & Jacklin, 1974). On the average, females surpass their male peers on standardized measures of verbal ability but come out second best on standardized tests of mathematical aptitude. Hyde (1981) combined the results of most of the published studies of sex differences in these abilities and found that the average correlation between gender and mathematical ability was approximately .10; the same average correlation existed between gender and verbal ability. Since, when taken as an aggregate, these studies represented thousands of observations, the correlation of .10 is statistically significant. But how much practical significance does it have? That is, how much information on abilities do we get from a knowledge of gender? Squaring the correlation would answer this important practical question. When Hyde did this, the result was $.10^2 = .01$. Only 1 percent of the variation in math and verbal ability, respectively, is accounted for by sex differences—a trivial amount indeed.

A Comment on Causal Interpretation. Regardless of its size, a correlation coefficient, by itself, doesn't provide information on cause-and-effect. Although a large and statistically reliable r may tempt you to assert that changes in variable X produce changes in variable Y, don't fall into that trap. Unless the correlation is derived from the data of a well-controlled experiment, in which variable X is systematically manipulated while all other influences on Y are held constant, any one of three causal interpretations could be invoked:

1. X is causing Y to vary.
2. Y is causing X to vary.
3. A third variable, Z, is causing X and Y to covary.

While it is sometimes feasible to rule out the possibility that Y is causing X—for example, differences in verbal ability couldn't be producing gender differences—it is very difficult to eliminate the **third variable problem**: the possibility that some unobserved variable is responsible for the covariation between X and Y. For example, does the biological fact of gender produce small but reliable differences in verbal ability? Or is it more probable that sex-linked social expectations, sex-linked differences in opportunity, or some other third process is responsible for the observed correlation? I would opt for the third-variable interpretation in this case, even though I have no idea what "it" or "they" may be.

Beyond Linear Association: Eta

To the degree that the relationship between two variables is nonlinear, r will underestimate the extent of association present. It is for this reason that you should always construct and examine your scatter diagram before calculating r.

When your scatter plot shows obvious curvilinearity, you can still calculate a numerical index of the strength of association between X and Y. The index is Eta and is referred to as the **correlation ratio**. Like r, Eta is bounded by the values of 0.00 and 1.00, and the stronger the relationship, the larger the value of Eta. But unlike r, Eta cannot be negative. Eta^2 may be interpreted as the proportion of variance in Y accounted for by variation in X for the sample of data under consideration. Eta may be utilized regardless of the scale of measurement that variable X is on, but variable Y should be on either an interval scale or a ratio scale (see Nunnally, 1967).

The logical basis of Eta is as follows: Compute a numerical index of *total variation on variable Y*. Next, compute a second value representing the *variation on Y that is associated with variation on X*. Then divide the latter value by the index of total variation on Y. The square root of the resulting quotient is Eta. In other words,

$$Eta = \sqrt{\frac{Y \text{ variation due to } X}{Total \text{ variation on } Y}}$$

It should be clear from the previous equation that Eta^2 is the proportion of total variation in Y that is accounted for by variable X.

In the computation of Eta, variation in variable Y is represented numerically by quantities called **Sums of Squares**. So the previous equation can be expressed as:

$$\text{Eta} = \sqrt{\frac{\text{Sum of Squares due to X}}{\text{Total Sum of Squares}}} = \sqrt{\frac{SS_x}{SS_{\text{Total}}}}$$

This formula would be useful for measuring the strength of association between X and Y in the sample of data that appears in Table 6–9. Raw scores on Y are arranged in four columns that represent four levels of variable X. Variable X is measured on an ordinal scale, and variable Y is on an interval scale.

The pattern of the column means suggests that Y varies as a curvilinear function of X. As X changes from level 1 through level 4, the mean of Y first increases, then levels off and, finally, decreases. The curvilinear pattern is verified when the raw scores on Y are plotted against their associated levels of X. This scatter diagram appears in Figure 6–10.

Computation of Eta is fairly straightforward when the procedure utilizes arithmetic means. The first mean to compute is the **grand mean**, $\overline{G}$, which is the *mean of all raw scores in the sample*. Thus,

$$\overline{G} = \Sigma Y/n, \text{ where}$$
Y is the symbol for raw scores on variable Y,
ΣY is the sum of all scores in the sample, and
n is the total number of scores in the sample (i.e., sample size).

For the n = 20 values shown in Table 6–9, $\overline{G} = 150/20 = 7.5$.

The next step is to compute the mean of the Y scores *for each level of X*. These are the column, or "group," means. Each column mean is calculated through use of the following expression:

$$\overline{Y}_{x_j} = \Sigma Y_{,x_j}/n_{x_j}, \text{ where}$$
$\overline{Y}_{x_j}$ is the mean of Y for the jth level of variable X (here, j = 1, 2, 3, 4),
ΣY_{x_j} is the sum of raw scores at the jth level of variable X, and
n_{x_j} is the number of raw scores at the jth level of X.

TABLE 6–9

Raw Scores, Raw-Score Sums, and Means on Variable Y at Each of Four Levels of Variable X

	X_1	X_2	X_3	X_4
	3	15	11	7
	5	12	10	5
	3	5	15	3
	7	10	5	5
	7	8	9	5
(Sums) ΣY_{x_i}	25	50	50	25
(Means) $\overline{Y}_{x_i}$	5	10	10	5

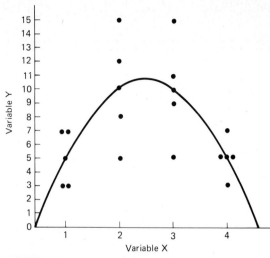

FIGURE 6–10

Scatter Diagram Showing Curvilinear Relationship Between Raw Scores on Variable Y and Levels of Variable X

In the present example, there are four levels of X, each having $n_{x_j} = 5$ observations. So the four column means are:

$$\overline{Y}_{x_1} = \Sigma Y_{x_1}/n_{x_1} = 25/5 = 5$$
$$\overline{Y}_{x_2} = \Sigma Y_{x_2}/n_{x_2} = 50/5 = 10$$
$$\overline{Y}_{x_3} = \Sigma Y_{x_3}/n_{x_3} = 50/5 = 10$$
$$\overline{Y}_{x_4} = \Sigma Y_{x_4}/n_{x_4} = 25/5 = 5$$

Once the grand and column means are available, it is a simple matter to calculate the two Sums of Squares needed to determine Eta.

To get the Total Sum of Squares, subtract the grand mean from each of the n raw scores, square the difference, and "sum the squares." Hence,

$$
\begin{aligned}
SS_{Total} &= \Sigma(Y - \overline{G})^2 \\
&= (3 - 7.5)^2 + (5 - 7.5)^2 + \ldots \text{etc.} \ldots + (5 - 7.5)^2 \\
&= (-4.5)^2 + (-2.5)^2 \quad + \ldots \text{etc.} \ldots + (-2.5)^2 \\
&= (20.25) + (6.25)^2 \quad + \ldots \text{etc.} \ldots + (6.25) \\
&= 259
\end{aligned}
$$

To obtain the Sum of Squares due to X, subtract the grand mean from each column mean, square the difference, multiply the squared difference by the number of observations in the column, and sum the products. Hence,

$$
\begin{aligned}
SS_x &= \Sigma(n_{x_j}(\overline{Y}_{x_j} - \overline{G})^2) \\
&= 5(5 - 7.5)^2 + 5(10 - 7.5)^2 + 5(10 - 7.5)^2 + 5(5 - 7.5)^2 \\
&= 5(-2.5)^2 \quad + 5(2.5)^2 \quad + 5(2.5)^2 \quad + 5(-2.5)^2 \\
&= 5(6.25) \quad + 5(6.25) \quad + 5(6.25) \quad + 5(6.25) \\
&= 31.25 \quad + 31.25 \quad + 31.25 \quad + 31.25 \\
&= 125
\end{aligned}
$$

Using the formula for Eta, we see that:

$$Eta = \sqrt{SS_x/SS_{Total}}$$
$$= \sqrt{125/259}$$
$$= \sqrt{.4826}$$
$$= .69$$

Within the framework of magnitude interpretation, there seems to be a strong curvilinear relationship between variables X and Y. Practical significance also looks good. For this sample, the proportion of variance in Y accounted for by X is: $Eta^2 = .69^2 = .48$.

To test the statistical reliability of Eta, an F test should be used. If you don't know how to do an F test, see Chapter 13 of this book, or consult any standard text on statistics.

SUMMARY

After the results of an investigation are in hand, the next step in the research process is to look in the data for relationships, which may appear in many forms: Frequency counts as a function of response category, percentages as a function of response category, mean differences on variable Y as a function of classification on variable X, and ordered pairs of matched X and Y values.

There are many ways of representing data in a graph. The *scatter diagram* is the type of graph that results from plotting raw scores on Y (the vertical axis) against corresponding values of X (the horizontal axis), when data are arranged in ordered pairs. A scatter diagram can reveal any one of a variety of relationships between two variables: *direct, inverse, linear,* and *curvilinear*. Relationship strength is reflected by the degree to which points in a scatter diagram lie close to the *line of best fit*.

Mean differences can be shown on a *line graph*, in which each point represents the intersection of the mean of variable Y with its corresponding classification on variable X.

Linear relationships may be statistically represented and assessed by the *Pearson Product-Moment Correlation Coefficient*, which indexes the strength and direction (direct or inverse) of covariation between two variables. The Pearson r statistic is evaluated in terms of its size and statistical significance, as well as in terms of the proportion of variance that it accounts for. Curvilinear relationships may be statistically represented by a statistic called *Eta*.

REVIEW QUESTIONS

1. Make up examples of research studies in which the data would take the form of frequencies, mean differences, and pairs of scores, respectively.

2. Describe the kinds of data characteristics you would examine in searching for numerical relationships when the data are:

   a. three columns of raw scores, where the column labels represent levels of the independent variable in an experiment.

   b. two columns of paired scores.

   c. frequencies arranged in a 2(rows) × 3(columns) contingency table.

3. Construct a scatter diagram of hypothetical data that show:
   a. a negative linear relationship.
   b. a null relationship without restriction of range.
   c. restriction of range on variable X.

4. Construct a scatter diagram for the following pairs of scores (Y, X): (10, 1); (8, 2); (1, 9); (2, 5); (7, 2); (8, 3); (2, 10); (3, 6); (4, 3); (5, 3). Be sure to label the vertical and horizontal axes. Would you describe the relationship as:
   a. linear or curvilinear?
   b. strong, moderate, or weak?
   c. positive or negative?

5. In a study of the relationship between body weight and taste sensitivity, an investigator laces some vanilla ice cream with quinine to make it slightly bitter. She finds that, on the average, overweight subjects eat 2 ounces of the ice cream, while "normal subjects eat 8 ounces and underweight subjects consume 5 ounces. Construct an appropriate graph of these results. Pay careful attention to correct labeling of the ordinate and abscissa. How would you describe the relationship shown in the graph?

6. State the logic and basic procedure involved in testing the statistical reliability of an empirical relationship.

7. Compare and contrast the characteristics and uses of r and Eta.

8. For what reasons are magnitude interpretations of correlation coefficients sometimes inadequate?

9. If the linear correlation coefficient for the relationship between variables X and Y is .98, is it safe to conclude that either X is causing Y to vary or that Y is causing X to vary? Explain the rationale behind your answer.

10. Briefly define or describe:
    contingency table
    restriction of range
    practical significance
    null relationship
    line of best fit

Notes

[1] Any study involving deception poses a potential ethical dilemma (see Chapter 3). An additional complication in this investigation was that half of the subjects were made to feel rejected by another human being. We used this kind of experimental manipulation only after various alternatives had been considered and judged to be inappropriate or ineffective in regard to the theoretical question being asked. We also conducted a lengthy debriefing session with each subject right after she finished writing her essay about Mary. In that session, we first explained the true purpose of the study and the rationale of the experimental treatments. The male accomplice was present to assure each "rejected" subject, in particular, that his behavior during the experiment was only part of a staged role and that he thought the subject was nothing short of marvelous for putting up with him.

[2] Designating a variable as X or Y is pretty much an arbitrary matter, and the information provided by the data would have been the same had the designations been reversed. By convention, however, the independent variable is usually labeled X and the dependent variable Y.

[3] Other types of percentage analysis are possible. For example, you could divide each cell frequency by its *row* total to find out what proportion of subjects preferring a certain book-carrying style is female or male. Or you could divide each cell frequency by the grand total, 361, to ascer-

tain what proportion of the total observations is represented by each gender/style combination. The way you elect to compute percentages in a contingency table will depend on the type of information you are seeking.

⁴If these data were real, they would not be very useful, because the sample size is hopelessly small. Psychological experiments normally require that treatment groups contain several times the number of observations shown in the table. The data presented here are only meant to serve as a simplified example.

⁵The term "regression line" is derived from the statistical theory of straight-line relationships. The rationale for the term is beyond the scope of this book, but is clearly explained in Hays (1981).

⁶But when r is used to make statements about the population from which the sample was drawn, a rigid set of assumptions must be met, including the assumption that the scale of measurement is at least at the interval level.

⁷The circumstances that must apply are: The data are on an interval or ratio scale of measurement; variable Y and variable X are normally distributed in the population from which the data were sampled; the variables are linearly related; values of Y are normally distributed around each value of X all along the regression line (Hays, 1981; Snedecor & Cochran, 1980).

7

INTERPRETING RELATIONSHIPS

Ms. M., a college student who is double-majoring in psychology and communications, broadcasts a show for children from the campus radio station. The show, called "Just for You," is presented daily and is intended to stimulate creative thinking in preschoolers.

Ms. M. decides to test her hypothesis that "Just for You" increases creative thinking ability in the youngsters who listen to it regularly. Her subjects are 40 children enrolled in a campus preschool program sponsored by the college. Having obtained written permission from the subjects' parents and the administrators of the preschool program, she randomly assigns 20 children to a "listeners" group and the remaining 20 to a "nonlisteners" group. She then contacts the parents of the listeners and asks them to have their preschoolers dial in "Just for You" five days a week for a period of six weeks. She also asks parents of the nonlisteners to make sure that their children don't listen to the program during the six-week interval. Fortunately, all of the parents are enthusiastic about the study and agree to cooperate.

At the end of the treatment interval, Ms. M. employs several testers (other college students) to administer a fairly reliable test of creative thinking to all 40 children. None of the testers knows which group each child belongs to.

Subsequent to the testing procedure it is revealed, to Ms. M.'s dismay, that some of the listeners had elected not to listen to the radio show; and, somehow, some of the nonlisteners had been tuning in regularly. To handle this contamination of experimental conditions, the unflappable researcher decides to omit from the statistical analysis all data of listeners who failed to listen and all data of nonlisteners who listened. Even after removal of the uncooperative subjects, the two groups are the same size (each n = 15).

Ms. M.'s statistical test indicates that the listeners obtained significantly higher creative-thinking scores than the nonlisteners. So she concludes that her radio program has the effect of enhancing this aspect of creativity in children who attend campus preschool programs.

Ms. M. conducted an empirical test of a hypothesis that was of much personal interest to her. She obtained evidence of a relationship, both numerically and statistically: Her experimental group scored significantly higher on the dependent measure than did her control group.

Like most scientists, Ms. M. wished to do more than merely discover a relationship. She wanted to make a substantial, theoretical statement about the relationship. That is, her aim was to be able to conclude that changes in variable X (Experimental Condition) *caused* changes in variable Y (Creative Thinking Scores), and perhaps to engage in some theorizing about why this was true. Accordingly, she used the experimental method, which, if properly carried out, will permit cause-and-effect conclusions. To ensure the validity of her findings, she equated the groups through random assignment and used testers who were unaware of which treatment group subjects belonged to.

But Murphy's Law is the dominant law of science: Anything that can go wrong will go wrong. In Ms. M.'s experiment, Murphy's Law was operating in the form of uncooperative subjects. The researcher's way of handling the resulting "contamination" of her conditions was to discard the data of the errant children. Did this solution work? Or did it simply substitute a second kind of data contamination for the original problem?

Isn't it possible that children who voluntarily listen to children's radio programs, in spite of being discouraged from doing so, have an unusual amount of creative imagination to begin with? Likewise, that children who refuse to subscribe to such programs, in spite of encouragement, are inherently lacking in creative imagination? If so, then Ms. M.'s act of discarding the data of certain subjects served to remove some of the more creative subjects from the nonlisteners group, while eliminating some of the less creative children from the listeners group. The effect of this action would be to allow *two* potential influences to vary together. That is, *both* amount of *inherent creativity* and *listening versus not listening* to the show would differentiate the two experimental conditions; the group that was exposed to the show would also be the group that was left with the more creative pool of subjects. Consequently, it is not possible to say with confidence which of the two associated influences—preexisting creativity or exposure to the show—produced group differences on the creativity test. Thus, Ms. M.'s conclusion is questionable.

CONFOUNDING AND THE INTERNAL VALIDITY PROBLEM

Confounding is the term used to label research situations in which *the independent variable is contaminated by one or more extraneous variables that are allowed to covary with it*, thus making it difficult to apply theoretical interpretations to empirical relationships. Theoretical interpretations almost always state or imply cause-and-effect processes, and confounding hampers the investigator's attempt to identify just what did produce changes in the dependent variable. Thus, if Ms. M. had thought carefully about her data, she would have realized that more than one potential influence on creativity scores had been allowed to vary between her experimental conditions, and she would then have been at a loss to determine which of the two factors was actually responsible for the group difference on the dependent measure.

Confounding reduces or destroys the **internal validity** of a study. While reading Chapter 4, you learned that a study is internally valid to the extent that changes in the dependent variable can be shown to be a result of changes in the independent variable. In practice, this usually means that the researcher has systematically manipulated only one potential influence (the independent variable), while holding constant all other influences—a situation difficult to obtain unless a true experimental design is employed. When such rigid control is implemented, only one hypothesis is plausible: that changes in X produced changes in Y. In contrast, situations involving confounded variables permit a number of plausible hypotheses to exist: the experimental hypothesis that X influences Y, plus one or more **plausible rival hypotheses** which assert that something different from (or in addition to) X is responsible for the covariation between X and Y (Campbell & Stanley, 1966). You'll recognize this dilemma as the third variable problem, which was discussed in Chapter 6. The major asset of the experimental method is that it gives scientists the capability to avoid the third variable problem and, hence, to rule out plausible rival hypotheses.

The remainder of this chapter covers the most common sources of confounding, as well as some possible ways to avoid or minimize the problems of confounding. It is important to bear in mind, however, that internal validity is not an either/or matter, but rather one of deciding how much confidence we can place in the assertion that changes in X produced changes in Y. While use of the experimental method often yields a quantum leap in the amount of confidence we can invest in the research hypothesis, other techniques, such as group-matching procedures and statistical control, can also increase our confidence to some extent.

The examples presented in this chapter repeatedly illustrate an important point about the process of scientific inquiry: *The conclusions drawn by an investigator are a matter that is separate from her research procedure and her data*, even though the procedure and data should temper the conclusions. As a rule, the method and findings are accepted as facts, but the researcher's interpretation of the research outcome is always subject to evaluation. To the extent that cause-and-effect conclusions are inconsistent with the "facts" of the study, a **research error** has been committed. It follows that to the extent that research errors can be ruled out, the study is internally valid.

COMMON THREATS TO INTERNAL VALIDITY

Any source of confounding is a threat to internal validity. And the circumstances that produce confounding are numerous. Campbell and Stanley (1966) identified several classes of confounding that plague behavioral research; here, we'll consider seven: *subject-selection bias, subject maturation, testing effects, instrumentation changes, statistical regression, subject histories,* and *subject mortality*. Although this list is not exhaustive, it will serve well as a framework for discussing threats to internal validity and some procedures for reducing these threats.

The seven categories of confounding can be classified according to the circumstances under which they are most likely to occur. For instance, many sources of confounding operate most commonly in situations where subjects are measured more than once on the same set of variables—that is, in **repeated-measurement designs**. But subject-selection bias may be a problem even when each subject is measured only one time. Still other categories of confounding, such as subject history, may affect the results of both single-measurement and repeated-measurement investigations.

Subject-Selection Bias in Single-Measurement Studies

Subject-selection bias probably is the most frequently encountered type of confounding in the behavioral-science literature. It exists in virtually every investigation that doesn't employ explicit procedures for "equalizing" subjects at different levels of variable X, in terms of possible confounding factors. Simply put, subject-selection bias means that *some systematic process, rather than chance, is responsible for subjects' being in particular treatment conditions or at particular levels of variable X* (the independent variable). Therefore, that systematic process, or something correlated with it, may be responsible for any observed changes or differences in variable Y. Since level of variable X is only one of several variables that are correlated with the subject-selection bias in such a case, many plausible rival hypotheses exist alongside the hypothesis that X is responsible for changes in Y.

Subject-selection bias is obvious in many investigations where the researcher is simply searching for correlations between variables. If scores on a self-esteem test are correlated with scores on a test of neuroticism, for instance, this relationship provides little, if any, information on cause-and-effect. Since, in a sense, the levels of neuroticism and self-esteem were *preselected by nonchance processes* in the subjects' lives, we have no way of knowing whether it is level of self-esteem that is influencing neuroticism or whether some set of variables correlated with self-esteem is responsible for the relationship. Or perhaps whatever it is that determines level of neuroticism also has a bearing on self-esteem. We simply can't tell from the correlation alone.

Nonexperimental approaches to research, such as that described in the above example, are inherently beset by subject-selection bias. This problem may occur in "experimental" research as well. Brady's (1958) "executive monkey" studies are a classic example of how experimenters can, and occasionally do, introduce subject-selection bias into their research designs. Brady wanted to examine the effect of psychological stress on the formation of stomach ulcers. He first trained monkeys to press a lever at least once during every 20-second interval to avoid receiving a painful electric shock. The monkeys learned this task quite readily, though they occasionally neglected to respond, and thus were periodically shocked. As a result of this shock-avoidance training, many of the subjects developed ulcers. But it was unclear whether the ulcers were produced by the psychological stress induced by the training situation or by the physical stress that resulted directly from the shock.

In a follow-up study, Brady attempted to separate the effects of physical stress from those of psychological stress. Pairs of monkeys were secured in restraining chairs. One member of each pair, the "executive monkey," had responsibility for controlling the fate of both animals; his lever was "live" and, if pressed at least once every 20 seconds, could prevent both monkeys from receiving a shock. If the executive monkey failed to press the lever, both subjects received a shock at the same time. The control monkey's lever was "dead"; it had no influence on the occurrence or nonoccurrence of shock. Hence both animals received the same number of shocks, but only one, the executive, suffered the psychological stress that was presumed to result from having control over the occurrence of shock.

Brady's executive monkeys developed ulcers, but the control monkeys did not. Thus, psychological, rather than physical, stress appeared to be leading to ulcer formation.

A neat study, indeed—except for one troublesome flaw. Brady had not randomly assigned members of each monkey pair to the executive or control conditions. Instead, he selected as his executives those animals that had shown the fastest learning in initial avoidance-training trials, and assigned the less responsive animals to the control condition (Seligman, Maier, & Solomon, 1971). Since the faster learners in the shock-avoidance task may have had a lower threshold for pain—or perhaps higher emotionality—some constitutional trait, rather than psychological stress, may have predisposed the executives to ulcer development.

In Brady's investigation, the researcher directly caused the subject-selection bias. In other situations, the subjects themselves bring about the selection bias. This happens whenever subjects are allowed to volunteer to be in one treatment condition or another—for example, to receive psychotherapy or decline it. Obviously, people who elect to enter therapy differ in some basic way from those who reject therapy opportunities.

Confounding in Repeated-Measurement Studies

When research subjects are measured more than once on any variable, either within a single research session or across several occasions, a host of potential confoundings must be considered. These include the effects of repeated testing, instrumentation changes, and statistical regression.

Testing Effects. This type of confounding, which is also known as **sequencing effects**, occurs in a variety of forms. A simple example is that of students who are given the same intelligence or achievement test on several occasions as part of a study of the effects of an innovative educational program. The students soon become "test-wise"; they learn how to do well on the tests because they have had so much practice in taking them. Naive program evaluators may attribute the progressively better test scores to the effects of the program, when, in fact, most of the improvement may be due to practice in test-taking. This type of confounding tends to be a problem in any **longitudinal study**—that is, one in which a single group of people is measured with the same or similar instruments on successive occasions (Kulka, 1982).

The effects of repeated testing may also contaminate the results of experiments in which subjects serve in more than one condition. Such experimental arrangements are referred to as **within-subjects designs**, since the independent variable is manipulated within each participant; that is, *each subject receives all levels of the independent variable*. This contrasts with **between subjects designs**, in which *each subject serves in one condition or another*—period—such that the various levels of variable X are represented by different groups of people.

As an example of a within-subjects design, suppose you want to compare the relative effectiveness of two types of psychotherapy in increasing the number of self-assertive statements that subjects make. Because you have only ten subjects altogether, you decide to use each subject in both conditions. So you first administer "positive-reinforcement" therapy, which consists of praising the subject whenever he or she makes a self-assertive statement. Using a tape recorder, you keep track of the number of such statements across 15 therapy sessions. Then you switch to "nondirective" therapy, in which you allow the subject to talk while you listen intently and occasionally repeat back what you think the subject has said. The nondirective approach is also used for 15 sessions.

Let's say that your records show a steady increase in self-assertive statements during positive-reinforcement therapy. However, the outcome of the nondirective therapy seems peculiar. The first couple of sessions seem to have produced a dramatic increase in self-assertive verbalizations, but the succeeding sessions were associated with an equally dramatic drop in such verbalizations. What would you conclude about the relative effectiveness of the two approaches? I hope you would conclude that, because of a confounded design, the results are not interpretable.

In the hypothetical study described above, it is quite likely that there were **carry-over effects**, which means that subjects' experiences and performance in the first experimental treatment carried over to the second treatment to bias the outcome. Experiencing positive-reinforcement therapy first would very likely influence how subjects later respond to nondirective therapy. Thus, chances are good that the results of such a study would be different if a between-subjects design were used. In the latter case there would be no carry-over effects, because each subject would receive either one type of treatment or the other, but not both. It is worth remembering, then, that within-subjects and between-subjects designs aimed at the same set of variables will produce different results to the extent that carry-over bias is a problem (cf. Poulton, 1982).

Instrumentation Changes.   In research that involves repeated measures on one or more variables, it is essential that the measurement instrument and measurement procedure remain constant across measurement occasions. As I pointed out in Chapter 5, random fluctuations in the measurement process make the data less reliable. But more important here are the occasional *systematic* changes in the measurement process which may produce misleading data and, hence, erroneous interpretations of the effects of variables.

Sometimes instrumentation-change confoundings are a result of systematic malfunctions in automated recording devices, as when a cumulative recorder fails to register every third response in an operant-conditioning experiment. But it is far more common for the human recorders—the observers—to change the way that they record or code observations. For example, an observer may become more skilled, discriminating, conservative, or liberal in classifying responses during the course of a study. This may create the illusion that the subjects are behaving differently when, in fact, it is the observer who has changed.

Statistical Regression.   This problem is sometimes referred to as the **regression toward the mean confounding**. It results from the fact that when subjects are measured twice on the same dimension, those who score extremely high *or* extremely low on the first measurement occasion tend to score relatively closer to the mean value on the second occasion. In short, they tend to "regress" in the direction of the average score.

This phenomenon can create interpretation difficulties when the subjects have been selected on the basis of their unusually high or low initial standings on the dependent variable. The average dependent-measure score of such an extreme group will often change substantially (from pretest to posttest) in the direction of the mean of the larger population that the subjects were selected from, even if the independent variable has no effect whatsoever. The regression artifact may be attributed erroneously to the influence of the independent variable.

The statistical-regression phenomenon seems to show up quite a bit in clinical research, probably because people with psychiatric diagnoses represent extreme subgroups of the general population. Consider a study that was reported by Selkin and Morris (1971). The subjects were suicide attempters who appeared at the emergency room of a general hospital during a 12-week period. All of the patients were pretested on several measures of psychological adjustment and depression. One month later they were post-tested with the same instruments. The investigators compared a subgroup of patients who had elected to undergo psychotherapy with a subgroup who had refused psychotherapy. Their results showed that all the patients had improved significantly—that is, had become "more average"—across the one-month interval. Compared to the pretest results, the posttest data indicated less stress, somatic anxiety, and depression, and more conformity and problem-solving behavior. Moreover, the no-therapy patients improved just as much as the therapy patients on most measures.

Commenting on the equal improvement shown by the treated and untreated groups, Selkin and Morris wrote: "It would appear that, for most people, the pull of homeostatic mechanisms acts as a counterbalance to highly charged emotional states. At the risk of being trite one is tempted to recall the aphorism, 'Time is the greatest healer of all'" (pp. 36–37).

A more realistic, and less trite, conclusion would have been: Statistical regression is the greatest healer of all. Obviously, suicidal patients are an extreme group in the general population, and they tend to get extreme scores on tests of adjustment and depression. Even if the therapy given to some of the patients did have an effect on the test scores, that effect could not have shown up in data that were subject to such powerful statistical-regression effects. It is quite likely that, upon retesting, many of Selkin and Morris' patients simply regressed toward the mean of the general population. Ironically, had all of the patients elected to enter therapy, the therapeutic procedure might have been credited for their improvement.

The statistical-regression phenomenon has been a subject of much confusion and misinterpretation. Many people view the phenomenon as a mysterious, self-moving process that gradually draws in the high and low extremes of a population, such that the population becomes ever more homogenous. But this is not the case. The term "statistical regression" simply refers to the fact that measurement procedures are not perfectly reliable, or that two measures are not perfectly correlated with one another (cf. Nesselroade, Stigler, & Baltes, 1980).

In Chapter 5, you read that many psychological measures contain random error renders them less than perfectly reliable. It should be added that extreme scores on a measure tend to have larger random-error components than less extreme scores. Thus, some extremely high scorers have had unusually "good luck," and some extremely low scorers have had unusually "bad luck" (Campbell & Stanley, 1966). But you know that luck, or random error, is fickle, so the size and direction of the error component is likely to change unsystematically from one measurement occasion to the next. Since people who score at the extremes on a dimension can hardly become more extreme due to random error, if their scores change on a posttest, the change is likely to be back toward the mean. Hence the tendency of extreme groups to regress toward the average.

Note that there would be no regression phenomenon in the pretest/posttest situation if the test were perfectly reliable, because in that case there would be no measurement error. You should also be aware that statistical regression doesn't progressively make a population of people more homogeneous. The same random process that produces regression of some scores also tends to cause other members of the population to move to the extreme positions on the second testing, so that the overall range, or spread, of scores remains relatively constant across testing occasions. Therefore, statistical regression is a problem of confounding only if a disproportionate number of subjects in a treatment group are extreme scorers in a particular direction.

An example of statistical regression is shown in Table 7–1. The fictitious data shown there are meant to simulate the results of pretesting (X_1) and posttesting (X_2) 18 subjects with a particular measure. But it would be just as appropriate to consider the data as representing the scores of 18 subjects on two different tests that are imperfectly correlated with one another. In either case, the scores are arranged in *ordered pairs*, such that each subject's identification letter, score on X_1, and score on X_2 appear in the same row of the table (e.g., subject c's X_1 score is 80, and his X_2 score is 60).

Since the linear correlation between X_1 and X_2 is substantially less than 1.00 ($r = .50$), regression effects should be evident in the table. To highlight the regression phenomenon, I have included the pretest and posttest means of subgroups of subjects. Notice that the subgroup that scored 90 on the pretest had a posttest mean of 80. An equal amount of regression toward the mean occurred for those having pretest scores of 50. Less extreme subgroups ($\overline{X}_1 = 80$ and $\overline{X}_2 = 60$) also regressed, but to a lesser degree.

Note that despite the existence of statistical regression in these data, the X_2 scores are not more homogeneous than the X_1 scores. There is an equal amount of dispersion in each set of scores. In fact, the same 18 values occur in each column. The so-called regres-

TABLE 7–1

Regression Toward the Mean*: Eighteen Ordered Pairs of Scores, Where r = .50

Subject		Measurement Occasion		
		Pretest (X_1)	Posttest (X_2)	
a	$\overline{X}_1 = 90$	90	90	$\overline{X}_2 = 80$
b		90	70	
c		80	60	
d	$\overline{X}_1 = 80$	80	80	$\overline{X}_2 = 75$
e		80	70	
f		80	90	
g		70	80	
h		70	70	
i	$\overline{X}_1 = 70$	70	80	$\overline{X}_2 = 70$
j		70	60	
k		70	70	
l		70	60	
m		60	60	
n	$\overline{X}_1 = 60$	60	50	$\overline{X}_2 = 65$
o		60	80	
p		60	70	
q	$\overline{X}_1 = 50$	50	50	$\overline{X}_2 = 60$
r		50	70	

*Mean of each column = 70.

sion phenomenon results solely from the fact that the subjects' scores tended to change from the pretest to the posttest. This observation brings us back to the earlier notion that statistical regression is synonymous with imperfect correlation. A general rule, then, is that *the extent of regression toward the mean will be an inverse function of the reliability of measurement.* The lower the test/retest reliability of a measure, the greater the amount of statistical regression from the pretest to the posttest.

Confoundings Affecting Both Single- And Repeated-Measurement Studies

History.   Although Campbell and Stanley (1966) define the history confounding as ". . . the specific events occurring between the first and second measurement in addition to the experimental variable" (p. 5), the same type of confounding may affect the results of experiments in which subjects are measured only once on the dependent variable. This is particularly true of studies in which all of the experimental subjects are tested at the same time *as a group*, and separately from the control group.

Suppose a researcher wishes to investigate the effect of the apparent size of a female's pupils on the general arousal level of male subjects who have viewed her picture. Using a between-subjects experimental design, the researcher randomly assigns half of her subjects to a group that is to view a picture of a female in which the pupils have been touched up by an artist so as to appear larger than normal. The remaining subjects are to view the same picture, except that the model's pupils are of normal size.

The "large-pupil" and "small-pupil" subjects are assembled into their respective groups and are simultaneously tested in separate, but identical, rooms. Both groups are instructed to spend one minute studying the model's picture, which is projected onto a screen at the front of the room, and then to rate her on a variety of traits, including intelligence, attractiveness, and social sophistication. They are also to rate the extent to which the picture makes them feel pleasant, threatened, and aroused.

Unbeknownst to the researcher, a bumblebee slips into the room where the large-pupil group is situated (such things do occur!), and buzzes menacingly about the heads of the participants. At this point the "histories" of the two groups of subjects have become unequal, and the results are thereby confounded. Even if pupil size has no effect on arousal, there is likely to be a group difference in rated arousal.

In studies that involve both pretesting and posttesting of subjects, any influential event that intervenes between the two testings can confound the results if it is unequally distributed between experimental groups. But, as the bumblebee example illustrated, the history confounding is not limited to repeated-measures situations.

Subject Maturation.   The subject-maturation confounding is defined as ". . .processes within the respondents operating as a function of the passage of time per se (not specific to the particular events), including growing older, growing hungrier, growing more tired, and the like" (Campbell & Stanley, 1966, p. 5). This category of confounding is most pronounced in single-group studies designed to assess the effect of special programs or treatments. Over the course of an educational program or group experience, for instance, participants almost always change psychologically, socially, or, in some cases, physically, as a result of general maturational processes. Consequently, posttest results will almost certainly differ from pretest outcomes. Unless an equivalent control group is employed, it is impossible to disentangle the effects of the treatment from the effects of maturation.

More subtle types of maturation can contaminate single-measurement experiments, even if a control group and random assignment to conditions are used. If a careless experimenter tests most of his experimental subjects right before lunchtime and most of his control subjects right after breakfast, his outcomes may reflect hunger as much as the influence of the independent variable.

Subject Mortality.   The mortality confounding is a problem whenever some of the subjects drop out of, or are lost from, a study. In effect, the same problem exists when a researcher decides to *nonrandomly* discard the data of certain subjects. You'll recall that the latter situation existed in Ms. M.'s study, which was described at the beginning of this chapter. Ms. M. felt that she had to eliminate the data of subjects who had not followed through with the procedure that was appropriate for their group. What she didn't realize is that subjects fail to cooperate for nonrandom reasons which may be systematically related to the dependent variable. Consequently, by eliminating subjects she made her empirical relationship uninterpretable.

Subject mortality is frequently a problem in repeated-measures investigations, especially if the measurements are taken across a span of several weeks, months, or years. The larger the time interval consumed by the investigation, the more likely it is that some subjects will die, move, change their research commitments, or become otherwise inaccessible to the researcher. Thus, across the repeated measures, an ever-shrinking group of subjects may show a systematic change in its average score on the dependent variable. But if most of the people lost from the study tend to be either high or low scorers on the dependent variable, we might well ask: Is the systematic change in the mean dependent-measure score mainly a result of the independent variable's influence or mainly a result of the systematic loss of certain subjects?

Consider a commonly cited example of this problem. In studies of human development that employ the longitudinal method, subject mortality is referred to as **attrition**. Attrition effects often confound the variable of age, because people are lost from the subject pool for systematic reasons. For instance, in longitudinal investigations of the relationship between age and intelligence, the mortality rate is higher for less intelligent subjects than for their more intelligent peers (Kimmel, 1974). This differential dropout pattern raises the average IQ score of the group over the years, giving the appearance that people get smarter as they go from middle age to old age. Experienced developmental researchers are aware of this problem, however, and routinely use statistical corrections to deal with it (see, for example, Schaie, 1982).

Subject mortality can also plague single-measurement experiments if, for some reason, one condition has a higher rate of subject loss than the other conditions. In a study of the effects of punishment, for example, a researcher might set up three levels of punishment severity and randomly assign an equal number of subjects to each condition. In such a situation, we could expect that a few subjects would object to the experimental treatment and refuse to complete their research commitments. If the dropout rate for the increasing levels of punishment severity were 10 percent, 15 percent, and 50 percent, respectively, then a circumstance of *differential mortality* would exist. That is, the independent groups would have undergone different amounts of attrition, so that only subjects with low "stress sensitivity" remain in the "most severe punishment" group. In contrast, the other two groups would still contain some subjects with moderate stress sensitivity. Therefore, the three groups would no longer be equivalent, even though they were initially equal in most respects. Further, if stress sensitivity influences scores on the dependent variable, then it would be impossible to tell whether group differences on the dependent variable are a result of the independent variable (punishment severity) or the confounded variable (stress sensitivity).

CONTROLLING CONFOUNDINGS

The diversity of subtlety of confoundings are exasperating to students and beginning researchers. It may seem that the researcher is hopelessly besieged by Nature's trickery. Of course, if Nature clearly laid out its causal sequences and laws, there would be little need for science, scientists, or education and training in psychology. And you and I might well be human-engineering technologists—a structured and comforting situation, but maybe a little ho-hum?

Paradoxically, perhaps, the excitement and rewards of scientific endeavors stem mainly from attempting to untangle the web of confoundings that presently may seem so frustrating to you. In fact, the chief differences between the scientist and the nonscientist are the scientist's greater acquired sensitivity to sources of data contamination and his higher level of sophistication in dealing with those problems.

Here, I'll briefly review the major tools and strategies that psychologists use to reduce or eliminate the various types of confounding discussed previously. Many of these principles and techniques will be given additional coverage in later chapters, within the context of specific research designs.

Subject-Selection Bias

Subject-selection bias and the interaction of this confounding with other types of confounding make up the most frequently encountered type of data contamination. Fortunately, there are several ways to avoid or deal with this threat to internal validity. The various approaches include random assignment to conditions, randomized matching, nonrandomized matching, and within-subjects manipulation of the independent variable.

Random Assignment to Conditions.   To be able to draw a conclusion about how a dependent variable is influenced by your independent variable, X, you first have to be confident that the groups of subjects representing various levels of the independent variable are, *on the average*, equal in all respects except X. The most widely accepted method of "equating" experimental groups on potentially confounding variables is to assign subjects randomly to the respective levels of X. Randomness is characterized by unsystematic change and unpredictability—in short, the operation of chance processes. Thus **random assignment** means that subjects are assigned to experimental groups entirely on the basis of a chance process.

Theoretically, if random assignment is used, then a subject's a priori probability of serving in a given group is equal to his a priori probability of serving in each of the remaining groups. To use the simple example of a completely randomized two-group design, the probability of serving in Group 1 equals the probability of serving in Group 2 = .50 (or 50 percent), *regardless of the subject's characteristics or personal history*. In other words, random assignment breaks up any systematic relationship that could exist between subject characteristics and the independent variable. The result of random assignment is that, on the average, the various experimental conditions contain approximately equal numbers of bright and dull subjects, male and female subjects, extroverted and introverted subjects, and so on. The latter statement becomes more accurate as sample size is increased.

I would hasten to add, however, that random assignment doesn't render the groups exactly equal, even when large samples are used. For example, when 100 subjects are randomly assigned to each of two conditions, the groups usually will differ slightly, sometimes appreciably, on the average level of IQ and other traits. But the statistical tests used to assess the impact of the independent variable take these sampling errors into account, so long as random assignment is used to determine group membership (Sohn, 1977). Therefore, a more precise statement about random assignment is that it usually makes the treatment groups "statistically equal." You should note, however, that randomization doesn't guarantee statistical equivalence of conditions; it only makes statistical equivalence highly probable.[1]

Random assignment may be carried out through a variety of devices that are well known to gamblers and all others who delight in games of chance. When there are only two treatment conditions, randomization may be implemented by successive, vigorous flips of a coin. If the coin comes down with heads showing, the subject for whom the coin was flipped goes to Group 1; if tails is the outcome, the subject is assigned to Group 2.

Consider the list of 20 hypothetical subjects that appears in Table 7–2. They are listed alphabetically by last name, and each subject's IQ and sex appear to the right of his or her name. Let's compare the result of assigning subjects to groups through flipping a coin to the result of assigning them on the basis of an alphabetical split. (Note that in the examples that follow, IQ and sex are neither independent nor dependent variables. They are merely "index variables" used to illustrate possible confounding factors. It isn't necessary to specify the independent and dependent variables in these hypothetical examples.)

Table 7–3 shows the outcome of arbitrarily assigning the first ten names in the alphabetical list to the Experimental Group and the last ten to the Control Group. Notice that the mean IQ of the experimental group is 118.3 and that the Control Group mean is

TABLE 7–2

Alphabetical Listing of 20 Subjects, Showing Their IQ's and Their Genders

Subject	IQ	Gender*
Argyle	105	F
Baxter	140	F
Carson	97	M
Donaldson	123	M
Ebber	126	F
Ferber	137	F
Gardner	110	M
Hagler	100	F
Ipswich	115	F
Johnson	130	F
Karten	124	M
Lashley	115	M
Morgan	117	M
Niedler	133	F
Orton	110	M
Pepper	100	M
Queen	130	M
Rather	90	F
Samuelson	93	M
Tompkins	90	F

*M = male; F = female.

TABLE 7–3

Alphabetically Assigned Groups

Experimental Group			Control Group		
Subject	*IQ*	*Gender*	*Subject*	*IQ*	*Gender*
Argyle	105	F	Karten	124	M
Baxter	140	F	Lashley	115	M
Carson	97	M	Morgan	117	M
Donaldson	123	M	Niedler	133	F
Ebber	126	F	Orton	110	M
Ferber	137	F	Pepper	100	M
Gardner	110	M	Queen	130	M
Hagler	100	F	Rather	90	F
Ipswich	115	F	Samuelson	93	M
Johnson	130	F	Tompkins	90	F
	$\Sigma X_1 = 1183$			$\Sigma X_2 = 1102$	
	$\overline{X}_1 = 118.3$			$\overline{X}_2 = 110.2$	
	F = 7			F = 3	
	M = 3			M = 7	

110.2—a difference of 8.1 IQ units, on the average. Gender is not especially well balanced across the groups either, since 7 of the 10 females are in the Experimental Group. Thus, if the dependent variable were subject to the influence of either intelligence or sex of the respondents, then a confounding problem would exist in the data obtained from this subject-assignment scheme. We wouldn't be able to tell whether any group difference on the dependent variable was due to the independent variable or to intelligence, sex, or something correlated with intelligence or sex.[2]

Table 7–4 presents the same pool of subjects after I allocated them to groups via a succession of coin flips. The mean IQ difference in this case is only 1.5 units, which is a much more satisfactory between-group balance than was achieved through the alphabetical split. I was lucky in this regard. With subject samples this small, a between-group difference somewhat larger than 1.5 units easily could have occurred despite the random assignment. But it is unlikely that a randomization procedure would produce as large a group difference (8.1 units) as was observed in Table 7–3. What is more important, however, is the fact that the usual statistical tests of mean differences can accommodate and correct for group differences due to random assignment but cannot accommodate group differences resulting from nonrandom assignment.

Also note that the gender variable is more evenly distributed across the groups when random, rather than systematic, assignment is used. Presumably, the potentially confounding variables, such as age, personality traits, and socioeconomic background, would also be statistically equated by the randomization procedure. Therefore, a statistically significant group difference on the dependent measure could be attributed to the influence of the independent variable rather than something confounded with the independent variable.

What randomization devices can be employed if there are more than two groups in a study? Any device that functions entirely on the basis of chance will do. If you have four levels of the independent variable, for example, the four suits of a thoroughly shuffled

TABLE 7–4

Randomly Assigned Groups

Experimental Group			Control Group		
Subject	IQ	Gender	Subject	IQ	Gender
Argyle	105	F	Baxter	140	F
Carson	97	M	Donaldson	123	M
Ebber	126	F	Ferber	137	F
Hagler	100	F	Gardner	110	M
Johnson	130	F	Ipswich	115	F
Karten	124	M	Morgan	117	M
Lashley	115	M	Orton	110	M
Niedler	133	F	Pepper	100	M
Queen	130	M	Samuelson	93	M
Rather	90	F	Tompkins	90	F
	$\Sigma X_1 = 1150$			$\Sigma X_2 = 1135$	
	$\overline{X}_1 = 115.0$			$\overline{X}_2 = 113.5$	
	F = 6			F = 4	
	M = 4			M = 6	

deck of playing cards would suffice (e.g., Hearts = Group 1, Spades = Group 2, etc.). Random assignment to conditions would be determined by the luck of the draw. If you have five or six conditions, you could roll a die to assign subjects to conditions. However, the best general randomization device is a random-number table. The numbers in such a table are strictly chance outcomes and help you to avert any coin-tossing or die-rolling biases you might inadvertently introduce into the subject-assignment procedure. A random-number table, together with instructions for its use, appears in the Appendix of this text.

Matching.   Random assignment to conditions is an effective general strategy for dealing with the problem of subject-selection bias, especially when sample size is at least moderate—for example, equal to or greater than 20 subjects per condition. But what if you are interested in the effects of an independent variable that cannot be randomly assigned—for instance, a clinical diagnosis? Or what if you have only a small pool of subjects to work with, but want to ensure that the treatment groups are reasonably similar on a particular confounding variable that is known to be strongly correlated with the dependent variable? In many such cases, the treatment groups can be matched on one or more potentially confounding variables *in advance* of data collection.

When the independent variable is a type that you can manipulate, it is possible to use a powerful matching technique with small samples. The technique is called **randomized matching**, because it combines random assignment with matching on a criterion measure.

Reconsider the pool of 20 hypothetical subjects represented in Table 7–2. Suppose you wanted to have these subjects participate in a study comparing the relative effectiveness of two approaches to teaching abstract concepts. Since concept-learning ability is known to be strongly related to general intelligence (e.g., Denny, 1966), IQ could be employed as a matching criterion to minimize the initial group difference in aptitude for concept formation. This would allow you to attribute a significant group difference in performance to the effect of your independent variable (technique of teaching concepts).

The randomized-matching procedure involves the following steps:

1. Select a **matching criterion** that has a strong correlation ($r \geq .50$) with performance on the dependent measure.
2. Obtain a score on the matching criterion for each subject. This may involve pretesting all subjects on the criterion measure. In the present example the IQ data are already available.
3. Arrange subjects into a criterion-measure hierarchy, from highest score to lowest score, or vice versa. Such a matching hierarchy is shown in Table 7–5. Note that the relative positions of subjects with tied scores was determined by a randomization device.
4. Using the criterion-measure hierarchy, designate the **matched pairs**,[3] as shown in Table 7–5. The highest and second highest subjects in the hierarchy make up the first matched pair, the third and fourth subjects the second pair, and so on. Note that two people with the same criterion-measure score may not fall into the same matched pair, depending on their ranks in the hierarchy.

TABLE 7–5

Matching Hierarchy

Pair	Subject	IQ	Gender
1	Baxter	140	F
	Ferber	137	F
2	Niedler	133	F
	Queen	130	M
3	Johnson	130	F
	Ebber	126	F
4	Karten	124	M
	Donaldson	123	M
5	Morgan	117	M
	Ipswich	115	F
6	Lashley	115	M
	Gardner	110	M
7	Orton	110	M
	Argyle	105	F
8	Hagler	100	F
	Pepper	100	M
9	Carson	97	M
	Samuelson	93	M
10	Rather	90	F
	Tompkins	90	F

5. Using a randomization device, a coin flip, for example, assign one subject in each pair to the "Experimental" or "Control" condition. This serves to randomize the effects of other potentially confounding variables that the subjects are not matched on.

The results of this matching procedure appear in Table 7–6. As you can see, randomized matching rendered the two groups almost identical in average IQ. The equivalence on this dimension is better than that achieved through the earlier random-assignment procedure, where the resulting mean difference was 1.5 units. Most of the time, randomized matching will result in a smaller group difference on the criterion measure than would simple random assignment. Also notice that, due to the randomization aspect of the matching procedure, the gender variable, too, is fairly well distributed across the two treatments.

Randomized matching, then, offers the advantage of establishing nearly perfect group equivalence on a variable that is strongly correlated with the dependent measure, while allowing other potential contaminators to be "randomized out." A second advantage is that the statistical tests normally applied to matched-pair data are more sensitive to the effects of the independent variable than are the tests that can be used with completely randomized designs (Kirk, 1968). This means that the test of statistical significance is more likely to detect a nonchance effect in the data when matching is used in lieu of simple random assignment.

But there are several disadvantages associated with randomized matching. First, it is sometimes difficult to find a matching criterion that is adequately related to the dependent measure. Matching usually is ineffective unless the linear correlation between the criterion and the dependent measure is at least .50 (Ary, Jacobs, & Razavieh, 1979; Kerlinger, 1973). Second, even if an effective criterion can be located, the matching procedure can be expensive and time-consuming if you must test each subject on the crite-

TABLE 7–6

Matched Groups Assembled Through Randomized Matching

	Experimental Group			Control Group		
Pair	Subject	IQ	Gender	Subject	IQ	Gender
1	Baxter	140	F	Ferber	137	F
2	Niedler	133	F	Queen	130	M
3	Ebber	126	F	Johnson	130	F
4	Karten	124	M	Donaldson	123	M
5	Ipswich	115	F	Morgan	117	M
6	Gardner	110	M	Lashley	115	M
7	Argyle	105	F	Orton	110	M
8	Pepper	100	M	Hagler	100	F
9	Carson	97	M	Samuelson	93	M
10	Rather	90	F	Tompkins	90	F

$$\Sigma X_1 = 1140 \qquad\qquad \Sigma X_2 = 1145$$
$$\overline{X}_1 = 114.0 \qquad\qquad \overline{X}_2 = 114.5$$
$$F = 6 \qquad\qquad\qquad F = 4$$
$$M = 4 \qquad\qquad\qquad M = 6$$

rion measure prior to starting the study. Third, the above problems are compounded when you attempt to match subjects on more than one criterion.

Matching procedures may be applied in situations where the independent variable is one that cannot be manipulated, but in such cases, confounding is only partially controlled. With **nonrandomized matching** the independent variable is represented by different levels of some *preexisting* characteristic of the subjects (in Chapter 2, this was referred to as an "organismic" independent variable); hence, subjects cannot be randomly assigned to levels of the independent variable. The researcher must locate research participants who differ from one another on the independent variable, and then try to assemble them into groups that vary on the characteristic of interest but are matched on other variables that might influence the dependent measure.

A study by Hare (1966) exemplifies this technique. Hare was interested in examining the relationship between the trait of "psychopathy"[4] and preference for immediate versus delayed punishment. He was able to match 12 psychopathic prison inmates, 12 nonpsychopathic prison inmates, and 12 college students on the dimensions of age, formal education, and IQ. This matching procedure eliminated any confounding effects that these three variables might have produced.

Hare's results showed that, compared to the two other groups, psychopaths preferred delayed punishment over immediate punishment significantly more often. Although the group differences could not have been due to age, formal education, or IQ, the relationship between the independent variable and the dependent variable is still difficult to interpret. The reason is that there may have been significant group differences on variables that were not controlled through the matching process; there is no randomization component in this approach to take care of potential confounds that subjects are not matched on. Hare's explanation of the results was based on a theory that states that psychopaths are less responsive to aversive conditioning than "normals." However, since he neither controlled for a number of confounding variables nor measured the subjects' conditionability, this interpretation is open to question. Thus, at best, nonrandomized matching permits the elimination of one or more plausible rival hypotheses, while allowing many other rival hypotheses to stand.

Within-Subjects Manipulation.   Still another approach to controlling subject-selection bias is to use subjects as their own "controls" by employing a within-subjects manipulation of the independent variable. The rationale for this is that there can't be initial differences among the various treatment conditions (levels of X) if the same people serve in all conditions. Within-subjects designs are also more economical than between-subjects designs, in the sense that within-subjects manipulations require fewer subjects. For example, if you wish to have 10 observations in each of 4 experimental conditions, a between-subjects design would require 40 subjects. But with a within-subjects manipulation, you would need only 10 subjects.

As is discussed below, however, there are potential confounding hazards that often attend the use of within-subjects manipulations.

Testing Effects

There are several classes of confounding associated with taking repeated measurements on subjects. One class is referred to as **progressive error**, defined as "any change in behavior which occurs as a consequence of continued experience or successive trials" (Underwood, 1966, p. 32). *Positive progressive error* can result from warm-up effects, practice effects, or, in memory experiments, recency effects; these factors can be expected to enhance subjects' performance, irrespective of the effect of the independent variable. *Negative progressive error*, which causes a deterioration in performance, is associated with the effects of boredom, fatigue, and proactive and retroactive memory interference.

Progressive error is a problem in within-subjects experimental designs when it is confounded with treatment conditions. The key to handling progressive error in this type of design is to balance it evenly across the various levels of the independent variable. The techniques of counterbalancing and randomization are two ways this may be accomplished.

Counterbalancing.   Suppose you want to attempt a replication of Triplett's (1897) classic experiment on "social facilitation," which was reviewed in Chapter 2 of this text. You may remember that Triplett was interested in finding out whether a simple task is performed more efficiently when people do it under conditions of competition rather than working alone. The simple task in this case was winding in fishing line via a special fishing reel apparatus. Triplett found that his subjects (all children) did wind the line at a faster rate in the Competition condition than in the Alone condition.

Let's say that your replication of Triplett's study will involve the same task and the same two conditions: Competition versus Alone. Since you will have only 10 subjects altogether, you decide to use a within-subjects design so that you will end up with 10 dependent-measure scores in each condition. In such a design, each participant will receive *8* one-minute trials in each condition, or 16 trials in all. In this kind of within-subjects experiment, you could normally expect an effect of both warm-up and practice. These two sources of progressive error would build up over the 16 trials to make the subjects more proficient performers. True, there may also be some negative progressive error across the 16 tests as fatigue and, perhaps, boredom set in. But since each trial lasts only one minute, you expect the positive effects of warm-up and practice to outweigh the negative effects of fatigue and boredom, yielding a positive progressive error, overall.

How can you avoid having positive progressive error confound the independent variable, Alone versus Competition? Somehow, you will have to ensure that the cumulative effect of the error is distributed in equal amounts between the two conditions. To accomplish this, perhaps you could alternate the Alone (A) and Competition (C) conditions in 4 "blocks" of 4 trials each across the 16 tests. With this arrangement, the treatment sequence would be: AAAA-CCCC-AAAA-CCCC. If *a* is used to represent a block of Alone trials and *b* is used to represent a block of Competition trials, then this is an *abab* pattern. Will this take care of the problem?

If progressive error is a positive *linear* function of experience with the task, then the expected effect of progressive error can be represented graphically, as shown in Figure 7–1.

The figure shows that the first Alone block will benefit from 2 units of progressive error, and the second Alone block will be enhanced by 6 units of progressive error, *for a total of 8 units*. In contrast, the number of units of progressive error for the two Competition blocks is $4 + 8 = 12$. Thus, relative to the Alone condition, performance in the Competition condition will be inflated by a progressive-error confounding. The same problem would exist even if you alternated individual trials in the following way: A, C, A, C, A, C, A, C, A, C, A, C, A, C, A, C.

Instead of using an alternating sequence, you might try a **counterbalanced sequence**, which utilizes the type of hypothetical scheme shown in Figure 7–1 to balance *linear* progressive error evenly across the treatments. If each block of four trials can be represented by *a* for the Alone treatment and *b* for the Competition treatment, then a counterbal-

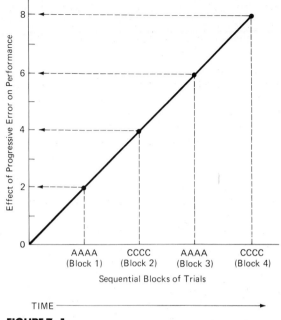

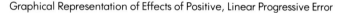

FIGURE 7-1

Graphical Representation of Effects of Positive, Linear Progressive Error

anced arrangement of trials would be *abba*: 4 trials in condition *a*, then 8 trials in condition *b*, then 4 in *a*. Using Figure 7–1 as a model, you can see that this would result in the following distribution of a progressive-error effects:

$$\text{Alone condition } (a) = 2 + 8 = 10$$
$$\text{Competition condition } (b) = 4 + 6 = 10$$

In other words, the effects of repeated experience with the task would be balanced evenly across the two levels of the independent variable; hence, no confounding would exist.

As you may have surmised by now, the essential characteristics of counterbalancing are: (1) Each treatment occurs equally often in the sequence of trials, and (2) each treatment precedes and follows every other treatment an equal number of times.

You should be aware of the fact that *this type of counterbalancing is effective only when you can assume that progressive error is a* linear *function of experience with the task*. When the relationship is *curvilinear*, this method will not remove all confounding effects. The problem is illustrated in Figure 7–2.

Examining the figure, you can see that progressive-error units sum to approximately 12.5 for condition *a* and approximately 14.5 for condition *b*, when the *abba* arrangement is used. But it is possible to employ a modified counterbalancing procedure to better distribute progressive error across conditions when the relationship between error and task experience cannot be assumed to be linear. You simply randomly assign half of your subjects to the *abba* sequence and the other half to a *baab* sequence. When the overall results are summed, this strategy will allow both conditions to benefit or suffer equally from the effects of progressive error.

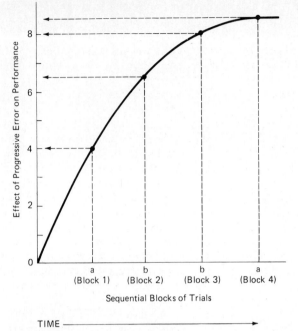

FIGURE 7–2

Graphical Representation of Effects of Curvilinear Progressive Error

Counterbalancing is easily extended to experiments with more than two treatments. In a three-treatment situation, for instance, the appropriate sequence of treatments would be *abccba*. What would be the correct counterbalancing sequence if there were four conditions?

As you may have realized by now, the number of experimental trials in a counterbalanced design must be some multiple of the number of blocks in the counterbalancing sequence. If an *abba* arrangement is employed, then 4, 8, 12, 16, or 20 trials would work, but 6, 10, 14, and 18 would not.

Randomization of the treatment sequence can often be substituted for strict counterbalancing and, if properly carried out, will distribute progressive error equally among the levels of X. For a 16-trial series involving two treatments, a series of coin flips would produce a sequence such as: *baaababbbbaabbaa*. Of course, a single random arrangement usually would not perfectly balance progressive error across the two conditions. Therefore, you would ideally generate a different random sequence for each subject in the study. Then by summing data across all subjects, you would allow the successive random variations in error to cancel out one another. If it is not feasible to provide a unique random sequence for each subject, several such sequences may be constructed and an equal number of subjects assigned, at random, to each arrangement.

Independent-Group Alternatives.   There are circumstances under which no counterbalancing scheme will remedy the confounding produced by repeatedly testing subjects. In such cases, some variety of **independent-groups design** should be used instead of a repeated-measures approach. The term "independent groups" means that different subjects have been randomly assigned to the respective measurement conditions, so that each subject serves in only one condition or is measured only once. The between-subjects experimental design is one kind of independent-groups design.

One type of situation that defies correction through counterbalancing is that involving a *carry-over effect* from one experimental condition to another. A carry-over effect is not simply a progressive error. When progressive error is the problem, then the sequencing effect produced by going from condition *a* to condition *b* is equal to the effect of going from *b* to *a*, at a particular point in the experiment. This is true because sources of progressive error, such as recency effects or warm-up effects, are general processes that are not tied to the specific nature of the experimental treatment. But when carry-over is operating, then *ab* is not equal to *ba*. Poulton (1982) has referred to this problem as **asymmetric transfer**, which means that subjects learn strategies or expectancies in one condition and use them in a subsequent condition where they are not appropriate. The consequence is that certain conditions have particular effects on behavior only when a repeated-measures design is used. In an independent-groups design, however, the same variables have a different relationship, or no relationship at all.

Carry-over would almost always be a problem when the same subjects served in two therapy or drug conditions. The effect of the first therapy or drug (*a*) condition probably would linger to affect how subjects responded to the second therapy or drug (*b*). Consequently the results obtained in an *ab* sequence would differ from those of a *ba* sequence. Because of the carry-over effect, condition *b* effectively becomes a different treatment when preceded by condition *a* than when it is presented by itself. For example, subjects who normally would respond well to nondirective therapy when it is the only approach they are exposed to may respond negatively to nondirective therapy if they have had prior experience with behavior-modification therapy. Moreover, an *abba* counterbalancing scheme isn't likely to correct the problem, because the nature and magnitude of the carry-over effect will be different for the *ab* sequence than for the *ba* sequence. In such cases, it is wise to use a between-subjects design.

Consider another type of research vulnerable to carry-over effects: longitudinal studies of human development. The problem is that the subjects become "test-wise." That is, the effect of earlier testing persists to influence the outcome of later testing. An independent-groups design may be used here also.

Let's suppose a researcher is interested in assessing changes in social and political attitudes of college freshmen during the course of the academic year. He has 300 randomly selected participants, and he wishes to measure attitudes at the start of the year, after the first semester, and at the end of the year. But he is aware that the experience of taking an attitude test can lead to an attitude change all by itself, even if there are no real developmental changes in the subjects. To avoid carry-over effects from earlier to later testings, he randomly assigns one-third (n = 100) of his subjects to each of the three testing occasions. This plan is illustrated in Figure 7–3. One hundred subjects are tested initially, 100 at midyear, and 100 at the year's end. Because of random assignment, each subgroup probably represents the larger group fairly well, and because no subject takes the attitude test more than once, there are no carry-over effects. Therefore, any differences in attitude scores among the three testing occasions probably represent developmental changes for this group of freshmen, and not merely the effects of repeated testing.

You should note that this technique is feasible only if the original sample size is quite large—several hundred subjects would be desirable. If the sample is small, the even smaller subgroups may differ substantially from one another due to sampling error associated with random assignment to subgroups. Sampling error becomes a less troublesome factor as the size of the original sample is increased.[5]

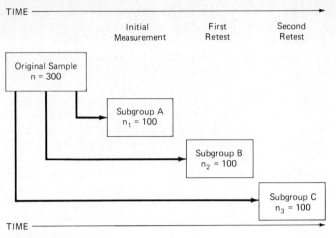

FIGURE 7–3

Schematic Representation of an Independent-Groups Longitudinal Design

Controlling Other Sources of Confounding

Instrumentation Changes. Confounding that results from malfunctioning equipment can be averted easily through periodically checking the instrument's accuracy. But instrumentation confoundings that stem from changes in the human observer are more difficult to control. It helps to develop and specify measurement procedures and criteria carefully in advance of the data-collection process, and then to give the raters or data recorders ample training before turning them loose in the research setting.

Pretraining data collectors has two advantages. First, it allows you to check the accuracy with which they apply the measurement criteria and procedures. Second, the training period affords the time and experience that are necessary for data collectors to develop and stabilize their skills, which, in turn, helps avoid systematic changes in how the data are recorded.

Statistical Regression. The best way to avoid the statistical-regression confounding is to avoid using subjects who represent an extreme sample on some dimension. If an extreme group must be employed, then half of the group should be randomly assigned to a control condition, which does not receive any special treatment. This procedure won't prevent the experimental group from regressing toward the mean of the general population, but it will at least expose the regression artifact. And since the experimental and control groups are likely to exhibit similar degrees of regression, a statistically significant difference between them on the posttest could be attributed to the influence of the independent variable (assuming that other potential confoundings have been controlled).

History. In the typical between-subjects experiment, involving randomly assigned experimental and control groups, it is imperative that steps be taken to ensure that the respective groups don't have differential experiences that are irrelevant to manipulation of the independent variable. It is such irrelevant differential experiences that make up the experimental-history confounding.

One of the most common techniques for avoiding the history confounding is to hold constant all potentially influential, but irrelevant, stimuli and circumstances. These include place of testing (and, if possible, time of testing), how general instructions are presented to the subjects, background noise, temperature, and physical setting. All of these, as well as other conditions, should be the same for all groups of subjects.

Since group-testing of subjects, using different places and/or times for the experimental and control subjects, invites a history confounding, it is best to avoid this type of procedure. But if subjects are to be tested individually, rather than in groups, how do you keep such things as time and temperature constant for all subjects? You can't in a literal sense. But you can in a statistical sense, by randomly assigning members of all groups to combinations of times, places, and data collectors, so that these factors are randomly distributed across the groups. For example, if you plan to test 60 subjects individually, say 20 in each of three conditions, then you will need to randomly assign each subject to one of 60 testing sessions.

Another type of history control is needed in some experiments in the field of physiological psychology. A common procedure in that area is to randomly assign animals to experimental and control groups, surgically alter or destroy a particular brain structure in the experimental animals, then look for behavior differences between the two groups. Any behavior differences can be attributed to the change or deficit in the specific brain structure that was surgically altered. Or can they? If the control animals were not operated on, then they differ from the experimental animals in two ways: The target brain structure was not altered in the controls, *and* the controls didn't undergo surgery. So are the postoperative group differences a result of change in a particular brain structure or a result of the general surgical procedure?

To avoid this kind of history confounding, investigations of this kind routinely include a second control group: A **sham-operation group** is subjected to the general surgical procedure, but the critical brain structure is not altered. Under these circumstances, the effects of a specific structural change can be separated from the general effects of surgery.

Unfortunately, there are some circumstances under which the effects of differential subject histories cannot be controlled. Such is the case when experimental and control groups are posttested several days, weeks, or months after they are exposed to their respective experimental conditions. In this kind of situation, you have no way of ensuring that the specific intervening experiences of one group will match those of another group.

Subject Maturation.   In pretest/posttest studies, the effect of subject maturation can be dealt with by using randomly assigned treatment groups. In an investigation of the impact of an educational enrichment program, for instance, only half of the students involved would be assigned to the special classroom. The remaining half would receive standard educational experiences. Because of random assignment, maturation effects probably would be statistically equal across groups. Thus, end-of-term differences between the two groups could be reasonably attributed to the enrichment program, assuming that other sources of confounding had been eliminated.

More subtle maturation variables, such as fatigue and hunger, can plague standard laboratory experiments. Fortunately, the effects of these variables can usually be evenly distributed across conditions by randomly assigning experimental and control subjects to testing times.

Subject Mortality.   The loss of certain subjects or data on those subjects can't always be avoided. But before you decide to discard data for any reason, make sure that such a radical act is necessary. Then consider what effect this act might have on the results of your study. You may decide that repeating the investigation is preferable to throwing out data.

Both long time intervals between treatment and posttest and the use of aversive treatments invite subject mortality. Therefore, it is a good idea to consider alternatives to these procedures when you design the investigation.

THE SOCIAL PSYCHOLOGY OF THE PSYCHOLOGY EXPERIMENT

To understate the matter a bit, eliciting responses from human subjects isn't quite the same as getting chemical reactions to occur in a test tube. Chemicals react to what you do with them. But human beings not only react, they also "act back" to influence the researcher's behavior (Rosenthal, 1967, 1976). Moreover, the human subject is as much engaged in problem-solving behavior as the researcher (Orne, 1962). These considerations have led to an ever-growing body of theory and research centered on the social-psychological aspects of the researcher-subject interaction.

Some of the interpersonal artifacts inherent in psychological research pose problems for establishing the external validity, or generalizability, of research results. These problems will be considered in Chapter 8.

Other social-psychological processes act to confound the independent variable in some studies and, hence, are a threat to internal validity. It is this second category of interpersonal influences that is of interest here.

Experimenter-Expectancy Effect

Although the idea that the researcher and her subjects can unintentionally (subconsciously?) collaborate to ensure a particular outcome is many decades old, the first systematic program of research on this topic was begun by Robert Rosenthal in the early 1960s (see Rosenthal, 1966 & 1976, for a comprehensive review of this line of investigation). A central theme in this research is the notion that data collectors who interact with subjects often hold strong biases, formalized in terms of their experimental hypotheses, regarding the type of behavior they expect subjects to exhibit; further, that these strong biases can lead the data collector to *unintentionally* communicate her expectations to the subject, who all too often acts in accordance with the perceived expectations. The result is that the independent variable under examination seems to be producing the expected effect when, in fact, something else is largely responsible for the effect. Essentially this is a variety of history confounding since, presumably, subjects in different conditions receive differential covert communications from the researcher.

Rosenthal's prototypical model of experimenter-expectancy effects is the case of "Clever Hans," a horse that reputedly could read, spell, and solve problems of musical harmony and arithmetic (Pfungst, 1911). Hans always indicated his "answers" by tapping his hoof an appropriate number of times (for example: "Hans, what does ten minus eight equal?" Answer: "tap, tap"). The word "hoax" immediately comes to mind when we hear of this type of phenomenon, yet a committee of experts had certified that Hans's performance was genuine—that the horse was not getting help from his questioners. How could a horse acquire so much human knowledge? How were these feats possible?

A series of experiments by Pfungst provided answers to these questions. Pfungst's careful observation revealed that Hans was receiving unintentionally emitted cues from his questioners. It was found that the typical questioner's first action upon asking Hans a question was to look expectantly at the horse's hoof. This signaled Hans to commence tapping. And then when Hans approached the expected number of taps, the questioners would almost imperceptively raise their eyes or heads in anticipation of the cessation of tapping. This, of course, tipped off the horse, and he would stop responding. Presto—a genius horse!

The upshot of the Clever Hans case was the realization that observers hold expectations, biases, if you will, that cause them to inadvertently send covert cues to the subject. The subject, in turn, picks up the cues and responds according to the perceived expectations.

Could this phenomenon be a widespread contaminating process in psychology laboratories? Rosenthal thinks so. A series of studies by him and his colleagues suggested that the expectancies of a psychological researcher can produce significant effects on the laboratory behavior of both rats and human beings (e.g., Rosenthal, 1966, 1967, 1976; Rosenthal & Fode, 1963; Rosenthal & Lawson, 1964). These results have occasionally been supported by other investigators working independently of Rosenthal (e.g., Johnson, 1970; Miller, 1970; Zobel & Lehman, 1969). What's more, Rosenthal (1964, 1967) cited evidence that similar, unintentional expectancy effects occur outside the laboratory, in survey research and public school classrooms, for example.

What is the nature of the covert mechanisms behind the experimenter-expectancy effect? Research by Rosenthal and others suggests that the researcher often communicates his or her expectations to the subject through "paralinguistic" cues, such as tone of voice, and through gestural, postural, and facial cues. Interestingly, the unintentional biasing effects apparently are greater for researchers who, upon meeting the subject, are more likable, dominant, personal, relaxed, and "important acting" (Rosenthal, 1967). Stronger expectancy effects are also obtained by researchers who are more professional in their manner while reading instructions to the subjects (Rosenthal, 1967).

Controlling the Experimenter-Expectancy Effect

Rosenthal (1966) lists 10 general strategies for minimizing the unintentional effects of researcher expectancies on subjects' behavior. Four are described here.

1. Use a large number of data collectors who differ in their expectations. This procedure will reveal experimenter-expectancy effects to the degree that there is an interaction between data collectors and the independent variable—that is, different researchers obtain different effects of the independent variable. Also, the researcher variable can be systematized as an "extra" independent variable, so that the effect of researcher expectancy may be statistically removed.

2. Use a **double-blind** approach to data collection. The typical research situation involves the single-blind approach, whereby the subject is "blind"—that is, doesn't know the research hypothesis or whether he is in the experimental or control group—but the data collector is not. In the double-blind approach, both the data collector and the subject are unaware of the research hypothesis and the subject's group membership.

Use of the double-blind method means that the **principal investigator**, that is, the person who formulates the hypothesis and designs the study, doesn't have direct contact with the subjects. Rather, he employs "naive" researchers to collect data from the subjects. Theoretically, the person who interacts with the subject cannot communicate the principal investigator's hypothesis to the subject because he or she (the data collector) doesn't know what those expectancies are. In practice, the double-blind procedure doesn't always work out this cleanly (see Rosenthal, 1966). Further, naive data collectors might have their own hypotheses, and if these are inadvertently communicated to the subjects, the results might be confounded anyway. For this reason, the ideal double-blind study employs several data collectors who are randomly assigned to conditions. That way, data-collector expectancies are randomized across levels of the independent variable.

3. Minimize researcher-subject contact. This can be accomplished by using automated data-collection systems and written, tape-recorded, televised, or telephoned instructions. A one-way mirrored window between researcher and subject may also be of some use in minimizing contact with the subject. The obvious problem with most of these techniques is that subjects may be offended by their impersonal nature. Also, subjects may be prone not to take the research seriously when the researcher seems to be making herself scarce.

4. Employ an expectancy control group. These special control subjects do not receive the same treatment as the experimental group, but the data collector is led to expect them to show the same behavior as the experimental group. Thus the effect of expectancy alone is isolated and may be compared to the results obtained with the experimental group.

Is Experimenter Bias Rosenthal's Bias?

Unintentional experimenter effects have received a lot of attention over the past two decades—enough to make conscientious researchers paranoid. Let's take a critical look at the evidence to see if such a reaction is justified.

The first aspect of the experimenter-bias notion that needs to be examined is its basic assumption: that most subjects will try to behave in a way that confirms the researcher's expectancies. Comprehensive reviews of the research literature on subject motives do not support this assumption (see Carlsmith, Ellsworth, & Aronson, 1976; Christensen, 1980). Rather than trying to confirm the researcher's expectations, most subjects seem to be primarily interested in presenting a positive image of themselves within the context of their research participation—that is, to come out looking competent and well adjusted. Thus the experimenter-expectancy effect might well be restricted to studies in which subject behaviors promoting positive self-presentation happen to coincide with behaviors that are being unintentionally encouraged by the researcher.

A second item requiring examination is the generality of empirical support for the existence of an unintentional experimenter-expectancy effect. Barber (1976) conducted a comprehensive survey of the literature on this question. All of the 55 investigations he reviewed were designed to experimentally induce an experimenter-expectancy effect. Barber found that 40 of the investigations failed to demonstrate the effect, and only 15 had produced any evidence at all for the phenomenon—often weak evidence at that.

Overall, then, available research suggests that unintentional experimenter-expectancy effects may not be as large a confounding problem as psychologists once thought. Does this mean that you should disregard the issue of controlling for experimenter bias? Certainly not! There is little to be gained by leading with your chin. Though apparently weak, there is evidence that your biases can contaminate your data. And these biases could become troublesome if you relax your vigilance too much. So it remains the better part of wisdom to incorporate safeguards against expectancy effects into your research design.

SUMMARY

Investigations lack internal validity to the extent that contaminating, or *confounding*, variables are allowed to covary with the independent variable. The existence of confoundings in studies makes relationships between variables difficult to interpret in cause-and-effect terms. Seven major categories of confounding were reviewed in this chapter:

Subject-Selection Bias: Subjects representing a particular level of the independent variable differ initially in some influential way from subjects representing other levels of the independent variable.

Testing Effects: The experience of being repeatedly measured causes subjects' behavior to change.

Instrumentation Changes: During the course of a study, the data collectors systematically change the way they record data.

Statistical Regression: From pretest to posttest, the dependent-measure scores of extreme groups of subjects will tend to gravitate toward the population mean regardless of the effect of the independent variable.

Subject History: The experimental and control subjects have differential experiences that are irrelevant to manipulation of the independent variable.

Subject Maturation: The effects of subjects' becoming older, hungrier, or fatigued during the course of the investigation may influence the dependent variable, irrespective of the impact of the independent variable.

Subject Mortality: Differential loss of subjects at different levels of the independent variable causes the treatment conditions to differ in ways other than that associated with manipulation of the independent variable.

Several techniques for dealing with these sources of confounding were examined.

Experimenter-expectancy effects can also confound the independent variable. Fortunately, there are various strategies for minimizing this type of confounding.

REVIEW QUESTIONS

1. Define *internal validity* and *confounding*, and describe the relationship between the concepts.

2. What sources of confounding are most prevalent in single-measurement situations? In repeated-measurement studies?

3. Make up original examples of the following types of confounding: subject-selection bias, testing effects, statistical regression, history, subject maturation, subject mortality.

4. In what sense is the statistical-regression artifact synonymous with imperfect correlation?

5. How might statistical regression account for the end-of-season "slumps" often shown by unexpectedly successful dark-horse sports teams?

6. Explain the logic behind randomization techniques. Why is randomization a preferred approach to the control of confoundings?

7. Compare and contrast within-subjects and between-subjects research designs. Include statements regarding the relative advantages and disadvantages of each type of manipulation.

8. Why is counterbalancing ineffective in controlling carry-over effects?

9. Describe a means of minimizing each of the following sources of data contamination: instrumentation changes, regression effects, history, subject maturation, and subject mortality.

10. Define the experimenter-expectancy effect, and describe four techniques that may be used to minimize it.

Notes

[1]When the 5 percent level of significance is used in the statistical test, the theoretical probability is .95 that the randomly assigned groups will be "statistically equal." This means that if a researcher uses the 5 percent level of significance throughout her professional career, approximately 95 out of every 100 randomized-groups experiments she conducts will start out with statistically equivalent treatment groups. Varying sample size would have no effect on this percentage, since most statistical-significance tests have a built-in correction for sample size.

[2]Sometimes assigning subjects to conditions according to their position in an alphabetical listing of last names may yield a result that is as good as random assignment. But you can't count on it.

[3]This matching system can be extended to experiments in which there are more than two treatments. If there are three conditions, for example, the top *three* subjects in the criterion-measure hierarchy are designated the first matched block; the next three are the second block, and so on. Each member of each block is then randomly assigned to one of the three conditions.

[4]The currently preferred term is "sociopathy." The trait is associated with a tendency toward habitually committing unlawful or immoral acts without experiencing the remorse, guilt, and fear that normally accompany such acts.

[5]There is still another problem with the procedure related to sample size. If you have randomly selected the original sample so that you can generalize your findings to the population from which you sampled, then you should be aware of the fact that each of the smaller subgroups provides a less precise estimate of the population mean than would the larger, original sample.

8

GENERALIZING

In his book *Science Is a Sacred Cow*, critical observer Anthony Standen posed a question that is both relevant and sobering:

> Consider this question: Can science disprove ghosts? In the supremely confident period, toward the end of the last century, when it was supposed that there was a conflict between Science and Religion, and Science was rapidly winning, it was the mark of an educated man to say "Science has proved that there are no such things as ghosts, they are merely the superstitions of the unenlightened." Education is always behind the times, and much the same attitude is prevalent today; you can still hear people say, "Surely science has proved that there are no ghosts." And yet, is that so? Suppose, just suppose for the sake of argument, that ghosts can occasionally appear when the psychological conditions are just right, and suppose, what might well be true, that one necessary condition for the appearance of a ghost is the *absence* of a scientist: well then, "Science" (that is to say, scientists) would go on investigating ghost after ghost, and would "disprove" every one of them, and yet ghosts would continue to appear whenever the scientists were not looking (Standen, 1950, pp. 32–33).[1]

The main point of Standen's example is clear: Not every issue or question can be approached through the scientific method.[2] But there is a second, perhaps paradoxical, point to be gleaned from Standen's argument: The systematic and rigorous methodology scientists employ for the purpose of discovering the most general laws of nature may actually limit the generalizability of scientific data (Argyris, 1980). What's more, this problem is most serious in fields where the "object" of study is the human being (see Wolman, 1971). See Box 8–1 for three points of view on this matter.

Using Standen's example metaphorically, we can think of the constructs and relationships of scientific psychology as peculiar types of "ghosts"—peculiar in the sense that they don't necessarily disappear in the presence of a scientific observer, but sometimes change their character or appearance when being scrutinized. Thus, the "ghosts" of the laboratory may not always look or act the same when encountered outside the lab. Furthermore, some of them may limit their domain of activity exclusively to the laboratory or to one type of observer or setting.

The point of the metaphor is that the discovery of relationships, even those with cause-and-effect status, does not complete the cycle of scientific inquiry. There is one more step that often proves to be a problem. The aim of science is not only to discover cause-and-effect relationships but also to establish that those relationships are *invariant* across time and a wide range of conditions; in other words, to move from tentative and localized principles to general laws. This aim pertains to the concept of **external validity** of research findings: "To what populations, settings, treatment variables, and measurement variables can this effect be generalized?" (Campbell & Stanley, 1966, p. 5). It also pertains, in an even more inclusive sense, to the concept of **reliability**, which refers to the replicability of data.

In this chapter, I will first outline the four major dimensions of generalizability and indicate how they might fall into a spatial versus temporal classification scheme. Next, I'll review the most common causes of external *invalidity* and follow up with a consideration of procedures designed to deal with these problems. Finally, I'll discuss the relationship of statistical significance and replication to the goal of generalizing across time.

SPATIAL VERSUS TEMPORAL GENERALIZATION

Going from Sample to Population

All of the people, settings, treatment stimuli, and time frames you wish to generalize to make up your **target population**. The people, settings, stimuli, and time frames you ac-

Box 8–1

ISSUES IN SCIENCE

Generalizing in the Behavioral Sciences:
Three Points of View

Viewpoint 1. Critic Anthony Standen makes the very strong assertion that the behavioral sciences are not really sciences at all, because there is nothing fixed or constant in their domain of observation (Standen, 1950). In contrast, he says, the physical sciences are true sciences, in the sense that they can rely on constants, such as the boiling point of water and the life cycles of certain insects.

Standen's reasoning is that since people are "infinitely variable," generalizations beyond the specific sample studied are hazardous; even the same sample of people may show entirely different results if the study is repeated a year later.

Standen concludes that, because of the large number of variables involved in human behavior, behavioral scientists can predict only the behavior of groups and not the behavior of an individual. He sees this as a serious limitation on the progress of the behavioral sciences.

Viewpoint 2. Psychologist Seymour Epstein (1980) asks, "How serious a limitation is imposed on psychology as a science if general laws cannot be used to predict particular instances of ordinary behavior?" (p. 795). His answer: Not very. And to the extent that prediction of the particular constitutes a barrier, the problem is certainly not limited to the behavioral sciences; even the physicist cannot predict the destination of a single molecule in space and time.

Epstein notes that the effectiveness of any science, behavioral or physical, stems from its ability to make *probabilistic* predictions of *average* outcomes, and not from an ability to predict particular events with certainty. Thus, when all is said and done, the major goal of any science is to discover general laws of nature. Accordingly, Epstein recommends that the behavioral sciences follow the example of the physical sciences by statistically averaging the results of many samples to discover the most general effects of variables.

Viewpoint 3. Psychologist Lee J. Cronbach's position on the issue of generalizing in the behavioral sciences is somewhere between the extreme views espoused by Standen and Epstein. Cronbach recognizes the importance of combining research results across studies in order to establish the most general effects of a variable. He suggests, however, that practical application of a general effect to a particular situation should be preceded by research which shows how local circumstances and incidental factors modify that effect. He argues that

Instead of making generalization the ruling consideration in our research, I suggest that we reverse our priorities. An observer collecting data in one particular situation is in a position to appraise a practice or proposition in that setting, observing effects in context. . . . As he goes from situation to situation, his first task is to describe and interpret the effect anew in each locale, perhaps taking into account factors unique to that locale. . . . As results accumulate, a person who seeks understanding will do his best to trace how the uncontrolled factors could have caused local departures from the modal effect. That is, generalization comes late, and the exception is taken as seriously as the rule. (Cronbach, 1975, pp. 124–125)

tually observe make up your **sample**, which is a subset of *some* population. To the extent that the sample is representative of the target population, you can say that your sample findings would hold true if you tested the entire population of interest—that is, you can generalize. This act of generalizing is referred to as making **inferences**, or educated guesses, about a population on the basis of sample data.

Many times, however, the sample you take does not represent the target population very well. Perhaps the subset of people, stimuli, etc., that you are observing does represent some larger set along these dimensions, but not the even larger set that makes up the target population. In this case, it is necessary to distinguish between the target population and the **sampled population**, that is, the population your sample actually represents. Plans and desires nothwithstanding, to the degree that there is a discrepancy between these two populations—and most often there is—it is legitimate to make inferences only about the sampled population.

For example, suppose your target population is the entire set of students presently enrolled at a college or university. You wish to assess that population's attitude toward neo-Marxist social policies. Accordingly, you *randomly* select 50 attitude-scale items from a pool of 760 items relevant to the topic, and you *randomly* select 500 students from the total set of 8,677 currently enrolled individuals. You mail out the 50-item attitude questionnaire to the (probably representative) sample of 500 people. Despite appropriate follow-up efforts on your part, only 400 of those polled cooperate by completing and returning the questionnaire. What population of people can you generalize to? Although the target population is all students at the school, you will be able to make strong inferences only about students at that school who return opinion questionnaires. The latter group is the sampled population. The reason for this limitation on your inferences is that people who don't cooperate in this type of study are likely to differ in reliable ways from those who do cooperate. Your target population consists of cooperators and noncooperators, whereas the sampled population consists of only cooperators. And it is quite possible that the political attitudes of the two groups differ.

Dimensions of Generalization

Ideally, researchers would like to generalize their sample findings across four dimensions (see Epstein, 1980): settings, treatment stimuli and tasks, subjects, and time.

Settings.   The research setting includes aspects of both the physical environment and the social environment. The physical environment is made up of such variables as place and circumstances of testing; surrounding objects, fixtures, and implements; temperature and noise. The social environment consists of the researcher and other persons or groups (except the measured subject) who happen to be involved in the research situation. If a set of findings represents general laws of behavior or experience, then the data should be relatively stable from one research setting to another and across different researchers.

Treatment Stimuli and Tasks.   This dimension includes the task and instructions given to the subject, the measurement instruments used, and any other event or circumstance related to the measurement of the independent or dependent variable. The question here is whether a given pattern of findings would hold up if the variables were manipulated or measured in several different ways.

Subjects.   Another aspect of external validity concerns the degree to which the particular subjects observed are representative of some larger set of people or animals. Findings relevant only to a particular subject pool or some other, narrow population are usually considered to be less useful than findings that apply to people in general or mammals in general, for example.

Time.   The random forces in nature sometimes combine in a fashion that produces a statistically significant fluke of chance. Such an unusual combination of events is theoretically and practically worthless, unless your hobby is collecting improbable events. But the data and apparent relationship associated with a fluky outcome certainly would look real enough at the time they occur. And, to be sure, many investigators have become excited about chance outcomes only to discover later that the outcomes were not replicable.

Thus, to be useful, findings must not be restricted to a brief time frame: They must be reproducible.

The four dimensions of external validity summarized above represent two fundamental questions about the utility of data: (a) To what extent can the results be generalized across "space"—from here to there, from these to those? (b) To what extent can the results be generalized across time—from now to then? Conceptually, **spatial generalization**[3] pertains to generalization across settings, treatment stimuli and tasks, and subjects, within a particular interval of time. In contrast, the concept of **temporal generalization** concerns the reproducibility of a particular finding from one interval of time to another, when settings, treatment variables, and the subject population are held constant.[4] Hence temporal generalization is intimately associated with the matters of statistical significance and "exact" replication.

Since spatial and temporal generalization are theoretically different aspects of external validity, the two concepts will be treated separately here. In practice, however, spatial and temporal generalization are confounded with one another to varying degrees. For one thing, it is impossible to hold all spatial dimensions perfectly constant even when you are attempting to conduct an exact replication of your own investigation (see footnote 4). Moreover, studies designed to test the relevance of prior findings to a new setting or population must, of necessity, be conducted at a later time than the original study; so the dimension of time would be confounded with the setting or population dimension. Furthermore, certain data-collection situations, such as preelection surveys of voters, expressly attempt to generalize across both space and time—namely, from a telephone conversation prior to the election to a voting booth on election day.

COMMON THREATS TO SPATIAL GENERALIZATION

Restrictions on spatial external validity may be thought of as *interactions* of certain generalization dimensions with the independent variable of interest. The concept of interaction means that the effect of a particular variable changes, depending on the circumstances that exist at the time the variable is studied. More precisely, the effect of one independent variable varies across levels of another variable. Therefore, to the extent that an independent variable influences behavior differently as settings, tasks, or subjects are changed, an interaction exists. And the generality of the relationship between the independent and dependent variables is thereby restricted.

An example will reinforce this point. A recurring question on college campuses concerns the meaning of students' end-of-term evaluations of their instructors. It has been found that students' grades are positively correlated with the ratings that they give their instructors (Costin, 1978). That is, when several different instructors teach the same course at the same school, and all sections of the course take the same exams, average exam scores of the various classes are positively related to average instructor ratings in those classes—the sections with the higher exam-score averages also rate their instructors more highly. But how should this relationship be interpreted? Does the correlation between grades and instructor ratings mean that instructor competence determines both course mastery and the instructor's ratings? Or do students who expect to get good grades (because they have been getting high test scores) simply feel obligated to reward their instructor, regardless of his or her performance (Blass, 1980)? The latter explanation implies that the students' subjective biases, rather than teacher competence, are responsible for the relationship between students' grades and how they rate their instructors.

Blass (1980) tested these alternative explanations. He had introductory psychology students complete a test of objective versus subjective reasoning and then divided the students into two groups: those who reason subjectively and those who reason objectively. At the end of the course he computed the correlation between students' course-exam scores and the ratings they gave the instructors, and compared the correlation produced by subjective students to that produced by objective students. Interestingly, the positive relationship between grades and instructor ratings was strong only for the subjective group; it was much weaker for the objective reasoners. If this finding can be consistently replicated, then it would suggest that the relationship between grades and instructor evaluations is due mostly to some subjective justification process and much less to teacher effectiveness. It would also mean that the variable of expected grade *interacts* with the variable of student subjectivity to determine instructor evaluations. And this interaction represents a limit on the generalizability of the student-grade/teacher-evaluation relationship: The relationship would exist only if many of the students who are rating the instructor are subjective reasoners. In classes where the students are predominantly objective reasoners, the relationship would all but disappear.

It will always be true that limits on the generalizability of findings represent an interaction of some sort; the threats to external validity discussed below should be viewed in that light.

Interaction Effects of Settings

Several characteristics of the physical and social environments of psychological investigations interact with the independent variable to limit the generality of findings. Some of the more important research-setting variables are the obtrusiveness of the research procedure, specific aspects of the physical setting, researcher attributes, and researcher expectancies.

Obtrusiveness of Scientific Trappings.   It is well established that people sometimes abandon their usual behavior when they become aware of their status as subjects in a scientific study (Jung, 1971). As a consequence of this, subjects' in-lab responses to certain stimuli or situations may differ considerably from their responses to similar stimuli or situations in everyday life. This phenomenon, referred to as "observational reactivity," was discussed at some length in Chapter 5.

It is reasonable to expect the amount of observational reactivity to vary as a direct function of the degree to which subjects are conscious of their roles as research participants. In turn, the role consciousness of subjects is influenced by the obtrusiveness of the research procedure. In naturalistic-observation studies, for instance, the presence of scientific observers and procedures is minimally conspicuous, and the subjects' behaviors are but minimally altered by the observation process. In contrast, most laboratory studies have a way of bringing the paraphernalia of science to the forefront of the subjects' consciousness. Therefore, observational reactivity may often be a troublesome factor in settings that are clearly earmarked as laboratories.

The naturalistic-observation approach and the stark laboratory experiment represent opposite extremes on the obtrusiveness dimension. Undoubtedly you can imagine many different research situations that lie between these extremes. And, other things being constant, you can expect the results of investigations to be generalizable to everyday circumstances to the extent that the subject's attention is directed away from his or her special role in the data-generation process.

The Physical Setting. Even when the general level of obtrusiveness is held constant, specific aspects of the physical research setting seem to affect the generalizability of findings. In one investigation of this matter, Rosenthal (1967) randomly assigned fourteen experimenters to eight laboratory rooms that varied in their "professionalness," "orderliness," and "comfortableness." Rosenthal's results indicated that subjects who served in the more "professional appearing" laboratory rooms perceived their experimenter as significantly more "expressive" (in voice, gestures, and facial expression) than did subjects who were tested in the less "professional appearing" rooms. If the perceived expressiveness of the experimenter influences performance on the dependent measure in any significant way, then it is conceivable that the apparent effect of an independent variable could change to some degree from one type of lab setting to another.

Even the experimenters in Rosenthal's study were influenced by the physical differences of the rooms. The experimenters took the experiment more seriously if they had been assigned to rooms that were both disordered and uncomfortable. Rosenthal suggested that disordered and uncomfortable lab rooms fit the stereotype of scientific research settings, thereby causing the experimenters to view their research activity as more authentic. But in any case, the setting's effect on the experimenter's attitude clearly could indirectly influence the subject's behavior. It is not too great a leap to suggest that experimenters who take the research seriously might get very different responses from their subjects than experimenters who exhibit a more casual attitude.

Researcher Attributes. The personal and professional traits of the researcher affect the character of the relationship between him and the subject. And it is likely that the subject-researcher relationship will interact with the research variables to place restrictions on the external validity of the outcomes. Let's consider the evidence that bears on this hypothesis.

In an experiment on verbal conditioning, Binder, McConnell, and Sjoholm (1957) employed two experimenters: a soft-spoken, petite young woman and a masculine-acting man who was a foot taller, 130 pounds heavier, and 12 years older than the young woman. Each experimenter verbally reinforced his or her subjects for uttering sentences containing hostile words. The results showed that the female experimenter's subjects emitted significantly more hostile words across trials than did the male experimenter's subjects. Although it is hard to tell which attribute—sex, height, weight, or manner—or attribute combination was responsible for the between-group difference in response rate, it is clear that researcher traits had an impact.

Other investigations examined the interaction of sex of researcher with sex of subject. In a study of the subjective experiences produced by sensory deprivation, subjects interviewed by an experimenter of the same sex reported more sexual feelings than did subjects queried by an experimenter of the opposite sex (Walters, Shurley, & Parsons, 1962). In another study, Harris and Masling (1970) found that while male experimenters obtained more projective-test responses from female subjects than from male subjects, female experimenters obtained approximately the same number of responses from subjects of each sex.

Obviously, sex of researcher isn't the only personal attribute likely to constrain the external validity of data. Just a few researcher traits implicated by research in this area include religion, race, warmth, likability, acquaintanceship with the subjects, anxiety, need for approval, personal values, psychological adjustment, and laboratory experience (see Barber, 1976; Rosenthal, 1963, 1967).

Researcher Expectancies. In Chapter 7, unintentional experimenter-expectancy effects were identified as a source of *internal* invalidity—that is, researcher expectancies can produce between-group differences even when the independent variable has no reliable effect. But unintentional experimenter-expectancy effects may also be viewed as a threat to external validity, in the sense that they could result in inconsistent findings from one research setting to another, depending on the biases of the respective investigators.

Interaction Effects of Stimuli and Tasks

Artificiality of Laboratory Experimentation.   As a technique of psychological investigation, the laboratory experiment has been variously exalted and attacked: exalted because it is capable of maximizing the internal validity of data; attacked because not only the laboratory setting but also the experimental stimuli and tasks tend to be obviously contrived and artificial, relative to subjects' everyday experiences (e.g., Harré and Secord, 1972; Wachtel, 1980). In many experiments on perception and memory phenomena, for instance, the stimuli are discrete and simple (e.g., isolated words or geometric sketches), in contrast with the continuous, complex, and highly meaningful information that human minds constantly process outside the lab.

Even in the more "relevant" experiments of social psychologists, treatment stimuli and experimental tasks sometimes bear little resemblance to everyday social stimuli and responses. In a study of the determinants of interpersonal attraction, for example, the "person" who is being evaluated by subjects might exist only in the form of a written or oral description of a hypothetical individual. And the subjects' expressions of liking or disliking might take the form of making checkmarks on a paper-and-pencil rating scale.

The argument that stems from these considerations is that, since many laboratory manipulations and measures are not representative of real-life events and behaviors, the data of laboratory experiments tell us little about what people are really like. Are there compelling counterarguments to this position? Berkowitz and Donnerstein (1982) think so. Their thoughts are summarized in Box 8–2.

Pretesting Effects.   An experimental design used with some frequency in the behavioral sciences is the two-group pretest/posttest design. Several years ago, an example of such a design came across my desk in the form of a master's-degree thesis proposal. The subjects were to be 36 cancer patients who were receiving medical treatment at the investigator's place of employment. She planned to randomly assign half of the patients to each of two conditions: a meditation group and a discussion group. In each group, subjects were to engage in the designated activity (meditation or discussion) several times a week across a period of three months. The dependent variable was the subjects' attitudes toward cancer and ill health in general. The hypothesis was that the meditation treatment would cause the subjects' attitudes to become more positive, whereas the group discussion would have little or no effect in this direction.

To check on the initial equivalence of the two groups, as well as to assess the *direction* of attitude change in each group, the investigator proposed to both pretest and posttest all subjects. Herein lay the possible threat to the external validity of the findings: *The effect of pretesting might interact with the independent variable* (meditation versus discussion) to yield results that would occur only in situations that combine pretesting with the treatments. Hence, even if meditation was associated with more positive attitude change than group discussion produced, we wouldn't know whether the same outcome would occur if pretesting were not used. The reason is that pretesting can lead subjects to view and react to the experimental treatment in unique ways, depending on the nature of the pretest. And it is possible that the effect of pretesting will produce different perceptual and

Box 8-2
ISSUES IN SCIENCE
In Defense of the Laboratory Experiment

Lab experiments have long been criticized for their presumed lack of *mundane realism*. Mundane realism exists to the degree that a situation resembles the "real world," at least on the surface. Because many experiments involve obviously contrived tasks and circumstances, as well as artificial or unrealistic stimuli, they tend to lack this quality. It is for this reason that several authors have questioned the generalizability of laboratory findings in psychology (e.g., Argyris, 1980; Gilmour & Duck, 1980; Wachtel, 1980). How valid is this criticism?

While not contending that the standard criticism of lab experiments is entirely invalid, Berkowitz and Donnerstein (1982) feel that it is overemphasized. Taking a hard look at the external validity issue, they offer the following replies to critics of the experimental method:

1. The main purpose of the experimental method is to test cause-and-effect hypotheses, not to make inferences about a large population of people, settings, stimuli, or what have you. Perhaps it is inappropriate to criticize the experimental method on the grounds that it may lack a characteristic (i.e., external validity) which is secondary to its major purpose, especially since it fulfills its primary function so well.

2. Since the experiment's "reason for being" is to demonstrate cause-and-effect relationships between theoretically important variables, it is more crucial that experimental manipulations produce their intended psychological effect than that they represent real-world conditions. Therefore, in the conduct of experiments, psychologists should stress *experimental realism* over mundane realism. A study has experimental realism if the experimental manipulation captures the subject's attention, engages him fully, and creates the psychological essence of the theoretical constructs under examination. Since experimental realism activates *fundamental* psychological processes, we might well expect the results of experiments possessing this quality to be universally applicable, *even if they lack mundane realism*. By definition, fundamental psychological processes occur in most people under a variety of circumstances.

3. It should not be automatically assumed that because a particular relationship has been demonstrated in a laboratory experiment, it won't be generalizable to naturalistic situations. The generalizability of laboratory findings is an empirical question; only further research can establish the range and limits of the phenomenon under investigation. What's more, there is considerable evidence suggesting that many relationships that were first revealed in the laboratory experiment hold up when they are investigated under more "representative" circumstances.

4. "We have now come to our central thesis: The meaning the subjects assign to the situation they are in and the behavior they are carrying out plays a greater part in determining the generalizability of an experiment than does the sample's demographic representativeness or the setting's surface realism" (Berkowitz & Donnerstein, 1982, p. 249).

cognitive biases when followed by meditation experiences than when followed by group-discussion experiences.

There is a way to test for the interaction of pretesting and treatments, and this technique will be discussed in a later section of this chapter.

Multiple-Treatment Carry-Over Effects. In the last chapter, I explained how carry-over effects hamper the internal validity of repeated-measurement studies. The carry-over contamination can also interfere with external validity, in the sense that certain results obtained with a within-subjects design would not generalize to between-subjects designs. This would be the case whenever a person's response to treatment B changes if he experiences treatment A before experiencing treatment B. For instance, Poulton (1982) reviewed several examples of published research which demonstrated that the effects of certain variables change when subjects receive several treatments (i.e., levels of the independent variable) rather than serving in only one condition or another. His examples were drawn from research in free-recall learning, choice reaction time, and letter-classification tasks.

As you may have discovered by now, the effect of pretesting that was described earlier is merely a special case of multiple-treatment carry-over. When a pretest is used, the experience of being tested can be thought of as treatment A, the effects of which may "carry over" to affect how subjects respond to the experimental condition (treatment B).

Another special case of carry-over effects concerns the "sophistication" of subjects. Ideally, researchers would like to employ subjects who are experimentally "naive"—that is, who haven't participated in previous psychological investigations. Most of the time, however, such subjects are difficult to find, especially on a college campus where dozens, or perhaps hundreds, of behavioral studies are conducted each year. Consequently, experienced, or sophisticated, research participants may comprise the majority of subjects in some studies, particularly those carried out late in the academic year. To the extent that earlier experience as a research participant carries over to influence subjects' reactions to subsequent research tasks, a type of multiple-treatment interaction effect exists. This means that the results of investigations employing experienced subjects may not generalize very well to experimentally naive populations. Perhaps this consideration can account for the occasionally reported performance differences between students who sign up for research participation early in the academic term and students who sign up late in the term (e.g., Richert & Ward, 1976; Richter, Wilson, Milner, & Senter, 1982). Additional evidence for the effects of subject sophistication is reviewed in Jung (1971).

Demand Characteristics.   It is possible that the specific instructions, stimuli, and tasks within some research settings contain unintentional cues which suggest a particular hypothesis to the subject. Presumably, cooperative subjects who pick up on the suggested hypothesis would then perform in ways that support the hypothesis, in order to fulfill their "obligation" to be "good subjects." The pattern of cues that may convey the research hypothesis is referred to as the **demand characteristics** of the research situation, because these cues implicitly "demand" that a "good subject" behave in accordance with the expectations that they point to.

Orne (1962), who formalized the concept of demand characteristics, noted that the demand cues can exist in campus rumors about the research, the behavior or traits of the experimenter, and various aspects of the research setting. However, he seemed to emphasize the research procedure (i.e., stimuli and tasks) as the principal source of demand cues: "A frequently overlooked, but nonetheless very significant source of cues for the subject lies in the experimental procedure itself, viewed in the light of the subject's previous knowledge and experience" (Orne, 1962, p. 779).

Demand characteristics threaten the generalizability of findings because they can modify or determine the results that are associated with a particular set of variables. For instance, manipulation of the independent variables of some experiments may be associated with certain changes in the dependent variable only when a unique pattern of demand cues is operating. Hence the results of such investigations may be hard to replicate should the demand characteristics change from study to study; also, the results may have little relevance to nonlaboratory situations, since the latter would probably lack the influential and essential demand cues.

To illustrate the concept of demand characteristics, Orne (1970) refers to the early experiments on the effects of sensory deprivation (e.g., Bexton, Heron, & Scott, 1954). In these studies, paid participants were kept, for hours or days, in barren rooms that were all but devoid of auditory, visual, olfactory, and tactile stimulation. In some investigations subjects were required to wear special goggles, earplugs, and padded attire in order to further reduce sensory input. Following several days of such isolation, many subjects exhibited deficits in concentration, visual perception, and problem-solving. And a few of them also reported auditory and visual hallucinations. But how much of this was due to sensory isolation per se?

Orne pointed out that several components of the treatment afforded sensory-deprivation subjects could have implicitly communicated to them that they were expected to experience strange and potentially harmful effects as a result of the isolation. For example, sensory-deprivation subjects are often required to undergo medical and psychological tests and to sign release forms prior to their participation. Also, they typically are shown an emergency signaling device, such as a panic button, which they are told to use if they need to get out of the situation in a hurry. All of these cues may cause suggestible subjects to expect weird or strange things to happen to them. And if many of the subjects wish to meet the researcher's "expectations," they may behave strangely on the posttests, thereby producing the dramatic effects sometimes reported in these studies.

Orne and Scheibe (1964) demonstrated the influence of demand characteristics by setting up a simulated sensory-deprivation situation. The experimental subjects were told that they were in a "Meaning Deprivation" condition and were asked to sign release forms. After being shown a panic button, they were allowed to sit in a quiet, but not soundproof, room for four hours, but were not sensorily isolated to the usual degree. The control-group subjects were given the same treatment except that they were told that they were a control group, had no panic button, and weren't required to sign release forms. Thus Orne and Scheibe's study had all of the demand characteristics of a sensory-deprivation investigation but didn't actually involve extreme sensory deprivation. Nonetheless the posttreatment tests showed some of the usual effects of sensory deprivation in the experimental group.

If demand characteristics played a major role in the dramatic findings of early studies of sensory deprivation, then it is perhaps not surprising that the most bizarre outcomes of these experiments proved to be difficult to replicate (see Beck, 1978).

Interaction Effects of Subject-Selection Bias

The generalizability of research findings is limited to varying degrees by the characteristics of the sample of subjects studied. Psychologists sometimes assume that "basic" processes of sensation, perception, learning, and memory are the same in diverse populations, simply because these processes are so intimately linked to brain structures and functions that are shared by all rats, monkeys, or people. Thus automatic generalizability of outcomes is frequently presumed in these cases. But even in regard to so-called "basic" phenomena, this presumption may not be warranted. For example, some optical illusions commonly experienced among North Americans and Europeans are much less commonly experienced by people of nonindustrialized cultures (e.g., Allport & Pettigrew, 1957).

When the phenomena under examination are of a complex nature, the characteristics of the sample are even more significant in determining the extent to which generalizing beyond the sample is justified. The causes of depression, for instance, vary as a function of age, even when culture is a constant. Self-directed anger and hostility appear to be major contributors to the condition in younger people. But personal loss seems to be the principal precipitating factor in depression among older persons (Busse & Pfeiffer, 1977).

Let's take a look at several sampling considerations that bear on the external validity problem.

Effects of Convenience Sampling.   A "convenience" sample consists of subjects who are available and willing to participate in a research project. College students who volunteer to be research participants are an example of a convenience sample. We employ them because they are readily available and often eager to advance the goals of science (and perhaps their grades in introductory psychology?).

Most of the samples of people and animals studied by psychologists are convenience samples, simply because it is impractical, and often unethical, to draft a scientifically selected sample that would adequately represent a larger population. The major problem created by the use of convenience samples is obvious: It allows subject-selection bias to influence the data. Human subjects who make themselves available for research purposes do so for systematic reasons.[5] Consequently, the people making up a "select" subject pool probably differ in systematic ways from people in general and from other subgroups of the general population. And the traits and experiences that set the convenience sample apart from the general population may interact with the variables of interest to produce results that have less than ideal generality. Thus, it is usually proper to qualify any general statements made on the basis of data taken from convenience samples.

Who Serves in Psychology Experiments?   In discussing the problem of population restrictions in psychological research, Jung (1971) wrote: "It sometimes seems as if psychology experiments are almost always done with either albino rats or college sophomores taking introductory psychology courses. Both types of Ss are convenient and relatively inexpensive. However, the cost of limiting ourselves to these types of Ss may be rather high in the long run because our generalizations may be quite limited" (p. 24).

How accurate was Jung's observation concerning the overuse of white rats and college sophomores in psychological research? Beach (1950) reviewed alternate-year issues of the prestigious *Journal of Comparative and Physiological Psychology* through 1948 and discovered a trend toward increasing use of the white rat in psychology experiments. Other reviewers have also noted this pattern of growing popularity for the white rat as psychological subject and have questioned the generalizability of a behavioral psychology that rests so predominantly on this species (e.g., Boice, 1973; Ehrlich, 1974).

Even the white rat runs a distant second to the college student when the whole gamut of psychological research is considered. In a review of the *Journal of Abnormal and Social Psychology* across the years of 1962–1964, Smart (1966) found that 73 percent of the studies therein had employed college students. His examination of the *Journal of Experimental Psychology* for the same years revealed that college students served as subjects in 86 percent of those studies. These findings were supported by subsequent reviews and surveys. For example, when Jung (1969) surveyed 44 college and university psychology departments regarding the source of subjects used in departmental research, the responses showed that 90 percent of the human subjects employed were college students. Further, nearly 80 percent of all human subjects were from introductory psychology courses. (Also see Levenson, Gray, & Ingram, 1976.)

A more recent examination of alternate-year issues of the *Journal of Abnormal and Social Psychology* (1960–1964) and the *Journal of Personality and Social Psychology* (1966–1980) showed little change in the incidence of utilizing college students as subjects. The combined results for the two journals indicated that 69 percent of the subjects were college undergraduates, with 35 percent of the total pool of subjects coming from introductory psychology classes (Ullman & Jackson, 1982).

Since most college students who serve as subjects in psychological research are fulfilling a course requirement (see Jung, 1971), perhaps they are fairly representative of a larger population of young people. After all, a diversity of people enroll in introductory psychology. But the matter is not that simple. For one thing, college students differ from noncollege populations on a variety of demographic, attitude, and value dimensions (Bereiter & Freedman, 1962). Second, even when fulfilling a course requirement, college-student subjects typically have a choice in the matter of which studies they sign up for. And it is likely that different "types" of students tend to select different types of investigations to participate in.

Characteristics of Volunteer Subjects. When researchers rely on the generosity of volunteers, rather than a course requirement, to procure their subject pool, the problem of generalizing results becomes even stickier. Jung's (1971) collation of available comparisons of volunteer and nonvolunteer subjects suggested that volunteers have a stronger need for social approval, more unconventional personalities, poorer personal adjustment, a higher need for achievement, and higher IQs (especially male volunteers). And, relative to nonvolunteers, volunteer subject pools tend to contain a higher proportion of first-borns (i.e., oldest children in their families). Thus, researchers who opt to employ true volunteers in their studies may encounter more external validity problems than researchers who rely on the tried and true course-requirement system for obtaining their subjects.

Effects of Subject Attrition. Even if a determined researcher shuns convenience sampling and invests a lot of time and expense to obtain a representative sample of subjects, she may not be completely free of subject-selection bias. Particularly when a study requires the use of "aversive" treatments or repeated measurements, or spans an interval of weeks, months, or years, some subjects will drop out of the investigation as a result of systematic influences. As a consequence, the final sample of subjects having complete data records may not fairly represent the original target population. This problem is especially acute in longitudinal research (Schaie, 1982) but is also encountered in other research designs.

MAXIMIZING SPATIAL GENERALIZATION

Since the early 1960s psychological researchers have become increasingly aware and sophisticated concerning the numerous constraints on external validity that often plague behavioral data (see, e.g., Berkowitz & Donnerstein, 1982; Epstein, 1980; Wachtel, 1980). This heightened sensitivity to issues of generalization has led to the application of a wide range of devices and strategies designed on the one hand to identify the constraints on external validity and on the other to maximize the external validity of data. Some of the more general strategies for accomplishing these goals include **probability sampling, conceptual replication, systematizing a generalization dimension**, and the **aggregation of findings**. In addition, there are several more specific procedures for dealing with such complex problems as demand characteristics and obtrusive measurement. I'll discuss these more specific procedures later, but first let's consider some of the more general approaches to the external validity problem.

Probability Sampling

Probability sampling means that sampling units (usually individual subjects) are selected in such a way that each sampling unit has a *known probability* of being selected (cf. Hamburg, 1979). Probability sampling always involves the use of random selection at one point or another in the sampling process. In fact, the most elementary form of probability sampling is **simple random sampling**, which means that the sample is chosen in such a way that every sampling unit has an *equal* and independent probability of being selected. For example, if you wished to obtain a simple random sample of five students from a class (i.e., population) of 10, you could do so by flipping a coin once for each student until you obtained five tails. The students who were associated with the tails outcome would be your sample. Probability, in this case, would be defined as *the ratio of the number of outcomes favoring selection* (five) *to the total number of outcomes* (five favoring selection + five not favoring selection), or probability = 5/10 = .5. Thus each student in the class would have a known and equal probability (.5) of being selected.

Probability sampling contrasts with convenience sampling in that in the latter case, subjects don't have a known probability of being selected. The potential subjects who are convenient, for whatever reason, are selected and the other members of the population are ignored—they aren't even considered in the sampling process.

Probability sampling has two advantages over convenience sampling. One advantage is statistical and will be discussed in Chapter 12. The other advantage is that probability samples have a better chance of fairly representing the target population than do convenience samples, because the random selection process involved in probability sampling avoids subject-selection bias. Sample membership is determined by chance rather than by systematic influences related to preexisting subject traits or behaviors. (See Chapter 12 for a discussion of additional techniques of probability sampling.)

Ideally, researchers would use some variety of probability sampling to select their subjects. A study by Page (1958) provides an example of this ideal. Page was interested in the effect that written comments on students' returned exams would have on their subsequent exam performance. Having obtained the cooperation of teachers in a large public school system, he randomly selected 74 classrooms to serve as his sampling units. This plan was designed to maximize the external validity of his data. To maximize *internal* validity, he then had each classroom teacher randomly assign one-third of her students to each of three conditions. In two of the conditions, "Personalized Comments" and "Standard Comments," the teachers wrote encouraging statements on students' exam papers, in addition to assigning grades to the papers. In a third, "No Comment" condition, the students' returned exams had only grades on them. Random assignment of students to the three conditions served to make the conditions statistically equivalent on potentially confounding variables at the beginning of the study.

Page's results were instructive. They showed that, relative to the "No Comment" condition, positive written comments on returned tests led to improved scores on the next exam. Furthermore, it didn't matter whether the comments were tailored to the individual student or simply standard, encouraging words, such as "Good work. Keep at it." The students responded positively in each case, and the test scores in the "Standard Comment" condition did not differ significantly from those in the "Personalized Comment" condition. Thus, Page's findings suggested that *any* encouraging comment from a teacher, be it ever so humble, can have a favorable impact on learning.

Since Page used probability sampling to obtain his sampling units, he could be reasonably confident about generalizing to the larger population of classrooms throughout the school districts involved in his study.

Page's investigation stands as a monument to good behavioral science. But, practically speaking, probability sampling is difficult to implement. First, it is expensive and time-consuming. Second, just because you randomly select subjects from a population doesn't mean that they will agree to participate in your investigation. Still, psychological researchers could be more creative than they often are in the recruitment of subjects. For instance, if all introductory psychology students at a particular school were required to serve in several psychology experiments, it would be possible for the researchers to work out a cooperative system for randomly allocating a certain number of subjects to each study scheduled in an academic term. Of course, there would be many details of planning and scheduling to be worked out. And, for ethical reasons, subjects would still have the right to refuse to participate in a study that they didn't think they would like. But such a system is possible and, for the sake of better "population validity," alternatives of this sort should be seriously considered.

In a similar vein, researchers who use animal subjects could arrange to order animals from several independent breeders instead of repeatedly sampling from the same supplier.

Probability sampling isn't necessarily limited to the subject dimension. In theory—and sometimes in practice—settings, stimuli, and, to a lesser extent, data collectors could be randomly selected, once the relevant populations were defined (Brunswik, 1956). Short of randomly sampling along these dimensions of generalization, researchers might at least attempt to investigate a range of values, situations, or types representing each dimension, either in a single large-scale study or in a series of "conceptual" replications.

Conceptual Replication

The traditional meaning of replication is that a study is repeated in exactly the same way that it was originally conducted. In other words, the subjects, setting, stimuli, tasks, and experimenter of later studies are, in theory, equivalent to those of the original investigation. This is called an **exact replication** (but see footnote 3).

An alternative type of replication is the **conceptual replication**: The same theoretical variables are studied in each repetition of the investigation, but the settings, populations, and the ways of measuring the variables change across the series of investigations. The purpose of conceptual replication is to find out if the theoretical concepts of interest have a constant relationship when the particulars of the methodology are allowed to vary—in short, to assess the range of the relationship's generality.

An example of conceptual replication was presented in Chapter 1 and concerned the transfer of training from one task to another. In a coordinated sequence of studies, Thorndike and his colleagues first investigated whether skill in estimating the area of rectangles would transfer to new area-estimation tasks involving other kinds of geometric figures. The subjects were college students. The investigators found that there was little transfer when these simple tasks and stimuli were used and concluded that old learning transfers to new learning only to the extent that the old and new tasks contain "identical elements"—i.e., require the same attitude, strategies, and techniques (Thorndike & Woodworth, 1901). To test the generality of his initial findings, Thorndike (1924) researched the transfer effects of various academic curricula (e.g., Latin, geometry, English, etc.) on general academic intelligence in high school students. Thus, though studying the same concepts, he changed the setting, the measures, and the subject population. Again he found little transfer of training, and his conclusions reiterated those drawn in connection with the simple area-estimation tasks of the original studies. What's more, the conceptual replication provided powerful support for Thorndike's earlier assertions about the nature of transfer effects; it was clear that the initial findings were not restricted to a particular method or population.

The use of "multiple converging methods," or "triangulation of methods," which was discussed in Chapter 4, is a version of conceptual replication. With this approach, several different research designs—for example, lab experiments, naturalistic observation, and the psychometric method—are utilized to explore a particular theoretical or practical question. If a certain relationship between variables shows up within the framework of several methods, the "robustness," or generalizability, of the relationship is supported. But should the relationship change or disappear across methods, the possibility of a method artifact must be considered.

Triangulation of methods has been successfully used in connection with a number of research topics in psychology. One such topic is the "weapons effect" in human aggression. Laboratory experiments by Berkowitz and his colleagues (e.g., Berkowitz, 1971) suggested that the presence of a weapon, such as a snub-nosed revolver, increases the level of aggression in people, especially if they are already angry with someone. Subsequent psychometric-type studies and field experiments, which sampled a variety of subject populations, indicated that the weapons effect possesses substantial generality (see Berkowitz & Donnerstein, 1982).

Systematizing a Generalization Dimension

Often the limits of a relationship's external validity can be directly assessed by incorporating a dimension of spatial generalization into the research design, in the form of an extra independent variable. One example of this is Blass' (1980) study of the relationship between students' course grades and their ratings of the instructor, which was summarized earlier in this chapter. Since Blass suspected that the relationship might be restricted to groups of students who tend to reason subjectively, he examined the correlation between grades and instructor ratings within a research design that included subjective versus objective reasoning as an "extra" independent variable. (The main independent variable was course grades, and the dependent variable was the students' evaluations of their teacher.) You'll recall that reasoning style interacted with course grades to determine instructor ratings; only for the subjective reasoners was there a strong correlation between grades and ratings. Thus this finding both supported Blass's hypothesis and revealed one limit on the relationship's external validity.

The strategy of systematizing a generalization dimension can also be used to deal with the problem of pretesting effects. You'll remember that the use of pretests restricts external validity when the effect of pretesting interacts with the independent variable to produce results that would not occur in the absence of pretesting.

The typical two-group, pretest/posttest design can be schematized as follows:

	Pretest	Special Treatment	Posttest
Experimental Group	Yes	Yes	Yes
Control Group	Yes	No	Yes

The fault of this simple design is that it doesn't allow you to separate the effect of the special treatment from the effect of the interaction of pretesting with the treatment.

By systemizing the pretesting variable, you get the following scheme, which is referred to as the **Solomon Four-Group Design** (see Solomon & Lessac, 1968):

	Pretest	Special Treatment	Posttest
Experimental Group: I	Yes	Yes	Yes
Experimental Group: II	No	Yes	Yes
Control Group: III	Yes	No	Yes
Control Group: IV	No	No	Yes

Normally subjects would be randomly assigned to groups, making the four conditions statistically equal at the outset; the two pretested groups would have similar mean scores on the pretest. Thus, the dependent variable in this design is *scores on the posttest*. Also, posttest means would be compared to pretest means to determine the *direction* of change in the dependent variable. The main independent variable is the special treatment versus no special treatment, and the "extra" independent variable is the generalization dimension that has been systematized within the design—that is, pretesting versus no pretesting.

Note that there are three possible effects to be analyzed in this design: (a) the effect of the special treatment, (b) the effect of pretesting, and (c) the effect of the interaction of the special treatment and pretesting. An interaction exists if the use of pretesting makes the effect of the treatment different from that obtained in the absence of pretesting.

To assess the effect of the special treatment, you average the posttest means of the two Experimental Groups $[(\overline{X}_I + \overline{X}_{II})/2]$ and the two Control Groups $[(\overline{X}_{III} + \overline{X}_{IV})/2]$. If the Experimental average is significantly different from the Control average, then the special treatment has had an effect.

To determine the effect of pretesting, you average the posttest means of the two pretested groups (I and III) and the two groups that were not pretested (II and IV). If the pretested groups scored significantly higher *or* lower than the nonpretested groups, then pretesting has influenced the posttest scores.

The effect of an interaction of pretesting with the special treatment is assessed in the following way:

1. Find the *difference* between the posttest means of the pretested Experimental and Control Groups—i.e., $(\overline{X}_I - \overline{X}_{III})$.
2. Find the difference between the posttest means of the nonpretested Experimental and Control Groups—i.e., $(\overline{X}_{II} - \overline{X}_{IV})$.
3. Compare the mean difference obtained in step 1 to that obtained in step 2.

If the difference between the Experimental and Control Groups is significantly greater *or* less when pretesting is used than when it is not used, or if the sign of the difference changes from positive to negative or vice versa, then an interaction exists. (Of course, the reliability of the numerical interaction would have to be established through a test of statistical significance.) Therefore, conclusions about the effect of the special treatment would have to be qualified to reflect the restriction that pretesting places on that effect.

Aggregation of Findings

In Chapter 5, I made the point that the reliability of measurement can be enhanced by increasing the number of observations that make up the measurement. This is true because a larger sample of behavior gives a better estimate of subjects' true scores on a variable than does a smaller sample. This follows from the fact that positive and negative random errors of measurement tend to be more evenly balanced against one another as the sample of behavior is made progressively larger. In effect, when a behavior sample is sizable, the positive and negative errors largely cancel out one another, leaving an overall value that is very close to the true score.

Conceptually, the generalizability of research findings pertains to the question of reliability. Findings that are generalizable are repeatable, or replicable, across time, stimuli and tasks, people, and settings—in a word, reliable.

Epstein (1980) has used the conceptual correspondence between reliability and generalizability to propose a strategy for dealing with the problem of external invalidity in psychological research. He notes, correctly, that there are many incidental, uncontrollable factors in psychological investigations that produce *systematic* errors in the findings. All of the threats to spatial external validity discussed in this chapter represent sources of such errors. These errors are what interfere with the generalizability of psychological data.

Epstein's interesting idea is that the various systematic errors that plague individual studies may be treated as *unsystematic* (i.e., random) errors when several studies of the same phenomenon are viewed collectively as a single investigation. The reason is that even systematic errors will vary in their direction and size across numerous investigations concerned with the same set of variables. That is, in some studies incidental factors will inflate the effect of the independent variable while reducing the true effect in other investigations. Thus, by statistically averaging the findings of the whole collection of studies centering on a particular question, we could effectively let the diverse errors cancel out each other.

Epstein uses the term **aggregation** to refer to the practice of combining the results of several investigations. He recommends that, for a given research question, results be combined across four dimensions of external validity: *subjects*; *stimuli and/or situations*; *measures*; *trials and/or occasions*. You'll recognize the first three dimensions as those pertaining to spatial external validity and the fourth as relevant to temporal generalization.

In most applications of aggregation, data consolidation would have to occur across more than one dimension at a time. For example, it would be impossible under most circumstances to aggregate data across studies employing different subject populations without also aggregating across occasions and settings.

The aggregation strategy accomplishes two major purposes: First, it reveals the "true" effects of variables by averaging out the influence of incidental factors. Second, by revealing the true effects of variables, aggregation allows us to determine how special circumstances modify those effects—for example, how the use of a sample of depressed people alters the effect of an independent variable relative to its average effect across dozens of "normal" and "abnormal" samples.

A good example of aggregation was published by Smith and Glass (1977). They were interested in finding out what effect, if any, psychotherapy has on the psychological well-being of people with problems of psychological adjustment. Using a special statistical procedure to standardize and combine many different kinds of data, they aggregated the results of 375 investigations. They found that some of the studies showed no effect of psychotherapy, some showed small effects, and still others suggested moderate to large effects. *On the average*, however, the typical client who received therapy was "better off" than 75 percent of clients who didn't receive therapy. Thus, when incidental and localized influences were canceled out through the averaging process, it became clear that psychotherapy does have a positive impact.

Smith and Glass were also able to examine how special circumstances change the effectiveness of therapy. For instance, they found that therapy effectiveness tends to increase with the IQs of clients and with the degree to which therapists are similar to their clients in age, ethnic group, and social level.

Assessing and Controlling Demand Characteristics

As was explained earlier, some investigations contain many cues, in both the setting and the procedure, that tip off the subject as to the researcher's hypothesis. To the extent that subjects wish to cooperate with researcher expectancies, they will alter their behavior to conform with these "demand characteristics." Such contrived behavior would not generalize to situations in which similar demand characteristics do not exist.

Available evidence indicates that it is questionable whether the dominant motive of research subjects is to cooperate with the perceived expectations of the researcher (see Carlsmith et al., 1976; Christensen, 1980). Nonetheless, it has been demonstrated that the demands of the procedure and setting can influence subjects' behavior in some cases (e.g., Orne, 1962; Page, 1973). Consequently, it is best to control or check for the effects of demand characteristics, unless prior research has shown that the specific procedure you are using is normally free of these biasing elements.

Demand characteristics may be avoided by using unobtrusive measurement procedures (see Chapter 5) or some variety of naturalistic or field research. In these situations, subjects are unaware of being measured and, therefore, do not have access to cues that would be provided by more obtrusive methods.

What alternatives are available when obtrusive research procedures must be used? Orne (1962) has suggested postexperimental interviews with subjects as one option. With this procedure, each subject is asked about his or her perception of the study immediately after the completion of the experimental session. Presumably subjects would refer to what they thought the researcher was "trying to prove" as well as to the cues that suggested "the hypothesis" to them. Subjects who report reacting to demand characteristics could then be eliminated from the data pool. But this creates a problem, in that eliminating a particular class of subjects will almost certainly bias the results even further. Perhaps those who are discarded under this procedure are more alert, intelligent, and perceptive than those who are retained.

Still another problem with the postexperimental inquiry is that it, too, is subject to demand characteristics. The researcher's manner of questioning, as well as the subject's perception of his or her role as a research participant, may serve as cues to suggest that "feigning naiveté is the proper thing to do." Thus, as Orne points out, the experimenter and the subject may innocently practice collusion in the form of a mutual "pact of ignorance": The experimenter assumes that the subject is telling the truth and doesn't press to check her assumption, and the subject assumes that the experimenter doesn't want to know the truth. For this reason, it may be wise to have someone other than the experimenter conduct the interview—preferably someone whom the subject sees as a "peer."

An alternative to the postexperimental interview is the preexperimental inquiry. With this technique, an extra control group is treated in exactly the same way as the experimental group, except that they do not actually complete the experimental procedure. However, they are told what the procedure involves and then are asked to indicate their perceptions of what would be expected of them if they actually went through the treatment. The assumption here is that since the subjects being interviewed haven't gone through the experimental procedure, they have less personal investment in falsely maintaining that there are no telltale signs in the experimental arrangements that could influence their responses. The shortcoming of the preexperimental inquiry is that verbal descriptions of the experimental procedure may not convey all of the demand cues that attend the experience of undergoing the procedure.

A third option is to employ a **simulation control group**. Subjects in such a group do not receive the experimental treatment but are given a description of the treatment and are told to *behave as though* they had actually been exposed to it. If their responses approximate those of the real experimental group, this suggests that demand characteristics may have been operating in the study. It doesn't prove the existence of demand cues, however, as the same responses may occur for different reasons in the simulation and experimental groups.

Orne (1962) used the simulation control group technique in a study of the effects of hypnosis. Interestingly, the behavior of subjects simulating hypnosis did not differ appreciably from that of subjects who were really hypnotized. This finding has also been reported by other researchers (see Barber, 1976) and suggests that demand characteristics play a major role in many hypnotic phenomena.

Approaches to the Obtrusiveness Problem

The impact of the obtrusiveness of research procedures and settings was first discussed in Chapter 5 (in the section called "Keeping Them Honest"), which was concerned with approaches to measuring behavior and experience. There I described several techniques and strategies for dealing with obtrusiveness, including the use of unobtrusive measures, instrumentation, validity scales, and the "bogus pipeline." Most of these "solutions" involved some form of deception.

Additional approaches to the obtrusiveness problem have been suggested. Sommer (1977) and Wachtel (1980), for example, have urged psychologists to do more systematic observation under natural circumstances and less laboratory experimentation. Others have suggested that psychology experiments be conducted with settings, tasks, and stimuli that are more representative of the "real world," so that subjects will respond in ways that are more representative of their everyday behavior (e.g., Brunswik, 1956; Harré & Secord, 1972; Stern, 1982).

Still another perspective on the problem suggests that you can sidestep obtrusiveness by using experimental tasks that are absorbing and ego-involving for the subject (Berkowitz & Donnerstein, 1982; Epstein, 1980). This is referred to as the creation of **experimental realism**. The rationale for this point of view is that if a laboratory task engages the subject's attention fully, he temporarily turns attention away from his role as subject and focuses on responding genuinely to the task at hand. Thus, the self-consciousness that usually dominates the behavior of a person who knows he is under scientific scrutiny is simply pushed into the background by a more "psychologically important" matter—a demanding, interesting, engaging problem. The subject responds as he would to any similarly demanding problem, regardless of the surrounding circumstances.

A cleverly designed investigation by Latané and Rodin (1969) provides a good example of the creation of experimental realism. These researchers wanted to find out how different kinds of social environments would affect a person's willingness to go to the aid of an accident victim. The subjects, who believed they were participating in a market research study, were seated in a testing room and asked to fill out a short questionnaire. Depending on their experimental condition, they filled out the questionnaire alone, with a friend, or in the presence of a stranger. During this time an apparent emergency occurred: A person in the next room had an accident and cried out for help. The research question was: Under which of the three social conditions would the subjects be most likely to go to the aid of the victim? To create experimental realism, Latané and Rodin used a tape recording to stage the following "emergency":

> If the subject listened carefully, he heard the representative climb on a chair to reach for a stack of papers on the bookcase. Even if he were not listening carefully, he heard a loud crash and a scream as the chair collapsed and she fell to the floor. "Oh, my God, my foot . . . I . . . I . . . can't move it. Oh . . . my ankle," the representative moaned. "I . . . can't get this . . . thing . . . off me." (p. 191)

The results of this study showed that people are most likely to offer help to the crisis victim if they are alone and least likely to offer assistance if they are in the presence of a stranger. The presence of a friend was associated with a moderately high tendency to intervene on the victim's behalf. For complex reasons, the presence of other people seems to inhibit our Good Samaritan instinct (see Latané & Darley, 1970). But of greater importance to the present discussion was the effect on the subjects' psychological state of Latané and Rodin's powerful experimental manipulation. So gripped were the subjects by the plight of the victim that their roles as research participants came to be of secondary importance, and their responsibility, or lack thereof, to the victim became their overriding concern. In fact, all of the subjects interpreted the apparent accident as a true emergency and, thus, placed themselves in a psychological state that required a decision on their part. This total absorption in a situation that demands to be dealt with is what is meant by experimental realism. The task at hand left little time, and practically no incentive, for contriving responses. Therefore, we would expect the subjects' behaviors to be generalizable to other such "emergencies."

TEMPORAL GENERALIZATION

Generalizing across time boils down to making an assertion about the reliability of your data. It amounts to an expression of confidence in the repeatability of the empirical relationship you have found. The decision to make such an assertion would normally be based on the outcome of a test of statistical significance. By declaring results statistically significant, you are implying that the average results of an indefinite number of replications of your study would agree with the pattern of findings you have obtained in a single investigation (Bakan, 1966). But in all cases, you should view testing for significance as only a preliminary step in the assessment of the reliability of a relationship. If you are serious about *confirming* the dependability of your findings, then your initial significance tests should be followed by replication studies.

The Meaning of Statistical Significance

The notion of statistical reliability (significance) was briefly introduced in Chapter 6. At this point, it will be helpful to consider the process and interpretation of significance testing in greater detail, so that you will know exactly what is meant when the concept of significance is used in later chapters and when it is applied to your own research.

Sampling Distributions. In Chapter 6, I stated that the assessment of statistical reliability involves computing a test statistic from your sample of data and comparing that nu-

merical value to a set of values representing chance outcomes. The test statistic is significant, suggesting reliable (i.e., nonchance) data, if it would rarely occur in the set of
chance outcomes.

The set of chance outcomes I referred to is called a **sampling distribution**. Most sampling distributions are abstract concepts derived from mathematical theories of random
processes. But they can be portrayed graphically by drawing a distribution curve that
shows the probabilities of the various random values. A graph of one sampling distribution is shown in Figure 8–1, which represents a probability distribution of an infinite
number of linear correlation coefficients that would be produced if only random processes determined the size of r. The distribution was generated by a mathematical formula that makes many assumptions about the data, two being that (a) each of the infinite
number of correlation coefficients is computed from a sample of exactly eight pairs of observations (i.e., sample size = 8) and (b) the observations were paired up entirely at
random.

The curve is drawn by plotting the probability of each possible value of r against that
value: The horizontal axis represents the value of r, and the vertical axis represents the
probability of r. The curve is smooth and continuous (i.e., has no breaks or steps in it)
because, theoretically, it is based on an infinity of outcomes, even though only 11 of the
possible r values are shown in the figure. Note that *the height of the curve corresponds to the
probability of a given r value*. Thus, when only chance operates to produce r, the most
likely value of r is 0.00 and the least likely is ± 1.00.

When dealing with continuous, theoretical distributions, it is better to work with the
probabilities of designated "areas under the curve" rather than attempt to determine the
probabilities of particular points under the curve. In this approach, probability is synonymous with the *proportion*, or *percentage*[6] of the curve contained within a designated range
along the horizontal axis. By examining Figure 8–1 closely, you can see that approximately 2.5 percent of the area under the curve lies between r = – .71 and r = – 1.00; an
equivalent proportion of the curve lies between r = + .71 and r = + 1.00. Together these
two regions of the distribution make up the "rarest"—that is, least likely, or most extreme—5 percent of the sampling distribution. Hence you would expect a correlation as
large as ± .71 or more only 5 percent of the time by chance alone. (Since r may be either
positive or negative, you usually would want to consider both the positive and the nega-

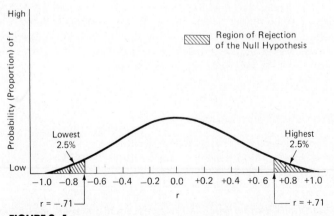

FIGURE 8–1
Sampling Distribution of r, When Sample Size = 8

tive extremes of the distribution to determine the "rarest" 5 percent of the possible chance outcomes.[7])

Suppose you actually compute a correlation between two variables on the basis of a sample of eight pairs of scores. How could you tell whether the relationship represented by the correlation coefficient is statistically significant? Applying the 5 percent criterion of "rareness," you would compare the correlation computed from the sample data to the distributions of randomly determined correlations shown in Figure 8–1. If the sample's correlation coefficient equals .71 or greater, regardless of whether it is positive or negative in sign, it would meet the criterion of rareness. Accordingly, you would declare it to be an unlikely event in a distribution of chance events—in other words, *statistically significant*, or "probably more than a chance event." And you would have some reason to believe that the relationship represented by the sample r is reliable.

Each type of test statistic used by researchers to assess statistical reliability has at least one sampling distribution that is used to separate significant outcomes from nonsignificant ones, and most test statistics have a "family" of sampling distributions associated with them. This is true of many of the tests described in this book, including r, t, F, and χ^2 (see chapters 9–14). In these cases, the particular distribution you refer to for making your decision about the reliability of the data will be determined by the size of your sample of observations. For example, the sampling distribution that appears in Figure 8–1 is a useful model of chance outcomes only when sample size equals eight pairs of observations. If sample size were seven or nine, a slightly different chance distribution would be required.

Null and Alternative Hypotheses.   In conducting a test of significance, a researcher pits two hypotheses against one another and, ultimately, decides in favor of one or the other. One hypothesis, *the one that is actually tested*, is the **null hypothesis**. The null hypothesis can assume many specific forms, depending on the kind of data collected and the question being asked. In its most general form, the null hypothesis states that *the sample data do not differ from those expected on the basis of chance alone*. If the 5 percent level of significance is used, this is the same as predicting that the test statistic will *not* fall into the most extreme 5 percent of the sampling distribution—in other words, that it will fall somewhere within the remaining 95 percent of the distribution, which is deemed the region of random events. Thus, the null hypothesis is the *hypothesis of chance*: It assumes that only random processes will operate to determine the value of the test statistic.

The hypothesis which directly opposes the null proposal is called the **alternative**, or **research**, **hypothesis**. It states that the sample data will differ from the data expected on the basis of chance alone. That is, this hypothesis predicts that the independent variable will have a "real" effect on the dependent variable or, more generally, that the research variables will be more strongly correlated with each other than can be accounted for by chance processes. The researcher usually will be more interested in the alternative hypothesis than in the null hypothesis, because the alternative hypothesis represents her expectations concerning the outcome of the study. In most cases, if she truly expected to find only chance outcomes, she probably wouldn't conduct the study.

Two common examples of null and alternative hypotheses are:

I. *Null*: The observed correlation is a member of a population of random correlations, in which the mean correlation equals zero.
   Alternative: The observed correlation is a member of a population of nonrandom correlations, in which the mean correlation is greater than zero.
II. *Null*: The observed mean difference between the experimental and control conditions is a member of a population of random differences, in which the average mean difference equals zero.

Alternative: The observed mean difference between the experimental and control conditions is a member of a population of systematic differences, in which the average mean difference does not equal zero.

About now, you're asking yourself what "populations" are being referred to in these hypotheses. After all, a researcher usually has only a *sample* of data to work with and, since most samples are not randomly selected, a larger population is not actually being tested by the study.

In the majority of research situations, the population that the null hypothesis refers to is the theoretically infinite population of random events represented by the sampling distribution.[8] Hence the sampling distribution is also called the **null distribution**. It is the distribution of outcomes expected if the null hypothesis is true. In contrast, the population that the alternative hypothesis refers to is an unknown and unobservable, but theoretically possible, distribution of nonchance outcomes. The purpose of conducting a test of statistical significance is to make a tentative decision as to which population of outcomes—chance or nonchance—your data are likely to belong to.

However, as mentioned earlier, a researcher tests only the null hypothesis, not the research hypothesis. Founded on a type of reverse logic, the rationale behind this is as follows: If you are interested in supporting research hypothesis A, you can do so by showing that its opposite, the null hypothesis, is false. Rejection of the null hypothesis doesn't directly "prove" the research hypothesis but does allow you to entertain the notion that the research hypothesis is true (Bakan, 1966). On the other hand, if the value of the test statistic is within the range predicted by the hypothesis of chance (i.e., the null), then your research hypothesis, which asserts that nonchance processes are operating, isn't likely to be true.

Why is this reverse logic used? Why not simply test the research hypothesis directly? The answer is twofold. First, it is logically easier to disprove an assertion than to prove it. For example, suppose I assert that all clinical psychologists are extroverts. If this proposition is true, it would be impossible to directly prove it without testing *all* clinical psychologists with a measure of extroversion. But if the proposition is false, it could be disproved simply by locating one clinical psychologist who is not extroverted. Similarly, it is much more feasible to attempt to disprove the opposite of your research hypothesis than to try a direct proof of the research hypothesis.

There is a second, and even more important, reason for testing the null, however. We know the shape, properties, characteristics, and values of the null distribution, otherwise known as the sampling distribution; this information has been provided by mathematical theories of random variables. Hence, research outcomes can be directly compared with the convenient and invariant models of chance that represent the null hypothesis. In most research situations, however, we have little, if any, idea about the nature and critical values of the alternative distribution of outcomes associated with the research hypothesis, as that distribution is literally unknown and unobservable. Consequently, we usually have no appropriate, invariant model of nonchance events to compare our data with. So we end up testing the hypothesis of chance instead.

Statistical Decisions and Decision Errors.   When you carry out a test of statistical significance, the only statistical decision you have to make concerns the truth or falsity of the null hypothesis. The *decision* is an either/or, or dichotomous, one. For a given investigation, the *reality* of the situation is also a dichotomous matter. *Regardless of your decision, the null hypothesis is either really false or really true.* The ideal in the practice of significance testing is to maximize the likelihood of matches between statistical decisions and reality.

When the two decision options are combined with the two possible states of reality, it becomes clear that there are four possible outcomes of a significance test:

1. A true null hypothesis is not rejected: correct decision.
2. A false null hypothesis is rejected: correct decision.
3. A true null hypothesis is rejected: Type I error.
4. A false null hypothesis is not rejected: Type II error.

Thus there are two ways to be right and two ways to be wrong in your decision about the null hypothesis.

The major concern here is with the possible decision errors. A **Type I error** occurs when you reject the null hypothesis even though it's true. What is the *theoretical* probability of doing this? Refer back to Figure 8–1. Recall that a test statistic is declared significant, and the null hypothesis is *rejected*, if the value of the test statistic falls into the most extreme 5 percent of the null distribution. It is for this reason that the area under the distribution curve representing "significant" events is often referred to as the **region of rejection**. But it is important to bear in mind that the entire sampling distribution, including the most extreme 5 percent, is a model of chance processes and actually represents the outcomes that are expected if the null hypothesis is true. Therefore, the theoretical probability of rejecting a true null hypothesis—that is, the theoretical probability of making a Type I error—equals the level of significance used in the test (in this case, 5 percent). Another way of putting it is to say that *the probability of a Type I error is equal to the proportion of the sampling distribution that has been designated to represent significant outcomes.*

One way to reduce the theoretical probability of a Type I error is to reduce the proportion of the sampling distribution that represents significant outcomes. For example, you could use the 1 percent level of significance rather than the 5 percent level. A sampling distribution of r showing the regions of rejection at the 1 percent level is illustrated in Figure 8–2. Since the areas under the curve associated with rejection of the null are considerably smaller in Figure 8–2 than in Figure 8–1, the probability of rejecting a true null hypothesis is also much smaller.

There is a problem, however, with using a more conservative criterion of significance in order to lessen the likelihood of a Type I error: This practice makes **Type II errors** more likely. That is, by reducing the proportion of the sampling distribution associated with a statistically significant outcome, you thereby decrease the likelihood of rejecting the null *regardless of its truth or falsity*. You'll notice, for instance, that when the region of rejection is "shrunken," a larger value of r is required for significance (compare Figures 8–1 and 8–2). Therefore, when the null is *actually false*, using a more conservative level of significance increases the probability of a Type II error—that is, failing to reject a false null hypothesis.

Fortunately, even when you use a conservative level of significance, you can give yourself some protection against a Type II error by using a larger sample of observations than you would normally employ. This is true because the likelihood of a Type II error decreases as sample size is increased.

What is the theoretical probability of a Type II error? Unfortunately, the answer cannot be as easily determined as the probability of a Type I error. The reason is that the likelihood of a Type II error is a function of three variables: (a) sample size, (b) the level of significance that you use (e.g., 1 percent or 5 percent), and (c) the amount of sampling error in the data. *The probability of a Type II error gets smaller as sample size and the level of significance are increased, and gets larger as sampling error increases.* Though the technical details of the procedure exceed the scope of this text, it is possible to estimate the probabil-

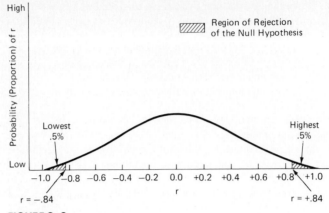

FIGURE 8-2

Sampling Distribution of r Showing 1 percent Regions of Rejection (Sample Size = 8)

ity of a Type II error by taking all three of these factors into account. It is also possible to estimate the sample size that will be necessary to achieve a desirable probability of making a Type II error. See Kirk (1968) for a description of these procedures.

It is always easy to lower the probability of a Type II error by using a larger level of significance—for instance, by employing the 10 percent criterion rather than the conventional 5 percent criterion. But this approach to the problem is not recommended, because it results in an increase in the probability of a Type I error. By far, the most generally effective strategy for avoiding Type II errors is to keep the level of significance fairly low—say, not higher than 5 percent—and use as large a sample of observations as your time and money permit.

Choosing a Level of Statistical Significance.   You may be wondering whether it is generally better to use the popular 5 percent criterion of significance or the more conservative 1 percent level (together with a larger sample)—or an even more stringent criterion, such as the .1 percent level. There is no simple and direct answer to this question. Your choice of a particular level of significance must be determined by the amount of risk of a Type I or Type II error that you are willing to take.

In doing theoretical, or "basic," research, the criterion of significance should reflect how improbable an outcome would have to be to convince *you*, the researcher, that the data could not be due to chance (Fisher, 1966). If you had more than the usual amount of doubt about the validity of your research hypothesis, for example, then your initial opinion would be that the null hypothesis might well be true in that particular area of research. Given such an a priori view on your part, you would want to afford the null hypothesis a good opportunity not to be rejected.[9] So you would use a significance level that favors the null hypothesis. Since the 1 percent level theoretically gives a true null hypothesis a 99 percent chance of not being rejected, whereas the 5 percent level provides the null only a 95 percent chance of escaping false rejection, you probably would opt for the 1 percent level in this case. Selecting such a demanding criterion of significance amounts to publicly stating that the evidence must be very convincing before you will be willing to declare the null hypothesis false. It also means that you are willing to accept a higher than usual risk of a Type II error in order to obtain the strong evidence that you need, but that you are not willing to accept very much risk of a Type I error.

Under the model of significance testing, the level of significance is supposed to reflect your standard for rejecting the null hypothesis *prior to data collection*. Therefore, the criterion of significance should be set in advance of data collection and should not be chosen or altered after the data are in (Bakan, 1966).

In applied research that could have important social and policymaking ramifications, the choice of level of significance should be determined by the seriousness of the consequences of a Type I error versus a Type II error. When studying possible ability differences between sexes, races, or ethnic groups, for example, a Type I error would be more serious than a Type II error. In this case, a Type I error would mean that you falsely assert that one group is higher in a particular ability than another group—a potentially troublesome mistake, indeed. To minimize the risk of this kind of error, you would employ a conservative criterion of significance (e.g., the 1 percent level or, safer yet, the .1 percent level).

In other kinds of applied research the Type II error may be the more serious one. For instance, if you were testing the effectiveness of a remedial education program for disadvantaged children, failing to reject a false null hypothesis could result in the discontinuation of a useful and sorely needed educational enterprise. In contrast, a Type I error in such a situation might simply result in the continuation of a program that, while not uniquely effective, does no harm. In research of this kind, then, it would be most reasonable to use a moderate level of significance, such as the 5 percent criterion, together with as large a sample as you can get. Taking these steps would minimize the probability of a socially costly Type II error.

Theoretical versus Realistic Interpretations of Significance. Psychology students often ask the following question: "If my results are significant at the 5 percent level, does this mean that I am 95 percent confident that the data represent a 'real' effect or relationship?" The answer is no.

The confidence that an investigator has in the "realness" of his results is a subjective matter that is separate from the theoretical probabilities of the significance-testing model (Rozeboom, 1960). That confidence is influenced not only by the significance test but also by the investigator's pre-investigation confidence in the research hypothesis, previous research on the question, theoretical framework, perception of the quality of the research design, and knowledge of related findings by other investigators. Although it is possible for a researcher to formulate a *subjective probability* of the validity of his research hypothesis in light of the data, that probability is likely to differ from the figure of 95 percent, sometimes markedly.

A related question that frequently pops up is, "If my results are significant at the 5 percent level, does this mean that the probability of my being wrong in declaring the results 'nonchance' is equal to .05?" The answer to this one is yes and no. There are two levels of reasoning to be considered here: theoretical and practical/realistic.

At the *theoretical* level, significance at the 5 percent criterion means that if the same study were independently conducted 100 times, results as extreme as those obtained would occur by chance alone just 5 times in the 100 trials. Thus, at the theoretical level, it is correct to assert that the probability of a Type I error is .05.

Practically speaking, however, you have conducted the study only one time. So viewing the matter *realistically*, when you assert that your results are "more than chance," *you are either right or wrong in that particular instance*, and there is no 5 percent wrong or 95 percent right to it.

If this seems a bit hard to accept, consider an example closer to home. If you are going to toss a coin one time, what is the *theoretical* probability of getting a heads outcome? The obvious answer: .50, or 50 percent. But when you flip the coin only once, the outcome is either heads or tails. The actual outcome of a single test is indifferent to theoretical probabilities.

The key to understanding the above point is to realize that the theoretical probabilities of the statistical-significance model serve as logical and objective decision criteria. But they pertain to the long run and the infinite, not to a particular case. Thus, each time you make a decision concerning the null hypothesis, you are either right or wrong that one time. In Bakan's (1966) words, "there is no probability associated with something that is either true or false" (p. 429). It is for this reason that replication is an essential component in the process of establishing the reliability of findings.

The Replication Net

Though not formally a part of the conventional model of statistical significance, the replication process can and should be used to corroborate tentative decisions about the reliability of data. "There is no more fundamental requirement in science than that the replicability of findings be established" (Epstein, 1980, p. 796).

There are two reasons for this "fundamental requirement." One has to do with the either-right-or-wrong character of individual statistical decisions that was discussed above. The only reasonable way to increase confidence in the accuracy of one statistical decision is to repeat the study, preferably more than once, and then reevaluate the initial decision in the context of the series of outcomes. Ideally, one or more replications of an investigation will serve to expose an initial statistical decision error. Thus, metaphorically, replication functions as a net designed to catch Type I and Type II errors.

A second reason for the necessity of replication is that the assumptions of the statistical-significance model are unrealistic. The model assumes an infinity of exact replications. But it is quite possible "that something happened in the specific [research] situation which was not likely a chance occurrence—and [this] does not establish that the effect can be attributed to the experimental variables of interest" (Epstein, 1980, p. 797). This means that, because actual replications are never perfectly exact reproductions of the original study, an effect can be "real" in the initial study but not be reproducible in other situations that differ in some small, but influential, detail. Again, to increase confidence in the reproducibility of the findings and, hence, the effect of the independent variable of interest, a researcher must show that the outcome of a particular study is not restricted to a unique set of circumstances.

The Logical Basis of Replication.   The theoretical rationale of replication is elegantly simple. Assuming a point of view that exists *prior to conducting any data collection on a question*, you could ask: If I conduct only one investigation and use the 5 percent level of significance, what is the theoretical probability of erroneously rejecting a true null hypothesis? If I conduct two independent replications of the study, what is the probability of making a Type I error *both times*? If I carry out three independent replications, how likely is it that I will make *three* Type I errors in a row?

If you can suspend reality for a moment and entertain the notion of completely independent, yet exact, replications, the theoretical answers to the above questions are as follow: With one study, the probability of a Type I error is .05. The probability of that kind of error in two investigations would equal $(.05) \times (.05)$, or .0025. And the probability of erroneously rejecting a true null hypothesis three times in a row would equal $(.05) \times (.05) \times (.05)$, or .000125. Thus, in the case of three independent occurrences of a particular investigation, wherein the significance criterion remains at 5 percent, the theoretical chances of making a Type I error in all three instances are fewer than 2 in 10,000. Note that, although the Type I error has been singled out to illustrate the logic behind replication, the series of replications would also be expected to reduce the overall probability of a Type II decision error, relative to that of one investigation.

When you return to reality, things aren't this neat and simple. Since most replications are not truly exact or independent, the theoretical probabilities given in the above examples would need to be modified, in most cases enlarged considerably. Even so, the theoretical probability of a Type I error for a *series* of replications, taken as a whole, would be substantially smaller than that of a single study.

For all practical purposes, when you get to the end of a sequence of replications and look back, your "final" decision about the null hypothesis will either be right or wrong. Nonetheless, if the outcomes of that sequence of tests are consistent, your confidence concerning the decision will increase.

What Makes a Good Replication? The quality and usefulness of a replication study depends on a number of factors. Rosenthal (1966) suggested that good replications have these characteristics:

1. A standard sample size is used in every one of the replications. This presumes that the standard sample size is also an adequate sample size.

2. Appropriate experimental and control groups are employed in each reproduction of the study. Furthermore, treatment of the experimental and control groups should be carried out in a way that ensures that the same variables are measured in every replication.

3. Ideally, each replication should employ the *double-blind* technique of data collection. You'll recall that in the double-blind situation, neither the subject nor the data collector is aware of the subject's treatment condition at the time of measurement. Effectively, this often means that the data collector knows that he is treating different subjects in two or more distinct ways but cannot relate the differential treatment to a particular hypothesis.

4. The replication of a certain investigation should be as independent of the original study as is practically possible. In Rosenthal's (1966) words, "We can state the general principle that a replication of that experiment which obtains similar results is maximally convincing if it is maximally separated from the first experiment along such dimensions as time, physical distance, personal attributes of the experimenters, experimenters' expectancy, and experimenters' degree of personal contact with each other" (p. 326).

SUMMARY

This chapter concerned the problem of generalizing the results of psychological research. The process of generalizing involves establishing the range and limits of a study's external validity.

Generalizing entails making statements about a *population* of events on the basis of a *sample* taken from that population. *Spatial generalization* refers to extrapolating across the dimensions of tasks, treatment stimuli, and subjects. *Temporal generalization* concerns the reproducibility of a finding from one time interval to another, and is tied in with the matters of statistical significance and replication.

Restrictions on spatial external validity may be thought of as *interactions* of research settings, procedures and stimuli, and subject characteristics with the independent variable of interest. Spatial external validity may be enhanced by employing *probability sampling*, *conceptual replication, experimental realism*, and the *aggregation of findings* from several studies concerned with the same phenomenon. Interactions between generalization dimensions and an independent variable may be explicitly assessed by systematically varying generalization dimensions as "extra" independent variables in an investigation.

The special problem of *demand characteristics* also threatens external validity; demand characteristics may be assessed through the use of preexperimental and postexperimental interviews with subjects.

The problem of temporal generalization was discussed within the context of *statistical significance* and *replication*.

REVIEW QUESTIONS

1. Distinguish among the concepts of *sample, target population*, and *sampled population*, and describe some events and influences that may produce discrepancies among these three groups.

2. List and describe the four main dimensions of generalization. In what sense are three of these dimensions "spatial" and the remaining one "temporal"?

3. Explain how limits on external validity may be thought of as interaction effects. What is interacting with what? Make up an example.

4. Summarize the evidence suggesting that the physical setting, researcher attributes, and researcher expectancies may interact with the independent variable to restrict external validity.

5. Describe some of the characteristics of laboratory experiments that are thought to make generalizing particularly difficult. Also, indicate techniques and strategies that may be used to deal with these special problems.

6. Define *probability sampling*, and contrast it with *convenience sampling*. What are some of the difficulties associated with implementation of probability sampling?

7. Characterize the typical subject in psychology experiments; also, the typical volunteer subject.

8. Briefly define or describe: obtrusiveness of measurement, pretesting effects, multiple-treatment carry-over effects, demand characteristics, subject attrition.

9. Describe the rationale underlying each of the following strategies: conceptual replication, systematizing a generalization dimension, aggregation of findings.

10. Describe three procedures used to reveal and assess the effects of demand characteristics.

11. Summarize the logic of statistical significance testing.

12. State two reasons for testing the null hypothesis rather than the alternative hypothesis.

13. Distinguish between Type I and Type II decision errors, and tell how you might reduce the theoretical probability of each type of error.

14. Describe and critique the "statistical logic" behind the practice of replication.

15. List some considerations in determining the quality of a replication study.

Notes

[1]From A. Standen, *Science Is a Sacred Cow*. New York: Dutton, 1950. Reprinted by permission of the author.

[2]Not even the staunchest advocate of the scientific method would deny that science has its limitations. However, I find that the domain of phenomena that are beyond the scope of the scientific method grows progressively smaller. Not two decades ago, a highly respected professor stood in front of a graduate class in research methods and confidently said, ''The limits of science are clear. We know, for instance, that science cannot study such things as the dark side of the moon and 'falling in love.' '' Since then, of course, both of the topics in question have been brought within the realm of the scientific method.

[3]Spatial generalization, as used here, is similar to Brunswik's (1956) concept of ''Ecological Validity'': the idea that data should be generalizable from the laboratory to everyday life.

[4]In practice, perfect constancy across spatial dimensions isn't possible, even if the same researcher repeats the same study. As Epstein (1980) points out, even the researcher will change in subtle ways from the initial study to the replication.

[5]Of course, animal subjects don't make themselves available for research participation. But they are nonetheless a select subject pool, in the sense that the researcher has chosen a particular species to study from a wide range of usable species. Beyond this, many laboratory animals have been selectively bred for malleability, ease of handling, and laboratory hardiness. Thus, we might expect the behavior of our friend, the albino rat, to be somewhat unrepresentative of her numerous wild cousins.

[6]Recall that percentage = proportion $\times$ 100.

[7]Some test statistics have sampling distributions consisting of only positive values. Therefore, when these tests are used, there is only one ''extreme'' portion of the distribution to consider. Also, there are some (infrequent) occasions on which a researcher might be interested in only the positive or negative extreme portion of a *bivalent* sampling distribution (one having both positive and negative values). Such one-sided interest is justified if the researcher's theory specifically predicts only a positive *or* a negative test outcome, and the opposite prediction would be theoretically meaningless (Kimmel, 1957). Except in this unusual kind of situation, both extremes of a bivalent sampling distribution should be considered in establishing the regions of statistically significant outcomes.

[8]When subjects are randomly selected from a target population, the null and alternative hypotheses also refer to that real population as well as to the hypothetical population of replications assumed by the model of statistical significance. In this case, statistical decisions concerning the sample are also assumed to apply to the target population from which the sample was chosen. Unfortunately, however, research samples are seldom randomly selected.

[9]Most statisticians prefer to say that one ''fails to reject'' the null hypothesis rather than that one ''accepts'' the null hypothesis. One reason for this preference is that it is just as difficult to directly ''prove'' that no real effect exists as it is to ''prove'' that an effect exists. A related reason for the preference is that, while no real effect of the independent variable may exist in your sample, it is possible that such a nonchance effect could exist in a different sample tested under different circumstances. Thus, it is inappropriate to make a general assertion that the null hypothesis is true.

PART
3

USING RESEARCH
DESIGNS

9

SYSTEMATIC OBSERVATION

Are you interested in singles bars? I mean the scientific study of singles-bar phenomena, of course! Since there isn't much scientific literature on the behavior of singles-bar patrons, and since significant social-psychological events reputedly take place in such establishments, a study in this area might prove to be a valuable contribution to psychological knowledge. How might you and your fellow students conduct such an investigation?

Let's consider some of the possibilities. You might approach the general topic experimentally in an attempt to manipulate variables of interest while holding constant all potentially confounding factors. This would require that you beg or rent space and obtain the funds necessary for constructing the setting and providing the fixtures and amenities that lend singles bars their special atmosphere. Of course, you would need to conform to local ordinances regulating entertainment spots and apply for a liquor license (the red tape may be cleared in time for your master's-degree project). When all of the patrons (subjects) finally arrive (they would be mostly singles, wouldn't they?), they would mingle with a dozen well-trained experimental confederates, who would help you manipulate the independent variables and . . . Well, maybe another method of research would be advisable for this line of inquiry.

Given the difficulties associated with an experimental design in this case, perhaps you could use the survey method. You could randomly select a large sample of people and interview them. After determining whether each respondent frequents, or has frequented, singles bars, you would proceed to ask a number of questions related to his or her nightlife experiences. (Do you think there might be certain categories of questions that many respondents would refuse to answer?) Assuming your respondents had accurate memories of their experiences, unscathed by the disruptive effects of alcohol molecules, you would hope (a) that you were asking questions that draw out the kind of information you're seeking and (b) that your respondents are being honest and forthright in relating what they experienced in bars. Perhaps a survey isn't the best way to start out on singles-bar research after all.

There will always be social-psychological phenomena that prove difficult to approach through the more obtrusive methods of science, such as the experiment and the survey. The study of singles-bar phenomena is simply a convenient example of this type of problem. Any of dozens of other "difficult" research situations could have been used as an illustration. Most of these situations are characterized by high "observational-reactivity potential." That is, any obvious attempt to research the people or animals involved is likely to make them behave so atypically that the data you get would not reflect what really goes on most of the time in that setting. This is an especially serious problem if the major aim of your research is to find out what a particular group of people or animals *does* under ordinary circumstances—that is, to maximize external validity.

Fortunately, there are data-gathering techniques that may be applied in the types of situations I'm referring to. In Chapter 4, these techniques were referred to collectively as **systematic observation**, which I will define as *the deliberate and planned recording of observations in a natural environment, in which the behavior of subjects is essentially unaffected by the observation process.* The techniques include **naturalistic observation** and **participant observation.** A variant of systematic observation is called the **field experiment**, which combines the unobtrusive character of systematic observation with control of extraneous variables and direct manipulation of independent variables.

These unobtrusive approaches to psychological research will be the focus of this chapter. You may think that they are a snap to carry out, but actually, considerable forethought is required for their successful implementation. So before you grab your notebook (which is obtrusive) or your napkins (which are less obtrusive) and stroll on down to the local nightspot, read on.

NATURALISTIC OBSERVATION

The "purest" form of systematic observation is **naturalistic observation**, in which the researcher unobtrusively records the behavior of unaware subjects in their natural environment. Thus, if naturalistic observation is carried out according to the book, the behavior of the observed individuals is not at all affected by the observation process. The subjects simply are unaware of their roles as subjects and the existence of the observation process. Hence, they go about their usual activities in the usual ways. The special advantage of the completely naturalistic study is obvious: This approach is the surest way to discover what the subjects of interest are really like and what they normally do in a particular setting.

The Case for Naturalistic Observation

During the past several years, there has been a growing outcry for a better balance between laboratory experimentation and naturalistic, or "field," research in psychology (e.g., Miller, 1977; Sommer, 1977; Wachtel, 1980). The position most often taken by the critics of laboratory research is not that field research should replace in-house experimentation, but that the two approaches should be used to complement, corroborate, and extend one another. The main thrust of this argument is that behavioral researchers must, at some point, attempt to establish the external validity of their laboratory findings. The following observations offered by Ellsworth (1977) make it fairly clear why we need to venture into naturalistic research if we are to accomplish this critical validation:

> The ethical requirement of weak treatments, with its attendant restriction of range, creates one major limitation on the kinds of question that can be studied successfully in the laboratory. Time constraints impose a second restriction. In general, laboratory studies are limited to studying the acute or reactive form of variables such as self-esteem, liking, or commitment. Chronic self-esteem, lasting friendship, or long-term commitment may have quite different effects from their reactive counterparts—they may not even involve the same underlying psychological processes; thus laboratory research based on acute manipulations may have very limited generality. (p. 607)

When you consider the above arguments, together with the fact (established earlier) that field observation may be the only feasible approach to some research questions, it becomes clear that naturalistic methods will remain an essential part of behavioral methodology well into the foreseeable future. In fact, recent trends in the philosophy of social/behavioral research suggest that field-type research will play a progressively larger role in the future work of research psychologists. With that possibility in mind, let's now look at some of the crucial considerations involved in setting up and conducting naturalistic-observation studies.

Three Examples of Naturalistic Observation

It will be helpful to view the various matters with which you will need to deal in any naturalistic study within the context of some representative investigations. Although other studies will be referred to, three such investigations will be the focus of discussion here.

Midwest and Its Children. Between July 1, 1951, and June 30, 1952, Barker and Wright (1954), with the help of a large team of observers, carried out the first comprehensive study of the "psychological living conditions" of people in a small American town. The Kansas town, dubbed "Midwest," had a relatively stable population of 707 residents at the beginning of the study. The major focus of Barker and Wright's pioneering effort was the day-to-day behaviors of the Midwest children under the age of twelve, but the researchers also collected an enormous amount of data on the lives of the adult residents. The principal research method in this study was direct observation of everyday behaviors in a variety of community settings. The primary goals of Barker and Wright's research were to classify the settings and activities normally entered into by Midwest's residents, to record the amount of time spent in these settings and activities, and to conceptualize the psychological significance of these settings and activities.

It is worth noting that although the main data-collecting activity of Barker and Wright's team spanned a one-year interval, the entire study, from conception to publication, required over eight years to complete. It was an *inductive* investigation in the purest sense of the word (see Chapter 2).

Gender and Book-Carrying Style.   Although this study was narrower in focus than the Barker and Wright investigation, it wasn't designed to test a particular hypothesis. Rather, this second study was simply an attempt to replicate earlier investigations of book-carrying styles as a function of gender (e.g., Jenni & Jenni, 1976; Scheman et al., 1978). These earlier studies, which involved systematic observation in natural settings, showed the following outcome: Males tend to carry books down at one side (about hip level) in one hand, whereas females tend to carry books against the abdomen or chest, frequently securing them with both hands.

Three students in my research methods class were intrigued by previous findings on this topic, so they decided to team up and attempt their own field study of book-carrying behavior in male and female college students. The student researchers were divided in their expectations regarding the likely outcome of such a study on their campus. Honorably, they made a pact to "let the data fall where they may."

Attractive Women in Singles Bars.   The third study serving as a primary example of naturalistic methods was reported by Glenwick, Jason, and Elman (1978; also see Horn, 1978). This investigation was designed to test a specific hypothesis. Previous research in social psychology had shown that, "idealistically," men prefer physically attractive women over "plain-looking" women. But the "matching hypothesis" of social intercourse suggests that men in general would expect a greater likelihood of rejection from attractive women than from less attractive women (Berscheid & Walster, 1974). This hypothesis would predict that many men who view themselves as "plain-looking" might actually avoid contact with attractive women, opting instead for women whose attractiveness level approximates their own.

Glenwick and associates tested the matching hypothesis in four singles bars in Rochester, New York. Posing as customers, they observed the frequency with which women of various attractiveness levels were approached by hopeful men; they also recorded the duration of those contacts. An "idealistic" hypothesis would predict a positive correlation between the attractiveness of females and the frequency and duration of attempts to woo them. However, the matching hypothesis would predict no correlation among these measures.

Planning a Naturalistic Study

Successful naturalistic studies are the product of much planning and advance decision-making. If you wish to conduct such a study, you will need to develop specific objectives and strategies relative to a number of items. Among other things, you will need to (a) decide what variables will be studied and what behaviors will be recorded, (b) develop data-recording techniques and data-recording sheets (if such sheets are appropriate), (c) plan your sampling design, and (d) train observers.

Deciding What to Observe.　The behaviors and variables you select for examination will be determined by the specific interests, questions, or hypotheses that motivated you to conduct the study. If you are attempting to replicate prior research, the choice of variables is a relatively simple matter. But if you're breaking new ground, or if your questions are very broad ones, then it is easy to become overwhelmed by the welter of possibilities. In these latter types of situation, a considerable amount of forethought is required.

Consider Barker and Wright's study of Midwest. Where does one begin in an attempt to study the "psychological living conditions" of a whole town, even a small town like Midwest? In deciding on their basic variables ("Ecological Units"), Barker and Wright first looked at what they termed "behavior episodes." A behavior episode was defined as a sequence of behavior with a clear behavioral end (i.e., goal) and a "unidirectional flow of the stream of action." As an example of a behavior episode, Barker and Wright referred to an instance of a boy's attempt to move an old wooden crate across a pit.

Of course, people are almost constantly engaging in behavior episodes. In fact, Barker and Wright estimated that the 119 children of Midwest engaged in approximately 100,000 behavior episodes per day. In addition to being incredibly plentiful, many of these episodes occurred only under limited or unique circumstances. Since the researchers were interested in reaching some general conclusions, they decided to focus on "ecological units" that were "larger" than the isolated behavior episode. The larger units decided upon were called "behavior settings," defined as recurring behavior episodes that are *independent of the particular individuals involved.* One example they cited was "shopping at a drugstore." Thus, the behaviors observed in a behavior setting are determined not by the particular persons in them but by the context in which those persons find themselves—by the places, objects, social functions, and times of the behavior episodes. In addition, to qualify as a behavior setting, a behavior episode had to be recognized as a significant aspect of town life by the residents of Midwest.

To help them identify the behavior settings of Midwest, the researchers relied on content analyses of occasions and events announced in church and school bulletins, on handbills, and in Midwest's newspapers. They also used direct observation to identify behavior settings. The result of this elaborate search for observational units was a "catalog" of 2,030 behavior settings that served as the focal points of the study. A list of the most important settings for Midwest's children appears in Box 9–1.

Box 9–1
HIGHLIGHT
Popular Behavior Settings of Midwest

School classes	Shoe repair shop	Hotels, rooming houses,	Music education groups
Trafficways	Drug, variety, and	and nurseries	Out-of-door athletic
Indoor entertainment	department store	Sunday-school classes	contests
Open spaces	Rest rooms	Indoor athletic contests	Church worship services
County jail and sheriff's	Classrooms: free time		
residence	Dining and lunchrooms		

Barker and Wright's behavior settings can be considered their units of observation. These units were thought to reflect several variables that were significant to the lives of Midwest's residents. One such variable was the percent of total behavior-setting time that was spent in each of the behavior settings. This variable was called the "Occupancy Index." For example, school classes were found to occupy approximately 31 percent of the children's total behavior-setting time, whereas indoor entertainment accounted for just over 6 percent of their time. Another variable represented in behavior settings was the "action pattern," defined as the general function served by a behavior setting. For instance, church socials and athletic contests served, among other things, a "social contact" function and a "recreation" function.

Compared to what Barker and Wright chose to research, an investigation of the behavior of singles-bar patrons may seem to be a simple undertaking. But consider for a moment the great variety of behavioral phenomena that could be observed and recorded in a singles bar. A few of the potential variables of interest are listed in Box 9–2. A glance at the list should make it clear that it is often necessary to make many advance decisions and plans even when the naturalistic study is confined to relatively narrow settings.

Fortunately, Glenwick and colleagues had some specific questions in mind in their study of singles-bar patrons: How attractive were selected women? How many men spoke to each selected woman? How long did these contact attempts last? How likely were the selected women to be rejecting toward men who approached them? Was the attractiveness of the women significantly related to any of the other variables? Accordingly, the researchers devised strategies for unobtrusively observing and measuring each

---

Box 9–2
HIGHLIGHT
A Sample of Potential Variables in Studies of
Singles-Bar Patrons

1. crowd density
2. sound intensity of music
3. sound intensity without music
4. ratio of males to females
5. proportion of same-sex couples
6. ratio of groups to couples
7. ratio of loners to groups and couples
8. proportion of women who are unaccompanied
9. proportion of men who are unaccompanied
10. ratio of attractive to plain males
11. ratio of attractive to plain females
12. proportion of nondrinkers
13. incidence of aggressive acts
14. incidence of flirtatious acts
15. incidence of attention-seeking behavior
16. incidence of romantic or sexual overtures

17. incidence of opposite-sex contacts initiated by females; by males
18. ratio of opposite-sex couples entering lounge to opposite-sex couples leaving lounge within a set time interval
19. ratio of male advances made toward attractive females to male advances made toward plain females
20. ratio of female advances made toward attractive males to female advances made toward plain males
21. average duration of contact attempts directed at attractive females; at attractive males
22. average duration of contact attempts directed at plain females; at plain males
23. proportion of romantic or sexual overtures initiated by females; by males

of the above variables in connection with 39 women who happened to be at the bars during the observation periods (you'll see how they accomplished this later in this chapter).

The team of students who set out to investigate the relationship between gender and book-carrying style had fewer decisions to make than did the researchers in either of the first two studies. Since the students were simply attempting a replication of earlier research, what they would observe and record was predetermined for them. But they still had to decide exactly how they would carry out the observation process and what kind of data-recording techniques they would use.

Data-Recording Techniques and Data-Recording Sheets.   Once the variables have been conceptualized and the target behaviors determined, the next step in planning a naturalistic study is to formalize your recording and measuring techniques. This involves developing measurement rules (see Chapter 5) and data-recording sheets and specifying exactly how these devices will be used.

As you might expect, the data-recording techniques employed by Barker and Wright in their study of Midwest were, by far, the most ambitious and laborious of the three field studies we are considering. Barker and Wright's principal data-generating device was called the *specimen record*, which was a detailed narrative (written) description on one or more behavioral episodes engaged in by a child. Such records were compiled via a "brute force" method: One or more observers would accompany or follow a child into a behavior setting and begin taking extensive notes on virtually every behavior sequence judged to be of psychological significance to the child. Typically these notes contained both literal descriptions of the child's behavior and commonsense inferences about the purpose of the behavior. Since Barker and Wright were conducting inductive research and wanted to obtain "theoretically neutral" data, the specimen record had to be a relatively complete account rather than a listing of psychological jargon and diagnostic terms. Consequently, a record describing a half hour's activity in a single behavior setting might be 15 to 20 pages long!

Occasionally Barker and Wright would have their research team compile a *day specimen record* on a child. This record contained an account of all of the child's behavior settings across an entire day. Normally this feat would require the assistance of seven to nine observers working in shifts, and the final narrative record would exceed 300 typewritten pages. Ultimately, the anecdotal data in such a record would be further analyzed, and hence expanded, in terms of the categories of behavior settings and action patterns that they represented. This approach to data recording clearly would not be feasible unless you have considerable clerical assistance and a sizable cadre of dedicated observers.

When the data of a naturalistic study are narrative in form, they are almost always voluminous. (This certainly was true of Barker and Wright's data.) Another problem with narrative or anecdotal data is that most often they are not suitable for quantitative analysis. For these reasons, it is a good idea to plan your measurement and recording devices in such a way that observations can be readily converted to numbers, such as ratings or frequency counts. Generally speaking, field observations will be quantifiable to the extent that your research question has been honed to specifics, and to the degree that you know precisely what behaviors you are looking for.

An example of a data-recording technique that yields frequency counts is provided by the research methods students' investigation of book-carrying behavior. Knowing that they wanted to cross-tabulate book-carrying styles and gender, the students devised a data-recording sheet similar to that shown in Figure 9–1. Notice that the sheet contains blanks for information identifying the observer, date, time, and place (in case any of these variables turns out to be a factor in the results). Also notice that the cells of the table pro-

Observer _____

Date _____

Time _____

Location code _____

Gender

Book-Carrying Style	Female	Male
A	//	//// /
B		///
C	//// ////	/
D	////	
E	//	///

FIGURE 9–1

Data Recording Sheet Used in Study of Book-Carrying Behavior

A: Books are carried down at the hip in one hand

B: Books are carried out from the side of the body, in one arm.

C: Books are carried against the chest or abdomen, secured in one arm.

D: Books are carried against the chest or abdomen, secured with both arms.

E: Style did not fit any anticipated category.

vide space for quick and simple classification of each subject according to the independent variable (gender) and the dependent variable (style). The line markings within the cells of the data sheet show how the instrument was used. Every book-carrying subject who walked through the observation area was represented by a line marking that summarized the coincidence of the subject's sex and his or her style of toting books. Thus, each book carrier was represented by one mark. The advantage of data-recording devices of this type is that they increase the efficiency of data collection while producing data that can be easily summarized and analyzed through statistical operations.

The Glenwick et al. study of behavior in single bars illustrates a number of measurement procedures that may be used to obtain quantitative data within a natural context. Both Glenwick and his co-researcher, Jason, participated in the data-collection process. After settling themselves within a high-density area of a singles bar, the two researchers selected an unattached female patron and unobtrusively observed her for five minutes. Working independently, each of the researchers (a) rated the woman's physical attractiveness on a 10-point scale, (b) counted how many other women were with her, and (c) counted the number of men initiating verbal contact with her. With the aid of concealed stopwatches, they also recorded the amount of time such verbal contacts lasted.

To obtain data on how receptive their subjects were to the contact attempts of men, Glenwick and Jason used a device that occasionally serves as a useful adjunct technique in field research: *researcher intervention*. After completing their observations of a particular subject, one of the researchers (both of whom were males) would walk up to the woman and say, "Hi. Having a good time?" Depending on how the woman reacted, the researchers rated her as either receptive or not receptive to overtures from men.[1] This example shows how, under favorable circumstances, it is possible to directly alter the stimulus situation of the subjects in a natural setting, for purposes of eliciting a particular kind of response, without sacrificing the unobtrusive character of the research.

Sampling Considerations.   As you read in Chapter 8, there are many sampling dimensions to be considered in any psychological investigation. These dimensions include *time, subject population, setting, measurement techniques, and even data collectors.*

In naturalistic-observation studies, the sampling of settings is often heavily influenced by the nature of the research aim or hypothesis. And sometimes particular settings must be used because they are the only ones available or feasible. When settings appropriate to the study's purpose are plentiful, however, you are faced with the question of which specific sites to select. In such a case the ideal strategy is to choose observation sites via some form of probability sampling (see Chapter 8). The idea, of course, is to obtain results that will be generalizable beyond specific locations and particular groups of subjects.

The team of student researchers investigating book-carrying behavior used simple random sampling to select their observation sites. Having decided that they would restrict their research activities to their college campus, they obtained a campus map to survey the possible observation points. The map appears in Figure 9–2. Since the observers planned to stand or sit in front of buildings during class-change intervals, they defined their population of sites as 15 campus buildings that students normally walked by on their way to, from, or between classes. This population consisted of the buildings numbered 1–4, 6–9, 11–16, 26, and 35 in the figure. The researchers used a random number table (see Table A–1 in the Appendix) to select 5 buildings as their observation points. The practice of sampling specific regions within a larger geographical space, as was done in this study, is called **area sampling.**

The next problem was to sample the time intervals during which the observations could be made. Simple arithmetic revealed that classes changed 29 times each week. Since each of the three observers in the team desired to collect observations once at each of the five sampled sites—15 observation episodes in all—it was decided that only 15 of the 29 time intervals would be used.

Whenever a behavior of interest occurs so often during the time span of a study that it is impossible to observe every instance of the behavior, researchers typically exercise the option of **time sampling.** This technique entails (a) dividing the time interval occupied by the study into a number of discrete units and (b) randomly selecting a desired proportion or number of those units to use as observation periods. This is exactly what the research methods team did. From the population of 29 10-minute class-change intervals, they randomly selected 15 intervals to serve as observation periods (see Table 9–1).

In sum, the generalization dimensions included in the student researchers' sampling design were observation sites, time, and subject population, which covaried with sites. Once again, the purpose of this elaborate sampling strategy was to allow the researchers to generalize their results to the whole population of students at their college.

With a rather modest problem to investigate, and a relatively small geographical area to cover, the students were able to be thoroughly "scientific" in their sampling procedures. However, naturalistic investigations aimed at numerous, open-ended questions and conducted in complicated environments frequently do not lend themselves readily to probability sampling. Such was the case in Barker and Wright's study of Midwest. At one level, Barker and Wright attempted to study an entire town, in an effort to catalog the various behavior settings of significance to the lives of Midwest's residents. But at another level, they were also trying to conduct intensive studies of the moment-to-moment

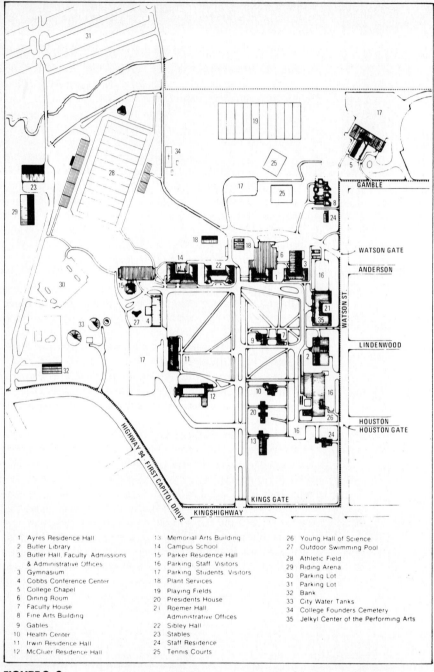

FIGURE 9-2

Map of Campus on Which Student Researchers Conducted a Study of Book-Carrying Behavior

1   Ayres Residence Hall
2   Butler Library
3   Butler Hall, Faculty Admissions
&   Administrative Offices
3   Gymnasium
4   Cobbs Conference Center
5   College Chapel
6   Dining Room
7   Faculty House
8   Fine Arts Building
9   Gables
10 Health Center
11 Irwin Residence Hall
12 McCluer Residence Hall

13 Memorial Arts Building
14 Campus School
15 Parker Residence Hall
16 Parking Staff, Visitors
17 Parking Students, Visitors
18 Plant Services
19 Playing Fields
20 Presidents House
21 Roemer Hall
    Administrative Offices
22 Sibley Hall
23 Stables
24 Staff Residence
25 Tennis Courts

26 Young Hall of Science
27 Outdoor Swimming Pool
28 Athletic Field
29 Riding Arena
30 Parking Lot
31 Parking Lot
32 Bank
33 City Water Tanks
34 College Founders Cemetery
35 Jelkyl Center of the Performing Arts

TABLE 9–1

Sample Frame of Class-Change Times in a Study of Book-Carrying Styles

		Day		
Monday	*Tuesday*	*Wednesday*	*Thursday*	*Friday*
[9–9:10]	9:30–9:40	9–9:10	9:30–9:40	[9–9:10]
10:10–10:20	[11:15–11:25]	[10:10–10:20]	[11:15–11:25]	10:10–10:20
11:20–11:30	[3–3:10]	11:20–11:30	3–3:10	[11:20–11:30]
[12:30–12:40]	[4:45–4:55]	12:30–12:40	[4:45–4:55]	12:30–12:40
[2:30–2:40]		[2:30–2:40]		2:30–2:40
3:40–3:50		3:40–3:50		[3:40–3:50]
[4:50–5]		[4:50–5]		4:50–5

Note: Bracketed times were randomly selected observation intervals.

activities of Midwest's children through the compilation of the hefty day specimen records. To achieve this second objective within realistic bounds, they had to focus on just a few children—in fact, they amassed daylong records on only 12 youngsters. Since Barker and Wright wanted the small sample to represent "all age, group, and sex categories of Midwest children," they couldn't rely on the disposition of chance (i.e., random) processes in their selection of the sample. So they used what is charitably referred to as **representative sampling**: The researchers handpicked a sample that, in their minds, consisted of individuals whose characteristics represented those of the whole population (cf. Mendenhall et al., 1971). The disadvantages of this sampling procedure are discussed in Chapter 12; the major problem is that representative sampling doesn't permit statements about the theoretical probability of being wrong in one's conclusions about the data. Nonetheless, in certain types of naturalistic research, representative sampling may be the best available option.

The third study of particular interest here, that conducted by Glenwick and his colleagues, appeared to use neither probability sampling nor representative sampling. Observations were taken at only four singles bars (selection criteria were not reported) and only on Friday nights between 10:30 P.M. and midnight. Perhaps these times and places were viewed as the most feasible circumstances for obtaining, within a short period of time, the type of data the researchers sought. If so, then the sampling technique would be referred to as **convenience sampling**: selecting situations and subjects on the basis of how readily available they are and how easily they can be studied. This is the least desirable sampling technique from the standpoint of generalizing the results. (What sampling strategy would you devise to ensure a more generalizable data base in an investigation of singles bars?)

Training Observers. Once you've thought through and carefully planned the matters discussed so far, you're about ready to begin observing behavior in a natural context. I say "about" because it is unwise to start your study without first ensuring that your observers have the necessary knowledge and skills to carry out the study. This is true even if you are the *one and only* observer in your study.

There are many things that can go awry in naturalistic-observation efforts. Are your observers aware of the desirability of their having no unnatural influence on the behavior of subjects? How will they be able to tell if they are disrupting the natural state of the target environment? How will they inconspicuously enter the environment and unobtrusively situate themselves? Is it possible to observe subjects in action without actually entering the setting? Are there bugs in the recording procedure? Are the observers thoroughly aware of the scheduling of observation times and sites?

These questions are best answered by conducting a *pilot study*, or dry run, prior to embarking on the actual study. Such a trial will reveal most of the flaws in the procedure and will also provide an opportunity for the behaviors and recording techniques of the observers to stabilize, thus minimizing, "instrumentation change" effects (see Chapter 7).

The pilot study has the additional advantage of giving you a chance to check the *interrater reliability* of the data-recording procedure. If two or more observers report vastly different data from the same trial, you've got problems: Remember, if your measurement procedure isn't yielding consistent results, you probably aren't measuring much of anything—and it's time to review and revise your measurement technique.

Some Results: An Interlude for Closure Purposes

Next we'll be looking into some techniques of unobtrusive data collection that are especially useful in naturalistic studies. By this time, however, you're probably wondering about the findings of Barker and Wright, Glenwick and associates, and the dauntless team of student researchers, whose planning and plotting we've graphically charted. Some of their results and conclusions appear in Boxes 9–3, 9–4, and 9–5.

Box 9–3
HIGHLIGHT
Midwest and Its Children: Some Conclusions

Barker and Wright's volumes of data on Midwest are replete with fascinating narrative records and quantitative indices that provide a fairly detailed sketch of the psychosocial systems operating in a small midwestern community. To fully appreciate the richness and value of their data, you should browse through *Midwest and Its Children* on some lazy Sunday afternoon. Their work is a genuine classic in social science research.

The findings and conclusions reviewed here represent a mere sketch of Barker and Wright's work; but even this brief summary suggests that the "psychological living conditions" of small-town children are diverse, challenging, and rewarding.

The 16 behavior settings that were entered most often by Midwest's children are shown below.

Some interesting statistics emerged from the investigation of Midwest:

1. Of the 2,030 behavior settings identified, 1,445 were "family" settings, the remaining 585 being "community" settings. Overall, then, family life was

very strong and psychologically important relative to other spheres of activity. But the relative amount of time spent in community settings increased from infancy to adolescence. Midwest's adolescents spent almost half of their waking hours in community behavior settings.

2. On an average weekday in Midwest, approximately 205 community settings of 70 different kinds took place in the town of just over 700 people!

Barker and Wright concluded that the average resident of Midwest was "under pressure to participate in a number of [community settings]," due to the large number of settings relative to the number of residents.

Some other conclusions were:

"In 1951/52, the variety of behavior settings available to Midwest children was limited; it was only a part of the total range occurring in American culture" (p. 459); but "the actual variety of psychological situations and behavior in which individual Midwest children engaged was, nevertheless, great. It may have

Box 9–3
HIGHLIGHT
Midwest and Its Children: Some Conclusions (*continued*)

Varieties of Community Behavior Settings Where Midwest Children Spent the Greatest Amount of Time

Variety *Number and Name*	*Prominent Behavior* *Characteristics*	*Children's* *Occupancy* *Index**
1. School classes	Formal teaching and learning	30.9
2. Trafficways	Traveling between behavior settings	7.4
6. Indoor entertainments	Attending and producing public entertainment	6.4
21. Open spaces	Playing	4.3
20. County jail and sheriff's residence	Punishing lawbreakers	3.9
13. Hotels, rooming houses, and nurseries	Providing temporary lodging	3.6
22. Sunday-school classes	Formal teaching and learning	3.2
11. Indoor athletic contests	Attending and participating in indoor athletic contests	3.0
27. Shoe repair shop	Providing and obtaining shoe repair	3.0
5. Drug, variety, and department store	Buying and selling clothing, household accessories, and medicines	2.5
25. Rest rooms	Washing, toileting	2.4
40. Classrooms: free time	Playing	2.3
30. Dining and lunchrooms	Providing and eating noon meal	2.3
31. Music education groups	Teaching, learning, and performing of music	2.1
16. Out-of-door athletic contests	Attending and participating in athletic contests	1.9
19. Church worship services	Attending and participating in church worship service	1.6

*Percent of total hours spent in community settings by infants, preschool, younger school, and older school children.

Source: R.G. Barker and H.F. Wright, *Midwest and Its Children: The Psychological Ecology of an American Town*. New York: Harper & Row, 1954. Reprinted by permission.

been greater than that of children living in the cities" (p. 459).

Also, "The levels of accomplishment of Midwest children were usually lower than those of which they were capable. Because they were under pressure to take part in so many diverse activities, Midwest chil-dren were able to attain in few of·them the maximal levels of which they were capable" (p. 460).

"The children of Midwest occupied positions of power and prestige; they were not a luxury in the community; they performed essential functions" (p. 460).

Box 9–4
HIGHLIGHT
Gender and Book-Carrying Styles

Were the student researchers able to replicate earlier findings on the relationship between gender and book-carrying behavior? As the data table shown below indicates, the answer is a resounding yes.

Book-Carrying Style	Gender	
	Male	Female
A: Down at side, one hand	148	21
B: Out at side, one hand	5	9
C: In front of body, one hand	1	33
D: In front of body, both hands	20	124
Totals	174	187

In line with the results of prior investigations, the students' data showed that males have a strong tendency to tote books in one hand slung down at one side of their bodies, just as one might carry an umbrella on a cloudy but rainless day. Almost as pronounced was the tendency of the females in this study to carry books in front of their bodies, frequently secured with both hands.

Once the results were in, a flurry of questions followed. What do the data mean? What is the reason, or reasons, for the sex differences in this particular behavior? Are the behaviors merely acquired preferences or are they forced or favored by anatomical differences between the sexes? Are college women simply more serious students than college men? If so, then women may tend to take more books along with them, thus requiring two hands rather than one. These questions point to a major limitation of naturalistic research: It normally lacks sufficient controls for isolating causal influences.

What specific research methods could you employ to get at some of the variables that contribute to sex-linked book-carrying styles?

Techniques of Naturalistic Observation

Systematic observation studies can be naturalistic studies only to the extent that the observer and the observation process don't cause the subjects' behaviors to deviate from what is typical for them in the particular environment being examined. This condition is met to the degree that (a) the observed individuals are oblivious of their roles as subjects in a scientific investigation and (b) the observation process doesn't create environmental situations or events that the subjects perceive as unusual, unexpected, or novel. Both of these criteria of unobtrusive observation apply in the case of human subjects, whereas criterion *a*, of course, is not relevant to investigations of animals.

Social and behavioral scientists use a large number and variety of strategies to implement unobtrusive observation. Some of these maneuvers were reviewed in Chapter 5. Four approaches, in particular, are widely used in naturalistic research: *blending in, hiding, employment of special surveillance devices, and creation of facsimile environments.*

Blending In.   When observers rely on the "blending in" strategy, they make little or no attempt to remain invisible to the subjects. Rather, the observers try to appear to be a normal, unremarkable, and expected part of the natural environment. The subjects may, in fact, be aware of the observers' presence, but, if blending in is successful, they don't become aware of their roles as subjects of observation. Blending in often works well in naturalistic studies of humans, but usually isn't a feasible method in investigations of animals. The natural environments of most animals would not contain humans on a regular basis.

BOX 9–5
HIGHLIGHT
Systematically Observing the Swinging
Singles

Recall that when Glenwick and his colleagues strolled into each of the four Rochester, New York, singles bars, they had a definite business purpose in mind: to test the relative accuracy of predictions stemming from two conflicting hypotheses. The "idealistic" hypothesis of heterosexual interaction predicted that the male bar patrons would attempt to interact with attractive women more often than with plain-looking women. The "matching" hypothesis, however, predicted that men who consider *themselves* to be plain-looking would approach plain-looking women more often than they would approach attractive women, their rationale being that attractive women would be more likely to reject them. Thus, assuming that the plain/attractive ratio is about the same for male bar patrons as it is for female patrons, the matching hypothesis predicted that there would be no correlation between women's attractiveness and how often they were ap-

proached. (This amounts to predicting the null hypothesis, which is always an awkward kind of prediction to make. See Chapter 8.)

Glenwick et al.'s evidence was consistent with the matching hypothesis. Women's attractiveness was not significantly correlated with how often they were approached by men. But if some of the men tended to avoid attractive women because of a fear of rejection, their fear may have been groundless: The researchers found that when *they* made contact with female bar patrons, the attractive women were just as receptive as the plain-looking women.

Other results were that the average duration of transient contacts between hopeful males and their quarry was just 7 seconds, and that, on the average, each observed woman was approached once every 15 to 20 minutes (see Horn, 1978).

Examples of the blending in technique are plentiful. One example, which was reviewed in Chapter 4, involved the study of how much beer is consumed by lone drinkers versus people who quaff in the company of friends (Sommer, 1977). The observers, Sommer and his students, simply posed as fellow beer drinkers in the numerous taverns and lounges they studied and made cryptic notes of their observations on napkins.

Not only was blending in the observation method of choice in the Glenwick study of singles bars, it was also the methodological objective of the observers in Barker and Wright's study of Midwest. However, one might well question how successful the strategy could be in the type of investigation represented by the Midwest study. It is likely that the town's children found it difficult to ignore both the degree of shadowing exhibited by the observers and the vigorous note-taking required by the format of specimen records.

If you conduct a naturalistic study that is amenable to the blending-in method, you will want to give special attention to your appearance, your entry into the setting, and your method of recording observations. Your attire and grooming should be selected with the aim of approximating what is normal for the people and situation you plan to observe. Your manner of entrance should be as nonchalant as possible. Signs of nervousness could blow your cover, but even nonchalance can be overdone. Generally, these aspects of your method will benefit from reconnaissance of the observation site and some careful planning as to the timing and manner of your entrance.

The third matter, recording observations, demands special consideration. Remember that in many settings, note-taking quickly arouses suspicion. In general, it is wise not to be an open note-taker, unless writing is a common activity in the environment being investigated. Seriously consider the possibility that you might have to rely on your memory or, at best, shorthand notes during the observational episode. You could then write thorough notes later in the day, in private.

Hiding. When it's not possible or easy to blend in, naturalistic observation can sometimes be conducted from a hidden observation point. Naturalists commonly use this observation strategy when they study animal behavior. The work of Jane Goodall is an example: In her investigation of the group behavior of chimpanzees in the Tanzanian forests, she was able to remain invisible to her subjects by observing them from behind a blind composed of a wall of underbrush cuttings (Van Lawick-Goodall, 1967). Thus, she could take notes, and even film animals in action, without altering their surroundings or attracting their attention.

The hiding approach to nonreactive observation is almost always necessary in naturalistic studies of animals. It is also a useful option in studies of humans, when blending in simply is not a viable method. Such a situation existed in Zimbardo's (1969) field study of vandalism. To examine the incidence and nature of vandalism in both a large-city setting and a college-town environment, Zimbardo deposited "abandoned" automobiles on selected streets in each type of setting. Then his observers stationed themselves in nearby buildings. From these hidden vantage points, the observers could watch and photograph anyone who attempted to vandalize the vehicles without being noticed by the villains.

Zimbardo's crew didn't have to wait long in the big city, where the first vandals descended upon the vehicle within 10 minutes after the stakeout. Only 7 minutes were required for them to scurry off with the car's battery and radiator. This opening assault was followed by a steady stream of adult-age vandals, each adding to the destruction in his own way—usually during daylight hours!

In contrast to the events observed in the city, no destructive acts were directed toward the car abandoned in the college town. Zimbardo attributed the setting differences to feelings of anonymity created by an urban environment, his theory being that anonymity encourages aggressive acts.

The hiding approach to unobtrusive observation requires just as much forethought as the blending-in method. Indeed, if the observers' invisibility is a necessary condition for the occurrence of natural behaviors, then you will have to take precautions to ensure that the observers remain unnoticed throughout the observation episode. As always, a pilot study would be an invaluable aid in the process of setting up the observation procedure.

One final caveat on hiding: Except when your subjects are small children, you can't count on the successful use of a one-way mirrored window as a device for implementing naturalistic observation. In almost any setting, except possibly that of a home environment, the presence of a mirror built into the wall immediately causes suspicion about being observed. And suspicious subjects will be guarded in their behavior and expressions.

Using Special Surveillance Devices. If it is not feasible to observe subjects directly from a hidden location, you can employ a variety of special instruments to do the observing for you. Such items as tape recorders and videotape cameras are generally expensive to purchase, but often your department, school, or organization will have a number of them available for borrowing.

If you plan to use special equipment to implement naturalistic observation, you will need to become very familiar with the operation and range limitations of such devices. Short of developing skills in this regard, you may be able to enlist the assistance of skilled audiovisual equipment operators. Needless to say, incorrect operation or the breakdown of such equipment can void an otherwise carefully planned study.

Using sophisticated automatic recording devices doesn't guarantee that the observation process will be unknown to the subjects. Inconspicuous placement and well-concealed location of cameras, microphones, and wires should be a major concern in setting up the investigation. Wires running across the bare floor or wall, as well as camera lenses jutting out from corners of the ceiling, are almost certain to draw attention. And, yes, people do look inside empty cups, and they might be both puzzled and threatened by a small microphone projecting from the bottom of the cup. Need I mention again the value of pilot studies?

Creating Facsimile Environments.   If it is difficult, expensive, or too inconvenient to study behavior in a natural environment but you are interested in *natural* behavior patterns, a compromise worth considering is to construct an environment that *simulates* the natural conditions that you are interested in. To the extent that your simulation is successful, subjects will behave in the contrived environment much as they would under natural circumstances. A definite advantage of using a facsimile environment is that such an approach makes it easy for you to systematically introduce discrete changes into the setting and then observe the effect of each change.

There are many instances of the use of facsimile environments in social-psychological research. The research on bystander intervention, discussed earlier (in Chapter 8), is a prime example of this. The staging of an emergency situation in such studies is designed to create a realistic social environment in which subjects lose sight of their research-participant roles as they focus on a real-life crisis. Role-playing exercises in industrial research also represent attempts to simulate natural circumstances (cf. Landy & Trumbo, 1980).

Facsimile environments have also proved useful in researching animal behavior. For example, Konrad Lorenz, a world-renowned ethologist, studied the territorial defense behaviors of fish through the use of aquariums designed to simulate the fishes' natural habitat (Lorenz, 1963). Knowing that behavior in a "naturalized" aquarium may be somewhat atypical, however, Lorenz later traveled to the coral reefs of Florida and observed the same species in completely normal circumstances. There, he was able to verify that most of the behavior patterns exhibited in the simulated environment also occurred in the sea.

Lorenz's excursion to Florida's coral reefs exemplifies a desirable practice: Ideally, researchers who use simulated environments should, at some point, check their findings against behaviors in the actual environments that have been simulated.

Evaluating Naturalistic Observation

Earlier in this chapter, I presented a number of arguments in favor of naturalistic observation. These arguments stressed the method's capacity for achieving external validity and permitting the investigation of situations that could not be studied through most other methods.

Though we haven't yet considered the limitations and shortcomings of naturalistic research, there are several. The most obvious limitation of the method is its susceptibility to confoundings. Because the researcher makes no attempt to control a host of extraneous variables that influence the dependent behavior, cause-and-effect conclusions based on naturalistic data are almost always subject to serious doubt.

Another commonly encountered problem is that the data of some naturalistic studies may not be easy to quantify. Particularly when the research questions are broad and the research inductive in nature, such as was true in the study of Midwest, most of the data may be in a narrative or anecdotal form. If so, they would not be suitable for analysis through the powerful statistical procedures that social scientists have come to depend on. Also, narrative data can quickly become so voluminous that data storage and summarization are rendered difficult.

A third general limitation concerns the ethics of the unobtrusive type of observation that characterizes naturalistic observation. The two ethical issues involved are: (a) observing and recording the behavior of individuals without their informed consent; (b) possible invasion of privacy.

Are these ethical issues realistic concerns? A poll on the general public's reaction to psychologists' use of unobtrusive methods suggests that they are. The results of interviews with 174 respondents showed that 38 percent of the sample thought that social scientists should "stop deceiving the public" with unobtrusive data-collection techniques. Further, approximately one-third of the respondents felt that such techniques constitute an invasion of privacy (Wilson & Donnerstein, 1977). Thus, to the extent that social scientists must grapple with the ethical costs of their methods, naturalistic observation, as a general approach to studying human behavior, may be more hampered by ethical problems than many of the alternative methods.

NATURALISTIC OBSERVATION WITH CONTROL AND MANIPULATION: FIELD EXPERIMENTS

At least one of the shortcomings of naturalistic observation—the relative lack of internal validity—can be remedied in some situations by exercising some control over variables within a natural context. In the ideal case, the unobtrusive nature of naturalistic observation is retained while an independent variable is systematically manipulated. When this combination of conditions is accomplished in a field-type investigation, the study is referred to as a **field experiment**. The field experiment represents an attempt to have the best of both worlds: the internal validity of a laboratory experiment and the external validity of the naturalistic-observation approach. In this respect, the field experiment is a hybrid method of investigation (see Chapter 4).

Sherif and Sherif's (1956) study of intergroup hostility in a summer camp for boys is a classic example of the field experiment (the study was summarized in Chapter 4). You may remember that the Sherifs successfully:

1. controlled confounding variables by using matched groups of subjects (the Rattlers and the Eagles) and by making sure that all subjects were exposed to essentially the same environmental conditions
2. directly manipulated independent variables, such as competition and cooperation, to identify the causes of intergroup hostility and harmony
3. established the generalizability (i.e., external validity) of their findings by using unobtrusive measurement techniques and conducting the study in a natural context

These three objectives—control of major confoundings, direct manipulation of variables, and nonreactive data collection in a natural setting—are the aims of all field experiments. To the extent that these goals can be realized, the field experiment is a powerful methodological tool for the social sciences. And all indications are that, because of the multiple advantages offered by the approach, social scientists will be utilizing the field experiment with increasing frequency in the future (see, for example, Bickman & Henchy, 1972; Reich, 1982).

If you are planning to set up a field experiment, you will need to consider all of the preparations and precautions that apply to naturalistic studies in general. Additionally, you will have to develop a strategy for directly manipulating your independent variable while exercising some control over potential confoundings. Possibly you will be able to employ matched groups, as the Sherifs did, but this isn't likely as the amount of control available to the Sherifs was unusual. It is more likely that your control of confoundings will have to be imposed through randomizing or counterbalancing levels of your independent variable over time and subjects. Let's suppose, for example, that you have 30 time-period/location combinations in a field experiment. If your independent variable has three levels, then you might randomly assign each level to 10 of the 30 combinations. Theoretically, this would "randomize out" potential confoundings due to setting-selection bias, subject-selection bias, and time of measurement effects.

Even though the field experiment can be a very advantageous research tool, no method is free of potential pitfalls and complications. All of the caveats and many of the potential shortcomings that apply to naturalistic observation also apply to field experiments. In addition, the following problems may limit the method's usefulness:

1. Just as some questions are not compatible with laboratory experimentation, many research problems are not open to study through field experimentation. Some restrictions on applicability are purely practical, whereas others represent ethical barriers.
2. The process of variable manipulation in field experiments may increase the probability that the natural conditions will be perceptibly altered and that the observation process will be detected by the subjects.
3. Usually, not all confounding variables can be controlled in a field experiment. Unexpected occurrences in the natural environment, such as a traffic accident or a weather change, can have uneven effects across the various experimental conditions, depending on when and where those occurrences happen.

Thus, the field experiment does not stand by itself as an ultimate solution to the external/internal validity dilemma. Like all other approaches, it must be supplemented by other methods.

PARTICIPANT OBSERVATION

Still another variation on naturalistic observation is **participant observation**. In this method, the observer attempts to assume a natural role within the social situation that she is investigating—to observe group behavior from "the inside out."

For example, if you wished to employ participant observation to study certain behaviors within an industrial setting, you would either actually get a job at the plant or obtain permission to function as an employee for a specified period of time. During that time, you would try to observe the behavior from the vantage point of a group member, while attempting to maintain scientific objectivity.

This approach is especially useful for obtaining detailed information on the personal motives and perceptions of individuals who function within a target group, as well as for gaining insight into the intricate interpersonal mechanisms that operate within social systems. Rosenhan's study of events inside psychiatric hospitals, which was summarized in Chapter 5, is an excellent example of the unique kinds of information obtainable via participant observation.

Participant observation is conducted at various levels of "openness." In some participant-observation studies, virtually all of the subjects know that the observer is occupying a dual role in the setting. This level of openness removes the burden of secrecy and deception from the shoulders of the researcher, but has the disadvantage of possibly causing some observational reactivity. A second level of openness exists when a few key members of the group are aware of the observer's dual role, but keep that knowledge to themselves. The advantage of this arrangement is that the informed individuals usually are powerful figures in the group who sympathize with the objectives of the study and thus have agreed to facilitate the group's acceptance of the observer. The third level of "openness" involves no openness at all: The observer joins the group under false pretenses, informing no one in the group of her purpose. Under these circumstances, the hope is that the group will accept the newcomer, not become suspicious, and hence, continue to behave in their usual fashion.

When Prophecy Fails

The third level of "openness" (complete deception) was employed in a study of a midwestern religious cult which was predicting the imminent end of the world by way of a flood (Festinger, Riecken, & Schachter, 1956). The researchers were almost certain that the world would not end on the designated day and were interested in observing how the cult members would handle the "disappointment." After all, most members had made heavy personal and financial sacrifices on behalf of the cult, with complete faith in the doomsday prophecy that had brought the group together.

To gain entry into the group, the three researchers posed as converts to the cult and participated in many of the activities of the real members. Presumably, little suspicion was aroused, allowing the group to function as they would have in the absence of their newly acquired recruits.

When the cataclysmic flood didn't occur at the appointed time, the cult members were observed to engage in a variety of cognitive and behavioral readjustments. For one thing, many of them were able to convince themselves that the world had been spared by their faith, a belief that was later "verified" by automatic writing on the part of the group's leader. Secondly, the group embarked on a vigorous campaign to recruit still more members for the cult. The researchers interpreted this proselytizing behavior to mean that the members of the cult were attempting to justify their unrequited faith by finding others who would profess the same degree of faith in the cult's purpose.

Evaluating Participant Observation

The principal advantage of participant observation is that it can reveal certain types of inside information about social groups that would not be obtainable through observation from a distance. Nonetheless, there are a number of practical limitations built into this method.

Webb and colleagues (1966) have noted that unless the participant observer joins the group on an incognito basis (i.e., dual role concealed), some degree of observational reactivity is likely to occur. When some group members know that the observer is recording observations, these individuals might very well alter their natural behavior in order to create a particular impression. And, of course, any such reactivity would militate against the purpose of observing in natural contexts.

A second limitation pointed out by Webb concerns the problem of instrument-change confoundings (see Chapter 7). The participant observer, holding certain beliefs or hypotheses, may selectively perceive and remember group events, or may change his method of measuring as familiarity with the group increases. For example, characteristics of individuals or activities that seemed distinct or unusual at first eventually may be perceived as unremarkable and thus fail to receive attention in later analyses. When this instrumentation change occurs, the observer's records tend to give the impression that the group has changed, whereas it is actually the observer who has changed.

Similarly, participant observers often become truly integrated into the group they are studying, at which time personal feelings and identification with the group may distort the data-collection process. For this reason, it is important for participant observers to be constantly aware of their feelings and the potential effects of those feelings.

Still another limitation of the participant-observation method hinges on the difficulty of gaining entry into and acceptance by the group of interest. Groups that are very cohesive or that presently are under threat or duress may be reluctant to assimilate new members, even if the newcomers seem to be legitimate entrants. In such situations, all new members tend to be distrusted or suspected of being spies or infiltrators with some ulterior motive. There are many ways to deal with such suspicion. One strategy, mentioned earlier, is to level with either the whole group or one or more of its influential members in the hope that they will accept and perhaps even promote your goals. Another tactic is to take your chances on an incognito basis, calmly dismiss or laugh off insinuations or accusations regarding your "real" motives for being in the group, and hope that, in time, you will be accepted. In the meantime, you may be able to speed up the acceptance process by befriending a group member who is respected by most of the others. Regardless of how you decide to handle the acceptance problem, observing must be done very discreetly until such time that group members start to feel comfortable in your presence and, thus, lower their vigilance.

ANALYZING DATA FROM SYSTEMATIC OBSERVATION STUDIES

A study is never complete until the data derived from it are organized and analyzed, either logically or statistically, or both. The ideal is to have quantitative data that can be subjected to statistical analysis. As was stated earlier, statistical analysis increases the amount of information you get from empirical investigations by (a) providing a clear and succinct picture of major trends in the data and (b) allowing you to tentatively decide whether it is likely that the data represent something more than chance outcomes. Let's now take a look at how you might organize and analyze data from a systematic observation study.

The Row × Column Contingency Table

If your data are on an ordinal, interval, or ratio scale of measurement (see Chapter 5), then they are in the form of numbers that represent points on a multi-point dimension. In that case, you will need to use one of the statistical procedures described in Chapters 14 and 15. As often as not, however, systematic observation studies yield either narrative data or frequency counts of subjects showing certain traits or behaviors. Consequently, the focus here will be on statistical methods that are applicable to frequency counts organized into categories, *where the categories represent particular combinations of the various levels of two variables measured on nominal scales.*

An example of frequency count data organized in this way is shown in Table 9–2, which represents data from a field experiment reported by Doob and Gross (1968). In that study, an experimental confederate frustrated automobile drivers on a Sunday afternoon by keeping his car at a stoplight for 15 seconds after the light had changed from red to green. There were two levels of the independent variable: High-Status Driver versus Low-Status Driver in the delinquent automobile. The apparent social status of the errant driver was manipulated by varying his attire and the make and condition of his automobile. Doob and Gross wanted to find out if people are less likely to honk their car horns at a sluggish driver when his social status is high than when it is low. Table 9–2 shows the number of automobile operators who responded in each of three ways to the high-status and low-status confederate, respectively.

Note that the two levels of the independent variable are represented by the rows of the table, and the three levels of the dependent variable (i.e., number of honks) are represented by the columns of the table. This kind of data-organizing scheme is called a 2×3 (Rows × Columns, or R × C) *contingency table*: it reveals whether values of the dependent measure are contingent upon levels of the independent variable and provides a basis for a test of statistical significance applicable to nominal data.

The Chi-Square Test

Purpose and Use. The test of statistical significance that is most commonly applied to frequency counts is the **chi-square statistic** (symbolized χ^2). A significant chi square means that the two variables represented in the table are more strongly related than would be expected on the basis of chance alone. The essence of the chi-square test is a comparison of the frequency counts actually obtained in a study with a set of frequencies expected on the basis of random variation alone. The latter frequencies are formally referred to as "expected" or "theoretical" frequencies, and each expected frequency is symbolized by f_e. If the *observed* frequencies (f_o) differ considerably from the expected (chance) frequencies (f_e), then χ^2 will be large. If χ^2 is sufficiently large, then it will exceed a *critical* χ^2, which is the value of χ^2 derived from a mathematical theory of random variation (see Chapter 8). Accordingly, you would declare your data to be more than a product of random variation—that is, statistically significant.

The *critical*, chance χ^2 for any contingency table can be found in Table A–2 of the Appendix. The appropriate critical value is a function of the level of significance you are using—we'll use the .05 level here—and the number of "degrees of freedom" in your

TABLE 9–2

Number of Frustrated Drivers Honking Car Horns Once, Twice, or Not At All (data from Doob & Gross, 1968)

	Number of Honks		
Status of Frustrator	*0*	*1*	*2*
Low Status	6	14	18
High Status	18	11	7

contingency table. When a chi-square test is applied to a contingency table, *degrees of freedom* refers to the number of cells in which the frequencies are "free to vary" once you have computed the row totals and the column totals. For the time being, I'll simply ask you to take the following statement on faith: The degrees of freedom in an $R \times C$ contingency table will always equal (number of Rows $- 1$) $\times$ (number of Columns $- 1$), or $(R - 1) \times (C - 1)$.

In this example,

$$
\begin{aligned}
df &= (2 - 1) \times (3 - 1) \\
&= \quad 1 \quad \times \quad 2 \\
&= 2
\end{aligned}
$$

If you consult Table A–2 and combine the .05 level of significance with 2 degrees of freedom, you'll find that the critical χ^2 needed for statistical significance in this problem is 5.99.

The Null Hypothesis.   One way of expressing the null hypothesis in a chi-square test is to state that observed frequencies will not differ from the expected frequencies by more than could be attributed to random variation. Symbolically, you might express the null hypothesis this way:

H_0: $F_0 = F_e$, where

H_0 is a symbol for the null hypothesis

The alternative, or research, hypothesis is then expressed as:

H_1: $F_0 \neq F_e$

These are shorthand expressions of the null and alternative hypotheses. They have to be taken with a grain of salt, since the observed frequencies would almost never be exactly equal to the expected frequencies, even when only chance is operating. In any case, remember that in a test of significance, it is the null hypothesis that you are actually testing and that you hope to reject (see Chapter 8).

Computing Chi Square.   The computational formula for χ^2 is:

$\chi^2 = \Sigma[(f_0 - f_e)^2/f_e]$, where
χ^2 is the symbol for chi square
Σ means add up the bracketed values
f_0 = observed frequency
f_e = expected frequency

The summation symbol (Σ) is well known to you by now. The bracketed expression is the crux of the formula. It simply means that for *each cell* in a contingency table, you are to (1) subtract the expected frequency from the observed frequency, then (2) square the difference, then (3) divide the squared difference by the cell's expected frequency. Once you have run through these three steps *for each cell in the table*, you can easily get χ^2 by adding up the results of step (3).

Table 9–3 is an abstract version of the contingency table from the Doob and Gross study (Table 9–2). Note that the rows represent independent variable A (with two levels,

TABLE 9–3

Observed Frequencies

Variable A	Variable B			Row Totals
	B1	*B2*	*B3*	
A1 (Row 1)	(A1B1) 6	(A1B2) 14	(A1B3) 18	38
A2 (Row 2)	(A2B1) 18	(A2B2) 11	(A2B3) 7	36
Column Totals	24	25	25	74 = *Grand Total*

A1 and A2), and the columns represent dependent variable B (with three levels, B1, B2, and B3). Also note that each cell represents a combination of one level of A with one level of B. Only the *observed frequencies* appear in Table 9–3.

The expected frequencies are given in Table 9–4. To get the expected frequency for any cell in a contingency table, use this formula:

f_e = [(Row Total) × (Column Total)]/Grand Total, where
Row Total = Sum of frequencies for the row that the cell is in,
Column Total = Sum of frequencies for the column that the cell is in, and
Grand Total = n, the total number of observations in the table (n = 74 in this example)

Thus:

f_e of cell A1B1 = [(Total of Row 1) × (Total of Column 1)]/n
= [(38) × (24)]/74
= 912/74
= 12.32

and:

f_e of cell A1B2 = [(Total of Row 1) × (Total of Column 2)]/n
= [(38) × (25)]/74
= 950/74
= 12.84

TABLE 9–4

Expected Frequencies

Variable A	Variable B			Row Totals
	B1	*B2*	*B3*	
A1 (Row 1)	(A1B1) 12.32	(A1B2) 12.84	(A1B3) 12.84	38
A2 (Row 2)	(A2B1) 11.68	(A2B2) 12.16	(A2B3) 12.16	36
Column Totals	24	25	25	74 = *Grand Total*

An important point to remember is that the *expected frequencies in a row of the contingency table must sum to the row total.* You can get the expected frequency of cell A1B3 through a process of subtraction:

$$f_e \text{ for cell A1B3} = (\text{Total of Row 1}) - (f_e \text{ of cell A1B1}) - (f_e \text{ of cell A1B2})$$
$$= 38 - 12.32 - 12.84$$
$$= 12.84$$

Likewise, *expected frequencies in a given column must sum to the column total.* Therefore:

$$f_e \text{ for cell A2B1} = (\text{Total of Column 1}) - (f_e \text{ of cell A1B1})$$
$$= 24 - 12.32$$
$$= 11.68$$

To verify the remaining expected frequencies in Table 9–4, use the subtraction method to obtain f_e for cells A2B2 and A2B3. *Note that even though the table has six cells, you had to calculate the expected frequencies of only two cells.* Because the row and column totals were fixed, the remaining four expected frequencies were not free to vary and therefore could be found through subtraction. This is precisely what is meant by the idea that the table has only two "degrees of freedom."

To complete the computation of χ^2, it is best to set up a *worksheet,* such as that shown in Table 9–5. Notice that each row in the worksheet represents one cell of the contingency table, and that each column represents a step in computing χ^2. Thus, for cell A1B1, (1) $f_o = 6$, (2) $f_e = 12.32$, (3) $(f_o - f_e) = -6.32$, (4) $(f_o - f_e)^2 = 39.94$, and (5) $(f_o - f_e)^2/\text{fe} = 3.24$.

After you go through these steps for each of the six cells, sum the figures in the last column. That sum $= \chi^2$; in this example, $\chi^2 = 11.13$.

Since the obtained χ^2 of 11.13 is greater than the critical (chance) χ^2 of 5.99, you would reject the null hypothesis and assert that frequency of horn honking is significantly related to social status of the delinquent driver: High-status drivers are honked at less than low-status drivers.

Finding the Strength of Relationship

Now that we know that the data are statistically significant, let's use a simple formula to compute the linear correlation (Pearson r) between the two variables in this study. This

TABLE 9–5

Chi-Square Worksheet

Cell	f_o	f_e	$(f_o - f_e)$	$(f_o - f_e)^2$	$[(f_o - f_e)^2/f_e]$
A1B1	6	12.32	−6.32	39.94	3.24
A1B2	14	12.84	1.16	1.35	.10
A1B3	18	12.84	5.16	26.63	2.07
A2B1	18	11.68	6.32	39.94	3.42
A2B2	11	12.16	−1.16	1.35	.11
A2B3	7	12.16	−5.16	26.63	2.19

$$\text{Sum} = 11.13 = \chi^2$$

correlation coefficient provides information on how strongly the two variables are related to one another. When used with contingency tables, r is called the *phi* coefficient.

Small Tables (1 or 2 Degrees of Freedom).   For 2×2, 2×3, or 3×2 contingency tables,

$$r = \text{phi} = \sqrt{\chi^2/n}, \text{ where}$$
$$n = \text{the grand total}$$

In this example:

$$\text{phi} = \sqrt{11.13/74}$$
$$= \sqrt{.15}$$
$$= .39$$

Thus, though the relationship between the variables is significant, its strength is only "weak to moderate." The proportion of variance in horn honking accounted for by status is phi^2, or $(.39)^2 = .15$ (refer to Chapter 6).

Larger Tables (More Than 2 Degrees of Freedom).   For 3×3 or larger contingency tables, the linear correlation is computed by the formula

$$\text{phi} = \sqrt{\chi^2/[n(L - 1)]}, \text{ where}$$
$$n = \text{the Grand Total, and}$$
$$L = \text{the number of rows } or \text{ the number of columns, whichever is } smaller \text{ (Hays, 1981)}$$

Restrictions on the Use of Chi Square

The application of any statistical procedure is limited by the assumptions of the mathematical model that underlies the procedure. This means that it is legitimate to use a chi-square test on your frequency counts only if you are confident that your data meet the fundamental assumptions of the chi-square model.

These assumptions are:

1. That every observation in the contingency table is *independent* of every other observation in the table. In practice, this usually means that *each person in your study can be represented in only one cell of the table*. If the same person contributes an "entry" to more than one cell, then it is not likely that those entries are independent of one another. Therefore, if person P serves in both condition A1 and condition A2, then the conventional chi-square test probably wouldn't be appropriate for those data. (See Hays, 1981, or Meyers & Grossen, 1978, for some alternatives to chi square.)

2. That when your contingency table has only one degree of freedom, no cell should have an *expected* frequency of less than 10; when the degrees of freedom equal two or more, then the expected frequency of each cell should be at least 5 (Hays, 1981).

Actually, the second assumption has been shown to be too conservative in many cases. Computer simulations of chi-square experiments suggest that the chi-square model is adequately fitted in most cases where your grand total (n) for the contingency table is at least *four* times larger than the number of cells in the table—that is, $n/(R \times C) \geq 4$—even when some of the expected values are well below 5 (cf. Faraone, 1982). Thus, if you had at least 16 observations in a 2×2 table, you'd probably be safe using chi square.

SUMMARY

Some questions asked by social and psychological researchers are difficult or impossible to study through the more obtrusive methods of science, such as the experiment or the survey. To gather data relevant to such questions, researchers may employ some variety of *systematic observation*. These techniques include *naturalistic observation, participant observation*, and the *field experiment*. All of these techniques have the advantage of high external validity.

In naturalistic observation, the researcher unobtrusively records the behavior of unaware subjects in their natural environment. Steps involved in the planning of a naturalistic-observation investigation include: deciding what variables and behaviors to study, developing data-recording techniques, developing a sampling strategy, and training observers. Two approaches to unobtrusive observation in naturalistic studies are "blending in" with the subjects and "hiding" from them. Also, special surveillance devices, such as videotape cameras, may sometimes be employed.

If it is too difficult or inconvenient to study behavior in a natural environment, it may be possible to set up a *facsimile* (simulation) of a natural environment, as is often done in the observation of animal behavior.

The major drawbacks of naturalistic observation include relatively low internal validity, difficulties in quantifying some types of observations, the unwieldy amount of data often yielded, and certain ethical problems.

In a field experiment, the setting is a natural environment, confoundings are controlled, and an independent variable is systematically manipulated. The field experiment, if properly conducted, has both high internal validity and high external validity.

In participant observation, the observer attempts to assume a natural role within the social situation that she is investigating. This approach is valuable for gaining insight into the interpersonal mechanisms that govern a social system.

There are many ways to analyze the data of systematic observation studies. If the data are in the form of *frequency counts* organized within a *contingency table*, then the *chi-square test* of significance usually is applied. This technique was described and illustrated in this chapter.

REVIEW QUESTIONS

1. State the major similarities and differences among naturalistic observation, participant observation, and the field experiment.

2. Design a replication of the Glenwick et al. study of singles-bar patrons; try to improve on the original procedure, giving special attention to the sampling of places, times, and subjects.

3. What are the principal questions that must be asked and answered in the planning stages of naturalistic research?

4. Compare and contrast the "hiding" and "blending-in" strategies of unobtrusive observation. With what kinds of research problem would hiding be preferable to blending in? Describe two or more types of research problems that would not be amenable to the hiding strategy.

5. What are the rationale and purpose of the field experiment? What specific provisions would you have to make to transform a naturalistic-observation study into a field experiment?

6. Summarize the advantages and possible pitfalls of participant observation.

7. Define or describe: specimen record, behavior setting, facsimile environment, area sampling, time sampling, Row × Column table, data-recording sheet.

8. Perform a chi-square analysis on the data obtained in the students' study of book-carrying styles; also, compute the phi coefficient. Were the results significant? If so, how strong was the relationship between the variables?

9. Summarize the purpose, use, and assumptions of chi square.

Note

[1]Although this study is being cited for illustrative purposes only, it would be unfair to ignore certain inherent limitations of the researchers' methods. First, the same people both rated the subjects' attractiveness and approached the subjects to ascertain their receptiveness to overtures from men. This method certainly would be vulnerable to a "self-fulfilling prophecy" effect. Second, the men who tested the subjects' receptiveness obviously were a limited, nonprobability sample (n = 2). Therefore, we cannot assume that the same subjects would have reacted in the same way to a different sample of "interested" men.

10

SINGLE-CASE RESEARCH

In a 1970 issue of *The International Journal of Social Psychiatry*, clinical psychologist Lawrence Simkins made a timely, if disturbing, observation about his field:

> It would seem that clinical psychology historically was an off-shoot of experimental psychology and as such was nurtured and controlled by an academic surrogate. The baby grew up and despite out-breaks of rebellion was always brought back into line again. In the meantime, the baby has gotten bigger and bigger but his academic parents still insist that he wear the same experimental clothes. (p. 180)

This statement, which more or less summarizes the gist of Simkins's article, refers to a reality that is often ignored or glossed over in the field of psychology: Though they are thoroughly trained in experimental methodology while in graduate school, the majority of clinical psychologists don't conduct conventional experiments in their day-to-day work. Nor do most counseling psychologists. The reason for this, of course, is that most clinical and counseling psychologists function primarily as service-oriented professionals rather than as researchers. And it often is considered unethical or infeasible to carry out well-controlled experiments with clients who have come to a psychologist's office for the sole purpose of receiving psychotherapy. After all, how many suffering individuals would knowingly pay $50 to $100 per hour to serve in a control or "placebo" group (even if determined by random assignment)? Apart from this ethical issue, there is the additional problem of controlling extraneous variables in the clients' lives that may confound a conventional experimental design.

Yet, as Simkins pointed out later in his article, it is important that service-oriented psychologists systematically collect data on their clients. How else could they evaluate the effectiveness, or lack thereof, of the techniques they use to help people cope with personal problems? In addition to the latter point, a review of psychology's history reveals that some of the great theories of personality and psychopathology were developed on the basis of clinical observations (cf. Hall & Lindzey, 1970). Thus it is indeed important for psychologists in the "service" areas of the profession to be data oriented, to do research, to accumulate evidence, and to critically evaluate that evidence.

It remains true that many of the research methods that academic and research psychologists take for granted and use daily are simply not appropriate for the counselor's or clinician's situation. So what methodological options are available to those professionals? Given that counselors and clinicians tend often to work with individuals more than with groups, the practical options fall into two related approaches: the **case study** and the **single-case experiment**.

The case study is an intensive investigation of the current and past behaviors and experiences of a *person* or an *organization*. The objective of the case study is to discover relationships between past events and present behaviors and experiences of the subject. Knowledge about such past-to-present relationships may be used to gain theoretical understanding or to solve practical problems in the subject's life, or both.

The single-case experiment is similar to the case study in its focus on the individual, but the similarity ends there. The single-case experiment tends to be much less oriented toward events in the subject's history; rather, the focus is on perhaps just two or three variables that are relevant to the subject's present and future functioning. In addition, the single-case experiment provides for the control and manipulation of variables, features that simply aren't part of a conventional case study. In a general sense, the single-case experiment represents a "hybrid method" designed to combine the advantages of the controlled experiment with those of the case study while sidestepping some of the disadvantages of each.

This chapter covers both the case study and the single-case experiment. By mastering the material, you will develop an appreciation of the uses and limitations of each method.

Before we get into the particulars, however, let's look at some additional reasons that single-case research techniques remain an important part of the psychologist's research armamentarium, even in an age when "group" research is the clear norm.

THE CASE FOR THE SINGLE CASE

The practical reasons for using the single-case approach in applied settings have already been discussed. There are also theoretical justifications for conducting single-case research rather than gathering data via methods that rely on large groups of subjects. It has been argued, for instance, that the case study may be the *only possible way* to investigate certain theories that were built upon clinical-case data (cf. Hilgard, 1962; Mujeeb-ur-Rahman, 1977). This position frequently has been taken in reference to tests of Freud's psychoanalytic theory. In presenting reasons for investigating psychoanalytic concepts exclusively through the case study, Mujeeb-ur-Rahman makes the following points:

1. The "subjective character" of psychoanalysis is not amenable to the conventional methods of science.
2. Psychoanalysis focuses on powerful emotional and motivational systems, such as sex, anxiety, aggression, and irrationality, all of which would prove difficult to manage in a laboratory.
3. A considerable number of psychoanalytic concepts are based on unobservable or unconscious processes that presently cannot be translated into convenient empirical definitions.

With regard to Mujeeb-ur-Rahman's third point, it has indeed proved difficult to operationalize "repression" in the context of experimental research (see Arkes & Garske, 1982). One might also expect to have "translation" problems in attempts to experimentally test concepts from several other clinically based personality theories, such as Jung's "Analytical Psychology," Adler's "Individual Psychology," and the "existential" models (see Hall & Lindzey, 1970). Perhaps the intensive case study would be the only reasonable way to assess and modify theories of this type.

A second frequently encountered argument for employing a single-case approach to research with human beings is that case studies reveal the richness, uniqueness, and complexity of the individual personality. By contrast, most other methods of research ignore or avoid these issues (see Allport, 1961). For example, it's useful to know that IQ is significantly correlated with many important traits and behaviors, such as grades in school, occupational level, health, and personal adjustment (Terman, 1925). But what do correlations based on group data tell us about Robert, a college sophomore who has an IQ of 157, was abandoned by his parents at the age of three, presently has a horrible self-concept, dislikes clinical psychologists, and is flunking out of college? Perhaps only an intensive study of Robert would help us—and Robert—to understand how these various facts fit together.

A third basis of support for single-case research stems from an often cited deficiency in traditional group experiments aimed at evaluating the effectiveness of psychological procedures. Suppose, for example, that you wish to test the effectiveness of psychological counseling as a device for relieving mild depression. If you used the traditional experimental approach, you would randomly assign half of your depressed subjects to a "treatment" group and administer the counseling to them. The remaining subjects would serve in an untreated control or "placebo" group. Putting aside some possible methodological

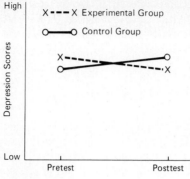

FIGURE 10–1

Results of a Hypothetical Pretest-Posttest Experiment on the Effectiveness of a Counseling Procedure in the Treatment of Depression

Note: Lower scores on the measure of depression represent less depression.

flaws in the procedure, let's further suppose that you pretest and posttest each group with some reliable measure of depression. If you actually carried out such a study, you might well obtain results such as those shown in Figure 10–1.

The data in Figure 10–1 represent hypothetical *group averages* on the pretest and post-test measures. Note that there is virtually no change from pretest to posttest in either group, and that the group means don't differ appreciably from one another. Based on group data alone, then, you would conclude that the counseling had no effect.

If you looked at how *individuals* fared in each condition, however, you might find results such as those shown in Figures 10–2 and 10–3. Figure 10–2 reveals that two of the four clients who received counseling did improve appreciably; that is, their depression scores declined from pretest to posttest. One client was unchanged, and client 4 got considerably worse. It was his large negative change that, in the *group* data, canceled out the positive effects of counseling shown by clients 1 and 2, and thereby made the treatment appear ineffective. By contrast, none of the control-group subjects changed much at all across testings.

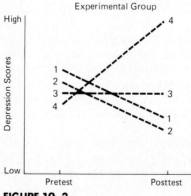

FIGURE 10–2

Results for Individual Subjects in the Experimental Group (n = 4)

Note: Each pretest-posttest function represents the results for one subject; each subject is identified by a number.

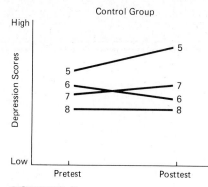

FIGURE 10–3

Results for Individual Subjects in the Control Group (n = 4)

Note: Each pretest-posttest function represents the results for one subject; each subject is identified by a number.

The point of this illustration is that group data, such as those obtained from conventional experiments, often conceal *interactions* between individuals and the treatment (Hersen & Barlow, 1976). However, if single-case experiments are used instead of group experiments for testing treatment effectiveness, then the effect of the treatment on each person can be assessed. Thus, it can be argued that the single-case experiment provides a fairer and more practical test of psychological procedures than do group experiments. Moreover, when it is found that treatments interact with individuals, further single-case research can be employed to determine what specific variables within a person's background are associated with a positive or negative response to the procedure. Theoretically, the end result of this approach would be that the practitioner would gain a considerable amount of information concerning which specific procedures are likely to work best with particular individuals (see Hersen & Barlow, 1976).

Several other functions of single-case research that recommend its use for specific purposes are described in the next section.

THE CASE STUDY

Uses of the Case Study

Demonstrating Unusual or Unique Phenomena.   No method of psychological research excels the case study when the purpose is to demonstrate or document rare or sensational phenomena. An example of this comes from an investigation of a pair of identical twins who had been separated within a few weeks after birth and didn't renew their acquaintance until the age of thirty-nine (Jackson, 1980).

Although both of the twins grew up in Ohio, they had been adopted and raised by different families and were not aware of each other's existence. When they were finally reunited as thirty-nine-year-old men, they were amazed to discover a number of remarkable similarities in their lives. Both had been named James by their adoptive families. Both Jims preferred Miller's Lite beer. The first wives of both men had the name of Linda, and the second wives of both were Bettys. Each had a son named James Alan, and both men had a dog named Toy. A psychologist tested the twins and discovered that their attitude and personality profiles were virtually identical. The coincidences continued: Both men enjoyed woodworking as a hobby, had served as sheriff's deputies, chain-smoked, chewed their fingernails, and drove Chevrolets. They could have swapped medical histories without affecting the content in either case. Each twin lived in a home that was the only house on the block. Both men's yards contained a white bench around a large tree.

This remarkable case study raised some tantalizing questions about the relative roles of heredity and environment in shaping people's lives. It is interesting because it is unique and sensational, and because it *suggests* that genetic factors can be an overwhelming determiner of lifestyles. But there are dangers built into this particular use of case studies: Individual illustrative cases can exploit very rare coincidences and create the erroneous impression that some general law of behavior has been discovered. How would you test the generality of the kind of findings that emerged from the study of the two Jims?

Demonstrating a Procedure.   The case study is often the method of choice for demonstrating the implementation and effects of a practical procedure. The work of French neurologist Jean Martin Charcot, carried out in the nineteenth century, provided many examples of this application of the case study (Reisman, 1966). Charcot believed that most neurotic symptoms were the product of "self-hypnosis" in hysterical people. To demonstrate to other physicians the effect of hypnotic suggestion on symptoms, he would select a good specimen of hysteria from his roster of patients, hypnotize the patient, and then suggest that the patient had certain afflictions. Characteristically, the patient would quickly develop the appropriate symptoms—perhaps a paralysis or a crying spell. Often during the same demonstration, Charcot would use hypnotic suggestion to remove the symptoms that he had earlier created.

Generating New Hypotheses.   Among research psychologists, the most widely recognized function of case studies is that of generating hypotheses. Hypotheses suggested through this means can often be translated into operational definitions that permit tests of the hypotheses by way of more rigorous research methods, such as the experiment.

Piaget's case-study research on cognitive development in children is an excellent example of the fruitfulness of the single-case approach as a source of research hypotheses. Through careful observation of each of his own children, Piaget was able to develop a comprehensive theory of intellectual change and growth. Today, Piaget's concepts and hypotheses are the focal points of a considerable amount of experimental research on cognitive development (see Navarick, 1979, Chapter 8).

Commenting on the contributions made by Piaget's case studies, Oppenheimer (1956) wrote:

> I have been immensely impressed by the work of one man . . . , Jean Piaget. When you look at his work, his statistics really consist of one or two cases. It is just a start; and yet I think he has added greatly to our understanding. It is not that I am sure he is right, but he has given us something worthy of which to enquire whether it is right. . . . (p. 132)

Theory Building.   Dozens of well-known psychological theories have been built upon case studies. I have already mentioned Piaget's theory. In addition, most of the classic theories of personality and psychotherapy that have been so thought provoking and useful to psychologists were the conceptual offspring of intensive investigations of individuals.

Disconfirming Generalities.   Although many important psychological theories have evolved from case studies, the case study, for reasons which will be discussed later, is not a very efficient method for establishing the validity of theoretical propositions. Nonetheless, a single case can be employed to *invalidate* general theoretical propositions, especially if such propositions are meant to apply universally.

A brief review of the demise of a theory of speech perception will illustrate this use of case studies. From the 1930s through the 1950s, several theorists working in the field of psycholinguistics held to a *motor theory* of speech perception. Very simply, the theory stated that a person can understand speech only by relating speech sounds to sensations associated with the muscle movements of his own speech apparatus. Thus, to understand a particular speech sound, you would have to have made the same sound yourself on some prior occasion (cf. Neisser, 1966). The implication of this theory is that people who have never made speech sounds could not possibly understand the spoken word. The generality of this theory was disconfirmed by a case study of an eight-year-old boy who, due to a "neurological deficit," had never uttered a word. Despite his complete lack of speaking experience, however, he understood speech sounds (Lenneberg, 1962).

Doing Case Studies

Although the case-study method is conceptually simple, actually doing a case study is a complicated task that requires both expertise and planning. Some of the most important items for consideration include:

1. deciding on the purpose of your study and what variables and behaviors you will focus on
2. selecting a target population
3. planning what sources and types of data you will utilize
4. planning a data-recording procedure

The "expertise" referred to above is most important in the matters of collating and interpreting your findings. It is particularly important to develop skill in using the **method of internal consistency**, a device that serves to cross-check various inferences and lines of evidence against one another. This will be discussed later in this chapter.

Deciding on Purpose, Variables, and Behaviors.   As true for all methods of research, the first step in conducting a case study is to develop a clear conception of the study's purpose. This is important because the main objective of the study will influence other decisions, such as selection of variables, target behaviors, and the target population.

If, for example, your aim is to look for evidence that might disconfirm a theoretical proposition, then the nature of that proposition will determine the specific class of behavior that you focus on. Likewise, if you intend to gather information for the express purpose of solving a client's practical problem, such as poor worker productivity, you will need to decide whether the real problem is one of morale, communication, or motivation before you select a set of variables to work with.

Other kinds of objectives, such as theory construction, require a more open-ended, inductive type of data collection. When theory construction is the goal, very often broad classes of variables are selected initially and then progressively narrowed down as the individual cases are worked through. Piaget's (1963) observations of problem-solving behavior in children fit into this category of single-case research. Piaget started his research with the objective of finding out how the general biological concepts of *adaptation* and *organization* apply to a child's intellectual development. As he began to accumulate observations on each of his cases, the data suggested to him that there were two general variables within the cognitive adaptation process:

1. *assimilation*, defined as the process of incorporating new experiences into existing knowledge structures
2. *accommodation*, defined as the process of changing existing knowledge structures to fit new experiences

Still later observations suggested that the assimilation process evolves through a sequence of four stages that are correlated with biological maturation. Each stage, in turn, was found to be characterized by its own set of variables and events.

Selecting a Target Population.   To the extent that the purpose of your case study includes reaching general conclusions about a phenomenon, it will be necessary for you to consider what population is represented by your "case" or sample of cases. If your subject is a person with a history of obsessive-compulsive symptoms, generalizing your findings beyond chronic obsessive-compulsives may not be either wise or warranted. If the subject is also still in his teens, then your generalizations may be limited to young obsessive-compulsives. In fact, if you work with only that case, and do not attempt replications with other persons reporting similar problems, then one might well question whether the data apply to anyone other than *the* subject. Freud's psychoanalytic theory is a case in point. A major criticism of Freud's theory is that his "sample" consisted largely of neurotic women who had been raised within a repressive system of Victorian morality. Although Freud reached general conclusions about the effects of people's sexual and aggressive problems, the population represented by his patients probably was much narrower than "people in general."

The latitude you have for generalizing will also depend on the nature of the processes and variables you investigate. For example, Piaget examined general problem-solving behaviors in young children. Despite the fact that his sample consisted of just two subjects (see Piaget, 1963), the behaviors he studied were so fundamental in child development that a certain degree of generalization to other normal children within the same age range was permissible—subject, as always, to later verification with other children.

Sources and Types of Data.   Many people think that interviews with and observation of the subject are the only sources of data in case studies. But there are several additional sources that may be tapped to increase the breadth of your data base.

If you are compiling a clinical-type case history, psychological tests may serve as useful data-generating devices. And don't overlook *personal documents*. Subjects who are cooperative and reasonably literate may be willing to write an autobiography for you or provide you with copies of diaries and personal letters—either those written by the subject to significant others or those sent to the subject by significant others (cf. Janis et al., 1969). These documents might reveal important events in the subject's life, or perhaps indicate her dominant values, needs, or concerns.

Also bear in mind that it is sometimes possible to interview friends and relatives of the subject, in order to obtain information that would validate the subject's recollections about her past. However, this latter data source should be used only with the subject's voluntary consent and written permission.

The data of case studies are most often in the form of narrative (i.e., written) summaries of significant observations, relationships, and inferences. But with some ingenuity and resolve on your part, it would be possible to compile some quantitative information as well, such as the frequency of self-assertive statements or the number of statements that refer to particular events in the subject's life.

Recording Data.   Because the intensive investigation of an individual or an organization is a complex undertaking, it is of little value to the investigator to make a mental note of a significant observation in a case study without also entering that note into a permanent record. Events, statements, and apparently important relationships between events quickly pile up and overload even the best of human memories. To avoid loss of significant data, then, your observations should be recorded in a permanent file as soon as possible. Furthermore, you should carefully document these records as to date, time, place, and participants.

Ideally, observations would be recorded as they are made, but many practitioners feel, as Freud did, that note-taking can be distracting to both the case researcher and the subject. The usual alternative to immediate recording is to rely on your memory until you have the opportunity to record the observations—at the earliest time on the same day that the observations are made.

Some single-case researchers find that tape-recording an interview with the subject is less distracting than note-taking; also, tapes provide a very reliable record of what occurred. However, this means of recording observations should be used only with the prior consent of the subject.

The Method of Internal Consistency.   Once you've compiled an interesting set of facts on a particular case, how do you go about organizing the data, extracting relationships between variables, and interpreting those relationships? Many case researchers rely on the **method of internal consistency** for helping them to derive conclusions from their data. Mujeeb-ur-Rahman (1977) describes the technique in the following way: "This method involves the continuous and repeated crosschecking of inferences drawn from evidence based on the many different aspects of the behavior of the [subject] . . . until the many facts and inferences fall into a coherent and meaningful pattern" (p. 14).

Let's look at how Kerckhoff and Back (1968) used the method of internal consistency to investigate the puzzling case of an apparent epidemic of sudden illness among employees of a clothing-manufacturing plant.

One afternoon in June 1962, plant officials at Montana Mills (fictitious name) had to close their plant. Eleven of their employees were admitted to a hospital for treatment of various symptoms, including nausea and a rash that covered their bodies. The affected workers believed that they were suffering from the bites of tiny insects that allegedly had been brought into the plant in a shipment of cloth from England. Before the epidemic subsided, 62 employees had been victimized by "the bug." But the puzzling aspect of this epidemic was that entomologists and state health officials who were called to the scene couldn't find any evidence of the mysterious insects.

After a thorough examination of the evidence, including psychological evaluations of the affected employees, Kerckhoff and Back concluded that the symptoms had been a physical manifestation of psychological stress—a type of defense mechanism that allowed the affected employees to deal with an anxiety-evoking situation. The researchers used the term "hysterical contagion" to label the phenomenon. This label reflected the fact that the physical reaction fitted the classic psychoanalytic model of hysterical "conversion reactions," and the fact that the reaction was socially contagious within a particular group of employees.

To arrive at this conclusion, the researchers cross-checked a number of items bearing on the outbreak. The following data fell into an internally consistent pattern:

1. The affected individuals interacted in a setting characterized by an ongoing atmosphere of *unresolved tension*. Though the working conditions and pay at Montana Mills were very good, the plant was new; communication channels,

expectations, and work procedures were not yet clear to the employees. The ambiguity of the situation generated considerable apprehension and anxiety, and, at the same time, the plant was so new that the employees had not yet developed a generally accepted method of dealing with work-related anxiety.

2. Sixty-one of the 62 affected employees worked on the *first shift and in the same department*—dressmaking. Since group hysteria is "transmitted" via a social network, this observation was consistent with the hypothesis that the outbreak was psychogenic in origin.

3. In line with the hysterical contagion hypothesis, employees who became sick had closer social relationships with one another than those who were not affected. This supported the notion that the outbreak traveled along social channels.

4. Eighty percent of the "victims" developed symptoms within two consecutive days. Group hysteria travels fast, much faster than most crawling or hopping insects could.

5. At the time of the outbreak, the dressmaking department had experienced increased pressure to produce. June, the month of the epidemic, is a *critical month* for producing fall fashions for women. Consequently, employees in the dressmaking department frequently had been asked, on short notice, to put in long overtime hours.

6. The characteristics of the affected employees suggested a special vulnerability to a hysterical outbreak. Compared to the other employees, the victims had worked more overtime, had less faith in their supervisors, were more likely to have small children at home, and exhibited "psychological profiles" that favored the development of conversion reactions—for example, denial coupled with psychological naiveté.

This example of the method of internal consistency shows how different sources and types of data may be integrated, through systematic cross-checking, to yield a coherent picture of a "case." But note that the cross-checking process wasn't entirely inductive; rather, it was guided by the researchers' *theory* about the nature of the phenomenon under examination. Indeed, researchers usually use this method within some theoretical framework (see Janis et al., 1969, pp. 628–629), which helps them make sense out of the relationships supported by the cross-checking process. As you will see in the next section, however, theories can also be cognitive straitjackets when they lead to *selective* gathering of evidence in a case study.

Evaluating the Case Study

We have considered the advantages and uses of the case-study method. Now let's consider its limitations and possible pitfalls.

Beware of "Operation Bootstrap."   The most common misuse of case studies occurs when the case researcher selectively perceives and records evidence that supports his theoretical assumptions and expectations, while ignoring instances of counterevidence. This is easy to do when you use only the case-study method to build and test a theory. Why? Because case studies, in general, tend to be open-ended and subjectively conducted; little control is exercised, and there may be considerable selectivity involved in the procurement of subjects and in decisions about what questions to ask and what observations to record. Thus, if a researcher believes strongly enough in his assumptions and hypotheses, it is almost always easy to pick out subjects and behaviors that conform to theoretical expectations. Unexpected behaviors may be perceived as unimportant "exceptions" or may be selectively forgotten. In the end, the researcher has a neat package of internally consistent assumptions, hypotheses, and results. But theoretical expectations have determined what observations were recorded and emphasized and, in turn, those observations are used to validate the expectations that led to their being selected—kind of like "pulling yourself up by your bootstraps."

The Reliability of Case-Study Data.   The usefulness of case-study data has been questioned on several grounds. One problem is that most case-study data are subjective, narrative accounts rather than quantitative indices. It is difficult to evaluate the reliability of narrative data, but the consensus among research psychologists is that such data probably are much less reliable than frequency counts of target behaviors and objective-test scores. One source of unreliability in narrative data is the inherent lack of precision in written language. Another factor contributing to error is the tendency of case researchers to use impressionistic statements that mean different things to different readers.

A second general reason for distrusting case-study accounts is that their accuracy is limited by human memory. First, the subject's memory is tapped in order to obtain historical information that pertains to the problem under examination. Then the researcher records his own recollections of the subject's recollections. Hence, it is possible for memory errors to enter at two levels in the data-collection process.

The Generality of Case-Study Data.   As was pointed out earlier, case studies tend to have limited external validity. This restriction is especially serious if the purpose of a study is to discover general laws of behavior. Not only is the sample size equal to one, but also the subjects of most case studies are selected for intensive examination precisely because they have a particular type of problem or characteristic that sets them apart from the general population. Therefore, case studies generally tend to have a built-in limitation on their external validity.

One feasible remedy for this shortcoming is to perform "replications" of a case study with as wide a range of subjects as practical considerations permit. Another approach to the external validity problem is to supplement case studies with other methods of data collection that are applicable to the question of interest and, at the same time, compatible with adequate sampling procedures.

The Case Study and Criteria of Causality.   The general problem of determining causality was discussed in Chapter 4. Perhaps you remember that the three principal criteria of causality are:

1. *covariation:* If X causes Y, then Y must be correlated with X
2. *time precedence:* If X causes Y, then X must always occur before Y
3. *nonspuriousness:* To assert that X causes Y, you must be able to rule out plausible rival hypotheses, such as Z causes X and Y to covary, but X has no influence on Y

To what extent can case-study data be used to satisfy these criteria? Often it isn't difficult to verify conditions of covariation and time precedence within the context of a case study, but it would rarely be possible to satisfy the nonspuriousness criterion on the basis of a case study.

Suppose, for example, that a clinical psychologist working with a depressed client decides to use a newly developed psychotherapeutic technique to help alleviate his client's suffering. The client is very dejected before the treatment is applied. But once therapy has

been under way for a few weeks, the therapist notes that the client's mood and voice in-
flection are starting to perk up. The client is also talking more, and reports a better appetite. Further, the frequency of somatic complaints is decreasing. All things considered,
the therapist concludes that the therapy was effective in bringing about a "recovery."

In this example, the data do provide evidence of covariation: Before the new therapy
was applied, there was little improvement, but after it was applied there was much improvement. In addition, since the beginning of the therapeutic procedure preceded the
client's positive change, the criterion of time precedence is also satisfied. But how convinced are you that the procedure was the cause of the change? Are there many plausible
rival hypotheses that would explain the results? The fact is that a single case study, such as
the one described above, fails to control for a number of the possible confoundings that
were reviewed in Chapter 7. In the above example, instrumentation changes, maturation
effects, the subject's "history," or regression effects could have been responsible for the
observed changes. There simply weren't any provisions for controlling or assessing these
influences, and the same shortcomings exist in most case studies.

Thus, the nearly universal weakness of the case study is the absence of adequate controls for establishing the internal validity of cause-and-effect conclusions. It is this limitation of case studies that single-case *experiments* are designed to remedy. Let's now look at
how well single-case experimentation succeeds in meeting this objective.

SINGLE-CASE EXPERIMENTS

Single-case experiments have a celebrated history in the field of psychology. When
Wilhelm Wundt founded the "new science" of psychology in 1879, the single-case experiment was the dominant method of investigation in his laboratory (see Boring, 1950).
The work of Ebbinghaus, Pavlov, and Skinner was also based on single-case experimental
designs. It is clear, then, that the single-case experiment contributed much to the early development of scientific psychology.

In the 1930s, however, psychologists generally began to abandon the practice of conducting experiments that involved only one subject and turned instead to group experiments, which were viewed as more reliable than single-case investigations. Another factor
in favor of group experiments is that they produce data that are easy to analyze statistically, whereas it is often difficult to apply statistical tests to the data of single-case experiments. As a result of such considerations, the group experiment has reigned supreme in
psychology.

In the past two decades, however, there has been a resurgence of interest in the single-
case experiment. Part of this renewed interest is a result of the growing popularity of behavioral therapies based on Skinner's operant conditioning model. More generally, many
applied psychologists are finding that the single-case experiment permits them to test the
effectiveness of their procedures in individual cases, with some degree of internal validity
(cf. Hersen & Barlow, 1976).

General Rationale of Single-Case Experiments

The single-case experiment is narrower in focus than the case study. While case studies
tend to stress the great number and complexity of variables that affect an individual's be-

havior, the single-case experiment usually concentrates on just two or three variables at a time—one that is manipulated and one or two that are observed and measured.

By definition, single-case experimental designs are "within-subject" designs (see Chapter 7). The subject serves in both the "experimental" and the "control" conditions, and usually her behavior is measured several times in each condition. Thus, the subject is her own "control." The typical procedure is first to measure the target behavior (i.e., dependent variable) under the control conditions, before any special treatment is applied. These initial observations may be taken over several days or weeks, in order to get a stable measure of the subject's baseline behavior, which is sometimes called the *baseline response rate*. The baseline data establish the average frequency of occurrence of the target behavior or the average value of the dependent measure under *usual*, or "control," circumstances. The baseline average, then, serves as a *standard* against which the effect of the experimental treatment can be compared. Normally the "experimental" condition is introduced only after a stable baseline has been established.

Although it is frequently difficult or impossible to apply statistical tests to the data of a single-case experiment, the results can be graphed to show how much the subject's behavior changes as she moves from the control condition to the experimental condition, or vice versa. In this type of analysis, the investigator's conclusions concerning the effectiveness of the experimental treatment will depend on (a) his confidence in the amount of control provided by the experimental design and (b) how dramatically the subject's behavior changes as a function of levels of the independent variable (i.e., experimental treatment versus control condition).

Recommended Procedures

Hersen and Barlow (1976) have suggested several ways to increase the internal validity of single-case experiments:

1. When possible, try to use several different measures of the dependent variable. For example, if the dependent variable is anxiety, you might measure it by recording external manifestations of tension, through a self-report device, or via physiological responses. If all of the dependent measures change in the expected directions at approximately the same time, this will increase your confidence in the effectiveness of the experimental treatment.

2. To maximize the reliability of your data, measure the dependent variable as often as is practical. For every measuring device applied, use a standard system for recording data each time measurements are taken. This practice minimizes contamination of the data by instrumentation changes.

3. Chart the baseline behavior until a "stable pattern" is observed. The observation process may cause the subject to behave atypically at first; in some cases, several weeks will pass before the baseline settles down. Unfortunately, the baseline behavior will sometimes begin moving in the direction predicted by the experimental hypothesis *before* the experimental treatment is applied. If the treatment is applied at that point, the results will be uninterpretable, as something other than the independent variable may have caused the predicted change.

4. Manipulate only one independent variable at a time. If more than one variable is changed at a particular point in the study, then a situation of confounding will exist.

Representative Designs

The degree of internal validity provided by a single-case experiment depends largely on the particular experimental designs you use. Although there are dozens of potential variations in such designs, most of the commonly used designs fall into three general classes: *reversal designs, multiple-baseline designs, and random time-series designs*. Only these three general models will be considered here; for information on additional designs, see Hersen and Barlow (1976).

Reversal Designs.   In a **reversal design** the experimenter first measures the subject's behavior under the control condition, then measures behavior while the experimental treatment is in effect, and then "reverses" the independent variable by resuming the control condition and taking further measurements. The experimenter monitors the pattern of the subject's behavior across the various phases of the experiment. If the independent variable is having an effect, then behavior changes should occur systematically with each change in that variable.

To demonstrate the rationale and value of reversal designs, let's first consider a pseudo-experimental design, which represents *just a portion of a reversal design*. This "pseudo," or sham, design is called the A-B model, where A represents the control condition and B represents the experimental condition. As an example, let's return to the hypothetical situation, described earlier in this chapter, in which a clinical psychologist is attempting to test the effectiveness of a new treatment for depression. Suppose the psychologist decides to use the number of "spontaneous verbalizations" made by the client as his dependent variable, his logic being that spontaneous verbalizations usually increase as a depressed person begins to "get better." The psychologist defines a spontaneous verbalization as a statement volunteered by the client in the absence of a question or prompt. The independent variable in this example has two levels: the new treatment versus a conventional clinical interview.

We will suppose that the study spans ten weeks, during which the client sees the psychologist once a week. The control, or A phase, of the study serves to establish a baseline and is implemented during the first five weeks. Then the psychologist applies the new treatment—the B phase—during each of the remaining five psychotherapy sessions.

The results of this hypothetical study are shown in Figure 10–4. By examining the figure, you'll see that the level of spontaneous verbalizations was quite low during the control phase, averaging only six per session. During the fourth and fifth sessions (weeks 9 and 10) of the "new treatment" phase, however, the number of verbalizations began to increase dramatically: The mean number of verbalizations for this phase was 9.4. Thus, although the new treatment may have been slow to take effect, it appears to have produced an increase in the level of the dependent variable. But how confident can you be that the change did, in fact, result from manipulation of the independent variable?

The shortcoming of the A–B pseudo-design is that the treatment changes only from the control (baseline) condition to the experimental condition and is never "reversed"— that is, the effect of changing from the experimental condition to the control condition is not assessed. Therefore, any number of confounding influences that happen to coincide with the onset of the new treatment may be responsible for the observed change in the dependent variable. Three possible confounding factors that may be operating in such a case are:

1. *Maturation*: Perhaps the client's brain biochemistry improved over the last weeks of the experiment. Brain biochemistry has been implicated in some types of depression (Levinthal, 1983).

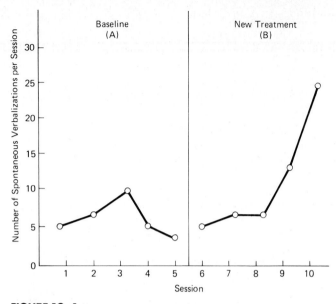

FIGURE 10–4

A-B Design. Number of Spontaneous Verbalizations Made by a Depressed Subject during the Baseline and Treatment Phases of the Experiment (Fictitious Data)

2. *History*: Perhaps the client has also been consulting a clergyman. If so, the outside counseling may be responsible for the client's improvement. Or maybe the client's spirits have been lifted by the discovery of a new love or by some exceptional luck at the race-track.

3. *Instrumentation changes*: Perhaps as the therapy progressed the clinical psychologist changed his criteria of what constitutes a spontaneous verbalization.

What could a single-case experimenter do in such a situation to increase his confidence in the internal validity of the findings? The answer lies in the rationale of a reversal design. The simplest reversal design is the A-B-A design, which is just an augmented A-B design that includes a switch back to the control condition once behavior has been measured under the experimental treatment. If the subject's behavior changes in one direction when the conditions change from A to B and then changes appreciably in the opposite direction when conditions are reversed from B back to A, then you can be more confident that the independent variable is responsible for the behavior changes.[1]

The case of "Mike" will illustrate how the A-B-A design is used. Mike (fictitious name) was a four-year-old autistic child who was receiving treatment from a clinical colleague of mine. Though some autistic children seem to have a defective speech apparatus which contributes to their communication problems, Mike's was okay. He could talk when he wanted to—but he rarely wanted to. The therapist desired to teach Mike that oral communication with other people can bring rewards. The strategy was to find out what Mike really liked and then use that item or activity as a reinforcer in an operant-conditioning type of therapy: Each time Mike answered the therapist's question, he was to receive a "small dose" of whatever the reinforcer turned out to be.

The first snag was encountered immediately. While Mike had many obvious preferences in life, nothing, not even candy or an opportunity to play an arcade game, seemed to be reward enough for talking. Then, while attempting to establish body contact with Mike, the therapist luckily hit upon the answer: Mike absolutely delighted in having his abdomen tickled! So "tummy tickling" became the reinforcer.

The procedure went as follows: An A-B-A experimental design was used. The operant-conditioning procedure was evaluated over a 12-day interval—4 days to establish a baseline (A), 4 days of the reinforcement procedure (B), and 4 days in the reversal phase (A), during which the reinforcement was withdrawn. During the course of each daily session, the therapist asked Mike 10 questions that had been randomly selected from a pool of 93 questions known to be within Mike's capacity to respond. During the treatment (B) phase, each time Mike gave a reasonable verbal response to a question, the therapist would hug and tickle him.

The results of the experiment appear in Figure 10–5, and they are fairly convincing. During the baseline phase, Mike responded verbally to an average of only 10 percent of the therapist's questions. That figure rose to 52.5 percent in the treatment phase, and then dropped back to 20 percent in the reversal phase.

When there is such a dramatic covariation between the dependent variable and levels of the independent variable, the investigator generally can be confident about the internal validity of his method-data package. But it is still possible that the results were confounded by some unknown variable, the effects of which just happened to coincide with the phases of the A-B-A sequence. To further increase internal validity, the investigator could add a second reversal to the procedure, producing an A-B-A-B design. If the dependent variable responds as expected in all four phases of an A-B-A-B sequence, then you can be very confident of the effect of the independent variable. Also, unlike the A-B-A design, the A-B-A-B model ends with a continuation of the helpful treatment, rather than

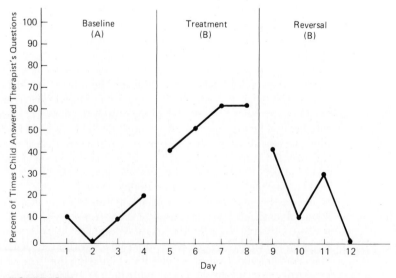

FIGURE 10–5
A-B-A Design. Percent of Questions Answered by an Autistic Child in Each of the Three Phases of a Reversal Design

leaving the subject in the baseline state. Thus, in practice, the A-B-A-B model is the reversal design that is used most often.

In fact, Mike's therapist did reinstate the B phase for a period of several weeks. In that time, Mike came to value the therapist so highly as a "playmate" that he (Mike) began to answer *and ask* questions even when no tickling was in the offing. Happily, in this case, the effects of this simple therapy transferred to Mike's home environment, where he began to speak spontaneously on a regular basis. Apparently he found that life with speech is generally more rewarding than a speechless existence.

Multiple-Baseline Design.   Very often, single-case experimenters cannot use reversal designs with certain types of problems. In some cases, it simply isn't ethical to withdraw a treatment that is alleviating a condition of suffering. In other situations, the effect of the experimental treatment may not be "reversible." This would be true, for example, if the treatment is effective in training the client in some skill, which would tend to persist even if the treatment were discontinued. Hence, it would be impossible to demonstrate covariation between the independent and dependent variables in a way that would rule out the influence of extraneous variables. In such situations, a multiple-baseline design may be a feasible alternative to the reversal model.

The **multiple-baseline design** typically involves the recording of *two or more behaviors* across time, first under the baseline (control) condition and then under the treatment (experimental) condition. But the switch from the baseline to the treatment condition occurs *at a different time* for each behavior. Since *all of the behaviors chosen for study are believed to be independently responsive to the treatment*, the following logic supports the design: (a) If each behavior changes in the expected direction only after the treatment is applied specifically to that behavior, then the independent variable is credited with the behavior change; (b) if all of the behaviors tend to change at the same time, even though the treatment is being applied to only one of them, then a confounding variable may be responsible for the behavior change. If outcome *b* occurs, then either all of the behaviors were influenced by an extraneous variable or the behaviors are not independent of one another. Regardless of the cause of outcome *b*, the internal validity of the results is in question when all of the selected behaviors change at the same time. On the other hand, if each of the selected behaviors changes only after the treatment is applied specifically to that behavior, then precise experimental control has been demonstrated, and you would have a lot of confidence in the internal validity of the data.

A multiple-baseline design was used by Fawcett and Miller (1975) to assess the effects of a three-module training program devised to enhance public-speaking skills. The three behaviors that were measured included making appropriate *eye contact* with the audience, making *effective gestures*, and engaging in a number of *good speaking behaviors*, such as greeting the audience, smiling, repeating critical questions, etc. Figure 10–6 illustrates the multiple-baseline design and shows the results that Fawcett and Miller obtained with one subject. Note that each of the three behaviors improved immediately after the training module was applied specifically to that behavior, and not before. Since the training was applied to each behavior at a different time, and since each behavior change covaried precisely with the time of application, the results strongly support the conclusion that the training procedure produced its intended effects.

Multiple-baseline designs may also be implemented across multiple situations and multiple subjects, following the same logic that underlies the use of multiple behaviors. See Hersen and Barlow (1976) for descriptions of these alternative applications.

Random Time-Series Design.   Suppose you desire to test the effectiveness of a relaxation-training procedure as a device for helping an insomniac client fall asleep. If the proce-

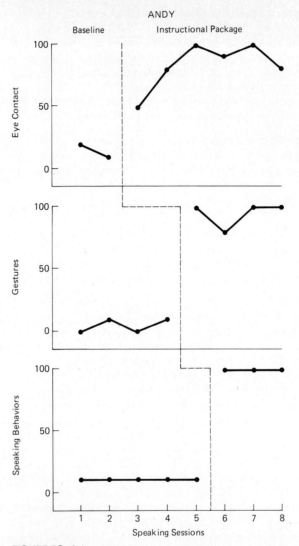

FIGURE 10–6

Multiple-Baseline Design. Percent Correct Responses Made by One Subject in Each of Three Categories of Public Speaking Behavior

Note: The vertical, dashed lines show the point at which the training module was introduced for each category of behavior. (Adapted from Fawcett, S. B., & Miller, L. K. Training public-speaking behavior: An experimental analysis and social validation. *Journal of Applied Behavior Analysis*, 1975, *8*, p. 129. Used with permission.)

dure works as you hypothesize it will and thus alleviates some of the client's sleeplessness, it probably would be unethical to "reverse" the treatment back to a baseline condition, even if that were feasible—and once the client learns the procedure, reversibility isn't likely, so a reversal design isn't a good strategy here. A multiple-baseline design probably wouldn't be possible either, as it would be very difficult to come up with a number of target behaviors relevant to insomnia yet independent of one another.

In research problems such as the one described above, it may be possible for you to employ a **random time-series design**. This model involves taking baseline measurements on a particular behavior and then introducing the treatment phase with no intention of reversing back to the control condition. The key to the design's rationale is that *the choice of the time at which the treatment is introduced is determined entirely at random*. Although it is possible that, by chance alone, a confounding factor may influence the subject's behavior at about the same time as the treatment is implemented, the probability of such a random coincidence is reasonably low. Therefore, if the dependent variable changes immediately after you introduce the experimental treatment, you would have a reasonable amount of confidence in the internal validity of your findings.

The results of a hypothetical random time-series investigation appear in Figure 10–7. The hypothetical problem was insomnia, and the dependent behavior was the number of minutes required for the subject to fall asleep on each of 15 nights. The first 5 nights were reserved for baseline measurements. Then one of the remaining 10 nights was randomly selected as the treatment-application night. In this example, night 9 was chosen. Earlier that day, the client was given training in the relaxation technique, and then he used it that evening at bedtime, as well as on all succeeding nights. As Figure 10–7 illustrates, time-to-slumber was lengthy up to night 9. But once the client began using the relaxation procedure to help him fall asleep, time-to-slumber dropped dramatically. This impressive change in the dependent variable represents either a positive effect of the treatment or a somewhat improbable chance event which had persistent effects. The tentative conclusion would be that the relaxation technique was effective. Subsequent replications with other insomniacs would support this conclusion.

Evaluating the Single-Case Experiment

The single-case experiment probably is the most powerful tool available to the everyday practitioner who desires to validate the usefulness of her procedures. The key to its effec-

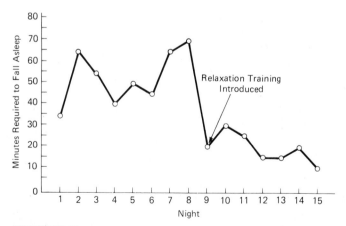

FIGURE 10–7

Random Time-Series Design. Effects of Relaxation Training on the Treatment of Insomnia: Time Required to Fall Asleep on Each of 15 Nights

Note: The treatment was introduced on Day 9, which was *randomly* selected (fictitious data).

tiveness resides in the elements of systematic measurement, manipulation, and control that characterize the single-case experiment. Although the approach doesn't yield the volumes of interesting and complex data that a conventional case study does, its precision of focus makes it much more amenable to quantification than most case studies are.

Several limitations do apply to single-case experiments:

1. Some dependent variables of interest, such as self-esteem, may not be capable of the relatively rapid change usually required for the assessment of treatment effects in single-case experiments.

2. It is usually impossible to avoid all major sources of confounding in single-case experiments. For example, carry-over effects may occur if a reversal design is used with the wrong kind of problem. If self-report measures are used to measure the dependent variable, then testing effects may accumulate across the course of the study, and these effects, if undetected, may lead to erroneous conclusions. Also, subject-expectancy, or placebo, effects are a universal threat to the internal validity of single-case experiments. Most subjects are well aware of changes from baseline to treatment and vice versa; they might change their behavior because they feel they are expected to change, not because of a specific effect of the independent variable.

3. As noted earlier, it is usually difficult, and sometimes impossible, to apply standard statistical tests to the data of single-case experiments. The major problem is that many statistical tests assume that the various data points are independent of one another, which may not be so when all of the data are based on the responses of one subject.

4. Like the simple case study, the single-case experiment may have little external validity. If you conduct a particular single-case experiment only once or twice, then very little generalization is warranted. When feasible, the best solution to the external validity problem is to replicate the experiment with several dozen subjects who have diverse characteristics and backgrounds. Of course, once that many replications have been conducted, the single-case approach begins to resemble a traditional group experiment that has been carried out in a piecemeal fashion.

SUMMARY

For practical and ethical reasons, many practicing psychologists are unable or unwilling to conduct well-controlled conventional experiments involving random assignment of subjects to experimental and control groups. The best methodological alternatives for these practitioners are the *case study* and the *single-case experiment*.

The case study is useful for a variety of purposes, including demonstrating unusual or unique phenomena, demonstrating a practical procedure, generating new hypotheses, theory building, and disconfirming general implications of certain theories.

In planning a case study, you need to consider the purpose of the study, the variables and behaviors to be observed, the target population, and the sources and types of data you will use. In conducting a case study, it is important that you compile *permanent records* of the data as the case progresses. Once data have begun to accumulate, hypotheses may be checked through the *method of internal consistency*.

The limitations of the case study include: its susceptibility to circular reasoning, its reliance on subjective data, restrictions on generalizability of findings, and its lack of control over confoundings.

The single-case experiment attempts to overcome the case study's vulnerability to confounding by incorporating controlled manipulation into the study of individuals. All single-case designs involve within-subject manipulation of the independent variable. The three designs discussed in this chapter were the *reversal, multiple-baseline*, and *random time-series* models.

Although more powerful than conventional case studies, single-case experiments rarely control for all sources of confounding. Expectancy effects and testing effects are always threats in these studies.

REVIEW QUESTIONS

1. Summarize the similarities and differences between the case study and the single-case experiment.

2. What ethical and practical considerations might encourage a scientist-practitioner to use single-case methods of research instead of the conventional group designs?

3. Summarize some of the typical arguments for and against single-case methods. Try to think of and develop additional points on both sides.

4. Describe at least four general uses of the case study within the field of psychology. Are some of the uses more valid or legitimate than others? Explain your response.

5. Tell why each of the following considerations is significant in the conduct of a case study: deciding on purpose, variables, and behaviors; selecting a target population; deciding on sources and types of data; recording data; using the method of internal consistency.

6. Summarize the major criticisms of the case study as a method of research, giving particular attention to the criteria of internal validity and external validity.

7. State the general rationale behind single-case experiments.

8. Make up one example of each of the following single-case experimental designs: A-B-A-B reversal; multiple-baseline; random time-series.

9. What is a "baseline," and what is its function in single-case experimentation?

10. Describe some potential shortcomings and pitfalls of single-case experiments. Be sure to address the issues of internal validity and external validity.

Note

[1]Because of ethical constraints and carry-over effects, it usually would not be feasible to use the A-B-A design to investigate a treatment for depression. There would be ethical problems associated with discontinuing a treatment that possibly has started to alleviate a client's depression. Apart from that consideration, it is likely that some of the effect of the therapy would "carry over" from the B phase to the A phase, rendering the data difficult to interpret. Possibly a random time-series design or a multiple-baseline design would be applicable in such cases (see text).

11

THE PSYCHOMETRIC METHOD

THE SCOPE OF PSYCHOMETRIC RESEARCH

ASSUMPTIONS OF THE PSYCHOMETRIC METHOD

USES OF THE PSYCHOMETRIC METHOD
Exploratory Research
Developing Predictors of Performance
Theory Building
Theory Testing

CONSTRUCTING AND VALIDATING AN OBJECTIVE TEST
Test Format
The Reliability Problem
Techniques of Test Validation

EVALUATING THE PSYCHOMETRIC METHOD

ANALYZING THE DATA FROM PSYCHOMETRIC STUDIES
Combining Predictors of a Criterion: Multiple Correlation
Dealing With the Third-Variable Problem: Partial r
Evidence for Directionality in a Relationship: Cross-Lagged Correlational Analysis

SUMMARY

REVIEW QUESTIONS

Psychologists use tests for a variety of purposes in basic research, applied research, and professional practice. Within the arena of psychological research, tests are frequently used to measure theoretical constructs such as self-esteem, hypnotic susceptibility, general intelligence, aptitudes, achievement motivation, and so on. In fact, it is not uncommon to see a research program that centers on *discovering the network of relationships between a particular test and a variety of other tests and behaviors*. This approach to scientific inquiry is referred to as the **psychometric method**, and we will explore its characteristics and applications in this chapter.

Some of the material discussed here represents an elaboration of measurement concepts that were developed in Chapter 5. In particular, special attention will be given to the various ways in which the reliability and validity of measurement are assessed.

THE SCOPE OF PSYCHOMETRIC RESEARCH

The word "psychometric" literally means pertaining to the measurement of the psyche, soul, or mind. In a broad sense, "psychometrics" refers to any operation used to measure psychological variables, but in general usage, the term usually is applied in the context of psychological testing.

Psychometric research is definitely "correlational" research. The approach primarily involves searching for correlations among tests or between tests and certain behaviors. For example, the psychometric method might be used to answer questions such as "What behavior patterns and personality traits are associated with the tendency to develop coronary artery disease?"; or "What traits are correlated with success in a sales career?" Thus, the emphasis is on obtaining evidence that *describes* relationships among theoretically important variables, and on *predicting* behavior from a knowledge of people's traits. But by itself, the psychometric method rarely supports strong cause-and-effect inferences: Psychometric researchers attempt to *measure what exists* in people and then relate these measurements to one another or to behavior, but there is usually no attempt to experimentally control or influence the level of the variables being assessed, as would be required for causal analysis. For instance, you might be able to measure IQ in your subjects and then find out what behaviors it is correlated with, but you could hardly randomly assign people to various IQ levels. Since IQ is confounded by a host of socioeconomic factors, you would not have an adequate basis to assert that IQ level directly causes something else. Nonetheless, it certainly is useful to know what behaviors are predicted by IQ.

Despite the fact that confounded variables are a fact of life in psychometric research, the approach serves many valuable functions in the social sciences. Later, I'll review those functions and how they are implemented. But first, let's examine the major assumptions underlying this method.

ASSUMPTIONS OF THE PSYCHOMETRIC METHOD

Psychometric research rests on four principal assumptions:

1. There are individual differences among people in regard to psychological traits.
2. These individual differences are consistent across time and situations.
3. It is possible to develop tests that yield reliable and valid measurements of these individual differences.

4. Test scores that reflect individual differences on traits are related in some systematic way to theoretically or socially significant behaviors outside the testing situation. (A corollary of this assumption is that the test scores can be used to predict the behaviors at a better than chance level.)

While few people would argue against the validity of the first assumption, the second one has been regularly challenged. Reviews of the evidence bearing on the consistency of personality suggest that although people's self-descriptions and abilities are fairly stable, their personality test scores and behavior patterns vary considerably across time and situations (cf. Fiske, 1979; Kimmel, 1974; Mischel, 1968, 1969). Since temporal and situational inconsistency in test scores adversely affects the reliability of those measures, the vulnerability of the consistency assumption also brings the third and fourth assumptions into question. While this problem has not prevented psychologists from doing fruitful research via the psychometric method, the consistency/inconsistency issue is certainly something to bear in mind as you conduct psychometric-type studies. The stability question also serves as a reminder of the importance of checking the reliability of your measures.

USES OF THE PSYCHOMETRIC METHOD

The field of psychometrics extends beyond research per se and includes many specific applications in the practice of counseling and clinical psychology. To stay within the bounds of this book's purpose, however, I'll discuss only the ways in which the psychometric techniques are employed in psychological research.[1]

Exploratory Research

One of the most common and important uses of the psychometric method is that of searching for significant relationships between an interesting behavior or trait and other traits. The goal of this application is to establish the psychological meaning of a trait by discovering what other variables are correlated with it. There are three basic steps in this process:

1. Develop a reliable measure of the behavior or trait of interest.
2. Measure a group of subjects on the target trait and on a large number of other variables.
3. Compute the correlation coefficient between the target trait and each of the other variables, to see what known traits are associated with the target trait.

Exploratory psychometric research frequently is maligned, being described as a "fishing expedition" or "tinkertoy research" (that is, you put everything together and see what you come out with). But such exploratory research is a necessary part of the scientific enterprise. It not only represents a possible first step in validating potentially useful constructs, but also may stimulate the development of new lines of inquiry within the social sciences. What's more, this particular application of the psychometric method has been known to lead to significant theoretical insights. Take an example from the field of experimental hypnosis: For years psychologists working in that area searched for a set of personality traits that would allow the accurate prediction of people's "susceptibility" to hypnotic suggestion. The mixed results were disappointing and led to the conclusion that personality traits have but minimal utility as predictors of "hypnotizability." But these findings led to other avenues of research which suggested that hypnotizability is largely a function of situational variables (e.g., specific instructions given to the subject) and the subject's hypnosis-specific attitude (e.g., what he expects from the hypnotic session) (cf. Barber, 1976; Diamond, Gregory, Lenny, Steadman, & Talone, 1972).

Developing Predictors of Performance

In the United States, psychologists who specialize in psychometric research often are called upon to develop or recommend tests that will allow business, government, or educational organizations to select employees or students who are likely to succeed at particular tasks. In the ideal situation, tests that are valid predictors of success at work or school are administered to applicants before final hiring or acceptance decisions are made. The organization then hires or admits only those applicants who score at or above a level usually associated with successful performance; the others are politely rejected. Because no psychological test is perfectly valid, this procedure usually results in a few errors: On the basis of test scores, some applicants who would have succeeded are rejected, and a few of the selected individuals do not succeed. To the extent that valid predictions of performance can be made, however, the *success ratio*—that is, (number successful)/(number selected)—is higher when the selection test is used than when it is omitted from the selection process. The ideal is to use the organization's time, effort, and money efficiently, while minimizing the incidence of failure experiences among those selected.

The basic steps in the development of a selection test will be presented here within the context of a program for selecting salespeople that was developed by psychologist David McClelland and his associates at McBer, Incorporated, a psychological consulting firm in Boston (see Goleman, 1981). The program was put together for a major retailer who wanted a salesperson selection program that would result in higher sales and fewer salespeople leaving the company. At the start of the study, the turnover rate in the sales force was 40 percent.

Developing a Job Description.   Selection tests and the performance criteria that are used to validate them are developed for specific jobs. Therefore, the starting point in mounting a selection program is the development of a **job description**. An adequate job description specifies the functions the employee is to engage in and the level of proficiency expected for each function performed. For example, a salesperson might be required to make 20 calls per week, clearly communicate the available product lines, articulate the advantages of the product relative to competing products, employ an effective sale-closing technique, achieve an average sales volume of $4,000 per week, fill out order forms, maintain sales ledgers and customer records, and attend at least two staff meetings per week.

There are a number of techniques for developing job descriptions (see, for example, Howell & Dipboye, 1982; Landy & Trumbo, 1980). The better approaches involve getting information on job requirements from both the present employees and their supervisors. In setting up the selection program for the retailing company, the McBer firm used a highly recommended procedure called the "critical incident" technique. This approach resulted in a job description that was so specific and concrete that a selection instrument was derived directly from its content. Let's examine how the critical incident technique was carried out.

Constructing the Selection Instrument.   There were two phases to McBer's application of the **critical incident technique**. First, with the aid of the retail company's officers, two criterion groups of employees were identified: a group of outstanding salespeople and a group of mediocre salespeople. Then the McBer psychologists interviewed both groups to identify "critical incidents" in job performance that distinguished the "greats" from the "also rans." That is, individuals in each criterion group were asked to describe in detail work situations in which they did something that was critical to successful performance or that was the cause of a serious failure on the job. Those job behaviors and competencies which the "greats" reported, but which were not found in accounts provided by their lessers, became the critical skills that the resulting selection instrument was designed to test for. In the McBer study, successful salespeople were differentiated from the mediocre ones by 15 critical behaviors. Four examples are:

1. *Efficiency:* If he couldn't make a sale in the first few minutes of interaction with a customer, the successful salesperson would refer the customer to another salesperson.
2. *Time-consciousness:* Successful salespeople were constantly aware of how much time activities ate up, and didn't like to waste time.
3. *Internal standards:* The "great" salespeople set up demanding internal standards for their own performance; these standards usually exceeded what the company expected of them.
4. *Productive use of spare time:* The better employees used a lot of their spare time in work-related endeavors—writing thank-you notes to customers, for example.

On the basis of the critical incident job analysis, the McBer psychologists developed a "behavior-event" interview (the selection instrument), which was designed to assess the 15 critical behaviors that characterized the most competent salespeople. This instrument was to be used to screen—that is, assess and select—new applicants for sales positions. In the behavior-event interview, an applicant would be presented with questions about different types of situations, and would then be asked what he would do in those situations or how he had handled similar situations in the past. Points would be awarded according to how many of the 15 critical behaviors he mentioned.

Developing a Criterion Measure.   In order to find out if a selection test successfully predicts job performance, you need to develop or decide on a performance criterion and measure that criterion. **Performance criteria** are the behaviors or pieces of evidence that constitute what you mean by successful performance; in other words, they are the operational definitions of "success." In the McBer study, two performance criteria were used to check the validity of the selection instrument: (a) dollar volume of sales for each salesperson; (b) turnover rate for sales personnel selected with the instrument versus the turnover rate that existed prior to using the instrument.

Testing the Predictive Validity of the Selection Instrument.   There are two general statistical procedures for assessing the validity of a selection test. Each allows you to determine whether scores on the selection test predict the level of job performance shown by employees. One method involves computing the linear correlation coefficient between the selection test scores and the performance criterion scores, and then evaluating the *statistical* and *practical* significance of the correlation coefficient (see Chapter 6).

A second approach to validity assessment is to divide the employees into criterion groups on the basis of their job performance: say, an outstanding group, an average group, and a below-average group. Then the mean of each group's selection-test scores is computed, and the differences between the group means are tested for significance. If the outstanding group has a significantly higher mean score on the selection test, then the test does predict job performance. The next step would be to set up "utility tables" that specify a selection cutoff point based on the relationship between certain test scores and the probability of succeeding at the job. See Brown (1976) or Howell and Dipboye (1982) for the details on how to set up utility tables.

The McBer psychologists used a variation of the second approach to validate the selection test. They compared the sales volume and turnover rates of employees hired on the basis of the behavior-event interview with the sales and turnover data of employees hired by all other methods.

Did the selection procedure work? You bet it did! After 12 weeks on the job the group selected via the behavior event interview averaged 15 percent higher sales volume than the other salespeople in the organization. Moreover, only 12 percent of the employees hired on the basis of the selection instrument quit their jobs during the first 12 weeks, which compared very favorably with the 40 percent overall turnover rate for salespeople during comparable time periods. This outcome clearly illustrates the value of psychometric research in the area of personnel selection.

Cross-Validation of the Selection Procedure.   Sometimes a selection procedure seems to work with the initially tested group of employees, but the good initial outcome is merely a result of chance. You might say that, on occasion, organizational psychologists get lucky the first time around. But since chance is fickle, the selection test may not be a valid predictor of performance for most succeeding groups of applicants. For this reason, it is necessary to **cross-validate** the initial results by periodically checking test scores against job performance with later samples of applicants. Encouragingly, research evidence suggests that most industrial selection tests hold up quite well under cross-validation (Howell & Dipboye, 1982).

Theory Building

Psychometric methods play an important role in theory development. In Chapter 2, a theory was defined as an internally consistent network of assumptions, constructs, operational definitions, relationships, and principles. Although the psychometric approach has trouble with the matter of cause-and-effect, it's quite handy for discovering relationships between variables, which is perhaps the largest part of theory construction.

As an illustration of how psychometric-type research can form the basis of a general theory, let's review a research program designed to develop a theory about the psychological traits of people who are prone to contract coronary artery disease. Early research with subjects who had been diagnosed as having coronary artery disease suggested the following psychological correlates: a pervasive sense of time urgency, an inability to relax without feeling guilty, the need to take one's work home, a competitive achievement orientation, and hostility. This constellation of traits is referred to as the Type-A, or coronary-prone, behavior pattern (e.g., Friedman & Rosenman, 1974). People who show the opposite behavior pattern are called Type-B individuals, and they have a much lower risk of developing coronary artery disease. A number of objective personality tests have been developed to measure the Type-A and Type-B patterns (cf. Glass, 1977). One intriguing finding in this line of research was that scores on objective tests of Type-A behavior are the single most efficient predictor of recurring heart attacks—better even than incidence of cigarette smoking, dietary habits, or levels of cholesterol in the blood (Jenkins, Zyzanski, & Rosenman, 1976.)

In an attempt to construct a useful psychological theory of Type-A behavior, Glass (1977) carried out several psychometric-type studies of Type-A and Type-B individuals. His subjects were college students, and he measured the extent to which they possessed the Type-A profile with a multiple-choice test designed to measure that behavior style. He then measured the subjects on a variety of other traits and behaviors, in order to gain additional insight into the Type-A personality. What were high Type-A scores associated with? Relative to the Type-B's, Type-A subjects showed a tendency to work at nearly maximum capacity in most laboratory tasks—yet they reported less fatigue. The Type-A's also had better retention in memory tasks, higher activity-level scores, greater impatience in tasks that involved periodic delay intervals, and significantly more hostility in reaction to rude comments about their performance during a difficult task. Glass concluded that:

> In contrast to B's, Type A's work hard to succeed, suppress subjective states (e.g., fatigue) that might interfere with task performance, exhibit rapid pacing of their activities, and express hostility after being harassed in their efforts at task completion—all, I submit, in the interests of asserting control over environmental demands and requirements. (pp. 181–182)

Thus, Glass's theory is that the Type-A person's dominant need is to maintain control over life situations. Based on other correlational evidence from the field of medicine, he further proposed that the Type-A's attempts to exercise "control" are associated with rises in the blood levels of noradrenaline, an endocrine hormone associated with stress. He cited additional evidence suggesting that the Type-A's noradrenaline levels decline markedly when attempts to control the environment fail and the Type-A feels "helpless." Glass' speculation is that the Type-A's frequent cycles of noradrenaline changes may be responsible for the link between behavior patterns and coronary artery disease. Of course, investigations that involve the direct control of critical variables, perhaps using animal subjects, will be required to assess the internal validity of this theory. Nonetheless, Glass's psychometric research has furnished the theory's basic structure.

Theory Testing

You can use the psychometric approach to test any theory that makes a clear prediction about a relationship between two or more variables. And, as was true of the case-study approach (Chapter 10), you can employ the psychometric method to disprove a cause-and-effect hypothesis, even though the method by itself isn't usually capable of confirming a cause-and-effect proposition. This is so because covariation between variables X and Y is one necessary condition for establishing causality, and if Y doesn't covary with X, psychometric techniques are capable of revealing that absence of covariation. On the other hand, a hypothesis, as well as the theory it was derived from, remains believable if a correlation between the relevant variables is shown.

CONSTRUCTING AND VALIDATING AN OBJECTIVE TEST

Chances are that if you carry out a study using the psychometric method, it will be necessary for you to construct one or more tests from scratch. In this section, I'll take you through such a procedure, using as an example a personality test that I constructed a number of years ago. This discussion also provides an excellent opportunity to consider the various kinds of reliability and validity checks that are part and parcel of test construction in particular and the psychometric method in general. You were exposed to the basic ideas behind the concepts of reliability and validity in Chapter 5. To refresh your memory, you might find it helpful to review that section before reading on.

The instrument I will use to illustrate test construction is the Personal Data Inventory. I developed this 41-item test to meet a special need that had been communicated to me by the campus counselor at a college where I was employed. Each year, the counselor helped dozens of students to cope with their personal problems, but some of the students who sought his help were so deeply "troubled" that they required professional services that exceeded what the counselor was able to offer. He tried to refer these cases to appropriate clinics or practitioners as quickly as possible. But often a very disturbed student would see the counselor for several weeks before the depth and complexity of the problem became apparent. Therefore, the counselor asked me to put together a short, quick-scoring test that would help him to detect some of the more serious cases before too much time elapsed. The result of my efforts was the Personal Data Inventory, which was designed to assess level of self-esteem.

Self-esteem is defined as the degree of positive feeling or positive attitude that a person has toward himself. If you feel good about who you are, then your self-esteem is high. People who have psychological problems or problems of personal adjustment often possess low self-esteem, expressed as guilt or negative self-feelings (cf. McMahon & McMahon, 1983). Although the correlation isn't perfect, people who score exceptionally low on a valid test of self-esteem probably have rather serious problems that require extensive psychological, and perhaps medical, treatment—the type of treatment that wouldn't be available in many college counseling centers. Therefore, referral would be indicated in these cases.

Test Format

It is worth noting that the Personal Data Inventory (PDI) is classified as an **objective test**. The term "objective" has nothing to do with the content of the test. Rather, it signifies the fact that *different test scorers usually agree with one another on what scores the test-takers made*. One criterion of test objectivity is that independent scorers should agree with one another on at least 90 percent of the test scores (Brown, 1976). Most objective tests achieve that status because the test items are written in a multiple-choice or true/false (or agree/disagree) format. If independent scorers use the same scoring key to tally the results of a multiple-choice or true/false test, they can hardly fail to agree on the test scores. The major advantage of objective tests is that they tend to be more reliable than tests that involve subjective judgment in the scoring process. Of all types of item format, multiple-choice probably is the most reliable (Nunnally, 1967).

The PDI consists of true/false items. The respondent marks either "A" (for agree, "true of me") or "D" (for disagree, "not true of me") next to each item. The test-taker receives 1 "self-esteem point" for each response that matches the corresponding scoring code on the test key (highest possible score = 41). Some items from the PDI are:

_____ 1. I feel satisfied with myself.
_____ 2. I am intelligent.
_____ 3. I feel that I am not contributing much to life.
_____ 4. I am capable of forming good relationships with other people.

A multiple-choice format could have been used on the PDI. For example, item #1 could have been written this way:

> 1. I feel _____ with myself.
>   a. happy b. satisfied c. dissatisfied d. disgusted

or

> 1. I feel satisfied with myself.
>   a. strongly agree b. agree c. don't know d. disagree e. strongly disagree

With a multiple-choice approach, a variable number of points could have been assigned to the subject's response to each item, depending on what alternative he selected. This probably would have made the test a little more reliable. But, as you will see, the agree/disagree format resulted in satisfactory reliability and made the test quicker to take.

Another objective-type test format is the **rating scale**, which might take this form:

> How do you feel about yourself?
> (Check One)
>
> ```
> :      :      :      :      :      :
> _____
> 1      2      3      4      5
> Very                 Very
> Dissatisfied         Satisfied
> ```

Subjective tests are those that must be subjectively scored. By definition, scorers of subjective tests often disagree on what the test scores should be. One format that tends to require subjective scoring is the completion, or fill-in-the-blank, format. Consider this example:

> 1. I feel _____ with myself. (Please fill in the blank with one word.)

How many self-esteem points would you add or subtract for each of the following responses?

> mellow
> down
> good
> sick
> satisfied
> unhappy
> crazy
> lonely
> okay

I'll bet that you and I would disagree on how points should be assigned to some of these responses. Such is the difficulty with subjectively scored tests. And keep in mind that scorer inconsistencies add random error variance to test scores, thereby lowering the test's reliability. The best way to minimize scoring error in subjectively scored instruments is to assign score points to several possible categories of response *in advance of* administering the tests—and then stick to the predetermined scoring code when assessing the results.

Sentence completion, another "subjective" format, is even more difficult to score. For example:

1. I feel _____.
(Please complete the sentence.)

What would you do with a response such as "like Alice in Wonderland"? In this case, it would be very difficult to specify a scoring code in advance of data collection, because there is such a diversity of possible responses to sentence-completion items.

Some subjective tests require essay or thematic responses. Generally, this type of item creates the greatest scoring problems. Example:

1. Mary is a college student. Write a short story about Mary.

This particular example would qualify as a **projective test**, since, presumably, any story you write about Mary would represent a psychological projection of your feelings, attitudes, values, and needs. Well-known projective tests include the Rorschach Inkblot Test and the Thematic Apperception Test (TAT), both of which require the test-taker to give personal interpretations of ambiguous pictures. Normally the scoring of these tests requires the scorer to exercise much subjective judgment. Although many psychologists profess a belief in the usefulness of such instruments (Wade & Baker, 1977), the reliability of those tests would not be sufficient for many research and applied uses (cf. Brown, 1976).

In sum, while there are many test-item formats available, the objective formats—multiple-choice, true/false, and self-rating scale—have the advantages of being reliable and easy to score relative to the subjective and "projective" formats. Therefore, when you have a choice, it would be wise to use an objective-test format in your psychometric studies. If a research problem can be approached only by way of a subjective measuring device, then by all means use that device, but, for the sake of adequate reliability, be sure to specify your scoring criteria in advance, write them down, and then refer to those criteria as you convert each subject's responses to numbers. This is essentially the approach that the McBer team used to select salespeople in the study discussed earlier in this chapter. They asked the applicants to give subjective answers to a particular set of questions; then they matched each applicant's answers against a set of 15 scoring criteria that were indicative of great selling ability.

The Reliability Problem

As you may recall from reading Chapter 5, reliable measurement is necessary (but not sufficient) for valid measurement. To review, **reliability** refers to the *consistency of results produced by a measurement operation*, such as a personality test. Unreliable variance in test scores represents the effects of unsystematic, or random, measurement error. Events that introduce random error into the testing procedure operate both *within* a test-taking session and *between* separate testing sessions. Examples of random error sources that operate within a testing session include item-sampling error (i.e., test items vary in how well they represent the target trait), guessing, item-to-item scorer inconsistencies, unsystematic fluctuations in the subject's physical or psychological state, distractions, misreading test items, inadvertent skipping of items, and careless or haphazard responding.

Item sampling error deserves further comment. It's important to remember that a test yields only a *sample of behavior*. Furthermore, any sample of items will evoke a somewhat imperfect sample of the behavior of interest. In general, the larger the number of items, and the more clearly they are written and presented, the better behavior sample they produce. Hence the better your estimate of the subject's "true score" and the higher your test's reliability.

The other category of random error, unsystematic variation *between testings*, can be a problem whenever your subjects are to be tested more than once. This is true whether they are tested twice with the same instrument or once with each of two different tests that you expect to be correlated with one another. Sources of between-testings error include unsystematic changes in the test scorer or the scoring criteria, random changes in the testing situation, and unsystematic changes in the subjects' physical or psychological states between occasions. Unfortunately, even *systematic* changes in subjects can adversely affect between-testings reliability, if different subjects change systematically in different directions.

We'll consider several methods of statistically assessing reliability. Some are limited to assessing consistency within one testing session, while other methods are designed to assess between-testings consistency. All rely on a statistical index you're already familiar with, the Pearson r. When used as a **reliability coefficient**, the linear correlation coefficient is symbolized r_{kk}, where the double-k subscript means that a measure is being correlated with itself, rather than an X variable being correlated with a Y variable. The reliability coefficient represents *the proportion of variance in a set of test scores that is true-score variance*. You'll recall that true scores are the scores that subjects would get if the test had no random measurement error in it. Thus,

$$r_{kk} = \frac{\text{True-Score Variance}}{\text{Total Test-Score Variance}} = \frac{\text{True-Score Variance}}{\text{True-Score Variance} + \text{Error Variance}}$$

Obviously, the higher the r_{kk} index, the better the test scores reflect the subjects' true scores, and the more reliable the test data will be.

Assessing Reliability Within a Single Testing Session.   The within-test reliability of a measurement instrument is determined by the amount of item-to-item consistency in the subjects' performance. Suppose you are administering a test to a particular group of subjects. If the test were almost perfectly reliable, then subjects' respective ranks in the group would be the same on each test item. As strange as it may seem, if the test were *ideally* reliable, then the person who ranked lowest in the subject pool on the first item would also rank lowest on all succeeding items. The second lowest person on item 1 would remain second lowest on the rest of the items, and so on. (What kind of total test score distribution would the "ideal" situation result in if the only possible score on each item were "0" [wrong] or "1" [right]?)

The ideally reliable psychological test doesn't exist. But the internal-consistency reliability of your test will be good to the extent that your subjects *tend* to behave consistently from one part of the test to another.

The simplest technique of indexing internal-consistency reliability is the **split-half method**. The procedure involves dividing your test into two equally long parts; let's say you consider the even-numbered items to be one half and the odd-numbered items to be the other half. You would tally two scores for each subject: (a) an even-half total and (b) an odd-half total. Next you would compute the correlation coefficient between the odd- and even-half scores, resulting in r_{oe} (o = "odd"; e = "even"). Finally, you would plug r_{oe}

into the Spearman-Brown "Correction Formula," to get the split-half reliability coefficient:

$$r_{kk} = \frac{2(r_{oc})}{1 + r_{oc}}$$

This formula adjusts the reliability correlation upward to "correct" for the fact that, in splitting your test, you have effectively reduced the size of the test to one-half of its original length. Remember that reliability is a direct function of the number of items on a test.

When the split-half reliability coefficient was computed for the Personal Data Inventory (PDI), using a sample of 22 college students, the result was:

$$r_{kk} = \frac{2(.835)}{1 + .835}$$

$$= \frac{1.67}{1.835}$$

$$= .91$$

This outcome was quite satisfactory, in view of the fact that a reliability of .80 is generally considered an acceptable coefficient for objective personality tests (Brown, 1976).

A more precise estimate of a test's internal-consistency reliability can be obtained by computing **Coefficient Alpha**. One formula for this second index of reliability is:

$$r_{kk} = \frac{k}{k - 1}\left(1 - \frac{k}{\Sigma r_{ij}} \right),$$

where, r_{kk} = Coefficient Alpha,

k = the number of items on the test,

Σ is the summation sign, and

r_{ij} represents the correlations among individual items on the test

Table 11–1 shows how Coefficient Alpha is computed. To use the formula given here, you must first compute the linear correlation between each test item and every other test item, and set up a correlation matrix, as shown in the table. Then, to get Σr_{ij}, you add up all of the correlations in the matrix. Finally, you insert the number of items wherever there is a k in the formula, and then compute Alpha.

Coefficient Alpha is a very useful measure of internal-consistency reliability. It can be shown mathematically that Alpha is the mean of all possible split-half reliability coefficients for a given test (Anastasi, 1968). In other words, if you divided the test in half via all possible methods (e.g., odd/even, first half/second half, various random splits, etc.) and computed the mean of all the resulting split-half reliabilities, that mean would equal Coefficient Alpha. Coefficient Alpha also represents the *expected* equivalent-forms reliability coefficient (see below), if both forms are the same length and are administered in immediate succession.

When Coefficient Alpha was computed for the PDI, the results were:

1. $r_{kk} = .86$ for a sample of 35 college students
2. $r_{kk} = .86$ for a sample of 187 college students
3. $r_{kk} = .83$ for a sample of 30 geriatric patients

Again, the reliability of the PDI was quite satisfactory.

TABLE 11–1

Correlation Matrix Showing the Pearson r Correlations among the Items in a Four-Item Test and the Computation of Coefficient Alpha (Fictitious Data)

		Item			
		1	*2*	*3*	*4*
	1	1.00	.40	.30	.50
Item	2	.40	1.00	.60	.20
	3	.30	.60	1.00	.30
	4	.50	.20	.30	1.00
Column Sums		2.20	2.20	2.20	2.00

$$\Sigma r_{ij} = 8.60 \quad k = 4 = \text{number of test items}$$

$$\text{Coefficient Alpha} = \frac{k}{k-1}\left(1 - \frac{k}{\Sigma r_{ij}}\right)$$

$$= \frac{4}{3}\left(1 - \frac{4}{8.60}\right)$$

$$= 1.33\,(1 - .465)$$

$$= 1.33\,(.535)$$

$$= .71$$

Assessing Reliability Across Testing Sessions. There are two operations for checking the reliability of a test across time. The simpler one is the **test-retest method**. The model is illustrated below:

$$\text{TEST} \xrightarrow{\text{(time)}} \text{RETEST}$$

The test is given to the same group of people on two separate occasions; the time between testings can vary from a few minutes to several months. The reliability coefficient, r_{kk}, is obtained simply by computing the linear correlation coefficient between the test scores and the retest scores. Usually the size of the test-retest reliability coefficient can be depended on to steadily decrease as the intertest interval is increased.

When the test-retest method was applied to the PDI, using a one-month interval, the resulting coefficient was .78. This isn't as impressive as the .86 and the .91 coefficients obtained with the internal-consistency techniques. However, since we would expect people to experience real changes in their self-esteem over a month's time, a .78 test-retest coefficient probably represents acceptable stability in this case. As you may have surmised by now, one problem with the test-retest method is that the resulting coefficient is made smaller by both random and systematic changes in people.

Another problem with this approach to reliability assessment is that if the intertest interval is short, the retest scores might correlate highly with the original test scores simply because subjects remember how they responded from one testing occasion to the next. Hence, it is possible for an unreliable test to appear reliable when this kind of analysis is employed. A potential solution to this shortcoming is to administer different, but *equivalent*, forms of the test on each occasion. The **equivalent-forms** reliability model looks like this:

$$\text{TEST} \xrightarrow{\text{(time)}} \text{RETEST}$$
$$\text{Form 1} \qquad\qquad\qquad \text{Form 2}$$

This procedure requires that you construct two tests that measure exactly the same trait in exactly the same way but contain differently worded items. The problem of memory carry-over is minimized because the subjects receive different questions or statements in the respective forms. The reliability coefficient is obtained by calculating the correlation of Form 1 with Form 2. Simple, right? Yes, except for the necessity of constructing two forms of the test that are, in fact, equivalent in what they measure, how they measure, average score yielded, and amount of score variation they produce. When equivalent forms can be successfully assembled, however, the equivalent-forms index of reliability can be very informative (cf. Brown, 1976; Nunnally, 1967).

One other type of reliability check, the interrater, or interscorer, method was discussed in Chapter 5 and will not be reviewed here. But you may find it useful to think of interscorer reliability as a special case of equivalent-forms reliability.

Techniques of Test Validation

To be useful, measures must be not only reliable but also valid. A test is valid to the extent that what it measures is *relevant* to what it is supposed to measure. You can establish the relevance of a test to a trait by way of both logical analysis and empirical studies. *Content validation* is based on logical analysis, whereas *criterion-related validity* is assessed through empirical investigations that examine what a test is correlated with. A third approach to test validation, called *construct validity*, combines both logical and empirical evidence. Let's take a look at how each type of validity analysis was applied to the PDI.

Content Validity.   **Content validation** of a test involves inspecting the psychological content apparently tapped by the measure and judging whether that content is relevant to the trait you are attempting to measure (APA, 1974). Hence, content validity is evaluated through "expert" judgment rather than through any kind of statistical analysis. People who presumably possess expertise in the content area of interest logically analyze the test items relative to the target trait, and then indicate whether they think the test items constitute a representative sample of the trait's content. Ideally, this rational assessment takes place during the construction of the test and not as an afterthought.

Content validity was built into the procedure used to construct the PDI. First, working with theoretical material from Rogers (1961) and Coopersmith (1967), I composed 180 statements that seemed to pertain to the construct of self-esteem. I then submitted these statements to three psychologists of differing theoretical orientations and asked each to indicate, for each statement, whether agreement with that statement would reflect high, average, or low self-esteem. The three "experts" unanimously agreed on the self-esteem ratings of 67 statements. I discarded the 26 statements that the judges had rated as representing average self-esteem. This left 41 statements that would most efficiently discriminate among different levels of the trait. These became the items of the PDI. Needless to say, I was very confident that the content of the items was relevant to self-esteem.

Criterion-Related Validity.   Often the specific content of a test is less important than what the test correlates with. In fact, some personality tests, such as the Minnesota Multiphasic Personality Inventory (MMPI), were validated solely on the basis of their correlations with behavioral criteria that they were intended to predict. The items on the Depression scale of the MMPI, for instance, were selected as "depression" items because the test constructors found that clinically depressed people responded differently to these items than "normal" people did. The specific content of the items was not a major consideration in the scale's development.

Criterion-related validity, often referred to as **predictive validity**, is especially important if the main purpose of a test is to predict people's future behavior. Such is the case for most aptitude tests, including the well-known Scholastic Aptitude Test, and predictive validity is always the primary concern in the development of employee selection tests.

Predictive validity is sometimes contrasted with a second type of criterion-related validity called **concurrent validity**. The validity is "predictive" if the performance criterion is measured sometime after the test scores are obtained. It is "concurrent" if the test data and criterion data are collected at the same time.

Since the PDI was designed as a "detection" device rather than a predictive device, I assessed its concurrent validity. I was interested in finding out what criteria the test was correlated with and whether the correlations made any sense within the framework of psychological theories of self-esteem. In effect, I used the criterion-related validity coefficients to help determine whether the PDI was actually measuring the theoretical construct it was designed to measure. So at this point I'll simply list the results of the criterion-validity studies, and later I'll show you how I used this evidence in assessing the PDI's "construct validity." PDI scores were found to be positively correlated with scores on Cattell's (1972) "ego strength" scale ($r = .49$) and with peer ratings of subjects' self-esteem ($r = .70$), and negatively correlated with Eysenck's (1968) "neuroticism" scale ($r = -.63$).

Construct Validity.   **Construct validation** involves the use of both logical and empirical analyses to establish the *psychological meaning* of a test (cf. Messick, 1980). In the process of construct validation, you attempt to show how your test of a construct—self-esteem, for example—fits into psychological theories that include that construct. This type of validation is a continuing process that starts with a rational analysis of how the test's content relates to theories about the target construct. For example, the PDI items were derived from Rogers' and Coopersmith's theories of self-esteem.

After the content analysis is complete, the next step is to find out what behavioral criteria and other tests are correlated with your test. As the evidence accumulates in support of the construct validity of your test, you may discover that the test is correlated with certain behaviors or traits that were not previously known to be related to the construct you're measuring. In that case, either the construct or the theories behind it may be revised to reflect the new evidence. In Kerlinger's (1979) words, "Construct validity . . . is the essence of science itself in its testing of deductions and implications derived from theory" (p. 141). In a real sense, construct validation incorporates all other kinds of validation.

There are many methods of gathering empirical evidence to establish the construct validity of a test. Two of the more common techniques are the **group separation method** and the **correlation method**, both of which were applied to the PDI.

In the group separation method, you first locate criterion groups of subjects known to differ from one another on traits that are theoretically related to the construct of interest. Then you administer your test of that construct to the criterion groups and compute the group means. If the means differ in the direction predicted by the theory behind the construct, then the validity of your test is supported.

Some theories of human development, such as that of Erik Erikson, predict that self-esteem should increase gradually in the years of late adolescence and early adulthood (ages eighteen to twenty-five). The enhancement of self-esteem is thought to result from individuals' consolidating their self-identities during that stage of development (cf. Gallatin, 1975). If that theoretical expectation is valid, *and* if the PDI measures self-esteem, then the average PDI scores of college students should increase from the freshman year through the senior year.

Table 11–2 shows the results of a study conducted to test this expectation. The subjects were a random sample of 187 college students who were attending day classes. By examining the table you can see that there was a definite tendency for mean PDI scores to increase with class standing. Though small, most of these mean differences were significant, the sophomore-junior difference being the only exception. Therefore, both the test's construct validity and Erikson's theory are supported by the data. If the groups had not differed from one another, the outcome would be hard to interpret. A negative outcome would mean that either the theory was wrong or the test wasn't valid, or both.

Another example of the group separation method comes from a study of the self-esteem of 14 clinically depressed patients. When I administered the PDI to these patients, their mean score was only 21 (the overall mean is 30 for people in general). The finding that the depressives had low self-esteem is entirely consistent with what is known about the characteristics of severely depressed people. Interestingly, however, when the same patients were retested exactly one week following the completion of electroconvulsive shock therapy, their mean PDI score rose to 29. This outcome had been predicted, since there is evidence to suggest that this type of therapy relieves most symptoms of severe depression (cf. Coleman, Butcher, & Carson, 1980). Again the results were supportive of the test's construct validity.

The *correlation* approach to construct validation was also used to evaluate the PDI. This involved having a group of people take several personality tests, including the PDI, and then computing the linear correlation of the PDI with each of several other tests. If the PDI does measure self-esteem, then the correlations should reveal two types of evidence for the PDI's construct validity:

1. **Convergent Validity**: The trait of interest should be significantly correlated with itself even when it is measured by two different methods. For example, self-esteem measured with the PDI should have a substantial correlation with a reliable peer-rating measure of self-esteem. The two different methods should *converge* on the same construct.

2. **Discriminant Validity**: The trait of interest should not be correlated with theoretically unrelated traits, even if the same measurement method is used to assess both the target trait and the irrelevant traits. Evidence for discriminant validity is important because part of construct validation involves demonstrating that a trait is distinguishable from other traits that supposedly have no theoretical connection to it. Thus, within the framework of construct validation, finding out what a test doesn't correlate with is just as important as discovering what it does correlate with.

TABLE 11–2

Mean PDI Scores of College Students as a Function of Class Standing

Class	Mean
Freshman	28.31
Sophomore	29.58
Junior	29.64
Senior	30.51

Note: n = 187

In between the conditions that satisfy convergent and discriminant validity there is a third type of outcome critical to construct validation: The trait in question should be significantly correlated with other traits that are theoretically related to it, regardless of the measurement methods used.

Why does the method of measurement figure into the question of construct validity? Very simply, because any measurement procedure is really a *trait-method unit*: The trait you are measuring contributes to the subject's score, but so does the specific measurement technique. It is for this very reason that some college students prefer multiple-choice tests, whereas other students prefer essay exams. Right?

In the process of construct validation, then, you must be able to show that the target trait's correlation with itself and theoretically related traits is not primarily a function of overlap in the methods used to measure the traits. One way of demonstrating this is to measure both the target trait and the other traits via *two or more methods* and then analyze the resulting correlations within a **multitrait-multimethod matrix** (Campbell & Fiske, 1959). Such a matrix was constructed for the PDI, and it appears in Table 11–3.

The table shows the results of a correlational study in which the subjects were 35 college students. Each student was measured on two traits—self-esteem and extroversion—by way of two different methods: objective personality tests and peer ratings. The objective test of self-esteem was the PDI, and the objective test of extroversion was the Extroversion-Introversion scale of the Eysenck Personality Inventory (Eysenck, 1968). Each student was also rated on each of the traits by three of his or her friends; a standardized 100-point rating scale was used in each case. My theoretical expectation was that the two measures of self-esteem would be strongly correlated with one another, and that the same would hold true for the two measures of extroversion. However, there is no psychological theory of self-esteem that would predict a strong relationship between self-

TABLE 11–3

Example of a Multitrait-Multimethod Matrix*

		Method			
		Objective Test		*Peer Ratings*	
	Traits	*Self-esteem*	*Extroversion*	*Self-esteem*	*Extroversion*
Objective Test	Self-esteem	(.86)			
	Extroversion	a .19	(.84)		
Peer Ratings	Self-esteem	[.70]	b .07	(.88)	
	Extroversion	.26	[.48]	a .34	(.91)

Note: (a) Correlations in *parentheses* are the *reliability* coefficients.

(b) Correlations in *brackets* are the *validity* coefficients.

(c) *Solid triangles* contain correlations between *different traits* measured by the *same method* (Different-Trait/Same-Method triangles).

(d) *Dashed triangles* contain correlations between *different traits* measured by *different methods* (Different-Trait/Different-Method triangles).

*Sample Size = 35

esteem and extroversion. Therefore, if the PDI's ability to correlate with other variables is not an artifact of method overlap, then there should be little correlation between self-esteem and extroversion even when both traits are assessed through the same method.

There are four outcomes to note in the table:

1. *Same-Trait/Same-Method Correlations*: These are represented by the correlations in parentheses. You will recognize these indices as the reliability coefficients of the four instruments used in this study. Thus, a reliability coefficient may be thought of as the correlation coefficient between maximally similar traits measured by maximally similar methods.

2. *Same-Trait/Different-Method Correlations*: These coefficients are bracketed in the table. They show that, as measured in this study, both self-esteem and extroversion have *convergent validity*. Self-esteem was strongly correlated with itself (r = .70) across the two methods of measurement; that is, the different methods "converged" on the same trait. The trait of extroversion exhibited a moderate amount of convergent validity (r = .48). What accounts for the difference between the size of the reliability coefficient (same-trait/same-method) and the size of the bracketed correlations (same-trait/different-method)? That's right, the contribution that specific measurement methods make to the test scores.

3. *Different-Trait/Same-Method Correlations*. You'll find these correlations in the solid-line triangles labeled "a." If the traits being measured have *discriminant validity*, then their correlations with theoretically unrelated traits should be relatively low, even when the variables are measured by the same method. These different-trait/same-method correlations should definitely be smaller than the bracketed coefficients if the traits are contributing more to the test scores than the methods. That is true in this case.

4. *Different-Trait/Different-Method Correlations*. Since these correlations are based on data that share neither traits nor measurement methods, they should be the smallest coefficients in the matrix. They appear in the broken-line triangles labeled "b." To the extent that these coefficients are lower than those in the different-trait/same-method triangles, the measurement methods are contributing to the test scores.

Overall, the multitrait-multimethod analysis of the PDI supports the validity of the test as a measure of the self-esteem construct. However, stronger validity evidence would be obtained if similar outcomes occurred in a study that included a large number of personality traits and perhaps a third measurement method.

Another line of evidence for a measure's construct validity concerns the extent to which the measure is correlated with tests of different traits that are theoretically related to the target trait. For example, self-esteem should be inversely related to the tendency to develop neurotic symptoms, since a nearly universal characteristic of "neurotics" is their negative self-regard (cf. McMahon & McMahon, 1983). In line with this theoretical expectation, I found that the correlation between PDI scores and scores on Eysenck's (1968) Neuroticism Scale was − .63. In still another investigation, the PDI was found to be positively correlated with Cattell's Ego Strength Scale (r = .49). High scores on the latter test are associated with emotional stability and realistic thinking, both characteristics of people who possess high self-esteem (cf. Rogers, 1961).

My overall impression, based on evidence to date, is that the PDI adequately measures the trait of self-esteem as generally defined in psychological theory. The PDI story won't end here, however, for construct validation, like the scientific method in general, is an ongoing process that continually corrects itself as it builds upon itself.

EVALUATING THE PSYCHOMETRIC APPROACH

The psychometric approach is a very efficient means of obtaining empirical evidence for the existence of a relationship. When variables such as personality traits or aptitudes are being investigated, direct manipulation of the variables is not possible. Still, for many applications in counseling, educational, and industrial psychology, we need to be able to *predict* the behavior of these variables or else to use measurements of them to predict people's future behavior. Thus, any method that helps us to discover and use predictive relationships is a valuable tool in the psychological professions.

The problems that the psychometric method has with internal validity have already been addressed. But how good is the *external validity* of the approach? Only as good as your sampling technique. In this respect, the psychometric method is similar to the survey method. If your sample of subjects is a probability sample, then your data probably are generalizable to some larger population. If a selective factor enters into your subject-selection process, however, your findings may have restricted applicability (see Chapter 8).

ANALYZING THE DATA FROM PSYCHOMETRIC STUDIES

Nearly every known statistical test has been applied to psychometric-type data. By far, however, the statistic most frequently used to analyze the data of psychometric research is the Pearson r. If you have read Chapters 5 and 6, then you already are familiar with the nature, meaning, and computation of r. But you still may not know how to test a correlation coefficient for statistical significance. Actually, there are several ways to accomplish this. The simplest procedure is to compare your computed correlation to a table of "critical" chance correlations, such as those which appear in Table A-3 of the Appendix. To use that table, you first decide on what level of significance you are going to employ (e.g., .05 or .01). Next you compute the degrees of freedom in your sample. Degrees of freedom (df) for a correlation coefficient are equal to $(n - 2)$, where n = the number of *pairs* of observations in your sample; in other words, n = the number of people in your sample.

For example, if you have measured 27 people on variables X and Y, then $df = (27 - 2) = 25$. To locate the critical value of r, you find the chance value of r in Table A-3 that lies at the intersection of the chosen level of significance and the degrees of freedom. If you used the .05 level of significance and df = 25, then the critical r = .38. If your *computed* r is larger than this value, the correlation is statistically significant.

There are many advanced applications of r that are often useful in psychometric studies. Three of these techniques will be reviewed here.

Combining Predictors of a Criterion: Multiple Correlation

In applied psychometric research, it is frequently advantageous to combine two or more predictor variables to forecast a particular criterion behavior. For instance, some college admissions committees will combine applicants' high school grade-point averages with their Scholastic Aptitude Test scores to predict the applicants' freshman-year college grade-point averages. Applicants whose predicted grades are below, let's say, a "C" level are normally not admitted to the college. In making these important decisions, admissions committees have found, through empirical studies, that a combination of predictor variables gives more accurate forecasts of students' actual grade-point averages than does any single predictor.

The basis for predicting a criterion from a combination of variables is a procedure called **multiple correlation**. The formula for computing a multiple correlation (R) of a combination of two predictors with a criterion looks like this:

$$R_{y.12} = \sqrt{\frac{r_{y1}^2 + r_{y2}^2 - [2(r_{y1})(r_{y2})(r_{12})]}{1 - r_{12}^2}}, \text{ where}$$

$R_{y.12}$ is the symbol for multiple correlation,
r_{y1} is the correlation between predictor 1 and the criterion, Y,
r_{y2} is the correlation between predictor 2 and the criterion, and
r_{12} is the correlation between predictors 1 and 2

It should be clear that you need to compute three linear correlations (r_{y1}, r_{y2}, and r_{12}) to use the multiple correlation formula.

Consider an example. Suppose you are a personnel officer in a large plant, and one of your jobs is to help select first-line supervisors for promotion to department supervisors. Past research has shown that two variables, in particular, predict the levels of performance attained by department supervisors: scores on a test of managerial skills (Predictor 1) and number of years with the company (Predictor 2). The relevant correlations are as follows:

$$r_{y1} = .50$$
$$r_{y2} = .40$$
$$r_{12} = .20$$

You could use Predictor 1 (test scores) to forecast performance and thus help you choose among the candidates for promotion. Or you could combine Predictors 1 and 2 to try to get a more accurate forecast of who will perform best in the department head's position. But is the combination of predictors actually more strongly related to the criterion than Predictor 1 alone? Plugging the three correlations into the formula for Multiple R, we get:

$$R_{y.12} = \sqrt{\frac{(.50)^2 + (.40)^2 - [2(.50)(.40)(.20)]}{1 - (.20)^2}}$$

$$R_{y.12} = \sqrt{\frac{.25 + .16 - (.08)}{1 - .04}}$$

$$R_{y.12} = \sqrt{\frac{.41 - .08}{.96}}$$

$$R_{y.12} = \sqrt{\frac{.33}{.96}}$$

$$R_{y.12} = \sqrt{.344}$$

$$R_{y.12} = .59$$

Clearly, the .59 correlation obtained with the combination of Predictors 1 and 2 is somewhat better than that resulting from Predictor 1 alone. So you probably would use the combination of predictors to help you make your decision about who should be promoted first.

The statistical procedure that utilizes information provided by Multiple R to make specific predictions about individuals is referred to as multiple regression. It's a fairly involved procedure; see Hays (1981) or Brown (1976) for a description. Note that more than two predictors can be used in multiple correlation and multiple regression; however, the first two predictors entered into the equation usually make the biggest difference in prediction accuracy. Because many predictors of a criterion typically are correlated with one another, the predictive information provided by a third or fourth predictor is often redundant with that furnished by the first two. Hence, adding a lot of predictors beyond the first two or, perhaps, three usually doesn't increase the multiple correlation by much.

The latter consideration leads to one final point about multiple correlation. Two predictors are better than one to the extent that they are *uncorrelated* with one another and thus provide independent information. In the above example, the predictors were almost independent of one another, since r_{12} was only .20. Had r_{12} been .50, the Multiple R would have dropped from .59 to .53. You might want to experiment with different values in the equation to see how R is affected.

Dealing with the Third-Variable Problem: Partial r

There are times when you might strongly suspect that a relationship between two variables is due to the influence that a third variable has on both of those variables. To verify or disconfirm your suspicion, you can employ a statistic called **partial correlation**, or partial r. Partial r indexes the strength of the linear relationship between two variables when the influence of a third variable has been statistically removed from both of them. The formula for partial r is:

$$r_{12.3} = \frac{r_{12} - [(r_{13})(r_{23})]}{\sqrt{1 - (r_{13})^2} \ \sqrt{1 - (r_{23})^2}}, \text{ where}$$

$r_{12.3}$ = the partial correlation between variables 1 and 2, with the influence of variable 3 "partialed out,"

r_{12} = the correlation between variables 1 and 2,

r_{13} = the correlation between variables 1 and 3,

r_{23} = the correlation between variables 2 and 3,

For example, suppose I've found a significant relationship between a personality trait called "cerebrotonia"—think of it as a characteristic of brainy people—and grade-point average (GPA), but I suspect that general intelligence might be responsible for the relationship. If cerebrotonia is variable 1, GPA is variable 2, and IQ is variable 3, the three relevant correlations might look like this:

$$r_{12} = .30$$
$$r_{13} = .40$$
$$r_{23} = .50$$

Applying the formula for the partial correlation between cerebrotonia and GPA when the influence of IQ has been removed from each of those variables, I get:

$$r_{12.3} = \frac{.30 - [(.40)(.50)]}{\sqrt{1 - (.40)^2} \ \sqrt{1 - (.50)^2}}$$

$$r_{12.3} = \frac{.30 - .20}{\sqrt{1 - .16} \ \sqrt{1 - .25}}$$

$$r_{12.3} = \frac{.10}{\sqrt{.84} \ \sqrt{.75}}$$

$$r_{12.3} = \frac{.10}{(.917) \ (.866)}$$

$$r_{12.3} = \frac{.10}{.79}$$

$$r_{12.3} = .13$$

This result shows that when the influence of IQ is subtracted from the relationship between cerebrotonia and GPA, there is very little relationship left. On the other hand, if "partialing out" IQ had had little effect on the correlation, then general intelligence would have been ruled out as a third variable responsible for the relationship.

Evidence for Directionality in a Relationship: Cross-Lagged Correlational Analysis

A major assumption of the scientific conception of causality is that "cause" precedes "effect"; in other words, that causal processes work forward in time. This assumption is the basis of the *time-precedence* criterion of causality that was discussed in Chapter 4. The time-precedence concept may be used to gather some support for the internal validity of a cause-and-effect hypothesis that is based on correlational data. Let's see how.

The correlational system that exploits the concept of time precedence for purposes of causal analysis is referred to as **cross-lagged panel correlation** or, more simply, **time-lagged correlation** (Kenny, 1975). The technique involves the computation of several correlations between two variables that are measured at *two different times*, with the same group of people serving as subjects on each measurement occasion. (You'll recognize this as a longitudinal method.) Then the correlation between variable X measured at time 1 and variable Y measured at time 2 is compared with the correlation between variable Y measured at time 1 and variable X measured at time 2. The strength of correlations between measurements at time 1 and measurements at time 2 is of special interest because *cause-and-effect is presumed to work in a forward direction.* If the X————————→Y correlation is much stronger than the Y————————→X correlation, then the hypothesis that changes in X cause changes in Y is supported. The rival hypothesis, that Y causes X to vary, would be supported if the Y————————→X correlation were stronger.

Examine the hypothetical example of a time-lagged correlation analysis shown in Figure 11–1. The hypothesis is that people's self-esteem during early adolescence influences the amount of "neuroticism" they exhibit later in life. That is, higher self-esteem is hy-

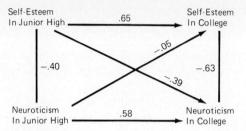

FIGURE 11–1

Time-Lagged and Contemporaneous Correlations Between Self-Esteem and Neuroticism (Fictitious Data)

pothesized to "protect" individuals from developing neurotic tendencies, whereas lower self-esteem is hypothesized to predispose individuals to the development of neurotic tendencies. Notice that self-esteem and neuroticism were measured twice—while the subjects were in junior high school and again when they were in college. This permitted the computation of the six correlation coefficients that appear in the figure. The correlation of each trait with itself across the time span is simply a long-term test-retest reliability coefficient. The two contemporaneous correlations show that the traits were negatively related to one another, both during the junior high years (r = − .40) and during the college years (r = − .63). But the correlations of particular value for causal analysis are the two time-lagged correlations that appear on the *diagonal lines* in the figure. There was only a negligible relationship between neuroticism in junior high school and self-esteem in college. Hence, the rival hypothesis, that neuroticism influences the development of self-esteem, is not supported. In contrast, self-esteem in the junior high years was a significant predictor of neuroticism in the college years. If the assumptions of the time-lagged model are correct, then, the more plausible hypothesis is that level of self-esteem influences the development of neurotic traits.

There are, however, some problems with the assumptions of the time-lagged correlation model. One difficulty is that the model assumes that the psychological processes that influence the individual subjects are unchanging over time. Rogosa (1980) has pointed out the possible fallacies in this and other assumptions on which time-lagged analysis is based. See his article for a thorough critique of time-lagged designs.

SUMMARY

Psychometric research is "correlational" research, in that its primary focus is on searching for relationships among variables without attempting direct manipulation or control of those variables.

The psychometric approach assumes that there are stable and measurable individual differences among people, and that test scores reflecting these individual differences are related to socially significant behaviors.

The psychometric method is employed for purposes of conducting exploratory research, developing predictors of performance in work or school situations, building theories, and testing theories.

When you construct and validate a test, the following matters must be considered: test-item format (objective or subjective?), reliability, and validity. Because they are more reliable, objective test formats, such as multiple-choice, are generally preferred over subjective formats. The reliability of a test may be measured through a variety of techniques, including the *internal consistency, test-retest,* and *equivalent-forms* methods.

A test that is reliable isn't necessarily valid. Validity is evaluated on the basis of test *content* and what *criteria* the test correlates with. *Construct validity*, which is important in theory development, combines both content validation and criterion-related validation. The following concepts were reviewed in connection with construct validity: *correlation method, group-separation method, convergent validity, discriminant validity.*

Almost any kind of statistical test potentially could be employed to analyze psychometric data, but the Pearson r is the most flexible and informative statistic in this approach to research. Special applications of r reviewed in this chapter include *multiple correlation, partial correlation* and *time-lagged correlational analysis.*

REVIEW QUESTIONS

1. What are the major characteristics of the psychometric method, and what are its principal uses in the social sciences?

2. List the four chief assumptions underlying the psychometric approach to research. Which of these assumptions has been most frequently questioned by research evidence? What does that evidence suggest?

3. Summarize the five steps in developing a psychometric device to predict performance in a job.

4. What functions are served by the psychometric method in theory building? In theory testing?

5. Evaluate the various test-item formats that may be used in psychological tests.

6. Distinguish among objective, subjective, and projective tests. What are the major advantages of objective tests?

7. Define: reliability; internal-consistency reliability; reliability across testing sessions.

8. Discuss the nature, advantages, and disadvantages of the four methods of computing reliability that were reviewed in this chapter.

9. Define: content validity; criterion-related validity; construct validity.

10. Differentiate between convergent and discriminant validity. Tell why each of these concepts is important in the process of construct validation.

11. Analyze the advantages and shortcomings of the psychometric approach, giving special attention to the issues of internal validity and external validity.

12. Summarize the purposes of multiple correlation, partial correlation, and time-lagged correlational analysis.

Note

[1] If you're interested in learning about the various applied uses of psychological tests, I suggest that you look into any of the many fine texts on psychological testing available at your college or university library.

12

THE SAMPLE SURVEY

In this chapter, we'll explore an approach to research that is notable for its external validity—the sample survey. Although the sample survey is similar in many ways to the psychometric method, the survey is distinguished from the latter by a greater concern with scientific sampling procedures and immediate generalization from "sample" to "population." The logic underlying these sampling procedures and the associated statistical analyses is elegantly simple, yet fascinating and powerful: That logical system will be a principal topic in this chapter.

Before I take you further into the survey method, let me quickly repeat some key definitions that were introduced in Chapter 8. These terms are especially important within the context of the present chapter.

Target population: all of the people, settings, treatment stimuli, and time frames that you wish to generalize your findings to. (Within survey sampling, the generalization dimension that receives primary attention is the people dimension.)

Sample: the people, settings, stimuli, and time frames you actually observe; a subset of *some* population.

Sampled population: the population your sample actually represents, which may or may not be the target population.

The aim of survey sampling is to ensure that the sampled population is nearly identical to the target population so that the desired generalizations to the target population can be made with confidence.

THE CONCEPT OF PARAMETER ESTIMATION

The major purpose of the sample survey approach is to estimate **population parameters** on the basis of the **statistics** compiled from a sample of data. Parameters are *statistical characteristics of populations*—for example, the *mean* IQ of the population of high school students in an urban school district; or, for another example, the *range* of annual income for the whole population of American accountants. If we were interested in finding out what these parameters are, it probably would be too expensive and time-consuming to collect data on every person in the target population. But, if we could use a sampling technique to obtain data on a few hundred people who fairly represent the population of interest, then we would be able to use the *sample statistics* (e.g., sample mean or sample range) to estimate the population parameters.

Overview of the Basic Procedure

Of central significance here is the idea that you can use a sample statistic to *infer*, or make an educated guess about, a population parameter that you are interested in. Hence, parameter estimation is one branch of the theoretical system called *inferential statistics*. And, as you will learn in later sections of this chapter, it is possible not only to estimate population characteristics on the basis of sample data, but also to calculate how far off your estimate of the population parameter might be.

A diagram of the fundamental idea behind parameter estimation appears in Figure 12–1. The figure suggests the following sequence of operations: (a) define the population of interest and the characteristic you wish to estimate; (b) draw a representative subset (i.e., sample) of people from that population; (c) measure the target characteristic in the sample of people, and compute a sample statistic; (d) use the sample statistic to estimate

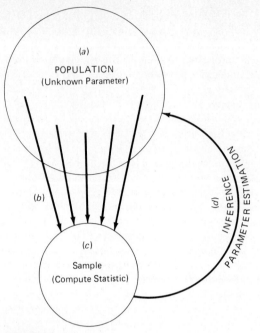
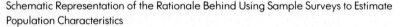

FIGURE 12-1
Schematic Representation of the Rationale Behind Using Sample Surveys to Estimate
Population Characteristics

the level of the characteristic in the population—that is, make an inference about the population parameter.

Uses of Parameter Estimation

You are probably already aware of some of the uses of parameter estimation in the social
sciences. Political scientists estimate the political opinions of populations from a study of
those opinions in samples of respondents. Commercial polling agencies, such as those of
Harris, Gallup, and Yankelovich, do the same thing prior to major elections, in an effort
to predict how voters will behave on election day. Economists study the behavior patterns and purchasing intentions of samples of consumers, in order to gauge what a population of consumers is doing or will be doing with their money. Marketing managers of
large businesses also have an ongoing interest in the latter use of survey sampling.

How is survey sampling used in psychology? Primarily to estimate attitudes and opinions of populations on such issues as abortion, drug use, euthanasia, sex roles, prejudice,
crime, and so on. Psychologists also employ this approach to gauge the behaviors and
traits of certain populations. For example, topics as diverse as factors affecting the quality
of life in America (Flanagan, 1978) and the achievement motivation of American women
(Veroff, Depner, Kulka, & Douvan, 1980) have been examined through the survey
method. Psychologists even use the survey approach to study their profession; for instance, a survey of 471 clinical psychologists examined how often these professionals use
objective tests versus projective tests in their day-to-day practice. In spite of the generally

poor reliability of projective tests, the survey revealed that clinical psychologists employ projective instruments just as often as the more reliable "objective" tests (Wade & Baker, 1977). In fact, the overall results suggested that the clinicians had a higher opinion of projective tests than of the objective measures.

More recently, the American Psychological Association surveyed a random sample of 100 chairpersons of psychology departments in regard to the special problems and issues facing undergraduate education in psychology. We will consider various aspects of that interesting study in later sections of this chapter.

Having considered the "what for" of the survey approach, let's now proceed to the matter of "how to."

TECHNIQUES OF SAMPLING

Sampling in the context of parameter estimation usually means selecting the individuals who will serve as subjects, or "respondents," representing some larger set of people. How you select the subjects is of paramount importance, because your *sampling design* will determine what population your findings will generalize to. An adequate sampling design, if implemented in your subject-selection procedure, will permit you to make inferences about a fairly broad population of people, for the use of proper sampling procedures will minimize the difference between the *sampled population* and the *target population*. In contrast, an inadequate sampling procedure will yield results that apply to a much narrower population than you intended to study.

In this section of the chapter, I'll review the major sampling designs used in survey research. They fall into two broad categories: *probability sampling designs* and *nonprobability sampling designs*. For reasons that will become clear as you read, probability sampling procedures almost always provide more useful information than their nonprobability counterparts.

General Steps in the Sampling Process

Regardless of the specific sampling procedures you use, there are three basic steps in the sampling process:

1. *Define the target population.* The first step in sampling should always be to decide exactly what the nature and bounds of your population are. If, for example, you desired to study student opinions concerning the dormitory facilities on your campus, would you want to sample from the entire population of students, perhaps selecting respondents from the registrar's master roster? Probably not, since commuting students may not possess sufficient information about dormitory life to contribute useful responses. Hence, you would perhaps define your target population as all students presently living in the university-owned dormitories. You may also wish to exclude freshman residents if your study is being conducted in the fall, as you may feel that they haven't had enough opportunity to evaluate the dormitory situation. The same might be true of new transfer students who are residing in the dorms. In the end, then, you might define the target population as "all current residents of university-owned dormitories, except those residents who are first-semester freshmen or first-semester transfer students."

2. *Compile or obtain a listing of your sampling units.* In order to identify and contact the specific individuals who will be your sample of respondents, you first need an exhaustive

and up-to-date list of all **sampling units** in the population. Sampling units are the entities that are directly selected in your sampling procedure. A sampling unit might be an organization, a building, a household, a person, or anything else that can be defined, distinguished as an independent unit, and listed. The listing of sampling units that you compile is referred to as the **sampling frame**. If your target population were all dormitory students at your school, for instance, perhaps the dean of students or the registrar could provide you with a relatively complete and accurate list of those students, together with their mailbox or telephone numbers. If so, the list itself would be the sampling frame.

If your target population consists of all adults in a particular town, city, or county, sometimes a telephone directory can be used as the sampling frame. Although there may be sampling biases associated with the telephone directory—not all people have telephones or listed numbers—that bias appears to be less troublesome today than it once was (see the discussion of telephone interviews below). Thus, the phone book is one possible and convenient sampling frame.

Many other sampling frames are available, depending on your specific purpose. Examples include housing-unit lists published by the U.S. Census Bureau, organization membership lists, and voter registration lists. With some ingenuity and official authorization, say from the university administration or a government official, you will be able to secure a sampling frame for practically any type of survey study you choose to undertake.

Note that the sampling frame may be either a list of the population members per se or a list of some larger units, such as households or formal groups, that contain those population members. As you will see below, the size of your sampling units will depend on the specific sampling design you employ. In all cases, however, it is wise to make sure that your list of sampling units is complete and up-to-date. Otherwise, your sample may not adequately represent the intended population.

3. *Select your sample.* The final step in the sampling procedure is to decide which units in the sampling frame should be selected. How this decision is made will be a function of your sampling design, so let's now consider the most commonly used sampling models.

Probability Sampling

When your sampling procedure is conducted in such a way that *every sampling unit has a known probability of being selected*, you are using some variety of probability sampling. One definition of "probability" given earlier in this book was "the number of outcomes favoring event A divided by the sum of outcomes favoring A and outcomes not favoring A." In shorthand, probability $(A) = A/(A + \text{not } A)$. For example, if there are 30 people in the sampling frame, and you plan to select 10 of them *at random*, then probability (of being selected) = (number of people to be selected)/(number of people to be selected + number not to be selected); probability $= 10/(10 + 20) = .33$. Thus, in theory, each sampling unit has a known probability of being included in the sample, and that probability is .33.

There are two important advantages associated with probability sampling. One is that it usually provides you with a sample that adequately represents the target population, something which can't often be said of "nonprobability" sampling. Second, by definition, probability sampling allows you to know the theoretical probability of selecting each sampling unit. With this knowledge, you can utilize a logical theory of probability to obtain a numerical estimate of the *likely maximal deviation* of your sample statistic from the population parameter it is supposed to represent. This theory of probability will be covered in the last section of this chapter. It is the same theory that permits the commercial polling agencies to publish statements such as: "In our sample, Candidate Bullwinkle leads Candidate Highhander by *seven* percentage points. However, due to sampling error, the actual percentage of vote commanded by each candidate may vary by *two* percentage points in either direction." Hence, the pollsters realize that the results of their sample may deviate from the population percentages by a few points, but they are confident that Bullwinkle leads Highhander by *at least* three percentage points in the population of voters. (What would be the largest likely difference between the candidates in this example?) If you follow the preelection polls much, you know that, as election day approaches, the pollsters' sample results become fairly accurate indicators of how the population of voters will actually behave.

There are dozens of variations on the basic concept of probability sampling, but most probability sampling designs fall into four categories: *simple random sampling, stratified random sampling, cluster sampling, and multi-stage area sampling*.

Simple Random Sampling.   In **simple random sampling**, *sampling units are chosen from the sampling frame in such a way that every possible sample of size n has an equal chance of being drawn*. When you use simple random sampling, each sampling unit has an *equal* and *independent* chance of being selected: equal because each person's inclusion in the sample is determined entirely by random processes, or chance; independent because the chance selection of a particular individual has no effect on the likelihood of another person's being selected.

You can conduct simple random sampling by listing members of a population in a sampling frame and using a random number table to select the units to be included in your sample. A large random number table is given in Table A–1 of the Appendix, along with instructions on how to draw a simple random sample using that table.

A generally acceptable substitute for simple random sampling is **systematic random sampling**. This procedure involves several steps. First, decide what proportion of the population you wish to sample. Suppose you decide to sample 100 people from a population of 700. In this case, then, the relevant proportion would be 1/7, and your "skip interval" would be *seven*. Next, using a random number table, select a number between 1 and 7. If the number 4 is selected, then the fourth person in the sampling frame is the first subject to enter the sample. Then take every *seventh* person thereafter; hence, the next several selected persons would be numbers 11, 18, 25, and so on. If you did your initial arithmetic correctly, then your 100th (and final) selection will be drawn from the last group of seven people in your list. This is an acceptable form of probability sampling, since every sampling unit has a known probability of being selected prior to your random selection of the entry point in the sampling frame.

Stratified Random Sampling.   If the population you're interested in appears to consist of two or more distinct subpopulations, such as commuter students and resident students, then you might wish to use **stratified random sampling** instead of simple random sampling. Stratified random sampling is schematically illustrated in Figure 12–2. In this design, you establish a separate sampling frame for each subpopulation, or *stratum*. Then you randomly select a predetermined number of sampling units from each stratum and compute separate sample statistics for each stratum. Finally, you combine the sample data of the separate strata to obtain an overall estimate of the population parameter—for example, the proportion of all students at an institution who hold a particular opinion on some issue. For a fixed number of subjects, stratified random sampling will give you a more accurate estimate of the population parameter than simple random sampling when the following two conditions hold: (a) the strata you have defined differ appreciably from one another on the variable that your survey is designed to measure; (b) people within

Population

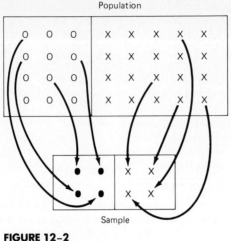

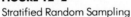

Sample

FIGURE 12–2

Stratified Random Sampling

Note: Separate samples of n = 4 were drawn randomly from each stratum. The probability of a person's being selected from each stratum is known, but the people in stratum 1 had a higher probability of being chosen (p = 4/12) than did the people in stratum 2 (p = 4/20).

each stratum don't vary much from one another on the measured variable. In short, between-stratum differences should be greater than within-stratum differences, on the average. See Figure 12–3 for a graphical illustration of these points.

If you use stratified random sampling, you may decide to sample the same percentage of people from each stratum. This is called **proportional allocation**. Suppose, for instance, that stratum 1 consists of 50 people and stratum 2 consists of 100 people. A 10 percent sample from each stratum would result in 5 people being drawn from stratum 1 and 10 being selected from stratum 2. However, it isn't necessary that you use proportional allocation. Especially if one stratum is very small, consisting, for example, of 17 Japanese students, you may need to sample a larger percentage of that stratum just to have a minimally adequate sample size to represent the small subpopulation. It's perfectly okay to do that. In fact, the hypothetical case of stratified random sampling represented in Figure 12–2 illustrates "disproportionate allocation": Thirty-three percent of stratum 1 was sampled, whereas only 20 percent of stratum 2 was sampled.

Cluster Sampling. If you are conducting a sample survey over a fairly large geographical area, such as a whole city, it can be both inconvenient and expensive to travel to and from selected households that are scattered widely across the targeted area. And most often a simple random sampling design would ensure that the selected sampling units are variously dispersed. To lessen their travel time and associated expenses, experienced sample surveyors often employ "cluster sampling." A **cluster sample** is *a simple random sample in which each basic sampling unit is a group of smaller units, called "elements."* To cluster sample, you first divide the population into a number of nonoverlapping groups, or "clusters," of sampling elements. All elements within a given cluster are situated close to one another. For example, a cluster might be a city block of homes, the "elements" of the cluster being all of the households located within that block. The next step is to randomly select a number of clusters. Finally, you interview every element—i.e., household

(a)

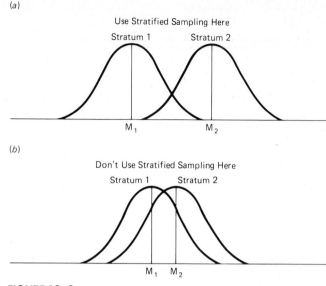

Use Stratified Sampling Here

Stratum 1   Stratum 2

M_1 M_2

(b)

Don't Use Stratified Sampling Here

Stratum 1   Stratum 2

M_1 M_2

FIGURE 12–3

When to Use and When Not to Use Stratified Random Sampling

Note: Stratified random sampling provides an advantage over simple random sampling when the respective strata can be assumed to be clearly different from one another on the measured dimension. The symbol M represents the mean of each stratum on the measured dimension.

or individual—within each cluster. A variation of this procedure involves interviewing a simple random sample of elements within each selected cluster, rather than attempting to get data from every member of the cluster. Since the selected elements are located close to one another within each cluster, the interviewing process is economical of time and money. Of course, you would want to sample a large enough number of clusters to ensure that the overall geographical area of the population is adequately represented in your sample data.

Multi-Stage Area Sampling.   When a survey is conducted across a *very large* geographical area, such as a state, or even a whole country, it is not feasible to begin the sampling procedure with a listing of individuals or housing units. This is the problem faced by all of the commercial polling firms, as well as by university-based survey centers that conduct state, regional, and national surveys. How do these organizations manage to obtain sample data that adequately represent these exceptionally large populations? Although specific techniques differ from one polling outfit to another, the general approach used in these cases is called **multi-stage sampling**: *A planned sequence of probability sampling is conducted in stages, with progressively smaller sampling units being used at each successive stage.* When the sampling unit reaches its smallest dimension, usually a household or a "housing unit," the interview is conducted with one person at each of the selected locations. The sampling strategy used by the University of Michigan's Survey Research Center illustrates the multi-stage approach to sampling:

> The United States is divided into primary areas, usually by counties. Using a probability sampling method, 74 of these areas are selected as the Center's sample of primary areas.

Then, particular *locations* (cities, towns, and rural areas) are selected within the primary areas.

Chunks (geographical areas containing from 16 to 40 [housing units]) are selected within each sample location.

The chunks are further divided into *segments* of from 4 to 16 [housing units].

A sample of [housing units] is drawn from segments. (*Interviewer's Manual*, p. 37)

Probability sampling, based on random selection, is used through the first three stages (through "chunk" selection), after which succeeding units are chosen according to specific criteria reflecting the purpose of the survey. For example, the purpose of some surveys might require that the oldest female of each household be interviewed; other surveys might require that the youngest adult be interviewed, and so on. The Survey Research Center's version of multi-stage sampling is illustrated in Figure 12–4.

Nonprobability Sampling

Many survey studies are not based on probability sampling. That is, the subjects are not selected through the use of a random draw at some point in the sampling process. Hence, in **nonprobability sampling**, *the theoretical probability of selecting a given sampling unit is not known.* This may not be a problem, so long as the purpose of such a survey is merely to reveal the characteristics, attitudes, or opinions of the particular group that is interviewed. Nonprobability sampling is a major drawback, however, if the purpose of the study is to estimate the characteristics of some larger group of people that the sample is supposed to represent. This is a problem because we can use probability theory to accurately estimate population parameters only if the sampling of respondents is based on *random* selection. There is no compromise on this matter: *The fundamental assumption of survey sampling statistics*—and the underlying theory of parameter estimation—*is that of random selection of events.* The statistical theory, as well as its practical applications, is useless when this assumption is violated. (Refer to Box 12–1 for further explanation.) Thus, it is very important for you to follow your probability sampling design to the letter if your survey study is a serious attempt to estimate the characteristics of a population. For an example of the kind of distortion that nonprobability sampling can produce, see Box 12–2.

For a variety of reasons, including time pressures, limited resources, and carelessness, survey researchers sometimes use nonprobability sampling techniques, even when the goal is to generalize to a population. The most commonly encountered nonprobability samples are the *convenience sample*, the *"representative" sample*, and the *quota sample*.

The Convenience Sample.   **Convenience sampling** has been referred to earlier in this book. To review, the term means that *the researcher uses particular subjects in her study because those subjects are readily available, perhaps eager to participate, and, in any case, easy to observe and measure.* Most subject pools in psychology experiments yield convenience samples. These pools usually consist of freshman and sophomore college students who must participate in a specified number of experiments to fulfill a psychology course requirement. However, for a variety of reasons that were considered in Chapter 8, the use of convenience samples is not necessarily undesirable within the context of the experimental method, but it can be disastrous in survey research designed to estimate something about a broad population of people.

The obvious problem with convenience sampling is that the "convenient" subjects have that status for reasons that set them apart from a large segment of the general popu-

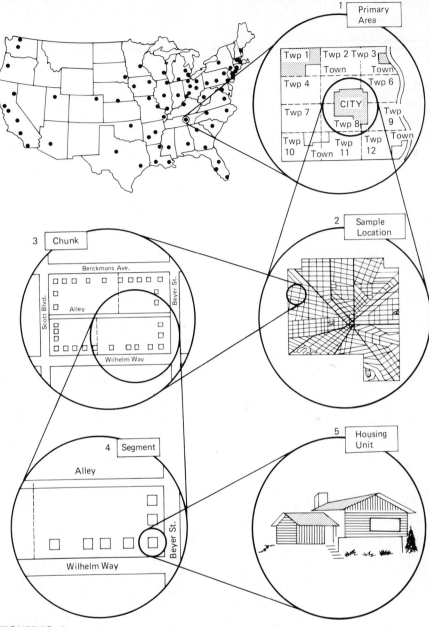

FIGURE 12–4

Sampling Sequence in Multistage Area Sampling

From *Interviewer's Manual* (rev. ed.). Ann Arbor, Mich.: Institute for Social Research, 1976. Reproduced with permission.

BOX 12–1
HIGHLIGHT
The Concept of "Error" Revisited

At many points in this book, you've encountered the notion of error and how it affects sampling, measurement, statistical decision-making, the interpretation of relationships, and the validity of generalizations. As it turns out, error is also a key concept in parameter estimation.

First, consider *unsystematic* or *random* error—the type that results from chance events. Random error can't be avoided in the sampling process; thus, it is an inherent aspect of estimating population parameters on the basis of sample data. Fortunately, however, mathematicians have developed an accurate model of random error which allows social scientists to know how random error affects their sample data. This random error model is built into the statistics of parameter estimation.

Probability sampling always involves the use of random selection at some point in the sampling procedure. Therefore, if probability sampling is used to select respondents in your sample, then the sampling error in your data will conform to the known model of random error. Consequently, you will be able to use the conventional statistics of parameter estimation to (a) infer the population proportion or mean that you're interested in and (b) calculate a number called the "bound on the error of estimation," which represents the *greatest likely deviation* of your sample esti-

mate from the true population parameter. Thus, sampling error presents no great problem when probability sampling is used.

However, *systematic*, or *constant*, error, which is normally caused by improper research procedures, is not accommodated by the conventional model of random error. Therefore, the statistics of parameter estimation would not give you accurate results if your data have been influenced by some systematic error. This is precisely why nonprobability sampling prevents you from accurately estimating population characteristics: It introduces systematic error into your sample data. An example would be interviewing anyone in the sampling frame who can be reached between 10:00 A.M. and 2:00 P.M. There are systematic differences between these people and the remainder of the general population: Perhaps this sample disproportionately represents unemployed, retired, and vacationing people, as well as people who are ill and persons who have unusual work schedules. This systematic error will affect your sample data in some unknown, nonrandom fashion. As a result, the mathematical model of random error will not apply to data obtained through nonprobability sampling techniques, and you will have no way of calculating how far off your estimate of the population parameter is from the "true" mark.

lation. Perhaps they are available because of factors such as age, sex, curiosity, desperation, their particular college curricula, work schedule, social role, or personality traits. Therefore, any results that hold true for a convenience sample may not hold true for the majority of their peers, let alone the majority of, say, the general adult population. It follows that your generalizations from a convenience sample may be restricted to some smaller, vaguely definable population of people who have the characteristics of "convenient subjects." In addition, of course, since random selection is not used in this approach to sampling, the statistics of parameter estimation cannot be legitimately applied to the data.

A special type of convenience sampling that disguises itself as "random sampling," at least to the untutored eye, is called **haphazard sampling**, defined as *the arbitrary and apparently unsystematic selection of sampling units that happen to be easily accessible.* The researcher who "hops" to different public areas on a couple of afternoons and interviews willing respondents on a catch-as-catch-can basis is using haphazard sampling. His disor-

BOX 12-2
HIGHLIGHT
To Call or To Be Called: That Is the Question
(Or How Badly Was Jimmy Really Whipped?)

It has become popular in recent times for political candidates to engage in face-to-face public debates, many of which are aired on national television. And televised debates between candidates for the American Presidency are of particular interest to most adult viewers. Of course, the overriding question immediately following each such debate is "Who won?" Although each viewer knows in his or her heart who "really" won and isn't afraid to say so, the bigger stakes ride on the overall opinion of the population of American adults. Enter, the sample survey.

During the 1980 presidential campaign, then incumbent President Jimmy Carter squared off in front of television cameras against his Republican challenger, Ronald Reagan. To get an on-the-spot indication of the American public's opinion on the debate, the American Broadcasting Company (ABC) network had worked out an arrangement with AT&T to have viewers immediately phone a computer-controlled switchboard and register their votes for the "debate winner." This is a case of respondents' selecting themselves for inclusion in a sample. Another interesting aspect of this sampling process was that each caller knew that he or she would be assessed a 50-cent fee for the call. A third factor possibly affecting the outcome of this "survey" was that operator-assisted calls from phone booths and hotel rooms could not get into the answering system.

Based on a sample of nearly 700,000 respondents, the results of ABC's nonprobability sampling system showed that 67 percent of the callers thought that Reagan had won the debate. How accurate was this figure? Fortunately, we have a basis for finding out. Three independent polling agencies used probability sampling techniques to gauge public opinion on the debate (Isaacson, 1980). In these cases, the polling agencies selected and phoned the respondents rather than letting the respondents select themselves. The results were:

Poll	Reagan	Carter	No Opinion
Wirthlin	45%	35%	20%
CBS News	44%	36%	20%
Associated Press	46%	34%	20%

Note how closely the probability samples replicated one another. This degree of agreement is not unusual when probability sampling is properly carried out. It attests to the usefulness of the statistical model of parameter estimation. The rather substantial difference between these data and those gathered in ABC's straw vote illustrates the inadequacy of nonprobability sampling, even when a very large sample is involved.

ganized and seemingly arbitrary way of buttonholing respondents may appear to be a random selection procedure, but the method is actually a type of convenience sampling. What kinds of biasing influences would affect the researcher's results if this technique were used? Would the probability of selecting a particular sampling unit be known?

"Representative" Sampling. The term "representative" sampling is sometimes used in connection with probability sampling. In that context, the term refers to the result of the sampling procedure rather than the sampling method used. But, as though to confuse matters, there is also a type of nonprobability sampling that goes by the same name; however, in this second case the label pertains to the *method* used, and certainly not to the less than desirable result. **"Representative" sampling,** as a nonprobability technique, involves "handpicking" available subjects on the basis of how well you think they collec-

tively "represent" the population of interest (cf. Mendenhall, Ott, & Scheaffer, 1971). Random selection is not involved in this process; you simply try intuitively to cover all bases in the selection of subjects. The following excerpt from a method section of a research report illustrates how the "representative" sampling method was implemented in a survey of public attitudes toward the topic of hypnosis. The researcher's intent was to obtain a sample that would adequately represent the public at large.

> [The sample consisted of] 101 elementary and secondary school teachers, 247 junior high students, 86 high school students, and 17 grade school students, 22 . . . college professors, 120 college students, 57 nurses and nursing students, 14 doctors, 12 police officers, and 213 other participants from the general population in the St. Louis County area. The questionnaires for the general population category were distributed through senior citizens groups, libraries, businesses, and community groups. . . . The sample fairly represented the area racially and in terms of the socio-economic strata. (Myers, 1981)

Actually, "representative" sampling is used more often in the social sciences than one likes to think. It is the most frequent substitute for probability sampling, perhaps because researchers find some comfort in the surface resemblance between the contrived diversity in handpicked "representative" samples and the natural diversity found in populations. But an objective evaluation of "representative" samples would place them in the general category of convenience samples. They also have the same general limitations as convenience samples.

Quota Sampling. **Quota sampling** is the practice of systematically selecting a specified number of subjects from each of several subsets of the target population. Suppose, for instance, that you want to sample a cross-section of the students on your campus that fairly represents the *proportion* of students belonging to each of several categories in the campus population. The following facts would dictate the number of students you would try to recruit from each category:

1. Your total sample size will be 200.
2. Sixty percent of the students are females (F).
3. Seventy percent are caucasian Americans (CA), 20 percent are black Americans (BA), 1 percent are Native Americans (NA), and the remaining 9 percent consist of a mixture of nationalities and races from several foreign states and countries (FS).

Taking these demographic variables into account, and ignoring, for the moment, other potentially relevant variables, the following sample "quotas" would be suggested:

$$
\begin{array}{llll}
60\%(F) & \times\ 70\%(CA) & \times\ 200\ = & 84\ \text{female caucasian Americans} \\
40\%(M) & \times\ 70\%(CA) & \times\ 200\ = & 56\ \text{male caucasian Americans} \\
60\%(F) & \times\ 20\%(BA) & \times\ 200\ = & 24\ \text{female black Americans} \\
40\%(M) & \times\ 20\%(BA) & \times\ 200\ = & 16\ \text{male black Americans} \\
60\%(F) & \times\ \ 1\%(NA) & \times\ 200\ = & 1\ \text{female Native American} \\
40\%(M) & \times\ \ 1\%(NA) & \times\ 200\ = & 1\ \text{male Native American} \\
60\%(F) & \times\ \ 9\%(FS) & \times\ 200\ = & 11\ \text{female "foreign" students} \\
40\%(M) & \times\ \ 9\%(FS) & \times\ 200\ = & \underline{\ 7\ \text{male "foreign" students}} \\
& & \text{Total}\ = & 200\ \text{(desired sample size)}
\end{array}
$$

Having predetermined these group "quotas" for various subsets of the population, you would then set out to interview the required number of individuals in each category. Once each quota is filled, the desired sample size of 200 will have been realized, and the resulting sample will fairly represent the target population along the dimensions used to define quota categories.

You can see that the sampling of population subsets is a feature that quota sampling has in common with stratified random sampling. But there is a definite difference between the two methods. In strict quota sampling, no effort is made to introduce random selection into the subject-procurement process. Rather, interviewers are given the required quotas and are then turned loose to fill them. Since it is quite likely that most interviewers meet their quotas via the easiest route, the typical outcome of quota sampling is a type of convenience sample that represents the target population along the dimensions used to specify quota categories, but not along other potentially important dimensions. Further, lacking the element of random selection, the quota sample does not lend itself to the statistical system that is conventionally used in parameter estimation.

In view of my generally negative evaluation of quota sampling, you may be surprised to learn that some of the large polling firms, such as the Gallup organization, use a quota sampling system in the final stage of a multi-stage area sampling procedure. That is, once a block of housing units has been selected, the interviewer simply proceeds in a *predetermined direction* along the block until a required quota of households has been interviewed. However, this is a legitimate use of quota sampling, because *all prior stages of sampling leading to the selection of a particular group of housing units are based on probability sampling* (see, for example, Gallup, 1977).

CONTACTING THE SAMPLE

Once you have prepared your survey questions, decided on a sampling procedure, and selected your respondents (at least on paper), you are ready to seek them out and enlist their cooperation in your project. When it comes to deciding on a mode of contacting the respondents and administering the survey, you have three options to choose from: the *face-to-face interview*, the *self-administered questionnaire*, and the *telephone interview*. Each technique has its advantages and disadvantages, as you'll see momentarily. What approach you choose will depend on the nature and purpose of your survey, the amount of help you have, the amount of time you have to conduct the survey, and, as always, your monetary resources.

The Face-to-Face Interview

As the name implies, the face-to-face interview involves walking up to the respondent, perhaps at her home or in some public area, persuading her to take the time to participate in your survey, orally presenting a set of prepared questions to her, and writing down her answers. Of all approaches to survey-data collection, the personal interview is the most highly regarded by social scientists—and rightly so. Its advantages are numerous and important. For one thing, you will usually get a very high response rate with this method. If interviewers are well trained, it is not uncommon for over 90 percent of the personally contacted respondents to agree to the interview. Needless to say, a response rate as high as this is necessary if the sample data are to fairly represent the target population, and if the sample is to retain its status as a probability sample.

A second strength of the face-to-face approach is that it normally permits a lengthy, in-depth interview. This is a significant consideration if your survey will require a lot of responses from the selected individuals, or when much detailed probing is required to get the specific information that you need.

A third major advantage is that, in a face-to-face interaction with the respondent, the interviewer can carefully monitor and guide the data-collection process. This means, among other things, that the interviewer can repeat instructions and questions that are not easily understood, use prepared, *standardized* "probe questions" to get more complete responses from the subject, and note possible reasons that the data from a particular subject might not be valid (e.g., the respondent might be addled, inebriated, emotionally unsettled, or otherwise incompetent to respond adequately). A practical implication of this feature of the personal interview is that even an illiterate subject can provide usable data, since all he needs to do is give oral answers to the interviewer's orally delivered questions. Beyond this, the personal interviewer can make sure that all questions are responded to, which would not be possible if the data were collected via a self-administered questionnaire.

You should note, however, that the ability of the face-to-face interviewer to monitor the data-collection process can be a double-edged sword. The advantages of the monitoring aspect are clear, but there are also potential drawbacks associated with the monitoring process. If the interviewer is not thoroughly trained and conscientious, she may deviate from the standard procedure and questions, effectively conducting different interviews with different respondents. For example, in an effort to clarify a question for a confused respondent, the interviewer may inadvertently or intentionally rephrase a question, or perhaps add material that is not germane to the purpose of the question. This adds error to the data which will not be handled by the statistical model typically applied to survey data. Also, interviewers have been known to occasionally skip questions, make recording errors, and fabricate interview data just to get done with an interviewing assignment (cf. Hyman, 1954). In addition, just as unintentional bias can affect the results of laboratory experiments (Chapter 7), so can unintentional interviewer bias influence the data one gets from respondents (Rosenthal, 1976).

Other shortcomings of the face-to-face interview are more obvious. The method involves considerable inconvenience and time. Some selected respondents will be so inaccessible that three or four callbacks may be necessary in those cases. And time usually translates into money, in terms of wages if you are using paid interviewers; in terms of travel expense if you are conducting your own interviews. Also, the personal interview is much less anonymous, psychologically, than other approaches, such as the telephone interview. Hence, it is sometimes difficult to get honest responses to sensitive questions that are delivered in person.

The Self-Administered Questionnaire

The self-administered questionnaire is basically the same type of instrument as a paper-and-pencil personality test or an attitude scale. The questionnaire is either mailed to the respondents or hand-delivered. The respondent answers items by marking his or her responses in blanks or boxes provided next to the item, or by writing "open-ended," thematic responses to unstructured questions (see "Choosing an Item Format" later in this chapter). Although questionnaires typically are completed in privacy and at the respondent's convenience, it is sometimes the case that the respondent fills in his answers in the presence of the person who delivered the questionnaire. This latter practice normally ensures a higher response rate than when the respondent is permitted to mark his responses at his leisure and return the instrument by mail.

The major advantage of the self-administered questionnaire is that it is convenient for both the investigator and the respondent. It requires little time on the researcher's part (once the instrument has been constructed), no travel, and no hired interviewers. Normally, the self-administered questionnaire can be completed more quickly than a face-to-face interview. There is also some evidence to suggest that people are more willing to honestly answer sensitive questions on a questionnaire than in a personal interview (Edwards, 1957). Finally, the self-administered questionnaire represents a *standardized* measuring device in that every respondent receives exactly the same questions, without interviewer variations.

What are the drawbacks of this method? For one, selected respondents who are illiterate or have a low reading level may not be able to complete the questionnaire without assistance; most often, they will simply throw away the device. Even for highly literate samples, the instructions and meaning of the items must be crystal clear, as there is no interviewer to clarify what is meant by a statement on the questionnaire.

The Achilles heel of the self-administered questionnaire is the low response rate it usually yields. A 10 to 30 percent return is typical, depending on how much interest the pool of respondents has in the issue being studied. Therefore, mail surveys aren't likely to produce probability samples, even if probability sampling is used to select questionnaire recipients.

How to Increase the Response Rate.   If you must use the self-administered questionnaire technique, there are a few steps you can take to maximize the response rate. One is to hand-deliver the instrument and request that the respondent complete it on the spot while you wait at a reasonably discreet distance. This, of course, saves little time over the face-to-face interview. Another ploy to maximize returns is to make the questionnaire as short and as interesting as possible. Brief forms, consisting of, say, both sides of a single sheet, are much more likely to be completed and returned than a multi-page document. Likewise, a simple multiple-choice or agree/disagree item format will bring more questionnaires back than essay-type questions.

The cover letter you send along with the questionnaire should also be brief. It should point out the importance of the survey and the significance of the recipient's cooperation; it might also suggest that the questionnaire will be quick and easy to complete. An excellent example of a questionnaire cover letter appears in Box 12–3.

BOX 12–3
HIGHLIGHT
Example of a Questionnaire Cover Letter

Dear Colleague:

I'm conducting this survey to obtain information on the relative popularity of different theoretical orientations among today's psychologists. You were selected via simple random sampling from the American Psychological Association's membership directory. Of course, your responses to my questionnaire will be anonymous.

The enclosed questionnaire asks you to respond to only 20 items and shouldn't take more than a few minutes to complete. I have also enclosed a stamped, addressed envelope for you to use in returning the questionnaire.

I look forward to receiving your responses and those of your colleagues. The outcome should be interesting, indeed, and I will be sending a copy of the resulting research report to everyone who is included in my sample.

Thanks so much for your help.

Sincerely,

You might try personalizing the cover letter—that is, addressing the respondent by first name rather than by "Dear Respondent." Also, you will usually get a slightly better return if you follow up your questionnaire mailing with one or two "reminders" sent to those who don't respond to the initial solicitation. If the questionnaire is anonymous, you will need to send a second packet to all subjects, with an apology to those who have already responded.

My final suggestion may seem obvious, but some survey researchers overlook it: *Don't forget to include an addressed, stamped return envelope in the packet that you mail.* Failing to provide your respondents with a convenient and free mode of returning the questionnaire invites almost certain disaster.

The Telephone Interview

Once thought to be a very biased approach to survey sampling, in recent years, the telephone interview has gained considerable respect and popularity. In fact, major polling firms will often use this approach when they need to obtain a measure of public sentiment very quickly—right after a political debate or a major event of national significance, for example. If a surveying organization subscribes to a Wide Area Telephone Service (WATS) line, which permits any number of long-distance calls for a flat monthly charge, then the telephone interview can be a very economical method as well as timely. Moreover, response rates in telephone surveys are usually quite satisfactory (Sudman, 1967). And apparently, even "sensitive" topics can be studied through this approach (e.g., Quinn, Gutek, & Walsh, 1980).

So why is the telephone survey generally not as highly regarded as the face-to-face interview? Chiefly because many researchers are still locked into older, unwarranted beliefs about the inadequacies of samples obtained over the telephone. One disproven belief is that telephone respondents aren't likely to let an interview go on for more than a few minutes. However, the accumulated evidence suggests that getting a 30-minute interview is usually no problem at all (cf. Kidder, 1981), and telephone interviews lasting much longer than half an hour apparently are feasible under some circumstances (Quinn et al., 1980).

A very serious objection to telephone surveys is that not everyone has a telephone, and many who do possess a telephone have unlisted numbers. Thus, you might expect a telephone sample to give biased results. This logical expectation doesn't seem to meet with the facts, however, since polling firms regularly obtain accurate predictions of population behaviors through telephone samples. As it turns out, only about 10 percent of the population is without phones; lower-income people who are socially isolated are least likely to subscribe to a telephone service (Leuthold & Schule, 1971). In some cases, this class of respondents might be interviewed face-to-face, with the balance of the sample being interviewed via phone. In other cases, the purpose of the survey may render the opinions of phoneless people insignificant; hence, their exclusion from the sample would be harmless.

There's still the problem of unlisted numbers, however. This matter is of particular concern, because the percentage of telephone subscribers with unlisted numbers appears to be rising (personal communication, Bell Telephone Company, 1983). Fortunately, serious sample surveyors can overcome this hurdle through a method called **random-digit dialing**, which involves appending sequences of four randomly selected digits to the known telephone exchanges in a given zone (e.g., *555-random digits*; *762-random digits*, etc.). This produces a list of randomly generated telephone numbers, and the owners of the numbers are a random sample of potential respondents. Of course, the random process that generated the numbers doesn't distinguish between listed and unlisted numbers. Contacting respondents selected in this way takes extra time because many nonworking numbers or business numbers are reached in the process. But it does allow you to sample people with unlisted numbers.

SPECIAL PROBLEMS IN SURVEY SAMPLING

Every method of research has its own set of nuisance factors. This section presents some of the more subtle problems associated with conducting a survey.

Biased Items

In Chapter 7, you read about the issue of unintentional researcher-expectancy effects and how they can contaminate your data. In survey studies, subtle researcher bias can enter into the data-collection process in two ways. First, if the face-to-face interview is used, it is possible for the interviewer to transmit to the respondent nearly imperceptible cues which communicate the interviewer's expectancies, just as is true of the experimenter-subject interaction (Rosenthal, 1966, 1976). Solutions to this potential problem are the same for the interview situation as for the experimental situation (refer to Chapter 7). Second, the wording of the items in an interview or on a questionnaire may also bias the results. In particular, you should check your survey items carefully to make sure that they aren't *loaded questions* or *leading questions*.

A **loaded question** (or statement) contains emotionally charged words that bias the respondent's interpretation of the item, so that he is more likely to give a particular response, regardless of his true opinion. For example, which of the following statements would you be more likely to agree with?

a. Universities should not require tuition-paying students to remit a campus-activities fee.

b. University administrations should not further exploit tuition-paying students by requiring them to contribute their hard-earned dollars to a campus-activities fund.

A **leading question** (or statement) is worded in such a way that a particular response seems most appropriate and socially desirable to most respondents; it encourages the respondent not to think about the issue raised, and effectively restricts her options. Here's an example of a leading question from a "health and wellness" questionnaire that was distributed on a college campus:

> "Obviously, since science (e.g., physics) can only deal with physical entities, it can have nothing to do with the 'spiritual' dimension of life." (Agree/Disagree)

Confusing Items

Confusing items add unnecessary random error to survey data, thereby making the results less reliable than they could be. By definition, confusing items are those that tend to be misunderstood by many of the respondents. Thus, the respondents' answers to such questions might not reflect their "true" stance on the dimension being measured. And if the respondents were tested and retested with confusing items, they might well vary their answers to those items from the first occasion to the next. Indeed, that is the source of the unreliability problem referred to above.

Confusing items tend to be of three types: *poorly worded items, double-negative items,* and *double-barreled items.* Here is an example of a poorly worded item from a "health and wellness" questionnaire:

> I have, in the past year, found and acted on significant information on one or more of the following five wellness dimensions (please mark the total number of dimensions you've acted on): 1. self-responsibility, 2. physical health, 3. psychological health, 4. environmental sensitivity, 5. spiritual well-being. Please mark the number, from 1 to 5, which ranks these five dimensions according to their importance to you.

The respondent who encounters such an item might very well skip it in frustration. Or he may respond haphazardly to it. Or he may bravely attempt to impose a subjective interpretation on the item and work out some systematic response pattern to what he thinks it might mean. The problem, of course, is that the item asks the respondent to perform at least two operations in response to the item, and neither operation is clearly specified. Moreover, with the present wording, many respondents are likely to confuse the two operations called for and attempt to integrate them into one. Trying out your survey items in a pilot study prior to the actual survey will help you to identify and revise poorly worded items.

A second category of confusing items are those containing two or more negative qualifiers. Double negatives are inherently difficult for people to understand, and items containing more than one negative qualifier probably will create unnecessary measurement error in a survey. An example of such an item is:

> "Are you opposed to not allowing department stores to open on Sundays?" (Check One)
>
> Yes _____
> No _____
> Uncertain _____

In view of the way the item is phrased, conscientious respondents might typically select "Uncertain," even if they have a definite opinion on the issue. The question would have been better phrased as:

> "Are you opposed to the law which requires department stores to be closed on Sundays?"

The third type of confusing items essentially requires the subject to respond to two or more possibly conflicting issues at the same time and is thus said to be "double-barreled." Consider the following example:

> "I brush and floss my teeth daily and get at least annual preventive dental check-ups."
>
> Yes _____
> No _____
> Uncertain _____

If the second part of the item is true of you, but the first part is not, how would you respond to the item? Perhaps by checking both "Yes" and "No"? If your questionnaire or interview contains an item that may be relevant to more than one dimension or topic, it is best to convert the item to two separate statements or questions.

Nonresponders and Absent Subjects

Because of the bias it introduces, the loss of subjects is always a concern in any approach to psychological research. But when parameter estimation is the primary goal of a research project, the problem of subject loss becomes particularly troublesome. Although you can sometimes salvage the study by replacing a few inaccessible subjects with randomly selected substitutes, even this practice leaves you with some bias in your sample. And the sample bias grows with the percent of the sample that consists of "substitutes." By now it should be obvious to you that the portion of your sample that evades or avoids being measured probably differs in some systematic ways from the subjects who are accessible and cooperative.

There are two causes of subject loss in survey studies. One is that some selected subjects may refuse to participate; the other, that a few members of the sample may be hard to track down for any of a variety of reasons.

Dealing With the Potential Nonresponder.   You can have a lot of influence on whether a subject will consent to an interview by approaching the subject with a confident, positive attitude. Being meek or tentative invites a refusal. Also, upon approaching the subject, be sure to identify yourself immediately and to enthusiastically communicate the purpose or importance of the survey. (See "Doing the Interview" later in this chapter.)

In spite of your best efforts, however, some subjects will show an initial reluctance to participate in your survey and will try to discourage you. Unlike most other types of research, a survey aimed at parameter estimation requires that you be intelligently persistent in the face of this reluctance. The University of Michigan's Survey Research Center suggests the following strategies for handling the problem (*Interviewer's Manual*, 1976):

1. Try to gracefully take leave of the subject before she gives you a final, irreversible "no." Perhaps you just caught her at a bad time. Try a "call back" on some other occasion, when she might be having a better day.

2. Don't allow another member of the household to decline participation for the subject. Wearing your finest diplomacy, explain to the person (who says the selected respondent wouldn't be interested) that your assignment requires that you talk to the respondent in person (and could you please have a time and place where you might just run the matter by the selected subject).

3. Try having your supervisor or sponsoring agency send a letter to the reluctant subject explaining the general purpose of the survey and why it is important to have her responses. Then, follow up with a "call back."

4. If other interviewers are involved in the study, arrange to have another person attempt to interview the subject. Sometimes, human nature being what it is, a particular subject may simply be unresponsive to a particular interviewer.

Pursuing the Absent Subject.   The "absent" subject is a somewhat different problem from the reluctant subject, even though both types of subject ultimately tend to create the same kind of deficiency in survey data. In dealing with the problem of the hard-to-find subject, perseverence is the most important general solution. You simply must plan on the necessity of making several attempts to contact a certain number of your subjects. Beyond that, there are some specific tactics you might want to try. One is to identify yourself and your purpose to neighbors and ask them what they think would be the best time to reach the respondent (*Interviewer's Manual*, 1976). If this proves unproductive, try calling again at a different time, or on a weekend if weekdays prove unfruitful.

You may also want to carry "form notes" that contain your name and telephone number and explain your need to get in touch with the subject. These should be left in a conspicuous place near the entrance of the subject's home or apartment.

Of course, the callback burden can be lightened if you have access to the absent subject's telephone number. If the subject's phone number is unlisted or otherwise unobtainable through the usual means, you may be able to find out where he works and phone him there.

HOW TO PREPARE AN INTERVIEW OR QUESTIONNAIRE

As you put together a questionnaire for a survey study, you will usually need to take care of six matters before beginning data collection:

1. defining the purpose of your study and the dimensions you will need to measure
2. constructing and sequencing questionnaire items
3. writing a "cover sheet" or, if you're using the interview approach, an introductory statement
4. deciding on what biographical information you will require from your respondents
5. conducting a pilot study
6. revising the questionnaire

Deciding on Purpose and Measurement Dimensions

As was true of other approaches to research already discussed, the initial task in preparing a survey is to develop a clear idea of just what the study is to accomplish. It is important for you to define your purpose at the outset, because the major goals of your study will heavily influence (a) what target population and sampling technique you select, (b) your decision concerning how you will contact the respondents, and (c) what measurement dimensions you will focus on.

First, determine the general question you wish to ask. It might be something such as "Do graduate students give their instructors higher or lower evaluations than undergraduates?" or "What does 'hypnosis' mean to the general public?" Then, consider your general question further, discuss it with your instructors and with other students, and try to narrow it down to specifics. For instance, if your question concerns possible differences in the favorableness of evaluations assigned to instructors by graduate and undergraduate students, respectively, then you might consider whether you want to compare only those graduates and undergraduates who happen to have the same instructors, or if you want to compare *overall* faculty evaluations given by the two sets of students, disregarding differences in the particular personnel who teach graduate and undergraduate courses. Are you interested only in faculty evaluations at your institution, or do you plan to sample from several institutions? Do you desire to generalize your results to a broad population, that is, to implement parameter estimation, or only to compare two specific samples?

Finally, put your specific purpose in writing. Revise it if it seems to be inadequate in some way, or if it seems to represent too large an undertaking for your time and money. The final written version of the purpose of your study should lead easily into a list of the general variables or dimensions you wish to measure in the survey.

Constructing and Sequencing Questionnaire Items

Choosing an Item Format.   The item format options available to you in questionnaire construction are pretty much the same ones you considered in the previous chapter on psychometric research—except that projective-type items would almost never be used in survey research. The two general classes of survey items are: (a) **open-ended items** (also known as "unstructured" or "open" items), which include the fill-in-the-blank, sentence completion, and essay formats; (b) **fixed-alternative items** (also known as "structured" or "fixed-choice" items), which use the multiple-choice, true/false (i.e., agree/disagree), and rating-scale formats.

Open-ended questions are useful when you're conducting an exploratory or information-gathering survey to identify people's concerns, problems, or preferences in regard to issues that haven't yet been clearly defined or researched. For example, the American Psychological Association (1983) used open-ended questions in a recent telephone survey of 100 undergraduate psychology departments. One purpose of the survey was to identify the most pressing problems currently faced by those departments in their efforts to provide quality education in psychology at a time of budgetary cutbacks and rapid socio-economic change. One open-ended question used in that survey was:

"What are the needs, problems, or issues facing your department that pertain to undergraduate education?"

Notice that the item simply probes the respondent for an opinion, which is to be delivered in an oral-essay format. The response options have not been preselected for the respondent; rather, they are freely generated by the respondent as he formulates his answer in the form of conversation. This feature is the hallmark of the open-ended question. The value of the open-ended format in this case was that the American Psychological Association had little prior information on what the relevant response dimensions might be, and the free-response aspect allowed the researchers to identify those dimensions.

A second advantage of the open type of survey question is that it doesn't force the respondent into a response category that misrepresents him. It can't because, in a sense, the respondent provides the response categories. A third advantage is that many respondents find the opportunity to freely voice their opinions to be much more interesting than selecting one of a list of preselected, fixed responses.

There is a major disadvantage associated with the use of an open-ended format. The volumes of data typically produced by this technique somehow have to be reduced to a relatively small set of numerical data, so that general trends can be identified and appropriate conclusions drawn. This task normally requires a substantial commitment of time and effort.

The process of converting qualitative responses to numbers is called **coding**. When you code open-ended responses, it is necessary to examine *all* of the responses obtained to a particular question and then to look for common themes that tie groups of responses together. A "theme" represents the content common to all of the responses that belong to a particular group of responses. Each theme becomes a coding category, which is given a numerical value. Often the numerical value assigned is simply the percent of the sample that gave a response in that category. In fact, this is the type of coding procedure that was used by the American Psychological Association to summarize the findings from their survey of psychology departments. The codes arrived at for the first question in the survey appear in Box 12–4.

Box 12-4
HIGHLIGHT
Results of a Coding System Applied to One
Open-Ended Survey Item

The following open-ended question was one of several in a survey of undergraduate psychology departments that was conducted by the American Psychological Association (1983): "1. What are the needs, problems, or issues facing your department that pertain to undergraduate education?"

On the basis of the oral-essay responses of department chairpersons, the following coding scheme was inductively developed.

Category	Percent*
a. Curriculum	65
b. Faculty	61
c. Employment of B.A. graduates	47

Category	Percent
d. Tight budgets	43
e. Facilities and equipment	35
f. Attracting and retaining students	26
g. Intra-institutional relations	22
h. Graduate school admissions	15
i. Poorly prepared students	14
j. Image or identity of psychology	12
k. APA policy toward undergraduate education	8
l. "Other" responses	5

*Percents far exceed a total of 100 because many respondents gave several different answers to the question.

You will find that developing a good coding system can be a very challenging task. It is important that a coding system have the following qualities:

1. *It must be exhaustive.* That is, there must be a coding category for every response given to each question, so that no data are disregarded.
2. *Coding categories must be mutually exclusive.* Mutual exclusiveness exists if each response falls into one *and only one* coding category. In other words, coding categories must not overlap.
3. *It must be reliable.* Once the coding categories are established, independent "classifiers" should agree most of the time on what categories responses belong to.

In contrast to open-ended items, **fixed-alternative items** do not require that you laboriously code survey responses. In effect, responses to fixed-alternative items are *precoded*: You have provided the respondent with a small number of alternatives to choose from in responding to each item, and you have a prepared "scoring key" that can be mechanically applied to convert the selected responses to a numerical scale. Obviously, this type of item will be convenient when you are able to identify the relevant response dimensions in advance of the study.

Having discovered some useful response categories in their initial survey of undergraduate psychology departments, the American Psychological Association will now be able to employ suitable fixed-alternative items in future surveys on the same topic. Some possible examples of fixed-alternative items for such a survey are as follows:

Agree/Disagree
1. Balancing the undergraduate curriculum is one of the most pressing problems facing your psychology department today.

Agree   Disagree

Multiple-Choice

1. Of the four problems listed here, which is the most pressing problem facing your psychology department today? (Check only one.)

☐ a. balancing the undergraduate curriculum

☐ b. inadequate employment prospects for the B.A. graduate

☐ c. small departmental budgets

☐ d. insufficient faculty size

If you plan to conduct a survey aimed at attitude assessment; you might wish to use some kind of rating-scale format, as rating scales often prove to be more sensitive to attitude differences among individuals than are simple agree/disagree items. The 5-point "Likert" scale, which was reviewed in Chapter 5, is a widely used measurement device in attitude surveys. An item representing this type of scale would look like this:

1. Motherhood is still a very important role in our society.

☐   ☐   ☐   ☐   ☐
Strongly   Agree   Uncertain   Disagree   Strongly
Agree   Disagree

Another type of item frequently used in attitude surveys is the **semantic-differential scale**: a multi-point rating dimension that is anchored at its extremes by *bipolar* (i.e., opposite-meaning) adjectives. The semantic-differential scale was first developed by Osgood (Osgood, Suci, & Tannenbaum, 1957) to measure the *connotative* meanings of concepts—that is, the meanings suggested by a concept that go beyond its literal definition. This kind of scale has proved to be an especially effective device for measuring the emotional/evaluative component of attitudes. A collection of three semantic-differential scales could be used to assess respondents' attitudes toward the concept of "motherhood" in the following fashion:

Please rate this concept on each of the scales appearing below it. Place a checkmark at the point on each scale that best represents what the concept means to you.

Motherhood

In this example the blanks given from left to right on each scale could be precoded with the values 1, 2, . . ., 6. A respondent's overall evaluation of "motherhood" would be represented by either the sum or the mean of her ratings.

Thus, you have a wide variety of fixed-alternative formats to choose from. The advantages of fixed-alternative items in a survey are that they are easy to score and that they usually yield an adequately reliable measure. Their major disadvantage is that they restrict the subject's latitude of response options and may thereby distort her true opinions or characteristics.

Screening Items.   The items in your survey should undergo an initial screening during construction of the interview or questionnaire. There are two aspects to this checking process. First, you will want to check each item's *content validity*, that is, the relevance of its content to the dimensions you wish to measure in the survey. The opinion of friends and co-researchers will be helpful here. Second, the *formal* quality of each item should be considered: Is it clearly written? Can it be easily understood by people not closely associated with your project? Does it seem to elicit the type of information you're after? Does it ask for only one piece of information, or is it double-barreled or multiple-barreled?

I also recommend a second screening of items in the context of a pilot study (see below).

Sequencing Items.　Where and in what order should individual items appear on the questionnaire? The following guidelines will help you decide.

1. If all of the items are intended to measure only one dimension or variable, it usually is a good strategy to order the items randomly. This procedure should tend to minimize (but not eliminate) carry-over effects from one particular item to another. An even better strategy when you are assessing only one dimension is to construct multiple forms of the questionnaire, with each having a different random ordering of items.

2. If several different dimensions are being measured, it usually makes sense to group together all items related to a particular dimension. This procedure avoids requiring the respondent to change his mental set from item to item. It also facilitates a smooth flow of communication during an interview. Within a given group of related items, you may wish to randomly order the items. In some cases, however, it may be wise to present the easy-to-answer items first and the more difficult or specific items last.

3. If your survey is aimed at one or more "emotional" or "sensitive" topics, you probably will increase the percent of subjects who complete the interview or questionnaire by starting out with the more general and least "touchy" questions and gradually working into the potentially more offensive questions. Once the respondent has answered a few questions, she is less likely to refuse to continue when the hot topics are reached.

Occasionally, not all of the items will be appropriate for every respondent. In other words, it will sometimes make sense to skip certain portions of the questionnaire when surveying certain respondents. In these situations, branching items should be incorporated into the scheme you use to sequence items. Branching items simply tell you or the respondent what items to go to next, based on the last response given. An example is shown in Box 12–5.

The Cover Sheet or Introductory Statement

An example of a cover sheet for a mailed questionnaire was shown earlier in this chapter (Box 12–3). If effectively written, the cover sheet is brief and clear, stimulates the respondent's interest, and provides structure and direction for the respondent. Generally, a cover sheet (also called a cover letter) should contain the following items:

1. your identification
2. the name of the organization for whom the survey is being conducted
3. the purpose of the study
4. how the respondent was selected (in *general* terms, e.g., "randomly")
5. the degree of confidentiality to be exercised in handling the data of individuals
6. the availability of feedback (e.g., a report of the results), if appropriate

Box 12–5
HIGHLIGHT
Example of "Branching" Questions

5. Have you ever received personal counseling from a professional counselor or therapist?

Yes _____
No _____

If you checked "no," go to Item 10. If "yes," to Item 6.

6. What type of professional administered the counseling?

Clinical Psychologist _____
Counseling Psychologist _____
Psychiatrist _____
Social Worker _____
Other _____
(Please Specify) _____
Don't Know _____

7. Approximately how many counseling sessions did you have?

1 _____
2–5 _____
6–20 _____
21–50 _____
Over 50 _____

* *

10. Have any of your college friends received personal counseling from a professional counselor or therapist?

Yes _____
No _____

If you checked "no," go to Item 15. If "yes," to Item 11.

Also, the cover letter should point out why the respondent's data are essential to the validity of the study. The letter might also suggest that the questionnaire will be quick and easy to complete, if you honestly believe this to be true. And a thank-you at the end of the letter is always appropriate.

If you are conducting your survey via personal interviews, then you will deliver this information orally. Such a face-to-face introduction is called an **introductory statement**. After constructing your introduction, you should memorize it and practice delivering it in a conversational fashion. An example of a general introductory statement is given in Box 12–6.

BOX 12–6
HIGHLIGHT
Sample Introductory Statement

Hello. I'm (Your Name), and I'm doing a series of interviews for the purpose of finding out what kinds of mental health services residents of Sunnyvale would like to have in their community. I work for Opinion Research Associates, Incorporated, and we are doing these interviews for the Sun County Association of Mental Health Professionals. To make sure we get an accurate indication of what Sunnyvale people really want in their town, we've used a scientifically devised random sampling technique to pick the people we interview. You were one of the 1,000 Sunnyvale residents selected by the sampling procedure. The answers that you give me will be completely confidential; in our analysis of the survey results, we'll be looking only at group averages, not at how individuals answered the questions. (I can send you a copy of our final report, if you like.) Do you have any questions before we start? [Answer respondent's questions.] Since it's very important that I accurately record your answers, we'll need to do the interview in a quiet room, where we can sit down. Which room of your home would be the best place for this?

The Question of Biographical Information

Biographical information, or demographic data in the case of group statistics, consists of data on the respondent's sex, age, marital status, socioeconomic class, income level, neighborhood characteristics, family structure, and so on. How much biographical information should you request from a respondent? The answer depends on the purpose of your study. The rule of thumb is to ask for only those pieces of information that are germane to your research question. In many surveys, most data of this type may not be needed.

Some survey researchers prefer to obtain biographical information first, before any other questions are presented. However, you may find that your respondents are more willing to divulge their age and other personal information if you request these items *last*, after you've firmly established good rapport and a willingness to cooperate.

The Pilot Study

It is always a good idea to pretest your questionnaire or interview in a pilot study. Pretesting will permit you to determine the approximate amount of time required to complete the questionnaire or the interview, so that you may be precise about this in your introductory statement. It will also provide an opportunity for you to carry out a final screening and revision of your survey items. Most importantly, however, the "dry run" will serve as a training experience for you and any other data collectors involved in the study. This is especially helpful if you are using either the telephone or the face-to-face interview method.

Who should serve as subjects in your pilot study? Ideally, you would use an informally chosen sample of persons who are members of the target population. If this is infeasible, however, friends, classmates, and even eccentric professors will suffice as stand-ins. In any case, listen carefully to the feedback your pilot subjects give you, and modify your method accordingly.

The Final Revision

If you've done a careful and conscientious job of planning and implementing all aspects of your questionnaire or interview, then only minimal revisions of materials or procedure will be suggested by the pilot study. Occasionally you will need to add a line or two to the instructions on a self-administered questionnaire, or to reword a few slightly ambiguous items. In making these revisions, be aware that small wording changes can sometimes alter the basic meaning of an item. It might also be worthwhile to recheck the sequence and flow of items to determine if any improvements can be made. Now, if you've already selected your sampling units, you're ready to begin data collection.

DOING THE INTERVIEW

The successful conduct of an interview is an art that depends on well-developed skills. Fortunately, you can acquire and refine critical interviewing skills through the practice of actually conducting interviews. You won't become a master interviewer simply by reading this book or any other book, as you simply have to get hands-on experience. Nonetheless, a knowledge of some basic guidelines and techniques may help you off to a good start in the development of interviewing proficiency.

Your Approach

When you begin ringing doorbells to secure your interviews, it is extremely important to maintain a confident attitude. Keep in mind that once respondents learn of your socially valuable purpose and lose their apprehension about your being a salesperson or a collection-agency employee, the majority of them will agree to let you interview them. As was mentioned earlier in the chapter, being timid, apologetic, or doubtful will only lessen the chances of securing interviews.

When a member of the household answers the door, immediately identify yourself and state why you have come to the person's home. This initial explanation of purpose will usually amount to an abbreviated version of your introductory statement. If necessary, show the person who greets you a letter of authorization from your supervisor or instructor. Most of the time, if the letter bears the letterhead of your organization, presenting it will dispel any doubts the person may have about your true purpose. Remember to remain relaxed, natural, and confident throughout this interaction. Try to be polite but firm in your pursuit of the interview.

If the person who greets you is not the individual who has been preselected as the respondent, explain that your assignment requires that you interview the selected individual and no one else. (You may also have to explain why in some difficult cases.) Then *state* that you'd like to come into the home and conduct the interview with the respondent. Most of the time, you will be invited in at this point; the respondent will be summoned, and you can give him or her your complete introductory statement.

In the process of getting respondents to agree to the interview, you should be prepared to answer certain questions without too much hemming and hawing. According to the University of Michigan's Survey Research Center, the following are questions that respondents frequently ask prior to granting permission for the interview:

1. "How did you happen to pick me? Who gave you our name?"
2. "I really don't know anything about this [so why would you want to interview me]?"

3. "Why don't you go next door?"
4. "What's all this about, anyway?"
5. "What good will this do?" (*Interviewer's Manual*, 1976, p. 8)

Delivering Questions and Taking Notes

It is important to deliver each survey question to the respondent exactly as it is written. Small ad-lib changes will add unnecessary error to the data. Articulate each item as clearly as possible and at a slightly slower pace than that of normal conversation. If the respondent asks for a clarification, try repeating the item, but don't alter the wording. Most often, the repetition will clear up any initial misunderstanding on the respondent's part.

If you use an open-ended item format, some respondents may occasionally give answers that are insufficiently short and, thus, do not provide the information you are seeking. You will normally be able to induce the respondent to elaborate on his answer by using an appropriate "probe," such as "Anything else?" or "Could you tell me more about your thinking on that?" (*Interviewer's Manual*, 1976, p. 16).

As you take notes in an open-ended interview, try to transcribe the respondent's answers fully and accurately. Write down every *essential* word in the respondent's answers. It's okay to leave out some articles and prepositions or to use shorthand symbols for these nonessential words, so long as your data coders are aware of the meaning of those symbols. But it will bias the data if you leave out some nouns, descriptive adjectives, and verbs, or if you substitute your own paraphrasing or interpretation of what the respondent says. Also, it is important that you write legibly, so that *you*, at least, will be able to decipher the response protocol accurately.

INTRODUCTION TO PARAMETER ESTIMATION

In this section, I'll present some of the elementary statistical concepts in parameter estimation but first, a reminder and two qualifications are in order. The reminder is that the statistics of parameter estimation assume that the sample used to estimate population characteristics is a *probability* sample. To review, probability sampling involves the *random* selection of sampling units from the target population, such that each sampling unit has a known probability of being included in the sample. Thus, the concepts and techniques described below apply only when you have, in fact, used probability sampling. They usually will not yield accurate population inferences if used with nonprobability samples.

Now for the qualifications: First, I will cover only parameter estimation from *simple random samples*. Although the general logic of parameter estimation presented here is relevant to other types of probability samples (e.g., cluster, stratified), the specific statistical formulas vary somewhat from one type of probability sampling to another. If you're interested in learning about the statistics of cluster and stratified sampling, I recommend that you consult a textbook that is devoted exclusively to survey sampling statistics (for example, Mendenhall, Ott, & Schaeffer, 1971). A second qualification is that, in consideration of space limitations, I will focus on estimating population *proportions*—for example, the proportion of people in the target population who hold a particular opinion—but you should be aware that the statistics of parameter estimation can also be employed to estimate population *means* via exactly the same logic and procedures (see Mendenhall et al., 1971).

The Sampling Distribution of the Proportion

At the very heart of parameter estimation lies a most important concept called the *sampling distribution*. You're already aware that two distributions are involved in parameter estimation: (a) the distribution of values or responses for the whole population (i.e., the "population distribution"); (b) the distribution of values or responses for the sample of people you actually observe and measure (i.e., the "sample distribution"). What you may not yet realize is that in order to estimate characteristics of the population from a knowledge of the sample, you must employ a third distribution, which exists only in statistical theory: The *sampling distribution of the proportion*, defined as *the distribution of sample proportions you would get if you drew an infinite number of simple random samples of a given size, n, and plotted the resulting sample proportions into a distribution* (based on X and Y coordinates).

The sampling distribution concept is a tough one to grasp. Let me express the basic idea in a semiconcrete example. Suppose you've measured a simple random sample of 100 psychology majors on their opinion about the desirability of requiring statistics in the psychology curriculum. Assume that the sample was drawn from a nationwide population. Also assume that the actual proportion of the entire psychology-major *population* favoring a statistics requirement is P = .50. (Bear in mind that the P, the population proportion, would be unknown at the time of your survey, but you would be trying to estimate it from your sample data.) Let's say the proportion of your *sample* favoring the statistics requirement is p = .55. Since you used probability sampling in your survey, you are fairly confident that the population parameter, P, isn't radically different from the sample proportion, p. But you know that every random sample is subject to *random sampling error*, and you would like to calculate how far off the actual population proportion could be from the sample proportion. How is this calculation made?

The *likely maximal deviation of the population proportion (P) from the sample proportion (p)* is called the **bound on the error of estimation**. The sampling distribution of the proportion can be used to determine the bound on the error of estimation. Mathematicians have employed a simple but powerful theory to generate sampling distributions of proportions for every possible sample size. For example, the sampling distribution for your hypothetical sample size of 100 appears in Figure 12–5. This distribution represents the results you would get if you:

drew a very large number—let's say ten thousand—simple random samples of psychology majors, where n = 100 in each sample,

computed the proportion of students favoring a statistics requirement *in each sample*, and

plotted the ten thousand sample proportions into a distribution, wherein the percent of occurrence (Y) of each sample proportion is plotted as a function of the value (X) of that sample proportion.

There are several features of the distribution to take note of:

1. The distribution is based entirely on a theory of random variation. This is precisely why probability sampling is a prerequisite to using the statistics of parameter estimation.

2. The distribution is a perfectly symmetrical, bell-shaped distribution, and it possesses all of the mathematical characteristics of what is known as the *normal distribution*.

3. The *mean* of the distribution of sample proportions is P, *the proportion of people in the population* who show the characteristic you are measuring. Thus, on the average, your sample proportion will equal the population proportion that you're trying to estimate. It follows from this that the best estimate of P will always be p.

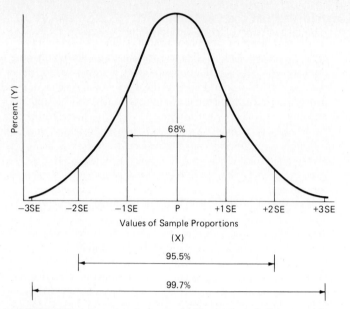

FIGURE 12–5

Sampling Distribution of the Proportion: Theoretical Chance Distribution That Would Result If an Extremely Large Number of Simple Random Samples of a Given Size, n, Were Drawn and Their p's Were Compiled into a Distribution

4. Random sampling error causes most of the sample proportions drawn from a common population to deviate in one direction or the other from the population proportion. Thus, even though the *expected sample proportion* is equal to P, the sample proportion will differ somewhat from the population proportion most of the time. As the "curve" of the sampling distribution suggests, however, the most frequent sampling errors are the smallest ones, and extreme sampling errors are very infrequent.

5. The variation of sample proportions about P is marked off in *standard units of variation*, called the **standard error of the proportion**, which is symbolized by SE. Figure 12–5 shows that there is a constant relationship between SE and the sampling distribution as a whole. It will always be true that:

1. 68 percent of the sample proportions will not differ from P by more than ± 1SE (refer to the figure).
2. 95.5 percent of the sample proportions will not differ from P by more than ± 2SE.
3. 99.7 percent of the sample proportions will be within ± 3SE of P.

At this point, you're probably thinking, "Wait a minute! This is all fine and dandy, but I won't be drawing ten thousand random samples. One sample at a time is all I can handle, thank you." You're exactly right about that. And your single sample proportion, if randomly selected, will be one tiny point in the whole sampling distribution of the proportion. Nevertheless, you can use a sampling distribution, such as the one shown here, to calculate how far your one sample proportion is likely to deviate from the population proportion and, by logical implication, *how far P is likely to deviate from p*. For example, just by looking at Figure 12–5 you can tell that at least 95 percent of the time a single sample proportion will not differ from P (what you're trying to estimate) by more than 2SE. Logically, this is equivalent to saying that *probability = .95 that P will not differ from your sample proportion by more than 2SE*. So if you have p (the sample proportion) and you can calculate SE, then the *lowest* that P is likely to be is (p – 2SE); and the *highest* that P is likely to be is (p + 2SE). Therefore, you can be very confident that the population proportion lies somewhere between (p – 2SE) and (p + 2SE).

I hope you can now see how the sampling distribution of the proportion is used to find out how far away P might be from your single sample proportion. In this example, 2SE is the *bound on the error of estimation*. Its numerical value equals the *likely* maximal deviation of your sample p from P. You already know that p is the decimal number that you get from dividing sample size into the number of people in the sample possessing the target characteristic. So to use this system to calculate the lowest and highest probable values of P, all that you need to learn is how to compute SE. You'll see how that is done in the next section.

Setting Up a Confidence Interval

The sample proportion, p, is called the **point estimate** of P, the population proportion. This is because p represents a single value (or point) in the sampling distribution that surrounds P. Point estimates of a parameter are of limited usefulness because sampling error causes them to be off the mark most of the time. For many applications of parameter estimation, such as predicting the outcomes of elections, we need to know how far off the mark our estimate might be. So, generally, parameter estimation requires setting up a **confidence interval**, a range of values that is likely (but not certain) to contain the population proportion. Confidence intervals are the basis of statements such as "We estimate that 65 percent of the voters favor the bond issue on the community mental health center but, due to sampling error, the true percentage could vary by 3 points in either direction." Thus, the *confidence interval* in this hypothetical case is 62 percent to 68 percent; the point estimate, however, is fixed at 65 percent.

The usual sequence of steps in setting up a confidence interval is:

1. Find p, the proportion of people in your sample who give the target response or exhibit the target characteristic.
2. Choose a **confidence level**. The confidence level is the theoretical probability that the confidence interval will contain P; also, it represents the *percent* of times that P, upon repeated random sampling, will lie somewhere in the confidence interval.
3. Calculate the SE (standard error) of the sampling distribution.
4. Multiply the value of SE times the number of SE's that corresponds to your confidence level. For example, if the confidence level were 95.5 percent, then SE would be multiplied by 2—as suggested by Figure 12–5. The resulting product is the *bound on the error of estimation*.
5. Subtract the result of step 4 from p (e.g., p – 2SE). This is the *lower boundary* of the confidence interval.
6. Add the result of step 4 to p (e.g., p + 2SE). This is the *upper boundary* of the confidence interval.
7. State the confidence interval—that is, (p – 2SE) to (p + 2SE)—and the associated confidence level.

To demonstrate parameter estimation, I'll now apply each of these seven steps to some sample data from the American Psychological Association's (APA) survey of undergraduate psychology departments. Recall that the APA used simple random sampling in that study; therefore, the statistics of parameter estimation are applicable to their data.

Find the Sample Proportion.   Consider the response of the APA's sample to the first question in the interview: "What are the needs, problems, or issues facing your department that pertain to undergraduate education?" In answer to this question, 65 percent of the department chairpersons in the sample cited the problem of "the undergraduate curriculum." Hence the sample proportion for that particular response was p = .65. This is also the *point estimate* of the proportion of the whole population of psychology chairpersons that would give this answer. But what is the likely maximal deviation of the population proportion, P, from .65? The confidence interval will give us an answer to this question.

Choose a Confidence Level.   The confidence level you select will depend on how confident you want to be that the population parameter actually lies within the interval of values you set up. The three most commonly used confidence levels are illustrated in Figure 12–6. As you study the figure, it will be apparent to you that 90 percent of the sample proportions are within ± 1.64SE's of P, whereas 99 percent of the sample proportions are within ± 2.58SE's of P. The upshot of these facts is as follows: If you use the 99 percent confidence level, your confidence interval will be quite large (p ± 2.58SE), but you will be quite confident in asserting that the interval of values you've set up does contain P; if you use the 90 percent confidence level, the interval you establish will be relatively narrow (p ± 1.64SE), but you won't be very confident that P is contained within it (after all, a 90 percent confidence level excludes 10 percent of the sampling distribution). Many survey researchers compromise and use the 95 percent confidence level. This standard yields a moderate-size interval (p ± 1.96SE) and a reasonable degree of confidence that the range of values established does contain P. We'll use this third confidence level in our statistical treatment of the APA's survey result.

Calculate the SE of the Sampling Distribution.   The formula for the standard error of the proportion is:

$$SE = \sqrt{(PQ)/n}, \text{ where}$$

P is the proportion of people in the population who exhibit the target trait or give the target response,
Q = (1 − P),
PQ = (P × Q), which is the *variance* of the population,
n = the number of units in the sample

What's new in this formula? You already know what P stands for, and that n is the symbol for sample size. Q is simply the arithmetic "complement" of P. For example, if P = .20, then Q = (1 − .20), or Q = .80. Then there's the matter of PQ, which was defined as the *population variance*. Depending on whether you've had a statistics course, the concept of a "variance" may be new to you, even though the concept of "variance in data" was explained in Chapter 5. The **variance** of a distribution is *a statistical index which reflects the amount of individual differences, or "disagreement," among people who contribute scores or values to a distribution*. A large variance means that there are many differences among values making up the distribution; a small variance means that people contributing scores

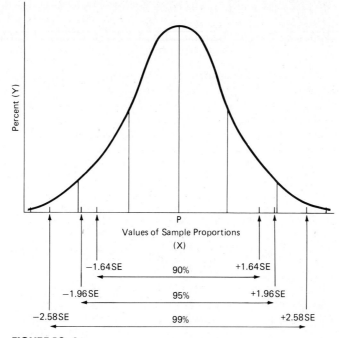

FIGURE 12–6

Sampling Distribution of the Proportion Showing Percentages of the Distribution Associated
With Three Standard Confidence Coefficients

to the distribution are very similar to one another on the measured trait or response.
When you are estimating proportions, the largest variance you can have is .25, which occurs when $P = .50$ (i.e., a 50–50 split among members of the population). The smallest
possible variance is .00, which would exist if $P = 1.00$ or $P = .00$—in other words, when
everyone in the population either agrees or disagrees with a survey question.

The only obstacle to computing SE is that you do not know what P is, since P is what
you're trying to estimate! So you won't be able to compute PQ—but you can still com-

Box 12–7
HIGHLIGHT

Confidence Coefficients for Three Confidence Levels*

If the Confidence Level Is:	Then the Confidence Coefficient Is:
.90	1.64
.95	1.96
.99	2.58

*These confidence coefficients are accurate only if sample size (n) is greater than 30.

pute SE by substituting an *estimate* of PQ. Just as the best estimate of P is p, the best estimate of PQ is pq, which is obtainable from your sample data. Just remember that $q = (1 - p)$.

For the sample data at hand, $p = .65$; $q = (1 - .65) = .35$; $pq = (.65)(.35) = .2275$.

Since we're using an estimate of PQ to get SE, the formula for SE must be slightly altered: we simply divide pq by $(n - 1)$ instead of n. Substituting the above values into the modified formula for SE, we get:

$$
\begin{aligned}
SE &= \sqrt{(pq)/(n - 1)} \\
&= \sqrt{.2275/(100 - 1)} \\
&= \sqrt{.2275/99} \\
&= \sqrt{.0023} \\
&= .048
\end{aligned}
$$

Find the Bound on the Error of Estimation.   You can calculate the likely maximal deviation of P from p by multiplying the value of SE (in this example, .048) times the number of SE's that correspond to your confidence level. Since we're using a 95 percent confidence level, a check of either Figure 12–6 or Box 12–7 indicates that we should multiply SE times 1.96. Thus, the **bound on the error of estimation** is: $(1.96)(SE) = 1.96(.048) = .094$.

Find the Lower Boundary of the Confidence Interval.   The lower boundary of the confidence interval is $[p - (1.96)(SE)] = [.65 - .094] = .556$. The theoretical probability is .95 that P will not be lower than .556.

Find the Upper Boundary of the Confidence Interval.   In a similar fashion, we obtain the upper limit of the confidence interval through $[p + (1.96)(SE)]$. Thus, the upper boundary $= [.65 + .094] = .744$.

State the Confidence Interval.   On the basis of our analysis of the response given by the APA's sample to the first question in the survey, we would make the following assertion: We think that about 65 percent of the population of psychology chairpersons would cite "the curriculum" as a major problem facing their departments; however, due to random sampling error, the true percentage could be as low as 55 or as high as 75. In any case, we are confident that more than half of the population would cite the curriculum problem.

Assertions such as the one just made are correct for approximately 95 out of every 100 surveys that are based on probability sampling and that use the 95 percent confidence level. You should note, however, that for any particular survey of this type, the confidence interval will either contain the population proportion or it won't. That is, confidence intervals help us to make decisions and ensure that across numerous surveys, most of the decisions are correct. But, as was true of tests of statistical significance (Chapter 8), for any one sample, your conclusion will be either right or wrong.

A Small Complication: Estimating SE When the Population Is Small

The formula for estimating SE that we've been using is based on the assumption that the sampled population is infinite—that is, that the population is so large that its sampling units could never be fully counted. However, most social science surveys deal with *finite*, or countable, populations. As it turns out, however, the standard formula for SE yields accurate parameter estimations for most of these finite populations. *The exceptions to the latter statement are those studies in which the size of the sample (n) equals 1/20 or more of the size of the population (N)* (cf. Hamburg, 1979). When $n/N \geq 1/20$, then the standard formula for the estimated SE provides too large a number, thereby making the confidence interval larger than it should be. Usually this is a problem only when you're dealing with very small populations.

Fortunately, this occasional problem can easily be corrected: When your sample size equals at least 5 percent of the population size, multiply your estimate of SE by $\sqrt{1 - (n/N)}$, which is called the finite population correction factor. Thus, in these special cases,

$$SE = [\sqrt{(pq)/(n-1)} \times \sqrt{1 - (n/N)}]$$

What Determines the Size of a Confidence Interval?

In parameter estimation, it is desirable to make the confidence interval as small as possible. The narrower the confidence interval, the less uncertainty you have about the true value of P. For example, you have a lot more information about the likely value of P when the confidence interval ranges between .48 and .52 than when it lies between .25 and .75. Examine the basic expression for the *bound on the error of estimation*: Z(SE), where Z is a standardized coefficient representing the number of SE's that correspond to your confidence level (e.g., Z may be 1.64, 1.96, or 2.58). Since the size of the confidence interval is determined by the magnitude of the bound on the error of estimation, anything that reduces the size of Z(SE) will give you a smaller, hence more precise, confidence interval. And since the estimated $SE = \sqrt{(pq)/(n-1)}$, the expression for the "bound" becomes:

$$Z[\sqrt{(pq)/(n-1)}]$$

If you study this expression carefully, you will realize that you can make the "bound" smaller by (a) decreasing Z, (b) decreasing pq, or (c) increasing n. Making Z smaller, say by using the 90 percent confidence level (Z = 1.64) instead of the 95 percent confidence level, is risky. By using a lower confidence level, you increase the likelihood that P will *not* lie in your confidence interval. Likewise, it isn't practical to look for a smaller variance. The sample variance, pq, is fixed once your sample is drawn; further, with probability samples containing at least 100 observations, pq would not be likely to change very much from one sample to the next. Therefore, the most practical way to decrease the size of the confidence interval is to increase n.

The Effect of Sample Size on SE. The fact that $SE = \sqrt{(pq)/(n-1)}$ means that the magnitude of SE is *inversely proportional to the square root of sample size.* Thus, as you *increase* n to $(n \times m)$, where m is some multiplier, the size of SE will *decrease* by a factor that equals the square root of m. For example, suppose that when n = 101, $SE = \sqrt{.25/(101-1)} = .0025 = .05$. Now increase sample size by a factor of approximately 100, so that n = 10,001 instead of 101. If you now compute SE based on the larger sample, you get .005. This figure is *one-tenth* the size of the previous SE (.05). Although you increased sample size by a factor of approximately 100, SE decreased by a factor of only 10, which is the *square root* of 100.

There are two morals to this story. One is that, since the size of the confidence interval is affected primarily by sample size, you should always use as large a sample as you can afford, which will maximize the precision of your parameter estimates. Second, the return in precision that you will get from increasing sample size will not be proportional to the numerical increment in n. Rather it will be proportional to the square root of the increase in n.

Choosing a Sample Size. Suppose that either your employer or the purpose of your study requires that you conduct a sample survey in which the bound on the error of estimation, and hence the confidence interval, *will not exceed a specified size*. Is it possible to control how large the confidence interval will be? It is, and you may exercise such control through choosing an appropriate sample size. If you consider that:

$$\text{Bound on the Error of Estimation} = Z[\sqrt{(pq)/(n-1)}],$$

then you can use algebra to solve for n, given a specified bound on the error of estimation. If you're not fond of doing algebraic derivations, you can calculate the sample size needed for any desired bound by using this equation:

$$n = \frac{Z^2(pq)}{(\text{Bound})^2} + 1, \text{ where}$$

Bound = bound on the error of estimation that you wish to impose on your parameter estimation, and

p = the likely proportion of the sample possessing the target trait or giving the target response

If you don't want P, the population proportion, to deviate from its estimate (p) by more than 3 percent, then set Bound = .03. If you think that around 90 percent of the sample will give the response of interest, then set p = .90. Assuming that the 95 percent confidence interval is being used, then Z = 1.96. Plug these values into the formula for calculating n, and you should get n = 385. This means that your sample would have to have at least 385 people in it to achieve an error of estimation that is not likely to be greater than ± 3 percent.

In Table 12–1, several sample sizes have been computed for you. Each entry in the table represents the minimal sample size needed to achieve a specified maximal error of estimation for a given p. Note that figures are provided for both the 95 percent and the 99 percent confidence levels. Note also that the required sample size decreases as the acceptable bound increases and as p deviates from .50.

The only possible complication in calculating an appropriate sample size is that you may not have any idea about what p will be (since you won't have collected the data at the point of planning a sample size). In that case, you will be safe by assuming that p will equal .50, since that figure will always result in the largest possible estimated sample size (refer to Table 12–1). Then, if p turns out to be larger or smaller than .50, having assumed that p = .50 will give you an even more precise confidence interval than you were counting on.

SUMMARY

The sample survey is distinguished from most other research methods by its emphasis on scientific sampling procedures and immediate generalization from a sample to a population. The major purpose of the sample survey is to estimate population *parameters*.

TABLE 12–1

Minimum Sample Sizes Required for Various Specified Bounds on the Error of Estimation: Sample Sizes Shown as a Function of Anticipated Sample Proportion and Confidence Level (.95 or .99)*

Maximum Bound	Value of p					
	.90 or .10		.75 or .25		.50	
1%	3458	(5968)	7203	(12433)	9604	(16577)
3%	385	(644)	801	(1382)	1068	(1842)
5%	139	(239)	289	(498)	385	(664)
7%	71	(122)	147	(254)	196	(339)
10%	35	(60)	73	(125)	97	(166)

*Sample sizes in parentheses are those required when the .99 confidence level is used. Sample sizes not contained in parentheses are those required when the .95 level is used.

The same results occur when $p = .90$ as when $p = .10$, because q is the complement of p (i.e., q = [1 – p]). Thus, the sample variance, pq, is the same when pq = (.10)(.90) as when pq = (.90)(.10).

Your method of selecting subjects, called the *sampling design*, will determine what population your sample data will generalize to. *Probability sampling* designs, which are based on random selection, include *simple random sampling, stratified random sampling,* and *cluster sampling*. Probability sampling designs permit the broadest and most valid generalizations to populations.

Nonprobability sampling does not involve random selection and, hence, usually introduces systematic bias into the sample data. *Convenience sampling* and *quota sampling* are examples of nonprobability sampling designs. These designs normally do not permit valid generalizations beyond the sample studied.

Once you have selected a sample of respondents, you have three options in regard to the method of conducting the survey: face-to-face interviews, self-administered questionnaires, or telephone interviews. The advantages and disadvantages of each method were discussed.

Special problems that must be dealt with in survey studies include: biased questions, confusing questions, absent subjects, and reluctant respondents.

In preparing an interview or questionnaire, you will need to attend to the following matters:

1. defining the purpose of your study and the dimensions or variables you will measure
2. constructing and sequencing questionnaire items
3. writing a cover sheet or introductory statement
4. deciding on what biographical information you will require from respondents
5. conducting a pilot study
6. revising the questionnaire

Several guidelines for the successful conduct of an interview were offered.

Once you have collected your sample data, you will want to estimate the population parameter of interest and use inferential statistics to place a *confidence interval* around the estimate. The confidence interval reflects the likely maximal error in your estimate. The best way to make a confidence interval narrow, and thus more precise, is to use as large a sample as you can afford.

REVIEW QUESTIONS

1. Define or describe: parameter, parameter estimation, statistic, target population, sampled population, sample, sampling unit, sampling frame.

2. Create an example of a research problem in which parameter estimation would be an appropriate objective.

3. Distinguish between probability sampling and nonprobability sampling. What is the key element in probability sampling?

4. Under what circumstances would you use each of the following types of probability sampling: simple random sampling, stratified random sampling, cluster sampling, multi-stage area sampling?

5. Define and evaluate each of these sampling techniques: convenience sampling, haphazard sampling, "representative" sampling, quota sampling.

6. Summarize each of the three principal techniques used to gather survey data from the selected respondents. What are the advantages and disadvantages of each approach?

7. Tell how you might avoid or minimize the following special problems in survey research: biased items, confusing items, reluctant respondents, absent respondents.

8. Discuss the value or significance of the following steps in constructing a questionnaire: deciding on purpose and measurement dimensions, the cover sheet, the question of biographical information, the pilot study.

9. Make up an example of a possible survey item in each of these formats: open-ended, multiple-choice, agree/disagree, semantic-differential. See if you can construct the items in such a way that all of them will elicit the same type of information on a particular issue.

10. What are the relative advantages and disadvantages of open-ended versus fixed-alternative survey items?

11. Define or describe: sampling distribution of the proportion, standard error of the proportion, bound on the error of estimation, confidence interval, confidence level, p, P, PQ.

12. What is the general relationship between sample size and the size of the standard error of the proportion? Between sample size and the width of the confidence interval?

13. For what reason is random sampling necessary for the successful construction of a confidence interval?

13

THE EXPERIMENT

In his delightful little book, *To Know a Fly*, ethologist Vincent Dethier wrote: "A properly conducted experiment is a beautiful thing. It is an adventure, an expedition, a conquest" (p. 18).

This kind of romantic enthusiasm for a research activity is hard for the uninitiated person to understand. But it is not unusual to meet experienced researchers who express the very same degree of excitement for experimentation. Without a doubt, in the minds of most research psychologists, the experiment is the preferred method in their science.

What is it about the experimental method that has raised it to such a high level of esteem among scientists while, at the same time, infecting many of them with a boundless enthusiasm for conducting experiments? For one thing, the elegant simplicity of the logic behind experimentation is very appealing to the rational mind. The basic idea of the experimental method is this: You conceptualize how an independent variable might influence a particular behavior (the dependent variable); that is, you develop a cause-and-effect hypothesis. Next you arrange the conditions of observation in such a way that all variables that could influence the target behavior are held constant. Then you directly manipulate the independent variable under these rigidly controlled conditions and carefully observe and record the target behavior. If the subjects' behavior changes significantly under these special circumstances, the change can be logically attributed to the one thing that was deliberately varied—the independent variable. And, *voilà!* You have isolated a causal sequence.

Apart from this compelling rationale, which doesn't always work out in practice quite as well as it promises to in theory, the experimental method allows you to exercise direct control over events and *make something happen*. This feature is not found in most of the other research methods covered in this book. Those methods generally require that you either wait for something to happen and then record it, or measure traits that already exist in subjects and look for correlations among those traits. In contrast, when you conduct an experiment, you ask, "What would happen if I created these specific conditions?"; then you grab hold of the environment, remake it to your theoretical specifications, and record the effect of what *you did*. This process of directly changing something to see what happens is reminiscent of the manipulative and exploratory play that engaged your attention so completely in early childhood. Perhaps some of that same sense of childlike adventure is resurrected when scientists conduct their experiments.

Beyond the aesthetic and emotional appeal of experimentation, there is a very important practical reason for the method's popularity: The experimental method presently is the only efficient means we have of isolating cause-and-effect processes with a high degree of confidence. If you've read the previous chapters in this book, the scientific significance of identifying causal sequences should be quite clear to you by now.

In this chapter, we'll consider the basic elements of experimentation and experimental research designs. Then you'll be ready to embark on the adventure that Dethier described.

GENERAL PROCEDURES IN EXPERIMENTATION

As was the case with other approaches to data collection, there is a typical sequence of steps that should be followed in planning and conducting an experiment. My discussion of these steps assumes that you have already formulated your research hypothesis and have decided on your specific independent and dependent variables (refer to Chapter 4).

Operationalizing Your Independent Variable

To review: The **independent variable** in an experiment is the set of conditions that you directly manipulate, or vary; your primary interest is in determining the effect that manipulating the independent variable has on a particular behavior. Although it is possible to manipulate more than one independent variable in the same experiment (see Chapter 14), in this chapter we'll focus on the simplest experimental case—that in which there is only one independent variable. Bear in mind that manipulation of the independent variable is accomplished by setting up different groups or conditions in your experiment—the "experimental" group versus the "control" group, for example. *The specific procedure you employ to establish the different treatment conditions is the operational definition of your independent variable.* Also note that the number of "levels" or "values" that your independent variable has will equal the number of treatment conditions that you set up.

Essentially, there are three ways to operationalize the independent variable in an experiment: by varying (a) the tasks or stimuli that subjects are exposed to, (b) the physical or social context of the experimental setting, or (c) the preexperimental explanation that you give your subjects. For certain kinds of research questions, you may also need to consider adding special control groups, such as a "placebo" group, in order to eliminate confoundings. Regardless of the specific way in which you operationalize your independent variable, your main initial consideration should be ensuring that the procedure used to manipulate the variable is logically related to the underlying psychological process of interest.

Task or Stimulus Manipulations.   Stimulus manipulations are the easiest to carry out. For example, if you're interested in the effect of the "meaningfulness" of words on subjects' ability to remember the words, you would simply arrange to have your subjects attempt to memorize lists of words that contain items of various levels of "meaningfulness." Likewise, if you're interested in the effects of stimulus complexity on visual attention, you could construct and present geometric figures of different structural complexities and measure how long subjects choose to view each figure (e.g., Berlyne, 1966).

You can also manipulate some independent variables by varying the task that you give different groups of subjects. For example, memory researchers often require different groups of subjects to apply different information-processing strategies to the words they are to memorize. Thus, some of the subjects might be required to orally report their judgments of the "pleasantness" of each word as it is presented, while other subjects are required to simply repeat each word several times while they study it. Still other subjects in the same experiment might be asked to count backward by three from a given number at the same time that they're attempting to memorize the words being presented. The idea behind this kind of task manipulation is to find out what kinds of information processing are beneficial or detrimental to long-term memory (cf. Craik & Lockhart, 1972).

Manipulation of the Preexperimental Explanation.   The purpose of your experiment might require that you manipulate subjects' mental sets or motivational states by varying the definition and explanation of the experiment that you give subjects when they arrive at the laboratory. For example, in a study of the effect of anxiety on the desire to affiliate with other people, Schachter (1959) was able to induce two different levels of anxiety by telling half of his subjects that they would be receiving a strong electrical shock, while telling the remaining subjects that their shock would be "very mild." His basic finding was that subjects who were anticipating a painful shock, and who were presumably more anxious, expressed a stronger desire to interact with other people than did the less anxious subjects. (No one actually received a shock in this study.) Apparently, when people become anxious they often will seek companionship, in the hope that other people will provide information that will help them to reduce their anxiety (Schachter, 1959).

Manipulation of the Physical or Social Context.   To obtain people's realistic responses to particular kinds of situations, experimenters in social psychology frequently use "staged" events or circumstances to manipulate the variables of interest. The studies of bystander intervention discussed in earlier chapters are classic examples of this mode of varying the independent variable. Staged manipulations of the social context almost always involve the use of an experimental confederate, or "stooge," who poses as a subject or, perhaps, "just another person" who happens to be in the vicinity. Of course, the stooge's acting ability will help determine the success of the manipulation.

An experiment on aggression by Berkowitz and LePage (1967) entailed manipulation of both the social context and the physical context. First, the social context was varied across treatment groups by having a confederate anger some of the subjects but not others. Then the physical context was varied by exposing some of the subjects to the presence of a snub-nose revolver while exposing others to the sight of a badminton racquet. The researchers found that angry subjects became more aggressive than nonangry subjects, and that the mere presence of a weapon greatly intensified these aggressive reactions.

Special Control Groups.   Two-group experiments based on one "experimental" group and a "control" group are quite common in psychology. Often this simple design is sufficient for answering a research question, but there are other situations in which the standard two-treatment model would result in nonequivalent groups, as a result of a hidden "history" confounding. In Chapter 7, you read about the usefulness of a *sham-operation* condition as an "extra" control group in physiological research.[1] This extra group allowed the physiological psychologist to separate the precise effects of a specific brain lesion from the general effects of undergoing surgery. If the sham-operation group had not been included along with the brain-lesion group and the unoperated control group, then the independent variable of "lesion versus no lesion" would have been confounded by the extraneous variable of "surgery versus no surgery."

For similar reasons, research in psychotherapy often requires a second control group, in addition to the standard experimental and control conditions. The experimental subjects in such a study actually receive two treatments: the therapeutic procedure *plus* the special attention associated with their status as the experimental subjects. Frequently the standard control group is placed on a "waiting list" and gets neither of those treatments. In this type of investigation, you can separate the general effects of special attention from the specific effects of the therapeutic procedure by including a third group, called the **placebo group**, which receives some sort of sham treatment which is not psychotherapy in the usual sense, but which does give the placebo subjects a sense of receiving attention and concern. Of course, these subjects would have to be led to believe that they were receiving therapy, a practice which certainly begs some ethical questions.

Would research that compares the learning ability of rats raised in an "enriched environment" with the learning ability of rats raised under "impoverished" conditions also require a special control group? If so, what would be the nature of the third condition, and what special evidence would it provide?

Operationalizing the Dependent Variable

A second important consideration in planning your experiment is how you will operationally define your dependent variable. Two criteria are especially important here. First, the dependent measure should be theoretically or logically pertinent to the psychological or social process you're trying to influence. You'll recognize this as the validity question. For instance, based on what we know about emotion, the Galvanic Skin Response (GSR) might be a valid measure of emotionality in subjects, self-ratings somewhat less valid, and ratings of subjects' facial expressions even less valid. Perhaps the best strategy in an experiment on emotional arousal would be to use both self-ratings and the GSR as measures of the dependent variable.

A second criterion to meet is that of *sensitivity*. A sensitive dependent measure is one that detects even small individual differences on the dimension you wish to measure. Sensitive measures are desirable because they are more likely than insensitive measures to reveal small, but reliable, effects of the independent variable. Moreover, in general, the most sensitive measures are also those which have the highest *reliability*. A number of procedures for maximizing the reliability and validity of psychological measures were presented in Chapter 5. You may wish to refer to them as guidelines in the process of developing your dependent measure.

Conducting a Pilot Study

Throughout this book, I've repeatedly emphasized the desirability of carrying out a dry run of your study prior to starting the "for keeps" data-collection process. There are a couple of reasons that a pilot study is particularly important when you are using the experimental method. First, the data-collection process during an experimental session usually is an intense event. A lot happens in the hour or so you spend with the subject and many things can go wrong, given all that must take place during that short time span. It's best to work out these frustrating bugs beforehand, lest they muddy your data.

A second very valuable function of the preexperiment pilot study is to check on the effectiveness of your manipulation of the independent variable. This statement doesn't mean that you should employ an extensive pilot study to "make sure" that the data you get in the actual experiment will confirm your hypothesis. Rather, a "manipulation check" should serve primarily to determine whether your method of varying the independent variable produces the intended psychological effect. Suppose, for example, that one of your manipulations involves having a confederate insult some subjects but not others, the purpose being to vary the level of *anger* between groups. In a brief pilot study, you could find out (a) whether the confederate's actions are indeed insulting, and (b) how most of the pilot subjects react to the insults—that is, whether they truly become angry or tend, instead, to feel rejected, defeated, and hurt. Similarly, in a study of the effects of different information-processing strategies on long-term memory, postexperimental interviews with pilot subjects could be used to find out if subjects are actually using the processing strategies that you instructed them to use.

Assigning Subjects to Conditions (or Treatment Sequences)

How well your experimental design controls confounding variables will often be primarily a function of how you assign subjects to conditions (in independent-groups experiments) or treatment sequences (in repeated-measurement studies). Most "true" experimental designs require that you assign subjects to conditions or treatment sequences on a *random* basis (see later sections on "true experiments"). The most practical way to accomplish random assignment in a smooth and timely fashion is to set up a random assignment sequence before you run any of your conditions. To do this, construct a **condition-**

assignment sheet *that contains as many numbered blanks as you will have subjects.* For example, if you have three experimental conditions (or treatment sequences)—A, B, and C—and 20 subjects will serve in each condition, then your condition-assignment sheet will contain 3×20, or 60, blanks numbered 1 through 60. Using either the random number table given in the Appendix or one of the randomization devices described in Chapter 7, assign one of your three treatments to each of the 60 blanks. You will get something that looks like this:

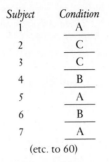

Subject	Condition
1	A
2	C
3	C
4	B
5	A
6	B
7	A

(etc. to 60)

This random sequence of letters means that the first subject you test will serve in condition A, the second in condition C, the third in C, and so on. The only constraint on the randomization sequence is that, if you want treatment groups of equal sizes, none of the three conditions can be allowed to occur more than 20 times in the random list that is formed. Once the list is constructed, you'll constantly know which condition each subject should be in before he or she arrives at the lab. Note that by following the random assignment sequence on this prepared list, you effectively are randomizing the three treatment conditions across subjects, date, time of day, weather conditions, your moods, and most other "nuisance" variables that could influence your results. The idea, then, is to ensure that potentially confounding variables influence all of your experimental conditions equally.

"Running" the Experiment

Having attended to all of the necessary preliminary steps considered so far, you're now ready to "run" your experiment. The expressions "running the experiment" and "running the subject" are commonly used in psychology. They came.into popular usage in the days when many experimental psychologists occupied their time by observing laboratory rats "run" through mazes or down alleys. There are three phases to running a subject: (a) administering the preexperimental explanation and instructions, (b) actual data collection, and (c) debriefing the subject.

In giving the subject his preexperimental instructions, you should briefly explain the nature and purpose of the study, explain exactly what the subject will be asked to do (minus information that must be withheld to accomplish manipulation of the independent variable), answer the subject's questions, and have him sign an "informed consent" form. The preexperimental instructions set the tone for the experiment, and will influence both how seriously the subject takes your experiment and how well he will follow your instructions. Be sure to plan this phase carefully and test it out in the pilot study.

The data-collection phase should proceed smoothly if you've planned ahead and practiced the procedure sufficiently. Be on guard against unintentionally communicating your theoretical expectations to the subject via gestures and tone of voice (see Chapter 7).

When the data collection is complete, debrief the subject in accordance with guidelines described in Chapter 3.

TRUE EXPERIMENTS VERSUS PSEUDO EXPERIMENTS

Recall the basic rationale of the experiment that was given in the first section of this chapter:

1. Hold all potentially influential variables constant.
2. Systematically change only one thing at a time (i.e., manipulate the independent variable).
3. Observe and measure the behavior of interest (i.e., the dependent variable) under each level of the independent variable (i.e., treatment condition).
4. If the target behavior changes systematically as the independent variable is varied, then the changes may be attributed to the influence of the independent variable since all else was held constant.

Clearly, the essential aspect and chief advantage of the experimental method is *control of confounding variables*. In fact, it is this very feature that gives the experiment its "power" to isolate cause-and-effect processes. Much was said about this matter in Chapter 7, where I discussed the various threats to internal validity and the procedures that can be used to eliminate, or at least minimize, these threats. Now you will see how the principles of control discussed earlier in the book are implemented within the context of specific experimental designs. To keep the discussion straightforward and basic, I'll present only those experimental designs that involve manipulation of a single independent variable. Then, in Chapter 14, I'll follow up with a review of designs that incorporate two or more independent variables within a single experiment.

It is important to note at the outset that not all so-called experimental designs represent "true experiments." A **true experiment** is designed and conducted in such a way that, theoretically, all sources of possible confounding are controlled or eliminated. The most common device for accomplishing this level of control is *randomization*, meaning random assignment of subjects to treatment conditions or treatment sequences. A second characteristic of true experiments is that they contain appropriate *control groups* or *control conditions* to rule out confounding influences that operate across time, such as subject maturation or the subjects' personal or experimental "history."

In contrast to true experiments, **pseudo experiments** are based on designs that lack either the randomization feature or the control-condition feature. Yet, to the untrained eye, pseudo experiments appear to be well-controlled studies—a state of affairs that product advertisers continually exploit.

The inadequacies of the three most common pseudo-experimental models will highlight the rationale behind the crucial control features of true experimental designs. Since the many types of confounding that were explained in Chapter 7 are germane to the present topics, I've constructed a summary of them for review. This appears in Box 13-1.

SINGLE-GROUP PSEUDO EXPERIMENTS

Single-group pseudo experiments are notorious for their lack of a control group. Since only one group is used in these studies, the question of random assignment to conditions is irrelevant.

Box 13–1
HIGHLIGHT
Review of Concepts: Sources of Confounding

Subject-Selection Bias: Some systematic process, rather than chance, is responsible for subjects' being in particular treatment conditions.

Testing Effects (also called Sequencing Effects): Prior testing or experience with the experimental task affects the subjects' performance on later testings in subsequent experimental treatments.

Instrumentation Changes: Systematic changes in the measurement process across time produce changes in the subjects' data that cannot be ascribed to the independent variable. These include changes in the data recorder and the data-recording technique, as well as possible changes in the recording equipment.

Statistical Regression: When subjects are measured twice on the same or correlated dimensions, those who score extremely high or extremely low on the first measurement occasion tend to score relatively closer to the mean of the population on the second occasion.

History: In a repeated-measurement study, specific events that occur between measurement occasions (apart from events associated with manipulation of the independent variable) may affect the subjects' behavior. Also, in a single-measurement experiment, the experimental subjects may experience different irrelevant events from those of the control subjects, such as differential expectancy cues from the experimenter.

Subject Maturation: General biological and psychological processes within the subjects, such as hunger, fatigue, or cognitive growth, can cause changes in the subjects' responses on the dependent measure, irrespective of the effect of the independent variable.

Subject Mortality: Subjects may drop out of, or become lost from, a study for nonrandom reasons that are related to performance on the dependent measure. This is especially serious if mortality rates differ substantially across treatment groups.

Single-Group Posttest Design

This design, also known as the **one-shot case study**, may be schematized in the following way:

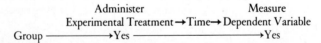

An example would be to administer a progressive educational curriculum to a class of disadvantaged kindergarten students and then measure their achievement level at the end of the term. The results would be hard to interpret for a number of reasons. First, since there was *no pretest*, we wouldn't really know whether the students have improved, stayed the same, or declined relative to their initial level of achievement. But let's say their end-of-term scores indicate that the class is functioning at an average level. This is actually better than we would expect of "disadvantaged youth"; so we'll hazard a guess that they must have improved over the term.

Was the improvement a result of the progressive curriculum? There's no way to tell, since an "equivalent, but untreated" control group was not included in the "experiment." Hence any one of the following sources of confounding may be responsible for results:

1. *Subject-selection bias:* Perhaps this particular group of youngsters was atypical in a way that caused their end-of-term achievement scores to be higher than usual for "disadvantaged" children.

2. *History:* Perhaps the special attention the subjects were receiving, or a new food program in the school district, or some other event irrelevant to the educational treatment was responsible for their "good" scores on the posttest.

3. *Subject maturation:* Perhaps many of these children were entering a "spurt" in their intellectual development just as the study began.

4. *Subject mortality:* Maybe the dullest children found the progressive curriculum too difficult and dropped out of the study, thereby leaving only the brightest of the disadvantaged kids for the end-of-term testing.

Single-Group Pretest-Posttest Design

A simple extension of the one-shot case study is to pretest, as well as posttest, the group who receives a special treatment. This yields the following model:

	Pretest on Dependent Variable	Administer Experimental Treatment →Time→	Posttest on Dependent Variable
Group———	→Yes ———	→Yes ———	→Yes

This is called the single-group pretest-posttest design. If this model were used with the hypothetical disadvantaged kindergarten students in the previous example, then we would indeed have information on whether the students' achievement levels increased or decreased across the school term. This is still considered to be a pseudo-experimental design, however, because no equivalent control group is used.

Since only one group is used, the pretesting aspect of this design may actually create more problems than it remedies. In addition to the four potential confoundings associated with the one-shot case study, the present design also invites:

1. *Testing effects:* The students may learn something on the pretest that influences their posttest scores in a systematic way, irrespective of the effect of the progressive curriculum.

2. *Statistical regression:* If the students were selected for the special class because they scored extremely low on the pretest, then their posttest scores might improve relative to the pretest outcome simply because the test is somewhat unreliable and the retest scores had no place to go but up. Only the inclusion of an equivalent but untreated control group would reveal the existence of this confounding.

A TWO-GROUP PSEUDO-EXPERIMENTAL DESIGN

Yes, there is such a creature as a psuedo-experimental design that employs a control group. In fact, it appears with fair frequency in the social science literature. Unfortunately, the inclusion of a control group in this case is deceptive in that it may create an unwarranted sense of confidence while allowing a major confounding to exist.

The two-group pseudo experiment usually takes the form of a static-group comparison design, also known as the **ex post facto design** ("ex post facto" literally means "from after the fact"). This model may be represented as follows:

	"Experimental" Treatment in Past →Time→	Measure Dependent Variable
Group 1	Yes, special trait	Yes
Group 2	No	Yes

The broken line separating Group 1 (experimental group) and Group 2 (control group) signifies that the groups are *not* equivalent on potentially confounding variables. The reason they cannot be assumed to be equivalent is that the members of each group were not randomly assigned to one condition or another. Rather, the subjects' personal histories determined their group membership. In the static-group comparison design, the "experiment" is conducted in the following way:

1. Locate a group of individuals who possess a critical trait or who have had a critical experience. This is the "experimental group."
2. Assemble a second (control) group of individuals who appear to be equivalent to the experimental group in all respects except that people in this second group do not possess the critical characteristic that is common to members of the experimental group.
3. Measure both groups on a dependent variable that you think is influenced by the critical characteristic, and compare the group averages.

Consider an example. Suppose you hypothesize that participating in the "Boy Scouts of America" organization during youth makes young men more patriotic. Accordingly, you locate a group of men between the ages of twenty and thirty who have been "cub scouts," "boy scouts," or "explorer scouts," and you measure them on a reliable and valid test of patriotism. You also measure an apparently equivalent control group of men who haven't had the scouting experience. And, indeed, the former scouts are much higher in patriotism. Is it reasonable to conclude that the scouting experience makes people more patriotic?

This design is plagued by both a subject-selection confounding and a subject-mortality confounding. First, it is likely that the subjects who entered the scouting organization came from more patriotic families, to begin with; hence the subject-selection bias. Subject mortality also enters the picture in that less patriotic boys may be more likely than their more patriotic counterparts to drop out of scouting soon after joining and to disclaim the scouting experience later in life. The end result would be that the scouting (experimental) group would be left with "superpatriots," whereas some scouting dropouts ("weak patriots") would be included in the control group.

These kinds of confounding are likely to exist whenever experimental and control groups are defined according to some "organismic" variable—for example, sex, IQ, personality traits—rather than being randomly assembled.

TRUE EXPERIMENTS: INDEPENDENT-GROUPS DESIGNS

True experiments fall into two categories: *independent-groups designs* and *correlated-groups designs*. **Independent-groups designs** always involve between-subject manipulations of the independent variable. To review: Between-subject manipulation means that each subject receives one, and only one, level of the independent variable. Also, the performance of subjects in a given condition is in no way correlated with the performance of subjects in any other condition; hence the term "independent."

Correlated-groups designs may use either between-subject manipulation of the independent variable—as in the *matched-groups* and *randomized-blocks* designs—or within-subject manipulation, as in the *repeated-measures* model. Also, in these kinds of experiments, the performance of subjects in one condition is correlated with performance in other conditions. Why this is the case will become clear later.

Generally speaking, correlated-groups experiments are harder to set up than independent-groups designs. Also, the repeated-measures model is subject to more possible confoundings than are independent-groups designs. However, correlated-groups experiments do have advantages, as you will see.

Now, let's consider two of the simpler independent-groups designs.

Completely Randomized Control-Group Design

The simplest true experimental design is the two-group completely randomized control-group design. In this type of experiment, the independent variable has only two levels—the experimental treatment and the control treatment—and subjects are randomly assigned to one level or the other. Since it is a between-subjects design, each subject serves in only one condition. This design may be schematically represented as:

	Administer Experimental Treatment →Time→	Measure Dependent Variable
Group 1	Yes	Yes
Group 2	No	Yes

In this example, the control group is Group 2, since those subjects will not receive the experimental treatment. In any such experiment, which group is considered the experimental group is somewhat arbitrary. Usually the control group is the group that receives a "standard treatment," or a treatment that has known, typical, or unremarkable effects. The experimental group, then, would consist of subjects who receive a new or nonstandard treatment.

In fact, when the completely randomized control-group design is extended to include three or more conditions, there will be either more than one experimental group or more than one control group, or, in some cases, more than one of each type of group. An example of a completely randomized *three-group* design appears in Table 13–1. In this hypothetical example, 10 of 30 subjects have been randomly assigned to each of three

TABLE 13–1

Completely Randomized Control-Group Design

Control Group	*Experimental Group 1*	*Experimental Group 2*
S1→X1	S11→X2	S21→X3
S2→X1	S12→X2	S22→X3
S3→X1	S13→X2	S23→X3
S4→X1	S14→X2	S24→X3
S5→X1	S15→X2	S25→X3
S6→X1	S16→X2	S26→X3
S7→X1	S17→X2	S27→X3
S8→X1	S18→X2	S28→X3
S9→X1	S19→X2	S29→X3
S10→X1	S20→X2	S30→X3

Key:
1. X1, X2, and X3 are the three experimental treatments (levels of the independent variable, X).
2. S1, S2, . . . , S30 represent the subjects.

independent treatments; two of the treatments are considered experimental conditions, and the remaining group is the control, in the sense that those subjects will receive some treatment that has known effects. The "S's" stand for subjects 1 through 30, and the "X's" represent the three treatments. Note that subjects 1 through 10 receive treatment X1, but not X2 or X3. The vertical lines separating the groups signify that they are independent, that is, uncorrelated.

The major advantage of the completely randomized design is that, if it is executed properly, it is usually free of confoundings. The key to this feature is the random assignment of subjects to conditions, which usually makes the separate groups "statistically equivalent" prior to the manipulation of the independent variable. The major disadvantage of this general model is that it isn't always possible to randomly assign people to levels of the independent variable of interest—being a boy scout, for example.

Completely Randomized Pretest-Posttest Design

Sometimes it is informative or necessary to both pretest and posttest subjects in a completely randomized experiment. For instance, pretesting can be used to check on the initial equivalence of the experimental and control groups—that is, to verify that the random assignment did what it was supposed to do. In other situations, the experimental hypothesis requires both a pretest and a posttest, because it predicts that one or more treatment groups will increase or decrease on the dependent variable as a result of the treatment. A completely randomized two-group pretest-posttest model takes this form:

	Pretest	Administer Experimental Treatment→Time→ Posttest	
Group 1	Yes	Yes	Yes
Group 2	Yes	No	Yes

If you are pretesting simply to verify the initial equivalence of groups, then it is not necessary to use exactly the same test on both occasions, but the pretest and posttest should be highly correlated with one another. Take an example. A colleague and I once used a completely randomized pretest-posttest experiment to assess the impact that personalized feedback on returned exams would have on subsequent exam performance (Evans & Peeler, 1979). We randomly assigned half of the students in three sections of my introductory psychology course to a "personalized feedback" condition; the remaining students were in the control condition and received only number grades on their exams. The first exam in the course was considered the pretest, and the final exam was treated as a posttest. Since different exams made up the pretest and posttest, pretesting in this case was used simply to verify the groups' initial equivalence.

The results appear in Table 13–2. Note that the pretest means of the two groups were *numerically* different. Did the random assignment not work? In fact, it did work, since the initial mean difference was not statistically significant; it was a "chance" difference. This is what is meant by the term "statistical equivalence." However, the mean difference between the groups on the final exam *was significant*, indicating that personalized feedback had a small but reliable effect on exam performance.

When pretesting is used for the purpose of assessing change over time due to the treatment, then *the same instrument must be used for pretesting and posttesting*. This creates a possible confounding, however, since pretesting may modify how the independent variable influences behavior. This possible confounding was reviewed in Chapter 7 and will not

TABLE 13–2

Means on Pretest and Posttest for Two Groups of Introductory Psychology Students

Group	Pretest (Exam 1)	Posttest (Final Exam)
Personal Feedback	35.39	34.33
Control	33.67	31.30
DIFFERENCE	1.72	3.03*

*Statistically significant difference at the .05 level of significance.

be explained again here, but perhaps you remember that a special experimental model, called the Solomon four-group design, can be employed to deal with it. We'll return to this useful design in Chapter 14.

TRUE EXPERIMENTS: CORRELATED-GROUPS DESIGNS

Recall that the distinguishing feature of correlated-groups experiments is that subjects' performance in one condition is correlated with subjects' performance in other conditions of the experiment. This situation exists either because members of matched pairs perform similarly in their separate treatments (in the matched-groups design) or because the same people serve in all conditions of the experiment (in the repeated-measures design). Correlated-groups designs have two chief advantages:

1. They do a better job of ensuring the initial equivalence of experimental conditions than do the independent-groups designs.
2. Relative to the independent-groups designs, correlated-groups experiments are more "sensitive" to the effects of the independent variable.

The second advantage refers to the fact that correlated-groups designs are very effective in detecting small, but "real," differences between conditions that might not be detected in an independent-groups experiment. This benefit stems from the more precise statistical tests that can be applied to data from correlated-groups designs. (I'll introduce you to those "more precise" tests in Chapter 14.)

Randomized-Blocks Design

A randomized-blocks experiment is simply a matched-groups experiment with more than two matched samples. In Chapter 7, you learned how to set up a matched-groups experiment. The randomized-blocks design is a straightforward extension of this logic and procedure in cases where you have three or more treatments in the experiment. If you have three conditions, for instance, after you establish the matching hierarchy you would parse it into adjacent groups of three people, or "triads." Each triad would be a *block* of subjects, which corresponds to the "matched-pair" concept in the two-group situation. And, as was true of the matched-groups design, members of each block of three would be randomly assigned to the three treatments.

TABLE 13–3

Randomized-Blocks Design

	Group 1	Group 2	Group 3
Block 1	S1→X1	S1a→X2	S1b→X3
Block 2	S2→X1	S2a→X2	S2b→X3
Block 3	S3→X1	S3a→X2	S3b→X3
Block 4	S4→X1	S4a→X2	S4b→X3
Block 5	S5→X1	S5a→X2	S5b→X3
Block 6	S6→X1	S6a→X2	S6b→X3
Block 7	S7→X1	S7a→X2	S7b→X3
Block 8	S8→X1	S8a→X2	S8b→X3
Block 9	S9→X1	S9a→X2	S9b→X3
Block 10	S10→X1	S10a→X2	S10b→X3

A randomized-blocks design is represented in Table 13–3. Subjects in each block are labeled similarly—for example, S1, S1a, S1b—to denote the fact that their performances on the dependent measure will be correlated as a result of the matching process.

Randomized-blocks experiments have the same advantages and disadvantages as matched-pair experiments. These designs usually ensure equivalent groups, and they are sensitive to even small effects of the independent variable. But they are time-consuming, and sometimes expensive, to set up because all subjects must first be measured on the matching criterion. Also, unless the criterion is known to be strongly correlated with the dependent measure ($r \geq .50$), the effortful matching process is a waste of time. Nonetheless, if successfully carried out, a randomized-blocks configuration is a powerful experimental design that is relatively free of confoundings.

Repeated-Measures Design

In repeated-measures designs, each subject receives all levels of the independent variable, and his performance is measured at each level. Since every subject serves in all of the treatment conditions, the independent variable is said to be manipulated *within subjects*.

A simple, three-condition repeated-measures design is represented in Table 13–4. You'll notice that this design bears a marked resemblance in its layout to the randomized-blocks design. There are functional similarities as well. For one thing, the performances of subjects are correlated across conditions, as is true of the randomized-blocks design. In fact, the correlation across conditions is even easier to understand here, since each subject performs in each condition and, effectively, is his own "control." Also, the statistical analysis which is applied to the data of repeated-measures experiments is exactly the same as that used to analyze the results of randomized-blocks experiments (see Chapter 14).

Advantages of Repeated-Measures Designs. A principal benefit of using the repeated-measures approach to experimental research is that such designs are economical of subjects, since every subject serves in all conditions. For example, in a three-treatment repeated-measures experiment, you would need only one-third the number of subjects that would be required in a comparable randomized-blocks experiment; in a four-condition experiment, only one-fourth as many, and so on. A second advantage of the repeated-measures approach is that subjects need not be premeasured on a matching criterion. The

TABLE 13–4
Repeated-Measures Design

	Condition 1	*Condition 2*	*Condition 3*
PERSON 1	→X1	→X2	→X3
PERSON 2	→X1	→X2	→X3
PERSON 3	→X1	→X2	→X3
PERSON 4	→X1	→X2	→X3
PERSON 5	→X1	→X2	→X3
PERSON 6	→X1	→X2	→X3
PERSON 7	→X1	→X2	→X3
PERSON 8	→X1	→X2	→X3
PERSON 9	→X1	→X2	→X3
PERSON 10	→X1	→X2	→X3

matching occurs automatically, since each subject is her own equivalent counterpart across conditions. And this point leads to a third major advantage of this design: Theoretically, since each person performs at every level of the independent variable, the initial equivalence of the various conditions is perfectly ensured.

Disadvantages of Repeated-Measures Designs. The major drawback of repeated-measures designs is their vulnerability to the testing effect, or *sequencing effect*. In Chapter 7, you learned that there are two general categories of confounding associated with sequencing effects: *progressive error* and *carry-over effects*. For purposes of review, these concepts are summarized in Box 13–2. Carry-over effects, of course, cannot usually be neu-

---

Box 13–2
HIGHLIGHT
Review of Concepts: Problems and
Procedures in Repeated-Measures Designs

Carry-Over Effects: Subjects' experience and performance in the early conditions of an experiment lead to the acquisition of a treatment-specific response bias which carries over to later treatments and biases the outcomes of those treatments—for example, information-processing strategies, coping mechanisms, persistent drug effects. The sequencing effect of going from condition *a* to condition *b* does not equal the effect of going from *b* to *a*.

Progressive Error: Any general change in the subjects' performance on the dependent measure that results from continued experience in the experiment. Examples include warm-up and practice effects, primacy and recency effects, boredom and fatigue effects, and the buildup of nonspecific memory interference.

The effect of a condition *a*→condition *b* order equals the effect of a *b*→*a* order at a given point in the experiment.

Counterbalanced Order of Treatments: A series of different treatments is ordered in such a way that each treatment occurs equally often in the sequence of experimental trials, and each treatment precedes and follows every other treatment an equal number of times.

Randomized Order of Treatments: A series of different treatments is ordered randomly across experimental trials. If several different randomized sequences of treatments are used in a repeated-measures study, then randomization has the same ''balancing'' effect as counterbalancing.

tralized or "balanced" across conditions in a repeated-measures design. Thus, when carry-over effects are likely to exist upon repeated testing, it is better to use a between-subjects manipulation of the independent variable than to risk a major confounding in a repeated-measures experiment.

Progressive error, which results from such processes as warm-up, practice, and recency effects, can often be handled through either counterbalancing (e.g., abccba) or randomizing the order of treatments within a repeated-measures experiment (see Box 13-2; also Chapter 7). You'll recall that the idea behind each of these strategies is to evenly balance the effects of progressive error across the various experimental treatments.

There is a third strategy, called **block randomization**, that you may use to balance progressive error. It is more generally useful than either simple randomization or counterbalancing of the treatment sequence. The basic procedure in block randomization is:

1. Divide the total number of experimental trials or stimulus presentations in your experiment by the number of levels of the independent variable. The result of this division is the number of stimulus or "trial" *blocks* you will expose each subject to. For example, if you plan to present 30 stimuli to each subject, and the stimuli represent three levels of the independent variable, then you will have 10 stimulus blocks, *each consisting of 3 stimuli*.

2. Within each block, present each level of the independent variable (e.g., each stimulus type) once; *randomize the order of the levels within each block*.

Here's an example. Suppose you wish to conduct a repeated-measures experiment to investigate how the "meaningfulness" of words affects subjects' ability to remember them. The independent variable, meaningfulness, has three levels: high, medium, and low. You plan to ask each subject to study a list of 55 words, and to subsequently attempt a free recall of as many words as he can remember. The first 15 and last 10 items in the list are "token" words; they simply fill up space and "absorb" the effects of primacy and recency effects in memory. The 30 words in the middle of the list represent the target stimuli. There are 10 each of high, medium, and low meaningfulness. So you actually have 30 stimuli representing the three levels of your independent variable.

You know that several sources of progressive error might operate across the middle 30 list positions to confound the results. To distribute progressive error evenly across the three meaningfulness levels, you could divide the 30 critical positions into 10 blocks of 3 words each. Within each block, you would present 1 word from each level of meaningfulness, and the order of the words would be randomly determined. The result of this balancing strategy appears in Box 13-3. Note how equitably the three levels of meaningfulness are distributed across list positions.

Box 13-3
HIGHLIGHT
Block Randomization

Below is an example of a block-randomized sequence of word stimuli for a hypothetical experiment in memory. The independent variable is meaningfulness of the words in the list. The list positions represented here are the middle 30 positions in a 55-word list. Note that each block of three list positions must contain 1 each of high (H), medium (M), and low (L) meaningfulness words.

Box 13–3
HIGHLIGHT
Block Randomization (*continued*)

	List Position	Meaningfulness		List Position	Meaningfulness
BLOCK 1	1	H	BLOCK 6	16	L
	2	L		17	H
	3	M		18	M
BLOCK 2	4	M	BLOCK 7	19	M
	5	L		20	L
	6	H		21	H
BLOCK 3	7	M	BLOCK 8	22	H
	8	H		23	M
	9	L		24	L
BLOCK 4	10	M	BLOCK 9	25	L
	11	L		26	H
	12	H		27	M
BLOCK 5	13	M	BLOCK 10	28	L
	14	H		29	M
	15	L		30	H

Block randomization is so effective in neutralizing progressive error that two or three "block-randomized" forms of the stimulus sequence normally will be sufficient to minimize this confounding. As a final step in the procedure, you would randomly assign subjects to forms of the stimulus sequence.

Unfortunately, dealing with sequencing effects won't always save the day for a repeated-measures experiment. The "instrumentation changes" confounding is always a threat when subjects are measured several times in an experiment. Also, if the repeated measures span a considerable time interval, say several hours or days, either subject maturation or subject mortality could also contaminate the data. Table 13–5 summarizes the various threats to internal validity for the repeated-measures approach, as well as for the other designs we've examined.

MAXIMIZING THE POWER OF EXPERIMENTS

The **power** of an experiment refers to how sensitive the experiment is to the effect of the independent variable. "Weak," or insensitive, experiments yield data suggesting no relationship between the independent and dependent variables even when such a relationship does exist and would be revealed by better-designed studies. What often happens in these cases is that the particular procedure used allows random error to become large relative to

TABLE 13–5

Summary of Confounding in Experimental Designs

					Sources of Internal Invalidity			
Design	Subject Selection Bias	Testing Effects	Instrumentation Changes	Statistical Regression	Interaction of Subject Selection with Other Factors	History	Subject Maturation	Subject Mortality
One-Shot Case Study	*					*	*	*	*
Single-Group Pretest-Posttest		*	*	*	*	*	*	*
Static-Group Comparison	*				*			*
Completely Randomized Control-Group						P		P
Completely Randomized Pretest-Posttest		*				P		P
Solomon Four-Group						P		P
Randomized Blocks						P		P
Repeated Measures		*	*			*	*	*

Key: * = definite threat to internal validity in the design; P = possible threat to internal validity.

small (but real) systematic differences between experimental treatments. As a result, the test of statistical significance that is applied to the data ends up indicating that only random error differences exist—that is, that the data are not "significant." Consequently, the researcher *fails to reject a false null hypothesis* and, thus, makes a Type II decision error (see Chapter 8).

There are some basic guidelines that you can use to maximize the power of your experiments and avoid the problem described above:

1. Use strong manipulations of the independent variable.
2. Use reliable measures of the dependent variable.
3. Use large sample sizes.
4. Use "more sensitive" experimental designs.

Strong Manipulations

Strong manipulations of independent variables tend to be of two types: extreme manipulations and multi-level manipulations. I learned about the value of extreme manipulations the hard way, during my tenure as a graduate student. I was attempting to discover what variables would influence the "spacing effect" in free-recall memory. To observe the "spacing effect," you must present a list of to-be-remembered words in which several of the words *occur twice at various spacing intervals.* For example, the second presentation of a word might occur after 0, 5, 10, or 20 intervening words since its first presentation. The usual finding in this type of study is that subsequent free recall of the repeated words increases systematically as the "spacing" interval between the first and second presentations increases (e.g., Melton, 1970). This fairly reliable finding is illustrated in Figure 13–1.

As Figure 13–1 suggests, free recall is lowest when the two occurrences of a word are back-to-back in the study list—that is, when the spacing interval is zero. As you increase the number of other items that are presented between the first and second occurrences of a repeated word, recall of that word increases.

Before I could investigate variables that might influence the spacing effect, I had to demonstrate that I could replicate the basic phenomenon. But at first, I was unable to replicate this fairly faithful effect! In the initial experiment, I used spacing intervals of 2, 10, and 20 and, to my dismay, obtained nonsignificant results. It was only after I carefully went back over the literature that I discovered my error: I had failed to use the *lowest extreme* in the range of possible intervals—that is, zero spacing. And, as Figure 13–1 correctly indicates, the greatest impact of the spacing of repeated words occurs as the spacing interval changes from zero to the first nonzero level. Fortunately, when I included a zero interval in subsequent experiments, the spacing phenomenon replicated strongly. The moral: Strong effects tend to be associated with extreme values of the independent variable.

The second approach to strengthening experimental manipulations is to *employ several levels of the independent variable*, rather than only two levels. There are a couple of reasons that this tactic often increases the sensitivity of experiments. One is purely statistical: Sta-

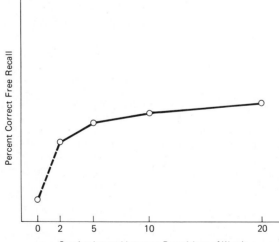

FIGURE 13–1

Long-Term Free Recall of Twice-Presented Words as a Function of Interpresentation (Spacing) Interval

Note: The figure illustrates the importance of using strong manipulations of the independent variable. Most of the so-called "spacing effect" is accounted for by the difference between the "zero" spacing interval and the first nonzero spacing interval (fictitious data).

tistical tests of multi-level experiments are more likely to detect effects than are tests of two-level experiments. (This fact is related to the concept of "degrees of freedom" in statistical tests; see Hays, 1981; Snedecor & Cochran, 1980.) Apart from statistical considerations, however, some relationships between psychological variables are *curvilinear* in form. This means that the direction of the relationship between the independent and dependent variables changes as a function of the particular set of treatment conditions used. A hypothetical example of a curvilinear relationship appears in Figure 13–2(a). Notice that values of the dependent variable (Y) first decrease from the first to the second level of the independent variable (X), then increase from level 2 to level 3 of the independent variable. Thus, if all three levels of the independent variable were employed in an experiment, the results would indicate a significant curvilinear change in Y as a function of the manipulation of X. This hypothetical three-level experiment represents a strong manipulation of the independent variable.

Now examine Figure 13–2(b), which represents a "weak" manipulation of variable X. Even though levels 1 and 2 of the independent variable might be "extreme" values, the results would suggest that the independent variable has no effect on the dependent variable. Had a third, "intermediate" treatment been included, a definite relationship between X and Y would have been shown to exist, and both the statistical decision and the experimenter's conclusions would have been dramatically different from those of the two-condition experiment.

Reliable Measures

The reliability of your procedures for measuring the dependent variable can greatly affect the power of your experiment. Unreliable measures add a lot of random error to your data, and in your test of significance, this extra random error will tend to "hide" small to moderate effects of the independent variable. This will lead you to declare the results nonsignificant even if there is a relationship between the independent and dependent variables. Therefore, to maximize the power of your experiment, use the principles and procedures described in Chapter 5 to ensure the reliability of your measurement operations.

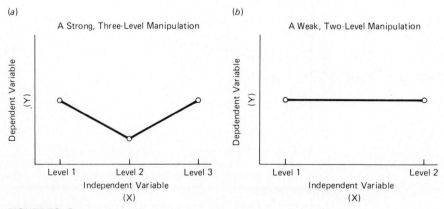

FIGURE 13–2
Hypothetical Cases of Strong (Multilevel) and Weak (Two-Level) Manipulations When the Dependent Variable Has a Curvilinear Relationship with the Independent Variable

Sample Size

Increasing the size of your treatment groups will increase the power of your experiment. The power of statistical tests to detect nonchance effects of the independent variable is directly related to the number of data points (i.e., people) in your study. Although a technical discussion of this matter goes beyond the scope of this book, it might be helpful to remember this general guideline: While increasing group size from n = 30 to n = 60 helps increase the power of your experiment to a small extent, increasing n from 10 to 30 will make a substantial difference in power (see Kirk, 1968, Table D.14).

"Sensitive" Experimental Designs

For reasons which will become evident in Chapter 14, the randomized-blocks and repeated-measures designs often are more powerful than independent-groups designs, for a given sample size. Indeed, the potential power of those designs is one of their major advantages. By now you know that it isn't always possible to use a repeated-measures or randomized-blocks design in your experiment; when it is, however, your study might benefit from the application of one of these models.

ANALYZING DATA FROM EXPERIMENTS

The specific statistical technique you use to analyze experimental data will depend on what scale of measurement your data are based on—that is, nominal, ordinal, interval, or ratio (see Chapter 5). If your data are frequency counts of subjects who either produce or fail to produce a particular response, then your measurement is of a *qualitative* (either/or) type, and the scale of measurement is "nominal." In such a case, you would apply a chi-square test of statistical significance. (That test was explained and illustrated in Chapter 9.)

Here I'll present a general significance test that may be used with interval or ratio data and a second test that is appropriate when you have an ordinal scale of measurement. *Both of these tests are applicable only to independent-groups designs that use only a single independent variable.* Tests that may be used with correlated-groups designs and multiple-variable designs will be covered in Chapter 14.

Analysis of Variance: A Significance Test for Interval Data

Analysis of variance—abbreviated ANOVA—is a widely applicable test of significance that may be applied whenever your experiment involves *two or more* conditions (i.e., levels of the independent variable) and your data have been measured on an interval or ratio scale. ANOVA yields a test statistic called the **F ratio**, which will be explained and illustrated below. Since the majority of psychology experiments assume an interval scale of measurement, ANOVA, or some variant of it, is the most frequently used significance test in experimental psychology.

The Logic of ANOVA.   The theory behind ANOVA is intimately tied to the logic of the experimental method. When you randomly assign your subjects to the treatment groups, you expect the "law of chance" to render the groups essentially equivalent at the start of the experiment. If you subsequently measure the subjects in all groups on the dependent variable and the group means are very close to one another, one of two conclusions is in order. Assuming that the dependent measure is reliable and valid, either (a) you haven't yet manipulated the independent variable or (b) you have manipulated the independent variable, but it had no effect on the dependent variable. Likewise, the statistical procedure called ANOVA assumes that you have randomly assigned subjects to conditions and that the treatment groups' means will be approximately equal if only chance is operating to determine scores on the dependent measure (i.e., if the independent variable has not been manipulated or has had no effect).

But recall that random assignment of subjects doesn't make the treatment groups exactly equal, only *statistically equal*. This means that even if the independent variable has no effect, the group means are likely to be somewhat different from one another, but not enough to be "statistically significant." The nonsignificant mean differences stem from random error processes that are inherent in random assignment. Therefore, average differences between groups after manipulation of the independent variable can be a result of one or both of the following:

1. Error (chance) effects resulting from random assignment itself. This may be thought of as a type of sampling error.
2. Real (nonchance) effects of the independent variable.

In fact, mean differences between experimental groups will always contain some random sampling error. The big question, then, is whether differences between the groups reflect any systematic effect of the independent variable *in addition to* normal sampling error.

If the results of an experiment show your group means to be "kind of different," but not overwhelmingly different, how can you know whether these results are a function of random error alone or primarily an effect of the independent variable? *You compare the between-group mean differences to an index of random error, that is, form a ratio of mean differences to error: If the between-group variance is much larger than the index of error variance, then it is likely that something more than chance is responsible for the difference between the group means.* In an unconfounded experiment, that "something more than chance" can only be the effect of the independent variable.

This critical comparison is called the **F ratio**, which is the end product of an analysis of variance procedure. Thus,

$$F = \frac{\text{Between-Group Variance}}{\text{Index of Error}}$$

You can see that as between-group differences get larger and larger relative to the index of error, F also becomes larger. In the theory of ANOVA, the larger the F, the more likely it is that the group differences represent a real effect of the independent variable, because large F ratios occur only when the size of the differences between group means diverges greatly from what is expected on the basis of a random error model. In such cases, it is only logical to conclude that some systematic process is responsible for the data.

The **between-group variance** referred to in the above formula is based on the differences among the group means. But what is the index of error? The proper term for the error index in ANOVA is the **within-group variance**, and it is based on the individual differences on the dependent measure within your various treatment groups. In statistical theory, differences among individuals in a sample are considered to be purely a result of random error. Thus, if you can compute an index of within-group individual differences, then you have a good *index of error*.

How big does the F ratio have to be in order to be declared a statistically significant result? That depends on the level of significance you use, the number of groups you have in the experiment, and the number of subjects within each group—as will become evident later in this section. But, ultimately, you will compare the F statistic you compute from your data to a sampling distribution of chance F statistics. If your level of significance is .05 and the probability that your computed F is a member of the chance distribution is less than 5 percent, then the results are significant. Accordingly, you would conclude that the independent variable had an effect on the dependent variable.

To summarize:

$$F = \frac{\text{Between-Group Variance}}{\text{Within-Group Variance}} = \frac{\text{Error + Systematic Variance}}{\text{Error Variance}}$$

When only chance determined your data:

$$F = \frac{\text{Error Variance}}{\text{Error Variance}} = 1$$

When the independent variable has influenced the dependent variable:

$$F = \frac{\text{Error Variance + Effect of Independent Variable}}{\text{Error Variance}} > 1$$

Assumptions of ANOVA.   Statistics textbooks disagree somewhat on the specific nature and relative importance of the assumptions underlying ANOVA (for example, compare Hays, 1981; Levin & Rubin, 1980; and Wolins, 1982). The following seems to be the consensus of opinion on what you must be able to assume in order to apply ANOVA to your data:

1. The scale of measurement is at the interval or ratio level.
2. The dependent variable tends to be normally distributed in the population that you sampled from (usually safe to assume).
3. All "errors" of measurement and sampling are independent of one another.

Assumption 2 becomes less important as sample size is increased. Usually, you can disregard this assumption if your groups contain at least 30 subjects each. Assumption 3 usually is satisfied in independent-groups designs by randomly assigning subjects to conditions and stimulus sequences. You must be fairly confident, however, that your dependent measure approximates an interval scale. If it doesn't, the F test you perform may not be valid.

An Example.   Let's now examine how you would carry out an analysis of variance and compute an F Test. Suppose you have conducted an experiment designed to investigate the effects of two different types of reinforcement on operant conditioning in preschool children. The children were given a bag of marbles of various colors. You told them that you wanted them to drop one marble at a time through a hole in a wooden box until you said "Stop." Unknown to the children, your aim was to see if you could use reinforcement techniques to get them to select mostly red marbles. There were *three groups* in this hypothetical experiment: Each subject in Group 1 received a piece of candy each time he or she dropped a red marble into the box; subjects in Group 2 received verbal praise for doing the same; Group 3 was an unreinforced control group. Assume that there were exactly five subjects in each group, or a total of 15 subjects. (These groups would be much too small for most real experiments, but let's keep things simple.)

The results of this experiment appear in Table 13–6. Under each group name in the table are the five raw scores for the subjects in that group. Raw scores are labeled "X." The *squared* raw scores appear in parentheses and are labeled "X^2." The table also displays:

1. T_i = the total of raw scores in each group
2. T_i^2 = the *square* of each group total
3. GT = the *grand total* of all raw scores in the table
4. GT^2 = the square of the grand total
5. ΣX^2 = the sum of all squared raw scores in the table
6. n_i = the number of subjects in the *ith* group

You will use all of these quantities to compute the F test.

TABLE 13–6

Raw Scores and Raw-Score Totals for Three Groups of Children in a Hypothetical Experiment on Reinforcement Effects

	Levels of the Independent Variable					
	Group 1 (Candy)		*Group 2* (Praise)		*Group 3* (Control)	
	X	X^2	X	X^2	X	X^2
	22	(484)	16	(256)	12	(144)
	18	(324)	15	(225)	10	(100)
	22	(484)	14	(196)	8	(64)
	18	(324)	16	(256)	8	(64)
	20	(400)	14	(196)	12	(144)
Totals	100		75		50	T_i
(Totals)^2	10000		5625		2500	T_i^2
Group Means	20		15		10	$\overline{X}_i$
Group Sizes	$n_1 = 5$		$n_2 = 5$		$n_3 = 5$	n_i

$$GT = 225$$
$$GT^2 = 5065$$
$$\Sigma X^2 = 3661$$

Key:
  X = any raw score
  X^2 = any squared raw score
  T_i = sum of raw scores in the *ith* group
  T_i^2 = square of sum of raw scores in the *ith* group
ΣX^2 = sum of all squared raw scores
  GT = grand total = sum of all raw scores
GT^2 = square of grand total

If you calculate the mean of each group through dividing each group total by the number of observations in that group, you'll obtain the following:

$$\text{Mean}1 = 20$$
$$\text{Mean}2 = 15$$
$$\text{Mean}3 = 10$$

The means are numerically different, and it appears that reinforcement produced more correct responses than "no reinforcement"; also, candy reinforcement appears to have been more effective than praise. The only question remaining is whether these mean differences are real (nonchance) or merely a result of sampling error. The F test will provide an answer.

The Null and Alternative Hypotheses.   In a three-condition ANOVA, the null hypothesis takes this form:

$$H_0: \mu_1 = \mu_2 = \mu_3$$

This is a symbolic way of asserting that all of the group means in an experiment come from the same population—the population of chance; therefore, all of the population means represented by the sample means are equal. Of course, if the independent variable has an effect, this hypothesis is false.

The alternative hypothesis is simply that not all of the population means represented by the sample means are equal—that is, the independent variable has an effect.

Remember that the hypothesis you actually test is the null hypothesis. A significant outcome means that the null is probably false.

Setting Up the ANOVA Summary Table.   In analysis of variance, it often makes sense to start at the end and work backward. The end of an ANOVA is the ANOVA summary table, which contains all of the essential data for arriving at the F statistic. Table 13–7 is a general example of an ANOVA sumary table. The table indicates that there are

TABLE 13–7

General ANOVA Summary Table for a One-Variable (One-Way) Analysis of Variance

Source of Variance	Degrees of Freedom	Sum of Squares	Mean Square	F
Between-Groups	$dfB = (k - 1)$	SSB	MSB	MSB/MSW
Within-Groups (Error)	$dfW = (\Sigma n_i - k)$	SSW	MSW	
TOTAL	$(\Sigma n_i - 1)$	SST		

Key:
k = number of treatment groups in experiment
n_i = number of subjects in the *ith* group
dfB = between-groups degrees of freedom
dfW = within-groups degrees of freedom
SSB = between-groups sum of squares
SSW = within-groups sum of squares
MSB = SSB/dfB = between-groups mean square
MSW = SSW/dfW = within-groups mean square

two sources of variation in the data of an experiment: between-groups variance, based on the difference among group means, and within-groups variance (i.e., error variance), based on individual differences among subjects within the three groups. *A useful point to remember is that between-groups figures and within-groups figures must always add up to the "total" figures* shown at the bottom of the summary table.

You will use two types of degrees of freedom in ANOVA:

1. Degrees of freedom for between-groups variation, symbolized dfB. You get dfB through $(k - 1)$, where k = the number of groups in your experiment. The logic of degrees of freedom here is similar to that used to determine degrees of freedom in chi square (Chapter 9). Given k group *totals* and a *fixed grand total* of raw scores, only $(k - 1)$ of the group totals are free to vary.

2. Degrees of freedom for within-groups variation, symbolized dfW. You obtain dfW through $(\Sigma n_i - k)$, which is the sum of all group sizes minus the number of groups. This is the same as saying that only $(n - 1)$ of the n raw scores in each group are free to vary, given a fixed group total.

Note that dfB and dfW must sum to total degrees of freedom, which can also be found directly through $(\Sigma n_i - 1)$.

Another column of the table contains *sums of squares*, one each for total (SST), between-group variation (SSB), and within-group variation (SSW). The sum of squares for total variation is what you would get if you found the *grand mean* of all 15 scores in the table, subtracted it from each of the 15 raw scores, squared the difference, and summed the squared differences. However, we'll use a simpler technique for computing SST. The sum of squares for between-group variation (SSB) is based on squared differences between the group means and the grand mean; and the sum of squares for within-group variation represents the sum of the squared differences between raw scores in each group and that group's mean. Remember, SST = SSB + SSW.

The *mean squares* in the table are the "means of the sums of squares." You get the between-group mean square (MSB) by dividing SSB by the between-group degrees of freedom: MSB = SSB/dfB. MSB reflects any systematic variance due to the effect of the independent variable (although MSB also contains some error variance). In contrast, MSW reflects only random error variance. You may compute MSW through SSW/dfW.

Finally, the F ratio is computed by dividing systematic variance by random error variance, or F = MSB/MSW.

Computing F.   As you perform an analysis of variance, you will sequentially convert each of the nine symbolic expressions in Table 13–7 to numbers. Let's now go through the "nine steps of ANOVA," using the data from Table 13–6. Be sure to refer to the figures in that table as we proceed:

1. Find total degrees of freedom:

$$dfT = (\Sigma n_i - 1)$$
$$= (5 + 5 + 5 - 1)$$
$$= 14$$

2. Find between-groups degrees of freedom, where k = number of groups in the experiment:

$$dfB = (k - 1)$$
$$= (3 - 1)$$
$$= 2$$

3. Find within-groups degrees of freedom:

$$dfW = (\Sigma n_i - k)$$
$$= (5 + 5 + 5 - 3)$$
$$= 12, \text{ or}$$
$$dfW = dfT - dfB$$
$$= 14 - 2$$
$$= 12$$

4. Find the total sum of squares. This is the index of *overall individual differences* on the dependent measure:

$$SST = \Sigma X^2 - (GT^2/\Sigma n_i)$$
$$= 3661 - (50625/15)$$
$$= 3661 - 3375$$
$$= 286$$

5. Find the between-groups sum of squares. This is the part of the overall individual differences that might contain a *systematic effect* of the independent variable:

$$SSB = [\Sigma(T_i^2/n_i)] - (GT^2/\Sigma n_i)$$
$$= [(10000/5) + (5625/5) + (2500/5)] - 3375$$
$$= [2000 + 1125 + 500] - 3375$$
$$= 3625 - 3375$$
$$= 250$$

6. Find the within-groups sum of squares. This part of the overall individual differences is definitely *error*. Recall that $SST = SSB + SSW$. Therefore:

$$SSW = SST - SSB$$
$$= 286 - 250$$
$$= 36$$

7. Find the between-groups mean square. This is the index of *error variance + systematic variance*:

$$MSB = SSB/dfB$$
$$= 250/2$$
$$= 125$$

8. Find the within-groups mean square. This is the index of *error variance alone*:

$$MSW = SSW/dfW$$
$$= 36/12$$
$$= 3$$

9. Find the F ratio. This is the comparison of between-group variance (error + ?) to within-group variance (error):

$$F = MSB/MSW$$
$$= 125/3$$
$$= 41.67$$

Now that we've computed all of the quantities represented by the symbolic expressions in Table 13–7, we can substitute numbers into the ANOVA summary table, as shown in Table 13–8. It is standard procedure to construct such a table when you do an ANOVA.

Testing the Significance of F.   Is the F of 41.67 significant? We certainly might hazard a guess that it is. When only random error is affecting the data, the *expected* F = 1.00 (i.e., error/error). And the computed F in this case is many times larger than 1. But most of the time, the F will be much smaller than the value we came up with here. Therefore, you will need to compare your obtained F statistic with some *critical values* of F taken from a sampling distribution of randomly determined F ratios. If your significance level is .05, and if your obtained F would occur less than 5 percent of the time in the sampling distribution, then it is significant.

Some critical values of F ratios for the .05 and .01 levels of significance are given in Table A–4 of the Appendix. To find the critical value of F for our hypothetical example, go to Table A–4. Next determine the degrees of freedom for the "numerator" in the F ratio, where the numerator is the between-subjects mean square. The degrees of freedom for the numerator is dfB, or 2. Then determine the degrees of freedom for the "denominator," which is dfW = 12. Finally, find the point in Table A–4 where the two types of degrees of freedom intersect. At that point, you will see that the critical, "chance" F for the .05 level of significance is 3.89. Since the computed F (i.e., 41.67) is *larger* than 3.89, it is significant. Consequently, you would reject the null hypothesis and conclude that the reinforcement variable did affect learning in the preschool children.

Tracking Down the Source of a Significant F.   When you do an F test on data from an experiment involving more than two groups, there are a number of specific mean differences that can cause the F statistic to be significant. For example, any two group means may be different from each other but not from a third mean; or all of the means may differ from one another. A statistical technique for detecting which specific mean differences are significant will be presented in Chapter 14.

A Few Comments on Tests for the Two-Group Situation.   If there were only two conditions in the above experiment, we could have used a statistic called the "t test" to assess the significance of the results. In fact, many textbooks recommend the t test for analyzing the data of two-group experiments. The t statistic is actually a special version of the F statistic: For the two-group situation, $F = t^2$. Both tests lead to the same conclusion, and F is usually easier to compute when you are starting out with raw scores.

TABLE 13–8

ANOVA Summary Table Containing the Results of an Analysis of Variance of Data from a Hypothetical Experiment on the Effects of Reinforcement

Source of Variance	Degrees of Freedom	Sum of Squares	Mean Square	F
Between-Groups	(3 − 1) = 2	250.00	125.00	41.67
Within-Groups (Error)	(15 − 3) = 12	36.00	3.00	
TOTAL	(15 − 1) = 14	286.00		

Kruskal-Wallis Test: A Test of Significance for Ordinal Data

Because analysis of variance assumes a normally distributed population and an interval scale of measurement, the F test is considered to be a **parametric test**. In other words, it is a test that *is dependent on the existence of certain characteristics in the population of observations that is sampled*. When you cannot assume that these characteristics exist, then you must use a **nonparametric test** to assess statistical significance. Nonparametric statistical tests are said to be "distribution-free," because they don't assume that the sampled population is normally distributed. Nor do they assume an interval scale of measurement.

A very useful and general nonparametric test is the *Kruskal-Wallis Test*, which yields the "K" statistic. You can use this test of significance when the data of your experiment are measured on an *ordinal scale*—that is, when you can rank the subjects from highest to lowest on the dependent measure but don't have information on the distance between ranks (see Chapter 5). Like the F test, however, the K test does depend on random assignment of subjects to treatment groups. In addition, the K test assumes that you have more than five subjects per treatment group (Hamburg, 1979).

An Example.   Suppose I wanted to use an independent-groups experimental design to investigate the relative effectiveness of three relaxation procedures: meditation, hypnosis, and progressive relaxation. I decide on a completely randomized design in which only a posttest is used. After randomly allocating six subjects to each of the three groups, I administer the treatments on an individual basis; after each session, I have the subject rate his or her depth of relaxation on a 100-point scale, where 99 is maximal relaxation and 0 is no relaxation at all. Since a simple rating scale such as this probably doesn't possess equal intervals—that is, $(90-80)$ probably doesn't equal $(50-40)$—I can assume only an ordinal scale of measurement. Therefore, I decide to test the significance of the results with the Kruskal-Wallis K statistic rather than with a standard ANOVA.

Setting Up the Ranking Hierarchy.   The first step in this statistical procedure is to arrange the subjects' scores in a hierarchy, from highest to lowest or vice versa, and display the ranks and the group identities next to the ranks. Such a hierarchy for this hypothetical study appears in Table 13–9. Note the symbols for meditation (M), progressive relaxation (PR), and hypnosis (H), which help us keep track of which group each score and rank goes with. The column labeled "Rank Position" simply serves as a reminder that the 18 subjects must fill up 18 "spaces" in the hierarchy. The critical data are in the "Rank" column. Thus, the top subject gave a relaxation rating of 95, so she receives the top rank of 18; she happened to be in the meditation (M) group.

Most often there will be *tied scores* in this type of analysis. *Tied scores must share the same rank*, and this rank must be the *average of the rank positions* occupied by the scores. For instance, the two scores of 85 occupy rank positions 15 and 14 in the hierarchy. Since the average of rank positions 15 and 14 is $[(15+14)/2]$, or 14.5, both of the subjects with scores of 85 are assigned a rank of 14.5. The same rank-assignment procedure had to be used for the three 65's and the two 42's.

Computing K.   A preliminary step in the computation of the K statistic involves rearranging the data in the ranking hierarchy into a rank sum table, which lists the subjects' ranks by treatment group. The rank sum table for the present example is Table 13–10, which provides the following information:

1. The original raw scores broken down by treatment group. At this point, the raw scores are used only for purposes of reference.

TABLE 13–9

Ranking Hierarchy from a Hypothetical Experiment on Relaxation

Rank Position	Score	Rank	Group
(18)	95	18	M
(17)	93	17	PR
(16)	90	16	H
(15)	85	14.5	M
(14)	85	14.5	PR
(13)	80	13	M
(12)	76	12	PR
(11)	74	11	PR
(10)	69	10	H
(9)	65	8	M
(8)	65	8	H
(7)	65	8	M
(6)	52	6	PR
(5)	50	5	H
(4)	48	4	PR
(3)	42	2.5	M
(2)	42	2.5	H
(1)	38	1	H

Key:
M = meditation-group subject
PR = progressive-relaxation-group subject
H = hypnosis-group subject

2. The subjects' ranks categorized by treatment group. These are the essential data to be used in computing K.
3. The sum of ranks (R_i) for each treatment group:
   $R_1 = 64.5$ (progressive relaxation)
   $R_2 = 64.0$ (meditation)
   $R_3 = 42.5$ (hypnosis)
4. The squares of the sums of ranks (R_i^2).
5. The number of subjects in each treatment (n_i).

Judging solely from the rank sums, it appears that progressive relaxation and meditation did not differ from each other on the relaxation ratings they received. The sum of ranks for hypnosis is numerically lower, however: Is this difference likely to have occurred by chance alone, or was hypnosis really a less efficient relaxation procedure in this study? The K statistic and its sampling distribution will provide the basis for answering this question.

The formula for K is:

$$K = \frac{12}{n(n + 1)}\left[\Sigma \frac{R_i^2}{n_i}\right] - 3(n + 1), \text{ where}$$

K = the test statistic for c groups of ranks
R_i^2 = the square of the *ith* sum of ranks
n_i = the number of observations in the *ith* treatment group
n = $n_1 + n_2 + \ldots n_c$ = total number of subjects,
      and 12 and 3 are constants

TABLE 13-10

Raw Scores, Ranks, and Sums of Ranks from a Hypothetical Experiment on Relaxation

	Treatment Groups				
Group 1 (P. Relaxation)		*Group 2* (Meditation)		*Group 3* (Hypnosis)	
Score	*Rank*	*Score*	*Rank*	*Score*	*Rank*
93	17	95	18	90	16
85	14.5	85	14.5	69	10
76	12	80	13	65	8
74	11	65	8	50	5
52	6	65	8	42	2.5
48	4	42	2.5	38	1
$R_1 = 64.5$		$R_2 = 64$		$R_3 = 42.5$	
$R_1^2 = 4160.25$		$R_2^2 = 4096$		$R_3^2 = 1806.25$	
$n_1 = 6$		$n_2 = 6$		$n_3 = 6$	

Key:
R_i = the rank sum of the *ith* group
R_i^2 = the square of the rank sum for the *ith* group
n_i = the number of subjects in the *ith* group

Plugging in the present values, I get:

$$K = \frac{12}{(18)(19)} \left[\frac{(64.5)^2}{6} + \frac{(64)^2}{6} + \frac{(42.5)^2}{6} \right] - 3(18 + 1)$$

$$K = \frac{12}{342} \left[\frac{4160.25}{6} + \frac{4096}{6} + \frac{1806.25}{6} \right] - 3(19)$$

$$K = .0351[693.38 + 682.67 + 301.04] - 57$$

$$K = .0351[1677.09] - 57$$

$$K = 58.7 - 57$$

$$K = 1.7$$

Testing the Significance of K.   The K statistic is distributed as chi square, with $(c-1)$ degrees of freedom, where c is the number of groups in the experiment. So Table A–2 of the Appendix, which contains critical chance values of chi square, may be used to assess the significance of K. With $(3-1)$, or 2, degrees of freedom, I would need a K greater than 5.99 for significance. Clearly, then, the actual K of 1.7 falls short and must be considered a chance event. Therefore, the data provide no evidence supporting the hypothesis that the three relaxation procedures differ in effectiveness.

SUMMARY

The experimental method is the most effective device available to social scientists in discovering and verifying cause-and-effect sequences in behavior. General procedures in experimentation include operationalizing the independent and dependent variables, conducting a pilot study, assigning subjects to treatment conditions, and "running" the experiment.

In an experiment, you can manipulate your independent variable by varying tasks or stimuli, the preexperimental explanation, or the physical or social context of the experiment. The effectiveness of variable manipulation should be checked in a pilot study.

True experiments always involve the use of random assignment and control groups. *Pseudo experiments* lack one or both of these features, making them vulnerable to a number of confoundings. The pseudo-experimental designs reviewed in this chapter were the *single-group posttest design*, the *single-group pretest-posttest design*, and the *static-group comparison design*.

True experiments fall into two categories: *Independent-groups designs* and *correlated-groups designs*. Examples of independent-groups designs include the *completely randomized control-group design* and the *completely randomized pretest-posttest design*. Correlated-groups experiments use models such as the *randomized-blocks design* and the *repeated-measures design*. Relative to independent-groups experiments, correlated-groups experiments are more sensitive to effects of the independent variable, but they are also subject to progressive error and carry-over effects.

The *power* of experiments can be increased by using strong manipulations of the independent variable, reliable measures of the dependent variable, large sample sizes, and "sensitive" experimental designs.

If the data of an experiment are on an interval scale of measurement, then *analysis of variance* may be used to test the results for statistical significance. If the data are on an ordinal scale, then the *Kruskal-Wallis K statistic* may be used.

REVIEW QUESTIONS

1. Summarize the basic rationale underlying the experimental method. (Hint: How is it that experiments can be used to isolate causal sequences?)

2. Describe three *general* ways in which an independent variable may be manipulated.

3. What important functions are served by a preexperimental pilot study?

4. Distinguish between pseudo experiments and true experiments, focusing on two major characteristics that true experiments have but pseudo experiments do not.

5. Evaluate the following designs, giving special attention to their vulnerability to confoundings: single-group posttest design, single-group pretest-posttest design, static-group comparison design.

6. Describe the specific steps you would go through to plan and set up a completely randomized control-group design.

7. Describe the specific steps you would follow in planning and conducting a randomized-blocks experiment.

8. Define or describe: between-subjects manipulation, within-subjects manipulation, block randomization, independent-groups designs, correlated-groups designs, power of an experiment, nonparametric statistics.

9. What are the special advantages and drawbacks of repeated-measures designs? Under what circumstances should a repeated-measures design definitely not be used?

10. Compare the theory behind analysis of variance with the rationale of the experimental method.

Note

[1] Recall that both the brain-lesion (i.e., experimental) group and the sham-operation (i.e., extra control) group undergo the general surgical procedure, but only the brain-lesion animals have a specific brain site destroyed.

14

COMPLICATING THE EXPERIMENT

In the last chapter, you learned about a very powerful method for discovering and verifying cause-and-effect sequences in human nature—namely, the psychology experiment with one independent variable. But human nature is complex, and experiments that examine the effect of only one independent variable at a time are not up to the task of revealing the more complicated relationships that characterize it.

Fortunately, however, social scientists have cleverly devised ways to complicate their experimental designs, so that the power of the experimental method can be used to reveal the *joint effect* of two or more independent variables. These more complicated experimental models are referred to as multi-variable designs or, more commonly, factorial designs. A factorial experimental design is defined by these features:

1. Two or more independent variables are manipulated ''simultaneously'' in the same experiment.
2. The various independent variables are manipulated independently of one another, in the sense that they do not confound one another. This is ensured by random assignment of subjects to treatments.
3. Each level of every independent variable is combined with each level of every other independent variable; hence, if you have two levels of independent variable A and three levels of independent variable B, then there are 2×3 combinations, resulting in six experimental conditions. Note that each of the six conditions represents the combination of one level of variable A with one level of variable B.
4. Every subject in the experiment receives at least one level of every independent variable.

Factorial designs are valuable for several reasons. They are more economical of time, effort, and money than are single-variable experiments. In addition, these designs avoid a potential confounding. For example, suppose you are interested in the effects of two independent variables, A and B, on dependent variable Y, and you decide to test the effect of each variable in a separate single-variable experiment. Each experiment would require its own planning, setup, and data-analysis time. Further, since the experiment involving the manipulation of variable A would be carried out first, and that involving manipulation of B later, the effect of each variable may be confounded by factors related to ''time of measurement.'' That is, the subjects you are able to recruit early in an academic term may differ systematically from those you can recruit later in the term, and these systematic differences between subject pools may contaminate any comparison of the effects of A with the effects of B. In contrast, if A and B are manipulated simultaneously within one experiment, then ''time of measurement'' is not a problem. Also, you would be required to plan and set up only one experiment to answer your questions about both A and B, and you would need to perform only one data analysis.

Perhaps the most important advantage of factorial designs is that they enable you to assess the unique joint effect of the *interaction* of two or more independent variables. This advantage has important implications not only for gaining a better understanding of human behavior and experience, but also for generalizing the results from laboratory to everyday life. After all, the behavior of people outside the lab is rarely a function of the effect of only one variable acting alone; almost always, several variables work together to influence a particular behavior. The factorial design allows you to see just how such joint action takes place, all within the framework of controlled observation and manipulation.

In this chapter, you'll encounter many of the interesting possibilities for combining multiple independent variables in a single experiment. You'll see how factorial designs may be set up to accommodate between-subjects manipulations, within-subjects manipulations, "organismic" independent variables, and various combinations of these different classes of variables. The concept of an interaction, which you've briefly encountered at several points in this book, will become clearer and more concrete. Also, you will learn how to perform tests of statistical significance on data from factorial experiments.

THE COMPLETELY RANDOMIZED FACTORIAL DESIGN

The most basic multi-variable design is the 2×2 completely randomized factorial design. This model consists of two independent variables, A and B, each having two levels. The combinations of two levels of each of two variables produce ($2 \times 2 =$) four experimental conditions, where *each condition consists of the combination of one level of A with one level of B*. Thus, the conditions would be: A1B1, A1B2, A2B1, and A2B2.

In a completely randomized factorial experiment, subjects are randomly assigned to the various conditions, and the independent variables are manipulated *between subjects*. That is, a given subject would receive one and only one level of A and one and only one level of B. For instance, a subject in condition A1B1 could not also serve in A1B2. Also, because of the completely random assignment to conditions, this type of experiment is an independent-groups design.

A schematic illustration of a 2×2 completely randomized factorial appears in Table 14–1. Notice that each experimental condition is represented by one cell of the table, and that five subjects have been randomly allocated to each of the four conditions. The X's stand for the various treatments that are administered. Thus, X11 signifies level 1 of variable A and level 1 of variable B, X12 is level 1 of A and level 2 of B, and so on.

TABLE 14–1

Abstract Configuration of a 2×2 Factorial Design with Five Subjects per Group

		Independent Variable B	
		B1	*B2*
		Treat. A1B1	Treat. A1B2
	A1	S1 → X11	S6 → X12
		S2 → X11	S7 → X12
		S3 → X11	S8 → X12
		S4 → X11	S9 → X12
		S5 → X11	S10 → X12
Independent Variable A		Treat. A2B1	Treat. A2B2
	A2	S11 → X21	S16 → X22
		S12 → X21	S17 → X22
		S13 → X21	S18 → X22
		S14 → X21	S19 → X22
		S15 → X21	S20 → X22

An Example

Now let's put the completely randomized factorial into the concrete terms of a specific example. Students are often required to memorize poems, passages, and speeches word for word. Some students use a "part-learning" method of memorization; that is, they first commit small segments of the material to memory and then, having mastered each component, attempt to connect all of the segments together in memory. Other students use the "whole-learning" approach, in which they attempt to memorize the entire body of material as a unit. This approach has the advantage of not requiring a final memorization of the correct order of a lot of isolated segments.

Which memorization strategy should teachers recommend to their students? Which strategy is more efficient in terms of the amount of time required to memorize material of a fixed length? You might be able to obtain a preliminary answer to this question by conducting a completely randomized two-group experiment in which whole versus part learning is the independent variable. The dependent variable could be the amount of time required to memorize a poem. But can the question be answered this simply? Certainly not. There are many factors to be considered, including the age and intellectual ability of the subjects, the type of material (e.g., poems versus technical rules), and, last but not least, the length of the unit to be remembered (cf. McGeoch & Irion, 1952). Perhaps the "whole" method would be more effective for memorizing short poems consisting of two to four stanzas, but with longer works, the "part" method may be more efficient. Certainly, in the case of longer poems, the part method would provide more frequent opportunities for feedback (i.e., "knowledge of results"), and it might also maintain interest better than the whole method.

What I'm suggesting is that a 2 × 2 completely randomized factorial experiment would be much more informative in this example than would a simple single-variable experiment. Not only would the factorial provide evidence on the overall effectiveness of the two memorization strategies, but also it would indicate whether the relative effectiveness of the strategies differs for material of different lengths.

Suppose that you have actually conducted this kind of factorial experiment. Length of materials was independent variable A (A1 = long poems; A2 = short poems), and learning strategy was independent variable B (B1 = part learning; B2 = whole learning). This 2 × 2 factorial required the following four groups (cells):

1. A1B1: subjects used part learning to memorize a long poem
2. A1B2: subjects used whole learning to memorize a long poem
3. A2B1: subjects used part learning to memorize a short poem
4. A2B2: subjects used whole learning to memorize a short poem

Let's further suppose that you randomly assigned five subjects to each of the four cells. You then administered the specified treatment to each subject and measured him on the dependent variable. Assume that the dependent measure was learning time, operationally defined as the number of minutes of study required to achieve one perfect recitation of the poem.

The hypothetical results are shown in Table 14–2. Each cell of that table contains the raw scores (in minutes) and means for the five subjects in a particular group. Note that, in addition to showing the group means, the table also exhibits the *overall means for each level of variable A* ($\overline{X}_{A1} = 37.5$; $\overline{X}_{A2} = 22.5$) and *each level of B* ($\overline{X}_{B1} = 30$; $\overline{X}_{B2} = 30$).

Now let's consider the type of information that we can derive from the data table. In factorial experiments, in general, the data will provide information on both the *main effect*

TABLE 14–2

Raw Scores, Cell Means, and Marginal Row and Column Means for a Hypothetical
2 × 2 Factorial Experiment on Part versus Whole Learning

		Learning Strategy		Means of Variable A
		Part Learning B1	Whole Learning B2	
		Cell A1B1	Cell A1B2	
		38	37	
		35	39	
	Long Poems A1	36	41	$\overline{X}_{A1} = 37.5$
		34	40	
		32	43	
		$\overline{X}_{A1B1} = 35$	$\overline{X}_{A1B2} = 40$	
Length of Materials		Cell A2B1	Cell A2B2	
		25	14	
		30	20	
	Short Poems A2	20	22	$\overline{X}_{A2} = 22.5$
		26	26	
		24	18	
		$\overline{X}_{A2B1} = 25$	$\overline{X}_{A2B2} = 20$	
	Means of Variable B	$\overline{X}_{B1} = 30$	$\overline{X}_{B2} = 30$	

Key:
$\overline{X}_{AiBi}$ = the cell mean for any combination of one level of Variable A with one level of Variable B
$\overline{X}_{Ai}$ = the row mean for either level of Variable A, averaged over both levels of Variable B
$\overline{X}_{Bi}$ = the column mean for either level of Variable B, averaged over both levels of Variable A

of each independent variable and the *interaction effect* of the combination of independent variables.

Main Effects

The **main effect** of an independent variable in a factorial experiment is *the effect that that variable has irrespective of the influence of the other independent variables.* The main effect of variable A, for example, literally is the effect of A *averaged* across all levels of all other independent variables in the experiment.

Take a "gut-level" example. Suppose that, in general, you like eating T-bone steak more than you like eating frankfurters. The preference for steak over frankfurters may have a greater influence on behavior when you're famished than when you're full. It may have a smaller effect when French fries are also served. But overall, averaging across all other influential factors and conditions, you definitely would choose steak over the frankfurter. That average outcome is the main effect of the meat preference variable.

In psychology experiments, there are three ways to assess the main effects of independent variables: (a) numerically, in terms of mean differences; (b) graphically; (c) through tests of statistical significance.

Numerical Mean Differences. A main effect can be *suggested*, though not verified, through a comparison of the overall means of the different levels of an independent variable. Notice in Table 14–2 that the overall means of A1 (Long Poems) and A2 (Short Poems) appear in the row margins of the table. In accordance with the definition of a main effect, these row means are what you get when you *average* the scores on the dependent variable across both levels of the other independent variable (B). Thus,

$$\overline{X}_{A1} = (\overline{X}_{A1B1} + \overline{X}_{A1B2})/2$$
$$= (35 + 40)/2$$
$$= 75/2$$
$$= 37.5$$

$$\overline{X}_{A2} = (\overline{X}_{A2B1} + \overline{X}_{A2B2})/2$$
$$= (25 + 20)/2$$
$$= 45/2$$
$$= 22.5$$

A main effect of A, however, is not represented by either $\overline{X}_{A1}$ or $\overline{X}_{A2}$ alone. Rather it is suggested by their numerical difference: $(\overline{X}_{A1} - \overline{X}_{A2}) = 37.5 - 22.5 = 15$. Hence, to no one's surprise, it appears that short poems were easier to learn than long poems. But it's important to keep in mind that this is a *numerical* difference rather than a statistical difference. The latter can be assessed only through a test of significance—an important point to remember, since many "numerical main effects" are not statistically reliable, and, according to the rules of the game, only statistically significant differences are "real" main effects. Nonetheless, without a numerical difference between the overall means of a variable, there can be no "statistical" main effect. For example, consider the overall means of B1 and B2, which appear in the column margins of Table 14–2. Since they are identical, there is no "numerical" main effect and, thus, there can be no "statistical" main effect of learning strategy. This means that, overall, part learning and whole learning were equally effective in the memorization of poems.

Graphing Main Effects. Main effects of variables may also be assessed on a tentative, visual basis by representing the marginal (overall) means of the independent variables in a line graph. This procedure will give you a "big picture" of the possible main effects and will be useful for quickly communicating your general findings to other researchers. Nevertheless, as was true of "numerical" main effects, the effects suggested by a line graph will need to be tested for statistical significance before they can be accepted as reliable outcomes. The line graphs for the main effects of variables A and B appear in Figures 14–1 and 14–2, respectively. Figure 14–1, which shows how dependent-measure means varied as a function of material length, reiterates the numerical information we considered earlier. The "tilted" function shows clearly that the subjects required fewer minutes of study to master short poems than they needed to master long poems. In contrast, Figure 14–2, which illustrates mean scores as a function of learning strategy, shows a function parallel to the horizontal axis. This means that the dependent variable did not change as the learning strategy varied. While the above example is somewhat trivial, it is important to remember that to the extent that a line function tends to run parallel to the

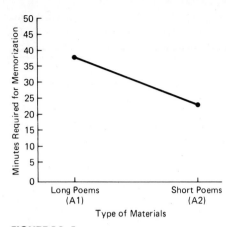

FIGURE 14-1

The Main Effect of Variable A (Type of Materials) in a Hypothetical Experiment on Memorization Strategies

Note: The overall means for A1 and A2 have been averaged across two levels of Variable B (Learning Strategy).

horizontal axis, the independent variable under consideration probably had no main effect.

Another important point is that graphs become more informative as the number of levels of the independent variable is increased. For example, when one or more variables have many levels, a graph of means can be used to get an idea of whether the relationship between the dependent variable and the independent variable is basically linear or curvilinear.

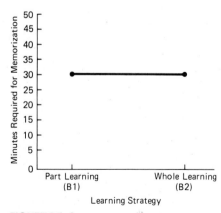

FIGURE 14-2

The Main Effect if Variable B (Learning Strategy) in a Hypothetical Experiment on Memorization Strategies

Note: The overall means for B1 and B2 have been averaged across the levels of Variable A (Type of Material).

"Statistical" Main Effects.　　The ultimate and most important assessment of a main effect in a factorial experiment is the test of significance that is applied to the overall mean differences between levels of an independent variable. Because of the possible influence of sampling error, all other evidence, be it numerical or graphical, is only suggestive. Later in this chapter, you'll learn how to carry out significance tests of main effects.

Interaction Effects

At several points in this book, you've come across the notion of an interaction of one independent variable with another. You can conceptualize an interaction from several angles:

1. An **interaction effect** means that the effect of one independent variable changes across different levels of other independent variables. For example, variable A might have one effect on the dependent variable when level 1 of independent variable B is present but have the opposite effect when level 2 of variable B is present. Thus, the stimulant drug called Ritalin has been shown to increase arousal in most "normal" children, but the same dose of drug apparently *decreases* arousal in some hyperactive children (cf. Cantwell & Satterfield, 1974). Another way of expressing this relationship is to say that the independent variable, "dosage of Ritalin," has opposite effects on behavior at the two different levels of the "child-type" variable.

2. Sometimes an interaction effect means that the *size* of the effect of variable A becomes larger or smaller at different levels of another independent variable. To use an earlier example, you might have a moderate tendency to choose steak over frankfurters in most situations, but the tendency might be greater than usual when you're very hungry—that is, preference interacts with hunger—and less than usual when French fries are also served or when your meal funds are meager. In a sense, then, the term "interaction" can often mean "different differences"—the difference between levels 1 and 2 of variable A is different at the respective levels of variable B (Schaefer, 1976).

3. If you are asked, "What effect does independent variable B have on dependent variable Y?" and your answer is "It depends," then you are referring to the existence of an interaction effect. Hence, if the question is, "Which technique of learning, part or whole, is more effective for memorizing poems?" your answer might well be, "That depends on whether the poems are long ones or short ones."

4. Finally, interaction can be conceived of as the *unique joint effect* of two or more independent variables. For example, when a dose of Ritalin is combined with the "hyperactive" category of children, the effect of the stimulant–child combination is indeed unique, in the sense that it is not found in connection with any other combination of conditions.

Providing information on interaction effects is perhaps the most valuable function of factorial designs. For one thing, this function enables you to answer the more complicated questions about cause-and-effect—for instance, if A1, B2, and C3 are present, what happens to Y? Beyond that, however, the factorial experiment also gives you a tool for simulating realistic situations while exercising experimental control. The "realism" stems from your ability to investigate the combined influences of two or more variables on a particular behavior. In "real life," of course, combined influences are the rule rather than the exception.

As was true of main effects, interaction effects in experimental data may be assessed numerically, graphically, and statistically.

Looking for "Different Mean Differences."　　You can conduct a preliminary assessment of a possible interaction by examining the *cell means* (not the marginal means) of your factorial data table. The basic procedure is as follows:

1. "Enter" the cells of the data table and compute the mean difference between the levels of variable A at the first level of B; for example, $(\overline{X}_{A1B1} - \overline{X}_{A2B1})$.

2. Compute the mean difference between the levels of A at the next level of B; for example, $(\overline{X}_{A1B2} - \overline{X}_{A2B2})$. Continue until the mean differences between levels of A have been computed for each level of B.

3. Examine how and to what extent the levels of A vary from one another at each level of B. If either the *sign* (i.e., positive versus negative) or the *size* of the differences between levels of A change from one level of B to another, then you have identified a possible interaction. That is, the levels of A have "different differences" at the respective levels of B.

Two comments are in order here. First, you could perform the same mean-difference analysis by comparing mean differences between levels of *B* at each level of A, rather than comparing the A conditions across B. Proceeding in either direction will yield information on the possibility of an interaction. Second, bear in mind that, even if an examination of cell means suggests an interaction, this is only a numerical analysis, and any apparent interaction effect is subject to verification through a significance test.

Let's carry out a mean-difference inspection of the cells in Table 14–2. Note that at the first level of independent variable A (Long Poems), part learning (B1) was more efficient than whole learning; that is, part learning required less study time. Thus, $(\overline{X}_{A1B1} - \overline{X}_{A1B2}) = (35 - 40) = -5$.

In contrast, at the second level of A (Short Poems), whole learning was more efficient than part learning: $(\overline{X}_{A2B1} - \overline{X}_{A2B2}) = (25 - 20) = +5$. In this case, then, the *sign* of the mean difference between B1 and B2 changed across different levels of A. And this type of outcome suggests a possible interaction effect in the data: The effect of learning strategy appears to depend on the length of the unit to be remembered. An interaction would also have been suggested had the size, rather than the sign, of the mean difference between B1 and B2 differed appreciably from one level of A to the other.

Graphing Cell Means.   Another way to detect and represent a possible interaction is to graph the cell means from a factorial data table. I've done this for the data in Table 14–2; the resulting graph appears in Figure 14–3. Note that the means of B1 and B2 have been plotted as a function of A1 and A2, resulting in four data points in all. It would have been just as informative, however, to plot the A means as a function of levels of B. In either case, all four cell means would be represented in the figure, and an apparent interaction effect would be evident.

In Figure 14–3, the interaction is suggested by the *crossing* of the B1 and B2 functions. This outcome reiterates our earlier numerical analysis of the cell means, which revealed that part learning is more effective than whole learning when long poems are being memorized, but it is less effective when the poems are short ones.

An important point illustrated by the figure is that crossing functions in a line graph of cell means usually indicate an interaction of the independent variables. Often, however, interactions are suggested not by crossing functions but by *diverging* or *converging* functions. Figure 14–4 illustrates a graphical interaction effect of the latter type. (Figure 14–4 is not related to the data in Table 14–2.) What Figure 14–4 shows is that the *size* of the mean difference between B1 and B2 is larger at the second level of variable A than it is at A1.

"Statistical" Interaction Effects.   Many apparent interactions suggested by numerical or graphical inspection are not statistically reliable, meaning that they are a result of chance

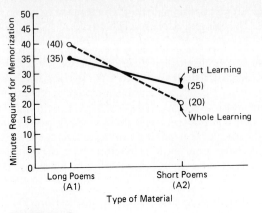

FIGURE 14–3

Learning Time Means as a Function of Length of Material (Variable A) and Learning Strategy (Variable B)

Note: Crossing lines suggest an interaction of the independent variables. There is a main effect of Variable A but no main effect of Variable B.

processes. Later in this chapter, you'll find out how to test the significance of interaction effects. For the time being, simply note that a significance test of an interaction in a 2×2 factorial basically assesses the extent of the difference between mean differences, as shown below:

$$\text{Interaction} = [(\overline{X}_{A1B1} - \overline{X}_{A1B2}) - (\overline{X}_{A2B1} - \overline{X}_{A2B2})]$$

If the difference between mean differences is too large to be accounted for by a model of random error, then the interaction is declared significant.

Other Possible Outcomes

We have only considered one of the many possible patterns of results that could occur in a 2×2 factorial. Since it is important for you to be aware of other patterns and their meanings, I've displayed several possible outcomes in Figure 14–5. The various combina-

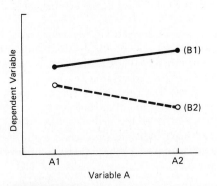

FIGURE 14–4

Interaction of Independent Variables A and B as Indicated by Diverging Functions in a Graph of the Group Means

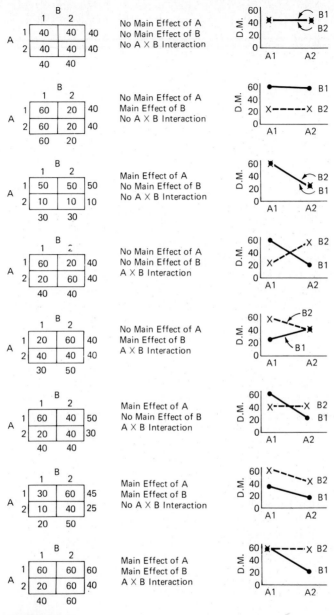

FIGURE 14–5

Possible Outcomes of a 2×2 Factorial Experiment

Note: Values represent either cell or marginal *means.* Graphs are plots of cell means; "D.M." stands for "dependent measure."

tions of main effects and interactions in a 2×2 design are represented graphically as well as in terms of cell and marginal mean differences. Note that an interaction effect is denoted by $A \times B$. Studying these configurations for a few minutes will strengthen your ability to apply the concepts covered thus far.

More Complex Designs

Adding Levels to Variables.   Very often, one or more variables in a factorial design will have more than two levels. For example, a 3×2 design is one in which variable A has three levels and variable B has two levels. How many experimental conditions does such a design require? The answer is always *the product of the numbers of levels*. In this case, there would be $3 \times 2 = 6$ conditions. If this design were a completely randomized factorial, then each of your subjects would be randomly and independently assigned to one of the six conditions.

Figure 14–6 illustrates two possible outcomes of a 3×2 factorial experiment. Panel (a) shows a main effect of each independent variable but no interaction. Don't be misled by the fact that the lines representing B1 and B2 "bend." It is tempting to view nonlinear functions as an instance of interaction, but note that the functions do not converge or cross. The mean difference between B1 and B2 is the same at all levels of A, and the functions are completely *parallel* to one another at all points in the graph.

In contrast, the variable B functions "converge" in panel (b), suggesting a possible interaction, as well as main effects.

Adding Variables.   Some factorial experiments involve more than two independent variables. In fact, you can occasionally find four- and five-variable factorials in the literature. Most researchers, however, are reluctant to combine more than three independent variables in a single experiment, because the higher-level interactions—for example, the interaction of $A \times B \times C \times D$—are difficult to conceptualize and interpret.

A three-variable factorial is represented in two ways in Figure 14–7. Each of the variables, A, B, and C, has two levels, producing a $2 \times 2 \times 2$ factorial with eight conditions.

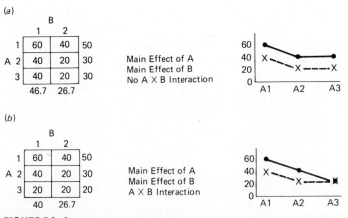

FIGURE 14–6

Results From a Hypothetical 3×2 Factorial Experiment

Note: The numbers within the cells of the tables are group means. The numbers in the margins are overall means for the respective levels of Variables A and B.

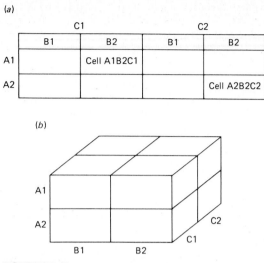

FIGURE 14–7
Two-Dimensional and Three-Dimensional Schematics of a 2×2×2 (Three-Variable) Factorial
Design

Panel (a) presents a two-dimensional representation of this design. Panel (b) is for those
whose minds are organized like Rubik's Cube: It portrays a three-dimensional organization of the design.

This type of design yields the following sources of variance, which must be statistically
analyzed:

Main Effects

A
B
C

Interaction Effects

A × B
A × C
B × C
A × B × C

What would a "three-way" interaction look like? One possibility is shown in Figure
14–8. The graph indicates that variables A and B interact at level 2 of C but not at C1.
Another possibility (not shown) would be that A and B interact differently at each level
of C. Would you care to try your hand at drawing and interpreting some four-way interactions?

SOLOMON'S DESIGN RECONSIDERED

In Chapter 8, you learned about a special kind of pretest-posttest experimental design
called the "Solomon Four-Group Design." What made it "special" is that two of the

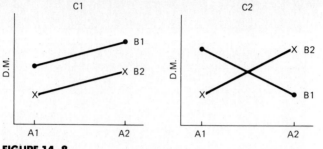

FIGURE 14-8

A Hypothetical Three-Way Interaction

Note: The interaction of variables A and B depends on the level of variable C. At C1, both A and B have a main effect on the dependent variable. At C2, neither A nor B has an effect, but A and B do combine to have an interaction effect.

four groups were included in the model specifically to assess whether the pretesting experience modified the effect that the independent variable had on the subjects' behavior. Recall that the Solomon design involved these four conditions:

1. an experimental group that is both pretested and posttested
2. a control group that is both pretested and posttested
3. an experimental group that is only posttested
4. a control group that is only posttested

The principal dependent measure in such a design is the posttest scores. A second possible dependent measure would be the difference between the pretest and the posttest scores.

You're now in a position to view the Solomon design as a completely randomized 2×2 factorial, in which variable A is the experimental versus the control treatment, and variable B is pretesting versus no pretesting. If you find that the effect of the experimental treatment is different when pretesting is used than when subjects are not pretested, that means that the effect of variable A is different at different levels of B. In other words, pretesting interacts with the main independent variable, and any conclusions drawn about the effect of the treatment must take that restriction into account.

Three possible outcomes in a Solomon-type design appear in Figure 14-9. These outcomes are represented both graphically and by mean differences on the posttest scores. Panel (a) shows what kinds of data you would get if the experimental treatment had an effect but pretesting did not. Panel (b) represents one type of outcome that could occur if both the main independent variable and pretesting influenced the posttest scores but did not interact. The most troublesome finding for generalization purposes appears in panel (c). Those outcomes suggest that the experimental treatment has an effect only when pretesting is used. This result, if replicated, would definitely represent a limit on the procedure's external validity; that is, the treatment could be expected to be effective only in situations where subjects are pretested.

REPEATED-MEASURES FACTORIALS

Are you long on variables and short on subjects? Depending on the specific nature of your independent variables, you may be able to manipulate one or more of the variables

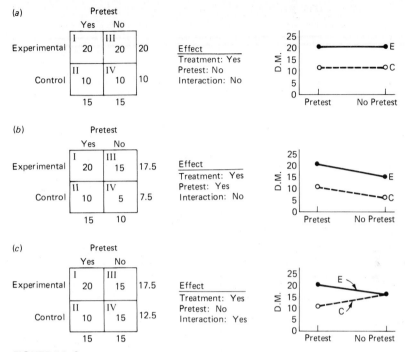

FIGURE 14–9

Solomon Four-Group Design as a 2×2 Completely Randomized Factorial

Note: E = Experimental Group; C = Control Group.

within subjects, which would permit you to conduct a factorial experiment with a relatively small sample of subjects. Moreover, your repeated-measures factorial experiment would be more sensitive to both main effects and interaction effects than a completely randomized factorial that employs between-subject manipulation. (See later section on repeated-measures ANOVA.)

The same rules that apply to repeated-measures designs involving one independent variable also apply to the repeated-measures factorial. For example, you would be wise not to use a repeated-measures factorial if one or more of the independent variables are vulnerable to carry-over effects. However, simple progressive error may be handled in the repeated-measures factorial just as it would be dealt with in a single-variable within-subjects design: You would use a counterbalancing or randomization scheme. Instead of counterbalancing or randomizing the order of the levels of one variable, however, you would apply one or the other of these strategies to the order of *treatment conditions* (e.g., A1B1, A1B3, etc.). Random assignment to treatment conditions would not be necessary, since every subject would receive every treatment combination. However, if you construct more than one counterbalancing or randomization sequence, then you would randomly assign subjects to the various sequences.

The configuration of a 3 × 2 repeated-measures factorial is shown in Table 14–3. Observe that the combination of three levels of variable A with two levels of variable B produces six treatment conditions altogether. Also note that each subject receives all six treatment conditions. Of course, the order of treatment combinations would not be as

TABLE 14–3

Example of a 3 × 2 Repeated-Measures Factorial Design

	Treatment Condition					
	A1		A2		A3	
Subject	B1	B2	B1	B2	B1	B2
Person 1 ⟶	→X11—	→X12—	→X21—	→X22—	→X31—	→X32
Person 2 ⟶	→X11—	→X12—	→X21—	→X22—	→X31—	→X32
Person 3 ⟶	→X11—	→X12—	→X21—	→X22—	→X31—	→X32
Person 4 ⟶	→X11—	→X12—	→X21—	→X22—	→X31—	→X32
Person 5 ⟶	→X11—	→X12—	→X24—	→X22—	→X31—	→X32
Person 6 ⟶	→X11—	→X12—	→X21—	→X22—	→X31—	→X32

displayed in this table. Rather, treatment combinations would be administered in one or more counterbalanced or randomized sequences.

Tomlinson, Hicks, and Pellegrini (1978) used exactly this kind of repeated-measures factorial to investigate how the pupil sizes of human models influence subjects' ratings of the models' "pleasantness" and "warmth." Variable A was pupil size (A1 = small; A2 = medium; A3 = large), and variable B was the gender of the model (B1 = female; B2 = male). Three snapshots of each model's face were retouched to vary apparent pupil size. Every subject then viewed the six resulting photos in a randomized sequence; a different random order was prepared for each subject. The experimental task was simply to rate the six photos on a 5-point scale of pleasantness and a 5-point scale of warmth. The two ratings were later combined into an overall "positiveness" rating.

The results of this experiment are graphically displayed in Figure 14–10. Would you say that either variable had a main effect? Does the graph suggest an interaction of the independent variables? Considering the fact that all of the subjects were female, what do you think the outcome means?

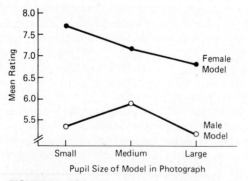

FIGURE 14–10

Positiveness of Ratings of Male and Female Photographs as a Function of the Model's "Pupil Size "

Source: Based on data from Tomlinson, Hicks, & Pellegrini, 1978.

MIXING THEM UP

The factorial experiment is a very flexible research tool. Its flexibility is aptly illustrated by the use of "mixed" factorial designs in the social sciences. The term "mixed factorial" has two meanings in psychology: Sometimes the term is applied to experiments that combine a between-subjects independent variable with a within-subjects independent variable; at other times, it means that one of the independent variables is a nonmanipulable, "organismic" variable, such as age, gender, or diagnostic category, and the other independent variable is a manipulable, "environmental" variable, such as a type of psychotherapy or task difficulty. We'll consider both types of mixed factorial here.

The Split-Plot Design

The practice of combining within-subjects and between-subjects variables in the same experiment is fairly common in experimental psychology. The usual reason for using this arrangement is to reduce the number of subjects required by some of the more complex experiments.

When an experiment involves at least one between-subjects manipulation and at least one within-subjects manipulation, the theoretical model is referred to as a split-plot design. A 3×3 split-plot model is shown in Table 14–4. By examining the table, you can see that variable A is the between-subjects variable; that is, different people serve at the respective levels of A. But variable B is manipulated "within subjects"; that is, each person in each group, or "plot," receives all levels of B. To use this type of design, you must:

1. construct several different counterbalanced or randomized orders of the levels of variable B to distribute progressive error evenly across the three levels of that variable
2. randomly assign subjects to the various levels of the between-subjects variable (A1, A2, and A3)

TABLE 14–4

A 3×3 "Mixed" Factorial Design in Which Variable A Was Manipulated Between Subjects and Variable B Was Manipulated Within Subjects

		Variable B		
Variable A		B1	B2	B3
A1	Person 1	→X11	→X12	→X13
	Person 2	→X11	→X12	→X13
	Person 3	→X11	→X12	→X13
A2	Person 4	→X21	→X22	→X23
	Person 5	→X21	→X22	→X23
	Person 6	→X21	→X22	→X23
A3	Person 7	→X31	→X32	→X33
	Person 8	→X31	→X32	→X33
	Person 9	→X31	→X32	→X33

3. within levels of variable A, randomly assign subjects to the various orders of the B treatments that you have constructed

I once used this type of 3×3 mixed design to investigate whether the "intent to learn" is necessary to produce the "spacing effect in free recall" (Evans, 1976). You learned about the spacing effect in the last chapter; to review, the term "spacing effect" refers to the fact that twice-presented words in a study list are remembered better if there is a long interval between their two presentations than if the interpresentation interval is short. In the mixed factorial experiment I'm referring to, it was convenient and economical to manipulate the variable of spacing interval within subjects. B1 was 0 spacing; B2 was a spacing of 4 intervening items between presentations; B3 was a spacing of 20 intervening items. Thus, every subject in the experiment studied repeated words at all three spacing intervals. To distribute any progressive error equitably across the three levels of B, I constructed three forms of the basic word list. Each form presented the spacing conditions and target words in a different random order.

Variable A was "type of learning instructions." Because of probable carry-over effects from one learning strategy to another, I decided to manipulate this variable between subjects. Group A1 received "intentional learning" instructions; they were told that they were to study the words in preparation for a free-recall test. Group A2 was an "incidental learning" group; these subjects were instructed simply to judge whether each word referred to something "active" or something "passive"; they did not expect to have their memory tested. Group A3 was the "intentional-control" group. They were asked to both make the perceptual judgments and prepare for a free-recall test. I randomly assigned 12 subjects to each group, and within each group, I randomly assigned 4 subjects to each list form.

Contrary to many theories of the spacing effect, the results of the free-recall test showed that the usual spacing effect occurred regardless of the specific information-processing strategy that was employed. In a sense, then, the spacing phenomenon represents an "automatic" cognitive process: It occurs whether or not people are actively engaged in an attempt to memorize material—even during incidental learning.

Combining Organismic and Environmental Variables

As was explained earlier in this book, the effects of organismic variables are inherently difficult to interpret because organismic variables are inherently confounded by a host of other factors. Since it isn't feasible to randomly assign subjects to age, intelligence, and gender categories, for example, these confoundings cannot be "randomized out." Nonetheless, practical questions in the social sciences often require that organismic variables be included as independent variables in factorial experiments.

Take a common example. One of the perennial questions in clinical research is "What techniques of psychotherapy work best with clients in particular diagnostic categories?" To investigate this type of question, clinical researchers typically use several different "client types," or diagnostic categories, as one independent variable and cross this variable with two or more techniques of therapy. Subjects can be randomly assigned to type of therapy in such a study but, of course, not to diagnostic category. While it may be difficult or impossible to apply a cause-and-effect interpretation to the effect of "diagnostic category," such a design can provide valuable information from a practical point of view.

MULTI-VARIABLE ANALYSIS OF VARIANCE

In the last chapter you learned how to use a procedure called analysis of variance (ANOVA) to test the statistical significance of mean differences between experimental conditions. That specific procedure is known as one-way ANOVA, because it applies only to the one-variable experiment. In this chapter, you'll learn how to carry out a two-way ANOVA on the data of two-variable factorial experiments.

The rationale and assumptions of two-way ANOVA are exactly the same as those of single-variable ANOVA (refer to Chapter 13). The only difference is that the between-groups variance in two-way ANOVA must be *partitioned* into three parts:

1. variance due to the main effect of A
2. variance due to the main effect of B
3. variance due to the interaction effect of $A \times B$

The between-groups variance in a factorial ANOVA is referred to as the between-cells variance. The reason this variance must be partitioned into several parts is that all of the sources of variance referred to above contribute to variation between the experimental groups, or "cells," in the data table. You will be interested in assessing the independent effects of A, B, and the $A \times B$ interaction; therefore, you will need to compute three F tests in two-way ANOVA—one each for the effect of A, B, and $A \times B$, respectively.

The within-groups, or within-cells, variance is still the "error term," just as it was in one-way ANOVA, and it is computed in exactly the same fashion. To obtain the three F ratios of interest, you will divide the mean square of A, the mean square of B, and the mean square of the $A \times B$ interaction, respectively, by the within-cells variance.

Although I'll present an example that applies specifically to the 2×2 completely randomized factorial, this basic procedure is easily extended to data sets with more levels per variable and more than two independent variables (see, for example, Hays, 1981; Kirk, 1968).

Setting Up the Data Table

As is true of any data analysis, your factorial ANOVA will be easier to carry out if you first arrange the data systematically in tabular form. Let's use the data from the hypothetical experiment on part versus whole learning that was discussed earlier in this chapter. These data now appear in Table 14–5, the content of which includes:

1. the raw scores on the dependent measure, symbolized X
2. the *squared* raw scores, symbolized X^2
3. the raw-score total for each group (cell), $T_{A_iB_i}$
4. the *squared* raw-score total for each cell, $T_{A_iB_i}^2$
5. the marginal totals for levels of variable A, T_{A_i}
6. the marginal totals for levels of variable B, T_{B_i}
7. the *squared* marginal totals for A, $T_{A_i}^2$
8. the *squared* marginal totals for B, $T_{B_i}^2$
9. the grand total of all raw scores, GT
10. the *squared* grand total, GT^2
11. the sum of all squared raw scores, ΣX^2

TABLE 14–5

Data Table for a Two-Variable (Two-Way) ANOVA Applied to a Completely
Randomized 2×2 Factorial Experiment

	Learning Strategy			
	Part (B1)		Whole (B2)	

	Cell A1B1		Cell A1B2		
	X	X^2	X	X^2	
Long	38	1444	37	1369	
Poems	35	1225	39	1521	
(A1)	36	1296	41	1681	
	34	1156	40	1600	
	32	1024	43	1849	
	$T_{A1B1} = 175$		$T_{A1B2} = 200$		$T_{A1} = 375$
	$T^2_{A1B1} = 30625$		$T^2_{A1B2} = 40000$		$T^2_{A1} = 140625$
	Cell A2B1		Cell A2B2		
	X	X^2	X	X^2	
Short	25	625	14	196	
Poems	30	900	20	400	
(A2)	20	400	22	484	
	26	676	26	676	
	24	576	18	324	
	$T_{A2B1} = 125$		$T_{A2B2} = 100$		$T_{A2} = 225$
	$T^2_{A2B1} = 15625$		$T^2_{A2B2} = 10000$		$T^2_{A2} = 50625$
	$T_{B1} = 300$		$T_{B2} = 300$		
	$T^2_{B1} = 90000$		$T^2_{B2} = 90000$		

$$GT = 600 = \text{Grand Total}$$
$$GT^2 = 360000$$
$$\Sigma X^2 = 19422 = \text{sum of all squared raw scores}$$

Also note that all group sizes (n_i) equal 5, and that the total number of observations is
$\Sigma n_i = 20$. You will use all of the squared quantities, as well as the data on group sizes, in
conducting a factorial ANOVA.

Establishing the Null and Alternative Hypothesis

The null hypothesis in factorial ANOVA is that all of the cell, or group, means come
from the same population—the population of chance; therefore, that all of the population means represented by the cell means are equal. Symbolically, the null hypothesis
would look like this:

$$H_0: \mu_{A1B1} = \mu_{A1B2} = \mu_{A2B1} = \mu_{A2B2}$$
where μ is the Greek symbol for a population mean

The alternative hypothesis is simply that not all of the population means represented by the cell means are equal.

Finding the Degrees of Freedom

There are 13 procedural steps in a 2×2 factorial ANOVA. The first 3 steps involve determining the degrees of freedom for each of the sources of variation.

Step 1: Find the Total Degrees of Freedom. If we have Σn_i observations altogether, then only $(\Sigma n_i - 1)$ of the observations are "free to vary," given a fixed sum of all observations in the data table. Therefore, total degrees of freedom = $dfT = (\Sigma n_i - 1) = (20 - 1) = 19$.

Step 2: Find and Partition the Between-Cells Degrees of Freedom. Since we have a levels of variable A and b levels of variable B, the number of groups or cells is $a \times b$, or 2×2. Given that there are four cells, only $(ab - 1)$, or $(4 - 1)$, of the cells are "free to vary." So $df(\text{Cells}) = 3$.

Keep in mind, however, that the between-cells variance is actually made up of three sources of variance. Therefore, we next "partition" $df(\text{Cells})$ into its three components:

1. $dfA = (a - 1) = (2 - 1) = 1$
2. $dfB = (b - 1) = (2 - 1) = 1$
3. $df(A \times B) = (a - 1) \times (b - 1) = 1 \times 1 = 1$

Step 3: Find the Within-Cells Degrees of Freedom. Since $dfT = df(\text{Cells}) + dfW$, the within-cells, or error, degrees of freedom may be found through subtraction: $dfW = dfT - df(\text{Cells})$. A formula for directly computing this quantity is $dfW = (\Sigma n_i - ab)$, where Σn_i is the sum of the group sizes and $ab = (a \times b) =$ the number of groups. In this example, $dfW = (20 - 4) = 16$; that is, within each cell $(5 - 1)$ observations were free to vary, and pooling across all four cells, we get $(5 - 1) \times 4 = 16$.

Finding the Sum of Squares

The most efficient sequence for computing the various sums of squares is:

1. Compute total sum of squares.
2. Compute between-cells sum of squares [SS(Cells)].
3. "Partition" between-cells sum of squares: $SSA + SSB + SS(A \times B) = SS(\text{Cells})$.
4. Compute within-cells sum of squares (SSW).

Step 4: Find the Total Sum of Squares. To obtain this quantity, representing the total amount of variation among all raw scores: Sum all of the squared raw scores (ΣX^2), compute the "correction factor" $(GT^2/\Sigma n_1)$, and subtract the correction factor from the sum of squared raw scores.

Hence:

$$\begin{aligned} SST &= \Sigma X^2 - (GT^2/\Sigma n_i) \\ &= 19422 - (360000/20) \\ &= 19422 - 18000 \\ &= 1422 \end{aligned}$$

Step 5: Find and Partition the Between-Cells Sum of Squares.   The between-cells sum of squares is found in the same way that the between-groups sum of squares was computed in Chapter 13:

1. Square each cell (group) total and divide the result by the number of observations in the cell (n_i); then add up the results of the four divisions.
2. Compute the correction factor ($GT^2/\Sigma n_i$).
3. Subtract the result of step 2 from the result of step 1.

Thus:

$$
\begin{aligned}
SS(\text{Cells}) &= [\Sigma(T^2_{A_iB_i}/n_i)] - (GT^2/\Sigma n_i) \\
&= [(30625/5) + (40000/5) + (15625/5) + (10000/5)] - 18000 \\
&= [(6125 + 8000 + 3125 + 2000] - 18000 \\
&= 19250 - 18000 \\
&= 1250
\end{aligned}
$$

We now parse the SS(Cells) into its component parts: SSA, SSB, and SS(A × B). Keep in mind that $SS(\text{Cells}) = SSA + SSB + SS (A \times B)$.

The sum of squares for the main effect of variable A is:

$$SSA = [\Sigma(T^2_{A_i}/bn_i)] - (GT^2/\Sigma n_i)$$

where $T^2_{A_i}$ is the squared marginal total for any one level of A,

   b is the number of levels of variable B (2 in this example), and

   n_i is the number of observations in any one cell

Therefore:

$$
\begin{aligned}
SSA &= [(140625/10) + (50625/10)] - 18000 \\
&= [(14062.5) + (5062.5)] - 18000 \\
&= 19125 - 18000 \\
&= 1125
\end{aligned}
$$

Likewise:

$$
\begin{aligned}
SSB &= [\Sigma(T^2_{B_i}/an_i)] - (GT^2/\Sigma n_i) \\
&= [(90000/10) + (90000/10)] - 18000 \\
&= [(9000) + (9000)] - 18000 \\
&= 18000 - 18000 \\
&= 0
\end{aligned}
$$

Since SSB + SSA + SS(A × B) must sum to SS(Cells):

$$
\begin{aligned}
SS(A \times B) &= SS(\text{Cells}) - SSA - SSB \\
&= 1250 - 1125 - 0 \\
&= 125
\end{aligned}
$$

Step 6: Find the Within-Cells Sum of Squares.   Since the between-cells and within-cells sum of squares must add up to the total sum of squares (i.e., $SST = SS(\text{Cells}) + SSW$), the within-cells sum of squares can now be computed through simple subtraction:

$$
\begin{aligned}
SSW &= SST - SS(\text{Cells}) \\
&= 1422 - 1250 \\
&= 172
\end{aligned}
$$

Finding the Mean Squares

It will be necessary to compute four mean squares (i.e., variances) in this example: MSA, MSB, MS(A×B), and MSW (error). As was true of one-way ANOVA, each mean square in factorial ANOVA is the result of dividing a sum of squares by its degrees of freedom.

Step 7: Find the Mean Square for Variable A. MSA = SSA/dfA = 1125/1 = 1125.

Step 8: Find the Mean Square for Variable B. MSB = SSB/dfB = 0/1 = 0.

Step 9: Find the Mean Square for the A×B Interaction. MS(A×B) = SS(A×B)/df(A×B) = 125/1 = 125.

Step 10: Find the Mean Square for Within-Cells (Error) Variation. MSW = MS(Error) = SSW/dfW = 172/16 = 10.75.

Computing the F Ratio

Because a 2×2 factorial provides for the assessment of three "effects," three F ratios must be computed in a two-way ANOVA: F_A, F_B, and $F_{(A×B)}$. Recall that an F ratio represents the ratio of two mean squares, where the denominator is always the "error term" in the analysis.

Step 11: Compute the F Test for the Effect of Variable A. Since the MSW is the error term in factorial ANOVA, the F ratio for the main effect of variable A is: F = MSA/MSW = 1125/10.75 = 104.65.

Step 12: Compute the F Test for the Effect of Variable B. The formula for the F test of the main effect of B is MSB/MSW. In this example, that F would have to be zero, since MSB = 0.

Step 13: Compute the F Test for the Interaction of A and B. F = MS(A×B)/MSW = 125/10.75 = 11.63.

Setting up the ANOVA Summary Table

The results of a factorial ANOVA are best evaluated and communicated via a summary table, such as that in Table 14–6. There are two items, in particular, that you should note: First, the "between-cells" source of variation has been subdivided into the three sources of variation that contribute to between-cells differences; second, the figures in the "between-cells" row of the table are in parentheses because those quantities are entirely redundant with the quantities associated with A, B, and (A×B). Thus, A + B + (A×B) + Error = Total, disregarding the parenthetical between-cells figures. In other words, the between-cells entries are only computational steps, and no F test need be computed for the between-cells row in the table.

Testing the Significance of F

In a factorial ANOVA, each F ratio is individually evaluated. To find the critical F ratio needed for significance, we must first decide on the level of significance. Suppose we de-

TABLE 14–6

ANOVA Summary Table for a Two-Variable Experiment

Source of Variation	df	SS	MS	F
Between Cells	(3)	(1250)		
A	1	1125	1125	104.65*
B	1	0	0	0
A × B (Interaction)	1	125	125	11.63*
Within Cells (Error)	16	172	10.75	
TOTAL	19	1422		

*Significant at the .01 level.

cide to use the .05 level for this experiment. Then, consulting Table A–4 of the Appendix, we find the critical F ratio needed for significance by locating the point in the table where the degrees of freedom for an "effect" intersect with the degrees of freedom for "error." In the present example, the degrees of freedom for the "numerator" will be 1 in the case of all three "effects" (A, B, and A×B), and the denominator degrees of freedom will be 16. Each of the three F statistics must exceed 4.49 to be significant at the .05 level. Thus, both the main effect of "length of materials" (A) and the interaction of length with learning strategy (A×B) had significant effects on performance—as was expected on the basis of earlier considerations of the data.

ANALYZING THE DATA FROM CORRELATED-GROUPS DESIGNS

In the last chapter, I covered correlated-groups designs (i.e., repeated-measures and randomized-blocks) but referred you to this chapter for information on how to analyze data from correlated-groups experiments. The reason for postponing the analysis of correlated-groups data is that this type of analysis is better understood after you have become familiar with factorial designs. In fact, a correlated-groups ANOVA is conceptually a two-way ANOVA, very similar to the kind we just performed.

An Example

The data shown in Table 14–7 represent the results of a hypothetical repeated-measures experiment with three experimental conditions. You may also consider it a randomized-blocks experiment, as the ANOVA procedure is the same for both correlated-groups designs.

By now, the type of information provided in the data table is quite familiar to you. Included are the raw scores, the squared raw scores, the totals (T_{Ci}) and the squared totals for each condition, the grand total (GT) and the square of the grand total, and the sum of the squared raw scores (ΣX^2). Also note that the totals (T_{Ri}) and squared totals have been tallied for each person (or "block") in the table. This was done because, in a correlated-

TABLE 14–7

Data from a Hypothetical Correlated-Groups Experiment*

	Condition 1		Condition 2		Condition 3		Person Totals	Squared Totals
	X	X²	X	X²	X	X²		
Person 1	6	(36)	11	(121)	5	(25)	T_{R1} = 22	(484)
Person 2	1	(1)	5	(25)	3	(9)	T_{R2} = 9	(81)
Person 3	2	(4)	5	(25)	3	(9)	T_{R3} = 10	(100)
Person 4	2	(4)	3	(9)	1	(1)	T_{R4} = 6	(36)
Person 5	4	(16)	7	(49)	7	(49)	T_{R5} = 18	(324)
Person 6	3	(9)	5	(25)	5	(25)	T_{R6} = 13	(169)

TOTALS T_{C1} = 18 T_{C2} = 36 T_{C3} = 24
T_{C1}^2 = 324 T_{C2}^2 = 1296 T_{C3}^2 = 576

GT = 78 = Grand Total
GT^2 = 6084
ΣX^2 = 442

*This particular example illustrates the results of a repeated-measures experiment.

groups experiment, *the subjects are considered to be a second independent variable* in the ANOVA. Therefore, for statistical purposes, what we have here is a 6×3 factorial in which the row (R) variable is "people," with six levels, and the column (C) variable is "experimental treatment," with three levels. Accordingly, as you carry out the ANOVA, you will analyze three sources of variation:

1. variance due to people
2. variance due to treatments
3. variance due to the interaction of people and treatments

The row × column (people × treatments) interaction is the error term in correlated groups ANOVA. If the data are really correlated from treatment to treatment, then people will perform similarly across conditions, and the row × column interaction, that is, the error term, will be small, because the "effect" of a person will not change from one treatment level to the next.

The Null Hypothesis

The null hypothesis to be tested here is:

$$H_0: \mu_1 = \mu_2 = \mu_3$$

The alternative hypothesis is that the means of the populations represented by the treatments are not all equal. It's clear that the treatment means differ numerically: Mean1 = 3; Mean2 = 6; Mean3 = 4. The ANOVA will reveal whether these differences are reliable.

Computational Steps

Step 1: Find the Degrees of Freedom.   If c = the number of columns in the data table and r = the number of rows, then:

$$\text{Columns degrees of freedom} = \text{dfC} = (c - 1) = (3 - 1) = 2,$$
$$\text{Rows degrees of freedom} = \text{dfR} = (r - 1) = (6 - 1) = 5,$$
$$\text{Interaction degrees of freedom} = \text{df}(R \times C) = (r - 1)(c - 1) = 10, \text{ and}$$
$$\text{Total degrees of freedom} = \text{dfT} = (rc - 1) = [(3)(6) - 1] = 17$$

Step 2: Find the Sums of Squares.   We will need to compute the total sum of squares (SST), the columns sum of squares (SSC), the row sums of squares (SSR), and the interaction (error) sum of squares [SS(R × C)]:

$$
\begin{aligned}
\text{SST} &= \Sigma X^2 - (GT^2/rc) \\
&= 442 - (6084/18) \\
&= 442 - 338 \\
&= 104
\end{aligned}
$$

$$
\begin{aligned}
\text{SSC} &= [\Sigma(T^2_{Ci}/r)] - (GT^2/rc) \\
&= [(324/6) + (1296/6) + (576/6)] - 6084/18 \\
&= [(54) + (216) + (96)] - 338 \\
&= 366 - 338 \\
&= 28
\end{aligned}
$$

$$
\begin{aligned}
\text{SSR} &= [\Sigma(T^2_{Ri}/c)] - (GT^2/rc) \\
&= [(484/3) + (81/3) + (100/3) + (36/3) + (324/3) + (169/3)] - 338 \\
&= [(161.33) + (27) + (33.33) + (12) + (108) + (56.33)] - 338 \\
&= 398 - 338 \\
&= 398 - 338 \\
&= 60
\end{aligned}
$$

$$
\begin{aligned}
\text{SS}(R \times C) &= \text{SST} - \text{SSC} - \text{SSR} \\
&= 104 - 28 - 60 \\
&= 16
\end{aligned}
$$

Step 3: Find the Mean Squares.   As usual, mean squares are found by dividing degrees of freedom into sums of squares:

$$
\begin{aligned}
\text{MSC} &= \text{SSC}/\text{dfC} \\
&= 28/2 \\
&= 14
\end{aligned}
$$

$$
\begin{aligned}
\text{MSR} &= \text{SSR}/\text{dfR} \\
&= 60/5 \\
&= 12
\end{aligned}
$$

$$
\begin{aligned}
\text{MS}(R \times C) &= \text{SS}(R \times C)/\text{df}(R \times C) \\
&= 16/10 \\
&= 1.6
\end{aligned}
$$

Step 4: Compute the F Ratio. The F ratios are found by dividing the mean square of the row × column interaction into the mean squares for people and treatments, respectively. The resulting F statistics appear in Table 14–8. Since only the differences between treatments are of theoretical interest (not the people differences), we'll only assess the significance of the F ratio for treatments. Accordingly, the relevant degrees of freedom for the "numerator" equal 2, and the degrees of freedom for the "denominator" of the F ratio equal 10. Consulting Table A–4 of the Appendix, we find that with a significance level of .05, the F ratio must exceed 7.56 to be significant. Therefore, we reject the null hypothesis and conclude that the effect of the independent variable is reliable.

Why Correlated-Groups Designs Are "Powerful"

In Chapter 13, I stated that a major advantage of correlated-groups experimental designs is that they are more "powerful," or "sensitive," than independent-groups designs. Power, in this sense, means that correlated-groups experiments are more likely to detect a real effect of the independent variable, even if that effect is relatively small. Having mastered the concepts and procedures of factorial designs and factorial ANOVA, you are now in an intellectual position to understand why correlated-groups designs possess this advantage.

The key to the extra power lies in the nature of the statistical analysis that is applied to correlated-groups data. Refer to the ANOVA summary in Table 14–8, and note that of the total sum of squares of 104, 60 units are due to differences between people. Fortunately, these individual differences were systematically separated from the rest of the variance in the process of doing the correlated-groups ANOVA. Had the ANOVA procedure not permitted us to isolate and "remove" the effects of people differences, then the 60 units of between-people sum of squares would have become part of the error sum of squares.

The effect of *not* "partitioning out" between-people variance is shown in Table 14–9, where the same data have been analyzed as though they were derived from a completely randomized independent-groups design. Note that the independent-groups ANOVA produces the same treatment SS but does not yield a people SS. Where did the 60 units of variance due to people go? Into the error term! Notice that the error SS is now 76 instead of 16, and that this results in a much smaller, *nonsignificant* F ratio, even though the earlier analysis revealed that the treatment effect was reliable.

You should now be able to see why correlated-groups designs tend to be more sensitive than independent-groups designs: Correlated-groups designs usually reduce the

TABLE 14–8

ANOVA Summary Table for a Correlated-Groups Design

Source of Variation	df	SS	MS	F
Between People	5	60	12	7.5
Between Treatments	2	28	14	8.75*
People × Treatments (Error)	10	16	1.6	
TOTAL	17	104		

*Significant at the .05 level.

TABLE 14-9

ANOVA Summary Table for a Correlated-Groups Data When They Are Treated as Independent-Groups Data

Source of Variation	df	SS	MS	F
Between Treatments	2	28	14	2.77*
Within Treatments (Error)	15	76	5.06	
TOTAL	17	104		

*F ratio is not significant.

amount of error in the F ratio, thereby increasing the probability of rejection of a null hypothesis that is really false.

TRACKING DOWN THE "SOURCE" OF A SIGNIFICANT F RATIO

When there are more than two means in an ANOVA, it may be difficult to directly interpret a significant F test, because the F test simultaneously tests all possible mean differences in a set of k means. So, if you have three groups of subjects, then a significant F ratio based on the three groups of data could mean any of the following:

1. Mean1 is different from Mean2 (but not from Mean3).
2. Mean2 is different from Mean3 (but not from Mean1).
3. Mean1 is different from Mean3 (but not from Mean2).
4. Possible combinations of outcomes 1, 2, and 3 above.
5. All three means differ significantly from one another.

Given all of the possible patterns of mean differences that could result in a significant F ratio when the number of conditions is greater than two, a significant F test frequently is simply a signal that it is worthwhile to start looking for the "source" of the significant outcome.

Looking for the source of a significant F means doing pairwise comparisons of means in your data table to find out which specific mean differences are significant (e.g., Mean1 versus Mean3, Mean2 versus Mean3, etc.). "Pairwise," then, means that you are comparing two means at a time.

There are more than half a dozen different statistical procedures for conducting pairwise tests of means after a significant F is found. Most of these procedures are reviewed in Hays (1981) and Snedecor and Cochran (1980). Here we'll consider the most generally useful pairwise test, which is the Tukey "Honestly Significant Difference" (HSD) test.

The number of possible pairwise comparisons for k treatment conditions is computed by $[k(k-1)]/2$. If you have three treatments in your experiment, there are $3(3-1)/2$, or 3, possible pairwise comparisons. With four means there are $4(4-1)/2$, or 6, possible comparisons.

We'll apply the Tukey HSD to the three treatment means in the correlated-groups ANOVA that we just carried out. Those means were: Mean1 = 3; Mean2 = 6; Mean3 = 4. Since the overall F was significant, we now want to find out which specific mean differences are responsible for the significant outcome.

Step 1: Set Up the Pairwise Difference Table

Table 14–10 is a "pairwise difference table." The three treatment means are arranged from smallest to largest along the rows and columns of the table. The numbers inside the table are the differences between pairs of means. For example, (Mean3 – Mean1) = 1. Hence, the number 1 is placed at the point where Mean3 and Mean1 "intersect" in the table.

Step 2: Obtain the "q" Statistic

The q statistic is a value that is necessary for computing the "Honestly Significant Difference" (HSD). To get the appropriate q for this example, we (a) decide on a level of significance, let's say .05, (b) get the degrees of freedom for error from our previous ANOVA [df(R × C) = 10], (c) note the number of means in the analysis (k = 3), and (d) go to Table A–5 of the Appendix. The q statistic is found by locating the point of intersection of df(R × C) and k in Table A–5. Note that, at the .05 level, q for 10 degrees of freedom and 3 means is 3.88.

Step 3: Compute HSD

$$\text{HSD} = q\sqrt{\text{MSE}/n}, \text{ where}$$

q = the value from Table A–5,
MSE = the mean square for error found in the ANOVA, and
n = the number of observations summed across to get each treatment mean

In this example:

$$
\begin{aligned}
\text{HSD} &= 3.88\sqrt{1.6/6} \\
&= 3.88\sqrt{.267} \\
&= 3.88(.516) \\
&= 2.00
\end{aligned}
$$

Step 4: Compare Pairwise Mean Differences to HSD

Every pairwise difference in Table 14–10 that equals or exceeds HSD (i.e., 2) is a significant difference. Referring to Table 14–10, you can see that the difference between

TABLE 14–10

Pairwise Differences among Three Means Ordered by Magnitude

	Mean1 = 3	Mean3 = 4	Mean2 = 6
Mean1 = 3	0	1	3*
Mean3 = 4		0	2*
Mean2 = 6			0

*Significant at the .05 level.

Mean1 and Mean3 is not significant, but the other two differences are. Hence, the significant F was due to (Mean2 – Mean1) *and* (Mean2 – Mean3), but not to (Mean3 – Mean1).

SUMMARY

This chapter was concerned with experiments that manipulate more than one independent variable at a time—*factorial* experiments. Factorial experiments are economical of time, effort, and money, because they allow you to examine the *main effect* of more than one variable in a single study. Factorial designs also enable you to see how two or more variables *interact* to produce unique joint effects on behavior. Both main effects and interaction effects may be assessed in three ways: through examination of numerical mean differences in a data table, through graphing those means, and through tests of statistical significance.

Although this chapter focused mainly on the 2×2 factorial, factorial experiments can be much more complex than that, sometimes involving up to four or five independent variables or variables with many levels.

The most common type of factorial experiment is the independent-groups factorial, which involves between-subjects manipulation of the independent variables. Some factorial experiments manipulate independent variables entirely within subjects; these designs are called repeated-measures factorials. Other factorials are "mixed" designs in the sense that a between-subjects variable is combined with a within-subjects variable (i.e., "split-plot" designs).

The data of factorial experiments are usually analyzed via a multi-variable analysis of variance.

REVIEW QUESTIONS

1. Define and make up an example of a completely randomized factorial experiment.

2. What are the two chief advantages of factorial experiments relative to single-variable experiments?

3. Define or describe: main effect, interaction, Solomon Four-Group Design, "statistical" main effect, pairwise comparisons.

4. Describe two kinds of "mixed factorials"; make up one example of each type.

5. How would you go about controlling "progressive error" in a repeated-measures factorial?

6. Create line graphs that illustrate each of the following outcomes: in a 2×3 factorial, a main effect of both independent variables, but no interaction; in a 3×3 factorial, no main effect of A, a main effect of B, and an interaction; in a 2×2 factorial, an interaction of A and B, but no main effect of either variable.

7. In a factorial ANOVA the between-cells variance must be parsed into its component parts. What are these parts in a two-variable experiment?

8. In what sense is the ANOVA performed on the data from a single-variable correlated-groups experiment the same as a factorial ANOVA?

9. For what reason is it often necessary to conduct pairwise comparisons subsequent to obtaining a significant F ratio?

15

SELECTED TECHNIQUES IN APPLIED RESEARCH

In the first chapter of this book, I drew a distinction between *applied research* and *basic research*. To briefly review, basic research is performed primarily for the sake of gaining new knowledge, irrespective of the possible practical value or implications of the investigation. In contrast, applied research is conducted on problems and questions that have immediate relevance or social value. Throughout this text, I've presented numerous research examples from both of these general categories. In many ways, however, applied research warrants still further consideration, the principal reason being that there are more snags and extraordinary situations to be dealt with in applied research than in most basic research. Some of these extra problems are purely methodological, having to do with the issues of internal and external validity. Others are practical glitches, in the sense that scientists investigating a current social problem may have numerous social and political barriers to surmount.

In this chapter, I'll review several special problems and methods in applied research, in an attempt to round out the strong foundation you've developed in research theory and methodology. I'll start with a discussion of the uses and limitations of some "almost-experimental" designs that have proved useful in providing tentative or circumstantial evidence on many practical matters. Next, I will cover the creative use of unobtrusive measures in the examination of some sensitive social problems. The third section of this chapter is devoted to outlining the special difficulties and techniques that you'll encounter in research on human development. Finally, I'll introduce you to a branch of applied research that is playing an increasingly important role in our society—program evaluation.

QUASI-EXPERIMENTAL DESIGNS

Many questions of great importance to psychologists, and to society, are not easily researched through the conventional experiment, even though experimental methodology may be the most desirable approach to those particular questions. In such cases, certain features of the experimental method must be adapted to the problem of interest, rather than following the usual practice of adapting the problem to the method. You might say that necessity is often the mother of inventive research designs. The research designs I'm referring to are called **quasi-experimental designs**, the prefix "quasi" meaning "as if." Quasi-experimental investigations are *experimentlike studies in which the researcher is either unable to randomly assign subjects to conditions or unable to control the scheduling of events, or both*; some quasi-experimental studies have only one group or condition in them. Perhaps it has occurred to you that the "pseudo-experiments" discussed in Chapter 13 are types of quasi-experimental designs. Two other varieties of quasi-experiments that are fairly common in applied-research situations will be discussed here.

As a collection of research methods, quasi-experimental designs tend to be plagued more by sources of internal *invalidity* (i.e., confoundings) than are "true" experimental designs, but often these designs are the best possible options that applied researchers have in a particular situation. Therefore, it is important that you become aware of how you can use these approaches to gather "circumstantial" evidence that bears on a research question when more rigorous approaches are not feasible. However, it is equally important that you become familiar with the shortcomings of these designs. Because of these shortcomings, no one quasi-experiment can be very convincing by itself but, as Campbell and Stanley (1966) point out, quasi-experimental approaches can *collectively* provide convincing evidence. This would be true, for example, if several different quasi-experimental studies on a particular problem all pointed to the same conclusion. You'll recognize this as an instance of "multiple converging operations," a term which has been referred to and illustrated at several points in this book.

Here I'll review two of the more frequently used quasi-experimental methods: the time-series design and the nonequivalent control-group design.

Time-Series Design

The time-series design involves taking repeated measurements on a particular sample or population and, at some arbitrarily or randomly chosen point in the series of measurements, introducing an experimental treatment. If the measurements change distinctly and dramatically right after the treatment occurs, then that change can logically be attributed to the effects of the treatment. You can see, then, that this design is similar in rationale to the random time-series single-case experimental design discussed in Chapter 10.

Take an example. A state may reinstate capital punishment in an arbitrarily chosen year. The incidence of capital murder could be charted for the ten years that preceded reinstatement of the death penalty and for several years following its reinstatement. If capital murder in that state decreases dramatically in the first two or three years following the statute change, then the drop would support the effectiveness of capital punishment as a deterrent to homicide.

Sometimes unforeseen events in the environment set up a naturally occurring "interrupted time-series" experiment. Clever and perceptive researchers often exploit such unforeseen events to let nature test their theories in what might be called "natural experiments." An example of an interrupted time-series study was reported by Berkowitz (1970), who was interested in the effect that a nationally publicized violent crime would have on the subsequent incidence of violent crime in the United States. In a nutshell, Berkowitz's hypothesis was that the witnessing of violence makes people in general more violent. To test his hypothesis, Berkowitz charted the data on violent crime for the years 1960 to 1966, which included the 1963 assassination of President John F. Kennedy. The results of this study appear in Figure 15–1. It is clear that the sudden rise in violent crime after November 1963 supports the "violence begets violence" hypothesis.

Since you're now sophisticated in the matter of threats to internal validity, you've probably surmised that the time-series design is vulnerable to the "history" confounding. That is, theoretically irrelevant events that coincide with the critical "treatment" may be responsible for the change in the dependent variable. The best protection against this confounding is to take measurements on a "control group" that is not exposed to the critical treatment but that is subject to the same irrelevant historical influences as the treatment group. Sometimes this is possible to do, and sometimes it isn't. In the case of the study of the effects of capital punishment, for example, you could chart the incidence of capital murder in a "control" state that does not use capital punishment but is otherwise similar to the "experimental" state. In the case of the Kennedy assassination, however, no such control group would exist, since the assassination received international attention.

Nonequivalent Control-Group Design

Another frequently encountered quasi-experimental design is the nonequivalent control-group design. In this model, two groups which differ initially in some systematic way are

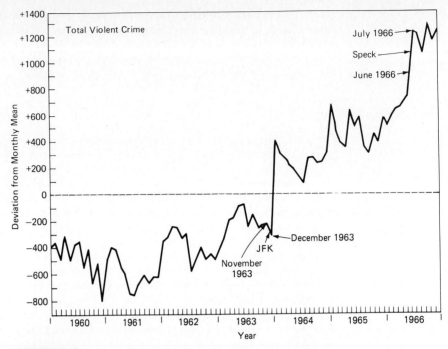

FIGURE 15–1

Deviations From Monthly Mean for Sum of Violent Crimes, 1960–1966.

Source: L. Berkowitz. The contagion of violence. An S-R mediational analysis of some effects of observed aggression. In W. J. Arnold & M. M. Page (Eds.), *Nebraska symposium on motivation* (Vol. 18). Lincoln: University of Nebraska Press, 1970. Reproduced with permission.

pretested and posttested on the dependent measure. Between testings, one of the groups receives a special program of treatment aimed at changing scores on the dependent measure. If the pretest shows that the groups are statistically equivalent on the dependent variable at the outset, but they differ from one another on the posttest, the change is ascribed to the effects of the treatment. Thus, the design may be represented as follows:

	Pretested	*Special Treatment*	*Posttested*
Group 1	Yes	Yes	Yes
Group 2	Yes	No	Yes

An example comes from a recent study of the influence of biofeedback training on the rehabilitation of juvenile delinquents, which was reported in a local newspaper. A group of young male "offenders" was offered the opportunity to enter biofeedback training to combat stress. Several of the clients *volunteered* to undergo the training, while the remainder of the group declined treatment. Because bureaucratic restrictions prohibited using random assignment, the volunteers thus became the experimental group, and those who declined served as the control group. The groups were equivalent on a pretest of "adjustment," but the treatment group was significantly higher on the same test when it was administered several weeks following the onset of biofeedback training.

These results, while encouraging, must be interpreted with caution. This particular design is loaded with possibilities for confounding influences, including a testing effect and a "Pygmalion" (positive expectancy) effect (see Campbell & Stanley, 1966). But the primary problem, which you have undoubtedly detected, is that of subject-selection bias: The subjects themselves determined who would serve in the respective groups. And chances are good that the biofeedback volunteers were the very clients most likely to improve in "adjustment" regardless of subsequent treatments. Nonetheless, given that the subjects could not be randomly assigned to conditions in this project, the research represents a first step in evaluating a potentially valuable rehabilitation technique. With appropriate opportunity, the program evaluators will be able to do further tests of the technique under better-controlled conditions.

SPECIAL APPLICATIONS OF NONREACTIVE DATA-COLLECTION TECHNIQUES

At several places in this book, you've read about various techniques of "unobtrusive" data collection, including clandestine observation, participant observation, hidden monitoring devices, and archival research. Because these approaches avoid or minimize "observational reactivity"—people's tendency to behave atypically when they are aware of being observed—unobtrusive methods of data collection are also known as **nonreactive techniques**. As you might imagine, such techniques are of immense value to applied researchers who have chosen to examine "sensitive" topics or behaviors that are difficult to investigate in a straightforward and open manner. Let's look at some of these special applications of nonreactive measurement.

Physical Traces

A wealth of information about human nature can often be found in the little traces of themselves that people deposit here and there as they go about their daily lives. When you systematically note, record, or count these "traces," you are using what Webb, Campbell, Schwartz, and Sechrest (1966) called **accretion measures** of behavior: accumulated deposits of material that may reflect systematic behavior patterns. Fingerprints are perhaps the best-known example of accretion measures.

Accretion measurements are inherently "nonreactive" because they are taken after the "depositors" have departed from the observation site. Therefore, these pieces of evidence can be very useful in the study of reactive topics. Consider, for example, an investigation designed to discover behaviors that predict who is likely to drop out of college during the first couple of years of enrollment. Clearly, this type of investigation calls for indirect approaches to data gathering. Very few entering freshmen believe that they will quit college, and the few who do probably would be reluctant to admit their socially undesirable expectations. In view of these considerations, four environmental psychologists at the University of Utah decided to look for clues to the dropout syndrome within the dormitory rooms of 83 freshmen (Brown, Vinsel, Foss, & Altman, as reported by Cohen, 1979). The researchers photographed the decorations that these students had hung on the walls of their rooms, and then kept track of which students eventually left college in spite of adequate academic records. Twenty-four of the "subjects" did leave the university within 18 months after the pictures were taken.

The decorations, which can be considered accretion measures, turned out to be fairly informative. Relative to students who stayed in school, the dropouts hung a larger number of decorations, but the types of decorations that they used were less varied than those of the "stay-ins." Altogether, the researchers noted 39 possible types of decorations (e.g., news articles, caps, beer-can tabs, etc.); but those who would eventually leave college showed an average of only 3.7 types of decorations, while their abiding counterparts displayed an average of 5.4 varieties. Also, while the "stay-ins" hung a larger number of decorations that indicated a commitment to the university, the dropouts displayed a much larger number of items related to their homes and hometowns.

The possibilities for ingenious uses of accretion measures in the investigation of "sensitive" behavior patterns are practically limitless. Do you want an "honest" index of variation in on-campus alcohol consumption across different segments of the academic year? Try counting the empty beer, wine, and liquor bottles in randomly sampled refuse cans around campus at different times of the year. Admittedly, this could be a somewhat unpleasant form of data collection, but it probably would provide more valid data than would periodic surveys on the same topic. To consider another possibility, what could you learn about the mood of the student body from a systematic examination of graffiti on the walls of college lavatories?

Private Documents

When people with unusual characteristics or problems die, they often leave behind a number of personal documents, such as letters, notes, and diaries, which potentially can provide circumstantial evidence pertaining to the origin of their special traits. For instance, Freud used biographical documents to conduct a posthumous psychoanalysis of President Woodrow Wilson. Obviously believing in the adage "Turnabout is fair play," Carl Jung, a close student of Freud, later contributed psychological analyses of various letters that Freud had written to him (Jung, 1963). Employing similar techniques, psychologist Gordon Allport carried out a very comprehensive personality assessment of a woman named "Jenny," based on 301 letters that she had written to a married couple during the last 12 years of her life (see *Letters From Jenny*, Allport, 1965).

The systematic study of personal documents is one application of a more general method of data collection called *content analysis*. Content analysis, of course, is an entirely "nonreactive" technique, since the authors of the "content" presumably created the documents of interest with no anticipation of scientific scrutiny. It is probably obvious to you that content analyses can yield valuable qualitative and impressionistic data. But quantitative analysis is also possible: Recurring themes can be counted, tabulated, and statistically analyzed.

Quantitative techniques have been applied to the content analyses of suicide notes. Specifically, researchers have tabulated and analyzed the major themes in hundreds of suicide letters and notes (left by "successful" suicide attempters), in the hope that these documents would reveal commonly occurring emotional and cognitive states associated with that drastic final act. One of the foremost researchers in the field of suicidology is Edwin S. Shneidman. Working in cooperation with legal authorities and families of the deceased, Shneidman and his co-researchers found that a relatively large number of suicide letters and notes contained one or more of the following features (summarized by Frederick, 1969):

1. strong emotion
2. a pervasive quality of forlornness

3. an overwhelming need for love
4. a disappointing relationship
5. specific instructions to those who are to be left behind
6. "unusual" thought processes (i.e., illogical chains of reasoning)

This type of research may aid our understanding of the dynamics of suicide. Potentially, it could also help mental health professionals to identify people who are most likely to carry out a suicide threat.

Public Records

The touchy topic of suicide has also been approached through the examination of data from public records. The systematic investigation of documents or records that are accumulated and maintained by individuals or organizations is referred to as **archival research**; the records themselves are the "archives."

The Cook County Study. Using a moderate amount of ingenuity and persistence (see below), Maris (1969) was able to obtain copies of the death certificates of all suicides committed in Cook County, Illinois (which includes Chicago), from 1959 to 1963—2,153 certificates in all. He was also skillful enough to gain access to the Cook County Coroner's inquest records that pertained to these death certificates. With this wealth of archival evidence in hand, he then proceeded to examine the data within the framework of a comprehensive theory of suicide that had been developed by Emile Durkheim, a nineteenth-century philosopher/sociologist.

The most important general hypothesis in Durkheim's theory is that the likelihood of suicide decreases as the strength of people's interpersonal and social-group bonds increases. Basically, this hypothesis asserts that strong relationships, family ties, and membership in stable social groups serve as prophylactics against suicide. A specific implication of this assertion is that married people are less likely to commit suicide than are people who have never been married.

To examine this particular implication of Durkheim's theory, Maris extracted data on marital status, sex, and age from the death certificates of the suicides and computed the *ratio* of suicide rates of the never-married to those of the married. The results of this descriptive-statistical analysis appear in Table 15–1. If marriage affords some protection against suicide, then the suicide rates for the never-married should exceed those of the married portion of the sample, which means that the ratios in Table 15–1 should exceed 1.00. You can see that the expected outcomes occurred for most age/sex combinations. Therefore, this particular set of data was consistent with Durkheim's major hypothesis.

A Note on the Use of "Indirection" in Archival Research. Maris' Cook County study is an interesting illustration of how public records and similar "archives" may be used to investigate questions that might otherwise be impossible to address empirically. It is important to note, however, that depositories don't always eagerly open important archives to scientific inquirers. To the contrary, it is frequently difficult for even the most legitimate and well-intentioned investigator to gain access to certain records. Indeed, Maris encountered bureaucratic resistance in his initial efforts to gain access to the needed death certificates. The first state official contacted denied Maris' request on the grounds that such an incursion into sensitive records would violate both state statutes and the privacy rights of the families of the deceased.

Knowing that copying state records was, in fact, not a violation of Illinois law, Maris pursued his research goals through what he termed "indirection": He contacted a sec-

TABLE 15-1

Ratio of Suicide Rates of the Never-Married to the Married by Sex and Age, Cook County, Illinois, 1959–63

Age Group	Males	Females
0–14	—	—
15–24	1.0	0.74
25–34	3.3	2.5
35–44	2.2	2.1
45–54	1.6	0.91
55–64	1.5	1.5
65–74	1.7	—
75 +	1.9	—

SOURCE: R.W. Maris. *Social Forces in Urban Suicide*. Homewood, Ill.: Dorsey Press, 1969. Reproduced with permission.

ond, influential state official who worked in a different, but related, department. In a subsequent interview, Maris convinced the second official that the potential benefits of the study outweighed other concerns. In turn, the second official cleared the way for the study.

Maris' intelligent persistence is instructive. There usually is more than one route to sensitive records that are not legally designated "classified" documents. Hence, if your first overture to a custodian of records is unproductive, you should not abandon your initial research plan. Rather, try one or more different tacks—access to the data may be just around the corner.

TECHNIQUES IN DEVELOPMENTAL RESEARCH

Much of what is termed "applied research" is aimed at investigating human development. Educators and mental health professionals, in particular, are often interested in discovering the problems, processes, and influences associated with growth, maturation, psychosocial life stages, and aging. By better understanding these factors, the human service professions can increase their ability to help people maximize their productivity and satisfaction in life.

As you will learn in this section, developmental research is a very challenging area of psychology because it involves untangling true developmental processes from a number of ever-present confoundings.

Fundamentally, developmental researchers have three goals:

1. identification of age differences
2. identification of age changes
3. discovery of variables and events that are responsible for age differences and age changes

Preliminary progress toward these goals is often accomplished through the application of *cross-sectional* and *longitudinal* research designs.

Cross-Sectional versus Longitudinal Studies

If you conduct developmental research you will be interested in how age-related and maturation-related processes affect people's behavior, experience, and capabilities. But before you can delve into the underlying processes in human development, you will first need to identify the characteristics of people (behaviors, attitudes, aptitudes, etc.) that seem to be correlated with the variable of age.

One approach to the identification of age-related characteristics is to test groups of people for age *differences*. Presumably, if a human characteristic is affected by the biological, psychological, and social processes that are related to maturation and aging, then various groups of subjects that differ in age should also differ in the characteristic. For example, if general intelligence is an age-related trait, then raw scores on an IQ test should vary systematically from one age-group to another. Thus, the average raw score of twenty-year-olds may be higher than the average raw score of ten-year-olds, and also higher than the average raw score of octogenarians (people between eighty and ninety years of age).

Cross-sectional studies enable you to identify such age differences. In a **cross-sectional investigation**, you *measure several age-groups one time*, with all measures being made at about the same time. In a sense, then, your sample would be a "cross-section" of the age dimension. Ideally, the various age-groups you employ would be randomly selected from a clearly defined population. After the different "age" samples are selected, you then measure the members of each group on some characteristic, compute group means, and compare those means in an attempt to detect possible age differences on the measured dimension. If there are significant age differences in the data, then the characteristic of interest merits further investigation as a developmental variable.

The results of a hypothetical cross-sectional study of IQ are shown in Table 15–2. Note that three age-groups—fifty-year-olds, sixty-year-olds, and seventy-year-olds—were measured on general intelligence on *one occasion* in 1970. All of the subjects born in a given year are considered **birth-year cohorts**; that is, they are developmentally "associated" with one another by virtue of having been born at about the same time. Notice, also, that the average IQ score is lower for the sixty-year-olds than for the fifty-year-olds, and lowest for the seventy-year-olds. Although the data in this example are fictitious, this age-related IQ pattern is a fairly typical outcome in cross-sectional studies of general intelligence in the "elderly" (cf. Birren, 1966; Kimmel, 1974). Keep in mind, however, that cross-sectional studies do not provide evidence on age changes per se; such studies reveal only age *differences* between different groups of birth-year cohorts. This is a significant point, as will be explained below.

TABLE 15-2

Results of a Hypothetical Cross-Sectional Study: Intelligence Quotients for Three Birth-Year Cohort Groups Measured in a Single Year

(Cohort Group) Year of Birth	Measured IQs in 1970	Age at Time of Measurement
1900	110	70 years
1910	118	60 years
1920	120	50 years

If you're interested in studying *age changes*, then you must use a **longitudinal design**, in which *a single group of birth-year cohorts is measured more than one time at progressively greater ages*. Since you study the same group of people at several different times in their lives, the longitudinal approach reveals how these people change with increasing age. For reasons which will become clear shortly, developmental investigations that assess age changes often suggest different conclusions about human development than do studies that assess age differences (i.e., cross-sectional designs). For example, the hypothetical longitudinal data shown in Table 15–3 suggest that, up to a point, people may get smarter, not duller, as they grow old. The group means suggest that the 1910 cohort group became brighter between the ages of fifty (1960) and sixty (1970) and, further, that their increased intellectual ability held up at age seventy (1980). This hypothetical outcome is not far out of line with the actual findings of some longitudinal studies (for example, see Botwinick, 1967).

Advantages and Disadvantages of Developmental Designs

Cross-Sectional Studies.   The major advantage of the cross-sectional approach to developmental research is that it is a quick, easy, and relatively inexpensive way to identify potentially important age-related traits and behaviors. The method requires that subjects be measured on only one occasion; thus, this type of design averts the record-keeping and follow-up effort that is necessary in a longitudinal study. Also, cross-sectional studies are not plagued by the influences of testing-to-testing carry-over effects and attrition effects than can contaminate longitudinal data.

But there are significant disadvantages associated with this approach. First, cross-sectional methodology provides for the identification of age differences only. You wouldn't be able to assess actual aging "trends" in your subjects from year to year or decade to decade. Nor would you be able to assess how one developmental event (e.g., retirement or menopause) influences subsequent changes in a group of people.

By far, however, the most serious drawback of the cross-sectional method is that "age effects" are confounded by cohort effects. Cohort effects are *characteristics of people that are a result of the cultural and historical factors that are somewhat unique to their time of birth*. For example, people born just before or during the Great Depression of the 1930s may see money as a very sensitive and important matter. Now that these people are in their "middle years," you might be tempted to conclude that people in general become cautious and "uptight" about money as a result of middle-years developmental processes. In fact, however, the observed "cautiousness" about money may be mainly a result of their early

TABLE 15-3

Results of a Hypothetical Longitudinal Study: Intelligence Quotients for a Single Birth-Year Cohort Group Measured Three Times at Ten-Year Intervals

	Year of Measurement		
Year of Birth	*1960*	*1970*	*1980*
1910	113	118	117
Age at Measurement	50 years	60 years	70 years

cohort culture rather than any general psychological or social phenomenon of development. Likewise, people born in 1910 received less formal education than people born in 1930; therefore, the lower IQ scores obtained by some older groups, relative to their younger counterparts, may be largely attributable to differences in the amount of formal education rather than to the ravages of old age. In fact, this conclusion is suggested by much of the available data on this matter (Kimmel, 1974).

Longitudinal Studies.　　The chief advantages of longitudinal investigations are as follows:

1. Since each subject serves as his own "control," age changes can be observed directly.
2. The multi-point measurement across time allows for assessment of aging "trends"; that is, increasing, decreasing, linear, or nonlinear functions.
3. Potentially, the effects of one kind of age change on other age changes can be considered.
4. Longitudinal designs avoid the confounding effects of cohort differences, because the birth-year cohort variable is held constant; that is, the same cohort group is measured on each occasion.

There are, however, numerous disadvantages associated with longitudinal research:

1. Longitudinal studies often require a long time to complete and, because of the extensive record-keeping, subject-tracking, and follow-up effort needed, these designs tend to be expensive.
2. Retesting subjects several times may make them "test-wise," producing sequencing effects in the data, which may get confused with developmental effects (see Chapter 7).
3. Attrition of subjects may progressively bias the sample as the study continues. For example, the least well-adjusted, least healthy, and dullest subjects may tend to be the first to be lost from the investigation, leaving you with a sample of the best and the brightest. Thus, careful monitoring of the characteristics of "dropouts" is indicated.
4. The age variable is confounded by time-of-measurement variables.

The last disadvantage, time-of-measurement confounding, warrants further discussion, since it can be a subtle but powerful confounding influence. Just as there are cultural and historical factors associated with the time of the subjects' birth, so are there many extraneous events associated with the time at which the subject is measured. For instance, the tumultuous social and economic changes of the 1960s and early 1970s undoubtedly affected the attitudes and values of many Americans, and adults participating in a longitudinal study that spanned those decades may have exhibited marked changes in some measures of attitude and personality as a result of those unique developments. Unless the developmental researchers are constantly monitoring such influences, the resulting changes in subjects may be mistakenly attributed to general developmental processes thought to be independent of specific times. Similarly, the extensive "continuing-education" (or "adult-education") movement of the sixties and seventies resulted in many middle-aged and older adults returning to school or college. With more formal education, those adults would also exhibit increased IQ scores. If some of them happened to be taking part in a longitudinal study of intelligence at that time, the sample would appear to have become smarter. It would therefore be tempting, but perhaps incorrect, to conclude that increasing age brings with it increased intellectual aptitude.

Beyond Longitudinal and Cross-Sectional Designs

Both the longitudinal and the cross-sectional approaches to developmental research have potentially serious confoundings built into them: time-of-measurement confoundings in the longitudinal designs and cohort confoundings in the cross-sectional model. Apart from these fundamental problems, neither cross-sectional nor longitudinal research, alone, yields information on the independent variables that are responsible for age differences or age changes. Essentially, then, these designs *identify* significant age-related phenomena, but to discover the causes of these phenomena, you will need to employ additional research procedures.

In this section, we'll first examine a developmental research design that deals simultaneously with the inherent confoundings of the longitudinal and cross-sectional models. Then we'll consider a research method that can sometimes be used to discern the causal processes behind age differences and age changes.

The Longitudinal-Sequential Design.   Although a major and sometimes expensive undertaking, the ideal developmental research model combines the longitudinal and cross-sectional approaches in a single study. In the **longitudinal-sequential design**, *several different birth-year cohort groups are studied longitudinally over the same measurement period*. An example of this design appears in Table 15–4.

If you carefully inspect Table 15–4, it will quickly become apparent that each column in the table represents the results of a cross-sectional study, and each row shows the results of a longitudinal study.

There are many ways to analyze the data of a longitudinal-sequential design (see Nesselroade & Baltes, 1974), each of which is aimed at unmasking the confounding influences of time-of-measurement, cohort effects, or a combination of these factors. For instance, the example presented in Table 15–4, which is a hypothetical study of intellectual development and change, reveals a cohort effect: In 1960 the sixty-year-olds (1900 cohort) have a much lower average IQ score than the fifty-year-olds (1910 cohort), suggesting that general intelligence declines from age fifty to age sixty. The longitudinal results contradict this conclusion, however. The second row of the table shows that the 1910 cohort group *increased* in IQ scores between age fifty (1960) and age sixty (1970). And row 3 shows that the general intelligence of the 1920 cohort group remained stable from age fifty (1970) to age sixty (1980). Thus, overall, the "positive" longitudinal results indicate that the "negative effects" of aging suggested by the cross-sectional age differences probably represent the influence of a year-of-birth factor, perhaps level of formal education.

TABLE 15-4

Results of a Hypothetical Longitudinal-Sequential Design: Intelligence Quotients for Three Different Birth-Year Cohort Groups Compared Across the Same Longitudinal Period

Year of Birth	Year of Measurement		
	1960	1970	1980
1900	106	110	100
1910	113	118	117
1920	115	120	120

The longitudinal-sequential data also suggest a time-of-measurement confounding in the *longitudinal* data: All three cohort groups show an increase in average IQ score from 1960 to 1970, *regardless of their age at the time of measurement*. In contrast, a "true aging effect" would consistently produce the same change from one age to the next, but not from a particular time of measurement to another particular time of measurement. Apparently, cultural/historical events occurring between 1960 and 1970 served to boost the general intelligence of all of the age-groups, irrespective of underlying biological and psychological changes.

I hope that the advantages of the complex longitudinal-sequential model are now clear to you: In a single study, you get information on age differences, age changes, and the two major confoundings that typically plague developmental research. Also, as the example used here illustrates, the longitudinal-sequential mode usually will show that the "truth" about developmental changes lies somewhere between what is indicated by cross-sectional data and what is suggested by longitudinal data.

The Age-Simulation Method.   As stated earlier, most developmental-research designs serve only to identify age-related behavior and characteristics that are worthy of further investigation. Once the pertinent characteristics have been discovered, the next task is to find out what basic causal processes bring about age-related changes in those characteristics. This is a very challenging task for the developmental researcher because most developmental changes are the result of a number of interacting variables. Baltes and Goulet (1971) have proposed an interesting technique for making inroads into the "causes" of age effects. In their **age-simulation technique**, *you systematically manipulate the independent variables that could be contributing to age changes or age differences and observe which variables seem to control the age effects of interest.* The following example from Kimmel (1974) illustrates this promising approach:

> . . . If we find that 65-year-old men perform less well in a dart-throwing experiment than 20-year-old men, we have no idea what may have caused this age difference. But if we manipulate the amount of light so that the 20-year-olds perform as poorly as the 65-year-olds when the light is very dim, but the 65-year-olds perform as well as the 20-year-olds when the lighting is increased, then we know that this age difference reflects differences in perceptual ability and indicates that the older men require more light to see as well as the younger men. Alternatively, it might be that lighting makes no difference, but when the older men are allowed to stand closer to the board, they score as well as the younger men, suggesting that physical strength is the important factor; thus we might simulate these age differences (i.e., experimentally cause the young men to perform like the old men and vice versa) by varying the distance the dart must be thrown. Again, it might be that if the older men are allowed to practice for an hour, they do as well as the young men, suggesting that the age difference really involves practice effects. (p. 33)

PROGRAM EVALUATION

An unmistakable sign of the growing importance of social/behavioral research in our society is the recent upsurge in the number of "accountability" and "effectiveness" studies being conducted in various sectors of American life. Today, it is not sufficient for educational, industrial, and therapeutic programs to look good on paper or in theory; increasingly, they must also survive empirical tests of their effectiveness. And psychologists who have skills in applied research are playing a major role in the growing enterprise of program evaluation.

Program evaluation is a very broad term that has been attached to a variety of effectiveness studies in the applied areas of the behavioral and medical sciences. Principally, program evaluation research has two general goals: (a) assessment of the correctness of application of a procedure that is designed to bring about a practical outcome (*formative* evaluation); (b) assessment of the degree to which the desired outcome of a procedure is achieved (*summative* evaluation). Beyond these two goals, an additional function of program evaluation is to determine the economic feasibility and cost effectiveness of an apparently successful procedure.

Program evaluation studies might be employed to answer relatively narrow questions, such as: To what extent are the client-centered counselors of a university clinic exhibiting empathic responses, reflection of feeling, and unconditional positive regard for clients? Is client-centered counseling effective in reducing the discrepancy between the clients' actual and ideal self-concepts? Does the new manager-training program at CFR Industries improve the participants' active-listening skills? Are the programmed instruction modules being properly administered at Millroad District Junior High Schools?

Program evaluation has also been applied to programs as broad as the federally funded Project Head Start for disadvantaged preschool children; the U.S. government's Comprehensive Employment Training Act (CETA) program, which is aimed at upgrading the job skills of the occupationally disadvantaged; and the general system of public education in America. Potentially, then, research on program effectiveness can be applied to virtually any human enterprise, regardless of scope, assuming that there is adequate need, money, and human resources. But actually carrying out program evaluations is almost never a simple and straightforward matter. Let's see why.

Evaluation Research: Does the Traditional Model Apply?

Although most of the research techniques examined in this text are applicable to program evaluation, there are definite differences between conducting program evaluation and conducting behavioral research in the traditional sense. Sommer (1977) has outlined several of the ways in which evaluation research deviates from the more familiar traditional model of research:

1. When you conduct research, you usually can afford the "luxury" of avoiding or withholding value judgments concerning the worthiness or quality of the phenomenon or question you are addressing. But, by definition and in fact, program evaluation is inherently oriented toward value judgment: "Good," "better," and "best" are the kinds of judgments evaluation studies are designed to produce.

2. Evaluation research often is much more problem-oriented and hurried than traditional research. In most cases, the program evaluator, herself, will be evaluated partly on the basis of whether she can come up with the answer to a particular practical question within a limited amount of time. Since evaluation deadlines frequently are unreasonable to begin with, there may be no time to pursue interesting *new* questions and possibilities suggested by the early data.

3. Since most evaluation projects are originated by someone other than the evaluation researcher, manipulation of variables often will not be possible, and the evaluator will have to settle for an analysis of what others have already done in the way of a "research design." For the same reason, originality is not encouraged in evaluation research as it is in "traditional" research.

4. Unlike traditional research, program evaluation is intrinsically "political." First, the people being evaluated frequently will not be receptive to the goals or procedures of the research, and the evaluators will need to exercise some skillful persuasion to obtain their cooperation. Second, evaluation criteria are always open to "partisan" criticism by special-interest groups affected by the outcome (for example, what are the criteria of effective teaching?). Furthermore, the originators and funders of the project usually have a vested interest in the study's "coming out right" and will apply various types of pressure to ensure this. Hence, in addition to having a diversity of well-developed research and quantitative skills, the evaluation researcher must also possess effective interpersonal skills and be politically astute.

As you can see, program evaluation can be an entirely new game, even for the veteran researcher. With that in mind, let's now consider the basic steps in a program evaluation.

Stages of Program Evaluation

In their excellent book, *Evaluation: A Systematic Approach*, Rossi, Freeman, and Wright (1979) outline four stages through which most program-evaluation studies progress: (a) planning the program, (b) monitoring the program's execution, (c) assessing the program's impact, and (d) evaluating the program's cost-effectiveness.

I'll describe each of these stages within the context of a hypothetical evaluation study of a program of client-centered counseling, the method developed by Carl Rogers (also called "Rogerian" therapy). Briefly, the approach involves setting up a special, "permissive" atmosphere, in which the client feels "safe" enough to explore formerly "unacceptable" aspects of his personality and experience. The major role of the counselor is to be emotionally genuine (providing a model for the client), remain nonjudgmental, empathize with the client, and verbally "reflect" back the feelings that the client seems to be expressing. An important aim of client-centered counseling is to help the client become more accepting of himself.

Planning the Program. In the initial stage of evaluation research, you need to define the problem and population to be investigated, establish the goals of the program, and decide on the specific procedures that will be used to monitor the program's progress and assess the outcomes.

Let's say that the evaluation of client-centered counseling will be conducted at a university counseling center, and that the target population will be college students who come to the center for help with personal problems of adjustment and coping. The program's application will be monitored via videotaping the counseling sessions and performing a content analysis of the tapes to see if the counselors are successfully implementing the special conditions of client-centered counseling. Since a major goal of client-centered counseling is to help clients raise their self-esteem, program effectiveness will be assessed in the following way: Prior to counseling, each client will rank a number of self-referring statements according to how closely the statements describe his *actual self*. He will then rank the same statements according to how accurately they describe his *ideal self* (the person he would like to be). The discrepancy between the actual-self ranking and the ideal-self ranking is a measure of the extent to which clients have low self-esteem—that is, the degree to which they are dissatisfied with themselves. After several weeks of counseling, the clients will repeat the same two ranking procedures. If the counseling is effective, the discrepancy between the "actual" and "ideal" self-descriptions should diminish from the pretest to the posttest.

Several control groups will be employed: a group that doesn't need counseling, a group that needs counseling but doesn't receive it, and two groups that receive other methods of counseling. Members of each control group will also take the pretest and posttest (i.e., self-description rankings).

Monitoring the Program.   When the program has begun, it is the evaluator's job to monitor the application of the target procedures. Are the procedures being implemented as planned? Do some features of the procedures require modification? Do some parts of a procedure conflict or interfere with other parts? Do the subjects in the program seem to be changing in the direction of the anticipated outcome?

The monitoring aspect of program evaluation is often referred to as **formative evaluation**, since it is aimed at assessing the program's formation and development. Formative evaluation is more *process-oriented* than it is outcome-oriented. The main concern is with ensuring that the implementation of the program proceeds smoothly and accurately. Unlike traditional research, formative evaluation may result in a program procedure's being altered during the course of the study.

In the case of the client-centered counseling program, formative evaluation might be implemented through videotaping the counseling sessions. Then, independent judges could rate the degree to which counselors are exhibiting empathy, reflection of feeling, a nonjudgmental attitude, and so on.

Assessing the Program's Impact.   Program outcome or impact comes under the label of **summative evaluation**, since the objective at this stage is to assess the sum of the procedure's influence on the people involved, at the "summation" (end) of the program's trial period. Relevant questions are: Did the procedure work? If so, how well? To what degree did the program result in the attainment of its specific goals? What were the major shortcomings?

Data analyses and statistical tests become a major aspect of the evaluation at this point. Following the appropriate analyses, conclusions concerning the program's effectiveness are reached. This information, together with data from the formative evaluation, then serves as a basis for recommending abandonment, adoption, or modification of the program, subject to a cost-effectiveness analysis (see below).

In the summative portion of the evaluation of client-centered counseling, the posttest results would be compared with the pretest results for each group or condition in the study, and the different conditions would be compared with each other. Conclusions and recommendations would then be drawn concerning the relative effectiveness of client-centered counseling as a means of raising self-esteem.

Evaluating Cost-Effectiveness.   The cost-effectiveness of a procedure is almost always a consideration in program evaluation. A program may shine at both the formative and summative levels of evaluation but be so expensive relative to slightly less effective procedures that the small advantage it brings does not warrant its adoption.

For example, client-centered counseling may be slightly more effective than behavior modification counseling in raising clients' self-esteem, but if the client-centered counseling sessions must be twice as long as the behavioral counseling sessions, then the client-centered procedure might not be deemed "cost-effective." That is, twice as many "cases" could be handled if the counselors used behavioral counseling, and the outcome would be almost as satisfactory as that of the less time-efficent client-centered approach. Since time translates into money, in effect the behavioral counseling would cost only half as much.

Clearly, then, the costing-out feature of program evaluation distinguishes it still further from traditional research, in which the procedure with the largest effect usually is viewed as the one most worthy of further attention—cost and efficiency notwithstanding.

SUMMARY

This chapter presented several techniques and strategies that are particularly useful in applied research. It was pointed out that, in many ways, applied researchers often have more practical and methodological obstacles to overcome than does the "basic" researcher.

As a result of the nature of particular phenomena or the inability to use random assignment, applied researchers sometimes employ *quasi-experimental* designs to obtain preliminary or circumstantial evidence on certain problems. The lack of proper control conditions is the common characteristic of quasi-experimental studies. The *time-series design* and the *nonequivalent control-group design* were presented as examples of quasi-experimental research.

Applied researchers can occasionally use nonreactive data-collection techniques to obtain evidence on socially sensitive topics or issues that otherwise would not be researchable—the topic of suicide, for example. Examples of nonreactive data sources include *physical traces, private documents*, and *public archives*.

Human development and aging are major areas of investigation in applied psychology. *Cross-sectional* research involves the study of the characteristics of different age-groups at a given point in time. *Longitudinal* studies measure the characteristics of a particular group of subjects at several points in time. The *longitudinal-sequential* approach combines the features of both cross-sectional and longitudinal methodology. The *age-simulation method* is designed to uncover the "causes" of age differences and age changes.

The fourth area of applied research covered in this chapter is *program-evaluation* research, which is aimed at assessing the processes, outcomes, and costs of special procedures and new techniques in education, industry, and therapeutic enterprises. A distinction was made between *formative evaluation*, which is process-oriented, and *summative evaluation*, which is outcome-oriented.

REVIEW QUESTIONS

1. What characteristic do all quasi-experimental designs have in common? For what reasons would any researcher want to use a quasi-experimental design?

2. How could you use an interrupted time-series design to study the relationship between the occurrence of a full solar eclipse and the incidence of suicide?

3. Define or describe: physical traces, private documents, archives, "indirection" in archival research, cross-sectional design, longitudinal design, longitudinal-sequential design, age-simulation method.

4. Compare and contrast cross-sectional and longitudinal research, citing the specific advantages and disadvantages of each.

5. What type of information can you get from cross-sectional and longitudinal research, respectively?
6. What are the chief goals of program-evaluation research?
7. In what ways does program evaluation differ from "traditional" research?
8. Summarize the four main steps in a program evaluation.

PART

4

COMMUNICATING SCIENCE

16

PUTTING TOGETHER A RESEARCH REPORT

Early in this book, I emphasized the *public* character of the scientific enterprise, as well as the main reasons for that publicness. Science is an ongoing, collective effort. To promote objectivity and correct thinking, the individual scientist's work needs to be reviewed, commented on, criticized, and replicated by his colleagues. In addition, the individual scientist's theorizing and research planning are nourished, tempered, and modified by the publicized work of other researchers. Science functions well as a system of inquiry only if scientists are willing to share their research; therefore, it is the responsibility of every serious researcher to communicate his research activities and findings to the scientific community as clearly, accurately, and promptly as circumstances permit.

In this chapter, you will learn how to transform your research into a manuscript suitable for presentation to the scientific community. As you learn how to construct a research report, you will simultaneously increase your ability to understand and evaluate journal articles that you read, all of which started out as "research report" manuscripts.

Like other skills, the ability to write scientific manuscripts responds well to practice. And *informed* practice is most beneficial. This means that you will need to seek critical feedback on your work from your course instructor and other students. You should realistically expect to write at least three or four drafts of your first research report. Your efforts will be generously repaid, as there is much personal satisfaction and, eventually, many career benefits to be derived from practicing this craft.

WHAT A RESEARCH REPORT SHOULD BE AND DO

A scientific manuscript should be a succinct, clear, and accurate history of a study that the writer has conducted. The "historical" account should include the theoretical rationale or purpose of the investigation (often including a statement of specific hypotheses), the precise method used to investigate the question, the data obtained, and the conclusions and implications developed on the basis of the data.

An effective research report meets two essential criteria: (a) It describes what you did in enough detail so that another researcher could conduct an exact replication of your study solely on the basis of information contained in the report; (b) it clearly points out the major contributions that your study makes to the body of knowledge called scientific psychology. In fact, these are the principal criteria used by journal editors in deciding whether to publish or reject a manuscript.

Your research report should be geared to the appropriate audience, that is, fellow researchers, not the lay public. Therefore, it should be written at a level that assumes a knowledge of general psychological concepts and terms, as well as an understanding of basic statistics. The goal of your writing should be to inform rather than to entertain.

GETTING ORGANIZED

Actual writing time can be dramatically reduced by getting certain things in order before you start pushing the pencil or pounding the typewriter keys. When you begin writing your research paper you should have already prepared the following items and arranged them in this order:

1. *An outline of the paper*. The outline headings should follow the topical structure of a journal article. The four main parts of a journal article include, in this order, (a) Introduction, (b) Method, (c) Results, (d) Discussion.

Under the Introduction heading of your outline, jot down notes on the major problem or purpose of the study, the names of other authors whose prior research you wish to refer to in the Introduction, and a tentative statement of the expectations or hypotheses that you had prior to collecting the data.

Under the Method heading, list, in abbreviated fashion, the number and characteristics of your subjects, how subjects were selected and assigned to conditions, your independent and dependent variables, and the nature of any apparatus or special materials you used. Also, include notes on how you manipulated the independent variable, how you measured the dependent variable, and the steps you went through in the data-collection procedure.

Under the Results heading, list notes on the specific data you wish to present, including reference to tables or figures you have constructed. Also note the kinds of descriptive statistics (e.g., means, percentages, etc.) and statistical tests you plan to report.

Under the Discussion heading, construct a logical sequence of the major points you desire to make in light of your findings. Include notes on conclusions and implications for possible future research projects.

2. *A set of note cards or sheets of paper containing information on prior research that your study is related to*. Each card or sheet should include complete bibliographic information on the sources of this information (e.g., books, journals). Arrange these in an order that will lend itself to a logical flow of ideas in the Introduction section.

3. *Data sheets, tables, figures, and results of statistical analyses*. Arrange these items in the order that you plan to refer to them in the Results section of the manuscript.

Now you are ready to plug in your coffeepot and begin writing. (But please read the rest of this chapter first!)

TIPS ON WRITING THE MANUSCRIPT

Writing a scientific paper is not the same as writing a short story or a chapter in a novel or textbook. The latter narratives are suited to an expansive style of expression and often must entertain as well as inform the reader. Though a scientific manuscript need not be dull, its primary function is to be objectively informative. This function requires both a thrifty writing style, in which much attention must be given to precise wording, and careful documentation of statements about previous research and conclusions derived from your study.

Below I'll highlight several critical considerations in scientific writing. For a much more thorough discussion of these points, consult the *Publication Manual of the American Psychological Association*. Your college bookstore or library may have copies of this excellent guide. If not, you may obtain a copy (for a fee) by writing to the American Psychological Association, 1200 Seventeenth Street, N.W., Washington, D.C. 20036.

Scholarship

The research report is a scholarly document. Scholarly writing is responsible, honest writing, based on rational argument, data, and documentation of points.

Rational argument in the Introduction section of the research paper involves a *logical* development of your hypothesis on the basis of previous research and theorizing that pertain to your topic. Rational argument in the Discussion section of the paper expresses the chain of reasoning that relates your conclusions to the total package of hypothesis, method, and results that preceded it. In short, *rational argument means developing a logical consistency throughout the paper*. It leaves no glaring gaps in your sequence of reasoning as you go from introduction to conclusion, and it carefully excludes statements founded mainly on personal prejudices, intuition, whim, and emotional appeals.

It is also good scholarship to stick close to your data in drawing conclusions. Conclusions that go beyond your method and findings will be viewed as speculation or, worse, naiveté, by knowledgeable readers. Journal editors perceive such speculation as a "research error," in that the conclusions reached are not consistent with the method/data package.

A related issue is the accuracy of your data. Conscientious writers of scientific reports double-check their scoring, coding, and statistics to ensure accuracy. And they don't alter or fabricate data to fit their hypotheses.

One final aspect of scholarship deserves special emphasis. It is absolutely essential that you credit other authors for any of their material that you use in your paper. Thus, if you refer to someone else's findings, theories, or ideas, you should "cite" that person at that point in your report. When you use citation correctly, the reader has no doubt about the origin of the material being discussed. Failing to properly document your sources is called **plagiarism**—presenting another person's material as though it were your own—a practice that is always deemed unethical and often considered illegal. For guidance on how to cite and refer to the works of others, see the sections "Introduction" and "References" later in this chapter.

Verb Tense

In regard to verb tense, the rule of thumb in scientific-report writing seems to be: (a) Use past-tense verbs to describe the "historical" information in your report; (b) use the present tense to express generalizations. Thus, reference to previous studies and findings, as well as the description of your method and results, should be expressed in the past tense, as these components of the report are essentially historical accounts. But when drawing general conclusions or discussing theories (either your own or others'), the present tense is more appropriate, as conclusions and theoretical statements presumably refer to processes that operate in the present.

ANATOMY OF A RESEARCH REPORT: AN EXAMPLE WITH COMMENTARY

Since you are now familiar with the general aims and characteristics of a research report, this is a good time to look at some of the specific items that should go into the report. The components of virtually every research report include: *title page, abstract, introduction, method section, results section, discussion section, references, tables,* and *figures*—in that order. I'll discuss each of these components in turn. Following the commentary on each part of the manuscript, I'll present an example of that part, taken from a student-written research paper. In every case, I'll be describing the major guidelines and practices recommended in the *Publication Manual of the American Psychological Association*. Reports structured and written in accordance with that manual are said to be in "APA format."

Title Page

Choosing a Title.   The title you select for your report should say a lot in a few words. It should include key terms that immediately inform the reader of the general area of your research (e.g., personality, memory, etc.), the specific topic or theory that was examined in your study, and the chief variables investigated. For example, on the sample title page shown below, the title is:

Unusual Experiences in Altered States of

Consciousness: An Experimental Comparison of Hypnosis,

Meditation, and Progressive Relaxation

By examining that title, the reader would be able to tell that the general area of research was "altered states of consciousness" and that the specific aim was to compare three methods of achieving altered states, in terms of the unusual experiences that they produce. This title also tells the reader that the experimental method was used, and suggests what the independent and dependent variables were (can you pick them out?).

It is a good practice to avoid "catchy" or "cute" titles, such as "Three Ways to Freak Out without Drugs." Such titles tend to be uninformative and to suggest a lack of seriousness on the author's part.

How long should a manuscript title be? Generally, the titles of research reports have to be longer than titles of nonscientific documents in order to incorporate the key pieces of information described above. However, the APA *Publication Manual* recommends a maximum length of 12 to 15 words.

Title Page Format.   Refer to the sample title page below. Note the three items that must appear on the title page:

1. the title, which is centered on the page and typed in uppercase and lowercase letters
2. the author's name and his or her institutional affiliation (i.e., school, business, or organization), which are also centered
3. the "running head," a shortened version of the title, which is centered at the bottom of the page and is useful to indexers, should your manuscript be published

Notice that double-spacing is used in typing the title page. *Double-spacing is used throughout the manuscript.*

Abstract

The second page of your manuscript should bear a 100- to 175-word summary of your report. This summary, called the abstract, adds information to that given in the title. It states the major problem investigated and briefly describes your method of investigation, your most important findings, and your conclusions. Even though the abstract is positioned on the second page of the manuscript, you will find that it is easier to write your abstract after you've completed the main body of the paper.

''Unusual'' Experiences in Altered States of Consciousness:

An Experimental Comparison of Hypnosis,

Meditation, and Progressive Relaxation

Cheryl A. Brolin

Lindenwood College

Running head: ''Unusual'' Experiences in Altered States of Consciousness

"Unusual" Experiences

1

Abstract

In an experiment involving 60 high school students, hypnosis, meditation, progressive relaxation, and a control condition were compared along six dimensions of unusual experience that are commonly thought to characterize the "hypnotic trance." A completely randomized, independent-groups design was used. After being exposed to their respective treatments, subjects completed an open-ended questionnaire, which asked them to describe any of 7 categories of unusual experience that they may have had during the treatment sessions. Subjects were also asked to indicate whether they thought they had been "hypnotized." The results showed that the "unusual experiences" traditionally associated with hypnosis are reported with equal frequency in any situation in which subjects expect to experience an altered state of consciousness. Furthermore, the incidence of reports of unusual experiences was not related to the incidence of believing that one has been "hypnotized."

The abstract gives the reader an overview of your report and helps him decide whether the report contains the information he is looking for. An example of an abstract appears below. Note that the abstract is the first page of text, and it is numbered as such.

Introduction

Format Considerations. The Introduction section begins the body of the research report. As you refer to the sample Introduction given below, there are several format features to note. One is that the Introduction starts on page 2 (the abstract was on page 1). Second, an abbreviated "running head" is typed above the page number. This shortened running head also appears above the page number on each of the remaining manuscript pages. Third, the complete title of the article appears again, four spaces above the beginning of the text of the Introduction. Finally, unlike other sections of the paper, the Introduction has no heading. That is, it is not necessary to type the word "Introduction" at the start of the section.

Content. As you write your Introduction, the guiding principle should be *continuity*. Begin with a statement of the *general* problem or purpose; next, *narrow* the focus somewhat by working in a brief review of the research literature that is relevant to the purpose of your study; finally, combine the general problem with the preexisting research or theory to logically derive your *specific* hypothesis, prediction, or purpose.

As the above overview suggests, the typical introduction is implicitly made up of three segments. The opening statement of the general problem, which should not require more than one or two paragraphs, conveys the context of your research project. It provides the reader with structure and orientation. Notice how the study of "unusual experiences" is introduced in the first paragraph of the sample introduction shown below.

The second segment of the Introduction involves a brief review of theories and past research that bear on your project. As you develop this part of the Introduction, your aim should be to use the research literature to proceed in a logical progression from the general problem to the specific purpose or hypothesis behind your study. Thus, you should be somewhat selective about which articles and books you cite; try to refer to the most significant prior work that bears directly on your purpose or hypothesis, but don't include everything that has been written on the topic. The selection process is easier if you have prepared note cards on your references.

In the literature-review section of the Introduction, there are two ways to credit authors whose work you are referring to. The first is to refer to the author's (or authors') last name (or names) in the text of the sentence and then give the year of publication in parentheses. Example: "A study by Barber and Calverley (1976) examined whether it is necessary to . . ." The second method of citation involves referring to the author's hypothesis, findings, or conclusions in the text of your paper and then giving both the author's name and the year of publication in parentheses. Example: "Advocates of the 'unique state of consciousness' position tend to view hypnosis as a trance or trancelike state that differs in important ways from ordinary waking consciousness (Bramwell, 1903; Hilgard, 1965; Gill & Brenman, 1959)."

The final segment of the Introduction tells how the specific hypothesis or purpose of your study stems from the combination of the general problem and the preexisting literature. The link between the background material and the focus of your study must be clear to the reader. You should state what your study was designed to examine or test and, in general terms, how you planned to conduct the test. In this brief preview of the study, designate your independent and dependent variables and present your hypothesis or predictions, if you had any prior to data collection. Some investigations are "What if?", or exploratory, studies and, thus, are not directed toward any particular hypothesis.

"Unusual" Experiences in Altered States of Consciousness:

An Experimental Comparison of Hypnosis,

Meditation, and Progressive Relaxation

For decades, a controversy has raged over the question of whether a person who is hypnotized experiences alterations of conscious experience that are unique to hypnosis. Advocates of the "unique state of consciousness" position tend to view hypnosis as a trance or trancelike state that differs in important ways from ordinary waking consciousness (Bramwell, 1903; Gill & Brenman, 1959; Hilgard, 1965). Specifically, in contrast to persons in ordinary states of consciousness, hypnotized individuals are said to experience such abnormal subjective phenomena as alterations in size of body or body parts, disappearance of body or body parts, changes in equilibrium, feelings of unreality, changes in experienced temperature, and distorted perception of the "distance" of the hypnotist's voice (see Barber, 1976). Theorists holding the "unique state of consciousness" view also assume that a specific procedure--the hypnotic induction technique-- is required to create this constellation of altered experiences. Or, short of making such a strict assumption, they may insist that hypnotic induction is necessary if the altered states associated with hypnosis are to be experienced maximally (Hilgard, 1965).

Barber, (1976) questions the assertion that hypnotic consciousness differs from ordinary consciousness. He also disagrees with the supposition that a special hypnosis-induction procedure is necessary for either generating those experiences or maximizing them. Barber's view of hypnosis is that it represents a label for a set of relationships between independent and dependent variables that are commonly investigated by psychologists working in a diversity of fields. He contends that, while the term "hypnosis" has been shrouded in mystery and superstition since the nineteenth century, most of the phenomena of hypnosis

eventually will be explained in terms of subjects' task-attitudes, task-expec-
tations, and task-motivation. All of these variables are already being studied
in a variety of fields within psychology. According to Barber, systematic experimental research will reveal how general psychological knowledge about these
kinds of variables can be used to account for the behavior and experience of hypnotized subjects.

Barber's interpretation of "hypnotic" experiences was supported by the
results of an investigation conducted by Barber and Calverley (cited in Barber,
1976). That study examined whether it is necessary to use a formal hypnotic-induction procedure to induce the various unusual experiences historically attributed to the hypnotic trance. Their three conditions were: (a) a hypnotic-induction group that was given a standard 15-min induction procedure; (b) a
place-yourself-in-hypnosis group in which subjects were told to simply close
their eyes and "place themselves in hypnosis"; (c) a control group in which subjects were only instructed to close their eyes for 5 min. The results showed that
the place-yourself-in-hypnosis subjects reported just as many unusual experiences as the "hypnotized" subjects. Overall, both of these groups reported more
unusual experiences than the control group.

Barber and Calverley's study clearly demonstrated that people do not have to
be formally "hypnotized" in order to report having "hypnotic" experiences. But
their study also begs a question: Were the reports of "hypnotic experiences" a
result of the subjects' desire to give responses that "good hypnotized subjects
should give," or were the reports valid reflections of strange experiences that
people actually have when they expect to enter an altered state of consciousness?

The present investigation was an attempt to answer the above question. Most of
the subjects in this study were led to believe that they might experience altered
states of consciousness. Then they were exposed to 1 of 4 treatments: Hypnosis,
meditation, progressive relaxation, or a control condition. The hypothesis was

"Unusual" Experiences

4

that the hypnosis, meditation, and progressive relaxation conditions would not differ in the number of reported unusual experiences, but that all of these conditions would elicit a larger number of reports of unusual experiences than the control condition. This hypothesis was based on the assumption that the expectation of altered states, rather than hypnotic role-playing, is the critical determiner of reports of "hypnotic" experience.

[*Note:* The "Method" section normally would begin at this point on the page. Although the parts of a research report have been segmented here for the purpose of illustration, the text of an actual research report should be continuous.]

Method

The Method section describes, in specific terms, how you operationalized and implemented your investigation. The measure of a good Method section is whether a reader who is not personally familiar with your work could conduct an "exact" replication of your study. Therefore, you should write this section with enough detail to permit such a replication.

Many Method sections are subdivided into three principal parts: subjects, apparatus or materials, and procedure; but there are many variations on this basic structure. I recommend that you consult a few research journals to become familiar with some of the variations.

Subjects.   Include a description of the population of subjects that you sampled from. For example, did you use college students only? If so, what type of college or university did you sample from? In what part of the country? Were your subjects primarily freshmen? Also, provide information on how you obtained the participants, the number of subjects in the sample, and the general characteristics of the sample (e.g., sex, approximate age range, experimental sophistication).

In the interests of indicating possible restrictions on the generality of your findings, it is a good practice to mention any inducements you used to procure subjects, such as promises of money or extra course credit. For the same reason, it is important to state the number of subjects who failed to complete the study and any special characteristics that seemed to set the dropouts apart from those who completed the study.

Apparatus or Materials.   Describe all laboratory equipment, tests, and measuring devices that you need. If you employed equipment or tests that are commonly used in psychological laboratories, simple reference to them, by trade name, is usually sufficient. However, materials or apparatus that were specially developed or modified for your study should be described in detail.

Procedure.   In the procedure subsection, describe, step-by-step, the sequence of events that you and the subjects went through in the conduct of the study. Attempt to relate all major parts of the procedure to your variables and hypotheses. It is especially important to communicate (a) how variables were manipulated, if any were, (b) how conditions were controlled, (c) how variables were measured, and (d) time intervals between and during steps in the procedure.

If you randomly assigned subjects to conditions, start with a description of exactly how this was done, including reference to the randomization device used (e.g., random-number table). Then, describe the following aspects of your procedure:

How the subject was contacted or greeted.

What instructions or explanations were given. Relate these to manipulations of the independent variable, if appropriate.

What stimuli were presented, and how stimuli were related to the variables under examination.

How stimulus conditions were randomized or counterbalanced to control for confoundings.

The time of stimulus exposure and rate of stimulus presentation, if appropriate.

When and how the dependent variable(s) was(were) measured.

What the subjects were told upon completion of their participation. Include a description of the debriefing session and any postexperimental inquiry.

Method

Subjects

The subjects were 60 high school students, 41 females and 19 males, who were
randomly selected from the rosters of psychology classes being offered at a local
school. A random-number table was used to implement the selection process. Participation by the chosen subjects was entirely voluntary; the only incentive was
the promise of experience as research subjects in a study of "methods of altering
consciousness." Three students in the original sample declined participation
and were replaced by three new subjects selected at random.

Materials

The hypnotic-induction procedure printed in Appendix B of Barber (1976) was
used to administer the hypnosis treatment. This procedure is a standard approach
to hypnosis induction, employing repetition of verbal suggestions of drowsi-
ness, heaviness, and the desire to cooperate.

To help create an atmosphere of authenticity during the hypnotic-induction
procedure, a metronome was employed. At various times during the induction process, the hypnosis subjects were asked to concentrate on the metronome as it
"blinked" and "ticked" in cadence with the hypnotist's voice.

The meditation subjects were given instruction in the use of Benson's (1970)
"relaxation response" technique. The technique is based on common meditative
strategies, such as assuming a passive attitude, sitting quietly with eyes
closed, and thinking only of a simple stimulus--the number "one," for example.
Instructions to the meditators emphasized regular breathing and the importance
of coordinating the simple thought with exhalation.

The progressive relaxation subjects were administered the modified progressive relaxation procedure described in Bernstein and Borkovec (1973).

Posttreatment reports of unusual experiences were elicited via a seven-item
open-answer questionnaire containing the following queries: (a) Did you experi-

ence any alteration in the size of your body or body parts? If so, please explain.
(b) Did you feel as though your body or any of its parts were disappearing? If so,
please explain. (c) Did you experience any changes in equilibrium (dizziness,
lightheadedness, body imbalance, etc.)? If so, please explain. (d) Did you experience any feelings of unreality (psychological disorientation, journeying in-
ward, or floating)? If so, please explain. (e) Did you experience any changes in
temperature (feeling either unusually warm or cold)? If so, please explain. (f)
During the experiment, did the experimenter's voice seem either very close or
very far away? If so, please explain. (g) Did you have any other unusual experiences that we have not asked you about? If so, please explain.

The questionnaire, which was adapted from Barber and Calverley (cited in Barber, 1976), was printed on two 8½" × 11" pages. Subjects gave written responses.

Procedure

A random number table was used to assign 15 subjects to each of 4 treatment conditions: hypnosis, meditation, progressive relaxation, or control. After subjects had been assigned to one of the treatment conditions, the members of each
treatment group were randomly assigned to subgroups of five participants each.
Thus, each of the treatment groups was made up of three subgroups; this yielded 12
subgroups altogether. All five members of a given subgroup received their particular treatment at the same time. To avoid confoundings due to sequencing effects, the 12 subgroups were randomly assigned to 12 testing sessions distributed across three days. Three experimenters (all females) administered the
various treatments. Each experimenter was randomly assigned to four of the testing sessions, subject to the restriction that each experimenter be scheduled to
conduct each of the four conditions one time only.

All participants experienced their treatments in comfortable chairs in a
quiet room inside the school building. Each treatment required 20–22 min to administer. Prior to being exposed to their respective treatments, the subjects

were given a description of the procedure they were to undergo, but they were not aware at that time that they would be asked to complete a postsession questionnaire on unusual experiences. After an experimenter determined that all subjects in a subgroup understood the nature of their treatment, she had them sign informed-consent forms, which stated that they were free to leave at any time (none did).

The hypnosis subjects were told that they were going to be hypnotized and were asked to assume a comfortable position. Barber's hypnotic-induction procedure (described above) was administered.

The meditation subjects were informed that they would be meditating for about 20 min. Benson's "relaxation response" procedure (described above) was explained to them. Then they were asked to close their eyes, get comfortable, and meditate, using the technique that had been recommended.

The progressive relaxation subjects were told that they would be guided into a state of profound relaxation. The relaxation procedure was briefly described to them, and then the experimenter took them through the relaxation sequence.

The control subjects were told that they were in the control group, and that they were to simply close their eyes and relax for about 20 min.

Immediately following their experimental sessions, all subjects completed a 7-item questionnaire (described above) designed to assess the frequency and specific nature of any unusual experiences they may have had during their treatments. The questionnaire also asked the subjects in all conditions to indicate whether they thought they had been "hypnotized."

Results

Contents.   The Results section of your report presents three categories of information: brief verbal descriptions of the statistically significant group differences or correlations in the data; "descriptive" statistical indexes, such as means, frequencies, or percentages, that represent the significant outcomes; the numerical values of the statistical tests used to substantiate the significance of the outcomes.

It should be clear to the reader how each outcome you refer to bears on the aims of your study, as they were stated in the Introduction. Thus, in most cases, the first question raised in the Introduction should be the first one addressed in light of the results; data related to the second question should be presented next, and so on.

It is a common, and often helpful, practice to use data "tables" and "figures" (i.e., graphs) to supplement the presentation of your results (see the sample "Table 1," later in this chapter). By summarizing your data in a small, well-structured space, these visual displays of your frequencies, percentages, or means help the reader to grasp the major trends in the results. When used wisely, they can also reduce the length of your Results section. Observe how the table references are used in the sample Results section shown below.

Two other points deserve special attention. First, it will be necessary to support every outcome described in the Results section with the data that it is based on. In other words, don't claim a result without linking it to a specific statistical index or test value. Second, the Results section should describe only what you found. Save theoretical interpretations of your findings for the Discussion section.

Format Considerations.   You have some leeway in how you structure certain aspects of the Results section. First, you may describe how you scored and analyzed your data in the Results section (as was done in the example shown below), or you may include a "Scoring and Analysis" subsection in the Method section. Second, you may subdivide your Results section, using appropriate subheadings (see example) or, if your results are few and straightforward, you may present them as an undivided unit. Third, if you use the same level of significance for all statistical tests, this probability need be stated only once, at the start of the Results section. If the significance level varied from test to test, however, then it must be presented with each test statistic referred to. Example: "Length of employment was significantly correlated with job satisfaction, $r(158) = .22, p < .01$." Note that the "degrees of freedom" in the test (158) are shown in parentheses immediately following the test-statistic symbol (r).

Discussion

The Discussion section is the place to present your interpretation of the data within the network provided by previous research on the topic, your hypothesis, your method, and your data. Ideally, the points you wish to make will be ordered in accordance with the flow of ideas and information established in the Introduction and Results sections.

The first paragraph or two of the Discussion should summarize the extent to which hypotheses were supported or disconfirmed by the data, or the ways in which the purpose of the study was fulfilled. The next part of the Discussion might be used to compare your results to those of other researchers or to predictions made by particular theories.

Toward the end of the Discussion, state what you think are the major conclusions or implications that may be derived from your findings. Try to stay close to your data/ method package here, so that you don't commit a "research error," that is, draw a conclusion that cannot be justified by what you did and found. If you feel there were significant flaws or shortcomings in your method, you might also point these out in a final, "disclaimer" paragraph, perhaps with some suggestions for future research on the topic.

"Unusual" Experiences

8

Results

To be counted as an instance of an unusual experience, a subject's "yes" response to a questionnaire item had to be supported by his or her vivid written description of that experience. In other words, subjects' descriptions had to convince the scorer that the subjects genuinely believed that they had had the
specific category of experience referred to. In no case was a simple "yes" response sufficient, by itself, for inclusion in the tally of unusual experiences.
A total of five affirmative responses (one in the hypnosis group, three in the
meditation group, and one in the progressive relaxation group) had to be counted
as negative responses ("nos") because they lacked supportive descriptions. All
questionnaires were independently scored by two experimenters, who were unaware
of which group the questionnaires were from. There was 100 percent agreement on
their classification of responses.

All data were in the form of frequency counts: number of unusual experiences
per group. Therefore, all group differences were tested for significance via the
chi-square statistic. The .05 level of significance was used in all tests. When
all four groups were included in the test, χ^2, with 3 degrees of freedom, was significant if it exceeded 7.82. When the control group was omitted from the analysis, χ^2, with 2 degrees of freedom, had to exceed 5.99 for significance.

Frequency of Reports of Being Hypnotized

In the hypnosis group, 14 of the 15 participants indicated that they thought
they had been hypnotized. In contrast, only 2 persons in the meditation group, 3
persons in the progressive relaxation group, and 1 person in the control group
thought that they had been in a hypnotic state. The four groups differed significantly on this variable, $\chi^2(3) = 32.6$. This result suggests that, by and large,
the meditation, progressive relaxation, and control subjects did not view their
role as that of hypnotized subjects. In contrast, the participants in the hypnotism condition clearly saw themselves as having served in that role.

Reported Unusual Experiences: Group Totals

    Since 15 subjects in each group responded to seven queries about unusual expe-
riences, the maximum number of unusual experiences that could have been reported
by each group was 105. When each group's responses were summed across the questions, the number reported was: hypnosis = 69; meditation = 64; progressive relaxation = 70; control = 26. When all four groups were included in the data analysis, the chi square indicated significant group differences in the overall
incidence of unusual experiences, $\chi^2(3) = 50.78$.

    The raw frequency data suggested that this significant outcome may have been
due to the large discrepancy between the control group's frequency and the remaining frequencies. Indeed, when the control group's data were removed from the
analysis, the remaining treatment groups did not differ significantly from one
another, $\chi^2(2) = .86$.

Reported Unusual Experiences: Specific Queries

    Additional chi-square analyses were conducted to test for significant group
differences in the frequency with which each of the seven unusual experiences was
reported.

    The chi squares were not significant in the case of question 2 (Did you feel as
though your body or any of its parts were disappearing?), $\chi^2(3) = 3.89$, question 5
(Did you experience any changes in temperature?), $\chi^2 = 7.75$, or question 7
(Did you have any other unusual experiences that we did not ask you about?),
$\chi^2(3) = 3.75$.

    As is shown in Table 1, the treatment groups did differ significantly on the
remaining four questions, when the control group's data were included in the
analyses.

Insert Table 1 about here

It is clear that the "altered states" treatment conditions elicited a large number of reports of unusual experiences relative to the control group.

The next question to be answered was whether the three "altered states" conditions differed significantly on the frequency with which they reported any of the specific experiences. As is shown in Table 1, only question 3 (changes in equilibrium) was associated with group differences when the control group's data were not included in the analysis. Moreover, the hypnosis group gave fewer affirmative responses to that item than the other two "altered states" groups.

[*Note:* The "Discussion" section in an actual research report should begin here.]

Discussion

The results of this investigation were consistent with the stated hypothesis: that the three "altered states" treatments would not differ from one another in the number of reports of unusual experiences that they elicit, but that all three would elicit a greater number of such reports than a control condition in which subjects do not expect to enter an "altered state of consciousness."

The present outcome was in agreement with that of Barber and Calverley (cited in Barber, 1976). Their study also showed that a formal hypnotic-induction procedure is not necessary for producing a high frequency of reports of unusual experiences. This kind of result contradicts theories of hypnosis that hold that a formal hypnotic-induction procedure yields a unique "trance" state characterized by a unique pattern of conscious experience.

The results also answer a question that was raised by the Barber and Calverley experiment: Should reports of unusual experiences under hypnosis be attributed to subjects' desire to give responses that they think are expected of hypnotized subjects, or should such reports be viewed as valid accounts of phenomenological events that people experience when they expect an altered state of consciousness? Since 14 of the 15 hypnosis subjects in the present study believed they had been hypnotized, perhaps their reports could be interpreted as hypnotic role-playing. But the data of the meditation and progressive relaxation groups suggest otherwise. Although only a very small number of those subjects believed they had been hypnotized, the frequency with which they reported "unusual experiences" matched that of the hypnosis group. In light of this outcome, it is worth noting that all of the "experimental" subjects, regardless of their specific treatment, were led to expect that they would experience "altered states of consciousness." This expectation was held in common by the hypnosis, meditation, and progressive relaxation subjects but not by the control subjects. Therefore, it appears that the unusual experiences historically associated with "being

"Unusual" Experiences

12

hypnotized" will tend to be experienced under any circumstances in which people expect to have their consciousness altered.

Of course it is possible that subjects in all three of the "altered states" groups were casting themselves in the roles of hypnotized, meditating, and profoundly relaxed subjects, respectively, and were giving posttreatment reports that they thought would meet perceived expectations. But there are two lines of evidence that argue against this interpretation of the findings. The first one is the remarkable similarity in the frequency with which specific kinds of experience were reported. The three "experimental" conditions differed significantly on only one unusual experience (changes in equilibrium). If the posttreatment reports represented attempts of independent subjects to play distinct roles, one would expect a larger number of heterogeneous response patterns among the groups.

Second, the posttreatment questionnaire required subjects not only to say whether they had had a particular category of experience but also to describe that experience. In scoring the responses, the experimenters tallied a response in the unusual-experience column only if the subject was able to vividly describe the nature of that experience. Those descriptions were most often elaborate, colorful, and convincing. Since the subjects had no external incentive for taking the trouble to relate their experiences in such vivid detail, it seems most plausible that they were providing accounts of genuine experiences.

It is possible that the type of results reported here and in Barber and Calverley is restricted to the specific kinds of posttreatment questions used in both investigations. Therefore, future research in this area should focus on the effects of varying the format and content of the postexperimental assessment device.

References

Although the Reference section of your paper comes right after the Discussion section, *it should begin on a new page*. Type the word "References" at the top (center) of the page. Then, *alphabetically*, according to author's last name (see the example of a Reference section presented below), list only the references you cited in the paper. Each reference should include the following information in this order:

1. *Author's (or authors') last name(s)*, followed by first initials. For example, Barber, T. X., or Jones, H. L., & Seeveforce, T. M.

2. *The year of publication in parentheses.*

3. *The title of the book or article cited.* For example, Hypnosis: A scientific approach (book), or Repetition effects in memory (article). Note that, in each title, only the first letter of the first word is capitalized; exceptions to this practice include words that follow a colon and proper names. Also note that though the titles of books are underlined, article titles are not.

4. *Additional bibliographic data.* When referencing a book, include the city where the book was published, and the publishing company. For example, Jungs Station, Ill.: Jackson Press. When referencing a journal article, include the title of the journal, and the volume and page numbers. For example, Journal of Comparative Phrenology, 14, 377-382. Note that all nouns and descriptive adjectives in the journal title are capitalized, and that the title and the volume number are underlined.

Here are some examples of the most frequently cited types of reference:

1. Journal article (note use and placement of ampersand—&):

> Small, A. C., Hollenbeck, A. R., & Haley, R. L. (1982). The effect of emotional state on student ratings of instructors. Teaching of Psychology, 9, 205-208.

2. Book (note placement of "edition notation"):

> Hays, W. L. (1981). Statistics (3rd ed.). New York: Holt, Rinehart and Winston.

3. Chapter or article in edited book:

> Weinberg, J. (1975). Psychopathology. In J. P. Howells (Ed.), Modern perspectives in the psychiatry of old age (pp. 234-252). New York: Bruner/Mazel.

4. Chapter or article in edited multivolume document:

> Bigelow, R. (1972). The evolution of cooperation, aggression, and self-control. In J. K. Cole & D. D. Jensen (Eds.), Nebraska symposium on motivation (Vol. 20, pp. 1-57). Lincoln, Neb.: University of Nebraska Press.

Notice that, in every reference, all lines except the first one are indented three spaces from the left margin.

"Unusual" Experiences

13

References

Barber, T. X. (1976). Hypnosis: A scientific approach. New York: Psychological Dimensions.

Benson, H. (1974). Your innate asset for combating stress. Harvard Business Review, 52, 49-60.

Bernstein, D. A., & Borkovec, T. D. (1973). Progressive relaxation training: A manual for the helping professions. Champaign, Ill.: Research Press.

Bramwell, J. M. (1903). Hypnotism. London: Grant Richards.

Gill, M. M., & Brenman, M. (1959). Hypnosis and related states. New York: International University Press.

Hilgard, E. R. (1965). Hypnotic susceptibility. New York: Harcourt, Brace, & World.

Tables

Data tables may be used to summarize a lot of data in a small space. The chief purpose of a table is to allow the reader to quickly and conveniently compare the results of different treatments or the effects of different variables.

Tables should supplement your Results section, not restate the information already present in that section. If you include data tables in your report, be sure to refer to them by number (e.g., Table 1, Table 2, etc.) as you describe the outcomes that they contain (see example on page 394).

It requires a fair degree of skill to construct a table properly, and often you will need to go through several drafts before you get it right. Some essential format considerations to remember are:

- Each table must be constructed on a *separate page of the report*, and the pages should be numbered consecutively as continuations of the body of the report. For example, if your references end on page 20, then the first table would appear on page 21.
- Each table must have a heading that briefly describes its contents. The heading should be centered and double-spaced.
- All lines of type in the table should be double-spaced, and the table, as a configuration, should be centered on the page.
- Column and row headings in the table should clearly indicate the treatment conditions and/or variables they represent.

Figures

Graphs, such as those presented in Chapter 6, are another way of presenting data in a research report. These pictorial representations of your results are referred to as "figures" in the text of the Results section and are numbered consecutively (e.g., Figure 1, Figure 2, etc.). If you wish to use figures, follow the guidelines of graph construction given in Chapter 6. Use the horizontal axis to represent the independent variable (X) and the vertical axis to represent the dependent variable (Y). Using permanent black ink, make all lines and markings "heavy," and set labels and descriptions of variables with some brand of press-on lettering. Each figure must be presented on its own page.

TECHNICAL MATTERS

Headings

The use of headings and subheadings in scientific manuscripts both clarifies the organization of the report and facilitates the reader's understanding of the material. You should employ two or three levels of headings, depending on the complexity of the report.

A manuscript that requires only two levels of headings, such as the sample report in this chapter, contains *main headings and side headings*. For example:

Method

Subjects

Table 1

Frequency of Subjects' Responding "Yes" to Each of Four

Questions Regarding Altered States of Consciousness, and

Results of Chi-Square Analyses of the Frequencies

	Question #			
Group	1	3	4	6
Hypnosis	11	8	9	13
Meditation	8	11	13	10
Progressive R.	7	15	11	11
Control	1	4	2	2

	Question #			
Statistic	1	3	4	6
$\chi^2(df = 3)^a$	14.21^c	18.66^c	11.28^c	19.45^c
$\chi^2(df = 2)^b$	2.37	8.97^c	4.20	1.69

[a]Control group included in the chi square

[b]Control group not included in the chi square

[c]Significant at the .05 level

Notice that the headings are capitalized and underlined. The main heading (Method) is centered, and the side heading (Subjects) is flush with the left margin.

The third level of headings is the *paragraph heading*. It is used whenever a side-heading topic needs to be subdivided. Paragraph headings are indented five spaces. They are underlined and end with a period. Only the first word is capitalized. For example, the side heading "Subjects" might be follow by:

<u>Subject sample 1</u>. The first sample was randomly drawn from . . . etc.

<u>Subject sample 2</u>. The second sample consisted of volunteers

from . . . etc.

Units of Measurement

The growing trend in scientific writing is to express physical measurements—e.g., weight, length—in metric units. In fact, most scientific periodicals either presently require use of the metric system or are moving in that direction. Thus, if your initial measurements are in U.S. Customary Units (e.g., ounces, inches), you should obtain a measurement-unit conversion table and determine the metric equivalents (e.g., grams, centimeters). Most standard dictionaries provide such information.

Numbers

In the text of your paper, numbers should be expressed in *figures* rather than words—for instance, "15" rather than "fifteen"—when the numbers are 10 or larger. Numbers from zero to nine should be expressed as words. There are many exceptions to this convention, however. For example, you should always use a word to represent a number that starts a sentence. The other exceptions may be found in the APA *Publication Manual*.

SUMMARY

Because science is a collective, "public" enterprise, scientists have a responsibility to share their research efforts and findings with one another. The research report is the preferred medium for doing this. To be suitable for presentation to the scientific community, however, a research report must meet several content, stylistic, and format criteria.

A scientific manuscript should be a succinct, accurate, and scholarly history of a study you have conducted. It must be objectively informative rather than primarily entertaining. Most research reports in the field of psychology follow the stylistic and format guidelines recommended in the *Publication Manual of the American Psychological Association*. Many of those guidelines were described and illustrated in this chapter.

Most research reports that are written in "APA format" are organized according to the following structure:

1. Title Page
2. Abstract
3. Introduction

4. Method Section
5. Results Section
6. Discussion Section
7. References
8. Tables (if any)
9. Figures (if any)

APPENDIX
STATISTICAL TABLES

TABLE A–1
ARRAY OF 7000 RANDOM DIGITS

The numbers in Table A–1 (pp. 000–000) were generated entirely on the basis of a random process. There is no predictable pattern to be found in them. The random sequences in these numbers are useful when you wish to randomly assign subjects to experimental conditions or stimulus sequences, and when you desire to randomly select a sample of subjects from some population.

Note that *you may arbitrarily assign any denomination to sequences of these random digits*. For example, consider the digits in *Row 0* of *Field 0*: 38 26 12 12 04. Each digit (e.g., 4) may stand by itself in the case where you are assigning 10 or fewer subjects to experimental conditions. Or the digits may be paired up (from 00 to 99) when you have up to 100 subjects to assign. If you are randomly selecting subjects from a population of, say, 10,000 people, then the digits could be combined to form numbers from 0000 to 9999 (e.g., 3826, 1212, etc.). The main consideration in using the table is to start at some arbitrary point and then move in any direction (horizontally, vertically, or diagonally), until all subjects have been assigned or selected. When you get to the beginning, end, or edge of the table, resume the process at some other arbitrarily selected point.

Instructions for Randomly Assigning Subjects to Conditions

1. List your experimental sessions by date and time; let's suppose that you have 60 sessions to run, altogether.
2. Plan on dividing the total number of sessions into an equal number of sessions for each treatment; let's say you have three treatments, so 20 sessions would be assigned to each treatment.
3. Using the table of random digits, assign random numbers to each of the 60 sessions.
4. Consider the 20 sessions with the lowest numbers to be Treatment 1 sessions; the 20 sessions with the highest numbers to be Treatment 3 sessions; the remaining 20 sessions to be Treatment 2 sessions.
5. As subjects arrive for their research participation, assign each to the treatment that was randomly attached to his or her session.

Instructions for Simple Random Sampling

1. Assign a random number to each sampling unit (usually a person) in your sampling frame (see Chapter 12).
2. If you need to draw a sample of, say, 200 units, select either the 200 units with the lowest numbers or the 200 units having the highest numbers.

TABLE A–1

Array of 7000 Random Digits

Row	Field 0	Field 1	Field 2	Field 3
000	38 26 12 12 04	89 66 62 07 35	04 90 90 46 10	71 70 58 41 19
001	80 70 88 33 76	17 46 14 87 84	27 27 68 40 15	66 07 75 45 55
002	57 65 22 01 29	93 95 40 94 32	45 52 51 12 08	58 09 24 56 98
003	05 73 99 86 34	43 89 39 97 96	86 58 79 90 39	04 10 55 84 69
004	25 55 16 81 74	48 63 02 30 20	60 54 59 16 78	35 02 22 29 28
005	32 04 02 18 31	85 55 99 38 46	29 70 54 20 52	66 30 30 13 24
006	73 25 58 86 09	48 21 59 03 86	96 46 80 63 93	77 22 64 34 56
007	28 17 17 93 36	27 89 16 69 54	17 98 32 18 63	74 48 33 38 54
008	29 48 14 09 25	97 03 71 22 59	03 37 59 84 19	88 47 48 44 89
009	07 50 52 63 35	00 67 39 47 39	17 26 80 89 10	48 18 58 67 03
010	34 03 45 28 16	45 72 97 46 38	64 02 36 16 55	08 23 28 82 33
011	22 52 73 66 72	04 67 11 41 43	80 95 10 95 40	89 62 81 39 86
012	71 94 37 30 93	21 85 02 36 56	32 38 46 24 05	32 39 14 22 73
013	29 62 61 20 81	24 92 24 39 12	14 19 43 51 64	36 45 12 01 80
014	77 13 60 06 62	28 55 61 43 12	25 08 78 58 36	68 42 91 57 58
015	18 68 22 69 79	21 11 10 77 17	85 86 29 27 62	64 57 73 42 78
016	83 25 17 51 80	21 39 61 17 88	49 77 53 70 11	74 98 51 29 29
017	50 15 40 70 42	58 56 67 20 61	67 59 13 45 31	56 20 88 98 32
018	26 30 27 96 02	03 33 41 70 70	53 14 01 18 53	19 07 98 95 86
019	07 67 57 35 03	28 76 19 05 79	56 27 99 87 21	82 83 62 48 45
020	04 85 50 36 86	49 51 83 92 12	68 73 65 68 03	80 92 47 91 33
021	53 65 91 33 34	83 93 35 27 32	54 05 28 64 69	54 25 86 94 51
022	12 82 20 80 46	25 77 95 37 25	79 85 47 17 67	97 55 73 54 54
023	09 30 31 63 38	34 92 22 68 60	33 70 16 28 07	17 11 48 14 04
024	80 50 57 87 10	71 64 68 96 91	92 25 65 20 20	48 10 29 23 01
025	26 40 37 02 69	40 83 59 45 21	68 46 02 18 96	21 16 75 81 28
026	45 94 21 29 36	25 68 84 68 00	51 37 89 52 23	47 80 43 07 89
027	87 04 08 62 64	56 64 93 39 81	79 89 23 99 19	48 79 21 90 35
028	10 81 75 44 02	07 13 68 66 41	60 03 30 36 80	97 11 65 68 27
029	01 80 82 55 22	90 54 90 73 85	67 26 76 45 90	79 58 46 00 45
030	85 94 45 70 02	66 21 40 28 63	80 23 46 77 43	74 71 60 92 62
031	74 27 64 72 73	09 87 86 05 56	38 51 39 73 52	53 96 29 86 34
032	19 59 19 18 38	86 26 05 29 87	04 01 16 55 49	68 02 76 13 40
033	16 82 99 81 16	58 45 68 31 20	17 67 43 77 56	22 15 09 47 25
034	59 38 38 79 29	91 74 64 74 38	06 45 54 44 43	42 08 22 92 76
035	72 02 41 68 15	50 46 17 86 93	29 84 08 13 30	65 42 40 43 69
036	05 54 39 44 06	25 88 38 98 91	02 50 37 03 81	48 37 18 62 91
037	95 36 83 46 91	51 06 83 39 25	19 68 92 09 55	55 43 61 09 01
038	30 94 06 22 46	01 54 86 96 52	66 59 58 46 09	76 69 83 87 19
039	47 22 08 20 58	12 94 15 95 02	58 48 95 34 70	47 34 49 08 02
040	75 58 41 39 75	96 32 54 47 16	92 45 72 94 36	78 76 31 86 15
041	93 73 93 33 25	31 44 03 39 56	57 43 01 53 53	91 27 03 67 55
042	05 72 24 59 59	96 66 92 83 00	91 85 07 57 18	84 18 46 21 95
043	46 61 84 12 63	71 28 89 68 11	82 02 88 97 58	31 89 69 65 60
044	48 99 52 72 25	49 55 26 08 09	73 47 35 41 63	43 88 91 41 22

Row	Field 0	Field 1	Field 2	Field 3
045	69 03 92 44 18	57 52 45 33 58	08 02 95 66 06	93 29 85 74 35
046	58 62 03 68 72	19 98 61 66 98	02 80 04 48 06	10 28 45 41 70
047	52 17 07 38 45	83 67 69 42 61	02 28 82 08 31	51 36 43 38 92
048	11 83 95 24 47	91 73 29 10 66	67 75 39 42 97	61 93 07 05 57
049	82 89 29 90 95	69 09 19 44 58	47 98 44 13 96	61 00 85 89 96
050	04 39 43 28 57	94 08 72 84 70	99 08 07 89 37	69 49 06 51 42
051	39 91 99 25 36	71 93 72 18 99	89 69 33 27 85	78 19 06 35 38
052	40 96 16 45 23	76 89 32 96 37	31 03 08 40 63	21 33 41 87 60
053	67 77 54 28 93	05 91 45 92 21	61 09 79 12 45	62 05 90 32 31
054	52 45 64 19 62	46 72 06 09 05	36 20 03 13 53	54 71 99 83 72
055	74 24 43 30 50	31 14 82 66 01	67 64 53 59 66	49 01 58 78 07
056	92 75 87 26 61	18 23 69 17 90	18 60 53 98 49	85 28 34 59 88
057	57 14 66 13 25	04 76 67 23 09	98 54 55 29 51	01 64 45 79 61
058	08 51 27 93 47	78 96 71 43 07	61 47 50 74 95	18 31 81 94 37
059	68 35 63 58 38	57 65 45 96 08	84 57 39 20 23	67 35 72 33 37
060	96 40 07 24 92	09 27 80 58 04	71 04 12 30 33	38 47 35 20 27
061	56 71 47 99 72	80 80 24 00 16	73 63 84 01 89	68 57 31 65 19
062	53 94 23 20 37	86 34 71 66 76	61 15 55 16 04	41 69 23 44 11
063	61 25 62 63 34	85 90 08 87 90	25 84 81 07 34	36 96 99 85 54
064	58 14 29 15 78	12 23 40 96 81	92 94 04 52 12	19 18 43 59 26
065	56 46 52 90 54	44 88 55 77 99	30 06 79 48 64	27 39 62 19 97
066	61 49 19 16 57	41 28 89 20 32	80 89 64 91 52	79 44 17 30 06
067	16 56 78 44 89	39 93 37 56 73	08 25 12 87 37	55 83 87 49 73
068	03 82 35 09 69	18 21 07 22 81	52 27 40 20 33	81 66 92 18 88
069	90 50 13 49 17	46 98 35 29 06	33 16 98 44 83	09 91 16 89 21
070	41 73 86 46 30	66 09 83 69 40	69 63 28 00 31	51 50 46 09 89
071	59 23 61 71 16	70 36 24 53 24	36 51 61 42 63	70 65 94 44 67
072	36 98 07 09 44	92 15 67 69 37	37 67 65 99 31	42 34 83 41 89
073	64 89 69 78 81	60 51 01 88 91	67 29 19 68 01	57 10 46 93 58
074	77 93 63 90 70	83 74 81 64 15	51 29 45 80 93	59 60 67 15 60
075	66 51 81 88 40	40 50 38 24 44	90 77 06 59 58	73 71 11 07 72
076	48 64 73 11 01	20 40 55 13 08	37 35 33 45 46	09 90 83 17 60
077	71 71 93 52 93	95 28 09 97 22	95 71 31 55 78	66 57 87 19 85
078	82 79 61 50 29	21 54 66 31 24	94 49 93 39 02	52 70 36 52 82
079	97 75 87 50 27	55 09 44 90 86	62 18 63 70 70	77 72 51 51 07
080	78 14 78 78 24	46 40 36 07 42	08 80 80 29 61	67 23 91 07 89
081	72 67 16 90 76	72 86 80 64 29	55 87 51 62 52	24 32 99 26 53
082	11 65 42 34 85	62 26 36 67 87	66 45 17 86 40	56 82 97 72 28
083	21 16 66 63 89	87 57 76 23 23	32 25 59 47 13	72 44 37 22 45
084	65 28 72 01 23	80 03 59 83 07	57 15 84 93 41	18 26 92 18 21
085	42 95 82 52 57	29 26 74 03 82	78 28 85 90 00	03 32 39 66 73
086	71 85 94 66 98	51 11 53 45 41	22 34 82 83 59	98 78 75 45 37
087	65 08 61 46 05	94 10 01 44 38	10 51 44 13 77	45 42 38 96 26
088	77 35 50 51 57	39 41 27 45 31	39 03 50 39 71	11 39 45 95 76
089	22 31 72 23 14	35 88 41 67 70	46 22 63 35 37	63 07 19 05 18
090	59 10 81 87 92	10 63 86 08 58	68 36 72 85 45	55 73 63 88 24
091	53 25 13 79 50	93 05 90 45 27	21 26 68 38 02	77 21 50 76 35
092	25 65 36 73 89	59 03 78 81 13	56 41 04 22 63	33 08 68 29 48
093	17 35 40 66 89	46 29 19 82 90	44 73 09 17 08	96 27 66 38 98
094	87 70 95 56 82	34 71 36 60 13	92 09 95 55 92	16 39 15 55 09

Row	Field 0	Field 1	Field 2	Field 3
095	26 93 64 29 23	54 67 05 13 68	05 65 37 23 58	89 15 47 36 57
096	84 03 03 80 99	14 58 20 19 99	96 37 22 69 02	81 06 92 81 82
097	57 91 69 20 29	85 47 75 79 34	61 20 26 50 93	16 97 22 83 48
098	27 95 43 04 21	86 49 88 17 02	82 36 87 90 60	97 94 11 59 53
099	21 84 10 91 20	16 34 75 43 53	02 99 02 33 14	83 61 40 64 33
100	37 36 95 90 53	79 97 63 43 74	11 15 34 80 06	38 94 35 85 33
101	96 20 02 72 50	29 70 59 50 83	74 19 74 96 90	94 17 04 23 06
102	66 67 64 17 02	18 89 61 21 61	20 37 35 22 22	52 09 92 67 71
103	67 10 19 55 24	39 09 22 30 66	94 41 81 43 74	12 10 52 71 08
104	55 87 63 70 85	70 15 02 81 16	52 67 63 84 19	15 33 31 41 46
105	82 60 66 35 68	79 63 32 14 41	38 00 11 72 48	10 06 02 18 13
106	18 18 14 68 28	89 37 81 48 54	61 69 64 10 39	86 51 83 51 53
107	32 71 57 70 01	01 47 70 97 58	62 16 41 11 05	55 91 49 97 53
108	06 22 26 02 11	11 38 31 58 68	08 81 69 01 12	22 22 52 66 66
109	08 92 82 02 57	06 14 13 14 25	39 91 59 26 88	14 87 06 05 29
110	28 57 06 77 00	59 57 05 94 97	42 82 99 89 85	79 30 89 55 64
111	80 20 44 80 40	46 70 61 50 42	04 64 36 05 53	96 23 21 08 19
112	80 54 85 43 53	44 43 65 46 84	29 36 99 17 30	27 63 53 78 31
113	01 26 88 38 10	37 28 58 99 58	98 00 11 11 39	61 54 08 40 25
114	75 52 43 73 96	26 99 79 68 11	48 26 92 46 46	39 66 89 97 95
115	14 18 53 25 89	89 45 28 72 12	22 45 57 50 20	25 25 20 24 28
116	71 97 11 27 14	17 93 93 44 06	63 23 54 91 75	31 18 05 89 06
117	79 56 01 61 35	50 88 93 22 56	92 57 13 74 62	28 96 70 67 62
118	10 90 24 23 48	96 19 22 92 06	37 82 88 16 33	80 42 27 83 66
119	98 43 63 74 49	80 26 62 32 40	78 66 09 69 91	41 21 37 80 57
120	06 99 50 34 45	31 19 96 46 99	27 96 05 02 20	46 58 85 38 11
121	40 04 53 40 54	71 97 24 39 09	07 97 53 60 00	34 21 39 06 97
122	62 57 89 21 98	00 38 82 51 28	64 39 71 14 35	31 57 98 99 17
123	91 66 03 07 10	73 05 38 96 10	71 21 70 35 12	81 69 80 73 95
124	06 64 44 77 37	16 04 10 15 95	94 90 93 88 21	71 03 23 80 87
125	70 13 81 06 84	07 88 14 16 01	15 04 14 86 94	80 48 04 07 66
126	89 08 04 90 90	23 59 88 46 45	94 91 18 04 43	85 82 86 13 82
127	35 29 28 61 60	84 81 39 79 94	63 97 46 27 68	56 72 41 95 75
128	43 70 43 60 91	97 78 95 94 82	62 21 66 63 02	66 84 88 87 76
129	02 01 19 19 06	82 97 52 87 01	78 69 37 72 95	87 54 11 12 36
130	24 04 33 99 91	34 19 10 81 73	48 56 83 57 01	42 84 32 18 25
131	55 54 50 32 74	47 44 05 56 95	88 24 19 82 33	02 47 73 88 30
132	71 52 89 63 39	67 33 28 87 90	89 24 81 16 92	11 16 24 99 96
133	88 26 27 12 56	84 41 50 35 13	50 64 89 46 44	75 38 67 36 04
134	37 84 12 88 89	09 07 72 59 27	09 44 77 90 49	54 09 03 71 99
135	76 68 42 12 57	60 47 12 62 49	02 36 63 31 33	13 86 45 77 70
136	48 44 59 90 57	54 39 71 24 07	10 48 01 22 27	42 31 14 39 69
137	93 46 67 70 73	37 21 88 27 97	79 08 55 26 51	27 07 47 36 37
138	38 50 06 44 40	64 33 23 86 24	80 27 75 05 30	55 86 83 52 33
139	89 04 08 40 95	85 03 12 96 44	06 98 56 82 50	52 12 22 45 26
140	35 73 73 38 52	91 69 47 26 92	30 47 63 02 80	16 13 99 03 38
141	63 34 16 01 62	05 26 14 66 75	71 99 77 92 42	92 43 59 48 44
142	62 13 52 08 28	16 42 18 02 84	90 54 79 13 62	31 12 12 07 72
143	82 14 90 49 94	58 51 68 83 24	91 40 16 37 87	52 51 88 14 70
144	08 56 78 15 69	41 17 59 55 92	23 11 32 50 89	15 06 67 69 93

Row	Field 0	Field 1	Field 2	Field 3
145	18 24 58 03 19	79 10 67 10 13	26 08 03 01 40	85 92 74 65 84
146	84 31 16 28 85	12 96 40 82 09	65 89 71 13 27	90 51 31 29 68
147	57 93 36 97 90	76 58 23 88 01	71 86 19 41 91	47 22 71 20 26
148	86 74 16 31 52	34 12 74 07 44	15 14 92 45 69	03 93 23 90 75
149	39 23 29 90 23	97 58 53 73 12	34 71 27 26 60	28 82 89 46 02
150	39 42 42 86 66	40 46 41 60 89	69 89 94 66 33	43 14 14 95 73
151	90 03 84 68 47	88 62 01 66 43	15 58 25 55 78	45 46 10 10 67
152	30 24 23 68 90	58 26 98 69 82	75 67 89 38 28	71 52 08 64 27
153	63 89 36 63 53	33 09 81 19 78	06 48 29 02 79	12 79 87 41 30
154	84 69 67 91 81	88 10 18 30 81	74 46 87 42 70	37 21 09 50 29
155	57 78 68 11 41	45 63 42 33 54	60 59 92 80 01	55 29 47 07 66
156	45 35 84 06 66	26 50 14 82 09	22 37 88 13 71	87 10 28 90 62
157	47 23 15 57 97	13 26 40 60 64	82 15 46 05 01	99 87 61 47 86
158	56 25 89 77 66	74 40 47 56 53	58 12 23 98 57	96 79 13 10 56
159	93 23 82 04 49	61 65 13 90 98	34 80 68 61 94	09 65 43 10 43
160	93 44 54 15 46	71 50 27 03 16	96 61 82 46 09	77 75 08 02 40
161	76 63 24 99 96	11 35 63 89 72	19 10 87 57 22	97 36 16 69 20
162	33 56 96 74 77	75 31 18 24 44	27 97 88 51 64	30 99 28 79 82
163	79 00 04 35 80	73 51 57 86 55	04 21 86 55 69	48 25 69 81 42
164	92 36 59 50 81	28 56 01 03 70	70 41 37 21 90	39 14 50 42 01
165	14 80 97 50 27	13 20 79 49 81	87 66 95 82 57	36 80 85 58 89
166	99 98 68 60 61	26 17 25 86 32	09 23 29 48 95	47 53 04 99 35
167	97 71 58 47 41	79 66 96 44 55	53 41 06 38 03	00 25 03 29 74
168	53 52 16 53 54	95 28 72 24 58	99 52 55 68 42	31 61 56 96 03
169	50 15 68 40 38	14 52 52 71 90	19 73 02 81 35	62 96 75 37 57
170	00 70 06 65 70	51 70 54 30 98	85 64 97 77 71	69 05 89 43 61
171	33 20 31 28 13	10 48 09 91 61	89 96 70 03 76	61 67 56 36 84
172	60 18 45 74 17	17 07 59 96 27	28 51 46 18 90	91 72 50 90 16
173	52 83 70 69 06	72 30 11 32 66	72 05 30 88 38	65 26 84 59 13
174	03 09 42 53 88	08 57 17 54 99	10 73 09 45 40	50 93 74 57 82

TABLE A–2

Critical Values of Chi Square

	Level of Significance		
Degrees of Freedom	*.10*	*.05*	*.01*
1	2.706	3.841	6.635
2	4.605	5.991	9.210
3	6.251	7.815	11.341
4	7.779	9.488	13.277
5	9.236	11.070	15.086
6	10.645	12.592	16.812
7	12.017	14.067	18.475
8	13.362	15.507	20.090
9	14.684	16.919	21.666
10	15.987	18.307	23.209
11	17.275	19.675	24.725
12	18.549	21.026	26.217
13	19.812	22.362	27.688
14	21.064	23.685	29.141
15	22.307	24.996	30.578
16	23.542	26.296	32.000
17	24.769	27.587	33.409
18	25.989	28.869	34.805
19	27.204	30.144	36.191
20	28.412	31.410	37.566
21	29.615	32.671	38.932
22	30.813	33.924	40.289
23	32.007	35.172	41.638
24	33.196	36.415	42.980
25	34.382	37.652	44.314

SOURCE: Adapted and abridged from Table IV of *Statistical Tables for Biological, Agricultural and Medical Research* by R.A. Fisher and F. Yates (Edinburgh: Oliver & Boyd, 1938). Reprinted by permission of authors and publisher.

TABLE A-3

Critical Values of the Pearson r at the 5% and 1% Levels of Significance

Degrees of Freedom	5%	1%	Degrees of Freedom	5%	1%
1	.997	1.000	16	.468	.590
2	.950	.990	17	.456	.575
3	.878	.959	18	.444	.561
4	.811	.917	19	.433	.549
5	.755	.875	20	.423	.537
6	.707	.834	25	.381	.487
7	.666	.798	30	.349	.449
8	.632	.765	35	.325	.418
9	.602	.735	40	.304	.393
10	.576	.708	45	.288	.372
11	.553	.684	50	.273	.354
12	.532	.661	60	.250	.325
13	.514	.641	70	.232	.302
14	.497	.623	80	.217	.283
15	.482	.606	90	.205	.267
			100	.195	.254

Note: Degrees of freedom = $(n - 2)$, where n is the number of ordered pairs in the sample.

Source: Adapted and abridged from Table VI of *Statistical Tables for Biological, Agricultural and Medical Research* by R.A. Fisher and F. Yates (Edinburgh: Oliver & Boyd, 1938). Reprinted by permission of authors and publisher.

TABLE A-4

Critical Values of the F Ratio

					.05 Level of Significance					
df1 df2	1	2	3	4	5	6	7	8	9	10
1	161.4	199.5	215.7	224.6	230.2	234.0	236.8	238.9	240.5	242.9
2	18.51	19.00	19.16	19.25	19.30	19.33	19.35	19.37	19.38	19.40
3	10.31	9.55	9.28	9.12	9.01	8.94	8.89	8.85	8.81	8.79
4	7.71	6.94	6.59	6.39	6.26	6.16	6.09	6.04	6.00	5.96
5	6.61	5.79	5.41	5.19	5.05	4.95	4.88	4.82	4.77	4.74
6	5.99	5.14	4.76	4.53	4.39	4.28	4.21	4.15	4.10	4.06
7	5.59	4.74	4.35	4.12	3.97	3.87	3.79	3.73	3.68	3.64
8	5.32	4.46	4.07	3.84	3.69	3.58	3.50	3.44	3.39	3.35
9	5.12	4.26	3.86	3.63	3.48	3.37	3.29	3.23	3.18	3.14
10	4.96	4.10	3.71	3.48	3.33	3.22	3.14	3.07	3.02	2.98
11	4.84	3.98	3.59	3.36	3.20	3.09	3.01	2.95	2.90	2.85
12	4.75	3.89	3.49	3.26	3.11	3.00	2.91	2.85	2.80	2.75
13	4.67	3.81	3.41	3.18	3.03	2.92	2.83	2.77	2.71	2.67
14	4.60	3.74	3.34	3.11	2.96	2.85	2.76	2.70	2.65	2.60
15	4.54	3.68	3.29	3.06	2.90	2.79	2.71	2.64	2.59	2.54
16	4.49	3.63	3.24	3.01	2.85	2.74	2.66	2.59	2.54	2.49
17	4.45	3.59	3.20	2.96	2.81	2.70	2.61	2.55	2.49	2.45
18	4.41	3.55	3.16	2.93	2.77	2.66	2.58	2.51	2.46	2.41
19	4.38	3.52	3.13	2.90	2.74	2.63	2.54	2.48	2.42	2.38
20	4.35	3.49	3.10	2.87	2.71	2.60	2.51	2.45	2.39	2.35
21	4.32	3.47	3.07	2.84	2.68	2.57	2.49	2.42	2.37	2.32
22	4.30	3.44	3.05	2.82	2.66	2.55	2.46	2.40	2.34	2.30
23	4.28	3.42	3.03	2.80	2.64	2.53	2.44	3.37	2.32	2.27
24	4.26	3.40	3.01	2.78	2.62	2.51	2.42	2.36	2.30	2.25
25	4.24	3.39	2.99	2.76	2.60	2.49	2.40	2.34	2.28	2.24
26	4.23	3.37	2.98	2.74	2.59	2.47	2.39	2.32	2.27	2.22
27	4.21	3.35	2.96	2.73	2.57	2.46	2.37	2.31	2.25	2.20
28	4.20	3.34	2.95	2.71	2.56	2.45	2.36	2.29	2.24	2.19
29	4.18	3.33	2.93	2.70	2.55	2.43	2.35	2.28	2.22	2.18
30	4.17	3.32	2.92	2.69	2.53	2.42	2.33	2.27	2.21	2.16
40	4.08	3.23	2.84	2.61	2.45	2.34	2.25	2.18	2.12	2.08
60	4.00	3.15	2.76	2.53	2.37	2.25	2.17	2.10	2.04	1.99
120	3.92	3.07	2.68	2.45	2.29	2.17	2.09	2.02	1.96	1.91
∞	3.84	3.00	2.60	2.37	2.21	2.10	2.01	1.94	1.88	1.83

					.01 Level of Significance					
df1 df2	1	2	3	4	5	6	7	8	9	10
1	4052	4999.5	5403	5625	5764	5859	5928	5981	6022	6056
2	98.50	99.00	99.17	99.25	99.30	99.33	99.36	99.37	99.39	99.40
3	34.12	30.82	29.46	28.71	28.24	27.91	27.67	27.49	27.35	27.23
4	21.20	18.00	16.69	15.98	15.52	15.21	14.98	14.80	14.66	14.55
5	16.26	13.27	12.06	11.39	10.97	10.67	10.46	10.29	10.16	10.05
6	13.75	10.92	9.78	9.15	8.75	8.47	8.26	8.10	7.98	7.87

					.01 Level of Significance					
df1 df2	1	2	3	4	5	6	7	8	9	10
7	12.25	9.55	8.45	7.85	7.46	7.19	6.99	6.84	6.72	6.62
8	11.26	8.65	7.59	7.01	6.63	6.37	6.18	6.03	5.91	5.81
9	10.56	8.02	6.99	6.42	6.06	5.80	5.61	5.47	5.35	5.26
10	10.04	7.56	6.55	5.99	5.64	5.39	5.20	5.06	4.94	4.85
11	9.65	7.21	6.22	5.67	5.32	5.07	4.89	4.74	4.63	4.54
12	9.33	6.93	5.95	5.41	5.06	4.82	4.64	4.50	4.39	4.30
13	9.07	6.70	5.74	5.21	4.86	4.62	4.44	4.30	4.19	4.10
14	8.86	6.51	5.56	5.04	4.69	4.46	4.28	4.14	4.03	3.94
15	8.68	6.36	5.42	4.89	4.56	4.32	4.14	4.00	3.89	3.80
16	8.53	6.23	5.29	4.77	4.44	4.20	4.03	3.89	3.78	3.69
17	8.40	6.11	5.18	4.67	4.34	4.10	3.93	3.79	3.68	3.59
18	8.29	6.01	5.09	4.58	4.25	4.01	3.84	3.71	3.60	3.51
19	8.18	5.93	5.01	4.50	4.17	3.94	3.77	3.63	3.52	3.43
20	8.10	5.85	4.94	4.43	4.10	3.87	3.70	3.56	3.46	3.37
21	8.02	5.78	4.87	4.37	4.04	3.81	3.64	3.51	3.40	3.31
22	7.95	5.72	4.82	4.31	3.99	3.76	3.59	3.45	3.35	3.26
23	7.88	5.66	4.76	4.26	3.94	3.71	3.54	3.41	3.30	3.21
24	7.82	5.61	4.72	4.22	3.90	3.67	3.50	3.36	3.26	3.17
25	7.77	5.57	4.68	4.18	3.85	3.63	3.46	3.32	3.22	3.13
26	7.72	5.53	4.64	4.14	3.82	3.59	3.42	3.29	3.18	3.09
27	7.68	5.49	4.60	4.11	3.78	3.56	3.39	3.26	3.15	3.06
28	7.64	5.45	4.57	4.07	3.75	3.53	3.36	3.23	3.12	3.03
29	7.60	5.42	4.54	4.04	3.73	3.50	3.33	3.20	3.09	3.00
30	7.56	5.39	4.51	4.02	3.70	3.47	3.30	3.17	3.07	2.98
40	7.31	5.18	4.31	3.83	3.51	3.29	3.12	2.99	2.89	2.80
60	7.08	4.98	4.13	3.65	3.34	3.12	2.95	2.82	2.72	2.63
120	6.85	4.79	3.95	3.48	3.17	2.96	2.79	2.66	2.56	2.47
∞	6.63	4.61	3.78	3.32	3.02	2.80	2.64	2.51	2.41	2.32

Note: df1 = degrees of freedom for the numerator of the F ratio.
       df2 = degrees of freedom for the denominator of the F ratio.

SOURCE: Adapted and abridged from Table 18 of *Biometrika Tables for Statisticians*, Vol. 1 (3rd ed.), edited by E. S. Pearson and H. O. Hartley. Reproduced with the permission of E. S. Pearson and the trustees of *Biometrika*.

TABLE A–5

Critical "q" Statistics for the Tukey HSD Test: Percentage Points of the Studentized Range

Error df	α	\(k = \) Number of Means Being Compared									
		2	3	4	5	6	7	8	9	10	11
5	.05	3.64	4.60	5.22	5.67	6.03	6.33	6.58	6.80	6.99	7.17
	.01	5.70	6.98	7.80	8.42	8.91	9.32	9.67	9.97	10.24	10.48
6	.05	3.46	4.34	4.90	5.30	5.63	5.90	6.12	6.32	6.49	6.65
	.01	5.24	6.33	7.03	7.56	7.97	8.32	8.61	8.87	9.10	9.30
7	.05	3.34	4.16	4.68	5.06	5.36	5.61	5.82	6.00	6.16	6.30
	.01	4.95	5.92	6.54	7.01	7.37	7.68	7.94	8.17	8.37	8.55
8	.05	3.26	4.04	4.53	4.89	5.17	5.40	5.60	5.77	5.92	6.05
	.01	4.75	5.64	6.20	6.62	6.96	7.24	7.47	7.68	7.86	8.03
9	.05	3.20	3.95	4.41	4.76	5.02	5.24	5.43	5.59	5.74	5.87
	.01	4.60	5.43	5.96	6.35	6.66	6.91	7.13	7.33	7.49	7.65
10	.05	3.15	3.88	4.33	4.65	4.91	5.12	5.30	5.46	5.60	5.72
	.01	4.48	5.27	5.77	6.14	6.43	6.67	6.87	7.05	7.21	7.36
11	.05	3.11	3.82	4.26	4.57	4.82	5.03	5.20	5.35	5.49	5.61
	.01	4.39	5.15	5.62	5.97	6.25	6.48	6.67	6.84	6.99	7.13
12	.05	3.08	3.77	4.20	4.51	4.75	4.95	5.12	5.27	5.39	5.51
	.01	4.32	5.05	5.50	5.84	6.10	6.32	6.51	6.67	6.81	6.94
13	.05	3.06	3.73	4.15	4.45	4.69	4.88	5.05	5.19	5.32	5.43
	.01	4.26	4.96	5.40	5.73	5.98	6.19	6.37	6.53	6.67	6.79
14	.05	3.03	3.70	4.11	4.41	4.64	4.83	4.99	5.13	5.25	5.36
	.01	4.21	4.89	5.32	5.63	5.88	6.08	6.26	6.41	6.54	6.66
15	.05	3.01	3.67	4.08	4.37	4.59	4.78	4.94	5.08	5.20	5.31
	.01	4.17	4.84	5.25	5.56	5.80	5.99	6.16	6.31	6.44	6.55
16	.05	3.00	3.65	4.05	4.33	4.56	4.74	4.90	5.03	5.15	5.26
	.01	4.13	4.79	5.19	5.49	5.72	5.92	6.08	6.22	6.35	6.46
17	.05	2.98	3.63	4.02	4.30	4.52	4.70	4.86	4.99	5.11	5.21
	.01	4.10	4.74	5.14	5.43	5.66	5.85	6.01	6.15	6.27	6.38
18	.05	2.97	3.61	4.00	4.28	4.49	4.67	4.82	4.96	5.07	5.17
	.01	4.07	4.70	5.09	5.38	5.60	5.79	5.94	6.08	6.20	6.31
19	.05	2.96	3.59	3.98	4.25	4.47	4.65	4.79	4.92	5.04	5.14
	.01	4.05	4.67	5.05	5.33	5.55	5.73	5.89	6.02	6.14	6.25
20	.05	2.95	3.58	3.96	4.23	4.45	4.62	4.77	4.90	5.01	5.11
	.01	4.02	4.64	5.02	5.29	5.51	5.69	5.84	5.97	6.09	6.19
24	.05	2.92	3.53	3.90	4.17	4.37	4.54	4.68	4.81	4.92	5.01
	.01	3.96	4.55	4.91	5.17	5.37	5.54	5.69	5.81	5.92	6.02
30	.05	2.89	3.49	3.85	4.10	4.30	4.46	4.60	4.72	4.82	4.92
	.01	3.89	4.45	4.80	5.05	5.24	5.40	5.54	5.65	5.76	5.85
40	.05	2.86	3.44	3.79	4.04	4.23	4.39	4.52	4.63	4.73	4.82
	.01	3.82	4.37	4.70	4.93	5.11	5.26	5.39	5.50	5.60	5.69
60	.05	2.83	3.40	3.74	3.98	4.16	4.31	4.44	4.55	4.65	4.73
	.01	3.76	4.28	4.59	4.82	4.99	5.13	5.25	5.36	5.45	5.53
120	.05	2.80	3.36	3.68	3.92	4.10	4.24	4.36	4.47	4.56	4.64
	.01	3.70	4.20	4.50	4.71	4.87	5.01	5.12	5.21	5.30	5.37
∞	.05	2.77	3.31	3.63	3.86	4.03	4.17	4.29	4.39	4.47	4.55
	.01	3.64	4.12	4.40	4.60	4.76	4.88	4.99	5.08	5.16	5.23

GLOSSARY

The number in parentheses that follows each definition indicates the chapter in which the term was introduced.

Abscissa the horizontal axis of a graph.(6)

Absolute determinism the idea that perfect prediction and control of events are possible.(2)

Accretion measures accumulated deposits of material that may reflect systematic behavior patterns.(15)

Age-simulation technique systematic manipulation of the independent variables that could be contributing to age changes or age differences.(15)

Aggregation of findings combined results of several studies of a particular phenomenon.(8)

Alternative hypothesis the hypothesis that the sample data and resulting test statistic will differ from expectations based on chance alone.(8)

Anecdote a verbal description of a behavior pattern or episode.(5)

Applied research research that has immediate relevance to social problems or immediate social value.(1)

Archival research the systematic investigation of documents or records that are accumulated and maintained by individuals or organizations.(15)

Area sampling the practice of sampling specific regions within a larger geographical space.(9)

Arithmetic mean the number which results from dividing the sum of a set of raw scores by the total number of raw scores.(6)

Assumed consent an alternative to deception research; if subjects in a pilot study find the research procedure to be acceptable, it is assumed that the actual subjects would willingly consent to the procedure.(3)

Asymmetric transfer a process by which subjects learn strategies or expectancies in one condition and use them in a subsequent condition where they are not appropriate.(7)

Attrition loss of subjects from a study.(7)

Basic research research which is undertaken primarily for the sake of generating new knowledge, irrespective of the social relevance of the research problem.(1)

Between-group variance variance based on the difference between group means.(13)

Between-subjects designs experiments in which each subject serves in one and only one condition, such that the various levels of variable X are represented by different groups of people.(7)

Birth-year cohorts in a cross-sectional study, all subjects born in a given year.(15)

Block randomization in a repeated measures design, the process of dividing the total number of experimental trials into k blocks and randomizing the order of treatments within each block.(13)

Bound on the error of estimation the likely maximal deviation of the population proportion from the sample proportion.(12)

Carry-over effects a result in which subjects' experience and performance in early treatments carry over to subsequent treatments to bias the outcomes.(7)

Case study an intensive investigation of the current and past behaviors and experiences of a person or an organization.(10)

Chi-square statistic a statistical test commonly applied to frequency-count data organized by categories of response or characteristics.(9)

Cluster sample a simple random sample in which each basic sampling unit is a group of smaller units, called "elements."(12)

Coding the process of converting qualitative responses to numbers.(12)

Coefficient Alpha an internal consistency index of reliability that is based on the average intercorrelations among test items.(11)

Conceptual replication a practice by which the same theoretical variables are studied in each repetition of an investigation, but the specific measures, populations, and procedures are varied across investigations.(8)

Concurrent validity a term applied to criterion-related validity when the test data and criterion data are collected at the same time.(11)

Condition-assignment sheet a list of the order of experimental conditions across experimental sessions.(13)

Confidence interval a range of values likely to contain the population parameter that you are estimating.(12)

Confidence level the theoretical probability that the confidence interval contains the population parameter.(12)

Confounded variables extraneous variables that covary with the independent variable of interest.(4)

Confounding the independent variable is contaminated by one or more extraneous variables that are allowed to covary with it.(7)

Constant an object, event, or process that has only one fixed value.(2)

Construct an inferred characteristic or process that forms part of the conceptual content of a theory.(2)

Construct validation use of both logical and empirical analyses to establish the psychological meaning of a test or measure.(11)

Content validation use of the judgment of "experts" to establish that the psychological content tapped by a measure is relevant to the trait or process that the measure is designed to assess.(5)

Contingency table a row × column table containing frequency counts.(6)

Control science's goal of applying theories and procedures in order to influence natural events; also refers to control of conditions and variables in research.(2)

Convenience sampling selection of situations and subjects on the basis of how readily "available" they are and how easily they can be studied.(9)

Convergent validity significant correlation of the trait of interest with itself even when measured by two different methods.(11)

Correlated-groups design configuration in which performance of subjects in one condition is correlated with performance in other conditions.(13)

Correlation method validation of a test by showing that it is correlated with other tests that measure traits which are theoretically relevant to the target trait.(11)

Correlation ratio a statistical index of the combination of linear and nonlinear relationship between two variables; Eta.(6)

Cost/benefit orthodoxy the philosophy that the ethical status of a research project is determined by the relative balance it strikes between the researcher's obligations to society and her obligations to her subjects.(3)

Counterbalanced sequence each treatment occurs equally often in the sequence of trials, and each treatment precedes and follows every other treatment an equal number of times.(7)

Criterion-related validity the extent to which a measure is correlated with other measures that it is supposed to be related to.(5)

Critical incident technique a method of constructing personnel-selection tests that focuses on discovering the particular skills and behaviors that are critical to successful performance on the job.(11)

Cross-lagged panel correlation a correlational system that exploits the concept of time precedence for purposes of causal analysis.(11)

Cross-sectional investigation the measurement of several age-groups at one time.(15)

Cross-validate to replicate the initial results of a psychometric study with a different sample of people.(11)

Curvilinear relationship the direction of relationship between variables X and Y changes as X values vary from low to high.(6)

Debriefing session a post-investigation explanation given to the subject by the investigator; fulfills both a dehoaxing and a desensitizing function.(3)

Deductive logic prediction of a specific event from some general ideas (or theory) that you started out with.(2)

Demand characteristics the pattern of cues in a research procedure that may convey the research hypothesis to subjects.(8)

Dependent variable the specific behavior of subjects that is observed and measured; also the underlying construct reflected in the behavior.(2)

Description science's goal of labeling, defining, and classifying natural objects, events, and situations.(2)

Determinism assumption a basic premise of science which holds that all events have causes.(2)

Direct relationship as scores on variable X change in a particular direction (higher or lower), corresponding scores on variable Y tend to vary in the same direction; a positive relationship.(6)

Discriminant validity the trait of interest is not correlated with theoretically unrelated traits, even if the same measurement method is used to assess both the target trait and the irrelevant traits.(11)

Double-blind situation in which both the data collector and the subject are unaware of the research hypothesis and the subject's group membership in the experiment.(7)

Duration the amount of time that a subject engages in a particular response.(5)

Empiricism a reliance on observation to answer questions.(2)

Environmental independent variable conditions that are external to the persons serving as subjects in a study; can be manipulated.(2)

Equivalent-forms reliability the correlation between two forms of a test.(11)

Exact replication a study repeated in exactly the same way that it was originally conducted.(8)

Experimental realism use of experimental tasks that are absorbing and ego-involving.(8)

Ex post facto design a pseudo experiment in which membership in the experimental and control groups is determined by subjects' personal histories.(13)

External validity the generalizability of findings.(4)

Field experiment an experiment conducted in a natural setting.(4)

Finite causation a basic assumption of science which asserts that the number of causes of any event is limited.(2)

Fixed-alternative item a test or questionnaire item in which the response alternatives have been predetermined by the researcher; multiple-choice, matching, and true/false (agree/disagree) items.(12)

Formative evaluation the monitoring aspect of program evaluation.(15)

F ratio the ratio of systematic variance to error variance; test statistic used in an analysis of variance.(13)

Grand mean the mean of a set of means.(6)

Group separation method validation of a test by showing that groups known to differ on the trait measured by the test also differ on their average test scores.(11)

Haphazard sampling the arbitrary and apparently unsystematic selection of sampling units that happen to be easily accessible.(12)

Hypothesis a proposed relationship.(2)

Hypothetical construct *see* **Construct**.(2)

Independent-groups design experimental design in which different subjects have been randomly assigned to the respective measurement or treatment conditions.(7)

Independent variable a variable thought to influence or cause changes in another variable; the variable that you systematically manipulate.(2)

Inductive logic drawing general conclusions from particular observations.(2)

Inference an educated guess about a population made on the basis of sample data.(8)

Interaction effect the effect of one independent variable changes across different levels of other independent variables.(14)

Internal validity the extent to which changes in the independent variable can be deemed responsible for changes in the dependent variable.(4)

Interrater method a method of reliability assessment that checks the consistency of results produced by independent scorers of a test.(5)

Interscorer method *see* **Interrater method**.(5)

Interval scale a scale of measurement that has equal scale intervals.(5)

Intervening variable a construct that is operationally defined on both the independent-variable and dependent-variable sides of a relationship.(2)

Introductory statement a face-to-face explanation of the purpose and source of a survey.(12)

Inverse relationship relationship in which variables X and Y tend to change in opposite directions, such that higher scores on Y tend to be associated with lower scores on X, and vice versa; a negative relationship.(6)

Job description a written specification of what functions an employee is to engage in and the level of proficiency expected in each function.(11)

Latency the amount of time that it takes a subject to respond to a stimulus situation.(5)

Leading question a questionnaire item worded in such a way that a particular response seems most appropriate and socially desirable.(12)

Linear correlation coefficient a numerical index, varying between 0 and 1, which measures the strength of a straight-line relationship between two variables; the Pearson r.(5)

Linear relationship a straight-line pattern of covariation.(6)

Line graph the graph that results from plotting the mean of variable Y as a function of classifications of X and then "connecting" the points.(6)

Line of best fit the line which best summarizes the pattern of relationship in a scatter diagram.(6)

Loaded question a questionnaire item that contains emotionally charged words that bias the respondent's interpretation of the item.(12)

Longitudinal design research design in which a single group of birth-year cohorts is measured several times at progressively greater ages.(15)

Longitudinal-sequential design research design in which several different birth-year cohort groups are studied longitudinally over the same measurement period.(15)

Longitudinal study measurement of a single group of people with the same or similar instruments on successive occasions.(7)

Magnitude estimation a self-report method of measurement in which the subject is asked to represent psychological magnitude on a physical scale.(5)

Main effect the effect that an independent variable has irrespective of the influence of the other independent variables in a factorial experiment.(14)

Matched pairs subjects paired up on the basis of similar scores on a criterion that is strongly correlated with the dependent variable.(7)

Matching criterion the measure used to form matched pairs or blocks of subjects.(7)

Mean difference the quantity remaining after the mean of one treatment condition is subtracted from the mean of another condition; often employed as an index of treatment effects.(6)

Measurement use of an unambiguous set of rules to convert observations to a numerical scale.(5)

Method of internal consistency cross-checking of various sources of data and inferences against one another in the conduct of a case study.(10)

Model an abstract conceptual framework that helps to stimulate and guide theory development.(2)

Multiple-baseline design a single-case experimental design that involves recording two or more behaviors across time, first under the baseline condition, then under the treatment condition.(10)

Multiple correlation the correlation of the combination of two or more predictor variables with a criterion variable.(11)

Multi-point rating scale a rating scale that has more than two values.(5)

Multi-stage sampling a planned sequence of probability sampling that is conducted in stages, with progressively smaller sampling units being used at each successive stage.(12)

Multitrait-multimethod matrix a table containing the correlations among two or more traits measured by two or more methods.(11)

Narrow operationism the idea that a particular set of observation or manipulation procedures is the one and only definition of a variable.(2)

Naturalistic observation a type of systematic observation in which the researcher unobtrusively records the behavior of unaware subjects in their natural environments.(4)

Negative relationship an inverse association between two variables.(2)

Nominal scale a scale of measurement that carries information only on categorical or qualitative differences.(5)

Nonparametric test a statistical test that does not assume a normally distributed population or an interval scale of measurement.(13)

Nonprobability sampling sampling technique in which the theoretical probability of selecting a given sampling unit is not known.(12)

Nonrandomized matching procedure by which members of matched pairs are assigned to treatment conditions on the basis of their preexisting characteristics.(7)

Nonreactive techniques unobtrusive data-collection methods.(15)

Null distribution the distribution of outcomes expected if the null hypothesis is true; a sampling distribution.(8)

Null hypothesis the hypothesis that the sample data and resulting test statistic do not differ from expectations based on chance alone.(8)

Null relationship the nonexistence of a relationship; zero covariation.(6)

Numerical ranks numbers representing subjects' relative positions on an ordinal scale of measurement.(5)

Objective test test on which different scorers usually agree with one another on what scores the test-takers made.(11)

Observation the act of systematically noting or recording instances of behavior that fall into a preselected behavioral category.(5)

Observational reactivity subjects' tendency to behave atypically when aware of being observed.(5)

One-shot case study a single-group posttest design.(13)

Open-ended item test or questionnaire item that allows the respondent to determine the response category; completion or essay format.(12)

Operational definition a specification of the operations used in observing, manipulating, or measuring a variable.(2)

Order assumption a basic premise of science which holds that natural events obey a discoverable set of laws.(2)

Ordinal scale a scale of measurement that contains information on both differences and ranks.(5)

Ordinate the vertical axis of a graph.(6)

Organismic independent variable a characteristic of subjects that cannot be altered during the course of a study.(2)

Parametric test a statistical test that is dependent on the existence of certain characteristics in the population of observations that is sampled.(13)

Parsimony the doctrine that states that, other things being equal, the simplest explanation of a phenomenon is preferred over more complicated accounts.(2)

Partial correlation an index of the strength of linear relationship between two variables when the influence of a third variable has been statistically removed from both variables.(11)

Participant observation research stance in which the observer attempts to assume a natural role within the social situation that he/she is investigating.(9)

Pearson Product-Moment Correlation Coefficient a standardized index of linear association between two variables.(6)

Percentage a proportion multiplied times 100.(6)

Performance criteria the behaviors or pieces of evidence that constitute what is meant by successful performance of a job.(11)

Pilot study a type of practice run that precedes the actual study.(5)

Placebo group in psychology, a control group that receives some sort of sham treatment which is not psychotherapy but which gives the placebo subject a sense of receiving attention and concern.(13)

Plagiarism presenting another person's material as though it were your own.(16)

Plausible rival hypothesis an assertion that something different from, or in addition to, the main independent variable is responsible for the covariation between the independent variable and the dependent variable.(7)

Point estimate a single sample value used to estimate a population parameter.(12)

Population the total set of people and situations that a researcher is interested in studying.(2)

Population parameter a statistical characteristic of a population.(12)

Positive relationship *see* **Direct relationship**.(2)

Power the sensitivity of an experimental design or statistical test to the effects of the independent variable.(13)

Practical significance the amount of information conveyed by a correlation coefficient; often measured by the square of the correlation index.(6)

Prediction science's goal of forecasting new events from theories.(2)

Predictive validity the extent to which a test predicts behaviors that it is supposed to predict; a type of criterion-related validity.(11)

Principal investigator the person who formulates the hypothesis and designs the study.(7)

Principle a simple statement that summarizes a body of evidence.(2)

Probabilistic (or relative) determinism the idea that when certain known causal conditions are present, a particular event has a known probability of occurring.(2)

Probability sampling sampling method in which sampling units are selected in such a way that each unit has a known probability of being selected.(8)

Program evaluation use of the research techniques of behavioral science to assess the application and impact of a remediation, training, or educational program.(15)

Progressive error any change in behavior that occurs as a result of continued experience with an experimental task.(7)

Projective test test in which the subject composes an oral or written interpretation of an ambiguous stimulus; in theory, the subject's composition is a projection of his fantasies, motives, and traits.(11)

Proportion the ratio of the frequency of occurrence of a particular outcome to the total number of outcomes.(6)

Proportional allocation in stratified random sampling, drawing the same percentage of sampling units from each stratum.(12)

Pseudo experiment a defective experiment

that lacks either the randomization feature or the control-condition feature of true experiments.(13)

Psychometric method the approach to research that focuses on discovering the network of relationships between a particular test and a variety of other tests and behaviors.(11)

Qualitative variable a variable that can vary only in kind, not amount.(2)

Quantify to convert observations to numbers.(2)

Quantitative variable a variable that may vary by amount or degree along a number scale that often can take on an indefinite number of values.(2)

Quasi-experimental design an experiment-like study in which the researcher is either unable to randomly assign subjects to conditions or unable to control the scheduling of events, or both.(15)

Quota sampling the practice of systematically selecting a specified number of subjects from each of several subsets of the target population.(12)

Random assignment procedure by which subjects are assigned to experimental treatments entirely on the basis of chance.(7)

Random-digit dialing selecting telephone-sample respondents on the basis of randomly determined telephone numbers.(12)

Randomization ordering treatments entirely on the basis of chance.(7)

Randomized matching procedure by which members of matched pairs of subjects are randomly assigned to their respective treatments.(7)

Random time-series design a single-case experimental design in which, following completion of the baseline observations, the experimental treatment is introduced at some randomly selected time.(10)

Rating scale an objective-type test format which requires the subject to express the strength of feeling or opinion by selecting a number from an ascending or descending quantitative scale.(11)

Rational sciences sciences that answer questions largely through logical analysis and rational argument.(2)

Ratio scale a scale of measurment that has both equal scale units and an absolute zero point.(5)

Raw score a number representing a subject's performance or standing on a dependent measure.(6)

Region of rejection area under the sampling distribution that represents statistically significant outcomes.(8)

Regression line the line of "best fit" in a scatter diagram.(6)

Regression toward the mean confounding when subjects are measured twice on the same dimension, the tendency of those who score extremely high or extremely low on the first measurement occasion to score relatively closer to the mean value on the second occasion.(7)

Relationship an instance of association or co-variation between two variables.(2)

Reliability the extent to which a measurement procedure measures something consistently.(5)

Reliability coefficient the correlation of a measure with itself; the proportion of test-score variance that is true-score variance.(5)

Repeated-measurement designs research designs in which subjects are measured more than once on the same set of variables.(7)

Replicate to repeat a previously conducted study to find out if the initial results are reliable.(2)

Representative sampling sampling method in which the researcher "handpicks" a sample which, in his mind, consists of individuals whose characteristics represent those of the whole population of interest.(9)

Research error an inconsistency between a researcher's conclusions and her method/data package.(2)

Research hypothesis *see* **Alternative hypothesis**.(8)

Response set the tendency to select test-item responses for the purpose of presenting an invalid image of oneself.(5)

Restriction of range situation in which the range of values on variable X, variable Y, or both is so small that one variable cannot possibly show much systematic change as the other variable increases or decreases in value.(6)

Reversal design repeated presentation and withdrawal of the experimental treatment in a single-case experiment.(10)

Role-playing approach an alternative to deception research; fully informed subjects simulate the behavior of deceived subjects.(3)

Sample the people and situations that the researcher actually observes and measures; a subset of a population.(2)

Sampled population the population your sample actually represents.(8)

Sampling distribution an abstract distribution of the values of a random variable.(8)

Sampling distribution of the proportion the distribution of sample proportions you would get if you drew an infinite number of simple random samples of a given size and plotted the resulting sample proportions into a distribution.(12)

Sampling frame the listing of your sampling units.(12)

Sampling units the "entities" that are directly selected in your sampling procedure.(12)

Scale of measurement the level of mathematical sophistication attained by the data of a measurement operation.(5)

Scatter diagram a configuration of points that results from plotting the points of graphical intersection of ordered pairs of X and Y values.(6)

Scientific law a principle that is widely accepted by the scientific community.(2)

Self-reports measurement techniques that generate data through asking the subject to describe his behavior, experience, or traits.(5)

Sequencing effects the confounding effect of repeated testing or the subject's continued experience in a study.(7)

Semantic-differential scale a multi-point rating dimension that is anchored at its extremes by bipolar adjectives.(12)

Sham-operation group in physiological research, the group of subjects that is subjected to the general surgical procedure without alteration of the target brain structure.(7)

Simple random sampling sampling procedure by which sampling units are chosen from the sampling frame in such a way that every possible sample of size n has an equal chance of being drawn.(8)

Simulation control group subjects who do not receive the experimental treatment but are given a description of the treatment and are asked to behave as though they had been exposed to the treatment.(8)

Single-case experiment systematic manipulation of an independent variable within a study of a single person.(10)

Skepticism   the doctrine which states that, because perfect knowledge is impossible and even partial knowledge is elusive, we should doubt the truthfulness of any assertion of knowledge.(2)

Slope   the average amount of change in variable Y for every unit change in variable X.(6)

Solomon four-group design   an experimental model that includes extra experimental and control groups to assess the effects of pretesting.(8)

Spatial generalization   generalization across settings, treatment stimuli and tasks, and subjects.(8)

Split-half method   an internal consistency technique of assessing a test's reliability; involves computing the correlation between scores on two halves of a test.(11)

Standard error of the proportion   the standard unit of variation in the sampling distribution of the proportion.(12)

Statistic   a numerical index used to summarize and describe a set of data or to make an inference about a population based on sample data.(12)

Statistical reliability   the outcome of a statistical test leads to the expectation that the same pattern of results would occur if the study were to be repeated.(6)

Statistical significance   *see* **Statistical reliability**.(6)

Stratified random sampling   dividing a population into several subgroups and drawing simple random samples from each of the subgroups.(12)

Subjective test   any measurement instrument which employs a subjective scoring procedure; scorers of a subjective test often disagree on what the test scores should be.(11)

Subject-selection bias   aspect of subject-selection method by which some systematic process, rather than chance, is responsible for subjects' being in particular treatment conditions.(7)

Summative evaluation   research designed to assess the outcome or effect of a program.(15)

Sum of squares   a sum of squared deviations used in computing various statistical indexes.(6)

Systematic error   constant error; same error appears in each subject's datum.(5)

Systematic observation   the deliberate and planned recording of observations in a natural environment in which the behavior of subjects is essentially unaffected by the observation process.(9)

Systematic random sampling   entering a sampling frame at a randomly selected point and selecting every kth sampling unit.(12)

Systematizing a generalization dimension including a dimension of generalization as an extra independent variable in an experiment.(8)

Target population   all of the people, settings, treatment stimuli, and time frames you wish to generalize to.(8)

Temporal generalization   the reproducibility of a particular finding from one interval of time to another.(8)

Test-retest method   a procedure for checking the reliability of measurement by assessing the consistency of subjects' performances on the measure from one occasion to another.(5)

Test statistic   a numerical index that serves as a decision criterion in tests of statistical significance.(6)

Theory   an internally consistent network of assumptions, constructs, operational definitions, relationships, and principles.(2)

Third variable problem   the possibility that some unobserved variable is responsible for the covariation between variables X and Y.(6)

Time-lagged correlation   *see* **Cross-lagged panel correlation**.(11)

Time sampling   process of dividing the time interval occupied by a study into a number of discrete units and randomly selecting a desired number or proportion of those units to use as observation periods.(9)

True experiment   a study conducted in such a way that all sources of confounding are controlled; involves control conditions and randomization.(13)

Type I Error   rejection of a true null hypothesis.(8)

Type II Error   failure to reject a false null hypothesis.(8)

Understanding   science's goal of explaining a large body of apparently complicated observations by a simple principle or theory.(2)

Unsystematic error   random error.(5)

Validity   the extent to which a measurement procedure measures what it is supposed to measure; the relevance of a measure.(5)

Validity coefficient the correlation coefficient between a measure and a criterion that, theoretically, should be related to the measure.(5)

Validity scale a set of items embedded within a test for the purpose of detecting the influence of a response set on a subject's answers.(5)

Variable anything that can take on different values or qualities.(2)

Variance an abstract statistical concept that stands for the individual differences among values in a data set; a statistical index reflecting the amount of dispersion in a data set.(6)

Within-group variance variance based on individual differences on the dependent measure within treatment groups.(13)

Within-subjects design experimental design in which each subject receives all levels of the independent variable.(7)

REFERENCES

Allport, G. W. (1961). *Pattern and growth in personality*. New York: Holt, Rinehart and Winston.

Allport, G. W. (1965). *Letters from Jenny*. Harcourt, Brace, and World.

Allport, G. W., & Pettegrew, T. F. (1957). The trapezoidal illusion among Zulus. *Journal of Abnormal and Social Psychology, 55,* 104–113.

Allport, G. W., & Vernon, P. E. (1933). *Studies in expressive movement*. New York: Macmillan.

Anastasi, A. (1968). *Psychological testing* (3rd ed.). London: Macmillan, 1968.

APA (1974). *Standards for educational and psychological tests*. Washington, DC: American Psychological Association.

APA (1975, May). Proxmire speaks out on social science. *APA Monitor*, p. 6.

APA (1981). Ethical principles of psychologists. *American Psychologist, 36,* 633–638.

APA (1982). *Ethical principles in the conduct of research with human participants*. Washington, DC: American Psychological Association.

APA (1983). *Results: Phase I survey of undergraduate department chairs*. Unpublished report.

Argyris, C. (1980). *Inner contradictions of rigorous research*. New York: Academic Press.

Arkes, H. R., & Garske, J. P. (1982). *Psychological theories of motivation* (2nd ed.). Monterey, CA: Brooks/Cole.

Ary, D., Jacobs, L. C., & Razavieh, A. (1979). *Introduction to research in education* (2nd ed.). New York: Holt, Rinehart and Winston.

Asch, S. E. (1956). Studies of independence and submission to group pressure: I. A minority of one against a unanimous majority. *Psychological Monographs, 70* (Whole No. 416).

Asher, J. (1976, February). Geller demystified? *APA Monitor*, pp. 4, 12.

Ashmore, R. D. (1970). The problem of intergroup prejudice. In B. E. Collins, *Social psychology: Social influence, attitude change, group processes, and prejudice*. Reading, MA: Addison-Wesley.

Bakan, D. (1966). The test of significance in psychological research. *Psychological Bulletin, 66,* 423–437.

Bales, R. F. (1970). *Personality and interpersonal influence*. New York: Holt, Rinehart and Winston.

Baltes, P. B., & Goulet, L. R. (1971). Exploration of developmental variables by manipulation and simulation of age differences in behavior. *Human Development, 14,* 149–170.

Barber, B. (1962). Resistance by scientists to scientific discovery. In B. Barber & W. Hirsch (Eds.), *The sociology of science*. New York: The Free Press of Glencoe.

Barber, T. X. (1976a). *Hypnosis: A scientific approach*. New York: Psychological Dimensions.

Barber, T. X. (1976b). *Pitfalls in human research: Ten pivotal points*. New York: Pergamon.

Barker, R. G., Dembo, T., & Lewin, K. (1941). Frustration and regression: An experiment with young children. *University of Iowa Studies in Child Welfare, 18*, 1–43.

Barker, R. G., & Wright, H. F. (1954). *Midwest and its children: The psychological ecology of an American town*. New York: Harper and Row.

Baron, J., and Treiman, R. (1980). Some problems in the study of differences in cognitive processes. *Memory & Cognition, 8*, 313–321.

Bartz, W. H. (1968). *Readings in general psychology*. Boston: Allyn and Bacon.

Baumrind, D. (1971). Principles of ethical conduct in the treatment of subjects: Reaction to the draft report of the committee on ethical standards in psychological research. *American Psychologist, 26*, 887–896.

Beach, F. A. (1950). The snark was a boojum. *American Psychologist, 5*, 115–124.

Beck, R. C. (1978). *Motivation: Theories and principles*. Englewood Cliffs, NJ: Prentice-Hall.

Bereiter, C., & Freedman, M. B. (1962). Fields of study and the people in them. In N. Sanford (Ed.), *The American college*. New York: Wiley.

Berkowitz, L. (1970). The contagion of violence: An S-R mediational analysis of some effects of observed aggression. In W. J. Arnold & M. M. Page (Eds.), Nebraska symposium on motivation (Vol. 18). Lincoln, NE: University of Nebraska Press.

Berkowitz, L. (1971). The "weapons effect," demand characteristics, and the myth of the compliant subject. *Journal of Personality and Social Psychology, 20*, 332–338.

Berkowitz, L., & Donnerstein, E. (1982). External validity is more than skin deep: Some answers to criticisms of laboratory experiments. *American Psychologist, 37* 245–257.

Berkowitz, L. & LePage, A. (1967). Weapons as aggression-eliciting stimuli. *Journal of Personality and Social Psychology, 7*, 202–207.

Berlyne, D. E. (1966). Curiosity and exploration. *Science, 153*, 25–33.

Berlyne, D. E. (1967). Arousal and reinforcement. In D. Levine (Ed.), *Nebraska symposium on motivation* (Vol. 15). Lincoln, NE: University of Nebraska Press.

Berscheid, E., Baron, R. S., Dermer, M., & Libman, M. (1973). Anticipating informed consent: An empirical approach. *American Psychologist, 28*, 913–925.

Berscheid, E., & Walster, E. (1974). Physical attractiveness. In L. Berkowitz (Ed.), *Advances in experimental social psychology* (Vol. 7). New York: Academic Press.

Bettleheim, B., & Janowitz, M. (1964). *Social change and prejudice*. New York: The Free Press.

Bexton, W. H., Heron, W., & Scott, T. H. (1954). Effects of decreased variation in the sensory environment. *Canadian Journal of Psychology, 8*, 70–76.

Bickman, L., & Henchy, T. (1972). *Beyond the laboratory: Field research in social psychology*. New York: McGraw-Hill.

Binder, A., McConnell, D., & Sjoholm, N. A. (1957). Verbal conditioning as a function of experimenter characteristics. *Journal of Abnormal and Social Psychology, 55*, 309–314.

Birren, J. E. (1964). *The psychology of aging*. Englewood Cliffs, NJ: Prentice-Hall.

Blass, T. (1980). What do positive correlations between student grades and teacher evaluations mean? *Teaching of Psychology, 7*, 186–187.

Boice, R. (1973). Domestication. *Psychological Bulletin, 80*, 215–230.

Bolles, R. C. (1967). *Theory of motivation*. New York: Harper and Row.

Boring, E. G. (1950). *A history of experimental psychology* (2nd ed.). New York: Appleton-Century-Crofts.

Brady, J. V. (1964). Behavioral stress and physiological change: A comparative approach to the experimental analysis of some psychosomatic problems. *Transactions of the New York Academy of Science, 26*, 438–496.

Brehm, J. W., & Cohen, A. R. (1962). *Explorations in cognitive dissonance*. New York: Wiley.

Brown, F. G. (1976). *Principles of educational and psychological testing* (2nd ed.). New York: Holt, Rinehart and Winston.

Broyler, C. R., Thorndike, E. L., & Woodward, E. (1927). A second study of mental discipline in high school students. *Journal of Experimental Psychology, 18*, 377–404.

Bruner, J. S., & Goodman, C. C. (1947). Value and need as organizing factors in perception. *Journal of Abnormal and Social Psychology, 42*, 33–44.

Brunswik, E. (1956). *Perception and the representative design of psychological experiments*. Berkeley, CA: University of California Press.

Buros, O. K. (Ed.). (1978). *The eighth mental*

measurements yearbook (Vols. 1 & 2). Hyland Park, NJ: Gryphon Press.

Burt, C. (1966). The genetic determination of differences in intelligence. *British Journal of Psychology, 57,* 137–153.

Busse, E. W., & Pfeiffer, E. (1977). Functional psychiatric disorders in old age. In E. W. Busse & E. Pfeiffer (Eds.), *Behavior and adaptation in late life* (2nd ed.). Boston: Little, Brown.

Campbell, A. A. (1947). Factors associated with attitudes toward Jews. In T. M. Newcomb & E. L. Hartley (Eds.), *Readings in social psychology.* New York: Holt.

Campbell, D. T., & Fiske, D. W. (1959). Convergent and discriminant validation by the multitrait-multimethod matrix. *Psychological Bulletin, 56,* 81–105.

Campbell, D. T., & Stanley, J. C. (1966). *Experimental and quasi-experimental designs for research.* Chicago: Rand McNally.

Carlsmith, J. M., Ellsworth, P. C., & Aronson, E. (1976). *Methods of research in social psychology.* Reading, MA: Addison-Wesley.

Cattell, R. B. (1972). *Manual for the 16 PF.* Champaign, IL: Institute for Personality and Ability Testing.

Christensen, L. B. (1980). *Experimental methodology* (2nd ed.). Boston: Allyn and Bacon.

Cohen, D. (1982, June). Eysenck finds quick thinkers have higher IQs. *APA Monitor,* p. 29.

Cohen, D. R. (1979, April). The dormitory life of the future college dropout. *Psychology Today,* pp. 101–102.

Coleman, J. A. (1958). *Relativity for the layman.* New York: The New American Library of World Literature.

Coleman, J. C., Butcher, J. N., & Carson, R. C. (1980). *Abnormal psychology and modern life* (6th ed.). Glenview, IL: Scott, Foresman.

Cooper, J. (1976). Deception and role playing: On telling the good guys from the bad guys. *American Psychologist, 31,* 605–610.

Coopersmith, S. (1967). *The antecedents of self-esteem.* San Francisco: Freeman.

Corso, J. F., (1967). *The experimental psychology of sensory behavior.* New York: Holt, Rinehart and Winston.

Costin, F. (1978). Do student ratings of college teachers predict student achievement? *Teaching of Psychology, 5,* 86–88.

Craik, F. I. M., & Lockhart, R. S. (1972). Levels of processing: A framework for memory research *Journal of Verbal Learning and Verbal Behavior, 11,* 661–684.

Cronbach, L. J. (1975). Beyond the two disciplines of scientific psychology. *American Psychologist, 30,* 116–127.

Dember, W. N., & Warm, J. S. (1979). *Psychology of perception* (2nd ed.). New York: Holt, Rinehart and Winston.

Denny, J. P. (1966). Effects of anxiety and intelligence on concept formation. *Journal of Experimental Psychology, 72,* 596–602.

Denzin, N. J. (1970). Triangulation: A case for methodological evaluation and combination. In N. K. Denzin (Ed.), *Sociological methods: A source book.* Chicago: Aldine.

Dethier, V. G. (1962). *To know a fly.* Oakland, CA: Holden-Day.

Diamond, M. J., Gregory, J., Lenny, E., Steadman, C., & Talone, J. M. (1972). Personality and hypnosis: The role of hypnosis-specific mediational attitudes in predicting hypnotic responsivity. *Proceedings of the 80th Annual Convention of the American Psychological Association, 7,* 865–866.

DiCara, L. V., Barber, T. X., Kamiya, J., Miller, N. E., Shapiro, D., & Stoyva, J. (1974). *Biofeedback and self-control.* Chicago: Aldine.

Dollard, J., Doob, L., Miller, N. E., Mowrer, O. H., & Sears, R. R. (1939). *Frustration and aggression.* New Haven, CT: Yale University Press.

Doob, A. N., & Gross, A. E. (1971). Status of frustrator as an inhibitor of horn-honking responses. *Journal of Social Psychology, 76,* 213–218.

Ebbinghaus, H. (1964). *On memory* (H. A. Ruger & C. E. Bussenius, Trans.). New York: Dover. ((Original work published 1885).

Edwards, A. L. (1957a). *Techniques of attitude scale construction.* New York: Appleton-Century-Crofts.

Edwards, A. L. (1957b). *The social desirability variable in personality assessment and research.* New York: Holt, Rinehart and Winston.

Edwards, A. L. (1970). *The measurement of personality traits by scales and inventories.* New York: Holt, Rinehart and Winston.

Ehrlich, A. (1974). The age of the rat. *Human Behavior, 3,* 25–28.

Ellsworth, P. C. (1977). From abstract ideas to concrete instances: Some guidelines for choosing natural research settings. *American Psychologist, 82,* 604–615.

Epstein, S. (1980). The stability of behavior II. Implications for psychological research. *American Psychologist, 35,* 790–806.

Errera, P. (1972). Statement based on interviews with forty "worst cases" in the Milgram obedience experiments. In J. Katz (Ed.), *Experimentation with human beings.* New York: Russell Sage Foundation.

Evans, J. D. (1976). Spacing effect in free recall as an obligatory phenomenon. *Psychological Reports, 38,* 1321–1322.

Evans, J. D., Nelson, L. A., & King, N. W. (1979, May). *Experimental induction of fear of success fantasies: Partial validation of Horner's construct.* Paper presented at the meeting of the Midwestern Psychological Association, Chicago, IL.

Evans, J. D., & Peeler, L. (1979). Personalized comments on returned tests improve test performance in introductory psychology. *Teaching of Psychology, 6,* 57.

Evans, P. (1976, December). The Burt affair . . . sleuthing in science. *APA Monitor,* pp. 4, 5.

Eysenck, H. J. (1968). *Eysenck personality inventory.* San Diego: Educational and Industrial Testing Service.

Faraone, S. (1982). Chi-square in small samples. *American Psychologist, 37,* 107.

Fawcett, S. B., & Miller, L. K. (1975). Training public-speaking behavior: An experimental analysis and social validation. *Journal of Applied Behavior Analysis, 8,* 125–135.

Feldman, M. P. (1966). Aversion therapy for sexual deviations: A critical review. *Psychological Bulletin, 65,* 65–79.

Festinger, L., Riecken, H., & Schachter, S. (1956). *When prophecy fails.* Minneapolis: University of Minnesota Press.

Fisher, R. A. (1966). *The design of experiments* (8th ed.). New York: Harper.

Fiske, D. W. (1979). Two worlds of psychological phenomena. *American Psychologist, 34,* 733–739.

Flanagan, J. D. (1978). A research approach to improving our quality of life. *American Psychologist, 33,* 138–147.

Foltz, D. (1980, June). Taking off on science. *APA Monitor,* pp. 4–5.

Forward, J., Canter, R., & Kirsch, N. (1976). Role-enactment and deception methodologies: Alternative paradigms? *American Psychologist, 31,* 595–603.

Frederick, C. J. (1969). Suicide notes: A survey and evaluation. *Bulletin of Suicidology, 3,* 17–26.

Friedman, M., & Rosenman, R. H. (1974). *Type A behavior and your heart.* New York: Knopf.

Gallatin, J. E. (1975). *Adolescence and individuality: A conceptual approach to adolescent psychology.* New York: Harper & Row.

Gallup, G. H. (1977, September). Ninth annual Gallup poll on the public's attitudes toward the public schools. *Phi Delta Kappan,* pp. 33–47.

Garfield, S. L. (1981). Psychotherapy: A 40-year appraisal. *American Psychologist, 36,* 174–183.

Gates, A. I. (1917). Recitation as a factor in memorizing. *Archives of Psychology, 6,* 40.

Gescheider, G. A., Catlin, E. C., & Fontana, A. M. (1982). Psychophysical measurement of the judged seriousness of crimes and severity of punishments. *Bulletin of the Psychonomic Society, 19,* 275–278.

Ghiselli, E. E. (1964). *Theory of psychophysical measurement.* New York: McGraw-Hill.

Glass, D. C. (1977). Stress, behavior patterns, and coronary disease. *American Scientist, 65,* 177–187.

Glasser, R. J. (1976). *The body is the hero.* New York: Random House.

Glenwick, D. S., Jason, L. A., & Elman, D. (1978). Physical attractiveness and social contact in the singles bar. *Journal of Social Psychology, 105,* 311–312.

Goleman, D. (1981, January). The new competency tests: Matching the right people to the right jobs. *Psychology Today,* pp. 35–36, 39–40, 42, 44, 46.

Gouldner, A. W., & Gouldner, H. P. (1963). *Modern sociology: An introduction to the study of human interaction.* New York: Harcourt, Brace & World.

Grose, R. F., & Birney, R. C. (1963). *Transfer of learning.* New York: Van Nostrand, 1963.

Gruen, G. E. (1965). Experiences affecting the development of number conservation in children. *Child Development, 36,,* 963–979.

Hall, C. S., & Lindzey, G. L. (1970). *Theories of personality.* New York: Wiley.

Hamburg, M. (1979). *Basic statistics: A modern approach* (2nd ed.). New York: Harcourt Brace Jovanovich.

Hanaway, T. P., & Burghardt, G. M. (1976). The development of sexually dimorphic book-carrying behavior. *Bulletin of the Psychonomic Society, 7,* 267–270.

Hansel, C. E. M. (1966). *ESP: A scientific examination.* New York: Charles Scribner's Sons.

Hansel, C. E. M. (1980). *ESP and parapsychology: A critical reevaluation.* Buffalo, NY: Prometheus Books.

Hare, R. D. (1966). Psychopathology and choice of immediate versus delayed punishment. *Journal of Abnormal Psychology, 71,* 25–29.

Harré, R., & Secord, P. E. (1972). *The explanation of social behavior.* Oxford, England: Blackwell.

Harris, S., & Masling, J. (1970). Examiner sex, subject sex, and Rorschach productivity. *Journal of Consulting and Clinical Psychology, 34,* 60–63.

Hathaway, S. R., & McKinley, J. C. (1967). *Minnesota mutiphasic personality inventory: Manual for administration and scoring.* New York: Psychological Corporation.

Hays, W. L. (1981). *Statistics* (3rd ed.). New York: Holt, Rinehart and Winston.

Henle, M., & Hubbell, M. B. (1938). "Egocentricity" in adult conversation. *Journal of Social Psychology, 9,* 227–234.

Hermann, D. J., & Neisser, U. (1978). An inventory of everyday experiences. In M. M. Gruneker, P. E. Morris, & R. N. Sykes (Eds.), *Practical aspects of memory.* New York: Academic Press.

Hersen, M., & Barlow, D. H. (1976). *Single case experimental designs: Strategies for studying behavior change.* New York: Pergamon Press.

Herzberg, F. (1968). One more time: How do you motivate employees? *Harvard Business Review, 46,* 53–62.

Hilgard, E. R. (1962). The scientific status of psychoanalysis. In E. Nagle, P. Suppes, & A. Tarske (Eds.), *Logic, methodology, and philosophy of science.* Stanford, CA: Stanford University Press.

Holmes, D. (1972). Repression or interference: A further investigation. *Journal of Personality and Social Psychology, 22,* 163–170.

Holmes, D. S. (1976a). Debriefing after psychological experiments: I. Effectiveness of postdeception dehoaxing. *American Psychologist, 31,* 858–867.

Holmes, D. S. (1976b). Debriefing after psychological experiments: II. Effectiveness of postexperimental desensitizing. *American Psychologist, 31,* 868–875.

Horn, J. C. (1978, December). The seven-second singles scene. *Psychology Today,* p. 32.

Horner, M. (1968). Sex differences in achievement motivation and performance in competitive and non-competitive situations. Unpublished doctoral dissertation, University of Michigan.

Horner, M. (1970). Femininity and successful achievement: A basic inconsistency. In J. M. Bardwick, E. Souvan, M. S. Horner, & D. Gutmann (Eds.), *Feminine personality and conflict.* Belmont, CA: Brooks/Cole.

Howell, W. C., & Dipboye, R. L. (1982). *Essentials of industrial and organizational psychology.* Homewood, IL: Dorsey Press.

Hull, C. L., (1943). *Principles of behavior.* New York: Appleton-Century-Crofts.

Hulse, S. H., Egeth, H., & Deese, J. (1980). *The psychology of learning* (4th ed.). New York: McGraw-Hill.

Hyde, J. S. (1981). How large are cognitive gender differences? A meta-analysis using w and d. *American Psychologist, 36,* 892–901.

Hyman, H. (1954). *Interviewing in social research.* Chicago: University of Chicago Press.

Interviewer's Manual (rev. ed.) (1976). Ann Arbor, MI: Institute for Social Research.

Isaacson, W. (1980, November 10). Now, a few words in closing. *Time,* pp. 18, 20.

Jackson, D. D. (1980, September). Reunion of identical twins, raised apart, reveals some astonishing similarities. *Smithsonian Magazine,* pp. 48–58.

Jacoby, L. L., & Bartz, W. H. (1972). Rehearsal and transfer to LTM. *Journal of Verbal Learning and Verbal Behavior, 11,* 561–565.

Janis, I. L., Mahl, G. F., Kagan, J., & Holt, R. R. (1969). *Personality: Dynamics, development, and assessment.* New York: Harcourt, Brace and World.

Jenkins, C. D., Zyzanski, S. J., & Rosenman, R. H. (1976). Risk of new myocardial infarction in middle-aged men with manifest coronary heart disease. *Circulation, 53,* 342–347.

Jenni, D. A., & Jenni, M. A. (1976). Carrying behavior in humans: Analysis of sex differences. *Science, 194,* 859–860.

Johnson, R. W. (1970). Subject performance as affected by experimenter expectancy, sex of experimenter, and verbal reinforcement. *Canadian Journal of Behavioral Science, 2,* 60–66.

Jones, E. E., & Sigall, H. (1971). The bogus pipeline: A new paradigm for measuring affect and attitude. *Psychological Bulletin, 76,* 349–364.

Jones, M. C. (1924). The elimination of children's fears. *Journal of Experimental Psychology, 7,* 382–390.

Jourard, S. M. (1969). The effects of experimental self-disclosure on subjects' behavior. In C. Spielberger (Ed.), *Current topics in community and clinical psychology.* New York: Academic Press.

Jung, C. G. (1963). *Memories, dreams, reflections* (A. Jaffe, Ed.; R. Winston & C. Winston, Trans.). New York: Vintage Books.

Jung, J. (1969). Current practices and problems in the use of college students for psychological research. *Canadian Psychologist, 10,* 280–290.

Jung, J. (1971). *The experimenter's dilemma.* New York: Harper and Row.

Kahneman, D., & Tversky, A. (1972). Subjective probability: A judgment of representativeness. *Cognitive Psychology, 3,* 430–454.

Kahneman, D., & Tversky, A. (1973). On the psychology of prediction. *Psychological Review, 80,* 237–250.

Kazdin, A. E. (1975). *Behavior modification in applied settings.* Homewood IL: Dorsey Press.

Kelman, H. C. (1967). Human use of human subjects: The problem of deception in social psychological experiments. *Psychological Bulletin, 67,* 1–11.

Kelman, H. C. (1972). The rights of the subject in social research: An analysis in terms of relative power and legitimacy. *American Psychologist, 27,* 989–1016.

Kenny, D. A. (1975). Cross-lagged panel correlation: A test for spuriousness. *Psychological Bulletin, 82,* 887–903.

Kenny, D. A. (1979). *Correlation and causalty.* New York: Wiley.

Kerkhoff, A. C., & Back, K. W. (1968). *The June bug, a study of hysterical contagion.* New York: Meredith Corporation.

Kerlinger, F. N. (1964). *Foundations of behavioral research.* New York: Holt, Rinehart and Winston.

Kerlinger, F. N. (1979). *Behavioral research: A conceptual approach.* New York: Holt, Rinehart and Winston.

Kidder, L. H. (1981). *Selltiz, Wrightsman, and Cook's research methods in social relations* (4th ed.). New York: Holt, Rinehart and Winston.

Kimmel, D. C. (1974). *Adulthood and aging: An interdisciplinary, developmental view.* New York: Wiley.

Kimmel, H. D. (1957). Three criteria for the use of one-tailed tests. *Psychological Bulletin, 54,* 351–353.

Kirk, R. E. (1968). *Experimental design: Procedures for the behavioral sciences.* Belmont, CA: Brooks/Cole.

Kulka, R. A. (1982). Monitoring social change via survey replication: Prospects and pitfalls from a replication of social roles and mental health. *Journal of Social Issues, 38,* 17–38.

Landy, F. J., & Trumbo, D. A. (1980). *Psychology of work behavior.* Homewood, IL: Dorsey Press.

Latané, B., & Darley, J. (1970). *The unresponsive bystander: Why doesn't he help?* New York: Appleton-Century-Crofts.

Latané, B., & Rodin, J. (1969). A lady in distress: Inhibiting effects of friends and strangers on bystander intervention. *Journal of Experimental Social Psychology, 5,* 189–202.

Lenneberg, E. H. (1962). Understanding language without ability to speak: A case report. *Journal of Abnormal and Social Psychology, 65,* 419–425.

Leuthold, D. A., & Scheeley, R. (1971). Patterns of bias in samples based on telephone directories. *Public Opinion Quarterly, 35,* 249–257.

Levenson, H., Gray, M., & Ingram, A. (1976). Current research methods in personality: Five years after Carlson's survey. *Personality and Social Psychology Bulletin, 2,* 158–161.

Levin, R. I., & Rubin, D. S. (1980). *Applied elementary statistics.* Englewood Cliffs, NJ: Prentice-Hall.

Likert, R. (1932). A technique for the measurement of attitudes. *Archives of Psychology, 140,* 1–55.

Lorenz, K. (1963). *On aggression.* New York: Harcourt, Brace and World.

McClelland, D. C., Atkinson, J. W., Clark, R. A., & Lowell, E. L. (1953). *The achieve-*

ment motive. New York: Appleton-Century-Crofts.

McGeoch, J. A., & Irion, A. L. (1952). *The psychology of human learning*. New York: Longmans.

McGuire, W. J. (1973). The yin and yang of progress in social psychology: Seven koan. *Journal of Personality and Social Psychology, 26*, 446–456.

McMahon, F. B., & McMahon, J. W. (1983). *Abnormal behavior: Psychology's view*. Homewood, IL: Dorsey Press.

Maccoby, E. E., & Jacklin, C. N. (1974). *The psychology of sex differences*. Stanford, CA: Stanford University Press.

Maris, R. W. (1969). *Social forces in urban suicide*. Homewood, IL: Dorsey Press.

Maslow, A. H. (1970). *Motivation and personality* (2nd ed.). New York: Harper and Row.

Melton, A. W. (1970). The situation with respect to the spacing of repetitions and memory. *Journal of Verbal Learning and Verbal Behavior, 9*, 596–606.

Mendenhall, W., Ott, L., & Scheaffer, R. L. (1971). *Elementary survey sampling*. Belmont, CA: Duxbury Press.

Messick, S. (1980). Test validity and the ethics of assessment. *American Psychologist, 35*, 1012–1027.

Meyers, L. S., & Grossen, N. E. (1978). *Behavioral research: Theory, procedure, and design* (2nd ed.). San Francisco: W. H. Freeman.

Middlemist, R. D., Knowles, E. S., & Matter, C. F. (1977). Personal space invasions in the laboratory: Suggestive evidence for arousal. *Journal of Personality and Social Psychology, 35* 122–124.

Milgram, S. (1963). Behavioral study of obedience. *Journal of Abnormal and Social Psychology, 67*, 371–378.

Milgram, S. (1964). Issues in the study of obedience: A reply to Baumrind. *American Psychologist, 19*, 848–852.

Milgram, S. (1974). *Obedience to authority: An experimental view*. New York: Harper & Row.

Miller, B., & Gordon, B. (1978, August). The right to say no. *APA Monitor*, p. 2.

Miller, D. B. (1977). Roles of naturalistic observation in comparative psychology. *American Psychologist, 32*, 211–219.

Miller, D. R., & Swanson, G. E. (1960). *Inner conflict and defense*. New York: Holt, Rinehart and Winston.

Miller, K. A. (1970). *A study of "experimenter bias" and "subject awareness" as demand characteristic artifacts in attitude change experiments*. Unpublished doctoral dissertation, Bowling Green State University, Bowling Green, OH.

Miller, N. E. (1969). Psychosomatic effects of specific types of training. *Annals of the New York Academy of Sciences, 159*, 1025.

Miller, N. E., & DiCara, L. (1967). Instrumental learning of heart rate changes in curarized rates: Shaping and specificity to discriminative stimulus. *Journal of Comparative and Physiological Psychology, 63*, 12–19.

Mischel, W. (1968). *Personality and assessment*. New York: Wiley

Mischel, W. (1969). Continuity and change in personality. *American Psychologist, 24*, 1012–1018.

Mixon, D. (1972). Instead of deception. *Journal for the Theory of Social Behavior, 2*, 146–177.

Mujeeb-ur-Rahman, M. (Ed.) (1977). *The Freudian paradigm: Psychoanalysis and scientific thought*. Chicago: Nelson-Hall.

Myers, S. A. (1981). A survey of conceptions of hypnosis. Unpublished manuscript, Lindenwood College, St. Charles, MO.

National Science Foundation funded projects controversy: Senator William Proxmire vs. social scientists (1975). *Wisconsin Sociologist, 12*, 72–86.

Navarick, D. J. (1979). *Principles of learning: From laboratory to field*. Reading, MA: Addison-Wesley.

Neisser, U. (1967). *Cognitive psychology*. New York: Appleton-Century-Crofts.

Nesselroade, J. R., & Baltes, P. B. (1974). Adolescent personality development and historical change: 1970–1972. *Monographs of the Society for Research in Child Development, 39* (1, Whole No. 154).

Nesselroade, J. R., Stigler, S. M., & Baltes, P. B. (1980). Regression toward the mean and the study of change. *Psychological Bulletin, 88*, 622–637.

Nisbett, R. E. (1968). Determinants of food intake in human obesity. *Science, 159*, 1254–1255.

Nunnally, J. C. (1967). *Psychometric theory*. New York: McGraw-Hill.

Olds, J., & Milner, P. (1954). Positive reinforcement produced by electrical stimulation of septal area and other regions of the rat brain. *Journal of Comparative and Physiological Psychology, 47*, 419–427.

Oppenheimer, R. (1956). Analogy in science. *American Psychologist, 11,* 127–135.

Orne, M. T. (1962). On the social psychology of the psychological experiment with particular reference to the demand characteristics and their implcations. *American Psychologist, 17,* 776–783.

Orne, M. T., & Scheibe, K. E. (1964). The contribution of nondeprivation factors in the production of sensory deprivation effects: The psychology of the "panic button." *Journal of Abnormal and Social Psychology, 68,* 3–12.

Osgood, C. E., Suci, G. J., & Tannenbaum, P. H. (1957). *The measurement of meaning.* Urbana, IL: University of Illinois Press.

Ozar, D. T. (1983). An alternative rationale for informed consent by human subjects. *American Psychologist, 38,* 230–231.

Page, E. B. (1958). Teacher comments and student performance: A seventy-four classroom experiment in school motivation. *Journal of Educational Psychology, 49,* 173–181.

Page, M. M. (1973). Effects of demand cues and evaluation apprehension in an attitude change experiment. *Journal of Social Psychology, 89,* 55–62.

Pfeiffer, E. (1975). Sexual behavior. In J. G. Howells (Ed.), *Modern perspectives in psychiatry* (Vol. 6). New York: Bruner/Mazel.

Pfungst, O. (1911). *Clever Hans (the horse of Mr. von Osten): A contribution to experimental, animal, and human psychology* (C. L. Rahn, Trans.). New York: Holt.

Piaget, J. (1963). *The origins of intelligence in children* (Margaret Cook, Trans.). New York: Norton.

Popper, K. R. (1964). *The poverty of historicism.* New York: Harper and Row.

Poulton, E. C. (1982). Influential companions: Effects of one strategy on another in the within-subjects designs of cognitive psychology. *Psychological Bulletin, 91,* 673–690.

Quinn, R. P., Gutek, B. A., & Walsh, J. T. (1980). Telephone interviewing: A reappraisal in a field experiment. *Basic and Applied Social Psychology, 1,* 127–153.

Reese, H. W., & Overton, W. F. (1970). Models of development and theories of development. In L. R. Goulet & P. B. Baltes (Eds.), *Life-span developmental psychology: Re-search and theory.* New York: Academic Press.

Reich, J. W. (1982). *Experimenting in society: Issues and examples in applied social psychology.* Glenview, IL: Scott, Foresman.

Reisman, J. M. (1966). *The development of clinical psychology.* New York: Appleton-Century-Crofts.

Resnick, J. H., & Schwartz, T. (1973). Ethical standards as an independent variable in psychological research. *American Psychologist, 78,* 134–139.

Richert, A. J., & Ward, E. F. (1976). Experimental performance and self-evaluation of subjects sampled early, middle, and late in an academic term: Sex and task. *Psychological Reports, 39,* 135–142.

Richter, D. O., Wilson, S. D., Milner, M., & Senter, R. J. (1980, November). *Some differences among students volunteering as research subjects.* Paper presented at the meeting of the Psychonomic Society, St. Louis.

Robinson, G. M. (1980, November). *People as scientists: Converging operations in judgments under uncertainty.* Paper presented at the meeting of the Psychonomic Society, St. Louis.

Rodin, J. (1975). Causes and consequences of time perception differences in overweight and normal weight people. *Journal of Personality and Social Psychology, 31,* 898–910.

Rogers, C. R. (1961). *On becoming a person.* Boston: Houghton Mifflin.

Rogers, C. R. (1963). Actualizing tendency in relation to "motives" and to consciousness. In M. R. Jones (Ed.), *Nebraska Symposium on Motivation* (Vol. 11). Lincoln, NE: University of Nebraska Press.

Rogers, C. R., & Skinner, B. F. (1956). Some issues concerning the control of human behavior: A symposium. *Science, 124,* 1057–1066.

Rogosa, D. (1980). A critique of cross-lagged correlation. *Psychological Bulletin, 88,* 245–258.

Rosenhan, D. (1973). On being sane in insane places. *Science, 179,* 250–258.

Rosenthal, R. (1963). On the social psychology of the psychological experiment: The experimenter's hypothesis as unintended determinant of experimental results. *American Scientist, 51,* 268–283.

Rosenthal, R. (1964). Experimenter outcome-orientation and the results of the psychological experiment. *Psychological Bulletin, 61,* 405–412.

Rosenthal, R. (1966). *Experimenter effects in behavioral research*. New York: Appleton-Century-Crofts.

Rosenthal, R. (1967). Covert communication in the psychological experiment. *Psychological Bulletin, 67*, 356–367.

Rosenthal, R. (1976). *Experimenter effects in behavioral research* (2nd ed.). New York: Irvington.

Rosenthal, R., & Fode, K. L. (1963). The effect of experimenter bias on the performance of the albino rat. *Behavioral Science, 8*, 183–189.

Rosenthal, R., & Jacobson, L. (1968). *Pygmalion in the classroom*. New York: Holt, Rinehart and Winston.

Rosenthal, R., & Lawson, R. (1964). A longitudinal study of the effects of experimenter bias on the operant learning of laboratory rats. *Journal of Psychiatric Research, 2*, 61–72.

Rosenthal, R., & Rosnow, R. L. (1975). *Primer of methods for the behavioral sciences*. New York: Wiley.

Ross, L. (1974). Obesity and externality. In S. Schachter & J. Rodin (Eds.), *Obese humans and rats*. Potomac, MD: James Earlbaum Associates.

Rossi, P. H., Freeman, H. E., & Wright, S. R. (1979). *Evaluation: A systematic approach*. Beverly Hills, CA: Sage.

Roseboom, W. W. (1960). The fallacy of the null-hypothesis significance test. *Psychological Bulletin, 57*, 416–428.

Sahakian, W. S. (1972). Social psychology: *Experimentation, theory, research*. Scranton, PA: Intext Educational Publishers.

Salter, A. (1949). *Conditioned reflex therapy*. New York: Creative Age.

Samuelson, F. J. (1980). J. B. Watson's little Albert, Cyril Burt's twins, and the need for a critical science. *American Psychologist, 35*, 619–625.

Sanford, F. H. (1965). *Psychology: A scientific study of man* (2nd ed.) Belmont, CA: Wadsworth.

Satterfield, J. H., Cantwell, D. P., & Satterfield, B. T. (1974). Pathophysiology of the hyperactive child syndrome. *Archives of General Psychiatry, 31*, 839–844.

Schaar, K. (1979, February). Hutchinson v. Proxmire raises key issues for researchers. *APA Monitor*, p. 13.

Schachter, S. (1959). *The psychology of affiliation: Experimental studies of the sources of gregariousness*. Stanford, CA: Stanford University Press.

Schachter, S. (1971). Some extraordinary facts about obese humans and rats. *American Psychologist, 26*, 129–144

Schaefer, V. H. (1976). Teaching the concept of interaction and sensitizing students to its implications. *Teaching of Psychology, 3*, 103–114.

Schaie, K. W. (1982). Longitudinal data sets: Evidence for ontogenetic development or chronicles of cultural change. *Journal of Social Issues, 38*, 65–72.

Scheman, J. D., Lockhard, J. S., Mehler, B. L. (1978). Influences of anatomical differences on gender-specific book-carrying behavior. *Bulletin of the Psychonomic Society, 11*, 17–20.

Schuler, H. (1982). *Ethical problems in psychological research*. New York: Academic Press.

Schultz, D. P. (1970). *Psychology and industry*. London: Macmillan.

Schwartz, G. E. (1975). Biofeedback, self-regulation, and the patterning of physiological processes. *American Scientist, 63*, 314–324.

Seligman, M. E. P, Maier, S. F., & Solomon, R. L. (1971). Unpredictable and uncontrollable aversive events. In F. R. Brush (Ed.), *Aversive conditioning and learning*. New York: Academic Press.

Selkin, J., & Morris, J. (1971). Some behavioral factors which influence the recovery rate of suicide attempters. *Bulletin of Suicidology, 4*, 29–38.

Shaffer, L. S. (1977). The golden fleece: Anti-intellectualism and social science. *American Psychologist, 32*, 814–823.

Sherif, M., & Sherif, C. W. (1956). *An outline of social psychology* (rev. ed.). New York: Harper and Row.

Silverman, I. (1975). Nonreactive methods and the law. *American Psychologist, 30*, 764–769.

Simkins, L. (1970). Clinical psychology at the choice point: Coexistence, divorce or mutation. *International Journal of Social Psychiatry, 16*, 180–189.

Singer, B. F. (1971). Toward a psychology of science. *American Psychologist, 26*, 1010–1015.

Singer, J. L. (1974). Daydreaming and the stream of thought. *American Scientist, 62*, 417–425.

Singer, J. L. (1975). Navigating the stream of consciousness: Research in daydreaming and related inner expectations. *American Psychologist, 30,* 727–738.

Skinner, B. F. (1953). *Science and human behavior.* New York: Macmillan.

Smart, R. (1966). Subject selection bias in psychological research. *Canadian Psychologist, 7,* 115–121.

Snedecor, G. W., & Cochran, W. G. (1980). *Statistical methods* (7th ed.). Ames, IA: Iowa State University Press.

Snow, C. P. (1963). *The two cultures: And a second look.* New York: Mentor Books.

Sohn, D. (1977). The rationale for the practice of randomly assigning subjects to groups: Its treatment in textbooks in experimental psychology and some suggestions. *Teaching of Psychology, 4,* 87–88.

Solomon, R. L., & Lessac, M. S. (1968). A control group for experimental studies of developmental processes. *Psychological Bulletin, 70,* 145–149.

Sommer, R. (1977, January). Toward a psychology of natural behavior. *APA Monitor,* pp. 1, 7.

Sommer, R. (1977, April). No, not research. I said evaluation! *APA Monitor,* pp. 1, 11.

Standen, A. (1950). *Science is a sacred cow.* New York: E. P. Dutton.

Stern, W. (1982). Realistic experiments. In U. Neisser (Ed. and Trans.), *Memory observed: Remembering in natural contexts.* San Francisco: Freeman. (Reprinted from *Beitrage zur Psychologie der Aussage,* 1904, *1,* 1–31.)

Stevens, S. S. (1956). The direct estimation of sensory magnitudes—loudness. *American Journal of Psychology, 69,* 1–25.

Strahan, R. F. (1980). More on averaging judge's ratings: Determining the most reliable composite. *Journal of Consulting and Clinical Psychology, 48,* 587–589.

Stricker, E. M. (1976). Drinking by rats after lateral hypothalamic lesions: A new look at the lateral hypothalamic syndrome. *Journal of Comparative & Physiological Psychology, 90,* 127–143.

Sudman, S. (1967) *Reducing the cost of surveys.* Chicago: Aldine-Atherton.

Taylor, J. A. (1953). A personality scale of manifest anxiety. *Journal of Abnormal and Social Psychology, 48,* 285–290.

Terman, L. M. (1925). *Mental and physical traits of a thousand gifted children.* Stanford, CA: Stanford University Press.

Thibaut, J. W., & Kelley, H. H. (1959). *The social psychology of groups.* New York: Wiley.

Thomas, L. (1981, January). On basic research. *Discover,* pp. 42–43.

Thompson, C. P. (1980, November). *Memory for unique personal events under nearly optimal conditions.* Paper presented at the meeting of the Psychonomic Society, St. Louis.

Thorndike, E. L. (1924). Mental discipline in high school studies. *Journal of Experimental Psychology, 15,* 1–22.

Thorndike, E. L., & Woodworth, R. S. (1901). The influence of improvement in one mental function upon the efficiency of other functions. *Psychological Review, 8,* 247–261.

Tolman, E. C., & Honzik, C. H. (1930). Introduction and removal of reward and maze performance in rats. *University of California Publications in Psychology, 4,* 257–275.

Tolman, E. C., Ritchie, B. F., & Kalish, D. (1946). Studies in spatial learning: II. Place learning versus response learning. *Journal of Experimental Psychology, 36,* 221–229.

Tomlinson, N., Hicks, R. A., & Pellegrini, R. J. (1978). Attributions of female college students to variations in pupil size. *Bulletin of the Psychonomic Society, 12,* 477–478.

TRACES: Basic research links to technology appraised (1969). *Science, 163,* 374–375.

Triplett, N. (1897). The dynamogenic factors in pacemaking and competition. *American Journal of Psychology, 9,* 507–533.

Tversky, A., & Kahneman, D. (1971). Belief in the law of small numbers. *Psychological Bulletin, 76,* 105–110.

Ullman, D., & Jackson, T. T. (1982). Researcher's ethical conscience: Debriefing from 1960 to 1980. *American Psychologist, 37,* 972–973.

Underwood, B. J. (1957). *Psychological research.* New York: Appleton-Century-Crofts.

Underwood, B. J. (1966). *Experimental psychology.* New York: Appleton-Century-Crofts.

Van Lawick-Goodall, J. (1967). *My friends, the wild chimpanzees.* Washington, DC: National Geographic Society.

Veroff, J., Depner, C., Kulka, R., & Douvan, E. (1980). Comparison of American motives: 1957 vs. 1976. *Journal of Personality and Social Psychology, 39,* 1258–1271.

Wachtel, P. L. (1980). Investigation and its discontents: Some constraints on progress in psychological research. *American Psychologist, 35,* 399–408.

Wade, T. C., & Baker, T. B. (1977). Opinions and use of psychological tests: A survey of clinical psychologists. *American Psychologist, 32,* 874–882.

Walizer, M. H., & Weiner, P. L. (1978). *Research methods and analysis: Searching for relationships.* New York: Harper and Row.

Walster, E., Aronson, V., Abrahams, D., & Rottmann, L. (1966). Importance of physical attractiveness in dating behavior. *Journal of Personality and Social Psychology, 4,* 508–516.

Walters, C., Shurley, J. T., & Parsons, O. A. (1962). A difference in male and female responses to underwater sensory deprivation: An exploratory study. *Journal of Nervous and Mental Disorder, 135,* 302–310.

Wartofsky, M. W. (1968). *Conceptual foundations of scientific thought: An introduction to the philosophy of science.* New York: Macmillan.

Watson, J. B., & Rayner, R. (1920). Conditioned emotional reactions. *Journal of Experimental Psychology, 3,* 1–14.

Webb, E. J., Campbell, D. T., Schwartz, R. D., & Sechrest, L. (1966). *Unobtrusive measures: Nonreactive research in the social sciences.* Chicago: Rand McNally.

Weick, K. E. (1965). Laboratory experimentation with organizations. In J. G. March (Ed.), *Handbook of organizations.* Chicago: Rand McNally.

Westoff, L. A. (1979). Women in search of equality. *Focus, 6,* 1–19.

White, R. W., (1960). Competence and the psychosexual stages of development. In M. R. Jones (Ed.), *Nebraska symposium on motivation* (Vol. 8). Lincoln, NE: University of Nebraska Press.

Wilson, D. W., & Donnerstein, E. (1976). Legal and ethical aspects of nonreactive social psychological research: An excursion into the public mind. *American Psychologist, 31,* 765–773.

Wolins, L. (1982). *Research mistakes in the social and behavioral sciences.* Ames, IA: Iowa State University Press.

Wolman, B. B. (1971). Does psychology need its own philosophy of science? *American Psychologist, 26,* 877–885.

Wolpe, J. (1969). *The practice of behavior therapy.* New York: Pergamon Press.

Wright, B. D. (1968). Sample-free test calibration and person measurement. *Proceedings of the 1967 Invitational Conference on Testing Problems.* Princeton, NJ: Educational Testing Service.

Yukl, G., Wexley, K. N., & Seymour, J. D. (1972). Effectiveness of pay incentives under variable ratio and continuous reinforcement schedules. *Journal of Applied Psychology, 56,* 19–23.

Zajonc, R. B. (1965). Social facilitation. *Science, 149,* 269–274.

Zeller, A. (1951). An experimental analogue of repression: III. The effect of induced failure and success on memory measured by recall. *Journal of Experimental Psychology, 42,* 32–38.

Zimbardo, P. G. (1969). The human choice: Individuation, reason, and order versus deindividuation, impulse, and chaos. In W. J. Arnold & D. Levine (Eds.), *Nebraska symposium on motivation* (Vol. 17). Lincoln, NE: University of Nebraska Press.

Zobel, E. J., & Lehman, R. S. (1969). Interaction of subject and experimenter expectancy effects in a tone length discrimination task. *Behavioral Science, 14,* 357–363.

Zuckerman, M., & Wheeler, L. (1975). To dispel fantasies about the fantasy-based measure of fear of success. *Psychological Bulletin, 82,* 932–946.

NAME INDEX

SUBJECT INDEX